Encyclopedia of

Russian & Slavic

Myth and Legend

Encyclopedia of
Russian & Slavic
Myth and Legend

Mike Dixon-Kennedy

ABC-CLIO

Santa Barbara, California
Denver, Colorado
Oxford, England

Library of Congress Cataloging-in-Publication Data
Dixon-Kennedy, Mike, 1959–
    Encyclopedia of Russian and Slavic myth and legend.
        p.   cm.
    Includes bibliographical references and index.
    Summary: Covers the myths and legends of the Russian Empire at its
greatest extent as well as other Slavic people and countries.
Includes historical, geographical, and biographical background
information.
    1. Mythology, Slavic—Juvenile literature.   [1. Mythology,
Slavic.   2. Mythology—Encyclopedias.]   I. Title.
BL930.D58   1998
398.2'0947—dc21   98-20330
                                                                              CIP
                                                                               AC

ISBN 1-57607-063-8 (hc)
ISBN 1-57607-130-8 (pbk)

04 03 02 01 00 99 98   10 9 8 7 6 5 4 3 2 1

ABC-CLIO, Inc.
130 Cremona Drive, P.O. Box 1911
Santa Barbara, California 93116-1911

Typesetting by Letra Libre

This book is printed on acid-free paper ∞.
Manufactured in the United States of America.

For Gill

CONTENTS

PREFACE

Having studied the amazingly complex subject of world mythology and legend for more than twenty years, I have found few stories more stirring than those of ancient Russia. Regrettably for us, at the end of the twentieth century very few Russian pre-Christian (pagan) beliefs remain. Those that have survived have been Christianized, their pagan roots now long forgotten.

My introduction to Russian legend was the story of the witch Baba-Yaga, told me by someone whose identity I have since forgotten. Many years later, as I began to research world mythology and legend, Baba-Yaga resurfaced as I delved into the mysteries and delights of ancient Russian and Slavic folklore.

This book is a general guide to the myths and legends of the Russian Empire at its greatest extent, along with those of countries and peoples that can be broadly defined as Slavic or that have influenced and been influenced by Slavic cultures. Today, at the end of the twentieth century, Russia or Rus is a huge country that occupies a large part of Europe and Asia. Yet it was once a land of modest size that subsequently underwent centuries of expansion and change. Populations came and went, and each migration added to the culture base of the country as it progressed from one incarnation to the next—from principality to empire. All this movement has left the rich legacy of mythology and legend detailed in this volume—a legacy inherited by a land that covers approximately one-sixth of the earth's total landmass.

This volume is not unique. A good number of books have been published about the myths and legends of the ancient Russians and Slavs. However, as a quick look at the Bibliography will show, many of these are available only in languages other than English. Thus this book presents, possibly for the first time, the myths and legends in their translated form. In addition, a great deal of historical, geographical, and biographical information related to the Slavs and their mythology has been included so that readers may gain the deepest possible understanding of the myths and legends against their cultural and geographical background. A detailed map of the area covered by this volume has been included to make this last task easier; for even though certain places or countries described might be familiar, there are a fair number that are not so well known.

Russian and Slavic beliefs weave a rich tapestry between the real world and the world of pure fantasy. Here we have a culture that believed in a large number of supernatural and fantastical beings, from dragons to one-eyed or multiheaded monsters, from shape-changing wolves to soulless beings. We also find a curious mix of the pagan and the Christian; for even though Russia adopted Christianity as the state religion in A.D. 988, paganism remained popular until the end of the nineteenth century, and in more remote areas, even up to the present day. Thus we find Christian themes interwoven with pagan ideas: Dragons fight priests, saints encounter nymphs, and witches enter the kingdom of heaven.

It is my hope that by preparing this volume in the format in which it is presented, I have brought the myths and legends of the Russian and other Slavic peoples to a much broader readership, and by so doing, have increased readers' understanding of the cultures on which the volume touches. Obviously one such volume cannot begin to do justice to this subject. Although I have included as much information as possible within the physical constraints of the book, I hope readers will be inspired to undertake their own, further research and to carry it to new levels.

Whenever one writes a book, one obviously owes thanks to many different people for their help. To list all those who over the years have provided me with information, guided me as to where to look, and correct-ed my countless mistakes and assumptions would need a volume all its own. Needless to say, they all know just who they are, and to each and every one of them I say a great big "thank you."

My final thanks have to go to my long-suffering wife, Gill, and to Christopher, Charlotte, Thomas, and Rebecca, my four often "fatherless" children. For long periods of time over many years they have lost me to my research, my passion. Very rarely have they complained, and I hope that now they will be able to enjoy the results of their solitude. Whoever thinks writing is a solitary occupation should think of the writers' partners, for theirs is the true solitude.

Mike Dixon-Kennedy
Lincolnshire

HOW TO USE THIS BOOK

Although this book is arranged as a simple, straightforward encyclopedia, several conventions have been adopted to make cross-referencing easier and the text more decipherable.

1. Where headwords have alternative spellings, these are given under the main entry within the book preceded by *"Also."* When the variant spellings are widely different, variants are given their own, shorter entries that direct readers to the main entries. Where this is simply a matter of the omission or addition of a letter or letters, then those letters affected within the headword are enclosed in parentheses; e.g., Timofe(y)evna gives two versions of the patronymic, **Timofeyevna** and **Timofeevna**, both of which are acceptable transliterations from the Cyrillic.

Where the variation is a different ending, then the most common is given first. For instance, **Svarozhich (~gich)** indicates that the most common variant is **Svarozhich** and the less common is **Svarogich**.

Where the difference is a complete word, then that word is enclosed in parentheses. This occurs when an epithet or patronymic is part of the subject's name but is not commonly used, e.g., **Peter (Belyaninovich)**.

2. Where there is a separate entry for any of the people, places, or objects mentioned within an entry, a list of these will be found at the end of the entry preceded by *"See also."*

3. At the end of many entries, citations of sources in the References and Further Reading section will be found, preceded by *"References."*

SPELLING AND PRONUNCIATION

The spellings of Russian words and names that appear in this book are based on various commonly used systems of transliteration from the Cyrillic to the Latin alphabet. These word-spellings are phonetically based (see Appendix 2); thus, the words should be pronounced more or less as written, with every vowel and consonant being sounded (there are no silent e's, for example). The single prime sign (') has been used where the soft sign would appear in the Cyrillic word, indicating that the preceding consonant is palatalized. Appendix 2 shows the full modern Cyrillic alphabet and each letter's various possible pronunciations as well as its written equivalents in the Latin alphabet.

RUSSIAN TITLES

Russian rulers and their families were given titles that may be unfamiliar to the reader. Briefly, they were as follows.

tsar or **czar**—Russian emperor. The title was first used c. 1482 by Ivan Vasilevich, Grand Duke of Muscovy—better known as Ivan Groznyi, or Ivan the Terrible. Thereafter, it was used by the emperors of Russia until the 1917 Revolution. The word *tsar* is derived from the Latin *cæsar*.

tsarevich or **czarevich**—The son of a tsar. Historically the tsarevich was the eldest son, but the word applies to any son, not just the heir.

tsarevna or **czarevna**—The daughter of a tsar. Like the tsarevich, the tsarevna was usually the eldest daughter of the tsar; but the word may be correctly applied to any daughter.

tsarina or **czarina**—The wife of a tsar; an empress, but not necessarily a ruler in her own right. (Unlike a tsaritsa, she is empress merely by virtue of her marriage.)

tsaritsa or **czaritsa**—A woman who is empress and rules in her own right, regardless of whether she is married to a tsar.

A glossary of other terms used in the book may be found in Appendix 1.

BRIEF HISTORICAL AND
ANTHROPOLOGICAL DETAILS

THE BALTS AND SLAVS

Known to the classical writers of the first and second centuries as the Vanedi, a people living beyond the Vistula, the Balts and Slavs originated the northeastern Indo-European languages spoken in central and eastern Europe, the Balkans, and parts of north Asia. The Slavs are generally subdivided into three linguistic and cultural groups: the Western Slavs, including the Poles, Czechs, Moravians, and Slovaks; the Eastern Slavs, made up of Russians, Ukrainians, and Belorussians; and the Southern Slavs, comprising the Bulgars, Serbs, Croats, and Slovenes. The closely related Balts are also divided into three groups: Latvians, Lithuanians, and Prussians.

There is such a high degree of similarity among the Slavic languages that experts describe this linguistic group as a dialect continuum in which the speakers of one language understand much of what is said in the others. In their written form, the Slavic languages visibly differ in that some, such as Polish, are written in the Roman alphabet, while others, like Russian, employ the Cyrillic alphabet (see Appendix 2). These different alphabets are largely explained by the turbulent history of the Slavic regions, which were subdued by various empires and rulers at various times. Although the languages themselves continue to flourish despite political and cultural upheavals, very little of ancient Slavic mythology and legend survives today.

THE FINNO-UGRIC PEOPLES

Although closely related to both the Balts and Slavs, with whom they assimilated, the Finno-Ugric peoples do not belong to the Indo-European family. Their language grouping, a subfamily of the Ural-Altaic family, contains more than twenty different tongues that are spoken from Norway in the west to Siberia in the east, and to the Carpathian Mountains in the south.

The Finno-Ugric peoples may be subdivided into four main groups according to their geographical position. The first group includes the Finns, Lapps, Estonians (though Estonia is generally thought of as a Baltic country), Livonians, and Karelians. The second grouping comprises the Cheremiss-Mordvin peoples of the middle and upper Volga. The third includes the Votyaks, Permyaks, and Zyrians, who inhabit the Russian provinces of Perm and Vyatka, and the last, the Voguls and Ostyaks of western Siberia. The Magyar people of Hungary are normally included in the fourth grouping, as they originated in western Siberia, but they are generally considered a Turkic people.

The Finno-Ugric peoples were widely influenced by their Indo-European neighbors—the Balts, Slavs, and Norse/Teutons. Many of their legends bear direct comparison with those of both the Balts and the Slavs.

The legends of the Finnish peoples are not considered in this volume, as they are extensive enough to warrant a volume of their own. In addition, these legends do not exhibit any signs of cultural cross-fertilization and seem to have little bearing on the study of Russian and Slavic myth and legend.

OTHER PEOPLES

Yakuts

An indigenous people who live near the Lena River in northeastern Siberia, in one of the coldest regions on earth, the Yakuts speak a Turkic language in the Ural-Altaic family, closely related to Finno-Ugric. Very few of the beliefs of the ancient Yakuts have survived.

Tungus

An ancient Siberian people. Only one of the major Tungus legends has survived, which is unfortunate, as this story (Ivan the Mare's Son) is particularly fine.

Letts

Indigenous inhabitants of Latvia who were closely related to their neighbors the Lithuanians. Their language is Baltic with characteristics of both Latvian and Lithuanian.

Readers will find further detail on each of these groups under the respective headings in the main body of the book.

Encyclopedia of

Russian & Slavic

Myth and Legend

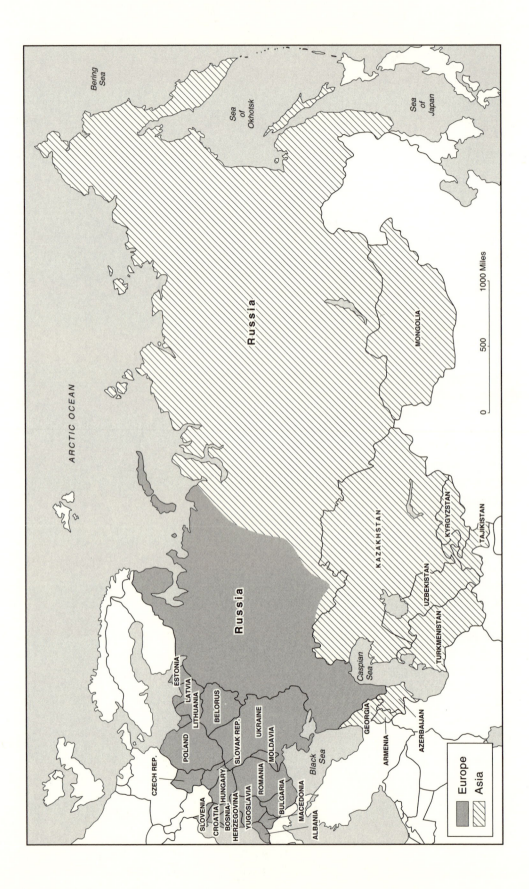

ADALBERT OF PRAGUE, SAINT

Prussia and Poland

The patron saint of Prussia and Poland, whose feast day is 23 April. Adalbert (c. 956–997) was born to a noble Bohemian family and baptized Voytech. At his confirmation, he took the name Adalbert, after his teacher of the same name in Magdeburg. When his teacher died in 981, Adalbert returned to Prague and was consecrated there in 982, becoming the first native bishop of the city. However, Adalbert encountered stiff opposition to his attempts to convert others to Christianity, and in 990 he withdrew from Prague to Rome, where he joined the Benedictine abbey of Saints Boniface and Alexis. Duke Boleslaus (Boleslaw I, "the Brave") of Poland petitioned Pope John XV (pope 985–996) for the return of Adalbert to Prague, and shortly thereafter Adalbert was sent back under papal decree.

Conditions appeared to have improved, and Adalbert founded the Benedictine abbey at Brevnov. The peace, however, was short-lived, and the populace once again grew hostile to him and his teachings when he attempted to give sanctuary to a woman who had been accused of adultery. The horde dragged the woman out of his church and summarily executed her, whereupon Adalbert promptly excommunicated everyone involved. Once again he was obliged to flee to Rome, from where he was yet again ordered to return, this time by Pope Gregory V (pope 996–999). However, in his absence, several of his family had been murdered, so it was decided, upon the suggestion of Duke Boleslaus, that Adalbert should undertake a mission to the pagan Prussians in Pomerania.

Adalbert went on to evangelize Hungary and possibly Prussia and Poland as well but was murdered in 997, along with his two companions Benedict and Gaudentius, by Prussians who suspected them of being Polish spies.

Adalbert's body was thrown into the water near Königsberg (modern Kaliningrad, a Russian city that is separated from the rest of the country by Lithuania) but was later recovered after it washed ashore in Poland. He was enshrined at Griezno, but his relics were forcibly repatriated to Prague in 1039. Saint Adalbert is usually depicted with a club and lances—the weapons used to murder him—and often with a two-headed cross.

See also: Bohemia; Hungary; Poland; Prussia

AFRON

Russia

The tsar of an unnamed realm, which some say lay in the Thrice-Ninth Kingdom, and the owner of the Horse with the Golden Mane. When Ivan Vyslavovich was caught trying to steal both the horse and its golden bridle (though the shape-changing wolf helping Ivan Vyslavovich had warned him not to touch the bridle), Afron gave him a chance to redeem himself. If Ivan Vyslavovich could bring him Elena the Beautiful, after whom Afron had lusted for quite some time, he would not only forgive Ivan Vyslavovich but would also give him the Horse with the Golden Mane and its bridle. If he failed, Ivan Vyslavovich would be branded a common thief.

Ivan Vyslavovich succeeded in abducting Elena the Beautiful with the help of the shape-changing wolf who had been helping him throughout his journey, which began as a quest assigned to him by his father, Tsar Vyslav Andronovich, to capture the Firebird. However, Ivan Vyslavovich fell in love with Elena the Beautiful, and vice versa, so the wolf assumed her shape when they came back to Afron's palace. Afron kept his word and gave Ivan Vyslavovich both the Horse with the Golden Mane and its golden bridle, and Ivan and the real Elena the Beautiful rode away on the horse. The wolf resumed its true form and rejoined them, thus leaving Tsar Afron with nothing.

> *See also:* Elena the Beautiful; Firebird, The;
> Horse with the Golden Mane, The; Ivan
> Vyslavovich; Thrice-Ninth Kingdom, The;
> Vyslav Andronovich

AGOG-MAGOG
Armenia

A mysterious monster with whom Badikan was said to have done battle. With Armenia lying so close to the Holy Land, it seems reasonable to assume that Agog-Magog was a derivation of Gog and Magog (Revelation 20:8), whose names would probably have been familiar to the common populace through the work of missionaries and travelers to and from the holy cities.

> *See also:* Badikan

AITVARAS
Lithuania

A mysterious and curious flying creature sometimes depicted as a cockerel and sometimes shown with the head of the lucky Zaltys (grass snake) and the fiery tail of a comet.

> *See also:* Zaltys

AJYSYT
Siberia—Yakut

The mother-goddess of the Yakuts, a Turkic people living near the river Lena in Siberia. Literally translated, her name means "birthgiver," though she is also referred to as "the mother of cradles" and was believed to be present whenever one of her devotees gave birth. As Ajysyt-ijaksit-khotan, she was the

"birthgiving, nourishing mother." She owned the Golden Book of Fate, which contained the names and destinies of every human being either living or yet to be born. She brought the soul of the newborn baby down from heaven so that a complete human being could come into existence and then entered the name of the new person in the Golden Book of Fate. It was only when the name had been entered in the book that the person became a fully fledged member of the human race. Other Siberian tribes thought the mother-goddess dwelt in heaven on a mountain that had seven stories. There she not only gave newly born people their lives but also determined the fate of all people and equipped them with the potential to do both good and evil.

The Altai Tatars acknowledged a similar deity known as the "milk lake mother," and the Yakuts themselves have a curious myth about a White Youth who encounters a calm "lake of milk" near the cosmic tree, the world pillar of Yryn-al-tojon, the "white creator Lord." After seeking the blessing of the tree, this youth felt a warm breeze, heard the tree creak, and saw a female divinity, Ajysyt, rise from the roots. She offered him milk from her full breasts, and after satisfying his thirst, the youth felt his strength increase a hundredfold. Thus, the milk-breasted mother of life, the mother-goddess, and the cosmic Tree of Life are combined into one sustaining and nourishing entity.

> *See also:* Golden Book of Fate, The; Lena,
> River; Siberia; Tatars; Tree of Life, The; White
> Youth; Yakuts; Yryn-al-tojon

AJYSYT-IJAKSIT-KHOTAN
Siberia—Yakut

"Birthgiving, nourishing mother," an aspect of the Yakut mother-goddess Ajysyt.

> *See also:* Ajysyt; Yakuts

AK MOLOT
Tatar

One of a pair of heroes who are described in a poem as engaged in mortal combat, the other hero being Bulat. Ak Molot managed to inflict numerous wounds on his enemy that would have killed any normal man, but Bulat was not normal, for he did not carry his soul. After three years of fighting, Ak Molot saw a golden casket hanging from the sky on a white silken thread. Ak Molot shot down the casket and opened it, whereupon ten white birds flew out, one of which contained Bulat's soul. While still fighting Bulat, Ak Molot shot the birds one after another, and then, as the tenth bird fell to the ground, Bulat died.

See also: Bulat

ALAKO
Slav—Romany

The god of the moon, formerly called Dundra. Sent to the earth by his father, Dundra taught the Romany people their laws and became their protector. When he had finished his task on earth he ascended into the skies, where he became Alako. He watches over his people and carries their souls to live on the moon after death. One day Alako will return from the moon and lead his people back to their lost homeland.

Alako was worshiped as recently as the late nineteenth century. Votaries carrying idols of Alako that showed him holding a quill in his right hand and a sword in his left would gather once a year at full moon, set up his idols, and offer songs and prayers to him. These rites were then followed by a feast. Alako was also central to the rites of passage. At Christian baptisms, a child would be baptized in the names of both Christ and Alako, and all newlyweds were consecrated to him.

See also: Dundra; Moon

ALANS
Russia

Iranian-speaking nomadic tribe of the barbarian peoples known as the Sarmatians, who inhabited Russia in Roman times. They first appeared in history north of the Caspian Sea, and between the second and fourth centuries A.D. migrated westward into the eastern provinces of the Roman Empire. They

then divided into two groups. One group of Alans continued to migrate westward with the Germanic peoples, appearing in Gaul, Lusitania (Portugal), and finally, North Africa, where they merged with the Vandals. The other group, wandering eastward, settled in the Caucasus Mountains. Their descendants, the Ossetes of the Republic of Georgia, tell a story similar to that concerning the passing of King Arthur. It is quite possible that the story of Arthur was carried to the region by the Romans, although this has never been proven. The story of Batradz the Ossete hero might also have been the source of the Arthurian legend, as it seems to be the older of the two.

See also: Arthur, King; Batradz; Caspian Sea; Caucasus; Georgia; Ossetes; Sarmatians

ALATNIR
Slav

A brilliant white stone that lies on the island of Buyan. Frequently mentioned as a potent force in magical spells and charms.

See also: Buyan

ALENKA
Russia

The daughter of an unnamed witch that some authorities identify as Baba-Yaga. The witch brought the lad Ivashko home for supper and ordered Alenka to cook him. However, when the witch went out again, Ivashko tricked Alenka, pushed her deep into the hot coals, locked the oven door, and hurried outside to hide in the forest canopy. The witch returned and berated her absent daughter for having left the meal unattended. She then sat down to dine with her friends, unaware that they were feasting on Alenka—a fact soon brought to light when Ivashko reappeared.

See also: Baba-Yaga (-Jaga, -Iaga); Ivashko

ALENUSHKA
Russia

Although of royal lineage, Alenushka and her brother Ivanushka were forced to wander like gypsies after their parents died. During their wanderings the pair came to a pond where a herd of cattle were grazing. Ivanushka rushed to the water to slake his thirst, but Alenushka stopped him, warning him that if he drank he would turn into a calf.

Next they came to a lake beside which a flock of sheep were grazing. Again Ivanushka ran to the water's edge, and again Alenushka stopped him from drinking, warning him that if he did he would turn into a lamb. Near the next stretch of water some pigs were rooting about. Alenushka once more stopped Ivanushka from drinking, this time warning him that he would become a piglet. By the time they reached the next watering hole, near which a herd of goats were grazing, Ivanushka's thirst was so great that he ignored his sister's advice. As soon as he drank the water, Ivanushka turned into a kid.

Alenushka harnessed her brother, and the two continued on their way. They eventually arrived at a royal palace, where Ivanushka ran off to eat the well-manicured grass. The royal guards brought Alenushka and her brother before the tsar, who was immediately captivated by Alenushka and asked her to marry him. She consented and she and her brother remained at the tsar's palace.

Some time later the tsar had to be away on business. While he was absent, a sorceress who had designs on his affections cast a spell on Alenushka, who fell ill, growing thinner and weaker each day. By the time the tsar returned, the flowers and the grass around the palace had died, and Alenushka was very wan. Awhile later, the tsar again had to leave the palace on business. This time the sorceress told Alenushka that she could cure herself if she went to the sea's edge at dusk and drank a little of the water. Alenushka went to the sea to drink, but as she bent down to the water, the sorceress tied a huge boulder around her neck and threw her far out to sea. The sorceress then assumed the likeness of Alenushka and returned to the palace, where

the tsar rejoiced to see his wife restored to full health.

Ivanushka remained by the water, bleating for his sister. In the palace the sorceress nagged the tsar to kill Ivanushka, saying that she had grown tired of the way he smelled. At first the tsar would not hear of it, but eventually he reluctantly agreed. Ivanushka, learning of his fate, asked the tsar for permission to go to the seashore. The tsar agreed.

There Ivanushka called out to his sister, but Alenushka replied that she could not come because of the boulder tied around her neck. Ivanushka returned to the palace, but at midday once more asked permission to visit the seashore, where he again called to his sister and received the same reply. As dusk began to fall Ivanushka asked permission of the tsar a third time. Once more the tsar agreed; but this time, his curiosity aroused by Ivanushka's strange behavior, he followed the kid to the edge of the water. There Ivanushka called to his sister, and this time she came bobbing to the surface.

The tsar immediately swam out to Alenushka, released the boulder, and carried her back to the palace. There he ordered his guards to light a huge bonfire. When the sorceress came out to see what they were doing, the tsar threw her onto the fire, where she burned to death. As the sorceress died, the gardens around the palace burst into flower once more, and Alenushka and Ivanushka lived out their days happily together.

See also: Ivanushka

ALEPPO
Armenia

City to which Martiros promised his dying father he would never travel to trade. He later broke his promise when he learned that the people of Aleppo paid exorbitant prices for goods, especially boxwood. Ancient Aleppo (today's Halab) is located in northern Syria.

See also: Martiros

ALESHA
Russia
Also: Aliosha

A bogatyr', the son of Leontii, a priest from Rostov, Alesha lived in Kiev at the court of Prince Vladimir Bright Sun. When Vladimir asked his knights which one would rescue the princess Zabava from the clutches of a dragon that had carried her away, it was Alesha who told the prince about Dobrynya Nikitich's pact with the dragon, thus making the prince command that knight to rescue the girl, or be beheaded.

Alesha was not always inept, as the story of his arrival at Kiev proves. Riding out from Rostov, Alesha and his squire Ekim chose to head for Kiev because they were certain that the other possible choices, Suzdal' and Chernigov, would lead them into trouble either from wine or from women. Arriving in Kiev, they immediately realized that all was not as it should be, for there were no grooms waiting in the courtyard to stable their horses.

Entering the royal palace, they presented themselves to Prince Vladimir Bright Sun, who had already heard of Alesha and bade him attend a banquet that night as a guest of honor. Alesha chose not to sit at the table but instead to perch himself on the stove in the banqueting hall, a position usually occupied by beggars and serfs. Shortly after the meal had got under way, the door to the hall was thrown open and a giant, brutish creature slithered in. This was Tugarin, a heathen creature with the girth of two fully grown oak trees, eyes set far apart in his ugly head, and ears that were nearly eight inches long. Without paying his respect to Vladimir, Tugarin seated himself between the prince and his wife.

Watching these events from his place on the stove, Alesha inquired as to how serious the argument must have been between the prince and his wife to allow such an ugly creature to sit between them. Ignoring Alesha, Tugarin plunged the blade of his knife into a roast swan that was set before him and ate it whole, spitting out the bones as he swallowed the flesh. Alesha once again taunted Tugarin, saying that his father, Leontii, once had a mongrel dog that choked to death on a swan's bone, and that he hoped Tugarin would do the same. Tugarin again ignored Alesha and devoured a huge game pie in a single bite.

Alesha once more commented, saying that his father had had an old cow that had rooted around in the dirt for food and had choked to death. He hoped that Tugarin's ill manners would lead to the same fate. At last Tugarin rose to the bait and asked Prince Vladimir Bright Sun who the ignorant peasant was. When he heard that it was none other than Alesha—for even Tugarin had heard of him—he threw his long knife at him. However, the agile Ekim caught the knife by its handle. Seeing this, Tugarin pushed the table over and challenged Alesha to meet him out on the steppe.

Alesha was only too happy to oblige and immediately set out on foot. Some distance from Kiev, he came across a pilgrim who was carrying a heavy staff weighing ninety poods (3,240 lbs, or 1,472 kg). Exchanging clothes with the pilgrim, Alesha also borrowed the staff. Soon afterward he caught sight of Tugarin astride a powerful horse, flying overhead on a set of paper wings he had made. Alesha prayed for a heavy shower of rain, and his prayer was answered almost immediately. As the rain fell, Tugarin's paper wings disintegrated and he crashed to the ground. Tugarin realized who the pilgrim was and galloped toward him, fully intending to crush him under his horse's hooves.

Alesha nimbly sidestepped the rushing horse and hid beneath its flowing mane. As Tugarin searched for Alesha the knight struck out with the staff, knocking Tugarin's head from his shoulders. Picking up the head, Alesha impaled it on the end of the staff and returned to Kiev riding Tugarin's horse.

See also: Bogatyr'; Chernigov; Dobrynya Nikitich; Dragon; Ekim; Kiev; Leontii;

Rostov; Tugarin; Vladimir Bright Sun, Prince; Zabava (Putyatichna), Princess
References: Astakhova 1938–51; Speranskii 1916

ALEXANDER THE GREAT
General
356–323 B.C. Greek Macedonian king, the son of Philip II of Macedon and Olympias. Alexander's place in Russian and Slavic legend is due to the fables of Vardan and Mekhithar Gosh.
See also: Mekhithar Gosh; Vardan

ALIOSHA
Russia
Variant spelling of Alesha. Although Alyosha is yet another variant spelling of the same Slavic name, the very different tales of Alesha/Aliosha and of Alyosha recorded in this volume should not be confused. The similarity between these two legends in certain details (e.g., both protagonists are the sons of priests) might or might not indicate a common origin.
See also: Alesha; Alyosha

ALKA
Lithuania
A collective term for sacred fields, springs, or groves that could not be plowed, fished, or felled. These Alka were holy places for the cremation of the dead and for votive offerings to the gods.

ALKLHA
Siberia
The personification of the darkness of the sky, a monster that filled the universe with a huge body and enormous wings of impenetrable blackness. Alklha fed on the moon each month, slowly nibbling away until the moon disappeared. However, the moon did not agree with Alklha, and the resultant irritation caused Alklha to vomit and thus return the moon to the night sky. Alklha also tried to eat the sun, but it was far too hot, so it disappeared only in part, or only for a short

Portrait of Alexander the Great (Library of Congress)

time. The gashes made by Alklha's fangs are clearly visible on the surface of the moon, and similar marks also could be seen on the sun if it were not so bright.
See also: Moon; Sun

ALKONOST'
Russia
A demoness, or *sirin*—half woman and half bird—who torments the damned. Possibly of Persian origin, Alkonost' lives in Rai, the abode of the dead, where her song tortures the souls of the dead who led evil lives, giving them no rest.
See also: Rai; Sirin; Underworld, The
References: Haase 1939

ALLELUIAH
Russia
Christian name given to one of the three female spirits that oversee the functions of human life—the Russian equivalents of the Greek Fates. Her companions were Miloserdnia and Miloslaviia.
See also: Miloserdnia; Miloslaviia
References: Bezsonov 1861

ALMAFI
Hungary—Magyar

"Son of the apple," the name of three children born miraculously to an old couple from three apples that fell from an apple tree, their only possession. As each of the three children was identical and each had the same name, the old couple referred to them as First Almafi, Second Almafi, and Third Almafi. When the children reached their eighteenth birthday, the old man called them to him, speaking initially to First Almafi, saying that the time had come for him to leave home and seek his fortune. His mother gave him a loaf of barley bread, and First Almafi set out.

As night fell, First Almafi sat down under a tree and took out the barley loaf and began to eat. He had only taken a couple of bites when an old man came up to him and asked for food. First Almafi said that he would gladly share his meager rations, whereupon the old man told the youth to watch for the rising of the scythe-star, and then go in the direction the shaft pointed him in. Along the way he would come to a fast-flowing stream. He was not to worry, as the stream's waters would bear his weight. In the midst of the stream grew the most beautiful water lilies. He was not to pick even a single one, as if he did he would be lost. When he had crossed the stream he would enter a field of silver, and after that, a field of gold. He was to cross both without picking even a single blade of the enchanted grass, as if he did he would perish. Finally, having crossed the fields, he would find his fortune.

First Almafi thanked the old man, who instantly vanished. Then he watched and waited for the scythe-star to rise, and set off in the direction it indicated once it was clearly visible. Before long he came to the stream, which he started to walk across, stopping when he came to the water lilies. Bending down, he picked one of the blooms, instantly turned into a fish, and was carried away by the fast-flowing waters.

Although it had been some time since First Almafi had set off to seek his fortune and no word had come from him, his father sent Second Almafi off to seek his fortune. Second Almafi took exactly the same road as his brother had, sat under the same tree, saw the same man, and received the same set of instructions. The old man, however, added that First Almafi had been tempted by one of the water lilies and had been lost. Second Almafi was almost tempted by the water lilies as he crossed the stream, but he remembered the words of the old man just in time and made it safely across. However, as he entered the silver field he was so enchanted that he stooped down and picked a silver flower for his buttonhole. Immediately he became a silver snake and slithered away.

Finally it was Third Almafi's turn to set out and seek his fortune. He followed the same road his brothers had, sat under the same tree, and received the same instructions from the same old man, who added that his two brothers had already succumbed to temptation. Third Almafi set off, crossed the stream and the silver field with ease, and was almost tempted to pick a flower as he crossed the golden field; but remembering what the old man had said, he resisted the urge and made his way safely through the field.

He found himself in a vast, empty desert that stretched as far as the eye could see. For three days he struggled through the deep sand, his feet sinking with every step. Finally he sank to the ground, exhausted. He lay there a long time, until he heard a loud humming in the sky, and looking up, saw a floating palace. As he watched the palace float by, he caught a glimpse of a beautiful maiden standing on a balcony. He hauled himself to his feet and hurried after the floating palace.

Exhaustion finally got the better of Third Almafi, who slumped to his knees, panting. As he knelt, a small chicken landed in front of him. Almafi watched it in amazement. He could easily have reached out and eaten the bird, but it looked as exhausted as he was, so he said that he would carry it so that they might seek refuge together. Instantly the bird turned into the old man, who told him that as his pity had overcome his greed, he could grant Third Almafi one wish. Third Almafi thought for a moment, then asked for his two brothers to be released from their enchantments. The old man told Third Almafi that they were already on the road home, and then he vanished once more.

Third Almafi continued on his journey, and after another day's travel, as exhaustion was again beginning to overtake him, he came to a huge castle with no windows, just a single small door. Inside he found a huge hall with a row of tables in it. The first table held a bowl of porridge and a note saying that whoever ate the porridge would never be hungry again. Third Almafi sat down and emptied the bowl, and afterward he felt as if he need never eat again.

He then moved to the second table, where he found a bottle of water along with a note saying that whoever drank the water would never feel thirst again. Without hesitation Third Almafi drank the water and then moved on to the third table, where he found a small jar containing some ointment, and a note saying that whoever anointed themselves with the ointment would be filled with the strength of a thousand men. Third Almafi duly anointed himself and then went to the fourth table. There he found a sword and a note saying that whoever wore the sword would be invincible. Third Almafi buckled on the sword and then went to the fifth table, where he found another small jar of ointment along with a note saying that whoever anointed their eyes with the lotion would see everything. Third Almafi applied the lotion and then lay down to rest, for now he knew that he had to find the mysterious flying palace and the maiden he had glimpsed.

For a full year Third Almafi wandered the world, looking for the flying palace, and through all that time he never felt hunger or thirst. During his travels Third Almafi came to the edge of an immense forest, where he sat down and fell asleep beneath a large oak, even though he didn't really need to rest.

His sleep was disturbed by a loud crowing from the branches above him. Sitting up, Third Almafi saw a large golden cockerel in the tree, the tone of its crowing telling Third Almafi that all was not well with the bird. Third Almafi asked it what the problem was, whereupon the cockerel told him that he was under an enchantment, having originally been a prince engaged to a beautiful maiden.

Third Almafi took pity on the plight of the prince and said that he would do whatever he could to help. The cockerel flew down from the tree and told Third Almafi that the enchantment had been placed on him by Deceit, who owned a well of enchanted water. If Third Almafi could obtain a cupful of the water and spray the cockerel with it three times without the bird's knowledge, the enchantment would be broken and the prince would be himself again. Third Almafi leaped to his feet and asked the cockerel to point him in the direction of the well, but the cockerel did not know its whereabouts. However, the cockerel told Third Almafi that he should travel to the Talking Mountain, and it would give him the directions he required. When Third Almafi asked how he was to find the mountain, the cockerel told Third Almafi to tear off a part of his crest, which would guide him.

Third Almafi did as he was told and set off after the piece of golden crest, which flew just ahead of him. For three days and three nights Third Almafi traveled without rest until he reached a vast forest in the middle of which rose a lofty mountain at whose foothills the crest stopped flying. Third Almafi found a cave on the slopes of the mountain and entered. Inside was a marble slab inscribed with instructions on how to awaken the voice of the mountain. Following the instructions, Third Almafi left the cave, uprooted twelve tall pine trees from the forest below, dragged them into the cave, and set them afire. Then he waited until the last embers died away, whereupon the mountain spoke, telling Third Almafi how to find both the well of Deceit and the beloved maiden of the cockerel prince.

Almafi traveled three weeks to reach the well, which was guarded by a twelve-headed dragon. Drawing his sword, Third Almafi quickly disposed of the vile monster and then lay down to rest. When he awoke he found that Deceit had bound him hand and foot and thrown him into a deep dungeon. Third Almafi waited three weeks in that dungeon before Deceit returned, surprised to find the prisoner still alive although he had had no food or water. Deceit moved closer to Third Almafi to have a better look. Third Almafi, who had loosened his bonds earlier, now tore them off and quickly bound Deceit hand and foot with them. Then Third Almafi carried Deceit out of the dungeon, built a huge bonfire, and burned Deceit to death. Then Third Almafi drew water from the well and made his way back to where the golden cockerel waited.

When the cockerel asked Third Almafi if he had succeeded in his task, Third Almafi said he had not. The cockerel dropped its head in despair, and Third Almafi sprayed the water over it three times, restoring the prince to his human form. The two of them then set out to rescue the prince's beloved from her place of imprisonment, which lay, as the Talking Mountain had told Third Almafi, beneath the sea, in a glass mountain.

At the edge of the sea Third Almafi dipped his head beneath the waves and saw the mountain far offshore. Then, calling all the animals of the sea to their aid, Third Almafi had them raise the mountain to the surface, for even he could not breathe under water. When the mountain surfaced, Third Almafi hauled it ashore and smashed it with a single, carefully aimed blow. The maiden stepped from the glass fragments and embraced the prince, and all three set off for the prince's kingdom, where Third Almafi acted as best man at the wedding. Then Third Almafi set out to resume his own quest.

After a long journey he came to the foot of an immense mountain and decided to climb it so that he might spy the flying palace in the distance. Seven days later he stood on the summit, far above the clouds, and saw the flying palace heading straight toward him. As it swept past, Third Almafi sprang upward and landed in the courtyard of the palace. Quickly searching through the palace, which was deserted, Third Almafi found the maiden chained to the balcony. Using his great strength, he tore the chains apart, and he and the maiden embraced. Then Third Almafi asked her what had happened.

She told him that her father, a king, once had the misfortune of wounding a terrible monster. The monster swore that one day he would steal away the king's most precious possession—his daughter. For a long time she had lived a virtual prisoner, but at length the king relaxed the guard and she was allowed to wander in the palace gardens. There, one day, she had heard a humming in the air, and looked up to see the flying palace heading down toward her. As it swept overhead the monster leaned out and took hold of her. She had been a prisoner for three years. Although at first the monster had allowed her to wander through the hundred rooms of the palace, he had chained her after she tried to escape.

Third Almafi searched the palace. In the hundredth room he came across the monster fast asleep and woke him with a swift kick. The two wrestled, the monster managing to throw Third Almafi only once before the youth got the upper hand and smashed the monster's head open. He returned to the embrace of the maiden, and together they pondered the manner in which they might leave the palace, which at that moment was flying on its two tremendous wings over a wide sea. Third Almafi decided that when they were over land again he would simply cut off the wings with his sword.

Some days later the maiden saw land in the distance. As they drew closer the maiden recognized the land, and soon she caught sight of her father's palace. Waiting until the appropriate moment, Third Almafi cut the wings from the flying palace, which floated to the ground next to the king's. The king celebrated the return of his daughter, and a little while later, he dispatched his messengers to bring Third Almafi's mother, father, and brothers to the kingdom, where preparations were being made for the marriage of the maiden to Third Almafi—who eventually would inherit the kingdom and would rule with kindness, compassion, and wisdom.

See also: Deceit; Dragon; Talking Mountain, The

References: Biro 1980

ALYONKA
Russia
See Alenka.

ALYONUSHKA
Russia
See Alenushka.

ALYOSHA
Russia

The son of a priest who was taught how to read and write by an old woman. One day, on his way home from his lessons, he passed the palace of the local, unnamed tsar and peered in through a window. There he saw the tsar's daughter, and as he watched, she took her head from her shoulders, washed and dried it, and then replaced it. Alyosha was astounded. He immediately realized that the princess was a witch. Worse for Alyosha, the witch had caught sight of him at the window and was plotting a way to keep her secret.

Feigning illness, the princess called the tsar to her bedside, eliciting his promise that when she died he would have the son of the local priest stand guard over her coffin three nights in a row. The tsar gave his word, and the very next morning the princess was dead. The tsar went to the home of the priest and told him that Alyosha must sit vigil

beside the coffin of his dead daughter for three nights, reading aloud from the Psalms.

Alyosha knew that the witch had faked her death. At his lessons that day he asked his teacher for advice. The old woman told Alyosha how he might protect himself; and thus prepared, Alyosha went to the church as night fell to begin his lonely vigil, first carefully inscribing a circle in the stone floor with a knife the old lady had given him. At the stroke of midnight, the lid of the coffin opened and the witch climbed out. She quietly made her way toward where Alyosha was seated with his back toward the coffin, reading the Psalms. However, as the witch reached the circle, she stopped, and no matter how hard she tried, she was unable to cross it; and so she spent the remainder of the night clawing helplessly at Alyosha's neck. Alyosha kept reading the Psalms and did not turn around, for turning would have broken the spell and he would have fallen prey to the witch. As the first cock crowed, the witch ran back to the coffin and tumbled in, and Alyosha went home.

The following night the very same thing happened, but when the witch reached the circle in the stone, she started to mouth eerie sounds. As these sounds filled the church, a huge wind blew up inside the sanctuary, and Alyosha felt as if his body were being invaded by a thousand creeping insects. Yet not once did Alyosha falter in his reading of the Psalms, and not once did he turn around; and at daybreak the witch had to return to her coffin.

The third night came and Alyosha returned to the church. This time he hammered nails into the coffin lid before sitting down to read from the Psalms. At midnight the lid of the coffin flew off and the witch sprang out, chanting strange spells that conjured up all the demons of hell. All through the night the demons tormented Alyosha, but not once did he falter or turn around, and at daybreak the terrible images faded away and the witch tumbled back into her coffin.

Then, as the cock crowed the second time, the tsar entered the church. He was alarmed to find his daughter face down in her open coffin. However, after Alyosha explained all that had passed, the tsar ordered the foul witch to be burned at the stake and buried beneath a heavy stone slab. In return for Alyosha's loyalty and faithful service, the tsar bestowed on him a vast treasure.

ALYOSHA POPOVICH
Russia

One of seven legendary bogatyri who assembled to go on a journey together. The other six were Vasilii Buslayevich, Vasilii Kazimirovich, Ivan Gostinyi Syn, Godenko Bludovich, Dobrynya Nikitich, and Il'ya Muromets. A legend that is purported to explain why the bogatyri disappeared from Holy Russia may be found in the entry for Vasilii Buslayevich.

Alyosha Popovich also puts in a brief appearance in the legends surrounding the wedding feast of Dunai Ivanovich and the Princess Nastas'ya, where he is described as the most valiant man in all Russia. The valor of Alyosha Popovich, however, is called into question when he recommends Dobrynya Nikitich to Prince Vladimir Bright Sun as the man most suited to go to the assistance of the King of Lithuania. Alyosha's intention was not to aid his prince or the besieged King of Lithuania but rather to rid Kiev of Dobrynya Nikitich so that he might marry Dobrynya's wife, Nastas'ya Nikulichna.

Several times over a period of several years Alyosha delivered news of the death of Dobrynya Nikitich, and each time, he asked Nastas'ya Nikulichna to marry him. She always refused, saying that she preferred to wait another three years. However, she eventually agreed, and preparations were made for the wedding. News of the impending ceremony reached Dobrynya Nikitich, who returned to Kiev in disguise and sang songs of celebration at the couple's wedding feast. In the end, Dobrynya Nikitich and his wife

were reunited, and Alyosha Popovich was shown in his true light.

See also: Bogatyr'; Dobrynya Nikitich; Dunai Ivanovich; Godenko Bludovich; Il'ya Muromets; Ivan Gostinyi Syn; Kiev; Lithuania; Nastas'ya, Princess; Nastas'ya Nikulichna; Vasilii Buslayevich; Vasilii Kazimirovich; Vladimir Bright Sun, Prince
References: Speranskii 1916; Ukhov 1957

AMBROSE
Hungary—Magyar

A young prince who was imprisoned beneath the earth, possibly in the underworld, by an old witch. The prince finally elicited from the witch the information that she kept her power in a shining beetle, and her soul in a black beetle. These beetles were to be found inside a box, inside a pigeon, inside a hare, all of which were inside a wild boar kept in a green field. If both beetles were killed, then she would die. After some time the prince managed to escape from his prison and found the boar, which he quickly killed. After he recovered the two beetles, he crushed the shining one first. At this, the witch took to her bed. The young prince confronted her there and crushed the second beetle, whereupon she died.

See also: Koshchei (the Deathless); Underworld, The

AMELF(I)A TIMOFE(Y)EVNA
Russia

The widowed mother of Vasilii Buslayevich and Dobrynya Nikitich, in the first case having been the wife of Buslai, and in the second case as the wife of Nikita. Amelfia Timofeyevna is depicted as a powerful and wealthy sorceress who constantly advised her sons—although her advice was seldom taken.

See also: Buslai (~y); Dobrynya Nikitich; Nikita; Vasilii Buslayevich
References: Speranskii 1916; Ukhov 1957

AMUR
Russia

This Siberian river originates at the junction of the Shilka and the Argun Rivers in southeastern Siberia, then runs east- and south-eastward until it nears the Songhua, a tributary flowing northward from China, where it turns again and heads northeastward along the Sikhote Alin mountains. The Amur empties into the northern end of the Tatar Strait, which separates mainland Russia from the island of Sakhalin. Today the modern city of Nikolayevsk-na-Amure lies at the river's mouth—the traditional homeland of a native Siberian people known as the Gilyaki (Nivkhi). The Amur holds the same great historical and cultural significance for the Gilyaki and other native people of the region as the Dnieper does for Russians and Ukrainians.

See also: Gilyaki (Nivkhi); Siberia

ANAHITA
Armenia

A goddess of Iranian origin, Ardva Sura Anahita ("the high, the powerful, the immaculate") was widely worshiped in Armenia, where she was commonly referred to as Anahita. Depicted as a young woman with an expansive bust, she wore a crown of stars, brocade and otterskin clothing, fine jewels, and golden sandals. Anahita was the goddess of all the waters—rivers, streams, lakes, and the sea, as well as the life-giving fluids of mankind, such as semen and mother's milk.

ANAITIS
Armenia

Goddess with a temple at Acilisena, where the unmarried daughters of noble families entered the goddess's service as temple prostitutes. After their term of service to the goddess, the young women commonly married without apparent difficulty.

ANASTASIA, SAINT
Russia

Connected with Saints Nedelia and Paraskeva. Twelve Fridays in the year were believed sacred to Paraskeva, and consequently also to Saints Nedelia and Anastasia.

On these days men and women young and old would strip naked and jump and shake themselves about, saying that they had seen Saints Paraskeva and Anastasia and had been ordered to honor them with their lascivious dances. These celebrations were condemned as pagan rituals in 1589 by the Patriarch of Constantinople. The Stoglav Council, set up during the latter half of the sixteenth century by Ivan the Terrible, also condemned the festivals, calling them orgies; but the cult remained active, especially in Ukraine, where Friday was considered the Sabbath until well into the eighteenth century.

See also: Constantinople; Ivan Groznyi; Nedelia, Saint; Paraskeva, Saint; Ukraine
References: Afanas'ev 1865–69; Bezsonov 1861; Haase 1939; Ralston 1872

ANDREW, SAINT
Russia

Patron saint of Russia, Scotland, and Achaia and of fishermen and old maids. Saint Andrew's feast day is 30 November. One of the twelve apostles, brother of Simon Peter, he was a fisherman converted and baptized by John the Baptist and became one of Jesus Christ's closest companions (see Mark 1:29 and 13:3; John 1:40 and 6:8; and Acts 1:13). Tradition holds that Andrew preached the gospel in Asia Minor and Scythia and was crucified in Achaia (Greece) on the order of the Roman governor. The belief that his cross was x-shaped dates from the tenth century but did not gain popularity until the fourteenth. Among Russia's patron saints in addition to Andrew are Saints George and Basil.

See also: Basil, Saint; George, Saint; Scythia

ANDRONOVICH, VYSLAV
Russia

See Vyslav Andronovich.

ANNA
Russia

The sister of Basil II, the Byzantine emperor. In 998, Vladimir I made the political decision

An icon of the apostle Andreas (Saint Andrew) from Macedonia, c. 1600 (collection of Professor D. Walter Moritz, Hanover, Germany; Erich Lessing/Art Resource, NY)

to accept Christianity as part of a pact with Basil. Another condition of this pact was Vladimir's marriage to Anna.

See also: Basil II, Bulgaroctonus; Byzantine Empire; Vladimir I

APPRENTICE, THE
Armenia

The unnamed son of the laborer Ohan. Having proved himself no good at anything, his father took him to the home of forty thieves to become their apprentice. The first task the thieves gave their apprentice was to fetch water from a nearby well. However, when the Apprentice leaned over the well and dipped his pitcher into the water, he found that he could not pull it out again. The Apprentice tugged with all his might, and the pitcher came out of the water with a pale white hand holding tightly onto it. Quick as a flash, the Apprentice took hold of the white hand and began to pull. A shriek emanated from beneath the surface of the water, from which another hand appeared holding a fantastic golden goblet. Not wanting to lose the pitcher, the Apprentice released the hand and snatched the goblet. He then made his way back to the home of the thieves, the pitcher full of water in one hand and the goblet hidden under his shirt.

The thieves were immensely surprised to see their apprentice return, for no one had ever succeeded in drawing water from the well before: Everyone who had tried had been pulled under the water and drowned. When asked where he had got the water, the Apprentice told his masters what had happened at the well, finishing up by showing them the goblet. Their eyes lit up when they saw the goblet, for they instinctively knew that it was priceless and that they should be able to sell it for enough to be able to retire and live in luxury for the rest of their days.

All forty thieves and their apprentice set off for the nearest city, and there they showed the goblet to the city jeweler, who offered to take it to the king for an assessment of its value. The thieves agreed. The jeweler then took the goblet to the king, claiming that it had once been his property but had been stolen by a band of forty thieves and that those thieves now were trying to sell it back to him. The king lost no time in having the forty thieves and their apprentice brought before him. The Apprentice told the king how he had come to have the goblet and said that he would bring his majesty eleven more like it to prove that the jeweler was lying.

The king agreed and freed the Apprentice but detained the forty thieves in case the Apprentice did not keep his word. The thieves were thrown into the king's dungeons, and the Apprentice set out from the city to find eleven more goblets just like the one from the well, although in truth he had no idea where to go or what to do.

After several days' ride the Apprentice came to a large city. There he found all the people shuffling around with sorrowful expressions etched on their faces. When the Apprentice asked an old woman what the problem was, he was told that the king's only son had died and that every night his grave was defiled and the people had to rebury the dead prince the following day. The Apprentice quickly made his way to the palace and sought an audience with the king, telling him that he would guard the grave of the prince and ensure that it was never again tampered with.

The king told the Apprentice that he would give him whatever his heart desired if he could make that so. The Apprentice kept vigil over the grave through the night. On the stroke of midnight three doves flew down, settled by the grave, and discarded their feathers to become three beautiful maidens. One of the maidens took out a tablecloth and a crimson wand, and tapping the cloth, a banquet was instantly laid. Then the maiden went to the gravestone and tapped it with the wand. The ground opened up, and the prince stepped out of his grave and sat down to eat with the three Dove Maidens.

The Apprentice watched from his hiding place, and then, taking careful aim, he fired an arrow at the Dove Maidens. The maidens hastily donned their feathers again and flew away, leaving behind the tablecloth and the crimson wand. The Apprentice made himself known to the prince, gathered up the cloth and the wand, and had the prince return to his grave, promising to release him from death very shortly.

When the king and his ministers came to the grave in the morning they were delighted to find that everything was just as they had left it the evening before. The king was even more delighted when the Apprentice struck the grave with the wand and the prince climbed out and embraced his father. However, when the Apprentice asked for eleven golden goblets just like the one he had gotten from the well, the king told him that one such goblet was worth more than his entire kingdom and that he could not give the Apprentice what he wished. Saddened by this, the Apprentice would not accept anything else from the king, and instead he resumed his travels.

After several days' ride the Apprentice came to another city, where he found all the people starving. When he asked the king of that city what the problem was, he was told that their food had to be brought to the city by ship, but that whenever a ship entered the harbor, a hand would reach out from the water and sink it. The Apprentice asked for a small boat, and having provided a feast for the entire city thanks to the tablecloth, he rowed out into the harbor to await the next consignment of food.

He did not have to wait long before a fleet of forty merchant ships sailed toward the harbor mouth. As the first ship entered the harbor, the Apprentice saw a pale white hand rise out of the water, a golden bracelet around its wrist. The Apprentice took hold of the bracelet and pulled with all his might, and the bracelet slipped over the hand, which then disappeared beneath the waves. When all forty ships had been unloaded and the people of the city had collected their food, the Apprentice went to the king and asked for eleven golden goblets as his reward. The king said he could not grant the Apprentice's request but he did know where the Apprentice might find such goblets.

The following morning the Apprentice set sail with one of the merchant ships, and after a journey of seven days and seven nights they came to the island of the king of the houris. On the island was a beautiful palace. The Apprentice walked boldly up to it, knocked on the door, and entered. Inside he found an old man preparing a stew, an old man who told the Apprentice to hide, as the houris would soon return, and if they found him there, they would tear him to pieces.

Sure enough, moments after the Apprentice had hidden, three white doves flew down into the courtyard, discarded their feathers, and sat down to dine. During the meal the first houri toasted the Apprentice who had managed to acquire her golden goblet. The second toasted the Apprentice who had secured her tablecloth and crimson wand, and the third toasted the Apprentice who now held her bracelet. When the Apprentice heard these toasts in his name, he made himself known and was welcomed to their table.

After they had eaten, the three houris sat in sad and silent contemplation. When the Apprentice asked them what was wrong, they told him that they had a brother who had been taken captive by the giant Azrail, and that no one had ever been able to set him free. The Apprentice said he would gladly perform this task if they would reward him with the eleven goblets he needed to set the forty thieves free. They agreed and took the Apprentice to see their father, the king of the houris. When the king asked the Apprentice what he needed to undertake his quest, the Apprentice asked for a horse from the king's stables, the use of the king's sword, a bow and arrows, and a large steel mace. So equipped, the Apprentice rode out to find the lair of the giant Azrail, guided by the king's chamberlain. After several days' ride they came to the foot of Mount Djandjavaz, the home of the giant.

Leaving the chamberlain at the foot of the mountain, the Apprentice rode onward and upward until he came to a group of huge buildings. When he approached them, he found his way barred by the two huge servants of Azrail; but having no time for them, the Apprentice spurred his horse, and in one swift swing of his sword, decapitated them both. As their huge heads fell from their shoulders, the Apprentice caught them and threw them onto an overhead balcony. The noise awakened Azrail, who came out to see what all the commotion was about.

When Azrail saw the Apprentice and the dead bodies of his servants, he roared a challenge, quickly armed himself, and came out to meet the Apprentice carrying seven maces, seven swords, and a bow with seven arrows. The Apprentice neatly dodged the first mace thrown by Azrail, picked it up, and hurled it back, telling Azrail to have another go. The giant threw all seven of his maces, all seven of his swords, and fired all seven of his arrows, but they all missed the Apprentice. Seeing the giant totally devoid of weaponry, the Apprentice urged on his horse, and at the gallop, let fly with his mace, which caught Azrail on the side of the head and knocked him to the ground. In a flash, the Apprentice sliced off the giant's head with his sword and then cleaved it in two with a second mighty blow. The head pleaded to be cut in half again, but the Apprentice refused, for he knew that a third blow would restore Azrail to life.

Instead the Apprentice tethered his horse and entered the home of Azrail, where he found the son of the king of the houris bound in chains. With a single swipe of his sword, the Apprentice set him free, and the two returned to the king of the houris. En route the houri prince told the Apprentice to ask as his reward not only the goblets but also the hand of the prince's youngest sister as his bride, and the ring of the king of the houris.

The Apprentice did as he was advised, and he was duly rewarded and married. The following day the Apprentice and his new wife returned to the palace of the king who held the forty thieves in his dungeons, and presented him with the eleven goblets. Seeing that the jeweler had indeed been lying, the king summoned the jeweler and had him executed. Then the king, who was elderly and lacked an heir, abdicated in favor of the Apprentice, who made the forty thieves his chamberlains and ministers.

See also: Azrail; Djandjavaz, Mount; Dove Maidens, The; Ohan

References: Orbeli and Taronian 1959–67, vol. 1

APRAKSI(I)A
Russia
See Evpraksiya (~ia), Princess.

ARCONA
Baltic Coast
Located on the Baltic coastline, the site of the god Svantovit's chief temple. Here the god was depicted on a carved wooden pillar, in four aspects, holding a bull's-horn cup in his right hand. A white stallion, sacred to the god, was kept either in the temple itself or in the temple precincts, together with its saddle and bridle and Svantovit's sword and battle flag.

See also: Baltic; Svantovit (~dovit)

AREVHAT
Armenia
A beautiful maiden who was caught and brought to the royal palace for the sole purpose of being fed to Odz-Manouk, the serpentine son of an unnamed king and queen. Arevhat was lowered through the roof of the chamber in which Odz-Manouk was held, and the trapdoor was shut.

Later in the day the king went to look in on his son, and he was astonished to find the girl still alive. His astonishment turned to bewilderment when he saw that Odz-Manouk was no longer a dragon but a handsome prince, having been transformed when

Arevhat spoke kindly to him and showed no fear. Released from the chamber, it was not long before Odz-Manouk and Arevhat were married.

Some days later, Odz-Manouk asked his new wife just exactly who she was. She told him that she was an orphan and had not always been the radiant woman he saw before him. Once she had looked quite ordinary; but one day, while she sat sewing out in the hills, her bobbin fell down a narrow ravine and into a crevice. She reached down into the crevice and could not reach the bobbin; but she saw an old woman at the bottom who told her how to enter her home in order to retrieve it.

Where Arevhat was inside, however, the door disappeared, and the girl realized that she was in the presence of a witch. The witch first asked Arevhat to clean her home, which she did, and then to comb her hair. Arevhat did these tasks with kindness, and then she allowed the old woman to rest her head in her lap while the old woman slept, having first given Arevhat instructions to wake her when she saw yellow water flowing. Arevhat did as instructed. When the old hag was awakened, she took Arevhat by the ankles and plunged her into the yellow water. Then she sent her on her way, transformed into a radiant beauty; and so it happened that she was brought to the palace.

See also: Odz-Manouk

References: Orbeli and Taronian 1959–67, vol. 1

ARKHANGEL'SK
Russia

The home of Ivan Savel'evich. The city of Arkhangel'sk (also known in English as Archangel) is located on the flatlands of the northern branch of the river Dvina, 28 miles (45 km) from the point where the river flows into the White Sea. English merchants first occupied the area near the river's mouth—a former Norse settlement—in 1584. Originally called Novo-Kholmogory, the city was renamed in 1613 in honor of the archangel Michael. Surrounded by dense forestlands, Arkhangel'sk was for centuries sustained by its wood, fur, and leather industries.

See also: Dvina, River; Ivan Savel'evich; White Sea

ARMENIA
General

A country in the Caucasus mountain region. People lived in historic Armenia by 6,000 B.C., the earliest societies there probably being tribal groups that lived by farming or cattle raising. In the eighth century B.C., a union of several tribes formed the kingdom of Urartu, introduced irrigation, and built fortresses, palaces, and temples. In the sixth century B.C., ancestors of the Armenians migrated, probably from the west, to the Armenian Plateau, where they settled alongside the native population. The kingdom of Urartu was conquered by the Medes, a people from what is now Iran, in the fifth century B.C.

Soon after Urartu fell to the Medes, the Medes themselves were conquered by the Persians. Armenia remained under Persian and then Greek rule for hundreds of years, while managing to maintain a degree of autonomy. King Tigran II, who came to power in 95 B.C., built an independent Armenian kingdom that reached from the Caspian Sea to the Mediterranean Sea; but the Romans defeated Tigran in 55 B.C., and Armenia became a part of the Roman Empire. In the early third century A.D., Armenia became the first nation to adopt Christianity as its state religion. The Armenian alphabet was developed in the early fifth century A.D. by an Armenian cleric, and in 451 the Armenians, under Vartan Mamikonian, defended their religion against the Persians in the Battle of Avarair.

Arabs conquered Armenia in the seventh century A.D., and in 884, an independent Armenian kingdom was established in the northern part of the region. Seljuk Turks conquered the country in the mid-eleventh century, but Armenians established a new state in Cilicia on the Mediterranean coast—the last Armenian kingdom, which fell to invading Mamluks (a powerful political class that dominated Egypt from the thirteenth century until their massacre in 1811) in 1375.

By 1514, the Ottoman Empire had gained control of Armenia, and it would rule western Armenia until its defeat in World War I, in 1918. Persia gained control of eastern Armenia in 1639 and ruled it until 1828, when the region was annexed by Russia. It became independent in 1991, after nearly 70 years as a part of the Soviet Union, and today it is a member of the Commonwealth of Independent States, a loose association of former Soviet republics.

See also: Caspian Sea; Caucasus; Russia

ARTHUR, KING
General
Semimythologized, legendary ruler of Britain whose exploits with the Knights of the

Head of King Arthur, from The Beautiful Fountain *(Germanisches Nationalmuseum, Nuremberg, Germany; Scala/Art Resource, NY)*

Round Table are known throughout the world. The only connection between King Arthur and the heroes (legendary or otherwise) of Russian and Slavic myth and legend stems from the similarity of a story told of Batradz, a hero of the Alans, as well as a possible connection to the Serbian Prince Marko, who, it is said, lies asleep awaiting a time when his services are once more required.

Although the similarities in these stories may be purely coincidental, it is commonly assumed that either the legend of Arthur was carried to Slavic regions by Roman soldiers or the stories of Batradz were taken to Britain and subsequently attached to the already growing folklore regarding King Arthur. The connection between Arthur and Prince Marko is more tenuous: In this case, it seems likely that the legend of King Arthur led to that of Marko's enchanted sleep until the time of his country's greatest need.

See also: Alans; Batradz; Marko, Prince

AS-IGA
Siberia—Ostyak
"Old Man of the Ob'," a benevolent water spirit venerated by the Ostyak people who lived beside the great Siberian river.

See also: Ostyaks; Siberia

ASKOLD
Scandinavia and Russia
According to Russian tradition as recorded in the *Primary Chronicle,* internal dissension and feuds among the Eastern Slavs around Novgorod became so violent that they voluntarily chose to call upon a foreign prince who could unite them into one strong state. Their choice was Riurik, or Ryurik, a Scandinavian (or Varangian) chief, who in 862 became ruler of Novgorod. Two other Scandinavians, Dir and Askold, possibly legendary figures, gained control of Kiev. Later, the cities of Novgorod and Kiev were united under a common ruler.

See also: Dir; Kiev; Novgorod; *Primary Chronicle;* Riurik

ASLAN
Armenia

"Lion," the third name by which Zurab was known (after Zuro). Aslan is also the name of a king, the father of Gulinaz in the story of Samson. It is quite possible that the two Aslans are one and the same, although this can be neither proved nor disproved.

See also: Gulinaz; Samson; Zurab
References: Orbeli and Taronian 1959–67, vol. 4

ASTLIK
Armenia

A star, also described as the goddess of stars, and the wife of the god Vahagn. The couple's marriage might be interpreted as incestuous, as Vahagn created the stars.

See also: Vahagn

ASTRAKHAN'
General

A city on the Volga River delta, in southwestern Russia. The city, which extends onto several islands in the delta, is an important trading center because of its direct connections by waterway with ports on the Caspian Sea and the Volga River. Like Moscow, Astrakhan' is dominated by an old fortress, a kremlin. Astrakhan' once served as the capital of a Tatar state. The Mongol conqueror Tamerlane (1336–1405) destroyed the capital in 1395. However, it was later rebuilt, and in 1556, Ivan Groznyi captured the city and made it part of Russia.

See also: Caspian Sea; Ivan Groznyi; Kremlin; Mongols; Moscow; Tatars; Volga

ATHOS, MOUNT
Serbia

Serbian mountain where legend records that the body of Prince Marko was buried by a priest who came across the corpse beside the burial place of Sarac. It is also said by some to be the place where Prince Marko simply sleeps and awaits his return to the land of the living.

See also: Marko, Prince; Sarac

ATRIMPAASA
Scythia

The goddess of the moon.

AURORA BOREALIS
Russia

Nainas, the personification of this familiar and spectacular natural phenomenon, was betrothed to Niekia. However, the two were never married, due to the intervention of Peivalké and his father, the sun.

See also: Nainas; Niekia; Peivalké; Sun

AURORAS
Russia

The two primary stars, Zvezda Dennitsa and Zvezda Vechernyaya (Morning Star and Evening Star), daughters and attendants of Dazhbog and sisters to the two—some say three—Zoryi.

See also: Dazhbog; Evening Star; Morning Star; Zoryi; Zvezda Dennitsa; Zvezda Vechernyaya

AUSEKLIS
Baltic

The deification of the planet Venus seen in the morning sky shortly before sunrise, known as Auseklis in Latvia and as Ausrine in Lithuania.

See also: Morning Star; Venus

AUSRINE
Lithuania
See Auseklis.

AUTRIMPAS
Prussia

The god of seas and of lakes.

AVARS
General

A Mongolian people who conquered (c. A.D. 461) the Uighurs, a Turkic tribe sometimes called the pseudo-Avars, and with the Uighurs formed an alliance on the Volga steppes (in what later would be Russia). In the middle of the sixth century this confed-

The Northern Lights (Aurora Borealis) on a moonlit night (Abe Black/Archive Photos)

eration was almost annihilated by the Turks. The survivors, mostly Uighurs led by Avar chiefs, took the name of Avars and split into two bodies. One part remained in eastern Europe. The other moved westward until they reached the river Danube and settled in Dacia, whence they initiated raids of conquest.

At the end of the sixth century the territory of the Dacian Avars extended from the river Volga to the Baltic Sea, and they exacted enormous tribute from the Byzantine Empire. During this period, under Baian, their khagan, or khan, they were possibly the greatest power in Europe, and tremendously influenced the later development of a large part of Europe by driving most of the Western Slavs to the areas they have occupied ever since. After the death of Baian, the power of the western Avars declined under strikes by the Slavs and Bulgars, and in 795 and 796 they were crushed by Charlemagne (742–814). Later

they were almost completely exterminated by the Moravians, the survivors being absorbed by the Slavic peoples.

Of the Avars who remained in eastern Europe very little is known. However, the available evidence indicates that one of the twenty-seven Lezghian tribes of Dagestan, Russia, might be their descendants. Estimated to number more than 150,000, these modern Avars are Muslims and speak a language similar to Arabic.

See also: Byzantine Empire; Caucasus; Danube; Khan; Moravia; Volga

AVDOT'YA
Russia

The wife of Mikhail Potyk. The couple made a pact that if one of them died, the other would join the deceased in the tomb. Avdot'ya died first, and true to his word, her husband was lowered into the tomb beside her. First, however, he took the precaution of having a rope connected to the church bell so that if he changed his mind, he might summon assistance and be released.

Lighting a candle, Mikhail Potyk settled down beside the body of his dead wife in silent vigil. Around midnight a great many snakes entered the tomb, one of which turned out to be a fire-breathing dragon. Unafraid, Mikhail Potyk cut off its head and rubbed the body of his dead wife with it. Avdot'ya instantly came back to life. Mikhail then rang the church bell, and he and his wife were released to enjoy many more years together.

See also: Dragon; Mikhail Potyk

AZERBAIJAN
General

Azerbaijan is the most populous and the least urbanized of the three Transcaucasian republics (the other two being Georgia and Armenia). The official language of Azerbaijan is Azeri, a Turkic language of the Ural-Altaic family. Russian is also commonly spoken, although its use is declining. The traditional religion of the Azeris is Shiite Islam, which has experienced a revival in recent years. Orthodox Christianity is practiced to varying degrees among the Georgian, Armenian, and Slavic minorities.

The area of Azerbaijan was settled from about the eighth century B.C. by the Medes, and the region later became a part of the Persian Empire. A much-disputed territory, it was conquered in the late seventh century A.D. by Arabs, who introduced the Islamic culture. Turkic tribes controlled the area during the eleventh and twelfth centuries. Azerbaijan once again came under Persian control in the seventeenth century and was ceded by Persia to Russia through treaties in

Azerbaijani interior ministry special forces patrol an ancient Muslim cemetery outside Kazakh, Azerbaijan, 14 May 1991. (Reuters/Archive Photos)

1813 and 1828. In 1918, following the Russian Revolution, Azerbaijan became an independent state; and in 1920 it united with Georgia and Armenia to form the Transcaucasian Soviet Federated Socialist Republic (SFSR). When the Transcaucasian republic was dissolved in 1936, Azerbaijan became a constituent republic of the USSR. The collapse of communism in the USSR in 1991 led to the reassertion of Azerbaijan's political independence. The new republic joined the United Nations in 1992.

See also: Armenia; Georgia; Transcaucasia

AZNAVOR
Armenia

Mysterious demon defeated by Badikan. Little is known about his origins, his character, or his deeds, as the legend offers no details.

See also: Badikan
References: Khatchatrian 1933

AZOV, SEA OF
General

A large, shallow inland sea bounded by Ukraine and Russia. The Sea of Azov is connected to the Black Sea by the Kerch Strait and covers about 14,500 square miles (37,550 square kilometers). Its maximum depth is only about 48 feet (15 meters). Its western end is called the *Sivash,* or Putrid Lake, because of the numerous foul-smelling marshes and lagoons there—lagoons that yield important chemicals for industry. The Don River flows into the Gulf of Taganrog, which lies at the northeastern end of the sea.

See also: Black Sea; Don; Ukraine

AZRAIL
Armenia

A giant who lived on Mount Djandjavaz and who captured the brother of the three houris. Although many tried, none managed to defeat the giant. When the Apprentice heard of the plight of the houris' brother, he said that he would defeat the giant and release the captive, provided the brothers gave him eleven golden goblets, which he needed to free his friends. The houris agreed and took the Apprentice to see their father, who equipped the Apprentice with a horse, a bow and arrows, the king's sword, and a large steel mace. Thus outfitted, the Apprentice was led to the foot of Mount Djandjavaz by the king's chamberlain. Riding ahead alone, the Apprentice quickly killed the two giant servants of Azrail. The noise of battle woke Azrail, who came out of his huge castle to see what was going on.

When he saw the bodies of his servants, Azrail roared a challenge and quickly armed himself with seven maces, seven swords, and a bow with seven arrows. The Apprentice neatly dodged the first mace thrown by Azrail, picked it up, and hurled it back, telling Azrail to have another go. The giant threw all seven of his maces, all seven of his swords, and fired all seven of his arrows, but they all missed the Apprentice. Seeing the giant totally devoid of weaponry, the Apprentice spurred on his horse, and at the gallop, let fly his mace, which caught Azrail on the side of the head and knocked him to the ground. In a flash, the Apprentice sliced off the giant's head with his sword and then cleaved it in two with a second mighty blow. The head pleaded to be cut in half again but the Apprentice refused, for he knew that a further blow would restore Azrail to life.

See also: Apprentice, The; Djandjavaz, Mount; Houri
References: Orbeli and Taronian 1959–67.

BABA

Poland

"Old woman," the name given to the last sheaf harvested. Also, the spirit that was believed to live in this last sheaf. Sometimes the sheaf was composed of twelve smaller sheaves lashed together, the women racing each other as each bound her smaller sheaf, because the one who finished last was certain to have a child the next year. The Lithuanian counterpart is the Boba.

See also: Boba

BABA LATINGORKA

Russia

A sorceress related to the dragon Goryshche, she appeared to Dobrynya Nikitich in the guise of an old hag and challenged him to a fight, armed with a sword and lance that reached into the skies. Two versions exist of the fight. In one, Dobrynya was mortally wounded by Baba Latingorka and died in shame. In the second, he did not die until his wound had been avenged by Il'ya Muromets, who defeated the hag. Many authorities believe that Baba Latingorka is an incarnation of that most terrible of all Russian witches, Baba-Yaga.

See also: Baba-Yaga (-Jaga, -Iaga); Dobrynya Nikitich; Dragon; Goryninka; Goryshche; Il'ya Muromets
References: Astakhova 1938–51; Evgen'eva and Putilov 1977; Speranskii 1916

BABA-YAGA (-JAGA, -IAGA)

Russia

Possibly the best known of all Slavic legendary characters, this witch is known as Ienzababa or Jezda in Poland, and Jazi Baba to the Czechs (*baba* meaning "old woman" and *yaga* being Russian for "hag"). Baba-Yaga is usually portrayed as malevolent, but she is occasionally a benefactress. Like most Russian witches, Baba-Yaga is an immortal shape-changer, a true sorceress with a deep knowledge of everything in the world (the Russian word for witch, *ved'ma,* comes from the root *ved',* meaning "to know"). Baba-Yaga is the personification of death; she is the Devil's handmaiden. She is never portrayed as a goddess, for she is far too earthly to be considered a true deity. Yet in her earliest form, she displayed an aspect of the Great Goddess, the patron goddess of women, benevolent to all. Not until the Christian era was she downgraded to a fearsome witch, and even then she retained a wide following among women.

Post-Christian legends provide evidence of the importance of Baba-Yaga to women. One story says that an old couple had a daughter but could find no godmother for her. After much searching, they found an old woman who said she would act as the child's godmother. This old woman then revealed herself as Baba-Yaga and spirited the girl away to live with her. The girl later committed some unrecorded crime against Baba-Yaga, who, rather than eating the child as she would have done in pre-Christian stories, simply exiled her into the dark forest. There the girl was found by a prince who was out hunting. He took her back to his kingdom, where she subsequently bore him three sons, each with the moon and stars upon his forehead. Learning of her goddaughter's whereabouts, Baba-Yaga appeared, demanding that the three children be given her as expiation for the girl's misdeeds. She then made off not

A turn-of-the-century illustration of the Russian witch Baba-Yaga (Sovfoto)

only with the children but also with their mother. The prince, predictably distraught, set out to find them. After some time, he came to a clearing in the forest. In the clearing a bright fire was burning around which all manner of animals were gathered, blocking his passage. In the center, next to the fire, sat Baba-Yaga with the prince's wife and three sons. The prince pleaded to be admitted, but the animals let him pass only after the prince's wife asked Baba-Yaga's permission. The hag allowed the prince to carry off his three sons but not his wife. As the story developed, Baba-Yaga came to be equated with Mary, Mother of God, and the forest home of the witch became the kingdom of heaven.

The oldest surviving stories of Baba-Yaga suggest that she is an ancient deity with origins perhaps as long ago as Paleolithic times, when she was the patroness of herds and herdsmen, the goddess of horses, and the patron goddess of farmers and farming. Her oldest personification, however, is as mistress of all animals, a bird goddess as reflected by the chicken legs on her house, with which she is as one.

Although unnamed in the story of Ivan the Pea, the old crone who lives in the forest in a strange house that revolves in the wind is none other than Baba-Yaga. In that story she is far from the malevolent witch; but maybe even Baba-Yaga realized that she would have been no match for Ivan the Pea.

Almost every story about Baba-Yaga describes her dwelling as a cottage in the most remote and inaccessible part of a deep forest, which makes her the *khoziaika lesa* ("mistress of the forest"). This cottage sits on four sets of hen's legs, one at each corner, and revolves either freely in the wind or when some unheard word is spoken. Some versions of the legend say that the cottage was not fixed to the ground and could run around on its hen's legs. Others say that the hen's legs were simply supports for the four corners and that the center of the house was fixed on the spindle of a spinning-wheel, indicating

that Baba-Yaga also spins the thread of life from the bones and entrails of the dead. Any hero who looked inside the cottage would be likely to find Baba-Yaga crammed into every corner of the house, with her nose pressed hard against the roof.

Descriptions of Baba-Yaga vary widely. Some describe her only as an old crone and leave the details to imagination. Others describe her as an aged, ugly crone who is so emaciated that she is little more than skin and bone. Her teeth are long and very sharp, occasionally made of iron, and sometimes her canines are so long that they protrude over her lips. Her teeth need to be sharp, for Baba-Yaga is a cannibal, one gaze from her eyes usually being enough to petrify her victims—either turning them temporarily to stone so that she could take them home, unpetrify them, and eat them, or simply immobilizing them with fear. Her hair is a tangled mass of writhing snakes. This aspect, like her petrifying eyes, suggests a classical Greek influence, for these are both essential attributes of the Gorgon Medusa. Her nose and her breasts are made of iron. The bones of her victims form the gate and fence that surround her home, each post being adorned with a human skull, the eyes of which light up at night. These bones are symbolic not only of Baba-Yaga's association with death but also of her role as the source of new life, which she brews from the bones of the dead. Her soup often contains leftover body parts, such as fingers, toes, and eyes. The house itself is also said by some to be made of human bones, with legs for doorposts, hands for the bolts, and a mouth with razor-sharp teeth for the lock. Others say that these parts are associated only with the bone fence and that Baba Yaga's house resembles any other peasant hut—apart from its chicken leg supports.

In her benevolent guise, Baba-Yaga appears as a normal, aged peasant woman with luxuriant hair and a kindly face and disposition, and as often as not, wears the traditional headdress of a married woman. Her dualistic aspects are not as clearly defined as might be expected. Baba-Yaga is an immensely complex character who is perhaps best described as triune rather than dualistic, each of her three aspects perhaps best equated to the three Fates of classical Greece. In her first aspect, as a fertility goddess, she is benevolent, bringing new life into the world. In her second aspect she maps out the course of human life and is both benevolent and malevolent. In her third aspect she determines the date of human death, the role in which she is most commonly regarded. In her triune state, Baba-Yaga hovers over the birth of every new life, immediately threatening to take it back again. She has the power to send life into the earth and to recall it. She is the most terrible of the regenerative fertility deities, for she appears prone to fits of passion and whim. She demands the sacrifice of a child in return for wealth, for she, like the classical Pluto, controls all the riches of the earth. Baba-Yaga is thus a chthonic earth deity who encompasses life from conception through birth and life to death, and beyond—although her role in the underworld is merely that of guardian: According to her pleasure, she may redistribute souls to newborns or keep them in the underworld for all eternity, never to be reborn.

Some commentators insist that the bones around Baba-Yaga's house indicate that she has a very strong connection with the spirit world. Some even go so far as to say that her house guards the point where the two worlds—the world of the living and that of the dead—meet. This may explain why in some cases she is benevolent to humans, her purpose being not to send people into the afterlife but rather, like the Greek Cerberus, to stop the dead from escaping. Others say that she is a portrayal of the gates of hell themselves, lying in wait for her victims with her jaws agape, swallowing any who are unfortunate enough to seek shelter in her mouth with its razor-sharp iron teeth.

Baba-Yaga possesses truly awesome power, for time itself is in her hands: The Sun, the Day and Night, obey her implicitly, as do all the laws of nature. She controls the weather, an aspect she shares with Russian witches in general, and can devour the sun and moon, cause crops to grow or perish, and regulate the flow of milk from cows in the same way as she regulates the rainfall. She also has connections with the leshii, for she, like the wood sprite, kidnaps small children and wields power over the forest and the animals that live in it. In another aspect she is regarded as the guardian of the fountain that supplies the Water of Life and Death. She rides through the air in a mortar instead of the customary broomstick of the pan-European witch, propelling herself forward with a pestle and brushing away all evidence of her passage with a birch broom. The mortar and pestle represent the destructive and the protective aspects of Baba-Yaga, for Slavic peoples traditionally used these implements not only to grind grain (the destructive aspect) but also to prepare flax for spinning (the protective aspect). Perhaps unsurprisingly, the mortar and pestle also represent the human reproductive organs. Thus, the two objects are symbols of all three phases of human life—birth, life, and death—and thus of all three aspects of the triune deity. All evidence of Baba-Yaga's passage through human lives is swept away with a birch broom—a broom that may be regarded as further evidence of her all-pervading influence, a symbol of the inverted Tree of Life, reaching downward. Baba-Yaga rides the skies generating and nurturing life before sweeping it away again with the broom. As would befit a powerful fertility deity, Baba-Yaga has hordes of children, although their names are never revealed. They are all as strange as their mother—from the reptiles, animals, and spirits that cohabit with her, to her forty mare-daughters.

The mare-daughters appear in one story where a young man is told that he must travel to Baba-Yaga's home to secure a horse that will help him release his bride Maria Morena, who has been taken prisoner by some unnamed captor. When the young man arrives at the home of the witch he is confronted by the bone fence that surrounds it. On closer inspection, however, the young man sees that one spike on the fence has no skull on top. As he is inspecting the fence he is confronted by the witch, who informs him that the last picket has been reserved for his skull, although he can escape death and obtain what he came for if he completes a simple task—controlling the forty mare-daughters for twenty-four hours. Needless to say, the hero of this story completes the task, receives a supernaturally empowered steed from the witch, and completes his quest to free his bride.

Although Baba-Yaga may essentially be regarded as a feminine deity, she is equally at home in the world of men. She carries a wand with which she can transform herself and those at whom she directs its power, and she rules over the male genitalia. She is also more likely to appear in her benevolent guise to men than to women. She owns a fire-breathing, flying horse, giving her an aspect as the horse goddess, as well as a self-directing, self-cutting sword, both items being more readily lent to men than to women. She also will lend other, feminine articles to deserving youths, such as mirrors, rings, and balls of yarn. Baba-Yaga is also the patroness of wandering minstrels, for she owns a self-playing *gusli* that some allude to as the first instrument of the type ever made.

With links to the werewolf and vampire, Baba-Yaga and her kind, the volkhvy (seers), would perform their chief rites and cause the most trouble at midsummer, the same time that the female elders of villages would go into the fields at night to look for medicinal herbs and other plants. Baba-Yaga is the wolf goddess who devours all who try to enter her sphere. She induces nightmares and hallucinations as well as deadly diseases, all three relating to her role as the goddess of death and the underworld. She also is asso-ciated with the bear, who sometimes replaces her in the role of master of the forest, and the serpent—both animals to be feared and respected. She demands human sacrifice from her supplicants in return for the sustenance of life.

In Russian legend, Baba-Yaga is closely associated with serpents and dragons. Koshchei the Deathless, whose name derives from *kost'* ("bone"), is a dragon in human guise, his destiny and all he does guided by the dualistic aspects of Baba-Yaga. She confers on him immortality but also gives him a soul, thus making him mortal. Baba-Yaga is also the controlling force behind the multi-headed, fire-breathing dragon Chudo-Yudo, who sits watch over the Water of Life and Death, a role that has often led Chudo-Yudo to be considered a bizarre offspring of the witch and thus a brother to the forty mare-daughters.

In Belorussia, Baba-Yaga and her associates are held to drain the energy of the sun with their magical fires, destroy plants, and turn the power of the earth against mankind. Thus, in this region at least, Baba-Yaga and her sisterhood are seen as being in control of the elements of the earth. If humanity does not please or placate them, then Baba-Yaga and her kind will use their awesome powers to turn the earth itself against those it is meant to support.

One particular story, that of Vasilissa the Beautiful, clearly demonstrates both the malevolent and benevolent sides of Baba-Yaga and her powers. In this story the witch assigns the poor girl impossible tasks, telling her that she will be eaten if she fails; but when Vasilissa has completed all of the tasks, Baba-Yaga gives her a magical skull that rids her of her cruel stepmother and stepsisters. Another story about a Vasilissa—Vasilissa the Wise—demonstrates the compassionate nature of Baba-Yaga: In this story the witch tells Ivan the Young how he might regain his wife, Vasilissa the Wise, and keep her forever.

See also: Chudo-Yudo; Day; Devil, The; Dragon; Great Goddess; Ienzababa; Ivan the

Pea; Ivan the Young; Jazi Baba; Jezda; Khoziaika lesa; Koshchei (the Deathless); Leshii (~y); Maria Morena; Moon; Night; Sun; Tree of Life, The; Underworld, The; Vampire; Vasilis(s)a the Beautiful; Vasilis(s)a the Wise; Volkhv; Water of Life and Death, The; Werewolf
References: Afanas'ev 1974, Baroja 1964; Dal' 1957; 1957, and 1865–69; Matorin 1931; Newell 1973; Snegirev 1839; Wosien 1969; Zemtsovskii 1970

BAB'E LETO
Russia
Indian summer (literally, "old woman's summer"), a period of the Russian agrarian cycle that started officially on Saint Simon's Day (1 September), after the harvest, and culminated in the Pokrovskaia Subbota in October. Bab'e leto was marked by several significant household events: Old fires were extinguished and new ones laid and lit by the mistress in honor of the ancestral spirits. The dead were remembered, new spinning was started, new beer was brewed, and marriages were arranged. Although most of these rituals (e.g., the lighting of fires) were observed only on Saint Simon's Day, the "old woman's summer" would run throughout September, right up to the Pokrovskaia Subbota—the Feast of the Intercession, or Day of Protection. Bab'e leto was also a time when rulers would go out among the people, seeking their renewed support.
See also: Pokrovskaia Subbota
References: Snegirev 1837–39; Zabylin 1880; Zemtsovskii 1970

BAB'IA KASHA
Russia
"Old woman's gruel," the day after Koliada, on which a Russian family would eat a meal of *kut'ia* specially prepared in the bathhouse so that the family would receive the blessings of a good harvest, direct from the spirits of their ancestors. The *kut'ia* was a type of mush made of eggs and grain—foods symbolic of rebirth. In Ukraine the festival centered on a rite in which the entire family drank *kut'ia* from a horned vessel.

See also: Koliada
References: Propp 1963; Sokolov 1945

BABII PRAZDNIK
Russia
"Old woman's holiday." An alternative name for Radunitsa, used widely in Kievan Rus'. Babii Prazdnik, celebrated near Easter time, was dedicated to the god Rod and included a feast prepared and eaten in honor of the dead. During this feast, women decorated eggs—a practice that was incorporated during Christian times into the festival of Easter—and placed them on the graves of deceased ancestors, symbolizing rebirth.
See also: Radunitsa; Rod(ú)
References: Snegirev 1839; Sokolov 1945; Zabylin 1880

BABUSHKA-LYAGUSHKA-SKAKUSHKA
Russia
"Grandmother Hopping Frog," the frog that lived in the Green Marsh and was asked by Baba-Yaga to help Petrushka in his quest to find the place I-Know-Not-Where and the thing I-Know-Not-What. Babushka-Lyagushka-Skakushka said that she would help Petrushka, provided he carry her in a jug of fresh milk to the River of Fire, for she was old, and without the rejuvenating powers of that river, she would not have the strength. Baba-Yaga agreed and took the frog back to her home in her pestle and mortar. There she prepared a jug of fresh milk, placed the frog in the jug, woke her son-in-law, and told him what to do.

Petrushka took the jug with the frog in it, mounted Baba-Yaga's swiftest horse, and within a matter of a few minutes, stood beside the River of Fire. There Petrushka let the frog out of the jug and placed her on the ground. Placing one foot in the River of Fire, Babushka-Lyagushka-Skakushka started to grow until she was the size of Petrushka's horse. The frog told the archer to climb on her back and hold tight, which Petrushka did, while the frog continued to grow until she was taller than the tallest tree in any forest. The frog made sure that Petrushka was holding on tightly, and then she leaped through the air, landing in a foreign land and breathing out slowly until she resumed her normal size.

Babushka-Lyagushka-Skakushka informed Petrushka that they were now in I-Know-Not-Where. The frog then told Petrushka that he should go to the lowliest hut in a nearby village and hide there behind the stove, for within that hut lived I-Know-Not-What. Petrushka thanked Babushka-Lyagushka-Skakushka and set off. He found the hut with little difficulty and hid himself inside as instructed.

Though the legend does not say so, it is reasonable to assume that after delivering Petrushka to his desired destination, Babushka-Lyagushka-Skakushka returned to the Green Marsh.

See also: Baba-Yaga (-Jaga, -Iaga); Green Marsh; I-Know-Not-What; I-Know-Not-Where; Petrushka; River of Fire, The

BADIKAN

Armenia

The youngest of the forty sons of an unnamed king. As each son came of age, the king sent him off to a distant land to prove his worth and find a wife. Finally it was Badikan's turn to be likewise dispatched. The King gave him a sword, a bow and arrows, money and servants, and a magnificent horse, and then gave Badikan his blessing and sent him on his way.

Badikan traveled far and wide. He crossed the Kingdom of Darkness and the Kingdom of Light. He did battle with Agog-Magog and the demon Aznavor, overcoming them and many other beasts both natural and supernatural. However, his servants all were killed in these battles and his money was spent by the time he reached an enormous palace. The palace had been built in a time before man walked upon the earth, and it was so large that it would have taken Badikan a week to scale its walls.

As he wondered who might own such a building, the sun was blotted out by the shape of an enormous giant making its way toward the palace, a giant with armor of steel, a casque (helmet) and shoes of bronze, and a bow and arrows of wrought iron. As the giant reached the gates to his castle he stopped, sniffed, and proclaimed that he could smell human flesh. Unafraid, Badikan stepped out of the shadows and made himself known to the giant. The giant in turn introduced himself as Khan Boghu.

Badikan replied that he had heard of Khan Boghu and had traveled to his land to do battle with him. Khan Boghu laughed and told Badikan that if he were that great a warrior, perhaps it would be better if they became friends. Badikan laughed and agreed that he would live with the giant as his companion.

The following morning Khan Boghu told Badikan that he had a problem with which Badikan might be able to help. In the Kingdom of the East there lived a king whose daughter was the most beautiful maiden in all the world, and Khan Boghu had fallen in love with her. If Badikan could bring him the maiden, Badikan would be rewarded. Badikan assented, and armed and provisioned by Khan Boghu, he set off.

In the Kingdom of the East, Badikan found employment as a gardener in the palace gardens, and there he caught his first glimpse of the princess. Immediately he was smitten by her beauty, and she too, guessing that he was far more than a gardener, fell in love with Badikan. However, as the city was heavily fortified to protect it against attack, Badikan could not hope to escape with the princess. She, however, said that she would travel beyond the city walls, and there she would allow Badikan to abduct her.

Thus it was that several days later the princess left the city with a retinue of forty handmaidens. Badikan waited until the party was crossing a river in single file, and then he swooped down, plucked the princess from her mount, and sped off into the mountains with her, hiding her safely before returning to dispose of the soldiers sent by her father to track them down.

The princess was overjoyed to be in the company of Badikan, but her joy turned to despair when Badikan admitted that he had abducted her at the request of Khan Boghu. However, the princess gained a stay of marriage when she told Khan Boghu that she had promised her parents that she would refrain from marrying for seven years—a delay that Khan Boghu gladly consented to. From then on both the princess and Badikan conspired to discover why Khan Boghu remained invulnerable to all weapons.

The princess settled into a routine of appearing loving and caring toward Khan Boghu, and it wasn't long before Khan Boghu lapsed into a false sense of security. One night, while Khan Boghu was glowing in the light of the princess's compliments, he dropped his guard and told her that he could not be killed because he did not carry his seven souls with him. Those seven souls were hidden inside seven sparrows that could not be caught. The sparrows, in turn, were secure inside a mother-of-pearl box that could not be opened, and the box was inside a fox that could not be caught. If that were not enough, the fox was inside an ox that could not be overcome, and thus he was safe for all time.

When Khan Boghu went hunting the following day, the princess told Badikan how he might find Khan Boghu's soul and thus kill him. When Khan Boghu returned, Badikan asked whether he might be allowed to travel on an adventure, promising to return when he had satisfied his need, for he was bored doing nothing in Khan Boghu's palace. Khan Boghu consented, and Badikan made his farewells to the princess and set off on his fabulous horse.

His first stop was at the home of a group of sorcerers who told him that the ox could be overcome with seven barrels of strong wine. So equipped, Badikan rode for many days until he found the huge ox. Hiding behind some rocks, Badikan left the seven open barrels of wine in the open, and when the ox had drained them and had fallen into a drunken stupor, Badikan leaped forward and cut off its head. As the head fell, Khan Boghu, who was out hunting, stumbled and fell, and instantly he knew that the princess had betrayed him and the ox was dead. Khan Boghu staggered to his feet and hurried back to his palace as quickly as he could, considering the pain he was suffering for the very first time. Seeing him coming, the princess fled to the rooftops, fully intending to throw herself to her death if the need arose.

Badikan, meanwhile, had cut open the ox, caught the fox by its tail, and cut off its head. As the head rolled from the fox, blood began to flow freely from Khan Boghu's nose. Badikan then cut open the fox, took out the mother-of-pearl box, and broke its lock. As the lock broke, Khan Boghu began to cough up blood. Badikan then let out the seven sparrows. He strangled the first two, and Khan Boghu fell to his knees. He strangled two more, and Khan Boghu's arms and legs grew numb. He strangled two more, and Khan Boghu's heart and liver burst. Then Badikan caught the last sparrow and crushed it in his hands, and as he did, all life left Khan Boghu in a cloud of black smoke.

Badikan then hurried back to the princess. A few days later they were married, and for the rest of their days they ruled Khan Boghu's domain together.

This story should be compared with that of Koshchei the Deathless, for he too had his soul hidden outside his body so that he might remain invulnerable, and like Khan Boghu, he was tricked by a woman's wiles into revealing his secret.

See also: Agog-Magog; Aznavor; Boghu, Khan; Kingdom of Darkness, The; Kingdom of Light, The; Kingdom of the East, The; Koshchei (the Deathless)
References: Khatchatrian 1933

BADNIK
Russia—Novgorod Province
The name given to the log ritually burned to bring the Koliada festivities to a close.

The burning of the log symbolized death and rebirth, the sun, and the ancestors of the people.

See also: Koliada

References: Afanas'ev 1869

BAGPUTYS

Lithuania

A sea god who is particularly associated with storms, Bagputys rides the choppy seas in a boat with a golden anchor.

BALD MOUNTAINS

Russia

A mountain range near Kiev. In the legend of Ivan the Pea, these mountains were said to mark the boundary of the kingdom of the dragon that carried off Ivan's sister, Vasilissa of the Golden Braid, and killed his two brothers.

See also: Dragon; Ivan the Pea; Kiev; Vasilis(s)a of the Golden Braid

BALKAN(S)

General

The Balkan peninsula, located in southeastern Europe, stretches from the Black and the Aegean Seas in the east to the Adriatic and Ionian Seas to the west, and is bounded by the Mediterranean to the south. The plural form of the name refers to the lands that make up the region: Slovenia, Croatia, Bosnia and Herzegovina, Serbia and Montenegro, Albania, continental Greece, southeast Romania, Bulgaria, European Turkey, and the former Yugoslav Republic of Macedonia. The peninsula is linked to the rest of Europe by an isthmus that is 750 miles (1,200 km) wide between Rijeka on the west, and the mouth of the river Danube on the Black Sea to the east—a strategically important route from the Mediterranean Sea to the Black Sea.

The Balkans have been inhabited since c. 200,000 B.C. By the seventh millennium B.C., a distinctive Stone Age culture had evolved in the region. The peninsula was settled around 3,500 B.C. by seminomadic farmers from the Russian steppes, and later, sometime during the Bronze Age (c. 2,000–500 B.C.), by Celts. The Slavic peoples first arrived in the region around the third century A.D., and migrated to the peninsula in large numbers in the sixth century. There they were joined by Bulgar tribes during the seventh century, the Bulgars eventually assimilating with the Slavs. Slavic, Magyar, and Germanic settlements evolved in comparative isolation due to natural barriers of communication, and as a result, each of these groups developed its own religion, language, and customs. All suffered periodic persecution by the Turks. During the Byzantine era (395–1453), a form of Orthodox Christianity was established in parts of the Balkans, while Islam spread in those regions held by the Turks. From the late Middle Ages on, the Ottoman Turks gradually took control of almost the entire peninsula; but the balance of power in the Balkans changed again after the siege of Vienna (1683), when the Ottoman Turks were driven back by the Austrian Habsburgs and by Russia, both powers seeking access to the seas surrounding the peninsula.

In the nineteenth century, one Balkan nation after another developed strong nationalist movements, forcing Turkey to concede a degree of autonomy to each constituent nation. The Balkan League of 1912 was formed to counter Turkish rule in the area, and this led to the Balkan Wars. Two years later Pan-Slavism contributed to the outbreak of World War I when the heir presumptive to the Austrian emperor was assassinated at Sarajevo by a young Serbian nationalist named Gavril Princip. After World War I ended in 1918 and the Ottoman Empire was dismantled, Bosnia and Herzegovina, Croatia, Slavonia, and Carniola united with Serbia and Montenegro to form the Kingdom of the Serbs, Croats, and Slovenes, which was later renamed Yugoslavia.

See also: Black Sea; Bosnia; Bulgaria; Croatia; Danube; Herzegovina; Macedonia;

Magyars; Montenegro; Romania; Serbia; Slovenia

BALTIC
General
Name given to a sea and a geographical region. The Baltic Sea is a large, shallow arm of the North Sea that lies between the Scandinavian peninsula and the northern coast of Europe. It links Sweden, Finland, Russia, Estonia, Latvia, Lithuania, and Poland with the North Sea and the Atlantic. The Baltic Sea has an area of approximately 160,000 square miles (414,000 square kilometers). It is about 950 miles (1,530 kilometers) long and around 400 miles (640 kilometers) across at its widest part.

The name *Baltic* also is used to refer collectively to Estonia, Latvia, and Lithuania. Before 1918, these three countries were ruled by Denmark, Sweden, Poland, Germany, and Russia, but each maintained its own language, literature, and traditions. The Baltic lands were part of the Russian Empire until the Russian Revolution of 1917 deposed the tsar and made it possible for the three nations to assert political autonomy. Soviet forces occupied the three independent Baltic states in 1940 and annexed them to the Soviet Union. German troops invaded the Baltics in 1941, during World War II, but the Germans were driven out by the Soviets in 1944 and 1945. Until 1991, the Baltics remained constituent republics of the Soviet Union; but in September 1991, the three countries regained their independence during a period of political upheaval that led to the dissolution of the Soviet Union by the end of that year.
See also: Estonia; Latvia; Lithuania; Poland

BANDIT AND THE PRIEST, THE
Armenia
A bandit once attacked a priest and nearly killed him, but the priest prayed to God, was filled with great strength, and beat the bandit within an inch of his life. When the bandit complained that this was not how a priest

should behave, especially as priests always preached peace to one and all, the priest replied that that was exactly why he had so soundly beaten the bandit—so that others could live in peace, free from banditry.

One of the fables of Mekhithar Gosh.
See also: Mekhithar Gosh

BANNIK
Slavic
The spirit of the bathhouse (*banya*), described as a wizened little man with wild white hair and a long, straggly beard. Bathers could invoke the spirit in order to obtain a reading of the future by exposing their naked backs outside the bathhouse. If the future was to be pleasant, then Bannik could be felt stroking the back. However, if the future was to be unpleasant, Bannik would run his nails down the exposed spine. Every fourth bathing session belonged to Bannik, who would entertain his spirit friends in the bathhouse. If humans were foolish enough to enter while Bannik and his guests were there, they would be fortunate to escape with a simple drenching in boiling water. More likely they would emerge badly beaten or would be found dead inside the bathhouse, strangled or with a broken neck.
References: Pomerantseva 1975

BARDOYATS
Prussia
The god of ships and patron of sailors.

BARO(N)
Armenia
The traveling companion of Haron. Some sources suggest a blood relationship between the two, but it is never confirmed or denied explicitly. During their travels Haron went blind, and from that moment on Baron had to act as Haron's guide, a fact he often bitterly complained about. One night they camped under a tree in a forest at the foot of Mount Amarven. Baron climbed a tree to remain safe during the night, leaving Haron to fend for himself on the forest floor. As the

sun set, the two travelers heard a pack of wolves approaching, and as the howls grew louder, Baron was so frightened that his trembling caused him to lose his footing and fall from the tree.

Haron, however, remained calm and told Baron that they should simply sit beneath the tree and talk, giving the impression that they were just two of many. They did exactly that, and the wolves, thinking that they would be set upon by an unknown number of men, left them alone. The following night exactly the same situation arose, this time with a pack of bears, and again Haron and Baron deceived the bears into thinking that they were not alone, although Baron was still extremely scared.

Once again, as they made their camp the next night, Baron sought to make his bed in a tree, leaving Haron on the ground. Baron climbed down to eat, but when Haron grew thirsty, Baron refused to lead him to a nearby stream. Thus Haron had to guide himself to the refreshing water. There Haron heard a bird alight on a branch above him, a bird that told him to splash the water from the stream on his eyes. Haron did so, and his sight was immediately restored. Overjoyed, he rushed back to the camp to tell Baron, but all Baron could think about was bettering his already perfect sight, and he rushed down to the stream to splash water in his face. However, when he did so he was immediately struck blind. From that moment on their roles were reversed, and Haron had to lead Baron.

The following evening the two once again made camp in the shade of a tree. Haron did not seek to make his bed in the tree but stayed with Baron. As they settled to prepare their evening meal they heard the sound of a man on horseback approaching them, the hoof falls of the horse accompanied by the sound of many men on foot. As they listened to the men approaching, a huntsman on a white horse entered the clearing—a huntsman that Haron immediately recognized as the king of the land they were traveling through.

The king eyed the two suspiciously, thinking they were spies for his enemies, and had them bound and dragged off to his dungeons. There they were left for several days before being dragged into the presence of the king and his beautiful daughter. Haron was immediately smitten by her beauty, and she likewise by his countenance. The king questioned both Haron and Baron and, not believing their story, called on his guards to take them out and hang them. However, the king's daughter interceded, and the king allowed her to hear their stories and be their judge.

She listened to what both Haron and Baron had to say, and then went to her father, told him that she believed that they posed no threat, and asked that her father should call upon Loqmân the Wise to restore Baron's sight. This he did, and when Baron could see again, he pleaded with the King to take him out and hang him, as he could not stand to look Haron in the face after the way he had treated him. Haron and the princess lifted Baron to his feet, and Haron and Baron were reconciled. The king then consented to the marriage of Haron and his daughter, a wedding at which Baron served as best man.

See also: Haro(n)
References: Orbeli and Taronian 1959–67, vol. 10

BARSTUKAI
Lithuania

An underworld being sometimes described as a fairy, who was believed to influence the harvest and to perform household chores for those who had made offerings to Puskaitis. Offerings were left these fairies by farmers who would lay out tables of food in barns, where the Barstukai were believed to gather and feast at midnight.

See also: Fairy; Puskaitis; Underworld, The

BASIL, SAINT
Russia

One of the most famous of Russian saints, to whom the landmark cathedral in Red

Saint Basil's Cathedral, Red Square, Moscow, October 1996 (Reuters/Ulli Michel/Archive Photos)

Square, Moscow, was dedicated. Saint Basil is said to have started his life as a wandering nomad, and through that wandering he became as one with God. A historical character from the first half of the sixteenth century, Basil is said to have marched naked into Moscow, where he punished dishonest merchants as Christ had the money-lenders in the synagogue and reminded Tsar Ivan IV (dubbed *Groznyi,* "The Terrible") of his atrocities. Basil lived with a widow but never married her, and in so doing demonstrated that a man may protect the innocent, an act in direct contrast with the actions of the tsar. Basil openly reproached the tsar for his bloody repression, but because Basil died in 1550, he never witnessed the worst excesses of Ivan's reign.

Basil was buried in the church of "Our Lady of Kazan'," which Ivan had built to celebrate his victory over the Kazan' Tatars. In the seventeenth century the cathedral was renamed Saint Basil's, a name it bears to this day.

See also: Ivan Groznyi; Ivan the Terrible; Kazan'; Tatars

References: Fedotov 1960 and 1966

BASIL II, BULGAROCTONUS
Russia

Lived from c. 958 to 1025. The son of Romanus II and sister of Anna, Basil ascended the imperial Byzantine throne as sole ruler in 976. Within a few years, his rule was endangered by an uprising of nobles led by Bardas Sclerus, who was assisted by General Bardas Phocas. Basil put down this revolt, but the rebellion continued to simmer. The same two men led a second revolt almost a decade later, this time threatening to topple Basil.

The emperor was saved when he entered into an alliance with Vladimir I, who, as part of his pact with Basil, converted to Christianity and married Anna. Vladimir sent six thousand troops to Basil's aid, tipping the scales in his favor, and the Byzantine emperor defeated the uprising in 989. The troops sent by Vladimir became the core of the future Varangian Guard, an élite unit of the Byzantine army. Basil II fought a fifteen-year war against the Bulgars that culminated in his victory in the Belasica mountains. This victory earned him his epithet Bulgaroctonus ("Bulgar-slayer"), for he had thousands of prisoners blinded and then led back, in groups of a hundred, by a one-eyed man, to the Bulgar Tsar Samuel, who reputedly died of shock at the sight (1015). Bulgaria was annexed to the Byzantine Empire in 1018, and the eastern frontier of the empire was extended to Lake Van in Armenia. Basil II died seven years later, in 1025.

See also: Anna; Armenia; Bulgaria; Byzantine Empire; Vladimir I

BASIL THE GREAT, SAINT
Russia
Patron saint of Russia, with Saints Andrew and George. Born c. 329 at Caesarea to a wealthy, respected, and extremely pious family (all of the members of his family are venerated as saints), Basil was educated in the schools of Caesarea, Constantinople, and Athens. He taught rhetoric in Caesarea for a short time but soon followed his family into religious life, visiting holy sites and monasteries in Spain, Egypt, and Palestine before settling as a hermit on the shores of the river Iris at Annesi in 358. He quickly attracted a number of companions, and together they founded the first monastery in Asia Minor, establishing the principles on which Orthodox monasticism thenceforth would operate.

Ordained in 363, Basil left his monastic community in 365 to take administrative control in Caesarea under Archbishop Eusebius, whom he succeeded in 370, receiving

authority over fifty bishops in Pontus. Basil remained resolutely opposed to the heterodoxy of the Byzantine emperor Valens, whom he eventually forced to withdraw from Caesarea. After this victory, Basil founded a new town, Basilia, where his preaching consistently drew large crowds. He died on 1 January 379 at the age of 49, worn out by illness, austerity, and hard work. His feast day is 2 January.

See also: Andrew, Saint; George, Saint

BATRADZ
Russia
Hero of the Alans, Sarmatian ancestors of the Ossetes. The story of this hero's death is remarkably similar to that of King Arthur. Having sustained a mortal wound, Batradz called upon his two companions to throw his sword into the water. Twice they pretended to carry out the task, and twice their deceit was uncovered. When they finally complied, the waters turned blood red and the surface was whipped into a frenzy although no wind blew. Some have suggested that this is the origin of the return of Arthur's sword Excalibur to the Lady of the Lake—a plausible theory, as it is known that Sarmatian soldiers served in the Roman army in Britain under Lucius Artorius Castus.

See also: Alans; Arthur, King; Ossetes; Sarmatians

BATU KHAN
Russia
Historical twelfth-century leader of the Mongol hordes who, thanks to the internecine wars being fought in the area, conquered Ukraine and central Russia with little or no resistance.

See also: Mongols; Ukraine

BEL BELYANIN
Russia
The tsar of an unnamed kingdom, husband of Nastas'ya of the Golden Braid, and father of three sons—Peter Belyaninovich, Vasilii Belyaninovich, and Ivan Belyaninovich. One

Detail showing Saint Basil the Great, from a mosaic on the right wall of the apse, Duomo, Cefalu, Italy (Alinari/Art Resource, NY)

day when the three children were young, a huge gust of wind blew Nastas'ya away. Many years later her three sons set off on a quest to find their mother, a quest that Ivan completed.

> *See also:* Ivan Belyaninovich; Nastas'ya of the Golden Braid; Peter (Belyaninovich); Vasilii Belyaninovich

BELARUS'
General

See Belorussia.

BELOBOG
Slav

The name *Belobog* is derived from the Russian words *belyi* (white) and *bog* (god). The White God represents the beneficent forces of goodness, light, and life. He is eternally opposed by Chernobog, the Black God, who represents the forces of evil and is the cause of all misfortune. Belobog—as the White God was called in the Balkan lands (in Russia, he was known as Belun)—was usually represented as a venerable old man with a flowing white beard, dressed in white clothes. He roamed the countryside during the day, doing works of kindness—curing sick animals, seeing to it that a hunter made a good kill, finding lost items, or ensuring a good crop. Belobog and Chernobog are two of the oldest Slavic deities. They might well have originated with nomadic peoples in western Asia or the Himalayas, being closely related in character to Ahura Mazda and Ahriman in ancient Persian myth; but they also have counterparts in almost every culture around the world where beliefs in the duality of good and evil are found.

> *See also:* Belun; Black God; Chernobog

BELORUSSIA
General

Originally part of the Russian empire, Belorussia, or "White Russia," traces its history back to Kievan Rus'. During the fourteenth century this land was incorporated first into Lithuania and subsequently into the Polish realm. It remained under Polish rule until 1796, when Catherine II (the Great) recovered the lost territory. In 1918, Bolshevik troops invaded Belarus', and the following year they established a Communist government there. In 1922 Belorussia became a republic of the Soviet Union. From 1922 to 1991, the country was part of the Soviet Union, during which time it was called the Belorussian Soviet Socialist Republic, or simply Belorussia. It gained independence in 1991, when the Soviet Union ceased to exist. The language spoken by Belorussians is closely related to Russian and is sometimes referred to as "White Russian." The country's official name now is Belarus'.

> *See also:* Lithuania; Poland

BELUN
Russia

The Russian name for the White God, known in the Balkans as Belobog. The personification of goodness, light, and life, Belun was particularly important in Russia—a land situated in northern latitudes where much of the year passes in virtual darkness. Belun is represented as an old man dressed in white, with a flowing white beard, who can be seen only during the daylight hours, when he performs all manner of kind acts for people's benefit. Belun is also an alternative name for Buyan, although many sources consider the paradisal island of Buyan merely an earthly manifestation of the deity.

> *See also:* Buyan

BEREGINY
Russia

The nymphs of river, lake, and forest, whose name is related to *bereg* (shore) and *beregina* (meaning both "shore" and "earth"). The bereginy appear to be among the most ancient of hunting and fertility deities. Their cult was associated with the birch, which is the first tree to flower in spring. Later the bereginy were separated into individual classifications, such as the russalki or vili, the ptitsy-siriny, and the rozhanitsy. Some authorities assert that many later deities, such as the West Slavic goddess Zhiva, also originated with the bereginy.

See also: Ptitsy-siriny; Rozhanitsa; Rus(s)alki (~ulki); Vila; Zhiva

BESSARABIA
General

An east European region situated partly in Moldova and partly in Ukraine, covering 17,147 square miles (44,411 square kilometers). Bessarabia is bordered by the Dniester River to the north and east, the Black Sea and Danube River to the south, and the Prut River to the west. Russia gained Bessarabia from the Turks in 1812. Southern Bessarabia was awarded to the historical principality of Moldavia in 1856, at the end of the Crimean War (1853–1856), but was regained by Russia in 1878. After World War I, Romania controlled Bessarabia until 1940, when the Soviet Union seized the region during World War II. Romania reoccupied Bessarabia in 1941, but the Soviet Union regained the territory toward the end of the war. Bessarabia then became part of the Moldavian and Ukrainian republics of the Soviet Union. The Moldavian Republic was renamed the Moldovan Republic in 1990, and in 1991, the Soviet Union was dissolved, and Moldova and Ukraine became independent countries.

See also: Black Sea; Danube; Moldavia; Moldova; Romania; Ukraine

BIRD'S WAY, THE
Lithuania

Alternative name for the Milky Way, the heavenly bridge that the spirits of the dead cross to reach their eternal home, the moon.

See also: Milky Way, The; Moon

BLACK GOD
Slav

The literal English translation of the Russian name *Chernobog* (a compound of the words *chernyi,* meaning "black," and *bog,* "god").

The personification of evil, Chernobog is opposed by Belobog, the White God, who personifies goodness.

See also: Belobog; Chernobog; White God

BLACK MIRE
Russia

A foul swamp that lay on the road between Chernigov and Kiev and that sucked in anyone who attempted to cross it. Il'ya Muromets had to cross the Black Mire as he traveled along the road from Chernigov on his way to the court of Vladimir Bright Sun at Kiev.

See also: Chernigov; Il'ya Muromets; Kiev; Nightingale; Vladimir Bright Sun, Prince

BLACK SEA
General

In Russian, *Chernoe More.* A large body of water in southeastern Europe that is bounded by Ukraine, Russia, Georgia, Turkey, Bulgaria, and Romania. The Bosporus and Dardanelles Straits and the Sea of Marmara connect it with the Mediterranean Sea. The ancient Romans called the sea *Pontus Euxinus,* which means "friendly sea." The Black Sea covers approximately 173,000 square miles (448,000 square kilometers), an area greater than that of California. At its deepest it is 7,238 feet (2,206 meters). North of the Kerch Strait is the Sea of Azov, a large bay of the Black Sea. Several important rivers empty into the Black Sea, including the Danube, the Dniester, the Dnieper, and the Don.

See also: Azov, Sea of; Bulgaria; Danube; Dnieper; Georgia; Romania; Russia; Ukraine

BLACK STREAM
Russia

A small river that flowed into Lake Il'men' from the west. Long ago, a miller built his mill on this stream, which nearly dammed its waters. More importantly for the sake of this legend, the mill stopped the fish in the river from gaining access to Lake Il'men', a fact they bitterly pointed out to the river.

Appearing as a man dressed from head to foot in black, the Black Stream came to a man from Novgorod who was fishing in his waters, and offering to show him a place where the water teemed with fish, he asked the man to do him a favor. The man readily agreed, and having been led to the point on the river where the fish filled the water almost completely, the Black Stream gave the man a message that he was to pass on to a peasant whom he would meet in Novgorod, who would be dressed in a blue kaftan, blue trousers, and a blue hat.

After returning to Novgorod, the man duly found the peasant and passed on the message without realizing that the peasant was none other than the personification of Lake Il'men'. That night, in response to Black Stream's plea, Lake Il'men' sent a huge wave thundering up Black Stream, which washed the mill away.

This story seems related to the ancient custom of offering a human sacrifice to a water god whenever a new mill was built, in order to assure the effort's success.

See also: Il'men', Lake; Novgorod

BLAISE, SAINT
Slav

The patron saint of wool-combers, his name is invoked against sore throats. Very little is known about Saint Blaise, who seems to have been unknown prior to the eighth century. He is thought to have been an Armenian bishop and martyr—possibly the bishop of Sebastea in Cappadocia—and to have been executed during the persecutions of Christians in the early fourth century. His feast day is 3 February, and his iconographic emblem is a comb. In art he is usually shown with two candles—an iconography that led to the sixteenth-century practice (still current today) of placing two candles on a patient suffering from a throat ailment.

BLASIUS, SAINT
Slav

Alternative name for Saint Blaise.

BLUDOVICH, GODENKO
Russia

See Godenko Bludovich.

BOBA
Lithuania

The name given to the last sheaf harvested, the equivalent of the Polish Baba. The person who binds this last sheaf is the subject of much attention, for he or she is held to be imbued with the life-giving forces of the grain. The last sheaf is made into the figure of a woman, which is then carried through the village on the last wagon to leave the fields, and at the farmer's house, is drenched with water before everyone involved in the harvest dances around it.

See also: Baba

BOGATYR'
Russia

(pl. bogatyri) "Champion," the post-Christian Russian name for a knight of Holy Russia. These knights were revered by the folk as demigods who fought imps, demons, and other evil beings sent forth by the Devil. These knights usually appeared in the wonder tales, the *volshebnye skazki,* but also figure as heroes in other categories of Russian legends, especially the *byliny* and the *bylichki.* In the epic cycles that related the stories of bogatyri, pagan myths were mingled with the new Christian beliefs—accommodating the ancient religious system within the new one. One poem in particular, *Why There Are No More Bogatyri in Holy Russia,* can be seen as a concerted attempt to eliminate the bogatyri altogether, as it explains that these knights became too self-confident and attacked a large supernatural army referred to in some versions of the stories as the Kams. However, every time a supernatural warrior fell to the bogatyri, two more sprang up to take his place, and at last the bogatyri admitted defeat and fled to the mountains, where they were turned to stone.

See also: Bylichka; Bylina; Devil, The; Il'ya Muromets; Kams; Mikhail Potyk; Mikula

Armored bogatyri on horseback travel the countryside in search of evil in Bogatyri, *an undated Vasnetsov painting in the Tretyakov Gallery. (V. Vasnetsov/Sovfoto/Eastfoto/PNI)*

Selyaninovich; Sviatogor; Volkh Vseslav'evich; Volshebnye skazki

BOGHU, KHAN
Armenia

An enormous giant who is central to the story of Badikan. Khan Boghu was the possessor of seven souls, which he kept inside seven sparrows that could not be caught. The sparrows, in turn, were inside a mother-of-pearl box that could not be opened, which was inside a fox that could not be caught. If that were not enough, the fox was inside an ox that could not be overcome. With his seven souls thus protected, Khan Boghu believed himself secure from his enemies for all time. When Badikan discovered this secret, he set out to kill the giant.

Badikan's first stop was at the home of a group of sorcerers, who told him that the ox could be overcome with seven barrels of strong wine. So equipped, Badikan rode for many days until he found the huge ox.

Hiding behind some rocks, Badikan put out the seven open barrels of wine, and when the ox had drained them and fallen into a drunken stupor, he leaped forward and cut off its head. As the head fell, Khan Boghu, who was out hunting, stumbled and fell and instantly knew that he had been betrayed and the ox was dead. Khan Boghu staggered to his feet and hurried back to his palace as quickly as he could, considering the pain he now found himself suffering for the very first time. Seeing him coming, the princess, who had fallen in love with Badikan and told her lover of Khan Boghu's weakness, fled to the rooftops, fully intending to throw herself to her death if need be.

Badikan, meanwhile, had cut open the ox, caught the fox by its tail, and cut off its head. As the head rolled from the fox, blood began to flow freely from Khan Boghu's nose. Badikan then cut open the fox, took out the mother-of-pearl box, and broke its lock. As the lock broke, Khan Boghu began to cough up blood. Badikan then let out the seven sparrows. When he strangled the first two, Khan Boghu fell to his knees. When he strangled two more, Khan Boghu's arms and legs grew numb. When he strangled yet another two, Khan Boghu's heart and liver burst. Then Badikan caught the last sparrow and crushed it in his hands, and as he did so, all life left Khan Boghu in a cloud of black smoke.

See also: Badikan
References: Khatchatrian 1933

BOGORODITSA

Russia

"Birth-Giver of God," name for Mary, mother of Christ. A post-Christian cult was devised around the Virgin Mary by the early Russian Orthodox clergy to bring the pagan worship of goddesses into the sphere of Christian theology. The Virgin Mary soon became a central focus of Russian Orthodoxy.

References: Bulgakov 1932, 1944

BOHEMIA

General

Bohemia is a region in the western part of the Czech Republic that covers 20,374 square miles (52,768 square kilometers). Bohemia is a saucer-shaped plateau ringed by hills and mountains. The Sudeten Mountains form Bohemia's northeastern boundary, and the Bohemian Mountains the region's western boundary. Most Bohemians belong to the Slavic grouping known as Czechs. The first known inhabitants of Bohemia were the Boii, a Celtic tribe that lived in the region during the fourth century B.C., from whose name Bohemia is derived. The Czech word for Bohemia, *Cechy,* refers to the Czechs, who had settled in the region by about A.D. 500. In 1158, Emperor Frederick I of the Holy Roman Empire gave the title of king to the Duke of Bohemia. Bohemia reached its political and cultural peak in the 1300s, when Charles IV (1316–78) ruled as king (from 1346, he also was the elected king of Germany, and after 1355, Holy Roman emperor).

A period of civil wars began in 1419, following the execution of John Hus, a Bohemian religious reformer. Called the Hussite Wars, these were chiefly religious conflicts in which Hus's followers fought loyal Roman Catholics. The two sides managed to reach a compromise in 1436, after which most Bohemians gradually became Protestants. Bohemia came under the rule of the Catholic Habsburg family in 1526. The Bohemian Protestants overthrew the Habsburgs in 1618, but the dynasty regained power in 1620 and subsequently ruled Bohemia for almost 400 years, during which time Bohemia lost most of its religious and political freedom. Beginning in the late eighteenth century, Czech leaders in Bohemia worked for a rebirth of patriotism and culture. A revolt in 1848 was unsuccessful.

In 1918, following the conclusion of World War I, Bohemia became a province of the new independent republic of Czechoslovakia until the government of Czechoslovakia abolished the country's provinces in 1949. In 1992, after the Soviet Union collapsed and many nations of eastern Europe had reasserted political independence, the state of Czechoslovakia was voted out of existence and the independent countries of the Czech Republic and Slovakia were created in its place. Bohemia became a region in the Czech Republic.

See also: Czechoslovakia; Czechs; Slovakia

BORIS, SAINT

Russia

Russian Orthodox saint who according to some legends was a smith who, along with Saint Gleb, forged the first plow. This plow was of enormous proportions, and was forged with implements of like size. The two smiths were reported to have used twelve golden hammers, and tongs that weighed almost four hundredweight, or twelve poods. Other versions of this legend name the two saintly smiths as Saint Kuz'ma and Saint Dem'yan.

Boris and Gleb are Russia's oldest saints, sons of Prince Vladimir Bright Sun, and brothers of Sviatopolk. The earliest account of the martyrdom of the brothers dates from the twelfth-century *Primary Chronicle*. In this version, Boris hears of his father's death while he is fighting the invading Pecheneg hordes. Boris quickly returns to Kiev, where he learns that his older brother Sviatopolk plans to kill him and take his lands and inheritance. However, instead of acting against his brother in order to evade death, Boris makes things easier for Sviatopolk and submits to his fate. Gleb then learns that Sviatopolk plans the same end for him, and he too submits to the inevitable. The brothers are recorded as dying in 1015, and shortly afterward they were canonized as "Protectors of the Land of Rus'."

The cult of Boris and Gleb was not Christian in origin, but the church gave its blessing in order to satisfy the newly converted populace.

See also: Dem'yan, Saint; Gleb, Saint; Kiev; Kuz'ma, Saint; Pechenegs; *Primary Chronicle;* Sviatopolk; Vladimir Bright Sun, Prince
References: Bezsonov 1861; Cross and Sherbowitz-Wetzor 1953; Golubinskii 1903; Zenkovsky 1963

BORUSHKA MATUSHKA
Russia
One of the names of the magical horse owned by Il'ya Muromets, the other being Kosmatushka.

See also: Il'ya Muromets; Kosmatushka
References: Astakhova 1938–51

BOSNIA
General
Nearly three millennia ago, the territory now called Bosnia and Herzegovina formed part of Illyria, which became known as the Roman province of Illyricum in the first century B.C. Following the collapse of the Roman Empire, first the Goths and then the Slavs conquered the territory. Various petty Slav princes ruled the area until the twelfth century A.D., when Hungary made the area one of its dominions. The Hungarians later

made Bosnia a *banat* (province) under the control of a *ban* (viceroy). Ban Stephen Krotomanic extended Hungarian authority over the principality of Hum (also known as Zahumlje), later known as Herzegovina. Krotomanic's nephew and successor Stephen Tvtko further extended the boundaries, and in 1376 proclaimed himself king of Serbia and Bosnia. The kingdom began to disintegrate after the death of Tvtko, and a rebellious Bosnian chieftain seized the Hum region early in the fifteenth century and established it as Herzegovina, which means "independent duchy." By 1463 the Ottoman Empire had conquered most of Bosnia, and Herzegovina fell to them in 1483. The two territories remained provinces of the Ottoman Empire for the next 400 years, although unsuccessful uprisings against the Turks occurred frequently during the nineteenth century.

The population of the area included Roman Catholic Croats, Orthodox Serbs, and Muslims (Slavs who converted to Islam during Ottoman rule) by the late nineteenth century. Unrest among the various ethnic groups, coupled with the increasing deterioration of the Ottoman Empire, led to a general decline of the area. During the Congress of Berlin in 1878, the double monarchy of Austria-Hungary negotiated with other European rulers for administration rights over the area, and by 1908 it had annexed the two provinces. Austro-Hungarian rule did little to quell the ethnic tensions in the region. Bosnia became a center of nationalist agitation for political independence and cultural autonomy. Europe began to take sides in the disputes: Austria-Hungary and Germany opposed the growing Serbian nationalism, and Russia and Great Britain partially supported it.

In June 1914 the heir to the throne of Austria-Hungary, Archduke Francis Ferdinand, and his wife were assassinated in Sarajevo by Gavril Princip, a Serb student from Bosnia. This act precipitated World War I. During the war, Croats and Serbs mostly fought together, hoping to create a kingdom

"Young Bosnia" members on trial in Sarajevo. Gavril Princip, one of the group's members, shot the Austro-Hungarian regent, Archduke Ferdinand, and his wife on 20 June 1914. (Archive Photos)

that would unite all of the South Slavic peoples. On 1 December 1918, following the overthrow of the monarchy of Austria-Hungary at the close of the war, Bosnia and Herzegovina merged and became part of the independent Kingdom of Serbs, Croats, and Slovenes under the Serbian monarchy of King Alexander from 1921 to 1934. When conflict between Croats and Serbs led to greater national tensions, Alexander tightened control over the country, and in 1929 he renamed the kingdom Yugoslavia (which means "Land of the South Slavs").

See also: Herzegovina; Hungary; Serbia

BOUYAN
Slav
See Buyan.

BOYARS
Russia
Aristocratic landowners in Russia. These nobles wrested power in Novgorod from the merchant guilds in 1416 and remained in control until 1476, when the city came under the control of Ivan the Great. During the sixteenth century the boyars formed such a powerful group that they began to threaten the authority of the tsar. However, their influence was decisively broken by Ivan Groznyi in 1565 when the tsar confiscated most of their land.

See also: Ivan Groznyi; Ivan the Great; Novgorod
References: Zenkovsky 1963

BOZHENA
Russia
From *bog*, "god," *bozhena* was the name given to the bathhouse in Russian folklore, the home of the bannik. Marriages were often sanctified in the bathhouse, and those so sanctified were considered more sacred than those conducted in church, the bathhouse being the traditional center of prophecy, sorcery, and healing.

See also: Bannik
References: Arbatskii 1956

BRIANSK WOODS
Russia

Woods that lay on the road between Chernigov and Kiev and in which the brigand Nightingale had his nest. It was also in the Briansk Woods that Ivan the Soldier hung Death in a pouch until he was almost dead.

> *See also:* Chernigov; Death; Ivan the Soldier; Kiev; Nightingale

BRIGHT SUN
Russia

Epithet applied to the historical prince Vladimir I of Kiev, whose identity merged in the folk imagination with that of Vladimir II to form the legendary prince of Kiev, Vladimir Bright Sun.

> *See also:* Kiev; Vladimir I; Vladimir II; Vladimir Bright Sun, Prince

BUDAPEST
Hungary

City in northern Hungary, on the river Danube near the Slovakian border. Hungary's capital and largest city. Tree-lined boulevards and wide squares bordered by modern buildings make today's Budapest one of the most beautiful capitals of Europe. The city consists of the community of Buda on the west bank of the Danube and the community of Pest on the east bank. Built on a terraced plateau, Buda contains ruins dating from the Turkish occupation, including the former royal palace situated on the summit of the plateau, at the base of which are famous medicinal springs. Pest stands on a plain and is the site of the Houses of Parliament (opened in 1896), the Academy of Sciences, the Museum of Fine Arts, the Palace of Justice, the Eötvös Loránd University (1635), the Custom House, and the National Museum. Buda and Pest are linked by six bridges over the Danube, including one of the largest suspension bridges in Europe.

About 10 B.C. the Romans established the colony of Aquincum on the present site of Buda and near that of an earlier settlement. In A.D. 376 invading Vandals conquered Aquincum. During the next 500 years Slavs, Avars, and others settled on the sites of Buda and Pest, and in the latter half of the ninth century the Magyars took the towns. In 1241, during the Tatar invasion of Hungary, Pest was destroyed. In 1247 King Béla IV of Hungary repopulated Pest with Germans and colonists of other nationalities and established the city of Buda. Buda became the capital of Hungary and the home of the royal court in 1361, while Pest became a leading commercial center. During the Turkish invasion of Hungary, Pest was taken in 1526 and Buda in 1541. When the Turks were driven out in 1686 by a league of states under the leadership of Austria, both cities were almost in ruins. Because of the commanding position of Buda and Pest on the Danube and their resultant economic importance, the recovery of both cities was rapid. Both Buda and Pest continued to grow during the eighteenth century and made an extraordinary advance during the period preceding the last decade of the nineteenth century.

In the mid-nineteenth century, Hungarian patriots made Pest a center of culture and politics, and in 1848 Pest became the capital of Hungary. In 1873, Buda, Pest, Obuda, and Margaret Island were united to form a new capital city, which was christened Budapest.

> *See also:* Avars; Danube; Hungary; Magyars; Slovakia; Tatars

BULAT
Tatar

One of a pair of heroes who appear in a poem engaged in mortal combat each other, the other hero being Ak Molot. Ak Molot managed to inflict numerous wounds on his enemy—wounds that would have killed any ordinary man. However, Bulat was not ordinary, for he did not carry his soul. After three years of fighting, Ak Molot saw a golden casket hanging from the sky on a white silken thread. Ak Molot shot down the casket and opened it, whereupon ten white birds flew out, one of which contained Bulat's soul. While fighting Bulat, Ak Molot also managed to shoot down the birds, one after another, and as the tenth bird fell to the ground, Bulat died.

See also: Ak Molot

BULAT THE BRAVE
Russia

Found being flogged in a market square for owing a large sum of money to a merchant, Bulat was saved from further torment by Ivan, who paid the money Bulat owed to the merchant. Thinking nothing of this, Ivan walked away from the market square; but Bulat ran up to him, thanked him for saving him, and told him that if he had not helped him, Ivan never would have found the girl Vasilissa Kirbit'evna, who was prophesied to become his wife.

To fulfill his destiny, Ivan followed Bulat the Brave's instructions exactly. The pair rode a great distance until they came to the land of Tsar Kirbit. There, in a tower, just as had been foretold, they found the maiden. Purchasing some chickens, ducks, and geese, Bulat told Ivan to have them roasted and to hand him a wing whenever he returned from trying to capture the girl. Bulat then went to the tower and threw a stone to attract the attention of the girl, cracking the gilded roof of the tower in the process. Running back to Ivan, Bulat had him give him a chicken wing and then returned to the tower, where he offered it to Vasilissa Kirbit'evna.

Three times Bulat did this, each time offering the girl the wing he carried, first of chicken, then of duck, and finally of goose. As the maiden leaned out of the window to take the last wing offered, Bulat grabbed her, and the three made away as fast as their horses would carry them. The following morning, when Tsar Kirbit saw the damage to the tower and found his daughter missing, he and a number of his men gave chase.

Sensing their approach, Bulat pretended to have lost his ring and told his companions to continue on their way while he returned to look for it. Vasilissa Kirbit'evna tried to dissuade him by giving him her own ring, but although Bulat accepted the offered ring, he still returned along the route they had followed. Coming across his pursuers, he killed all but the tsar before returning to his companions.

Tsar Kirbit returned home and gathered together twice as many men. Bulat the Brave once again sensed their approach, and this time pretending to have lost his scarf, he returned and dispatched them all, leaving only the tsar alive to return home. Knowing that his daughter was lost to him forever, Tsar Kirbit gave up the chase and returned home to mourn her.

As night fell Bulat, Ivan, and Vasilissa Kirbit'evna made their camp. Bulat told Ivan that he would scout the area and ordered him to stay awake and watch over the maiden. Ivan managed to stay awake half the night but fell asleep soon after midnight. When Bulat woke him in the morning the girl was nowhere to be seen. Bulat scolded Ivan, telling him that Koshchei the Deathless had abducted her and that they would have to search for her.

After several days' ride they came across a herd of cattle being tended by two men. Having discovered from one of the herdsmen that the cattle belonged to Koshchei, they killed the men and dressed in the herders' clothing before driving the herd back to where Koshchei lived.

In order to maintain her beauty in such a dreary place, Vasilissa Kirbit'evna had taken to washing her face in goat's milk morning and night. As Bulat and Ivan drove the cattle into the yard a maid was just filling a cup with the goat's milk for Vasilissa Kirbit'evna. Bulat slipped the girl's ring off his finger and slyly dropped it into the milk. When Vasilissa Kirbit'evna found the ring she immediately knew who the two herdsmen were and rushed out to greet them. Bulat told the girl that she must discover where Koshchei kept his soul, for without it they could not kill him. Then he bade her quickly to help them hide. Scarcely were they secreted when Koshchei flew in.

Pretending to have missed him very much, Vasilissa Kirbit'evna snuggled up to Koshchei, telling him that she had been scared for him. He replied that she had no need to be frightened, for he did not carry his soul with him. It was hidden in a broom in the kitchen. When Vasilissa Kirbit'evna told Bulat this, he knew that Koshchei was lying, so he told the girl to be even more cunning.

That evening, when Koshchei returned, Vasilissa Kirbit'evna presented him with the broom, finely decorated, as a gift, telling him that his soul was too precious to leave lying around. Koshchei laughed. He then told her that his soul was in fact inside the goat that provided the milk she washed in. Again Bulat knew he was lying, so Vasilissa Kirbit'evna presented Koshchei with the goat, elaborately decorated. Koshchei once again laughed, and told her that his soul was not in the goat but rather in an egg, inside a duck, inside a hare, under a huge oak on a remote island in the middle of an endless ocean.

When Vasilissa Kirbit'evna relayed this to Bulat, he knew that at last Koshchei had told the truth. Immediately he and Ivan set off the find the island. En route they grew dangerously short of food. Coming across a dog, they made to kill it. The dog pleaded for mercy, saying that he would be of use to them. Bulat set the dog free. Next they came to an eagle, and the same thing happened. On the shore of the ocean they met a lobster, and exactly the same thing happened again.

Crossing the ocean took many days, but finally they came to an island on which a single, huge oak tree grew. Bulat unearthed the tree with ease, and the hare jumped out and ran away. Instantly the dog they had spared appeared and caught the hare. Out of the hare the duck flew high into the sky, where

it was pounced upon by the eagle Bulat and Ivan had spared. Out of the duck fell the egg, which rolled into the sea, whence it was recovered by the lobster. Having Koshchei's soul in their possession, Bulat and Ivan returned to Vasilissa Kirbit'evna. That evening, when Koshchei returned, they confronted him and smashed the egg on his forehead, killing him.

Ivan returned to his homeland, where he married Vasilissa Kirbit'evna in fulfillment of the prophecy and made Bulat the Brave his most trusted friend and adviser.

See also: Ivan; Koshchei (the Deathless); Vasilis(s)a Kirbit'evna

BULGARIA
General
A country of southeastern Europe that is bounded to the north by Romania, to the west by the former Yugoslavia, to the south by Greece, to the southwest by Turkey, and to the east by the Black Sea. In ancient times, as the Roman province of Moesia Inferior, the territory comprised Thrace and Moesia. It was inhabited by the Thraco-Illyrians. Beginning in the sixth century A.D. Slavic tribes migrated into the region and either absorbed or drove out the original inhabitants. In the latter half of the seventh century, the region was conquered by the Bulgars (a people of Turkic stock), who migrated from their domain on the east side of the Black Sea, crossed the lower reaches of the Danube River, and subjugated Lower Moesia, then a province of the Byzantine Empire. Imperial armies failed repeatedly to dislodge the invaders during the eighth century. Fewer in number than the Slavic population of Lower Moesia, the Bulgars gradually became Slavicized during this period, and by the end of the century they had annexed considerable additional territory and laid the foundations for a strong state under Khan Krum, who reigned from 803 to 814. The Krum armies inflicted a devastating defeat on an invading Byzantine force in 811 and almost suc-

ceeded in taking Constantinople in 813. Bulgarian-Byzantine relations were thereafter relatively peaceful and continued to be so during the first half of the ninth century. Khan Krum's immediate successors enlarged their dominions, mainly in the region of Serbia and Macedonia. However, in 860, during the reign of Boris I (852–889), Bulgaria suffered a severe military setback at the hands of the Serbs. Four years later Boris, responding to pressure from the Byzantine emperor Michael III, made Christianity the official religion of the khanate (865). Boris accepted the primacy of the papacy in 866, but in 870, following the refusal of Pope Adrian II (pope 867–872) to make Bulgaria an archbishopric, he shifted his allegiance to the Eastern Orthodox church. Under his son, Simeon (893–927), the country became a leading power. In the eleventh century Bulgaria came under Byzantium's rule, and even though a second independent Bulgarian empire was founded in the fourteenth century, Bulgaria formed a part of the Ottoman Empire for almost 500 years, until it became an independent kingdom in 1908. The term *Bulgar* may be correctly used to refer to any of the invaders from Asia who entered the region in the seventh century and conquered and subjugated the Slav population.

In the late ninth and early tenth centuries, during the reign of Boris's son Simeon, Bulgaria became the strongest nation in eastern Europe. A brilliant administrator and military leader, Simeon introduced Byzantine culture into his realm, encouraged education, obtained new territories, defeated the Magyars, and conducted a series of successful wars against the Byzantine Empire. In 925 Simeon proclaimed himself emperor of the Greeks and Bulgars. The following year Simeon conquered Serbia and became the most powerful monarch in contemporary eastern Europe. Simeon's reign was marked by great cultural advances led by the followers of Saint Cyril and his brother Saint

Methodius, the "apostles to the Slavs." During this period the Cyrillic alphabet was adopted, and the language known today as Old Church Slavonic became the first written Slavic language.

Weakened by domestic strife and successive Magyar raids, Bulgarian power declined steadily during the following half century. In 969, invading Russians seized the capital and captured the royal family, but the following year the Byzantine emperor John I, Tzimisces, alarmed over the Russian advance into southeastern Europe, intervened in the Russo-Bulgarian conflict. The Russians were compelled to withdraw from Bulgaria in 972, and the eastern part of the country was annexed to the Byzantine Empire. Samuel, the son of a Bulgarian provincial governor, became ruler of western Bulgaria in 976; but Samuel's armies were annihilated in 1014 by the Byzantine emperor Basil II, who incorporated the short-lived state into his empire in 1018.

Led by the nobles Ivan and Peter Asen, the Bulgarians revolted against Byzantine rule in 1185 and established a second empire. It consisted initially of the region between the Balkan Mountains and the Danube, but by the early thirteenth century it included extensive neighboring territories—most notably, sections of Serbia and all of western Macedonia. In 1204, following the Latin occupation of Constantinople, Ivan's and Peter's brother Kaloyan (reigned 1197–1207) temporarily broke with the Eastern Orthodox church and accepted the primacy of the pope. However, this act was renounced in 1234. Ivan Asen II (reigned 1218–1241), the fifth ruler of the Asen dynasty, added western Thrace, the remainder of Macedonia, and part of Albania to the empire in 1230.

Feudal strife and involvement in foreign wars caused the empire gradually to disintegrate after the death of Ivan Asen II. The Bulgarian armies were decisively defeated by the Serbs in 1330, and for the next quarter century the second empire was little more than a dependency of Serbia. Shortly after 1360 the Ottoman Turks began to ravage the

Maritsa Valley, completing the subjugation of Bulgaria in 1396. During the next five centuries the political and cultural identity of Bulgaria was almost destroyed. However, after a century of terrorism and persecution, the Turkish administration improved and the economic condition of the remaining Bulgarians rose to a level higher than it had been under the kingdom, although unsuccessful revolts against Turkish rule still occurred from time to time.

In the late eighteenth and early nineteenth centuries, with the revival of a literature glorifying Bulgaria's history, nationalism became a powerful movement. In 1876 the Bulgarians revolted against the Turks but were quelled. In an act of sadistic reprisal, the Turks massacred about 15,000 Bulgarian men, women, and children. In 1877, prompted by the desire to expand toward the Mediterranean Sea and by Pan-Slavic sentiment, Russia declared war on Turkey. As a result of the ensuing Russo-Turkish War, in which Turkey was defeated, a part of Bulgaria became an autonomous principality, and Eastern Rumelia, another region, was made an autonomous Turkish province.

> *See also:* Black Sea; Byzantine Empire; Byzantium; Constantinople; Cyril and Methodius, Saints; Danube; Macedonia; Magyars; Romania; Serbia

BUSI-URT
Finno-Ugric—Votyak
One of the classes of urt. The spirit of the grain field who protects the d'u-urt, the soul of the grain, and ensures a good harvest.

> *See also:* D'u-urt; Urt

BUSLAEV, VASILII
Russia
See Vasilii Buslayevich.

BUSLAI (~Y)
Russia
The husband of Amelfia Timofeyevna and father by her of Vasilii Buslayevich. Legends indicate that Amelfia Timofeyevna also was

married at one time to Nikita but do not mention whether this marriage occurred before or after Amelfia's marriage to Buslai, or how the marriage ended.

> *See also:* Amelf(i)a Timofe(y)evna; Vasilii Buslayevich

BUSLAVLEVICH, VOL'GA
Russia
See Vol'ga Buslavlevich.

BUSLAYEVICH, VASILII
Russia
Also: Busla(y)ev, Vasilii
See Vasilii Buslayevich.

BUYAN
Slav
An oceanic island described by some as paradise. The home of the North, East, and West winds, the soft west wind being known as Dogoda. These winds were the attendants of the Sun, who—according to some accounts—also lived on the island. Buyan is sometimes described as the home of the two Zoryi, the daughters of Dazhbog—Zorya Utrennyaya and Zorya Vechernyaya. Further accounts made Buyan a silent, subterranean city that was the eternal, peaceful home of the dead.

> *See also:* Belun; Dazhbog; Dogoda; Sun; Wind; Zorya Utrennyaya; Zorya Vechernyaya

BYLICHKA
Russia
(pl. bylichki) One of the three main types of Russian legend, the other two being the bylina and the skazka. Bylichki deal with the supernatural world and with beings that come from the land of the dead, the underworld. When pagan beliefs were at their strongest in ancient Russia, the common peasants half-believed the bylichki. These legends are generally short and told in the first person, being related from father to son and thence passed down through the generations.

> *See also:* Bylina; Skazka; Underworld, The

BYLINA
Russia

(pl. byliny; from *byl'*, meaning "fact" or "true story") One of the three categories of Russian legend, with the skazka and the bylichka. The byliny, or *stariny*, tell of the heroes of yore, such as Il'ya Muromets and Dobrynya Nikitich, and of their daring deeds in battle against the enemies of ancient Russia. They are formulated in verses intended to be sung or chanted and evidence a distinctive mix of the mythical and the historical. The earliest byliny date from the tenth or the eleventh century, but their content is undoubtedly of much earlier origin.

See also: Bylichka; Dobrynya Nikitich; Il'ya Muromets; Skazka
References: Chadwick 1964; Oinas 1978; Sokolov 1945

BYZANTINE EMPIRE
General

One of the most influential acts of Emperor Constantine was his decision in 330 to move the capital of the empire from Rome to "New Rome"—the city of Byzantium—at the eastern end of the Mediterranean Sea. The new capital, Constantinople (today, Istanbul), also became the intellectual and religious center of Eastern Catholicism. This move fostered a special relationship between church and state that combined elements of Eastern Catholicism with those of classical antiquity (a synthesis frequently described rather simplistically as "Caesaropapism"). At its worst, this culture led to the subjection of the church to state tyranny.

A collision between the church and the imperial power in the eighth century

Engraving of Saint Sophia in Constantinople, c. 1837 (Print and Picture Collection, Free Library of Philadelphia)

brought about a crisis. Emperor Leo III had prohibited religious images, thus precipitating a struggle in which Eastern Orthodox monks became the principal defenders of the icons. Eventually the icons were restored, and with them a measure of independence for the church. However, during the seventh and eighth centuries three of the four great Eastern Orthodox capitals were captured by the dynamic new faith of Islam. Only Constantinople remained immune for a time; however, besieged by the Turks, it finally fell in 1453.

Among the points of controversy between Constantinople and Rome was the evangelization of the Slavs that began in the ninth century. Even though several Slavic tribes—Poles, Moravs, Czechs, Slovaks, Croats, and Slovenes—did adopt the Western rites, the vast majority of Slavic peoples became Christians in the Eastern (Byzantine) church.

From its early foundations in Kiev, this Slavic Orthodoxy pervaded Russia, where the features of Eastern Christianity took firm hold. However, during the centuries-long rule of the Ottoman Turks in the Balkans some Christian populations were forced to embrace Islam.

See also: Byzantium; Constantinople; Kiev

BYZANTIUM
General

The name given by the Greeks to a city on the Bosporus. In A.D. 330 the Roman emperor Constantine the Great moved the capital of the Roman Empire from Rome to Byzantium and renamed the city Constantinople. The city became the seat of power for the Byzantine Empire. Today it is known as Istanbul, Turkey.

See also: Byzantine Empire; Constantinople

During the past several centuries, the Caspian has been shrinking in size because the rivers that empty into it (chiefly the Volga, Ural, Emba, Terek, and Kura) bring less water than it loses by evaporation. The Caspian Sea lies 92 feet (28 meters) below sea level and is drained by no natural outlets to the ocean. The waters of the Caspian are less salty than ocean waters and abound with both freshwater and saltwater fish.

CAIN
Armenia
   See also: Kayen.

CARPATHIAN MOUNTAINS
General
Part of the great mountain system of central Europe. The Carpathians extend about 900 miles (1,400 kilometers) along the border between Slovakia and Poland and into Ukraine and Romania, with most of the range being situated in Slovakia and Romania. The highest peak in the Carpathians is Gerlachovsky (8,711 feet, or 2,655 meters), in Slovakia's Tatra Mountains. The Carpathians are an extension of the mountain range that includes the Alps, although the Carpathian peaks are generally lower than the Alps and have fewer lakes, glaciers, and waterfalls.

CASPIAN SEA
General
A great salt lake below sea level, the Caspian is the largest inland body of water in the world. It lies between Europe and Asia east of the Caucasus Mountains and is bordered by Kazakhstan on the north and northeast, Turkmenistan on the southeast, Iran on the south, Azerbaijan on the southwest, and Russia on the west and northwest.
   The Caspian Sea covers 143,250 square miles (371,000 square kilometers). It is about 750 miles (1,210 kilometers) long at its greatest extent and varies from 130 to 300 miles (209 to 483 kilometers) in width.

CAUCASUS
General
A series of mountain ranges that extend 750 miles (1,200 km) between the Caspian and the Black Seas. The highest peak is Elbruz, which rises to 18,480 feet (5,633 m).

CAUTIOUS MOTHER CROW
Armenia
A mother crow once told her children to be wary of man, especially if they saw a man stooping to pick up a stone. One of the young birds asked his mother what they should do if they encountered a man already holding a stone, to which the mother replied that their question showed her that they were already cautious enough to go forth into the world and come to no harm.
   One of the fables of Vardan.
   See also: Vardan
   References: Marr 1894–99

CHARITY
Russia
The village that is home to the beautiful, half-naked spinning-woman who cures Peter of Murom of his sores in exchange for his promise of marriage. When Peter of Murom attempts to renege, his strength saps away and the sores reappear. Convinced that he has no choice, Peter of Murom marries the maiden, who reveals that her true name is Fevroniia.
   See also: Fevroniia; Peter of Murom

CHEREMISS-MORDVIN
General
Adjective describing the indigenous inhabitants of the region around the middle and upper Volga that is today the autonomous republic of Mordovia or Mordvinia. The region was conquered by Russia during the thirteenth century and did not regain political autonomy until 1930. Almost none of the Finno-Ugric–speaking Cheremiss-Mordvin indigenes have survived.

CHERKESS
General
Alternative name for Circassians. Cherkess is also the name of an autonomous oblast in today's Russian Federation.

CHERNAVA
Russia
Daughter of the Sea Tsar. Sadko was forcibly betrothed to her, having been detained beneath the oceans by her father: The Sea Tsar knew that if the couple consummated their marriage, Sadko would be forever under his spell. However, Sadko sought the help of Saint Nikolai of Mozhaisk, and in accordance with the saint's instructions he did not lie with the girl; thus, he was soon released from his bond. Chernava is also the spirit of the river of the same name, which flows near Novgorod and to which Sadko was transported when the Sea Tsar was forced to release him. In Russian legend, all rivers are described as children of the Sea Tsar—even those that spring from the blood of fallen heroes.

> *See also:* Nikolai of Mozhaisk, Saint; Novgorod; Sadko; Sea Tsar

CHERNIGOV
Russia
Port town on the River Desna in northern Ukraine, also the site of an eleventh-century cathedral. In the legend of Il'ya Muromets, the hero Il'ya freed the inhabitants of the town, who were under siege. They asked him to become their tsar, but Il'ya refused because he was only passing through, on his way to the court of Vladimir Bright Sun at Kiev.

> *See also:* Desna; Il'ya Muromets; Kiev; Ukraine; Vladimir Bright Sun, Prince

CHERNOBOG
Slav
The Black God, whose name is a compound of the words *chernyi* (black) and *bog* (god). He was the epitome and personification of evil, darkness, and death. Usually represented as a dark figure dressed all in black, he was reportedly seen only during the hours of darkness. His direct opposite is Belobog, the White God, the personification of goodness. Chernobog was particularly feared in northern Russia, where long periods of each year passed in virtual darkness.

> *See also:* Belobog; Black God; White God

CHUDO-YUDO
Russia
Fire-breathing, multiheaded dragon described in some accounts as the brother of Koshchei the Deathless, and thus the offspring of Baba-Yaga, and in others as a personification of the witch in her foulest form. Chudo-Yudo is one of the guardians of the Water of Life and Death, and his name traditionally was invoked in times of drought.

> *See also:* Baba-Yaga (-Jaga, -Iaga); Dragon; Koshchei (the Deathless); Water of Life and Death, The
> *References:* Afanas'ev 1865–69

CHUR
Slav
Alternative name for Rod(ú).

CHURILO PLENKOVICH
Russia
The best-dressed man in all Russia, according to the legends surrounding the wedding feast of Dunai Ivanovich and the Princess Nastas'ya.

> *See also:* Dunai Ivanovich; Nastas'ya, Princess

CILICIA
General
Also: Kilikia
Armenian state established on the Mediterranean coast in the mid- to late eleventh century. This kingdom fell to Mamluk invaders in 1375. The territory now is part of modern Turkey.

CIRCASSIANS
General
People of the northwestern Caucasus, also referred to as the Cherkess. They are found today chiefly in the Adygeya and Cherkess autonomous oblasts (political subdivisions of the Russian Federation) and in larger groups in Jordan, Turkey, and Syria. They belong to the Abkhaz-Adygei language group, a non–Indo-European group distantly related to Georgian, and are linguistically related to many other mountain peoples of the Caucasus and Transcaucasus. Since the seventeenth century they have been Muslims. Although Circassia was ceded to Russia in 1829, its fiercely independent inhabitants were not subjugated until 1864, by which time many had left the Caucasus and migrated to various parts of the Ottoman Empire.

CITY OF THE KING, THE
Russia
A city in the Kingdom by the Sea, in which Sviatogor's future bride had lived for thirty years on a dunghill.
    See also: Kingdom by the Sea, The; Sviatogor

CLAY CITY, THE
Armenia
One in a succession of cities that Habërmani's princess-wife traveled through on her quest to find her husband and be reconciled with him.
    See also: Habërmani
    References: Orbeli and Taronian 1959–67, vol. 4

CONSTANTINE
Slav
The given name of Saint Cyril, who did not adopt the name Cyril until he had become a monk. As he died soon afterward, in A.D. 869, he was known only a short time as Cyril.
    See also: Cyril and Methodius, Saints

CONSTANTINOPLE
General
"City of Constantine," the name by which Byzantium was known between A.D. 324, when the Roman emperor Constantine I chose the city as his capital, and 1453, when the Ottoman Empire conquered the city and renamed it Istanbul.
    See also: Byzantium

COPPER CITY, THE
Armenia
One of a succession of cities visited by Habërmani's wife on her quest to find her husband and restore him to her side.
    See also: Habërmani
    References: Orbeli and Taronian 1959–67, vol. 4

COPPER KINGDOM, THE
Russia
One of three kingdoms in the realm of Whirlwind, which was located on a plateau at the top of some tremendously high mountains. The tsaritsa of this kingdom had been imprisoned by Whirlwind in a copper palace that was guarded by dragons. She was set free by Ivan Belyaninovich, along with her sisters, the tsaritsas of the Silver Kingdom and the Golden Kingdom, when he killed Whirlwind and released his mother, Nastas'ya of the Golden Braid. She married Vasilii Belyaninovich, one of the two brothers of Ivan. Her sister the tsaritsa of the Silver Kingdom married Peter Belyaninovich, and Elena the Fair, the tsaritsa of the Golden Kingdom, married Ivan Belyaninovich.
    See also: Dragon; Elena the Fair; Golden Kingdom, The; Ivan Belyaninovich; Nastas'ya of the Golden Braid; Peter Belyaninovich;

Silver Kingdom, The; Vasilii (Belyaninovich);
Whirlwind

COSSACKS
General

A group of people in the former USSR,
chiefly of Russian and Ukrainian stock, who
lived principally on the steppes that lie to the
north of the Black Sea and the Caucasus
mountains and extend eastward to the Altai
mountains in Siberia. Some historians trace
the origin of the Cossacks to serfs who fled
the principality of Moscow in the fourteenth
and fifteenth centuries A.D. and established
wheat-growing and stock-raising communities in the valleys of the Dnieper, Don, and
Ural Rivers and in Siberia. The name *Cossack*
derives from the Turkish word *kazak,* which
means "free person." The individual Cossack
communities, like other Russian peasant
communes of the time, owned land in common. These communities were governed by
village assemblies that were presided over by
elected village elders called *ataman*s or *hetman*s. The chief *ataman* or *hetman* of a region
enjoyed great power and prestige, exercising
the authority of a military leader in times of
war and that of a civil administrator in
peacetime.

In the sixteenth century, as the tsars
extended their realm, the Cossacks were subjected to the authority of the Russian government, which tried to incorporate them
into the state on the same basis as the other
inhabitants of the country. As subjects of the
tsar, all Cossack males aged between 18 and
50 became eligible for military service. They
were most often conscripted as members of
the cavalry. Cossack horsemen became
famous in the wars of the tsars against the
Tatars in the Crimea and the Caucasus.

The Cossacks, however, cherished their
tradition of freedom, which frequently
brought them into conflict with the tsars. In
the seventeenth and eighteenth centuries the
Cossacks, supported by peasants, engaged in
two widespread revolts (1670–71 and 1773–
74) in the lower Volga Valley. In later years the

*The famine in Russia, 1892; a Cossack patrol near
Kazan prevents peasants from leaving their village.
(Wood engraving in the* Illustrated London News,
*from a sketch by a Russian officer; Library of
Congress)*

Russian tsars used the Cossacks as border
troops and as a special military and police
force for the suppression of internal unrest.
In the latter nineteenth and early twentieth
centuries the tsarist government used
Cossack troops to perpetrate pogroms (organized massacres, from *grom*—"thunder")
against Jewish people. Cossack troops were
employed on a large scale in the suppression
of the Russian Revolution of 1905, but they
refused to be used for the same purpose during the Revolution of 1917.

During the civil war that followed the
1917 Revolution, the majority of Cossacks
fought against the Bolshevik armies. The
establishment of the Soviet system brought
about many changes in Cossack life. The
richer Cossacks were deprived of their
wealth, and traditional forms of local admin-

istration were abolished. Cossack soldiers were relieved of their special military and police duties, and Cossack cavalry units were prohibited. Cossacks were forced to engage in collective farming. Many were deported from their lands and resettled in Kazakhstan or in Siberia. Nonetheless, Cossack customs and traditions continued to be practiced in several parts of Russia during the Soviet period, particularly in the regions of the Don and Kuban' Rivers.

During the last years of the USSR, Cossack organizations experienced a sudden revival. In 1990, Cossack associations were formed in traditional Cossack areas of the Russian south including the lower reaches of the Don River, the North Caucasus, and the Ural Mountains. The same year, a national union of various Cossack associations was founded in Moscow. After the USSR was dissolved in 1991, the movement spread to areas outside traditional Cossack lands, so that by the end of 1992, Cossack associations had appeared in several large northern cities, such as St. Petersburg and Moscow.

See also: Black Sea; Caucasus; Dnieper; Don; Kazakhstan; Moscow; Siberia; Tatars; Volga

CRIMEA
General

The Crimea is a peninsula in southern Ukraine that juts out into the Black Sea and the Sea of Azov. It covers about 10,400 square miles (27,000 square kilometers) and is joined to the mainland by the narrow Isthmus of Perekop.

See also: Azov, Sea of; Black Sea; Ukraine

CRNOJEVIC, IVAN
Serbia
See Ivan Crnojevic.

CROATIA
General

A constituent republic in the former Yugoslavia. Part of Pannonia in Roman times, the country was conquered by the Avars in the sixth century A.D. During the seventh century the Carpathian Croats ousted the Avars and were in turn conquered by the Franks. Later the region was made into a duchy. Croatia was an independent kingdom from 925 until the end of the eleventh century, when a period of anarchy led to intervention by Hungary. Except for periods of occupation by the Ottoman Empire, most of what is today the Republic of Croatia was an autonomous kingdom within the Habsburg Empire from 1102 until the Hungarian revolution of 1848–49. Dalmatia and Istria were dominated for a time by Venice and France, respectively. After the Hungarian revolution, Croatia and Slavonia became separate Austrian crown lands. In 1867 the Austrians and Hungarians created the dual monarchy of Austria-Hungary from the Habsburg Empire, and Croatia was assigned to the Hungarian crown the following year. Croatia gained its autonomy and was formally joined with Slavonia in 1881.

During World War I, Croats and Serbs fought side by side, hoping to create a kingdom that would unite all of the South Slavs. On 1 December 1918, following the overthrow of the monarchy of Austria-Hungary at the close of the war, Croatia became part of the independent Kingdom of the Serbs, Croats, and Slovenes under the Serbian monarchy of King Alexander I. When conflict between Croats and Serbs led to greater national tensions, Alexander tightened control over the country, and in 1929 he renamed the kingdom Yugoslavia ("Land of the Southern Slavs"). Tensions between the two ethnic groups continued, however, and the postwar history of the state was marked by the struggle of the Croats for greater political autonomy. Croatian extremists assassinated Alexander in 1934, and the fascist movement Ustaša began to garner support among discontented Croat peasants. In 1939 the approximate present boundaries of the republic were defined and the area was named Croatia.

See also: Avars; Hungary; Mongols; Pannonia

CRYSTAL CITY, THE

Armenia

One of the succession of cities that the wife of Habërmani traveled through on her quest to find her husband.

    See also: Habërmani
    References: Orbeli and Taronian 1959–67, vol. 4

CYRIL AND METHODIUS, SAINTS

Slav

Cyril and Methodius were brothers born in Thessalonica (Cyril in c. 826, Methodius c. 815 or c. 826) who achieved renown as the Apostles to the Slavs. Cyril was christened Constantine and was educated at the University of Constantinople, where he studied under Photius. Later, Cyril taught at the same university in Photius's place, while Methodius became the provincial governor of the Slavic colony of Opsikion.

In 861 the two brothers were sent by Byzantine Emperor Michael III ("the Drunkard") to convert the Khazars, a Tatar people of Russia who tolerated all faiths and whose ruler practiced Judaism. When they returned from this mission, Methodius became the abbot of a Greek monastery and Cyril went back to teaching. However, in 863, Rostislav, Duke of Moravia, wrote to the patriarch of Constantinople, Photius, requesting missionaries who could teach his people. Photius sent Cyril and Methodius because of their knowledge of the Slavic language.

The most significant achievement of these two brothers was their invention of the Glagolitic alphabet that is still used in a few isolated locales and that became the basis of the Cyrillic alphabet, which probably was the work of a later disciple. Due to this invention as well as their translations of many passages from Scripture and Christian liturgy, the brothers are regarded as the founders of Slavic literature. They won many Slavs to the eastern Catholic rite due to their knowledge of the language. Eventually, however, as they began to encounter stiff opposition from German bishops and missionaries, Cyril and Methodius withdrew to

Twelfth-century Romanesque embossed tin reliquary with the heads of Saints Cyril and Methodius, Castle Armory, Kreuzenstein, Austria (Erich Lessing/Art Resource, NY)

Rome, where they were received with honors by Pope Adrian II.

Cyril became a monk and adopted the name Constantine, by which he is commonly known, but died a short time afterward (869) and was buried at San Clemente in Rome. Methodius was consecrated as bishop of Moravia but later was imprisoned for two years, for his continuing opposition to German bishops. He was released upon the intervention of the pope, but in 879 he was called to Rome to answer charges of heterodoxy. Pope John VIII cleared him of the charges and appointed him bishop of Simium and Moravia with express papal permission to celebrate mass in the Slavic language. Methodius remained in his see until his death in 885. In 1880 the feast day of the brothers was extended to the universal church by Pope Leo XIII, and Pope Paul II named them patrons of Europe along with Saint Benedict. In church art the two brothers are depicted as holding up a church between them. Their feast day is 14 February on the Roman Catholic calendar, and 11 May on the Orthodox calendar.

See also: Byzantine Empire; Constantinople; Cyrillic alphabet; Opsikion; Tatars

CYRILLIC ALPHABET
General

Around A.D. 860, Greek missionaries from Constantinople came to Slavic lands to convert the people to Christianity. The people lacked a written alphabet, however, so the missionaries devised for them a unique system of writing known as Cyrillic, from the name of one of its inventors, St. Cyril. (Cyril and his brother St. Methodius, also known as the Apostles to the Slavs, are often credited with having created this alphabet.) The Cyrillic alphabet, like its Latin counterpart, has Greek roots, being based on the ninth-century uncial script. Additional characters, however, were devised to represent Slavic sounds that had no Greek or Latin equivalents. The Cyrillic alphabet originally consisted of 43 letters. Various smaller versions of this alphabet are currently used in Russia (32 letters), Ukraine (33 letters), Serbia (30 letters), and Bulgaria (30 letters), but not in Poland, the Czech and Slovak Republics, or Slovenia, where modified Latin alphabets are used. An interesting division exists in the Balkan countries, where the Roman Catholic Croats use the Latin alphabet but the Greek Orthodox Serbs employ Cyrillic for the same language.

Appendix 2 shows the modern Cyrillic alphabet as used in present-day Russia, along with its most common English transliteration.

See also: Bulgaria; Cyril and Methodius, Saints; Czechs; Poland; Serbia; Slovakia; Slovenia; Ukraine

CZECHOSLOVAKIA
General

A state in central Europe from 1918 until 1992. On 1 January 1993 the state of Czechoslovakia ceased to exist and was divided into the Czech Republic and Slovakia. Czechoslovakia was home to two closely related Slavic peoples, the Czechs and the Slovaks. Most of the Czechs lived in the western part of the country, in the regions of Bohemia and Moravia, whereas the Slovaks lived primarily in Slovakia, an area in the east.

Celtic and Germanic tribes also lived in what became Czechoslovakia more than 2,000 years ago. The first Slavic tribes settled in the region about A.D. 500. Several tribes united to form a state in the ninth century that became the core of the Great Moravian Empire, which soon covered much of central Europe. Hungarian tribes conquered the empire in 907 and ruled Slovakia for nearly 1,000 years.

In 1212, Bohemia became a semi-independent kingdom within the Holy Roman Empire, a German-based empire in western and central Europe. In 1526, the Austrian Habsburgs began ruling Bohemia, which during the ensuing decades gradually lost most of its powers of self-governance. In the late eighteenth century Czech intellectuals began actively to encourage a national identity among their compatriots. A similar movement that emerged around the same time in Slovakia was put down by Hungarian rulers. Not until 1993 were the nationalist aspirations of the two peoples realized.

See also: Bohemia; Czechs; Hungary; Moravia; Slovakia

CZECHS
General

The word Czechs as used in this book refers to people who speak the Czech language and who live in central Europe, roughly inside the bounds of the former Czechoslovakia (today, the independent Czech and Slovak republics). Czechoslovakia was created as an independent state after the breakup of the Austro-Hungarian empire at the end of World War I, in 1918. It comprised the Bohemian crown lands: Bohemia, Moravia, and part of Silesia, the three areas in which the Czech language originated; and Slovakia, a part of Hungary that was inhabited by Slavs.

See also: Bohemia; Czechoslovakia; Hungary; Moravia; Slavs; Slovakia

Early-twentieth-century photograph of Prague, the capital of Czechoslovakia, looking to the ancient Roman palace and Saint Vitus Cathedral (Archive Photos)

D

DACIA

General

The name given to the land today known as Romania, during the period prior to the Roman occupation in A.D. 106. Dacia also included parts of modern Hungary, but those areas did not become parts of Hungary until the modern borders were established; so it is correct to refer to Dacia as the ancient name for Romania. The Dacians— the earliest known inhabitants of the region—were living in Dacia by the fourth century B.C., although their origin and the exact date of their arrival are unknown. Trajan conquered Dacia in A.D. 106 and made it a province of the Roman Empire, and the country thereafter became known as Romania.

See also: Hungary; Romania

DADZBOG

Slav

See Dazhbog.

DALMAT

Russia

Tsar of an unnamed realm, he owned the Firebird that was the target of a quest by the sons of Tsar Vyslav Andronovich—Dmitrii, Vasilii, and Ivan (all of whom bore the patronymic Vyslavovich, meaning "son of Vyslav"). When Ivan Vyslavovich was caught trying to steal the Firebird and its gilded cage, Tsar Dalmat gave him a chance to redeem himself. If Ivan could steal for Tsar Dalmat the Horse with the Golden Mane,

which belonged to Tsar Afron, not only would Dalmat forgive Ivan but he also would give him the Firebird and its cage. Ivan Vyslavovich tricked Dalmat with the help of a shape-changing wolf who became the Horse with the Golden Mane, and after Ivan had ridden away on the real one, resumed his shape as a wolf and disappeared.

See also: Afron; Dmitrii (Vyslavovich); Firebird, The; Horse with the Golden Mane, The; Ivan Vyslavovich; Vasilii Vyslavovich; Vyslav Andronovich

DALMATIA

General

One of the two primary geographical regions of modern Croatia, the other being the Pannonian Plains. Dalmatia is a coastal region between the Adriatic Sea and Bosnia-Herzegovina. Once a state in its own right, it became a part of the former Yugoslavia when the Kingdom of the Serbs, Croats, and Slovenes was formed on 1 December 1918 from Bosnia-Herzegovina, Croatia, Dalmatia, Montenegro, Serbia, and Slovenia.

See also: Bosnia; Croatia; Herzegovina; Montenegro; Pannonia; Serbia; Slovenia

DANILO, PRINCE

Russia

Autocratic despot whose authority was challenged by an all-female army. Danilo engaged the female army in a singing contest, challenging them to sing about Il'ya Muromets. They refused, and instead they sang a song about how they would overcome Danilo. Having finished the song, Danilo ordered the guards to attack the female army; but before the guards could move, the people of Danilo's city rose up, drove the guards away, and then turned against Danilo and killed him.

See also: Il'ya Muromets
References: Chadwick 1964

59

Detail in marble from the Column of Trajan, Rome, showing the Roman campaigns against the Dacians, c. 106 B.C.–A.D. 13 (Alinari / Art Resource, NY)

DANUBE

General

The second-longest European river, flowing c. 1,776 miles or 2,858 kilometers. It rises on the eastern slopes of the Black Forest (in southwestern Germany) and flows across Europe to Romania, where it enters the Black Sea through a swampy delta. The river's Russian name is Dunai, stemming from the legend that the river sprang into life from the blood of Dunai Ivanovich after he impaled himself on his upturned spear for shooting his wife, Princess Nastas'ya, through the heart with a poisoned arrow.

The river has always been an important route between western Europe and the Black Sea. In the third century A.D. it formed the northern boundary of the Roman Empire in southeastern Europe. Early in the Middle Ages, Goths, Huns, Avars, Slavs, Magyars, and other migratory peoples crossed the Danube on their way to invade the Roman, and later the Byzantine, Empire. It served as an artery for the Crusaders into Byzantium (Constantinople) and from there to the Holy Land, and it later eased the advance (beginning at the end of the fourteenth century) of the Ottoman Turks into central and western Europe. During the nineteenth century it became an essential link between the growing industrial centers of Germany and the agrarian areas of the Balkans. At that time, most of the river's middle and upper course lay within the Austrian Empire and the lower part belonged to the decaying empire of the Ottoman Turks. As Turkish control over the Balkans weakened, Austria and other European powers moved to prevent Russia from acquiring the strategic Danube delta.

See also: Avars; Black Sea; Byzantine Empire; Byzantium; Constantinople; Dunai Ivanovich; Magyars; Nastas'ya, Princess; Nastas'ya Nikulichna; Romania

DARK PRINCESS, THE
Russia

The euphemistic name given to the wife of Paul, the ruler of Murom.

See also: Murom; Paul

DARKNESS
Russia

The personification of the night, which would hold the Sun captive without the daily intervention of Perun.

See also: Perun; Sun

DATAN
Poland

One of the three gods of the field, the others being Lawkapatim and Tawals. All three were invoked to ensure a good harvest, because if they were not called upon for their help, they could become malevolent and ruin the crop.

See also: Lawkapatim; Tawals

DAUSOS
Lithuania

Mysterious realm of the dead—possibly the moon—governed by Dievas. It was not a heaven or a paradise but simply a world that lay beyond the slippery high hill of the sky, which the dead had to climb. To stop themselves from slipping down again, the dead needed strong fingernails or claws like those of an animal. As the journey was believed to be very long, spirits were also said to have made the trip on horseback, in the smoke of cremation fires, by traveling along the Bird's

Way (the Milky Way), or in a boat such as that used by the Sun on his return trip to the east.

See also: Bird's Way, The; Dievas; Milky Way, The; Moon; Sun

DAWN
Russia

The rising sun, personified in the goddess Zorya Utrennyaya.

See also: Zorya Utrennyaya

DAY
Russia

Although there are no legends specifically focused on Day, the legends of Baba-Yaga describe Day as being under the witch's command, as are the Sun and the Night. In these tales Day is described as a horseman with a white face, dressed from head to foot in white, and riding a brilliant white horse that has a white saddle and harness. He is the brother of Night, who is his complete opposite. Day's relationship to the Sun is never revealed. Some specialists say that the Sun might be the father of both Day and Night; but this assertion appears in none of the stories that mention Day.

See also: Baba-Yaga (-Jaga, -Iaga); Night; Sun

DAZHBOG
Russia, Poland, Serbia
Also: Dadzbog

The son of sky god Svarog, brother to fire god Svarozhich, Dazhbog is god of the sun, happiness, destiny, and justice. He gradually superseded his father as the supreme deity in the Russian pantheon. The giver of warmth and light, he was much revered by the early Russians because much of Russia is covered by snow and ice most of the year and the winter nights are unendurably long. The disappearance of Dazhbog was always greeted with dismay, and occurrences such as eclipses, when Dazhbog was said to have been devoured by wolves, were taken as forewarnings of terrible times to come—of plague, famine, or war. The Russians believed that Dazhbog ruled over the twelve kingdoms of the zodiac and was served by two beautiful maidens, the two Zvezdy (Zvezda Dennitsa and Zvezda Vechernyaya)—the personifications of the Auroras—and by the seven planets; and that comets acted as his messengers. Daily he drove his golden chariot, which was drawn by a pair of fire-breathing white horses, across the sky from his golden palace in the east, while his balding old uncle Mesyats (the moon) awaited his arrival in the evening. Some stories, however, say that Dazhbog married Mesyats, who in this case would be female, and that their union begot the stars. Occasionally the genders of Dazhbog and Mesyats are reversed, making Dazhbog the sun goddess, and Mesyats the moon god. Later tradition said that Dazhbog lived in the sun, whence he ruled over twelve kingdoms—one for each sign of the zodiac.

In 988, when Vladimir I married Anna and converted to Christianity, Dazhbog's huge statue in Kiev was ceremonially toppled into the river, along with the statues of other pagan deities. Dazhbog then became increasingly identified with Lucifer, the bearer of God's light who fell from the sky to outer darkness.

Polish belief held that Dazhbog lived in the east, in a paradise of milk and honey, a land of eternal sunlight, whence he rode out each new morning in a golden chariot with diamond wheels that was drawn by twelve white, fire-breathing horses (some accounts say that his chariot was drawn by three horses—one of gold, one of silver, and one of diamonds). The Serbs saw Dazhbog as an upright young man who lived in a palace in the east, whence he drove his carriage out every morning. Again, some accounts say that he had twelve white horses, others that he had three made respectively of gold, silver, and diamonds. As the day wore on he grew steadily older before dying each evening as a red-faced, bloated, elderly gentleman. He was reborn the next morning as a young man.

See also: Anna; Auroras; Kiev; Mesyats; Moon; Sun; Supreme Deity; Svarog; Svarozhich (~gich); Vladimir I; Zvezda Dennitsa; Zvezda Vechernyaya
References: Gimbutas 1971; Ivanov and Toporov 1965

DEATH
Armenia and Russia

In the traditions and cultures of many peoples throughout the world, death is personified as a skeletal figure dressed in black. Nobody can cheat him when he calls. One Armenian story shows Death in an unusually benevolent light, although he certainly does not start off that way when he calls on a young man and tells him that he will die on his wedding day. The young man, terrified, takes to his heels. After several days of walking and worrying, the young man comes to the foot of Mount Biledjan, where he sees an old man sitting on a stone throne, a staff in his hand. The old man calls to the youth and asks him why he looks so troubled. When the young man replies that he is running from Death, who has warned him that he will die on his wedding day, the old man reveals himself as Time, adding that Death is under his control. The youth then begs to be spared from the clutches of Death, whereupon Time tells him to drink of a well in the distance, for the water of the well will free him of his fear so that he might live his life to the fullest, though not in his own hometown.

The young man drinks from the well, as instructed. Immediately his fear of Death vanishes, and the young man continues on his way until he comes to a town where he settles and over the years amasses a small fortune. However, after several years his thoughts turns to his parents, so he sets off for home, carrying his fortune with him. No sooner does he enter his parents' house than Death reappears and demands the young man's soul. Seeing Death, the young man's mother throws herself in front of her son, telling Death to take her soul instead. Death agrees and starts to draw the woman's soul

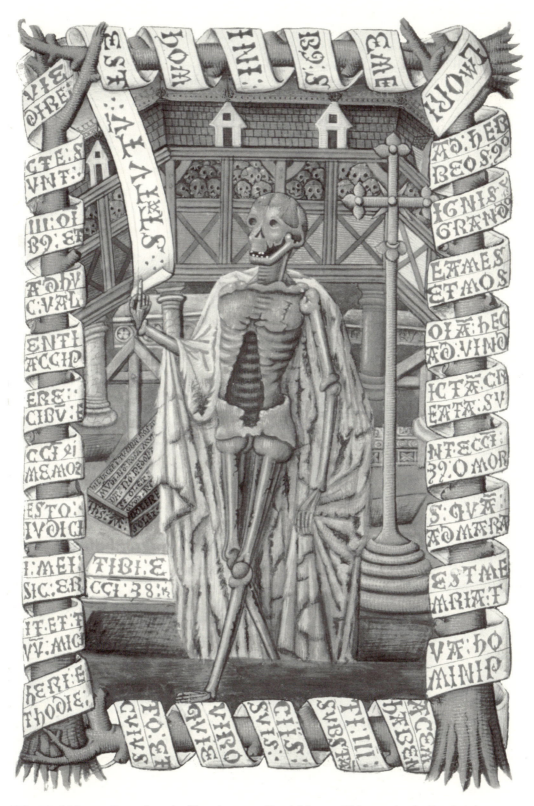

"The Final Moments," page from the fifteenth-century French Hours of Marguerite de Coetivy *(ms. 74/1088, folio 90, Musée Condé, Chantilly, France; Giraudon/Art Resource, NY)*

out of her mouth, but the pain is too much to bear, and the old woman begs for mercy, whereupon Death lets go. Next, the young man's father offers his soul, but with the same result. Seeing that his case is hopeless, the young man tells Death that he will gladly give up his own soul if the maiden he loves will not offer herself in his place. Death agrees, and the two go to the home of the young woman to whom the youth is betrothed. She immediately offers her soul; but when Death starts to draw it out of her, she complains that he is taking too long and that he should either let her live or take her soul at once, allowing her time only to kiss the man she loves one last time before she dies. Death marvels at the love and devotion of the young woman. No sooner has he removed her soul than he is filled with remorse—a very alien feeling for Death. He gives her back her soul and departs. The young man and the young woman are duly married, their wedding feast lasting three days and three nights, and from that day to this they are the only couple ever to have escaped the clutches of Death.

A Russian legend confirms that Death may be evaded but that the result might not be desirable: In the tale of Ivan the Soldier, Ivan captures Death in a pouch and hangs him in a tree in the Briansk Woods. Later, Ivan decides that his time has come to die. He returns to the Briansk Woods and releases Death from the pouch, but Death refuses to take the old soldier and quickly hurries away.

See also: Briansk Woods; Ivan the Soldier; Time
References: Orbeli and Taronian 1959–67, vol. 10

DEBESTEVS
Latvia

"Father of Heaven," the god of the sky. His Lithuanian counterpart is Dievas, and in Latvia he is known as Dievs. In Latvian belief, the sky god married the Sun—in this instance, female—and as a result controlled the destiny of all beings.

See also: Dievas; Sun

DECEIT
Hungary—Magyar

An evil sorcerer who placed a spell on a prince, turning him into a cockerel.

See also: Almafi; Talking Mountain, The

DED MOROZ
Russia

"Grandfather Frost," the friendly personification of frost, is the Russian counterpart to Father Christmas (Santa Claus). When unaccompanied by Wind, Frost is a jolly old fellow.

See also: Frost; Morozko; Wind

DEDY
Russia

"Grandfathers," the generic name applied to the spirits of revered ancestors, who were believed to be linked to the household spirits, such as the domovoi.

See also: Domovoi

DEKLA
Lithuania

Sister of Karta and Laima-Dalia in legends that describe three goddesses of fate. Usually Laima-Dalia was considered the sole goddess of fate. The three goddesses were believed to control the destinies of all living things, from a single blade of grass to a human being.

See also: Karta; Laima(-Dalia)

DEMIAN, SAINT
Russia
See Dem'yan, Saint.

DEM'YAN, SAINT
Russia

Russian Orthodox saint. According to legend, he was a smith who with the help of his brother, Saint Kuz'ma, forged the first plow (although other versions of this legend name the two smiths as Saints Boris and Gleb). The real Saints Kuz'ma and Dem'yan, however, had nothing at all to do with smithing: They were doctors who were martyred. Their connection with the legends surrounding smiths

An undated woodcut of Ded Moroz, the spirit of Frost, flying through the air (from the collections of Carol Rose; photo by David Rose)

stems from the fact that Kuz'ma sounds similar to the Russian word for a smithy, *kuznya*. As a result they became, in the Russian Orthodox calendar of saints, the patrons of smiths and craftsmen, guardians of the land and providers of fertility, and patrons of medicine and metallurgy. Churches dedicated to them were often found in the part of a town where smiths and craftsmen plied their trades.

The plow reputedly forged by Kuz'ma and Dem'yan was of enormous proportions and was forged with implements of like size. The two smiths were reported to have used twelve golden hammers, and tongs that weighed almost four hundredweight, or twelve poods. One Ukrainian story (see the entry on Kuz'ma, Saint) tells how this plow was first used. Given their putative talent in the art of welding, Kuz'ma and Dem'yan also came to be regarded as the patron saints of marriage in Russia.

See also: Boris, Saint; Gleb, Saint; Kuz'ma, Saint
References: Chicherov 1957

DENNITSA
Slav

The shortened, popularized version of Zvezda Dennitsa, the Morning Star.
See also: Morning Star; Zvezda Dennitsa

DEREVLIANE
Russia

A peaceful people whose prince, Prince Mal, sought to unite his house with that of Kiev by marrying the widowed Olga. What happened then is related in a folktale known as "Olga's Revenge."
See also: Kiev; Mal, Prince; Olga
References: Cross and Sherbowitz-Wetzor 1953

DESNA
Russia

River that flows through Ukraine. The capital city of Kiev lies at the confluence of the Desna and the Dnieper.
See also: Dnieper; Kiev; Ukraine

DEVANA
Czech

Goddess of the hunt, paralleling the Roman Diana. Among the Serbs she is known as Diiwica, and in Poland as Dziewona or Dilwica.
See also: Diiwica; Dilwica

DEVIL, THE
Russia

Although the Devil is not described in Russian legends in the same terms as he appears in other cultures, he is said, as he is elsewhere, to reside in the underworld, where he is the lord of the dead and of demons, witches, and serpents, and to bring misfortune to the living. Some authorities claim that the witch Baba-Yaga is the servant of the Devil, but there is no evidence in the legends to support this. One particular legend shows that the Devil could also have a compassionate nature, provided he was shown the respect he thought he deserved.

An unnamed smith once saw a frightening image of the Devil in a local church. Upon returning to his smithy, he commissioned a painter to re-create the likeness on the doors to his workshop. For ten years he always gave the Devil a cordial greeting as he came to work and bade him a good night every evening as he left. After the smith died, his son inherited the smithy, but the youth swore never to show something so hideous the respect his father had. Instead he used to hit the image with a large hammer, squarely between the eyes, every time he passed it. For three years the Devil withstood these insults, until he could bear it no longer.

Transforming himself into a young man, he went to the smithy, where he asked to be made the smith's apprentice. Having been taken on, the Devil soon proved his worth and was often left to mind the forge. On one such occasion the aging wife of a local landowner came to the smithy to have her horse shod. The Devil told her that they had just started a new line of business, the rejuvenation of old people. The vanity of the old woman got the better of her, and she paid the Devil in advance to renew her youth.

Gathering two pails of milk, the Devil took hold of the woman in his tongs and cast her into the middle of the furnace. When all that was left were her bones, the Devil removed these from the fire and placed them in a tub. He then poured the milk over the still crackling bones, and within a few minutes a young woman stepped forth. Returning to her husband, she persuaded him to go for the same treatment.

When the old man arrived at the smithy, the Devil had gone and the smith was back at the forge. Threatened with all kinds of punishment if he did not do for the landowner as he had done for his wife, the smith was obliged to do as he was asked. Throwing the landowner into the fire, he burned him until only his bones were left. These he placed in the tub and poured milk over them. Several hours passed and nothing happened. Anxious about her husband, the recently rejuvenated woman came to the smithy, and finding only the charred bones of her husband, she ran off to have the young smith arrested for murder.

After she left, the Devil reappeared, and the smith explained his predicament. The Devil then revealed who he was and told the smith that if he promised from that moment forth always to be civil to him and never to strike his image again, he would restore the man. The smith agreed, and by the time the woman had returned to have the smith arrested she was greeted by her rejuvenated husband.

See also: Baba-Yaga (-Jaga, -Iaga); Underworld, The

DEVIL AND THE SOLDIER, THE
Russia

An old soldier, on his way home after being discharged from the army of an unnamed tsar, was seated by a lake when he was confronted by a red-horned demon. The demon made a pact with the soldier that for the next fifteen years, in return for untold riches, the soldier would not wash, shave, comb his hair, cut his nails, wipe his nose, or change his clothes. However, if the soldier broke any of these rules even once, then the Devil would have his soul.

The soldier agreed, and had the demon bring him a sack of money and then transport him to Moscow in a flash. There the soldier quickly bought a wonderful mansion and settled down to pass the next fifteen years in splendid isolation. Every day the soldier's fortune continued to grow, and soon he found that he did not have enough room to store it all. Therefore he started to distribute his wealth among the poor of Moscow; but still his fortune continued to grow, and his fame began to spread far and wide.

The tsar heard of the old soldier's generosity, and being almost bankrupt, he called for the soldier to be brought before him so that he could solicit a donation from him. The soldier duly presented himself to the tsar, his hair and beard touching the floor in a matted mass, his nose constantly running, and his clothes in the most disgusting state. Worst of all was the smell, which was nauseating.

The tsar offered the old soldier the rank of a general in his army in return for a large sum of money. The soldier politely refused the post, but promised to give the tsar all the money he needed if one of the tsar's three daughters would become his wife. The tsar instantly agreed and called for his oldest daughter to be brought to him. However, as soon as she saw the hideous apparition before her, the girl said that she would rather marry the Devil—a comment noted by the demon who had struck the deal with the soldier.

The tsar's second-oldest daughter was brought in, and she retorted in exactly the same manner, and her name likewise was noted by the demon. Finally, the tsar's youngest daughter was brought into the hall, and although her initial reaction was one of disgust, she knew that her father was depending on her. Thus, with tears rolling down her fair cheeks, she agreed to marry the soldier.

Preparations for the marriage were soon in full swing, and the tsar had collected his gold, when the fifteen years the soldier had agreed to came to an end. The demon came to the soldier, and unable to convince the soldier to continue in the service of the Devil, restored him to his former self, and then rejuvenated him with the Water of Life and Death. Shortly afterward, the soldier and the tsar's daughter were married.

The demon returned to his master and reported all that had happened. The Devil was furious to think that fifteen years' wealth had been wasted on the soldier and

that in return he did not even possess the soldier's soul. His anger subsided, however, when he learned that the two elder daughters of the tsar had said they would rather marry the Devil than the soldier. The Devil rubbed his hands in glee and waited until in due course he was able to add their souls to his vast collection.

See also: Moscow; Water of Life and Death, The

DEVIL'S CASTLE
Armenia
The lair of Tapagöz, the oldest of the demons.
See also: Tapagöz

DIDA
Slav
The female counterpart of Dido, the pair likely to have been twins born to the deities Lada and Lado.
See also: Dido; Lada; Lado
References: Afanas'ev 1865–69; Znayenko 1980

DIDILIA
Poland
One of a pair of fertility deities, the other being Zizilia. The twin mothers of divine twins, Didilia and Zizilia were venerated as goddesses of erotic and maternal love.
See also: Zizilia
References: Afanas'ev 1865–69; Znayenko 1980

DIDO
Slav
The consort of Lada; or, according to some sources, the son of Lada. Dido had a female counterpart named Dida, and it seems likely that Dido and Dida were twins born to the deities Lada and Lado.
See also: Lada; Lado
References: Afanas'ev 1865–69; Znayenko 1980

DIEVAS
Lithuania, Latvia
"Heavenshine," the high god of the sky, ancestor of everything that exists, and the most ancient of gods. His name is cognate with the Sanskrit *dyut,* "to shine," and *deiuos,* "of the

sky," and can thus be related to both the Greek Zeus (originally Dieus) and the early Indian sky god Dyaus. He is called Debestevs in neighboring Latvia, where he is depicted as a handsome king dressed in a silver robe, cap, belt, and sword. He lives beyond the slippery high hill of the sky, far beyond the realm of Dausos, in an enclosed kingdom that may only be entered through three silver gates. Within the walls of his kingdom are his manor house, farms, sauna, and garden, the entire realm being surrounded by an impenetrable forest.

Every day Dievas leaves his home and drives very carefully down the slippery high hill of the sky in a chariot of gold, or on a copper sledge. He takes great care not to make the earth tremble or to disturb so much as a single dewdrop, for Dievas is primarily concerned with the promotion of the earth's fertility. Dievas stimulates the growth of crops and tramples weeds underfoot or under the wheels of his chariot. In association with Laima, Dievas is also responsible for determining man's fate. He is attended by his unnamed sons, the Dievo suneliai, and the moon god Menuo.

Although he is the most powerful of Baltic deities, he is not the king or ruler of the gods, having surrendered that role to Perun. He is rather primus inter pares, living on in his realm beyond the horizon, in celestial retirement, his home being shared by the dead. If they were lucky, the dead were carried there on the smoke of their funeral pyres, or climbed along the Milky Way; but if they were unlucky, they would have to crawl up the slippery high slope of the sky, clinging on with their fingernails. The variant name of Dievs is used mostly in Latvia.

See also: Dausos; Debestevs; Dievo suneliai; Laima (-Dalia); Menuo; Milky Way, The; Perun

DIEVO SUNELIAI
Lithuania

Collective name given to the unnamed sons of Dievas. They were their father's attendants, as was the moon god Menuo.

See also: Dievas; Menuo

DIIWICA
Serbia

The Serbian name for Devana, the goddess of the hunt.

See also: Dilwica

DILWICA
Poland

An ancient goddess of the hunt who rode with her followers and her hunting dogs through the forests. She was depicted as eternally beautiful and radiant and totally unapproachable. To stumble across Dilwica and her hunting party would mean almost certain death, possibly by being torn to pieces by her hounds. Some commentators have suggested that Dilwica (also known in Poland as Dziewona or Dziewana) is a version of the Roman goddess Diana, whom she certainly resembles. Others have suggested that Dilwica was originally an aspect of the Great Goddess common to many cultures and that the name Dilwica was given her only to protect her true, secret name.

See also: Devana; Great Goddess

DIMSTIPATIS
Lithuania

Alternative name for Zemepatis, the god of the homestead. This variant is derived from *dimstis* (home) and *patis* (father).

See also: Zemepatis

DIR
Russia

A Varangian who, along with Askold, gained control of Kiev at about the time Riurik became the ruler of Novgorod (A.D. 862). However, Dir and Askold may be purely legendary figures, whereas Riurik is known to be historical.

See also: Askold; Kiev; Novgorod; Riurik; Varangians

DIV
Russia

A magical bird that appears in the *Lay of Igor's Campaign* as the forces of nature combined into a single force that bars Igor's way, signals disaster, and leads Igor toward his enemies.

See also: Igor
References: Mann 1979; Zenkovsky 1963

DJANDJAVAZ, MOUNT
Armenia

The home of the giant Azrail.

See also: Apprentice, The; Azrail
References: Orbeli and Taronian 1959–67, vol. 1

DMITRII (VYSLAVOVICH)
Russia

One of the three sons of Tsar Vyslav Andronovich; brother to Vasilii Vyslavovich and Ivan Vyslavovich. When their father sent the three on a quest to locate and capture the Firebird, Dmitrii traveled with Vasilii, and Ivan traveled alone. When Ivan Vyslavovich was on his way home, having successfully completed the task, and bringing the Horse with the Golden Mane and the maiden Elena the Beautiful with him, his brothers ambushed and killed him. Then they returned home with the spoils, claiming Ivan's success as their own, and cast lots to determine each man's share. Vasilii won Elena the Beautiful, and Dmitrii won the Horse with the Golden Mane. Both brothers were thrown into the tsar's deepest dungeon after Ivan Vyslavovich returned, having been miraculously brought back to life with the help of the Water of Life and Death, sprinkled on him by the shape-changing wolf that had helped him earlier in his quest.

See also: Elena the Beautiful; Firebird, The; Horse with the Golden Mane, The; Ivan Vyslavovich; Vasilii Vyslavovich; Vyslav Andronovich; Water of Life and Death, The

DNIEPER
Russia

River, total length 1,400 miles (2,250 km), that rises in the Smolensk region of White Russia and flows south past Kiev, Dnepropetrovsk, and Zaporozhe to enter the Black Sea east of Odessa. The river features in many of the Russian legends that evolved around the court of Vladimir Bright Sun at Kiev. In the legend of Sukhman, the river is reported to have told the hero that the Tatar army was attempting to cross her to reach Kiev.

See also: Black Sea; Kiev; Sukhman; Tatars; Vladimir Bright Sun, Prince

DOBRYNYA NIKITICH
Russia

Friend of Dunai Ivanovich and his companion in travel from the court of Vladimir Bright Sun in Kiev to Lithuania, to bring back Princess Evpraksiya to be Vladimir's bride. In Lithuania he persuaded the king to allow Evpraksiya to marry Vladimir Bright Sun, whom the king held in very low esteem. Dobrynya brought the princess back to Kiev by himself after Dunai Ivanovich set off in pursuit of a mysterious marauder who had circled their camp at night.

Dobrynya, whose name is derived from *dobryi* (good), is probably best known as a dragon-slayer. Having slain the young of a she-dragon named Goryshche, Dobrynya was warned by his mother, Amelfia Timofeyevna, never to return to the Sorochinsk Mountains, where the dragon lived, and to stay away from the river Puchai. Dobrynya ignored what he thought were the ramblings of an old woman, and he was soon back in dragon-hunting country.

Tired and dusty from his long journey, Dobrynya stripped off his clothes, and leaving them with his horse on the bank, dived into the river Puchai. As soon as he entered the swiftly flowing waters, he saw fire and sparks leap into the air, accompanied by thick black smoke. Out of this smoke emerged the twelve-headed she-dragon Goryshche—the dragon whose offspring Dobrynya had previously killed. As the dragon asked Dobrynya what she should do with him, the knight saw his chance and dived beneath the waters, coming ashore on the bank opposite that on which his clothes and weapons lay, his horse having been frightened away when the dragon appeared.

Just as he thought he was finished, Dobrynya caught sight of a priest's hat lying in the grass. As a bogatyr', a knight of Holy Russia, he knew that this would make a formidable weapon; but when Dobrynya lifted it, he found that it was extremely heavy. As the dragon flew toward him, Dobrynya brandished the hat and severed the dragon's heads. As the dragon dropped to the ground, Dobrynya leaped onto her and readied himself to finish her off. Goryshche begged for mercy, promising never to raid the lands of Holy Russia again and never to carry off any more Russian people. Dobrynya likewise promised never to return to the Sorochinsk Mountains. Then he released the dragon.

Having lost his horse and his weapons, Dobrynya had to make his way home to Kiev on foot. When he arrived there he found that in his long absence a disaster had befallen the court of Prince Vladimir Bright Sun. The very dragon whom Dobrynya had spared had broken her word, and flying over the city, had carried away the Princess Zabava, Vladimir's favorite niece, holding her between her jaws. Vladimir Bright Sun called together his knights and challenged them to rescue the unfortunate maiden.

Alesha, the son of the priest Leontii, told Vladimir that Dobrynya appeared to be familiar with the dragon that was responsible, adding that he believed that the dragon regarded Dobrynya as her brother. When Vladimir Bright Sun heard this, he commanded Dobrynya to bring back the girl or be beheaded.

Dobrynya went home and told his mother what had transpired, complaining that he would have to walk to the Sorochinsk Mountains because he had no horse. His mother told him of his father's old chestnut, which stood mired in dung inside the stables. Telling her son to clean up the horse and feed it, she also advised him to get a good night's sleep. Dobrynya followed his mother's advice to the letter, and the follow-

ing morning, he mounted the chestnut and made ready to leave. Just as he was about to spur the horse on, his mother gave him a silken whip, telling him to whip the horse, should its strength begin to fail.

Placing the whip in his pocket, Dobrynya spurred the horse, which cleared the walls of the city in a huge leap and sped off faster than the eye could follow. In no time at all, they had reached the foothills of the Sorochinsk Mountains. There the ground teemed with the young of the she-dragon. Dobrynya set upon them, trampling them with his horse. After a while, having been bitten badly, the horse began to falter. Remembering the words of his mother, Dobrynya took the whip from his pocket and gently whipped his mount between the ears and hind legs. Instantly the horse's vigor returned, and they made their way to the cave of the she-dragon.

Needless to say, Goryshche was not happy to see Dobrynya. She complained bitterly about the death of her offspring, and even more so about the fact that Dobrynya, a knight of Holy Russia, had broken his word. Dobrynya retorted that it was she who had first broken their pact, and he demanded the return of Zabava. When the dragon refused, Dobrynya attacked her. For three days the pair fought, until finally Dobrynya was victorious. However, Dobrynya now found himself stranded in the middle of a vast lake that had formed from the dragon's blood, a lake that the earth would not soak up.

Calling on Mother Earth, he commanded her to open up and swallow the dragon's blood. Instantly a huge chasm appeared and the lake was drained. Dobrynya climbed down from his horse and entered the network of caves in which the dragon had lived. Inside he found, and released, many hundreds of Russians, before he found Princess Zabava in the very last chamber. Leading her outside, he perched her in front of him on his horse and returned to Kiev at the same speed with which he had departed. When he returned he was greeted as a great hero by Prince Vladimir Bright Sun and all the people of the city. He was also greeted at home by his horse Voroneyushka, "Little Raven," which had at long last returned to its stable.

Some time later, despite his great popularity in Kiev, Dobrynya Nikitich sat at his window brooding. When his mother, Amelfia Timofeyevna, asked him what was wrong, he replied that it was long past the time when he should have married but that all of the eligible maidens of the city had already been spoken for. His mother told him that if he were ever to find a bride, he would have to travel beyond the confines of the city—an idea that immediately appealed to Dobrynya. Even if he failed to find a wife, he was sure to have some adventure.

As Dobrynya left for the stables, his mother called after him, telling him to leave his own horse Voroneyushka behind and instead to take the horse that had belonged to his father, which had served him well in his quest to find the Princess Zabava. Dobrynya followed the advice of his mother, and armed himself before riding out from the city onto the steppes. A short time later he came across the tracks of another rider and hurried after them. Having ridden hard for a short distance Dobrynya spotted a *polianitsa* (female warrior) spurring her jet-black steed across the plains. Dobrynya quickly strung an arrow in his bow and let it fly. The arrow flew straight and true and struck her on the side of her helmet. Instead of hurting the rider, the arrow simply fell to the ground, and the woman rode on as if nothing had happened. Dobrynya let a second arrow fly, with exactly the same result; but the third arrow hit the woman's helmet again and caused her to stop and look around. Seeing Dobrynya, she lifted him from his horse by his hair and thrust him into a deep pouch that she always carried with her; and for three days he brooded there in silence as they rode across the steppes. On the fourth day the woman's horse stumbled and complained that it could no longer continue to carry a *polianitsa* and a bogatyr'.

The woman immediately climbed down from her horse and took Dobrynya out of her pouch, demanding to know who he was. She said that if he were older than her, she would kill him; if he were younger, she would consider him her brother; and if they were the same age, she would marry him. Dobrynya refused to tell the woman anything, but the horse had recognized him and told the woman that his name was Dobrynya Nikitich and that he was the same age as the woman. The latter then told Dobrynya that her name was Nastas'ya Nikulichna and that as they were the same age, they should marry. Dobrynya agreed, and the two of them rode back to Kiev.

Dobrynya's mother, the widow Amelfia Timofeyevna, welcomed the woman, and before long a great wedding had been arranged, which would be attended by Prince Vladimir Bright Sun and his wife Evpraksiya. For three days and three nights the wedding feast continued, and then Dobrynya and his new wife Nastas'ya returned to live with Amelfia Timofeyevna. After her marriage, Nastas'ya stayed at home, like any other Russian wife.

Some three years later Prince Vladimir Bright Sun arranged a great banquet in Kiev and invited all the bogatyri to attend. As the banquet drew to a close, Vladimir addressed the knights present, asking which of them would lead an army against the forces of an enemy who had attacked his father-in-law, the King of Lithuania. At first none of the knights responded, so Vladimir asked the question a second time. This time Alyosha Popovich stood and told the prince that there was none better qualified to serve the purpose than Dobrynya Nikitich, who had once served in the army of the King of Lithuania. Reluctantly Dobrynya agreed, and he went home to prepare for the coming expedition.

There his mother questioned him about what he was doing, and with great reluctance Dobrynya told her of his mission, telling her not to worry; for if he were killed, he would join his late father, Nikita, in heaven and would see her there one day. Amelfia Timofeyevna blessed her son and then ran to tell Nastas'ya, her daughter-in-law, of Dobrynya's impending departure. Nastas'ya ran to her husband, who told her about his mission, adding that she should wait for him for 12 years, and that if he had not returned by that time, she should divide his wealth equally between the church and the poor and then seek a new husband. However, Dobrynya advised her that she should not marry Alyosha Popovich, for the two men had exchanged crosses and were thus brothers in the eyes of God.

With that Dobrynya kissed his wife, mounted his horse, and left for Lithuania. Three years passed and Dobrynya did not return home. News of his death was brought to Kiev by Alyosha Popovich. Amelfia Timofeyevna wept for her son, but Nastas'ya refused to accept the news and continued her long vigil.

Three more years passed, and Alyosha Popovich once more rode into Kiev and brought news of the death of Dobrynya Nikitich, and again Nastas'ya refused to believe him.

Six more years passed before Alyosha Popovich came back to the court of Prince Vladimir Bright Sun, again bringing news of the death of Dobrynya Nikitich. This time, although Nastas'ya did not believe her husband was dead, she knew that she had honored his wishes, and so she agreed to marry Alyosha Popovich. Thus the city of Kiev prepared for the marriage of Alyosha and Nastas'ya, while at the Lithuanian border Dobrynya Nikitich slept a long and deep sleep.

As he awoke, two white doves flew into his tent and spoke of the wedding arrangements being made at that very moment in Kiev. Hearing the news, Dobrynya quickly gathered his possessions, mounted Voroneyushka, and rode like the wind all the way back to Kiev. There he was joyfully reunited with his mother. Then he dressed as a min-

strel and went to the palace to serenade the wedding guests. There, seated on the stove, the customary location for minstrels and beggars in the palace, Dobrynya sang songs in celebration of the marriage.

So touched was Nastas'ya by the minstrel's songs that she asked permission of Prince Vladimir Bright Sun to give him a drink. The prince agreed. Having accepted the drink from his wife, Dobrynya asked permission of Prince Vladimir Bright Sun to return the compliment. Vladimir gave permission, and Dobrynya gave Nastas'ya a cup of mead into which he had slipped his wedding ring. As soon as Nastas'ya found the ring, she fell to the floor and begged her husband's forgiveness.

The banquet fell silent at the sight of the bride begging the forgiveness of the minstrel, but it soon became apparent that the minstrel was none other than Dobrynya Nikitich, returned from Lithuania. Prince Vladimir Bright Sun welcomed him warmly, but all Dobrynya could think of was how he had been betrayed by his brother in God, Alyosha Popovich. Having forgiven his wife—for she could not have known the truth—Dobrynya turned to Alyosha, who also begged forgiveness. Dobrynya rejected Alyosha's pleas, and grabbing him by the neck, threw him to the ground, drew his sword, and raised his arm to strike—but was prevented from doing so by the great Il'ya Muromets. Dobrynya sheathed his sword and left the palace with his wife, refusing from that day forth to speak to Alyosha, and for the rest of their lives Dobrynya Nikitich and Nastas'ya Nikulichna lived in peace and happiness.

See also: Alesha; Alyosha Popovich; Amelf(i)a Timofe(y)evna; Bogatyr'; Dragon; Dunai Ivanovich; Evpraksiya (~ia), Princess; Goryshche; Il'ya Muromets; Kiev; Leontii; Lithuania; Mother Earth; Nastas'ya Nikulichna; Polianitsa; Puchai; Sorochinsk Hill; Vladimir Bright Sun, Prince; Voroneyushka; Zabava (Putyatichna), Princess
References: Astakhova 1961; Evgen'eva and Putilov 1977; Gil'ferding 1951; Rambaud 1879

DODOLA
Serbia

Goddess of rain, propitiated in times of drought by dressing a girl from head to foot in grass, herbs, and flowers so that even her face was hidden. This girl, now known as Dodola, would walk through the community in the company of a group of other girls, stop in front of every house, and dance. The retinue would form a circle around the girl and sing a propitiation song, while the lady of the house would come out and throw a bucket of water over Dodola.

DOGODA
Slav

The god of the west wind, he was perceived as the most gentle of the deities that personified the winds. He lived on the island of Buyan with the east and north winds, and according to some sources, the Sun.

See also: Buyan; Sun; Wind

DOJRAN, LAKE
Serbia

Shallow lake that straddles the border between Macedonia (in the southern part of former Yugoslavia) and northern Greece, east of the border town of Gevgelija.

According to Serbian legend, the lake was originally a dry hollow in the center of which there was a deep well safeguarded by 13 locks. A local girl named Dojrana, deeply in love with a local boy, was taken by the Turks. Preferring death to concubinage, Dojrana is said to have committed suicide by throwing herself into the well. The locks could not be closed after her suicide, and the water from the well gushed forth to form Lake Dojran, which was named in her memory.

See also: Macedonia

DOMANIA
Slav

Another name for the domovikha, or the kikimora.

See also: Domovikha; Kikimora

DOMOVIK
Slav

Alternative name for the domovoi, and the one that is perhaps most correctly used when referring to him in connection with his female counterpart or wife, the domovikha.

See also: Domovikha; Domovoi

DOMOVIKHA
Slav

The wife of the domovoi. This female household spirit lived in the cellar or henhouse, whereas her mate lived in the stove. The domovikha (also known as domania or kikimora) would help good wives by doing household chores for them and would annoy bad ones by tickling their children awake in the middle of the night.

See also: Domovoi; Kikimora

DOMOVOI
Slavic
Also: Kaukas; Majahaldas; Majasgars, Domovik, Tsmok

(pl. domovoi) The spirit of a family's founding ancestor who lived in the stove, the focal point of the Russian home. The domovoi's connections to familial ancestors (or *dedy*) guaranteed him a stable place in folk traditions, especially in rural communities, well into the modern era. The domovoi, whose name comes from *dom* (house), looked after the welfare of the family and was sometimes affectionately referred to as *dedushka* (granddad) or *chelovek* (fellow). His wife, the domovikha, lived in the cellar or henhouse and helped good wives by doing domestic chores, annoying slovenly ones by tickling their children to wake them in the middle of the night.

According to legend, the corps of domovoi staged a revolt against Svarog when the universe was created. Svarog drove them from his realm, whereupon they fell to earth, some into backyards, some down chimneys and into stoves, some into forests, and some onto the plains. Each group was domovoi, and each had the same characteristics; but over the years those outside the home disappeared or were assimilated with other spirits, leaving a single race of domovoi.

Very few people claim to have caught a glimpse of the domovoi, although everyone has heard him in the creakings and groanings of their house. Those who say they have seen this spirit describe him as a dwarfish, aging man covered with a long beard and soft, silky fur, even on the palms of his hands and the soles of his feet. The only parts of his body visible through this downy covering are his piercing eyes and his pointed nose. Sometimes he would also be depicted with horns and a tail, but he was usually conceived of according to peasant lore, as an animated haystack. Less approachable and much shier than the domovoi was the dvorovoi, the spirit of the household yard, who might have been a descendant of the domovoi.

Although mischievous, the domovoi would never harm the family with whom he lived unless he was offended in some way. During daylight hours the domovoi stayed hidden or used his shape-changing abilities to disguise himself as an animal while he roamed the fields and woods. At night he would return to his human hosts' home, eating the bread and salt that were left out for him, or upsetting pots and furniture if he felt in any way ill treated.

One story concerning the domovoi tells of two peasants who lived next door to each other. One owned horses that were well fed and well groomed, whereas the neighbor's horses were sickly and thin. Wishing to find out why his horses were so much finer than those of his neighbor, the peasant hid at night and caught the domovoi grooming, feeding, and watering his horses from the large water cask in the yard. The following day, not wanting his drinking water supply to be contaminated by an ugly spirit, he asked his jealous neighbor what he should do. The neighbor knew that a domovoi was surely helping this lucky fellow, and keen to see him reduced to the same terms as him-

self, he suggested that the man drill a large hole in the cask. He could then plug the hole during the day but let all the water out at night. The man foolishly followed this advice, and when the domovoi came to water the horses he found the cask empty. Enraged, he smashed the stables to pieces and killed all the horses.

The importance of the domovoi was reflected in the fact that every time the master of the house left, his wife would ensure that the mouth of the stove was covered so that the domovoi did not leave as well. Later traditions said that the domovoi lived not only in the stove but also in the cattle sheds and stables, for he was particularly fond of farm animals. At night he would feed the horses and then comb and groom them, neatly plaiting their manes and their tails. Every time the peasant bought a new animal he would lead it around the yard to make sure that the domovoi approved of his purchase, and would ask the domovoi to welcome the newcomer to his home. However, the spirit of the yard, including the stables and sheds, was usually referred to as the dvorovoi.

See also: Dedy; Domovik; Domovikha; Dvorovoi; Kaukas; Majahaldas; Majasgars; Svarog; Tsmok

DON
General
River that rises south of Moscow and flows 1,180 miles (1,900 kilometers) before entering the extreme northeastern extremity of the Sea of Azov. For almost four months of every year it is closed by ice. In its lower reaches the river is a mile (1.5 kilometers) wide, and its upper navigable reaches are connected to the Volga River by canal.

DONETS
General
The chief branch of the river Don, the Donets runs through the northeastern corner of Ukraine, an area known as the Donets Basin.

DORMITION, THE

Russia

Fifteenth-century church inside the walls of the Kremlin in Moscow. The church was dedicated to the Virgin Mary and traditionally was regarded as the heart of the capital city. This building was the symbol of Mary's power and protection; and because it was at the heart of the capital, its power and protection extended over the entire city and its people.

See also: Kremlin

References: Hapgood 1906; Lebedev 1881

DOVE MAIDEN

Russia

The form in which Masha was captured and nursed back to health by Petrushka.

See also: Masha; Petrushka

DOVE MAIDENS, THE

Armenia

Three supernatural maidens who used to fly down every night, raise a prince from his grave, and sup with him. The Apprentice frightened the Dove Maidens away and obtained from them a tablecloth and a crimson wand. With the wand the Apprentice restored the prince to life, and thus won favor with the rejuvenated prince's father.

See also: Apprentice, The

References: Orbeli and Taronian 1959–67, vol. 1

DRAGON

Russia

Dragons abound in Russian legends. They are usually described as serpentine in shape, as was the twelve-headed dragon dispatched by Dobrynya Nikitich. Other accounts, especially those from the era of byliny, tell of dragons with the head of a serpent and the body of a man, and flying on a winged horse, as did the dragon killed by Ivan the Pea to free his sister Vasilissa of the Golden Braid.

Although many Russian tales of dragons date from pagan times, the creatures continued to be associated with Christian knights and legends and are still popularly believed to be the cause of many natural phenomena. Eclipses of the sun or moon were taken to be caused by a dragon, their reappearance showing that even a dragon could not withstand their power—a reassuring sign that dragons could be defeated by righteous people.

Dragons were not the most intelligent of creatures and were easily tricked, as illustrated by the following story of the dragon and the gypsy:

A gypsy once wandered into a village the day after a particularly ferocious dragon had devoured all of the inhabitants save one. This survivor pleaded with the gypsy to leave before the dragon reappeared; but as they were talking, a huge shadow fell over them and the dragon landed right before their eyes.

When the monster made toward the gypsy, the fellow held up one hand and told the dragon that it would choke if it tried to eat him, for he was far stronger than the dragon. The dragon scoffed at this and suggested a test. Picking up a millstone, he proceeded to crush it into a fine powder. The gypsy applauded the dragon and then asked whether the creature could make water run from a stone. The gypsy picked up a muslin bag full of cream cheese and began to squeeze the whey from it.

Impressed, the dragon thought that it might be better to befriend the gypsy; so it asked him to bring back the fattest oxen he could find in the field for their dinner. The gypsy knew that he was not strong enough to do that, so he herded the cattle into one end of the field and began to tie their tails together. When the dragon came to see why the gypsy was taking so long, the gypsy told him that he thought it better to drag back the whole herd, for then they would not need to fetch any more food for a long time. Impatiently, the dragon skinned a large ox, threw it over his back, and carried it back to the village.

Having filled two cooking pots with fresh meat, the dragon gave the ox hide to the gypsy and told him to go to the well and fill it with water and then bring it back. The gypsy had trouble carrying the skin to the well, but once there, he started to dig a channel around it. Once again the dragon grew impatient and came to see what the delay was. The gypsy explained that he thought it better to bring back the whole well, for then they would never run out of water. The dragon, anxious to eat, filled the ox skin himself, carried it back, and poured the water into the cooking pots.

Now they needed firewood. The dragon sent the gypsy into the forest to collect a large oak tree. There the gypsy began to make a rope from the bark of the trees, which he had wound around twenty trunks by the time the dragon came to see what was taking so long. Again the gypsy explained that he thought it far better to bring twenty trees than a single one, for then they would never run out of firewood. The dragon laughed, tore up a huge tree, and strode back to the village and built a huge fire under the cooking pots. Soon the dragon began to eat, but the gypsy pretended to sulk and refused to eat.

When the dragon asked why he was sulking, the gypsy replied that the only way he would know that they were true friends would be if the dragon would come to meet his family. The dragon agreed, and hitched three fine horses to a large cart, and the pair drove back to the gypsy camp. There they were greeted by the gypsy's naked children, who ran noisily around the cart. The dragon asked who these children were, and the gypsy replied that they were his children, hungry as usual, and what a fine meal they would make of the dragon.

With that, the dragon leaped down from the cart and hurried away, never again to attack a human. The gypsy sold the horses and the cart, and he and his family lived comfortably on the proceeds for many years.

See also: Alesha; Bylina; Dobrynya Nikitich; Il'ya Muromets; Ivan the Pea; Vasilis(s)a of the Golden Braid

D'U-URT
Finno-Ugric—Votyak
The soul of the grain, which is protected while the grain is growing in the field by Busi-urt, the soul of the grain field.
   See also: Busi-urt; Urt

DUGNAI
Slav
An unusual, though important goddess with but a single responsibility—to make dough rise.

DUNAI, RIVER
Russia
Ancient Russian name for the Danube. Slavic legend describes how the river Dunai formed from the blood of Dunai Ivanovich.
   See also: Danube; Dunai Ivanovich

DUNAI IVANOVICH
Russia
A knight, or bogatyr', who offered to undertake a quest to secure the daughter of the King of Lithuania as the bride of Prince Vladimir Bright Sun. Dunai Ivanovich made this offer during a banquet at which the prince complained that he was the only unmarried man present. The knight offered to travel to Lithuania, accompanied only by his friend Dobrynya Nikitich (also a bogatyr'), to bring back the Princess Evpraksiya for Vladimir. For their mission, Vladimir offered them forty thousand men and ten thousand pieces of gold, which Dunai refused. Instead he asked for an unbroken stallion for each, with bridles and whips that had never been used, and a letter stating their mission. So equipped, the two rode from Kiev to Moscow and then on to Lithuania. Arriving at the court of the King of Lithuania, Dunai left Dobrynya in charge of the horses and entered the great hall, where he was cordially greeted.

However, when Dunai explained the purpose of their visit, the mood very quickly changed, for the King of Lithuania had a poor opinion of Vladimir Bright Sun. He also scolded Dunai for seeking the hand of his younger daughter in Vladimir's behalf, instead of that of his elder daughter. Just as he was about to have Dunai dragged off to the dungeons, one of the king's men rushed into the hall to tell the king that Dobrynya was bludgeoning the king's men to death. Taking this as a divine sign, the king quickly agreed to the suit and bade the three of them a safe journey.

That night, as they slept, they heard suspicious sounds nearby but were not attacked. The following morning Dobrynya and Princess Evpraksiya rode off toward Kiev, while Dunai tracked down the bandit that had been stalking them the previous night. When he caught up with the stranger, he knocked him from his mount and demanded to know where he was going. Looking down, Dunai saw that the person he had knocked from the saddle was a woman.

This woman told Dunai that she was Princess Nastas'ya, Evpraksiya's elder sister. She had been hunting when Dunai and Dobrynya left with her sister, and she had set out in pursuit, aiming to rescue her sister from her abductors. So taken was Dunai with her courage that he spared her life and asked her to become his wife. Quickly they rode to Kiev, and they were married at the same service at which Vladimir married Evpraksiya.

The wedding feast lasted twelve days, during which time a great many boasts were made. Dunai Ivanovich boasted that in the city of Kiev there was none who could compare with him. His new wife chided him, saying that even though she had only been in the city for a short time, already she had noticed that Churilo Plenkovich was the best-dressed man in all Russia and Alyosha Popovich was the most valiant. However, now that she had arrived in Kiev, there was no finer archer in the city than herself. Dunai rose to the boast and challenged Nastas'ya to a test of skill with the bow and arrow. A silver ring was to be placed on the head of one of them, and the other would then shoot an arrow down the blade of a knife and through the ring without disturbing it. Dunai bade his wife take the first turn, and three times she succeeded. Yet when it came to Dunai's turn, she pleaded with him not to attempt the feat, asking him to forgive her for her foolish challenge. When Dunai refused, she told him of their unborn child—a child with arms to the elbow that were of solid gold and legs of silver from hips to knees. Stars clustered around his temples; from every hair on his head there hung a pearl; the moon shone from his back; and the sun radiated from his eyes.

Unimpressed, Dunai proceeded with the contest, dipping the point of his arrow into the venom of a poisonous snake. However, he failed to make the target, and the arrow pierced Nastas'ya's heart. As she died, they cut the baby from her womb, and it proved to be every bit as wondrous as she had said it would be. Grief-stricken, Dunai sank the butt of his spear into the ground and fell onto its point. Two rivers sprang up from where husband and wife lay dead: One was the river Nastas'ya, and the other, the river Dunai—better known today as the Danube.

See also: Alyosha Popovich; Churilo Plenkovich; Danube; Dobrynya Nikitich; Evpraksiya (~ia), Princess; Kiev; Lithuania; Moscow; Nastas'ya, Princess; Vladimir Bright Sun, Prince
References: Evgen'eva and Putilov 1977

DUNAY (-USHKA)
Russia
Variant names for Dunai Ivanovich, Dunayushka being a familiar form that would have been used by family and close friends.
See also: Dunai Ivanovich

DUNDRA
Slav—Romany
The original name of the god of the moon, who later became known as Alako. Ac-

cording to legend, Dundra was sent to earth by his father, to teach the Romany people their laws and to serve as their protector. When he had finished his task on earth he ascended into the skies, where he became Alako. He watches over his people and carries their souls to live on the moon after death. One day Alako will return from the moon and lead his people back to their lost homeland.

See also: Alako

DUSK
Russia

The setting sun, personified in the goddess Zorya Vechernyaya.

See also: Zorya Vechernyaya

DVINA
General

The name of two rivers in eastern Europe. The Western Dvina, or Daugava, rises west of Moscow and flows into the Gulf of Riga in Latvia. This river is 633 miles (1,019 kilometers) long. The other, the Northern Dvina, is an important waterway in northwestern Russia, formed by the Sukhona and Vychegda Rivers. It is 455 miles (732 kilometers) long and flows into the White Sea at the port of Arkhangel'sk.

See also: Arkhangel'sk; Moscow; White Sea

DVOEVERIE
Russia

Literally, "double faith." Refers to the continuation of pagan traditions and rituals for centuries after the adoption of Christianity as the state-sanctioned religion, due mainly to resistance from women who far preferred matriarchal pagan religions to patriarchal Christianity. As a result, medieval Russia became a nation divided by class and religion, the upper class being (in the majority) Christianized and the peasants clinging to their pagan roots. To this day elements of dvoeverie remain in Russian culture, especially in the most remote regions.

References: Dal' 1957

DVOROVOI
Slav

The spirit of the household yard. Closely related to the domovoi, the dvorovoi lives in the sheds and stables, where he tends the animals. New animals brought to the house are introduced to him so that the dvorovoi can welcome them to their new home. However, the dvorovoi is believed hostile to animals with white fur, although he tolerates chickens with white feathers, for they have their own god.

The dvorovoi could be influenced in one of two ways: by bribery or by punishment. If a piece of bread and some bits of sheep's wool were left out, then the dvorovoi probably would do as he was bidden. He also could be made to do what was wanted by taking a long stick and a thread from the shroud of a dead man. This thread was to be tied to the stick and then used to whip the yard, in the process of which the dvorovoi was sure to be lashed. Those who could see the dvorovoi would pin him to a fence with a pitchfork. However, as the story of Katya shows, the dvorovoi was a jealous character who could exact his own revenge.

See also: Domovoi; Katya

DZIEWONA (~WAN[N]A)
Poland

The name by which the goddess of the hunt, Devana, was known to the Polish.

See also: Devana

DZULI
Siberia—Tungus
Also: Muxdi

The name given to a statuette of a revered ancestor who was thought to have gone to live with the gods and could thus be relied upon, if treated with respect, to bring good fortune to the household.

EARTH MOTHER

General

See Mother Earth.

EKIM

Russia

Alesha's squire. Ekim accompanied his master from Rostov to the court of Prince Vladimir Bright Sun at Kiev. There he caught the knife thrown at Alesha by the vile monster Tugarin.

> *See also:* Alesha; Kiev; Rostov; Tugarin; Vladimir Bright Sun, Prince

ELENA THE BEAUTIFUL

Russia

A princess from an unnamed kingdom who was abducted by Ivan Vyslavovich and his helper, the shape-changing wolf. Ivan Vyslavovich had been set the task of abducting Elena by Tsar Afron after he had been caught trying to steal Afron's Horse with the Golden Mane and its bridle—that being a task assigned Ivan by Tsar Dalmat, who had caught Ivan trying to steal the Firebird and its cage for his father (Tsar Vyslav Andronovich). Elena was abducted by the wolf, who helped Ivan Vyslavovich in recompense for having killed his horse. By the time they arrived at the kingdom of Tsar Afron, Ivan and Elena had fallen in love. The wolf assumed Elena's form so that the lovers could evade Afron. Ivan Vyslavovich and Elena rode away on the Horse with the Golden Mane and were later rejoined by the wolf.

Having completed all of the tasks assigned him, Ivan Vyslavovich was on his way home with Elena and the Horse with the Golden Mane when they were ambushed by Dmitrii Vyslavovich and Vasilii Vyslavovich, Ivan's jealous brothers. Ivan Vyslavovich was killed, and Elena fell by lot to Vasilii. The treachery of the two brothers was revealed after Ivan was restored to life by the wolf, who used the Water of Life and Death to resuscitate him. Dmitrii and Vasilii were thrown into a deep dungeon, and Elena the Beautiful married Ivan Vyslavovich.

> *See also:* Afron; Dalmat; Dmitrii (Vyslavovich); Firebird, The; Horse with the Golden Mane, The; Ivan Vyslavovich; Vasilii Vyslavovich; Vyslav Andronovich; Water of Life and Death, The

ELENA THE FAIR

Russia

The tsaritsa of the Golden Kingdom, one of three kingdoms in the realm of Whirlwind. She and her sisters, the tsaritsas of the Copper Kingdom and the Silver Kingdom, were the prisoners of Whirlwind. When Ivan Belyaninovich came to Whirlwind's realm to rescue his mother, Nastas'ya of the Golden Braid, whom Whirlwind had abducted years earlier, Elena told Ivan where he might find Nastas'ya, making him promise to return and free her as well. This he did, although his brothers Peter and Vasilii Belyaninovich tried to claim the credit for themselves and returned home with Elena and the other two tsaritsas, leaving Ivan stranded in Whirlwind's realm. After Ivan Belyaninovich returned home with the help of Lame and One-Eye, two servants of Whirlwind, it was Elena who first realized that someone had arrived who possessed magical powers from the realm of Whirlwind. Elena also devised the three tasks that uncovered the treachery of Peter and Vasilii. She later married Ivan Belyaninovich. Her sister, the tsaritsa of the Copper

Kingdom, married Vasilii Belyaninovich, and her other sister, the tsaritsa of the Silver Kingdom, married Peter Belyaninovich.

See also: Copper Kingdom, The; Golden Kingdom, The; Ivan Belyaninovich; Lame; Nastas'ya of the Golden Braid; One-Eye; Peter (Belyaninovich); Silver Kingdom, The; Vasilii Belyaninovich; Whirlwind

ELETSKOI
Russia

One of the earliest religious icons of the Virgin Mary that "miraculously" appeared. Dating from 1060, the Eletskoi icon was found in a forest near Chernigov. Modern thinking attributes the appearance of these holy relics to the early clergy who recognized the importance of associating the Virgin Mary with the nature goddesses that pervaded pagan religious belief. The clergy must have reasoned that icons found near pagan holy trees and water would be readily accepted and revered even by those least likely to convert to Christianity. All available evidence suggests that this ruse was successful.

See also: Chernigov
References: Matorin 1931

ELIAS
Russia

The Christian name with which the attributes of Perun became associated. Both legendary figures were believed to have power over rain and harvest.

See also: Perun
References: Frazer

ENVY
Armenia

A king once had two champions, each of whom was being eaten away by envy of the other. The king resolved to do something about this and summoned one of his champions. The king told the fellow that he could ask whatever he wanted and it would be his; but he warned that whatever the champion asked for, the other champion also would be given twofold. The champion thought for a moment and then asked the king to put out one of his eyes.

One of the fables of Vardan of Aygek.

See also: Vardan
References: Marr 1894–99

ERISVORSH
Slav

The god of storms. To the Czechs he was known as Varpulis, the god of storm winds and an attendant of Perun.

See also: Perun; Varpulis

ERLIK
Siberia, Lapland

"First life," the being created by the sky god Ulgan from a speck of mud found floating on the surface of the primordial ocean, for the single purpose of helping the sky god to create the rest of the universe. Ulgan sent Erlik to fetch more mud from the ocean floor, which he did, though he hid some of the mud in his mouth, fully intending to create a universe of his own from it. However, as Erlik chewed the mud, it started to swell until he was forced to spit it out, the mud and saliva mixture spraying across the land created by Ulgan to form all the damp and putrid places of the world—the swamps and marshes.

Meanwhile, Ulgan had created not only the land but also the first people, whom he fashioned out of the mud and then imbued with a divine spirit of life. However, Ulgan ran out of mud and left the people to dry out while he went to fetch some more, leaving a huge dog to guard them. Where this dog came from is not recorded, but he was probably created by Ulgan. Erlik saw the new people drying out and tried to bribe the dog to let him have them. The dog refused, whereupon Erlik spat on the new people, covering them in saliva. When Ulgan returned, he turned the new people inside out before finally bringing them to life, and mankind has been that way ever since—dry on the outside and foul and wet on the inside. Ulgan then banished Erlik to purgatory in the underworld; but before Erlik went, he snatched as many of the newly created people as he could to be his servants. Since that day the dead have been inside-out versions of the living. And Erlik, the first created being, became the god of death and ruler of the underworld.

See also: Ulgan; Underworld, The

ERMOLAI-ERAZM
Russia

A fifteenth-century monk who recorded a number of post-Christian legends. The monk is best remembered for his account of the legend of Fevroniia.

See also: Fevroniia
References: Zenkovsky 1963

ERZYA
General

The northern branch of the Mordvin people, their southern counterparts being the Moksha.

See also: Moksha; Mordvins

ESKERI
Siberia—Tungus

The creator, who plunged into the primeval waters and brought back a clump of mud from which he fashioned the earth.

ESTONIA
General

A republic of the Soviet Union from 1940 to 1991, Estonia and its Baltic neighbors Latvia and Lithuania are now independent states. Estonia, like the other Baltic countries, has had a turbulent history, and as a result very little remains of Estonian mythology and legend. The country was a democratic republic between 1919 and 1934, when the government was overthrown in a fascist coup. Unlike the languages of Latvia and Lithuania, the language of Estonia is not of Slavic but of Finno-Ugric origin, and it

therefore more closely resembles Swedish and Finnish than Russian.

See also: Finno-Ugric; Latvia; Lithuania

EVENING STAR
Slav

The personification of the planet Venus seen in the early evening sky. In Slavic mythology the Evening Star is Zvezda Vechernyaya, the sister to Zvezda Dennitsa, the Morning Star. Together the sisters are collectively referred to as the two Zvezdy, the daughters of Dazhbog, and sisters to the two, or three, Zoryi.

See also: Dazhbog; Morning Star; Venus;
Zoryi; Zvezda Dennitsa; Zvezda Vechernyaya

EVIL
Russia

The personification of all that is bad, although not equated with the Devil. Evil is usually feminine and personified as the aged hag One-Eyed Likho (*likho* being Russian for "evil").

See also: Likho, One-Eyed

EVPRAKSIYA (~IA), PRINCESS
Russia

Daughter of the King of Lithuania and sister to Princess Nastas'ya. She was brought from Lithuania to Kiev to become the bride of Vladimir Bright Sun by Dunai Ivanovich, who married her sister, and by Dobrynya Nikitich. She and her sister were married at the same service, and by virtue of their marriage became Christians. In some versions of the story, Evpraksiya and Nastas'ya are identified as the daughters of the Tatar khan.

See also: Dobrynya Nikitich; Dunai
Ivanovich; Khan; Kiev; Nastas'ya, Princess;
Tatars; Vladimir Bright Sun, Prince

EZERINIS
Lithuania

The god of lakes but apparently not of rivers and streams.

FAIRY
General

A supernatural being with magic powers who could help or harm human beings. In recent legend, fairies have been pictured as very small and sometimes as very lovely and delicate. In medieval stories, however, fairies were often of human size.

FARAONY
Russia

One of the many variant names applied to the russalki, others being mavki, navki, and vodianiani.

See also: Mavki; Navki; Rus(s)alki (~ulki); Vodianiani
References: Pomerantseva 1975

FEVRONIIA
Russia

Paul, the Christian ruler of the city of Murom, was visited by the Devil, who appeared to his wife, euphemistically referred to as the Dark Princess, in the form of a serpent. Only she could recognize the Devil; all those around her saw only the image of Paul. When she told her husband of the visit she had received in her bedchamber, Paul advised her to ascertain from the Devil the manner of Paul's death. She did as he asked, and found out that Paul's brother Peter of Murom would kill him. However, when Peter came to do the dirty deed, he succeeded only in killing the serpent that had assumed Paul's guise. At this point in the legend the Dark Princess ceases to be mentioned, from which

we may deduce that she was a servant of the Devil, and with her purpose at an end, she had returned to eternal damnation.

Peter, however, had been tainted by the blood of the serpent. Covered in sores, he set out in search of a cure for himself and his kingdom, which had been struck down as a result of his apparent fratricide. Traveling with a large coterie, Peter arrived at a village called Charity, where he was carried to an isolated cottage. There he was confronted by a very beautiful, half-naked woman, who sat spinning. The woman told Peter that she lived alone, the remainder of her family being long dead, and that she would cure him of his affliction on the condition that he married her. Peter immediately agreed. No sooner had he done so than his sores disappeared and his strength returned. However, Peter now saw no reason to marry the maiden and made ready to leave the cottage. As he did so, his strength sapped away and the sores erupted again. Convinced that he had no choice in the matter, Peter agreed to the union, and the couple were duly married.

At their wedding the woman told Peter that her name, or rather the name she had chosen to use as his wife, was Fevroniia. Together Peter and Fevroniia traveled back to Murom, where the influential boyars, angry because Peter had married a mere peasant, accused Fevroniia of poor manners at the feast thrown in honor of their prince. Fevroniia retaliated by performing a series of miracles, such as turning crumbs from the table into frankincense and myrrh. These acts, however, did not assuage the anger of the boyars, who demanded that she be banished from the court because as a powerful sorceress, she could hold their wives in thrall. Fevroniia agreed to leave Murom, provided that Peter accompany her.

So Peter, Fevroniia, and their retinue set out from Murom by boat. However, as they made camp that evening, Peter began to worry about their exile. Fevroniia assuaged

An early illustration of a fairy king and queen standing beneath a mushroom being entertained by the court (from the collections of Carol Rose; photo by David Rose)

his fears by performing another miracle: She took the branches that had been cut to fuel the cooking fire and blessed them, telling Peter that by morning they would be tall trees. True enough, the following morning Peter and his coterie awakened to find themselves in the midst of a great forest, whereas they had gone to sleep at the edge of a small wood the night before. Peter and Fevroniia remained there until they received news of a fratricidal war that had broken out among the boyars in Murom, who had asked for Peter and Fevroniia to return and rule over them. This the couple did; but Peter was merely a figurehead, the true ruler of Murom being Fevroniia.

Many years passed, during which the couple ruled Murom with wisdom. However, after Peter died and was buried in the cathedral, Fevroniia willed herself to die on the feast of Kupalo. She was buried outside the city walls, in keeping with her pagan and peasant origins; but the following morning the boyars discovered her grave beside that of her husband, inside the cathedral grounds.

Fevroniia, as shown through her transformation of the cut branches into a fully grown forest, is a personification of the pagan tree goddess. This story, which was recorded by the fifteenth-century monk Ermolai-erazm, demonstrates the coexistence of Christian faith alongside the ancient pagan religions—apparently acceptable to the clergy, so long as Christianity was seen to be the more potent force, as demonstrated by Peter's burial inside the cathedral and Fevroniia's burial outside the city walls. However, the supernatural migration of Fevroniia's grave to the cathedral demonstrates that no matter whether pagan or Christian, God accepts all into his kingdom after death.

See also: Boyars; Charity; Dark Princess, The; Devil, The; Ermolai-erazm; Kupalo; Murom; Paul; Peter of Murom
References: Zenkovsky 1963

FINLAND

General

Scandinavian country that is bounded to the north by Norway, to the east by Russia, to the south and west by the Baltic Sea, and to

The harbor market at Helsinki, Finland (Archive Photos)

the northwest by Sweden. The country was originally inhabited by Lapps, but they were driven northward by Finnic invaders from Asia around the first century B.C., into the area they occupy to this day. During the twelfth century the country was conquered by Sweden, and for the following two centuries the area was the scene of a great number of wars between Sweden and Russia. As a duchy of Sweden, Finland was allowed ever greater autonomy, becoming a Grand Duchy in 1581. In 1809, during the Napoleonic Wars, Finland was annexed by Russia. It remained under Russian imperial rule until 1917, when it declared independence during the Russian Revolution. Russia at first tried to regain its lost territory, but finally recognized Finland's independence in 1920.

The inhabitants of Finland speak Finnish, a Finno-Ugric language closely related to Estonian, Livonian, Karelian, and Ingrian. At

the beginning of the nineteenth century, Finnish had no official status, Swedish being the language of education, government, and literature in Finland. It was not until the publication of the *Kalevala* in 1835 that the Finns' linguistic and nationalistic feelings began to emerge.

See also: Baltic; Estonia; Finno-Ugric; Karelia; Lapps; Livonia

FINNO-UGRIC

General

Closely related to both the Baltic and Slavic languages, with which they became assimilated, the Finno-Ugric languages do not belong to the Indo-European family. Their language grouping, a subfamily of the Ural-Altaic family, contains more than twenty different tongues spoken from Norway in the west to Siberia in the east, and to the Carpathian Mountains in the south. The

Finno-Ugric peoples may be subdivided into four main groups according to their geographical position. The first group includes the Finns, Lapps, Estonians (although Estonia is generally thought of as a Baltic country), Livonians, and Karelians. The second grouping comprises the Cheremiss-Mordvin peoples of the middle and upper Volga. The third group includes the Votyaks, Permyaks, and Zyrians, who inhabit the Russian provinces of Perm and Vyatka; and the last group, the Voguls and Ostyaks of western Siberia. The Magyar people of Hungary are normally included in the fourth grouping because they originated in western Siberia, but they are considered a Turkic people.

The Finno-Ugric peoples were widely influenced by their Indo-European neighbors, the Balts, the Slavs, and the Norse, or Teutons, and as a result many of their legends bear direct comparison with those of both the Balts and the Slavs.

See also: Carpathian Mountains; Cheremiss-Mordvin; Estonia; Finland; Hungary; Karelia; Lapps; Livonia; Magyars; Mordvins; Ostyaks; Permyaks; Siberia; Voguls; Volga; Votyaks; Zyrians

FIREBIRD, THE
Russia
A fabulous bird described as having eyes that sparkled like crystal and golden feathers that

The image of a Firebird painted in miniature on a black lacquer plate (Sovfoto/Eastfoto/PNI)

shone as bright as day. Owned by Tsar Dalmat, the bird used to steal the golden apples that grew in the garden of Tsar Vyslav Andronovich. The latter set his three sons Dmitrii Vyslavovich, Vasilii Vyslavovich, and Ivan Vyslavovich the task of locating and obtaining the bird for him. Ivan succeeded in this quest; but his brothers ambushed and killed him, claiming that they had completed the quest when they presented the bird to their father. Their false claim was exposed when Ivan Vyslavovich was restored to life by the Water of Life and Death, which was sprinkled on him by the shape-changing wolf that had been helping him in his quest. The Firebird remained in the ownership of Vyslav Andronovich, for Dalmat had given the bird to Ivan after the latter completed a task that Dalmat had assigned him. Dmitrii and Vasilii were thrown into their father's deepest dungeon for their treachery.

See also: Dalmat; Dmitrii (Vyslavovich); Ivan Vyslavovich; Vasilii Vyslavovich; Vyslav Andronovich; Water of Life and Death, The

FIRST ALMAFI
Hungary—Magyar
See Almafi.

FOMA NAZARIEV
Russia
One of two cogovernors of the city of Novgorod, the other being Luka Zinoviev. The pair accepted a wager of thirty thousand rubles offered them by Sadko that the latter had amassed a fortune sufficient to buy everything that was for sale in the city. Sadko ultimately lost the bet because as soon as he had bought something, the governors brought in more goods to take the place of those purchased.

See also: Luka Zinoviev; Novgorod; Sadko

FOOL AND THE BIRCH TREE, THE
Russia
There once lived an old man who had three sons. The two elder sons were quick-witted, but the youngest was a fool. When their

father died, the two eldest made sure that the bulk of the estate went to them. A short time later, the local fair arrived, and all three sons set out to sell their goods. The two eldest took the finest cattle, calves, sheep, and lambs, whereas all the fool had was a bony old ox.

En route to the fair the fool passed through a wood. An old birch tree was groaning in the breeze—a sound that the fool took to be an offer for his ox. The fool bartered with the tree and finally agreed to a price of twenty rubles. The tree creaked again, and the fool agreed to leave the ox and return the following day for his money. Back at home, the fool told his brothers that he had sold his ox for twenty rubles. When they asked him to show them the money, he told them he had to return to collect it the next day. His brothers cursed him as a fool and left him alone.

The following day the fool returned to the wood and demanded his money. The tree creaked, which the fool took to be a request for one more day's credit, terms to which he agreed. That night, when the fool told his brothers what had transpired, they called him every bad name under the sun. Thus, when the fool returned the next morning, he took his ax with him, and when the tree was not forthcoming with his twenty rubles, he cut it down. As the tree fell, a horde of gold hidden at its roots by long-ago robbers tumbled out. The fool stuffed as much as he could into his pockets before returning home to fetch his brothers, there being far too much gold for him to carry.

The three brothers filled a number of sacks with the gold and were on their way home again when they encountered a greedy deacon who asked what they were carrying. The two smart brothers said that they had been gathering mushrooms; but the fool laughed, said that they were lying, and opened his sack to reveal the gold within. The deacon leaped down from his horse and began cramming his pockets full of the fool's gold. The fool took offense at this, took out his hatchet, and killed the deacon.

The two eldest brothers were aghast. They hurriedly took the body home and buried it in their cellar, telling the fool not to mention what had happened to anyone. Some days later the townsfolk came to the door and asked whether the brothers had seen the deacon. The fool immediately told them that the deacon was buried in their cellar. However, without his knowledge, his two brothers had dug up the deacon and buried a goat in his place. Thus, when the townsfolk dug in the cellar, all they found was the corpse of the goat; and from that day forward, no one ever believed the fool again.

FROST
Russia
In most Russian folktales and legends, Frost appears as a nameless demon. In the tale of Marfusha, Frost has the name Morozko. In another story, where he remains nameless, he appears to a peasant as a thin, hunched man with gray hair and bushy white eyebrows. Frost is usually a malevolent spirit; however, as the story of Marfusha illustrates, he can show compassion when he is so disposed.

See also: Ded Moroz; Marfusha; Morozko

GABIJ(I)A

Lithuania

The goddess of fire and the domestic hearth. Some accounts say that she was brought to earth by Perkunas; others, that she was carried by a swallow that was badly burned while carrying her.

See also: Perkunas

GENGHIS KHAN

General

(c. 1162–1227) A Mongol conqueror who founded the largest land empire in history and ruled an area that stretched across central Asia from the Caspian Sea to the Sea of Japan. Genghis (also Chinghiz) Khan was a political and military genius who united Mongol and other nomadic tribes into an effective, disciplined fighting force. Genghis's warriors were known for their use of terror to intimidate their opponents, and they frequently killed their prisoners.

Genghis Khan was an intelligent man with superior organizational abilities. He showed great generosity to his followers; and although he had little interest in cultural matters, he promoted literacy among his people, as well as establishing the first Mongol code of laws, called the *Yasa* or *Yasak*.

Genghis Khan's original name was Temujin, which means "ironworker." His father was the chief of a small Mongol tribe. Temujin inherited the position of chief around age 13, when members of an enemy tribe poisoned his father; but according to

The Secret History of the Mongols, a Mongol epic written during the mid-thirteenth century, the tribe for a time ignored its new chief. It was not long, however, before Temujin began to attract followers, form alliances, and build an army. He used harsh training and strict discipline to create a superior fighting force that was well equipped and that employed new tactics and weapons.

Temujin used his army to extend his power over neighboring tribes, and by 1206 he had become the ruler of Mongolia. That year, an assembly of Mongol chieftains proclaimed him Genghis Khan, a title that probably means either universal ruler or invincible prince. After becoming the ruler of Mongolia, Genghis Khan set out to conquer China. First he attacked a kingdom in northwestern China called Xi Xia, or Hsi

Nineteenth-century engraving of Genghis Khan (Print and Picture Collection, Free Library of Philadelphia)

Hsia. He then invaded northeastern China, and in 1215 he took Beijing (Peking), the capital of the Jin (Chin) Empire. In 1218, Genghis Khan broke off his assault on China and swept into central Asia, where he crushed the kingdom of Khorezm, or Khwārizm, which occupied an area roughly contiguous with modern Uzbekistan and Turkmenistan. In 1220, he destroyed the cities of Bukhara and Samarqand (Samarkand in present-day Uzbekistan), and Neyshabur (Nishapur in modern Iran). Two smaller armies of Genghis invaded the plains north of the Caspian Sea, and by 1223, they had conquered the Kipchaks and had defeated the Russians at the Kalka River. From 1225 until he died in 1227, Genghis Khan again laid siege to Xi Xia. His grandson, Kublai Khan, completed the conquest of China.

See also: Caspian Sea; Khan; Mongols; Turkmenistan; Uzbekistan

GEORGE, SAINT
Russia
Patron saint of Russia. His preeminence stems from his emergence in the sixteenth century. A warrior saint who embodied aspects of Perun and Svantovit, George was the dragon-slaying hero who awed the earth and its inhabitants. He was also a symbol of the consolidation of Muscovite sovereignty, and his warlike depiction in art, seated atop a great white charger and carrying a spear, suggested that the traditional sacrificial image of the Muscovite ruler had changed to that of an aggressive and self-assertive defender of the land.

Saint George first appeared as the patron of Russian rulers in 1415, under the Muscovite Grand Prince Vasilii II. This patronage was advanced under the rule of Ivan III ("the Great"), the successor to Vasilii II, and marked the transformation of the Kievan ideal of service into overlordship. For the first time the ruler was not seen as the servant of the people; instead, the people were seen as servants of the crown. Saint George was so popular in Moscow that forty-one churches there are dedicated to him.

Saint George's Day (23 April) marked the beginning of the agricultural year, a day on which George appeared in his fertility aspect. In Belorussia, as in other areas, the day was marked with a ceremony in which a young man who was called George for the day, and representing the saint, dressed in greenery and flowers and led an entourage of singing maidens into the fields to stimulate the fertility of the ground. In Ukraine the ceremony combined both Christian and pagan elements. There a priest led a company into the fields to bless the soil, and then the company, or in some cases the priest himself, would roll on the ground to imbue it with their own inherent fertility. Saint George supplanted the ancient fertility deities, being depicted as the guardian of all aspects of agriculture, from plants to cattle and beyond. He was described as winging his way across the land on his white steed, reviving the soil and all life that lay dormant within it, his powers allegedly given him by the Virgin Mary.

Russia was not the only country to adopt Saint George as patron saint. England, Portugal, and Greece all delegated this role to Saint George; but in Russia, the saint seems to have been more potent than elsewhere.

As with many saints, not much is known about George's life—indeed, it cannot be confirmed that he actually existed. It has been suggested that he may have been tortured and put to death by Diocletian at Nicomedia on 23 April 303. Some, however, prefer the idea that he died c. 250 at Lydda in Palestine, where his alleged tomb is exhibited. The famous story of George's fight with the dragon cannot be traced to an earlier source than *Legenda Aurea* by Jacobus de Voragine (1230–98), which was translated as *Golden Legend* by Caxton in 1483.

See also: Dragon; Perun; Saint George and the Deceitful Fox; Svantovit
References: Afanas'ev 1865–69; Bezsonov 1861; Delehaye 1927; Gimbutas 1971; Kazanskii 1855; Leroy-Beaulieu 1905; Tereshchenko 1848

Sixteenth-century Russian icon of Saint George and the dragon (Rubliev Museum, Moscow; Beniaminson/Art Resource, NY)

GEORGIA
General

A nation in the Caucasus region that became independent in 1991 after nearly 200 years of Russian and Soviet rule. Georgia has an area of 26,911 square miles (69,700 square kilometers) and lies mostly in Asia, with a small part in the north being located in Europe.

People have lived in what is now Georgia for thousands of years. The first Georgian state was established in the sixth century B.C., and by the third century B.C. most of what is now Georgia was united in a single kingdom. However, for most of its history Georgia was divided by powerful empires that wrangled over it. From the mid-first century B.C. until the eleventh century A.D. Georgia was invaded by Romans, Persians, Byzantines, Arabs, and Seljuk Turks. Georgia was Christianized in the third century A.D.

During the eleventh and twelfth centuries a series of Georgian rulers gradually freed the country of foreign control and centralized its government. Beginning in the early thirteenth century, however, Georgia again suffered attacks by other nations. Mongol armies, including those of Asian conquerors Genghis Khan and Tamerlane, frequently raided Georgian lands between the early thirteenth century and the early fifteenth century, sending the nation into a decline. Between the sixteenth and the eighteenth centuries the Ottoman Empire and Iran fought over Georgian territory.

In the late eighteenth century the ruler of one of the kingdoms in east Georgia accepted partial Russian rule in exchange for military protection; and by the early nineteenth century, all of Georgia had been incorporated into the Russian Empire.

See also: Caucasus; Genghis Khan; Mongols

GHOVT
Armenia

A she-devil, the demoness into which Koknas, the sister of Suren, was transformed.

See also: Koknas; Suren

GILYAKI (NIVKHI)
General

Ancient people who today number around 4,500 and inhabit a region of Russia in southeastern Siberia, near the mouth of the Amur River. The Gilyaki (Nivkhi) traditionally have made a livelihood hunting and fishing. Their native religion is a form of shamanism.

GIRAITIS
Lithuania

God of the forests. The fact that he is mentioned in seventeenth- and eighteenth-century manuscripts suggests that he might be a deity of comparatively modern invention.

GIWOITIS
Slav

Spirit who assumed the shape of a lizard and who was offered milk to drink.

GLASS MOUNTAIN, THE
Ukraine

The home of a ferocious dragon in the kingdom of an unnamed tsar. The kingdom was for many years a peaceful place to live, until the dragon took up residence, its home accreting under its feet. At first the mound was no more than a shiny hillock. However, the longer the dragon stayed there, feeding on the people, the larger the hillock grew, until a huge glass mountain dominated the kingdom. The tsar sent out his bravest warriors to kill the dragon, but none returned, and the glass mountain continued to grow until it occupied almost half the kingdom. The dragon, knowing that it was safe, swooped down on the palace and carried away the tsar's only daughter, locking her in a cave on the glass mountain.

In a neighboring kingdom lived a young tsarevich named Ivan who heard of the plight of his neighbor and set out to see if he could help. En route he was bitten by an ant that promised to help him if the young prince would spare its life. Ivan did so and continued on his journey, pondering the task that lay ahead. As he thought of the immensity of this task, he called out to the ant for help. The ant appeared and gave the prince a grain of wheat, which he told Ivan to place at the foot of the glass mountain. Ivan thanked the ant and rode on.

Having introduced himself to the tsar and told him his aim, Ivan rode to the foot of the glass mountain, which by this time covered almost three-quarters of the kingdom. Ivan tethered his horse to a tree and placed the grain of wheat at the base of the mountain. Then he hid among the trees and watched. As he looked at the grain of wheat, it began to glow, and a trickle of water began to flow from the base of the mountain. That trickle quickly became a raging torrent as the mountain continued to melt, and Ivan had to find higher ground or be swept away.

The dragon, on returning to his lair, saw water gushing from the base of the mountain and swooped down to see what was causing it. As the dragon landed, the torrent of water became even more intense, and a great wall of water dashed the dragon to its death and then carried its remains away. Ivan then rushed over to what remained of the mountain and released the princess, and together they hurried back to her father. Several days later Ivan—by then called Ivan the Dragon Killer—and the princess were married. Ivan inherited the kingdom some years later when the tsar abdicated in his favor.

See also: Dragon; Ivan the Dragon Killer

GLEB, SAINT
Russia
Russian Orthodox saint. According to legend, he and Saint Boris were smiths who forged the first plow. This plow was of gigantic proportions, and was forged with implements of like size. The two smiths were recorded as having used twelve golden hammers, and tongs that weighed almost four hundredweight, or twelve poods (a pood being an old Russian measure of weight roughly equivalent to 36 lbs, or 16.38 kg). Other versions of this legend name the two saintly smiths as Saints Kuz'ma and Dem'yan.

Boris and Gleb are Russia's oldest saints. They are described as sons of Prince Vladimir Bright Sun and brothers of Sviatopolk. The earliest account of the martyrdom of the brothers dates from the twelfth-century *Primary Chronicle.* In this, Boris hears of his father's death while he is fighting the invading Pecheneg hordes. Boris quickly returns to Kiev, where he learns that his older brother Sviatopolk plans to kill him and take his lands and inheritance. However, instead of attempting to avoid his death, Boris smooths the way for Sviatopolk and submits to his fate. Gleb then learns that Sviatopolk plans the same fate for him, and he too submits to the inevitable. The brothers are supposed to have died in 1015, and shortly afterward they were canonized as "protectors of the land of Rus'."

Although the cult of Boris and Gleb was not Christian in origin, the church sanctioned it in order to satisfy the needs of the newly converted populace.

See also: Boris, Saint; Dem'yan, Saint; Kiev; Kuz'ma, Saint; *Primary Chronicle;* Sviatopolk; Vladimir Bright Sun, Prince
References: Bezsonov 1861; Cross and Sherbowitz-Wetzor 1953; Golubinskii 1903; Zenkovsky 1963

GODENKO BLUDOVICH
Russia
One of the seven bogatyri who undertook a legendary quest together. The other six were Vasilii Buslayevich, Vasilii Kazimirovich, Ivan Gostinyi Syn, Alyosha Popovich, Dobrynya Nikitich, and Il'ya Muromets. This legend, which purports to explain why the bogatyri disappeared from Holy Russia, may be found in the entry about Vasilii Buslayevich.

See also: Alyosha Popovich; Bogatyr'; Dobrynya Nikitich; Il'ya Muromets; Ivan Gostinyi Syn; Vasilii Buslayevich; Vasilii Kazimirovich
References: Speranskii 1916; Ukhov 1957

Late-fourteenth-century Russian icon of Saints Boris and Gleb on horseback from the Cathedral of the Dormition, the Kremlin, Moscow (Tretyakov Gallery, Moscow; Scala/Art Resource)

GODINOVICH, STAVR
Russia
See Stavr Godinovich.

GOIK
Poland
The name given to a puppet that is used in a pagan ceremony traditionally performed during the Lenten season. The puppet, which represents death, is taken out into the fields and ritually dismembered, or carried on horseback and thrown into the local watercourse. This ceremony's purpose is not to safeguard the people of a village from death, which they must accept as inevitable, but it is thought to protect them from illness during the coming year.

GOLDEN BOOK OF FATE, THE
Siberia—Yakut
The book owned by Ajysyt, the mother-goddess of the Yakut people who live near the river Lena in Siberia. The book contains the names and destinies of every human being living or yet to be born. Ajysyt brought the soul from heaven so that a complete human being could come into existence at birth, and then the goddess entered the name of the new person in the Golden Book of Fate. It was only when the name had been entered in the book that the person became a fully fledged member of the human race.

See also: Ajysyt; Lena, River; Siberia; Yakuts

GOLDEN CITY, THE
Armenia
The last city visited by the princess in her quest to locate Habërmani. There she met the daughter of the witch nursing Habërmani, who was getting water at the well. The princess asked the girl if she knew where Habërmani was, and she was delighted to hear that he was in that city, although for seven years he had lived a life of torment in the clutches of a vile fever. The princess asked the girl for a drink from the pitcher, and she surreptitiously slid her wedding ring into the water as she drank. The princess

then sat down to wait while the witch's daughter took the pitcher to where Habërmani lay. As he drank the water, he found the ring and was immediately cured of his fever. Habërmani sent the witch's daughter to fetch the woman from the well. Thus Habërmani and his princess were reunited, although they had yet to escape the witch.

For the full story see the entry for Habërmani.

References: Orbeli and Taronian 1959–67, vol. 4

GOLDEN HORDE, THE
General
In 1237, Batu Khan, a grandson of the conqueror Genghis Khan, led between 150,000 and 200,000 Mongol troops into Russia and destroyed one Russian town after another. In 1240, the troops conquered Kiev and Russia became part of the Mongol Empire, being incorporated into an administrative area called the Golden Horde. The capital of the Golden Horde was at Sarai, near what is now Volgograd.

In the early fourteenth century, Prince Yuri of Moscow married the sister of the khan of the Golden Horde, and he was appointed the Russian grand prince about 1318. From that time on, Moscow grew stronger and richer while the Golden Horde grew weaker, chiefly because of struggles for leadership. In 1380, Grand Prince Dmitrii defeated a Mongol force in the Battle of Kulikovo, near the Don River. The victory briefly freed Moscow of Mongol control and proved that the khan's troops could indeed be beaten. However, Moscow was recaptured by the Mongols in 1382.

During the late fifteenth century, Moscow became the most powerful Russian city. Tsar Ivan III ("the Great") won control over Moscow's main rivals, Novgorod and Tver'. In 1480, Ivan made the final break from Mongol rule by refusing to pay taxes to the Golden Horde. The khan's troops moved toward Moscow but they never attacked, as they were forced to return in order to defend their own capital from Russian attack.

See also: Genghis Khan; Khan; Kiev; Mongols; Moscow

GOLDEN KINGDOM, THE
Russia

One of three kingdoms in the realm of Whirlwind, located on a plateau atop a tremendously high mountain range. The tsaritsa of this kingdom, Elena the Fair, a prisoner of Whirlwind, lived in a golden palace that was guarded by dragons. She was set free by Ivan Belyaninovich, along with her sisters, the tsaritsas of the Silver Kingdom and the Copper Kingdom, when he killed Whirlwind and released his mother Nastas'ya of the Golden Braid. She married Ivan, and her first sister, the tsaritsa of the Silver Kingdom, married Peter Belyaninovich. Her other sister, the tsaritsa of the Copper Kingdom, married Vasilii Belyaninovich (Peter and Vasilii being the two brothers of Ivan).

See also: Copper Kingdom, The; Dragon; Elena the Fair; Ivan Belyaninovich; Nastas'ya of the Golden Braid; Peter (Belyaninovich); Silver Kingdom, The; Vasilii Belyaninovich; Whirlwind

GOLDEN MOUNTAIN, THE
Ukraine

The tale of the Golden Mountain—a Ukrainian version of the story of Grishka and the Mountain of Gold—revolves around the unnamed, idle son of a rich merchant.

Having grown up amid a life of luxury where he had only to ask for a thing and it would be given, the merchant's son knew nothing about managing money and had no skill or profession. When his father suddenly died, the young man quickly squandered the large fortune his father had left him. Destitute and suddenly friendless, the young man sold the golden buttons from his coat, his last asset in the world, and with the money bought food and a spade. Then he went to the town square and waited for someone to come along and employ him. All day long the young man waited, but

although others were readily hired, he was passed over due to the softness of his hands.

He had almost given up hope when a golden carriage entered the square, those others still looking for work quickly taking to their heels, leaving the young man quite alone. The carriage drew up beside him and its owner, a wealthy merchant, offered him a job, good food, and fine clothes. The young man readily accepted the offer and climbed into the carriage. Minutes later the carriage stopped beside a golden ship, which they boarded. Several days later they landed on an island on which stood a magnificent golden mansion and a huge, glittering mountain.

As the ship moored, the merchant and the young man disembarked to be greeted by the merchant's daughter, a maiden of such beauty that the young man immediately lost his heart to her. All day long the young man labored, unloading the ship and carrying the provisions to the mansion. Then the merchant invited him to dine with himself and his daughter, for the following day the young man would start the work he had been hired to do.

The banquet laid out in the mansion was finer than the young man had ever seen in all his privileged youth. After the meal, the merchant poured two goblets of wine and pushed one toward the young man. As he did so, the merchant's daughter called to her father from outside the room, and he left. As he left by one door, the maiden came in through another and hurried over to the young man. She handed him a tinderbox, telling him that should he ever find himself in danger, he only had to strike the tinderbox and help would come.

The young man quickly pocketed the tinderbox and drank the goblet of wine. No sooner had he drained his goblet than he slumped across the table and fell into a deep sleep, for the wine had been drugged. The merchant got up from the table and went out into the stables, where he harnessed two strong horses to a cart and then killed an old nag, cleaned out the carcass, and loaded it onto the cart. Then he went back into the mansion and carried the young man out and sewed him up, with his spade, inside the body of the old horse. The merchant then drove to the foot of the Golden Mountain, where he unloaded the carcass and set his horses to graze while he hid behind some bushes. As dawn broke, a flock of ravens with iron beaks and claws flew down from the mountain and picked up the carcass and carried it to the summit. There they started to tear away the flesh of the old horse. As the sun broke over the horizon, they had picked the bones clean and were beginning to peck at the body of the young man inside.

The youth awoke as the pain chased away the last effects of the drugged wine, and he chased away the birds with his spade. Wondering where he was, he called out for help. From the foot of the mountain the merchant shouted that the young man should dig and roll the gold down the mountain. If by evening he had dug a cartload of gold, then the merchant would tell him how he might descend the mountain. If he had not, then the merchant would leave him there to be devoured by the ravens when they returned to roost at sunset.

All day long the young man dug into the mountain, and by evening the cart below was fully laden. However, as he stopped digging and looked down the mountain, he saw that the merchant was hitching his horses to the cart and making ready to leave. The young man shouted down to the merchant, asking to be told how to get down. The merchant simply laughed at him and told him that he would never get down and that he should enjoy the time he had left, for when the sun set the ravens would return and tear him to pieces. With that the merchant drove away, and the young man sat down to ponder his fate.

As he pondered, the sun began to set, and he saw the ravens in the distance. Just then he remembered the tinderbox, took it out, and struck it twice. Instantly two men (described in the legend as Cossacks) stood

before him and asked him what he desired. He immediately asked to be taken back to his hometown, and in a flash he found himself standing in the deserted market square where his journey with the merchant had started.

The young man lived quietly by himself until his hands had healed from the labor on the mountain, and then he went back to the market square to await the return of the merchant. He waited patiently every day for almost two months. Then the merchant reappeared and the young man stood his ground as those around him seeking honest employment fled. So it was that the young man once again found himself on the island. The merchant's daughter was amazed when she recognized the young man to whom she had given the tinderbox; but she bit her lip and said nothing to her father.

That evening, as the merchant poured the two goblets of wine, the young man passed some comment that made the merchant turn around, and as he did so, the young man swapped the goblets. Then, when the merchant fell into a deep sleep, the young man went out into the stables, hitched the horses to the cart, killed and gutted an old nag, and sewed the merchant and a spade inside. Then, just as the merchant had done, the young man drove to the foot of the mountain, unloaded the carcass, unhitched the horses, and watched from his hiding place as the ravens carried the carcass up to the summit of the mountain.

As the sun rose and the ravens began to tear at the merchant, he awoke and fought off the ravens with his spade. From the foot of the mountain the young man called up to him and told him to dig a cartload of gold before sunset. The merchant dug furiously all day, and by evening the cart was fully laden with gold. As the sun began to set, the young man drove away and left the merchant to his well-deserved fate. He drove the cart back to the golden mansion, where he took the merchant's place, married the merchant's daughter, and lived a life of ease, never employing any unfortunate lads to mine gold from the Golden Mountain.

> *See also:* Cossacks; Grishka; Mountain of Gold; Ukraine

GORYNICH
Russia

A terrible dragon that was the nephew of the sorcerer Nemal Chelovek.

> *See also:* Dragon; Nemal Chelovek

GORYNINKA
Russia

A sorceress related to Goryshche the dragon. She appears to Dobrynya Nikitich in the guise of an old hag and challenges him to a fight, armed with a sword and lance that reaches into the skies. Many authorities believe that Goryninka (also known as Baba Latingorka) is an incarnation of that most terrible of all Russian witches, Baba-Yaga.

> *See also:* Baba-Yaga (-Jaga, -Iaga); Dobrynya Nikitich; Dragon; Goryshche
> *References:* Astakhova 1938–51; Evgen'eva and Putilov 1977; Speranskii 1916

GORYSHCHE
Russia

(from *gora,* "mountain") A multiheaded she-dragon related to Baba Latingorka, or Goryninka, and Sviatogor. Goryshche's lair is in a cavern in the Sorochinsk Mountains, where she holds many Russians—her food supply—in captivity. Dobrynya Nikitich undertakes a quest to find Goryshche and end her murderous ways.

Having slain her young, Dobrynya is warned by his mother, Amelfia Timofeyevna, never to return to the Sorochinsk Mountains and to stay away from the river Puchai. Dobrynya ignores what he thinks of as the ramblings of an old woman, and he is soon back in dragon-hunting country. Tired and dusty from his long journey, Dobrynya strips off his clothes, and leaving them with his horse on the bank, dives into the river Puchai. Suddenly he sees fire and sparks leaping into the air, accompanied by thick

black smoke. Out of this smoke emerges the twelve-headed she-dragon Goryshche. While the dragon asks Dobrynya what she should do with him, the knight seizes the moment and dives beneath the waters, coming ashore on the bank opposite that where his clothes and weapons lie, his horse having been frightened away when the dragon appeared.

Just as he thinks the game is up, Dobrynya catches sight of a priest's hat lying in the grass. As a bogatyr', a knight of Holy Russia, he knows that this hat will make a formidable weapon; but when he lifts it, it seems extremely heavy. As the dragon flies toward him, Dobrynya brandishes the hat and severs all but one of the dragon's heads. The dragon drops to the ground and Dobrynya leaps astride her, preparing to finish her off.

Goryshche begs for mercy and promises never to raid the lands of Holy Russia again, and never to carry off any more Russian people. Dobrynya likewise promises never to return to the Sorochinsk Mountains; and having made their pact, the two part ways.

Absent his horse, Dobrynya must make his way home to Kiev on foot. When he arrives he finds that in his long absence a disaster has befallen the court of Prince Vladimir Bright Sun. The very dragon that Dobrynya spared had broken her word, and flying over the city, she had carried away the Princess Zabava, Vladimir's favorite niece. Vladimir Bright Sun calls together his knights and challenges them to rescue the unfortunate maiden.

Alesha, the son of the priest Leontii, tells Vladimir that Dobrynya seems to know the dragon quite well, adding that he believes that the dragon regards Dobrynya as her brother. When Vladimir Bright Sun hears this, he commands Dobrynya to bring back the girl or be beheaded.

Returning home, Dobrynya explains what has transpired to his mother, complaining that he will have to walk to the Sorochinsk Mountains because he has no horse. His mother tells him of his father's old chestnut, which is standing in the stable, mired in its own dung. Telling her son to clean up the horse and feed it, she also advises him to get a good night's sleep. Dobrynya follows his mother's advice to the letter. The next morning, as he mounts the chestnut and makes ready to leave, his mother hands him a silken whip, telling him to whip the horse with it if the beast's strength begins to fail.

Placing the whip in his pocket, Dobrynya spurs the horse, which clears the city walls in a single leap and speeds away faster than the eye can follow. In no time at all they reach the foothills of the Sorochinsk Mountains. There the ground is teeming with the young of the she-dragon. Dobrynya attacks them, riding over their dead bodies; but gradually, having been bitten badly, the horse begins to falter. Remembering the words of his mother, Dobrynya takes the whip from his pocket and gently lashes his mount between the ears and hind legs. Instantly the horse's vigor returns, and they finally arrive at the cave of the she-dragon.

Needless to say, Goryshche is not happy to see Dobrynya and complains bitterly about the death of her offspring, and even more so about the fact that Dobrynya, a knight of Holy Russia, has broken his word. Dobrynya retorts that it is she who first broke their pact, and demands the return of Zabava. When the dragon refuses, Dobrynya attacks her. For three days they battle, until finally Dobrynya triumphs. However, Dobrynya now finds himself stranded in the middle of a vast lake that has formed from the dragon's blood—a lake that the earth will not soak up.

Calling on Mother Earth, he commands her to open up and swallow the dragon's blood. Instantly a huge chasm appears and the lake drains away. Dobrynya climbs down from his horse and enters the network of caves in which the dragon lived. Inside he finds and releases many hundreds of Russians before he sees Princess Zabava in the very last chamber. Leading her outside, he perches her in front of him on his horse, and they return to Kiev at the same speed as that with which he departed. When he returns, he is greeted as a great hero by Prince Vladimir Bright Sun and

all the people of the city. At home, he is also greeted by the sight of his horse Voroneyushka, "Little Raven," which has at long last returned to its stable.

See also: Alesha; Amelf(i)a Timofe(y)evna; Baba Latingorka; Bogatyr'; Dobrynya Nikitich; Dragon; Goryninka; Kiev; Leontii; Mother Earth; Puchai; Sorochinsk Mountains; Sviatogor; Vladimir Bright Sun, Prince; Voroneyushka; Zabava (Putyatichna), Princess
References: Evgen'eva and Putilov 1977; Nechaev and Rybakov 1959; Speranskii 1916; Ukhov 1957

GRAMOVITSA
Russia
The personification of the Virgin Mary as "Mary the Thunderer," an aspect in which she appears as a column of fire—a characteristic previously attributed to Perun. In this aspect she is responsible for the rainbow bridge that connects heaven and earth, allowing the rain to flow freely over the fields.

See also: Perun
References: Afanas'ev 1865–69; Matorin 1931

GREAT BEAR
General
The common name for the constellation Ursa Major.

See also: Ursa Major

GREAT GODDESS
General
The head goddess of any pantheon, whether she be the goddess of the sun, the moon, or the earth. The Great Goddess was usually—but not always—the most respected female deity. In some cultures the Great Goddess was considered too remote or aloof to be interested in the affairs of mere mortals, and there her cult was weak.

See also: Moon; Sun

GREEN MARSH
Russia
The home of Babushka-Lyagushka-Ska-kushka ("Grandmother Hopping Frog"), the

oldest living creature. Baba-Yaga asked her to help Petrushka in his quest to locate the place I-Know-Not-Where and the object I-Know-Not-What.

See also: Baba-Yaga (-Jaga, -Iaga); Babushka-Lyagushka-Skakushka; I-Know-Not-What; I-Know-Not-Where; Petrushka

GREGORY OF SMOLENSK
Russia

A fourteenth-century ecclesiastical chronicler who boasted that he had heard the earth bemoaning the loss of her children to the Mother of God. These stories were obviously an attempt by the chronicler to convince others that even Mother Earth herself had accepted the inevitability of full conversion from paganism.

See also: Mother Earth

GRISHKA
Russia

A young and handsome yet very poor peasant who sought work by waiting among other men seeking employment in the market square of an unnamed town. Several men had been picked by the time a richly attired merchant drove into the square in a solid gold carriage. All the other prospective laborers turned on their heels and fled when they saw the merchant approach, but Grishka stood his ground. Thus he was the only man present when the merchant asked him if he was looking for work, and he was also able to command the princely sum of one hundred rubles a day for his services.

Grishka climbed into the merchant's carriage, and soon they had traveled the short distance to the harbor. There they boarded a magnificent ship and set sail. Eventually a small island came into sight, the merchant's golden palace shining like a beacon in the bright sunlight. As they sailed into the small harbor and moored, Grishka and the merchant were met by the merchant's wife and his beautiful daughter. Grishka immediately fell in love with the maiden, who likewise fell in love with him.

At a banquet that night, the merchant's daughter gave Grishka a tinderbox, telling him that if he ever had need of assistance, all he had to do was strike the steel against the flint, and help would be at hand.

The following morning the merchant led Grishka to the great Mountain of Gold that rose from the center of the island, but no matter how hard he might try, Grishka found it too steep to climb. The merchant clapped Grishka on the back and told him not to worry, and sat him down with a goblet of wine to refresh him so that he might try again. The wine was drugged, and Grishka soon fell into a deep sleep. As soon as he had dozed off, the merchant cut the throat of the horse that had accompanied them, gutted it, sewed Grishka up inside the carcass, and then quickly hid.

Two enormous black crows alighted, picked up the carcass, and carried it up to the top of the mountain, where they picked its bones clean. Grishka woke up and drove the crows away, and then called out to the merchant, who replied from the foot of the mountain. The merchant promised that if Grishka toiled hard that day, he would divine a means by which he could descend the mountain safely.

Grishka dug gold all day long, rolling it off the sheer sides of the mountain to the merchant below, who loaded it onto a series of carts. As night began to fall, Grishka called down that he had done enough for one day and was ready to come down. The merchant simply laughed, shouting back to Grishka that ninety-nine men before him had perished on the summit of that mountain and that he would become the hundredth. Then the merchant rode away, and Grishka sat down to ponder his predicament with the crows circling overhead.

It was then that Grishka remembered the tinderbox. He struck a spark from it and was immediately joined by two shining youths, who asked what he desired. Grishka asked them to get him off the mountain. In an instant Grishka found himself on the shore of the island, just as a boat was sailing past. Grishka called out to the sailors to rescue him, but they simply laughed and proceeded on their way. Grishka struck another spark, and an evil wind blew the ship back to the shore so that the sailors had no choice but to pick up Grishka and carry him home.

After he had returned home and rested a while, Grishka returned to the market square and waited for the merchant to arrive. Soon the gold carriage entered the square, and all the other men waiting took to their heels and fled. Grishka this time bargained a price of two hundred rubles a day, and once again he was taken to the merchant's island. However, when they again stood at the foot of the mountain and the merchant offered Grishka a drink to refresh himself, Grishka politely declined until the merchant himself had accepted a drink from his grateful employee. Grishka poured the merchant a drugged drink from his own flask, and when the merchant had fallen asleep, he cut the throat of the horse that had accompanied them, took out its entrails, sewed the merchant up inside, and hid.

The crows duly appeared, carried the carcass to the top of the mountain, and stripped its bones. Thus the merchant found himself at the top of the Mountain of Gold with no way down, and Grishka called up to him, saying that it would be the merchant and not he who became the hundredth man to die upon that summit. Grishka went to the merchant's palace and was joyfully reunited with the merchant's daughter, who agreed to become his wife. As the couple sailed away, the crows alit on the summit of the Mountain of Gold.

See also: Mountain of Gold

GUDIRI-MUMI

Votyak

"Mother of thunder," the goddess of thunder and lightning.

GULINAZ

Armenia

The daughter of King Aslan, who was abducted and imprisoned by a Tapagöz. Samson, who had seen her in a dream, set out to find and release her from the cave in which she was held captive. This he did, after killing the Tapagöz. Samson and Gulinaz then set out for home, where they were married in due course. For the full legend, see the entry for Samson.

See also: Aslan; Samson; Tapagöz
References: Orbeli and Taronian 1959–67, vol. 4

HABËRMANI

Armenia

A sorcerer prince who assumed the guise of a snake and hid in a bundle of firewood that had been gathered by an old peasant. That night he made himself known to the old man and his equally aged wife and was subsequently accepted into the family. One evening, the snake spoke to the old man and told him that the very next day he should go to the local king and ask for the hand of the princess for his son. The old man protested, but Habërmani insisted, and finally the man agreed to go.

All did not go well at the palace the following morning. At first the palace guards tried to throw the old man out on his ear; but he insisted that he had something important to ask the king, so they unceremoniously dragged him off and deposited him in a pile on the floor before the throne. The king asked him what he wanted, and the old man boldly asked the princess's hand for his son.

The king laughed to himself, thinking that the old peasant was mad; but he told him that he would give the hand of his daughter in marriage if by the following morning the peasant could build a fine palace that rivaled that of the king. If he failed, however, the king would have his head. Thus the old man trudged back to his ramshackle hut, sure that he was living his last few hours on the earth. Habërmani knew exactly what to do when the old peasant told him of the king's command. He instructed the old man to go into the forest, where he would find a well. At that well he should shout to Mother Earth and tell her what Habërmani wanted.

The peasant forlornly did as he was asked, and when he returned home he was amazed to find that his dilapidated old hut had become a palace finer than even that of the king. The following morning the peasant once again set out for the king's palace to repeat his request. The king was amazed when he saw the magnificent new palace, and he knew that forces were afoot about which he knew nothing and which he could not control. However, he was not ready to give up his only daughter so easily; so he told the old man that he must now go back and lay out gardens around the new palace, or he would lose his head.

Again the peasant related the demand to Habërmani, who told him to go back to the well and ask Mother Earth, as he had done before. This the peasant did. The following morning the peasant went back to the king, the gardens around the new palace being the finest any mortal had ever seen. Again the king would not give up his daughter without setting another task, this time telling the peasant, again under threat of losing his head, to provide a carpet that stretched between the two palaces.

Habërmani sent the peasant back to the well, and the following morning the old man trekked back to the king and told him that everything he had been asked to do, he had done. However, the king assigned him one last task: to provide seven invisible minstrels with pipes and drums, a demand that the old man easily complied with, thanks to Habërmani, Mother Earth, and the well. Finally, seeing that there was nothing that the old man could not achieve, the king relented and asked the old man to present his son. When the king saw that the youth was a snake, he was horrified; but as he had given his word, he gave the order for wedding preparations to begin.

The wedding feast lasted seven days and seven nights. When all the guests had departed and Habërmani and his new wife were left alone, Habërmani removed his snakeskin and revealed himself to be a handsome prince. He told his wife that he would only assume his manly guise when they were alone, and would live as a snake during the day. He also warned her not to breathe one word about his human form; for if she did, the magic spell would be broken and she would lose him, and everything would be as it was before.

Many weeks passed, and although sorely tempted on more than one occasion, the princess kept her bond, and she and Habërmani lived a life of happiness. However, the king then decided to hold a tournament in which all the nobles of his kingdom would take part. Habërmani stole away and shed his snakeskin. He then dressed in blue armor and rode to the tournament, where everyone was amazed by his prowess. The princess immediately guessed that this mysterious blue knight was none other than her beloved Habërmani. Many ladies of the court made fun of the princess, saying that her husband would not dare slither onto the tournament ground, for he would surely be trampled to death. At length their taunts became intolerable, and the princess retorted that her husband was the finest knight at the tournament that day.

No sooner had she spoken the words than Habërmani was struck by a lance and thrown from his horse. When he regained consciousness, his wife beside him, he told her that she had lost him. She could only recover him by binding iron sandals to her feet, taking up a steel staff, and traveling the world for seven years, during which time she would pass seven castles—one each year. Then Habërmani, the palace, its gardens, the carpet, and the pipers vanished, and the princess was left alone in the ramshackle hut that had once been the home of the old peasant and

his wife. Immediately resolving to find Habërmani, the princess strapped on iron sandals, took up a steel staff, and set out.

Habërmani, still wounded from the tournament, had traveled by magic to a realm ruled by a witch and her daughter whom the witch wanted Habërmani to marry. However, Habërmani was so in love with his princess that when his wound had healed, he succumbed to a fever that felt as if he were burning in the fires of damnation. The witch's daughter fetched pitchers of water from dawn to dusk in an attempt to cool the fever, but Habërmani simply lay there, writhing in agony.

The princess, on the other hand, was wending her way through the world, until she came to the Clay City. There she met a maid at a well, collecting water in a pitcher. She asked the girl if Habërmani lived in the city. The girl told the princess that she had not heard of Habërmani, and sent her on to the Crystal City, which lay one year's walk away. The princess tried that city and received the same response, this time being sent to the Copper City. From there she was sent to the Iron City, then the Steel City, then the Silver City, and finally the Golden City.

There she met the witch's daughter getting water at the well. The princess asked the girl if she knew where Habërmani was, and she was delighted to hear that he was in that city, although for seven years he had lived a life of torment in the clutches of a vile fever. The princess asked the girl for a drink from the pitcher, and surreptitiously slid her wedding ring into the water as she drank. The princess then sat down to wait while the witch's daughter took the pitcher to where Habërmani lay. As he drank the water, he found the ring and was immediately cured of his fever. Habërmani sent the witch's daughter to fetch the woman from the well, and thus Habërmani and his princess were reunited. However, they had yet to escape the witch.

That night the old witch asked the princess to massage her feet until she fell asleep, and then to sleep at the foot of her bed. Habërmani advised his wife that the witch intended to kill her with a powerful kick; so the princess placed a large log in her place after the witch had fallen asleep. Just as Habërmani expected, in the morning the log had been smashed. When the witch realized that she had been tricked, she tried to get the princess lost by sending her out to gather five sacks of feathers in the forest. However, Habërmani told the princess how she could gather them easily, and she quickly returned with the required amount. The witch then sent the princess to bring her twelve dresses like no others in the world. This time, when the princess told her husband of the task she had been assigned, Habërmani decided that the time had come for them to escape.

Having traveled a fair distance from the city, Habërmani told his wife to look around and see if they were being followed. She saw a cloud of dust in their wake, a cloud that Habërmani guessed would be the witch's daughter. He instantly turned his wife into a windmill and himself into a deaf miller. Thus, when the witch's daughter reached them, he could only respond with nonsense, and the witch's daughter returned to her city empty-handed. The witch guessed what had happened and sent her daughter out again.

Habërmani and his wife had traveled a good distance farther when the princess saw the cloud of dust again catching up to them. This time Habërmani turned his wife into a garden and himself into a deaf gardener. As before, the witch's daughter was thwarted and returned to her mother. This time it was the witch herself who set off in pursuit of Habërmani and the princess.

Having returned to their normal, human forms, Habërmani and the princess had traveled a good distance when they saw a huge cloud of dust following them. Habërmani told his wife to throw her comb on the ground. Instantly a huge forest sprang up around them. Habërmani turned his wife into a small sapling and himself into a small snake, winding himself around his wife to keep her safe. The witch came to the forest and knew that within its depths she would find Habërmani as a small snake wound around a fine young sapling that was his wife. However, from within the trees, Habërmani pleaded for mercy, and the witch agreed in return for a kiss from the snake. Habërmani agreed, whereupon the witch returned to her city, and Habërmani and his wife resumed their human forms again. They returned home, where they found the palace and its gardens restored, and there they lived out their days, Habërmani never again resorting to the use of his snakeskin.

See also: Clay City, The; Copper City, The; Crystal City, The; Golden City, The; Iron City, The; Mother Earth; Silver City, The; Steel City, The

References: Orbeli and Taronian 1959–67, vol. 4

HAHE

Siberia—Samoyed

Wooden idols that personified various household spirits. The idols would be carefully wrapped and carried on the household's hahengan, a sled especially reserved for this purpose. The hahe had various functions: One guaranteed wedded bliss; another was the patron of fishing; another the guardian of health and the patron of medicine; and another saw to the health and welfare of the reindeer herds.

When the services of the hahe were required, the idol would be taken from the hahengan and erected where the influence was required, such as in a wood, on the banks of a river, or in the house. Then the mouth of the idol would be smeared with oil or blood, and a dish of meat or fish would be set before it. In return for this food the hahe was expected to respond favorably to requests.

HAHENGAN

Siberia—Samoyed

The sled that was reserved to transport the hahe of a household or individual.

See also: Hahe

HANSEATIC LEAGUE
General

A forerunner of the modern European Union, the Hanseatic League (Ger. Hansa or Hanse) was a confederation of northern European trading cities that operated from the twelfth century until 1669. At its height in the late fourteenth century the league consisted of over 160 towns and cities, among them Lübeck, Hamburg, Cologne, Kraków, and Breslau. The basis of the league's power was its monopoly of Baltic trade and its relations with Flanders and England. The gradual decline of the league beginning in the fifteenth century was due to the movement of trade routes and the formation and development of national states.

The earliest confederation had its headquarters at Visby, Sweden, and included over thirty cities. It was quickly eclipsed by a similar league based at Lübeck. Both Hamburg and Lübeck established branch offices in London, in 1266 and 1267, respectively. These two German leagues were united with yet another based in Cologne, in 1282, to form the so-called Steelyard. There were three other branches of the Hanseatic League—at Bruges, Bergen, and Novgorod. The last general assembly, that of 1669, marked the League's end.

See also: Novgorod

HARO(N)
Armenia

The traveling companion of Baron, some sources suggesting a blood relationship between the two but never explicitly confirming or denying it. During their travels Haron went blind, and from that moment on Baron had to act as Haron's guide, a fact he often bitterly complained about. One night they made their camp under a tree in a forest at the foot of Mount Amarven. Baron climbed a tree to remain safe during the night, leaving Haron to fend for himself on the forest floor. As the sun set, the two travelers heard a pack of wolves approaching them; and as the howls grew louder, Baron grew so afraid that his trembling caused him to lose his footing and fall from the tree.

Haron, however, remained calm and told Baron that they should simply sit beneath the tree and talk, giving the impression that they were just two of many. They did exactly that; and the wolves, thinking that they might be attacked by an unknown number of men, left them alone. The following night exactly the same situation arose, this time with a pack of bears, and again Haron and Baron deceived the bears into thinking that the two were not alone (again, Baron was very frightened, and Haron was calm).

Once again, as they made their camp the very next night, Baron sought to make his bed in a tree, leaving Haron on the ground. Baron, however, had to climb down to eat. When Haron grew thirsty during the meal, Baron refused to lead him to a nearby stream. Thus Haron had to guide himself to the refreshing water. There Haron heard a bird alight on a branch above him, a bird that told him to splash the water from the stream on his eyes. Haron did so, and his sight was immediately restored. Overjoyed, he rushed back to camp to tell Baron. When Baron heard the news, all he could think about was bettering his already perfect sight, and so he rushed down to the stream to splash water in his face. However, when he did so he was immediately struck blind; and from that moment on, their roles were reversed, and Haron had to lead Baron.

The following evening the two once again made camp in the shade of a tree. This time, Haron did not seek to make his bed in the tree but stayed close to Baron. As they sat down to prepare their evening meal, they heard the sound of a man approaching on horseback, the horse's hoof falls accompanied by the sound of many men on foot. As they listened to the men approaching, a huntsman on a white horse entered the clearing—a huntsman that Haron immediately recognized as king of the land they were traveling through.

The king eyed the two suspiciously, and thinking them enemy spies, he had them bound and dragged off to his dungeons. There they were left for several days before being brought before the king and his beautiful daughter. Haron was immediately smitten by the princess's beauty, and she likewise by his countenance. The king questioned both Haron and Baron, and not believing their story, called on his guards to take them out and hang them. However, the king's daughter interceded, and the king allowed her to hear their stories and be their judge.

She listened to what both Haron and Baron had to say, and then went to her father and told him that she believed they posed no threat. She also asked her father to call upon Loqmân the Wise to restore Baron's sight. This he did; and when Baron could see again, he pleaded with the king to take him out and hang him because he could not stand to look Haron in the face after the way he had treated him. Haron and the princess lifted Baron to his feet, Haron and Baron being reconciled. The king then consented to the marriage of Haron and his daughter, a wedding at which Baron served as best man.

See also: Baro(n)

References: Orbeli and Taronian 1959–67, vol. 10

HAZARAN

Armenia

From the Persian *Hazârân,* "bird of a thousand songs," Hazaran is a fabulous nightingale who appears in a post-Christian legend.

An unnamed king had taken seven years to build a wonderful church. As it was being consecrated, a strong wind rose and a hermit appeared before the king, congratulating him on building such a fine church but adding that it was a pity just one thing was missing. The hermit then disappeared, and the king ordered that the church be destroyed and rebuilt.

Seven years later exactly the same thing happened. This time the king ordered that an even grander church be built, a church that took nine years in the construction. However, as the bishop was consecrating the church, the hermit reappeared with the same message. This time the king took hold of the hermit and asked him just what was missing. The hermit replied that the missing item was the nightingale Hazaran, and then he disappeared.

The king had three sons, and they eagerly volunteered to discover the whereabouts of the nightingale and bring it back to their father. Having ridden for a month, the three sons encountered a hermit at the junction of three roads. The hermit told the three that he who followed the first road would return, he who followed the second road may or may not return, and he who followed the third road had little chance of returning. The three brothers cast lots. Then the eldest took the first road, the middle son the second road, and the youngest the last.

After his two brothers had set off, the youngest brother asked the hermit why he had little chance of returning. The hermit told him that the road was beset with hazards, and then told the youth how he might overcome each one. Well prepared, the youngest brother set out.

Before long he came to the first obstacle, a river with poisonous waters and no bridge. The youth dismounted, took a drink, and declared, "the Waters of Life!" At that, a bridge appeared, and he crossed the river safely. A short time later he came across a huge thistle. This he picked, smelled, and declared "the Flower of Paradise." Riding on, the young man came across a wolf and a lamb tied to wooden posts, a heap of grass before the wolf, and a joint of meat in front of the lamb. The youngest brother gave the grass to the lamb and the meat to the wolf, and continued down the road. The last obstacle was a two-sided gate, one side open and the other side closed. Following the instructions of the hermit, the young man closed the open side and opened the shut side, and riding through, found the palace of the mistress of Hazaran.

Meanwhile, the eldest brother had ridden his road and come to a fine palace, where he had decided he would remain to live a life of luxury, in the service of its lord. The middle brother had likewise had an easy journey; but the palace he came to hid a danger to which he succumbed—a huge Arab who whipped the youth and turned him into stone.

The youngest brother, having entered the palace, encountered the mistress of the nightingale lying on a bed. As he watched, Hazaran flew down from its perch and alighted on the maiden's chest, where it started to sing, and in an instant the maiden fell asleep. As she did so the young man darted forward, snatched up Hazaran, kissed the maiden on the cheek, and made his way back along the road. Seven days later the maiden awoke from her sleep, and seeing that her bird had vanished, she commanded her traps along the road to stop the thief. They could not, for the spell that held them had been broken when the youth followed the advice of the hermit.

The young man made his way safely back to the crossroads, where he once again encountered the hermit and asked for news of his brothers. When the hermit told him that they had not returned, the young man gave Hazaran to the hermit for safekeeping and then set off down the first road. In the town surrounding the first palace, he found his brother working as a servant in an inn. He told him of his success, and together they rode back to the crossroads. Leaving his eldest brother there with the hermit and the nightingale, the youngest brother set off to find his other sibling.

At the second palace he too encountered the huge Arab; but when the whip was aimed in his direction, the young man simply stepped aside, took hold of the whip, and pulled it from the Arab's grasp. Then he turned the whip on the Arab, and turned him into stone. Guessing that the stones that lay all around had once been people, the young prince began whipping them, and they all turned back into people, who fled in all directions. The very last stone he whipped turned into his brother, and the two rode back together to the crossroads, where they were reunited with their eldest brother. They took Hazaran from the hermit, and set out toward home.

En route the three ran out of water. Luckily, a short distance farther down the road they came to a well. They lowered the youngest brother down to fetch water. While the young man was at the bottom of the well, the two other brothers discussed how they would look in their father's eyes if they allowed their young brother to take all the glory. As a result they left the unfortunate youth in the well and returned to their father with the nightingale, telling the king that their brother had perished along the way.

The king placed Hazaran in his church, but the bird would not sing and looked close to death. Several days later the maiden came to the king and demanded to know who had stolen her bird. The two brothers said that they had, and when asked what they had encountered on the way, they replied that they had encountered nothing. Immediately the maiden knew that they were lying, and so she seized the brothers and their father, threw them into a dungeon, and ruled in their stead.

In the meantime, the young prince had been rescued from the well and made his way back home on foot. When he arrived in the city he was told all that had happened, and he ran to the dungeon to release his father and his brothers. There he was confronted by the maiden, who asked him exactly the same questions she had asked his brothers. He told the maiden all he had encountered, and she immediately knew that he was telling the truth. A few days later the maiden and the young prince were married in the king's magnificent church, where Hazaran sits and pours out an endless stream of song.

References: Khatchatrian 1933

HELEN
Russia
Anglicized, alternative form of Elena.

HERZEGOVINA
General
Part of the land known as Bosnia-Herzegovina. This territory, originally referred to as Hum, was inhabited by Illyrians from about the third millennium B.C. In c. 11 B.C. the area became part of a Roman province. It was settled by Slavs during the late sixth and early seventh centuries. Control of the area shifted among the Byzantine Empire, Croatia, and Serbia from the tenth to the twelfth centuries. At this time Bosnia came under Hungarian rule, which continued until the fifteenth century, while Herzegovina changed hands between Serbia and Hungary until Bosnia seized control of the region from 1326 to 1448. In the latter year, the region's local ruler seized power and assumed the title *herzeg* (duke), hence the name *Herzegovina*. The Ottoman Empire gained control over most of Bosnia in 1463 and over Herzegovina in c. 1482, after which many of the Slav inhabitants converted to Islam. Bosnia and Herzegovina were made a single political unit by the Ottomans in the mid-nineteenth century.

> *See also:* Bosnia; Byzantine Empire; Croatia; Hungary; Serbia

HORSE WITH THE GOLDEN MANE, THE
Russia
Fabulous horse owned by Tsar Afron. Ivan Vyslavovich attempted to steal it for Tsar Dalmat, who had assigned him this task after Ivan was caught trying to steal the latter's Firebird and its gilded cage. Ivan was caught by Afron because he ignored the advice of the shape-changing wolf that was helping him, and also tried to make off with the horse's golden bridle.

Afron offered Ivan a chance to redeem himself, telling him to bring him the maiden Elena the Beautiful. If he did, then Afron would give him both the horse and the bridle. If he failed, he would be branded a common thief. Ivan succeeded with the help of the wolf, but fell in love with Elena the Beautiful on the way back to Afron's palace. The wolf assumed Elena the Beautiful's form and was presented to Afron, who kept his word and gave Ivan Vyslavovich both the horse and its bridle. Ivan rode away on the horse and met up with the real Elena the Beautiful, who had been waiting in a forest nearby. The wolf then resumed his true form and slipped away from Afron's palace to rejoin Ivan and Elena the Beautiful.

Ivan Vyslavovich was killed by his treacherous brothers Dmitrii and Vasilii Vyslavovich, after which the horse fell by lot to Dmitrii. It was, however, restored to Ivan after he was brought back to life by the wolf, using two small bottles of the Water of Life and Death. The two murderous brothers were incarcerated by their father.

> *See also:* Afron; Dalmat; Dmitrii (Vyslavovich); Elena the Beautiful; Firebird, The; Ivan Vyslavovich; Vasilii Vyslavovich; Water of Life and Death, The

HORSEL
Slav
See Ursula, of which Horsel is a variant.

HOURI
Armenia
The generic name for a nymph of any sort.

HOURI-PARI
Armenia
A paradisal nymph usually but not always connected with water.

HUNDRED SILVER PIECES, THE
Armenia
A poor man once prayed to God, asking for one hundred silver pieces and promising to spend ten of the silver pieces on oil for the lamps in the church. Later in the day the man

Undated illustration of a welcoming houri (from the collections of Carol Rose; photo by David Rose)

found ninety silver pieces, fell to his knees, and praised God for his wisdom in taking the ten silver pieces up front.

One of the fables of Vardan of Aygek.

See also: Vardan
References: Marr 1894–99

HUNGARY

General

A small, landlocked country in central Europe that was a large, independent, and powerful kingdom until the late fifteenth century. The Ottoman Empire ruled much of

Hungary from the early sixteenth to the late seventeenth centuries, after which the country became part of a huge empire ruled by the Austrian branch of the Habsburgs, a powerful European dynasty. The empire of the Habsburgs collapsed after World War I, in 1918, and Hungary lost about two-thirds of its land but regained its independence.

The history of the Hungarian state begins in the late ninth century when tribes of Magyars, led by a chief named Arpád, swept from the east into the middle Danube Basin. During the early tenth century, Magyar armies raided towns throughout much of Europe; but in 955, the German King Otto I defeated the invading Magyars, putting an end to their frequent raids.

Around 970, Arpád's great-grandson Geza became leader of the Magyars and began to organize the various Magyar tribes into a united nation. After Geza died, his son Stephen, a Roman Catholic, carried on his work. Stephen asked Pope Sylvester II (pope 999–1003) to give him the title King of Hungary, a proposition to which the pope agreed. Stephen I, Hungary's first king, was crowned in 1000. As king, Stephen made Roman Catholicism the country's official religion, and for this work, the Catholic Church declared him a saint in 1083, 45 years after his death.

In 1241, armies of the Mongol Empire invaded Hungary, and within a few months, they had overrun much of its territory. The death of the Mongols' ruler forced the invaders to withdraw the following year, leaving much of the country in ruins. However, under the leadership of the Arpád kings, Hungary gradually recovered.

After the death of the last Arpád king in 1301, Hungary remained an independent kingdom for another 225 years. John Hunyadi, a Hungarian nobleman of Romanian descent, led Hungarians in defeating the Ottoman Empire in 1456. Hunyadi's son Matthias Corvinus became king of Hungary in 1458. A period of conflict and disorder followed Matthias's death in 1490. Weakened

by these internal problems, Hungary was defeated by the Ottoman Empire in the Battle of Mohacs in 1526. The Ottomans seized central Hungary soon afterward and made the eastern third of the country, a region called Transylvania, a dependent principality. The Austrian Habsburgs, who had long wanted to make Hungary part of their empire, took the country's western and northern sections, and in the late seventeenth century drove the Ottomans out of most of Hungary. The Habsburgs gained complete control of the country in the early eighteenth century.

In the early nineteenth century, Count István Széchenyi led a movement to revive Hungarian culture and national pride and to promote economic and social reforms. In the 1840s, Lajos Kossuth became the most important leader of the reform movement and eventually turned it into a drive for Hungarian independence. In 1848 a government responsible to parliament was formed with Austrian consent. Other changes were also made, but disagreements between the two countries finally led Hungary to fight for its independence. Kossuth became head of a revolutionary Hungarian government, which declared the country's complete independence from Austria in April 1849; but the Austrians, aided by the Russians, defeated the Hungarian army in August of that year, and Hungary again came under Habsburg rule.

In 1867, a group of Hungarians led by Ferenc Deák was able to force the emperor of Austria, Francis Joseph I, to give Hungary equal status with Austria. Under this arrangement, called the Dual Monarchy, both countries had the same monarch and conducted foreign, military, and certain financial affairs jointly, but each country retained its own constitutional government to handle all other matters.

In 1914, a Serbian student from Bosnia-Herzegovina killed the heir to the Austro-Hungarian throne. Austria-Hungary suspected its southern neighbor Serbia of instigating the killing, and as a result, Austria-

Hungary declared war on Serbia—a move that marks the start of World War I (1914–1918). In the war, Germany, Bulgaria, and the Ottoman Empire supported Austria-Hungary, forming the Central Powers. The Central Powers fought Serbia, France, Russia, Britain, and other Allied forces—including the United States, which entered the war on the side of the Allies in April 1917.

A defeated Austria-Hungary signed an armistice on 3 November 1918. On 16 November, the Hungarian people revolted and declared Hungary a republic. Count Mihály Károlyi was made president. Hungarian Communists and Socialists joined together to form a coalition government in March 1919, whereupon Károlyi resigned and Béla Kun, leader of the Communists, took control of the new government as dictator.

Kun's rule lasted only a few months, collapsing largely because Kun could not defend Hungary against attacks from Romania, which sought Hungarian territory. In addition, most Hungarians did not support Kun's policies, which included taking over the country's factories and farms. Late in 1919, Admiral Miklós Horthy came to power. With Horthy acting as regent, Hungary again became a monarchy, although it had no king.

Hungary and the Allies signed the Treaty of Trianon in 1920. The treaty was part of the World War I peace settlements and stripped Hungary of more than two-thirds of its territory. Parts of Hungary went to Czechoslovakia, Romania, Austria, and the Kingdom of the Serbs, Croats, and Slovenes (later called Yugoslavia). Hungary's present boundaries are about the same as those set by the treaty.

See also: Bulgaria; Czechoslovakia; Danube; Magyars; Mongols; Romania; Serbia; Transylvania

HUZUL

Slav

Ancient people inhabiting the Carpathian Mountains about whom very little is known. From the scant records that do exist, they appear to have held great influence by means of taboos and magic. For example, the Huzul believed that if mice obtained the cut hair of an individual, that person would suffer bad headaches, and in severe cases might even go insane.

See also: Carpathian Mountains

I

I-KNOW-NOT-WHAT
Russia

An unidentified object that Petrushka had to obtain, being told that he could find it in I-Know-Not-Where. Petrushka had the help of the witch Baba-Yaga and the magical frog Babushka-Lyagushka-Skakushka in completing his seemingly impossible task. I-Know-Not-What turned out to be an invisible being by the name of Nobody. When asked where he came from, Nobody would reply, "I know not where"; and when asked what type of being he was, he would reply, "I know not what."

See also: Baba-Yaga (-Jaga, -Iaga); Babushka-Lyagushka-Skakushka; I-Know-Not-Where; Nobody; Petrushka

I-KNOW-NOT-WHERE
Russia

An unidentified place in which Petrushka had to obtain an object simply known as I-Know-Not-What. Petrushka had the help of the witch Baba-Yaga and the magical frog Babushka-Lyagushka-Skakushka in completing his seemingly impossible task.

See also: Baba-Yaga (-Jaga, -Iaga); Babushka-Lyagushka-Skakushka; I-Know-Not-What; Petrushka

IARILA
Russia

The feminine personification of the sun god Iarilo.

See also: Iarilo

IARILO
Russia

"Ardent Sun," the sun god who has a feminine personification in Iarila. Iarilo was just one aspect of a quadruple fertility deity—the other aspects being Kupalo, linked with water; Kostromo-Kostrobunko, linked with grain; and Lado, a name used in invocations of the fertility deity as a single entity. Each of these aspects also had a feminine personification—Kupalo becoming Kupala, Kostromo-Kostrobunko becoming Kostroma, and Lado becoming Lada. Iarilo and Iarila, like their other aspects, were considered Divine Twins. Their effigies were often burned together in a ritual suggestive of the marriage of brother and sister—a ritual thought to stimulate the fertility and potency of the aspect they represented (in the case of Iarilo and Iarila, the sun).

See also: Iarila; Kostroma; Kostromo (-Kostrobunko); Kupala; Kupalo; Lada; Lado; Sun

References: Snegirev 1837–39; Vernadsky 1959

IAROSLAVNA
Russia

The wife of Igor, a powerful sorceress who used her supernatural powers to protect her husband.

See also: Igor
References: Mann 1979; Zenkovsky 1963

IAROVIT
Baltic Coast

"Wrath," an alternative name for Svantovit.
See also: Svantovit (~dovit)

IENZABABA
Poland

Polish name for the witch Baba-Yaga.
See also: Baba-Yaga (-Jaga, -Iaga)

IGOR

Russia

The hero of the *Lay of Igor's Campaign,* husband of the sorceress Iaroslavna, who also appears as a chief protagonist. With his kingdom under threat from invaders, Igor gathers together his army—paying no heed to his wife's warnings and seeking no maternal blessings—and goes forth to do battle. En route he finds his path barred by the Div, which steers him relentlessly toward his enemies.

Following a great battle in which it is feared that Igor has been killed, Iaroslavna sets out to redress the balance by use of her powers. As she travels she invokes all the powers of nature and turns events soundly in favor of her husband. However, Iaroslavna neglected to invoke Mother Earth, who turns against the battling Igor, although the other forces of nature carry him to safety within the waters of the river Donets. Here Igor realizes how foolish he was not to seek approval from the maternal forces of nature for his campaign. Having first appeased the Donets, enabling him to cross, he seeks to appease all the other elements of nature who have come to his aid. Finally he invokes Mother Earth, presenting himself as her supplicant, and thus restores his land to peace and fertility and all the forces of nature to their rightful places.

See also: Div; Donets; Iaroslavna; *Lay of Igor's Campaign;* Mother Earth
References: Rambaud 1879; Zenkovsky 1963

IGOR, PRINCE

Russia

Historic prince of Kiev, the husband of Olga and son-in-law of Oleg. He was killed by an assassin during his attempt to subdue the Derevliane and bring them under the auspices of Kievan rule, and was succeeded by his wife. It seems likely that the historical Prince Igor is the prototype for the hero of the *Lay of Igor's Campaign.*

A miniature painting of Prince Igor defending his land against invaders (Sovfoto/PNI)

See also: Derevliane; Kiev; *Lay of Igor's Campaign;* Oleg; Olga
References: Cross and Sherbowitz-Wetzor 1953

IL'MEN', LAKE
Russia

Lake to the south of Novgorod. Personified as a venerable, bearded old man, the lake was respectfully referred to as Granddad Lake Il'men'. Both benevolent and malevolent, the lake was more likely to respond to the wishes of water spirits and fish than to those of man. On one occasion he sent a huge surge of water up a river known as Black Stream simply because a mill had been built on that river, and that mill had blocked the fishes' access to the lake. On this occasion a human messenger carried a message from Black Stream, and Lake Il'men' appeared as a well-built peasant dressed in blue kaftan, trousers, and hat.

See also: Black Stream; Novgorod
References: Gil'ferding 1951; Ukhov 1957

IL'YA
Russia

The Russian name for the Old Testament prophet Elijah, who following the adoption of Christianity by Russia, replaced the god of thunder Perun. Elijah, or Il'ya, shared many of Perun's powers and attributes, such as being able to call down rain and fire from heaven.

See also: Perun

IL'YA IVANOVICH
Russia

Also known as Il'ya Muromets. The patronymic, *Ivanovich,* means "son of Ivan," and *Muromets* means "man from Murom."

See also: Il'ya Muromets

IL'YA MUROMETS
Russia

A Russian knight, or bogatyr', who was a hero of the Russian epic tales, or byliny, although he appears to have originated in pre-Christian times as the giant Sviatogor. However, there appears to be some confusion here, as one story places both Il'ya Muromets and Sviatogor together, which obviously they could not have been if they were one and the same. Il'ya's surname is actually an epithet that simply means he came from the city of Murom, not far from Moscow. Il'ya was born in the village of Karacharovo, the son of a peasant named Ivan, and thus was given the patronymic of Ivanovich, his more common name of Muromets being used to identify him after he had left his hometown. Born a cripple, too weak to even move, he was miraculously cured at the age of 33 by a group of men, *kaleki* or pilgrims (some stories identify them as Jesus Christ and two of the apostles), who gave him a drink made of honey.

The pilgrims gave Il'ya advice on how he should spend his life, mentioning that he should avoid confrontation with Sviatogor and Mikula Selyaninovich and Volga Yaroslavich. They told Il'ya that although he might defeat Volga in battle, Volga's cunning would surely defeat Il'ya in the end. The pilgrims then vanished from sight, and Il'ya went to find his parents so that they might join him in celebrating his cure.

Shortly after his cure, Il'ya vowed to travel to Kiev, to offer his services to Prince Vladimir Bright Sun and his wife Evpraksiya. Attending mass in Murom before setting out, he vowed that he would neither fight nor spill blood before he reached Kiev that evening, where he would once again attend mass.

This vow meant that Il'ya intended to travel more than 500 miles in a single day—a feat that would have been impossible had it not been for his wondrous horse Sivushko, which galloped like the wind and cleared mountains in a single leap. Some sources state that a single leap of this wondrous animal covered fifty versts, a verst being the equivalent of approximately two-thirds of a mile (so fifty versts would be around 33 miles). Arming himself with his saber, his bow and arrows, his massive mace, and a long, very sharp lance, Il'ya set out on the most direct route to Kiev, which would take him past the city of Chernigov (although some sources identify the city in this particular episode as Smolensk).

As he approached the city he saw that it was under siege. Praying to God to release him from his vow, he charged the heathen hordes and killed the entire army. The people of Chernigov welcomed him as a hero and offered to make him their tsar. Il'ya refused, and instead asked them to point out to him the most direct road to Kiev. This they did, warning him that on that route he would have to cross the Black Mire, a swamp that pulled people down into its depths; ford the raging river Smorodina; and then in the Briansk Woods he would be ambushed by Solovei Rakhmatich, son of Rakhmat, a terrible brigand, half man and half bird, who was commonly known as Nightingale. Unafraid, Il'ya set out along the overgrown road. (It was overgrown because for the previous thirty years Nightingale had let no one pass, killing all who attempted the journey.)

Sivushko cleared the Black Mire in a single bound and then leaped across the raging torrent of the river Smorodina. Eventually Il'ya came to a stream called Smorodinka, beside which, in a nest in a tree, lived Nightingale (some sources say Nightingale's nest was so large that it covered the tops of seven trees). As Nightingale saw the knight approach, he whistled with all his might. All around him the trees and grass were flattened; and so strong was the blast that even Il'ya's horse stumbled. Chiding it to regain its feet, Il'ya fired an arrow at Nightingale, striking him on the temple and knocking him from his perch.

Il'ya leaped down from his horse and quickly bound Nightingale before he regained his senses. Then he tied him to the stirrup of his horse and continued on his way. A short distance down the road they were to pass the house in which lived Nightingale's daughters and sons-in-law. This house stood on seven pillars and covered an area seven versts by seven versts (about five miles long by five miles wide). When they saw Nightingale tied to the stirrup of Il'ya Muromets's horse, they rushed out of the house to attack. However, Nightingale made them put down their weapons and had them invite Il'ya into the house to be their guest. Il'ya guessed that as soon as he was inside the house he would be beaten; so wasting no time, he killed all of Nightingale's daughters and their husbands.

Il'ya came at last to Kiev and presented himself to Vladimir Bright Sun. He had arrived slightly too late to attend mass as was his intention. When he told Vladimir of all that had befallen him that day, the prince did not believe him; so Il'ya led the prince out into the courtyard where Nightingale was still tied to his horse. Vladimir commanded Nightingale to whistle, but he refused, saying that as Il'ya had defeated him fairly, only Il'ya could command him now. Il'ya ordered him to whistle, but only at half-strength. Nightingale put his fingers to his lips, and ignoring what Il'ya had said, whistled at full strength. All around, the guards and courtiers fell dead. Vladimir himself was blown around the courtyard.

Having been accepted by Vladimir Bright Sun as a great knight worthy of becoming a member of his court, Il'ya took Nightingale out onto the steppe and beheaded him. The human half of his body he fed to the wolves, and the bird half to the carrion crows. Then Il'ya returned to Kiev, and there he lived as a respected member of the court of Prince Vladimir Bright Sun, setting out frequently across the steppes to pursue many adventures.

On one occasion Il'ya Muromets traveled to the Holy Mountains (some sources say that these events took place while Il'ya was en route from Murom to Kiev after his miraculous cure). There Il'ya came across a huge white pavilion beneath an oak tree, inside which stood a huge bed. Some sources say the bed was ten fathoms long and six fathoms wide (80 feet by 48 feet). Curious about who owned such a bed, Il'ya tied Sivushko to the oak tree and lay down on the bed, where he slept for three days and three nights. Then the earth began to tremble. Sivushko stamped his feet and called out that the mighty Sviatogor was returning to his tent. Il'ya leaped up from the bed and untied his horse so that it might hide, and then he climbed the oak tree.

From his position in the oak tree Il'ya watched as Sviatogor approached his pavilion carrying a crystal casket on his shoulder. At the pavilion Sviatogor placed the casket on the ground. He unlocked it with a golden key from around his neck, opened it, and drew out a beautiful woman—his wife. The couple then ate a fine meal, after which Sviatogor grew sleepy and went to bed. His wife, however, did not immediately join him, having decided that she would first go walking. As she walked, she caught sight of Il'ya Muromets hiding in the tree. She bade him climb down, and threatening to wake Sviatogor, made the bogatyr' lie with her. Then she placed the knight in her husband's pocket and went to sleep next to the giant.

The following morning Sviatogor placed his wife back in her crystal casket, and mounting his mighty horse, set off to ride through the Holy Mountains. Before long his horse stumbled for the very first time in its life; and when Sviatogor chided it, the horse complained that once he had only to carry a bogatyr' and his wife but now he was forced to carry a wife and two bogatyri. Immediately Sviatogor guessed that his wife had been unfaithful to him, and taking her out of the casket, he cut off her head. Then he reached into his pocket and pulled out Il'ya Muromets, and the two rode on together, Sivushko having followed the party at a discreet distance.

Before long the two came across a huge stone casket. Dismounting, Il'ya lay down in the coffin, but he found it far too large and bade Sviatogor try it out. Even though Il'ya Muromets pleaded with him not to close the lid, Sviatogor did just that. However, when he asked Il'ya to remove the lid, Il'ya found it far too heavy. Three times he hit it with his mace; but each time he struck, a steel band closed around the coffin, securing the lid.

Sviatogor blew some of his strength into Il'ya so that the knight could use the giant's sword; but this just made matters worse, for two steel bands closed around the coffin every time Il'ya struck it with the sword. Resigning himself to his fate, Sviatogor had Il'ya tie his horse to the tree, so that it would die there beside its master. Il'ya did as asked and then sadly rode away from the coffin, knowing that Sviatogor, the last of the giants, would shortly be no more.

Il'ya returned to Kiev and served his prince faithfully for many years. One day, when he realized that his end was near, he departed the city one last time to ride across his beloved countryside. As he rode he came to a three-way crossroad. Each road was marked by a sign saying that one road led to certain death, the second led to certain marriage, and the last led to certain wealth. As he was old, Il'ya knew that he had no reason to marry and no need for wealth, so he took the first road, as it seemed the most appropriate.

Il'ya spurred on Sivushko. After riding three hours and covering a distance of three hundred versts (two hundred miles), he came to a huge palace, the home of more than forty thousand robbers. The robbers attacked him, but Il'ya simply rode among them and killed them all. He then returned to the signpost and changed the wording so that anyone who passed that way would know the road was now safe.

Il'ya turned Sivushko down the second road, rode another three hours and three hundred versts, and pulled up in front of a second palace. A beautiful maiden lived in the palace. She invited Il'ya to dine with her and spend the night, and if he did, then he would remain with her always, as her husband. Il'ya ate and then followed the maiden to her bedchamber; but instead of lying down when invited to, he took hold of the maiden and threw her onto the bed, guessing that this was some form of trap. Just as he suspected, the bed opened up and the maiden fell through to the dungeons beneath. Il'ya took the maiden's keys, went down into the dungeons, and released the many prisoners she had taken in this manner. Then he rode away, leaving the deceitful maiden locked in her own dungeons. Returning once more to the signpost, he altered its wording so that everyone would know that the road was now safe.

Finally Il'ya traveled the third road, again riding three hours and covering three hundred versts. At journey's end he came to a huge boulder in the middle of a field. This rock weighed 270 poods (around 9,720 pounds), but Il'ya easily lifted it to reveal a huge hoard of gold, silver, and precious stones. Il'ya distributed these riches among the poor and had enough left to build a small church. He then returned to the crossroads, where he once again altered the wording on the sign to let all who passed know what he had done. Then Il'ya returned to Kiev.

His last act was to build Kiev a cathedral. As soon as it was completed he died and his body turned to stone. Some versions of the account say that Il'ya became the last stone needed to complete the building.

See also: Black Mire; Bogatyr'; Briansk Woods; Bylina; Chernigov; Evpraksiya (~ia), Princess; Il'ya Ivanovich; Karacharovo; Kiev; Mikula Selyaninovich; Moscow; Murom; Nightingale; Rakhmat; Sivushko; Smorodina; Smorodinka; Solovei (~y) Rakhmatich; Sviatogor; Vladimir Bright Sun, Prince; Volga Yaroslavich
References: Astakhova 1938–51; Chadwick 1964; Gil'ferding 1951; Gimbutas 1971; Khudiakov 1863; Nechaev and Rybakov 1959; Rambaud 1879; Speranskii 1916

IMPS OF MISFORTUNE
Ukraine
See Misfortune, The Imps of.

INDIA
Russia
Having no connection with the real country, India is a fantasy land mentioned in many Russian legends. In one such legend, that of Volkh Vseslav'evich, India is ruled over by King Saltyk, whom Volkh kills, to rule in his stead.

See also: Saltyk; Volkh Vseslav'evich

IOANN THE LONG-SUFFERING, SAINT
Russia
According to a medieval tale, this Russian saint buried himself up to the chest for thirty years in order to discipline his body. The Devil lit underground fires in an attempt to move Ioann, but to no avail. Finally the Devil assumed the guise of an awesome dragon that threatened to burn the saint to death. One Easter night the dragon took the saint's head in its jaws and scorched his hair and his beard; but even this would not deflect the saint from his purpose. After this the Devil gave up.

See also: Devil, The; Dragon

IRON CITY, THE
Armenia
One of the succession of cities that the princess wife of Habërmani traveled through on her quest to find her husband and restore him to her side.

See also: Habërmani
References: Orbeli and Taronian 1959–67, vol. 4

ISTANBUL
General
The modern name for Byzantium, also known as Constantinople.

See also: Byzantium; Constantinople

ISTVAN
Hungary—Magyar
The elder of the two sons of a poor widower, the other son being Janos. Istvan was morose, lazy, selfish, and bad-tempered, whereas his brother was the complete opposite—cheerful, generous, kind, and good-natured. The family lived in a small kingdom beset by problems, for two seven-headed

dragons had taken up residence in the king's palace. One dragon was of copper and the other of iron, and both had refused to leave until the king's daughter consented to marry one or the other. They had compounded the problem by turning the unfortunate princess into a dragon as well. The king proclaimed that whoever could release the princess from the clutches of the dragons would receive her hand in marriage and half the kingdom as her dowry.

News of this proclamation reached Istvan's father, who told the boy to go and see if he could make something of his life by liberating the princess. Istvan grumbled continuously as he made his way to the royal palace. En route he sat down to eat and spied a colony of ants. Gathering up his food, as he did not want it contaminated, Istvan kicked the anthill and continued on his way until he came to a lake. There he sat down to eat again, only to be annoyed on this occasion by twelve ducklings playing in the reeds. Istvan picked up a handful of pebbles and threw them at the ducklings, which scattered.

Istvan traveled on. After spending an uncomfortable night in the open, which did nothing to improve his already foul temper, he arrived at the palace and knocked on a side door. Before long an old crone came to the door and asked Istvan what he wanted. When he said that he had come to free the princess, the old crone told him he had three tests to pass. With that, she threw a handful of millet on the ground, and told Istvan that his first test was to pick up every grain; but as he bent down to do so, an army of ants appeared and devoured the millet. The old crone slammed the door, and it remained closed the rest of the day, no matter how hard Istvan hammered on it.

The following morning, having spent yet another uncomfortable night in the forest, Istvan returned to the door and knocked hard. The old crone opened the door, took out twelve golden keys, and threw them into a lake, telling Istvan that he had to collect all twelve as his second test. Istvan stripped off

his clothes and dived in; but no matter how hard he searched, he could not find even a single key. Thus it was that Istvan had to spend another night in the open, this time frozen to the bone in his wet clothes.

As day broke Istvan went back to the palace and hammered on the small side door. The old crone appeared and told him to go away. However, he insisted that he be given the third test, so the crone took him to the king's chamber, where he saw the three dragons. The old crone told him to say which was the princess. Istvan had no idea and chose at random. He chose one of the real dragons, which instantly bellowed with all its might. A giant entered the hall, picked up Istvan, took him outside, and threw him onto the ground, which opened up and swallowed him.

Meanwhile, Istvan's father was waiting for news of his son. When none arrived, he sent Janos to see if he would fare any better. Janos traveled the same road as had his elder brother, and on the way he too sat down to eat. As had happened with his brother, a colony of ants gathered around the crumbs that fell from his food. However, instead of kicking the anthill, Janos took out a cake and broke it into fine crumbs, which he fed to the ants. He then continued on his way. Before long, he came to the lake on which the twelve ducklings were swimming. Seeing them, Janos reached into his bag, took out a loaf of bread, broke it into pieces, and threw the pieces to the birds. Then he made his way to the palace.

As his brother had done before, Janos knocked on the door. He was greeted by the old crone with the same challenge. She threw a bag of millet on the ground, and as Janos bent down to pick it up, a column of ants appeared and did the job for him. Next the old crone threw the twelve golden keys into the lake and closed the door. Before Janos even had time to take off his shirt, the twelve ducklings appeared with the keys in their beaks. The next time Janos knocked on the door he was greeted not by the old crone but by a beautiful maiden dressed in the crone's rags. She told him that she had been held under a spell, which he had broken through his kindness to the ants and the ducklings.

The maiden led Janos into the palace and told him how to distinguish the princess from the two real dragons. She then gave the young man a sword with which to kill the dragons, telling him that after he had disposed of them he must return to the palace and put on a pin-encrusted suit of clothes and stamp his foot three times, whereupon a giant would appear. This was the giant who held his brother Istvan in Thrall. Janos, the woman said, must then let the giant do as he wanted.

Janos thanked the woman, who instantly vanished. He entered the king's hall, where he correctly identified the princess and cut off the heads of the two dragons, thus releasing the princess from her enchantment and returning her to her human form. Then Janos went outside, put on the pin-studded suit, and stamped his foot three times. Beneath his feet a huge giant appeared, picked up Janos, and placed him in his mouth. The giant, however, could not swallow Janos because of the pins; nor could he spit him out, as Janos sat on the giant's tongue. The pain was more than the giant could endure, and he asked Janos to climb out of his mouth. Janos said he would, on three conditions.

The first was the release of Istvan, who was duly returned unscathed. The second was a promise to leave the kingdom and never return, and the third was for two huge beams of wood. The giant produced these, and Janos climbed out; but before the giant had time to close his mouth, Janos wedged in the beams, thus preventing the giant from ever closing his mouth again. The giant then ran away from the palace as fast as he could go, and he was never heard of again.

Janos and the princess were married that very day, the king gladly giving his new son-in-law half his kingdom as a wedding present and the remainder later, when he abdicated in Janos's favor. As for Istvan, his ordeal taught him a much-needed lesson; and from that day forth he was the most pleasant person anyone could hope to meet.

See also: Dragon; Janos
References: Biro 1980

ITUGEN
Mongolia
Mother Earth, the wife of Tengri and the mother by him of numerous children, all called Tengri. Her children live on earth as the spirits of everything in the world—from visible objects, such as trees or the flames of a fire, to abstract notions, such as law, order, and human nature. The wife of Tengri is sometimes referred to as Umai.

See also: Mother Earth; Tengri; Umai

IVAN
Russia
A peasant from the village of Karacharovo, near Murom, and the father of Il'ya Ivanovich, who was better known as Il'ya Muromets.

See also: Il'ya Muromets; Karacharovo; Murom

IVAN
Russia
A young tsarevich from an unnamed kingdom. As a youth he set out to find Princess Vasilissa Kirbit'evna, whom he had been prophesied to marry. On his way, he paid the debt of Bulat the Brave, who, indebted to the tsarevich, told him that had he not helped him, Ivan would never have found the maiden. Together they traveled to the kingdom of Tsar Kirbit, and there they found the girl in a tower with a gilded roof. Bulat the Brave captured the girl, and the three of them made away at full speed. When they were chased by Kirbit and his men, Bulat the Brave twice dispatched the pursuers, on each occasion leaving only the tsar alive.

One night as Ivan lay sleeping, Vasilissa Kirbit'evna was abducted by Koshchei the

Deathless. Dressing themselves in clothes belonging to two of Koshchei's herdsmen, Ivan and Bulat the Brave found Koshchei's abode and spoke with Vasilissa Kirbit'evna, advising her to trick Koshchei into revealing where he had hidden his soul so that the two men could put an end to him.

After a long journey, Ivan and Bulat came to the island where Koshchei's soul was safeguarded inside an egg that was inside a duck, which was in turn inside a hare. These three objects lay buried under a huge oak tree. With the help of three animals whose lives they had spared during their quest, Ivan and Bulat the Brave returned to the home of Koshchei with the egg that held his soul. Smashing the egg against Koshchei's forehead, they killed him and rescued the girl. Ivan married Vasilissa Kirbit'evna, and Bulat became his most trusted friend and adviser.

See also: Bulat the Brave; Kirbit; Koshchei (the Deathless); Vasilis(s)a Kirbit'evna

IVAN
Russia

The son of a merchant who was placed under the protection of Saint Nicholas (Saint Nikolai of Mozhaisk) and then made to keep vigil over the body of the local tsar's daughter, a witch. By reading the Psalms and with the help of Saint Nicholas, Ivan captures the witch when she rises from her coffin, and makes her pray to God for absolution. Even though she does this and is resurrected, she is not free of the evil inside her. Seeing this, Saint Nicholas pushes the girl into a bonfire and pulls her burning body apart. From her severed limbs, hordes of frogs, snakes, and other reptiles—the sources of her evil—come forth and are burned in the fire. Saint Nicholas restores the princess, thus exorcised, to life and baptizes her. He then marries Ivan to the princess. Many years later, Ivan ascends to the throne after the death of his father-in-law.

See also: Nicholas, Saint; Nikolai of Mozhaisk, Saint
References: Magarshack 1968

IVAN III
Russia
See Ivan the Great.

IVAN IV
Russia
See Ivan Groznyi.

IVAN BELYANINOVICH
Russia

The youngest son of Tsar Bel Belyanin and his wife Nastas'ya of the Golden Braid. Brother to Vasilii Belyaninovich and Peter Belyaninovich. Many years after Nastas'ya was blown away by a huge gust of wind, the two eldest sons, Vasilii and Peter, set out on a quest to find her. Some time later Ivan also set out on the same quest.

Riding through the forest, he met up with his unnamed uncle who lived in a splendid palace, and who gave him a magical ball to follow. This ball, Ivan was told, would lead him to where his mother was being held captive. Following the ball, Ivan caught up with his brothers, whom he persuaded to join him. Together they followed the ball until it came to a stop outside a cave at the foot of very steep, almost insurmountable mountains. Not wanting to risk their own lives, Vasilii and Peter sent Ivan on alone, promising to wait for him at the foot of the mountains.

Ivan entered the cave, where he found a huge iron door barring the way. Placing his shoulder against the door, he found that it swung easily open. Inside, just as his uncle had told him he would, Ivan found some metal claws, which he fixed to his hands and feet, and started to climb. After a month he reached the top, a vast plateau that stretched out as far as the eye could see. Following a faint path, he first came to a palace made of copper, the gates of which were guarded by dragons fettered with copper collars and chains. Nearby there was a well with a copper cup on a copper chain. Filling the cup with water, he gave it to the dragons, which immediately fell asleep, allowing him to pass by in safety.

Once inside, he was greeted by the tsaritsa of the Copper Kingdom. She did not know where Nastas'ya of the Golden Braid was kept, but she suggested that Ivan journey onward to the Silver Kingdom, for the tsaritsa of that kingdom, her middle sister, might know the whereabouts of Ivan's mother. The tsaritsa gave Ivan a copper ball to follow and bade him farewell.

Outside Ivan placed the ball on the ground and followed it all the way to the Silver Kingdom. There he placated the dragons that guarded the gates in the same way he had the others, and on entering, was greeted by the tsaritsa of the Silver Kingdom. She, like her sister, did not know the whereabouts of Ivan's mother, but she gave him a silver ball to follow.

This Ivan did until he came to the Golden Kingdom. Once more he quietened the dragons that stood on guard and entered the gleaming palace. Inside he was greeted by the tsaritsa of the Golden Kingdom, whose name was Elena the Fair. She knew exactly where Nastas'ya of the Golden Braid was being held. As had her two sisters, she gave Ivan a ball—this one made of gold—to follow, which would lead him to where his mother was being held by Whirlwind.

Ivan duly followed the ball until he came to a palace that was even more impressive than those he had just visited, this one shining with diamonds and other precious stones. Pacifying the six-headed dragons that guarded the gates, he entered the great hall of the palace, where he found his mother seated upon a magnificent throne and dressed in the most wondrous clothes Ivan had ever seen.

Amazed to see her son, Nastas'ya explained that the secret of Whirlwind's strength lay in a barrel in the wine cellars of the palace that contained a magical water, which bestowed tremendous strength on whoever drank it. She then told her son how he might defeat Whirlwind, who was due to return at any minute. Ivan took a drink from the barrel his mother had shown him, and

then he substituted a barrel of water that sapped the strength of those who drank it. He then hid beneath his mother's cloak to watch.

As Whirlwind returned and leaned over Nastas'ya, Ivan reached out and grasped the mace that Whirlwind always carried. Bearing Ivan high into the air, Whirlwind tried, without success, to shake him free. Returning to the palace, Whirlwind drank from the barrel which Ivan had exchanged for the strength-giving water, and his strength was completely sapped. Having drunk from the good barrel, Ivan was filled with tremendous power; and with a single blow of his sword, he decapitated Whirlwind. He burned the body and scattered the ashes. Then he quickly released his mother, and the two made their way back through the three kingdoms, with Ivan freeing each tsaritsa in turn. Finally all five came to the top of the mountain at the bottom of which Vasilii and Peter were still waiting. After Ivan lowered their mother and the three maidens down to Vasilii and Peter, the jealous brothers spurred their horses toward home, intending to claim Ivan's success as their own.

Ivan wandered back to the palace of Whirlwind, where he found a small whistle, on which he blew. Instantly two servants appeared, called Lame and One-Eye—for that is what they were. Ivan requested food, and the servants, who had served Whirlwind before, magically made a magnificent banquet appear. After he had eaten and slept, Ivan asked them if they could return him to his own land. The next moment, Ivan found himself standing in the middle of the marketplace outside his father's palace.

Instead of going straight home to find out what had happened to his two brothers, Ivan hired himself out as an apprentice to a shoemaker. That night, as Ivan and the shoemaker slept, Lame and One-Eye made a wonderful pair of shoes that the shoemaker went into the market to sell the very next morning. As Elena was soon to be married, having been brought back from the mountains by Vasilii and Peter, she needed new shoes for her wedding. Seeing the pair that Lame and One-Eye had made, she knew that they could only have been made by someone who had come from the kingdoms at the top of the mountains. She immediately bought them and instructed the shoemaker that he was also to make her wedding dress—the most magnificent dress anyone had seen—by the very next morning, or he would be hanged.

That night, having drunk himself into a stupor, the shoemaker slept and dreamed of his impending death, as Lame and One-Eye made the dress. The following day Elena came for the dress, and again she could tell instantly who had made it. To be absolutely certain, she set the shoemaker a final, impossible task. By the very next morning he was to have built her a palace out of gold that was to stand in the middle of the sea, connected to dry land by a golden bridge covered with a fine velvet carpet, with a garden on either side filled with trees.

That night the shoemaker became so drunk that he had to be carried to his bed; and when he rose the next day, he continued to drink, for he did not want to be sober when they came to hang him. However, Lame and One-Eye had once more completed the task. Elena asked the shoemaker how he had managed to complete such an impossible task. Not knowing what to say, the shoemaker in turn asked Ivan, and the truth finally came out. Tsar Bel Belyanin was so furious with Vasilii and Peter that he wanted to have them executed, but Ivan interceded. In the end, Ivan married Elena, Peter married the tsaritsa of the Silver Kingdom, and Vasilii married the tsaritsa of the Copper Kingdom. The shoemaker was made a general, and no land was ever bothered by Whirlwind again.

See also: Bel Belyanin; Copper Kingdom, The; Dragon; Elena the Fair; Golden Kingdom, The; Lame; Nastas'ya of the Golden Braid; One-Eye; Peter

(Belyaninovich); Silver Kingdom, The; Vasilii Belyaninovich; Whirlwind

IVAN CRNOJEVIC
Serbia

Heroic enemy of the invading Turks. Believed to be asleep in a cave near Obod in southern Montenegro, at the northern tip of Lake Skadar. There he lies in the arms of the *vile,* awaiting the time when he will awaken to defend his people. This story bears direct comparison with that of Prince Marko and might have been influenced by stories of King Arthur brought to the area by the Romans.

Thunder is, to this day, interpreted as the anger of Ivan Crnojevic; and the river named after him, the Rijeka Crnojevica, which flows into Lake Skadar a few miles from the cave, was said to have been formed by the tears he shed over his people's misfortune.

See also: Arthur, King; Marko, Prince; Montenegro

IVAN GOSTINYI SYN
Russia

One of the seven bogatyri that once assembled to go on a quest together. The other six were Vasilii Buslayevich, Vasilii Kazimirovich, Godenko Bludovich, Alyosha Popovich, Dobrynya Nikitich, and Il'ya Muromets. The legend of their quest, which purportedly explains why the bogatyri disappeared from Holy Russia, may be found in the entry for Vasilii Buslayevich.

See also: Alyosha Popovich; Bogatyr'; Dobrynya Nikitich; Godenko Bludovich; Il'ya Muromets; Vasilii Buslayevich; Vasilii Kazimirovich
References: Speranski 1916; Ukhov 1957

IVAN GROZNYI
Russia

The Russian epithet attached to this tsar—*Groznyi*—means "fearsome." This historical ruler of Russia, better known in English as Ivan the Terrible, was born in 1530 and was proclaimed successor to the throne after the death of his father, Grand Prince Vasilii, in 1533. Following a period when power was first in the hands of his mother, Elena, and then after her murder in 1537, of the boyars, Ivan finally took the throne in 1547 and became the first ruler to style himself *tsar'*—Russian for "Caesar." In an attempt to consolidate his absolute power and undermine anyone who was in a position to contest it, Ivan initiated a series of reforms that weakened the upper nobility—the princes and boyars—in favor of the minor gentry. In 1549 he convoked a legislative assembly and inaugurated a period of legal reform of both state and church that was to last for a decade, establishing a new code of law and a radical system of local self-government. In 1552 he liberated Kazan' from the Tatars, and two years later, in 1554, he occupied Astrakhan'. In 1558 he invaded Livonia and captured the important Baltic seaport of Narva.

In 1565, rumors of a boyar uprising brought about an offer by Ivan to abdicate; but he was reinstated by popular demand with sweeping powers to take whatever actions he deemed fit against his opponents. These powers led to a prolonged period of arrests and summary executions. In 1570 Ivan ravaged the city of Novgorod. In 1571 his capital city, Moscow, was overrun and burned by Crimean Tatars. (Ivan took bloody revenge against the Tatars the following year.) In the last years of his reign, in an attempt to redress some of his excesses, Ivan posthumously rehabilitated many whom he had executed during the middle period of his reign. However, in 1581 he accidentally killed his eldest son in a fit of anger, which left power in the hands of Ivan's sickly and feeble-minded second son Fyodor after Ivan's death in 1584.

Ivan Groznyi is featured in a story titled *The Tsar Resolves to Kill His Son*. This bylina opens during a feast held in Moscow in honor of the state's warriors both male and female. During the feast, Ivan Groznyi learns that Ivan Tsarevich, his son, has conspired against him. He immediately has him ar-

rested and dragged off to the banks of the Moskva River, where the executioner's block awaits him. The tsarina, Ivan Tsarevich's mother, goes to the house of her brother and tells him what has occurred. Her brother, Nikita Romanov, hurries to the banks of the river, where he stops the execution and then finds out who betrayed his nephew. Nikita Romanov then seeks out the informer and kills him. Ivan Groznyi acknowledges his mistake and rewards Nikita Romanov for preventing the death of the tsarevich. However, it is this very tsarevich whom history records as having been killed by his father in 1581; so even if the story is true and Nikita Romanov did manage to save the youth this once, Ivan Groznyi eventually accomplished the evil deed by his own hand.

See also: Astrakhan'; Boyars; Bylina; Crimea; Ivan IV; Ivan the Terrible; Ivan Tsarevich; Kazan'; Livonia; Moscow; Nikita Romanov; Novgorod; Tatars
References: Chadwick 1964; Chistov 1967

IVAN KUPALO
Russia

The feast of midsummer, occurring at the summer equinox, during which the fertility of Mother Earth and married women was celebrated. The entire community participated in rituals that symbolically linked the fertility of human mothers with that of the fields. The female members of the community led in the orgiastic celebrations, which involved ritual bathing by both men and women in lakes and rivers (*Kupalo* is derived from the verb *kupat'* [to bathe]).

The earliest records of the festivities of Ivan Kupalo come from twelfth-century church chronicles that almost always confuse them with the Rusaliia. These ancient writings say that the oldest unmarried peasant women would be dressed as brides and led to the banks of a river or lake. There they would dance and worship the goddess, then jump into the water, and later return to the village to sprinkle the houses with the sanctified water. After the water rituals, bonfires would be lit and the villagers would jump over and through the flames.

Kupalo, the deity central to these celebrations, had a female counterpart in Kupal'nitsa. In regions where different names were applied to the deity central to the festival, each likewise had a female counterpart. Thus, Lado was accompanied by Lada, Kostromo by Kostroma, and Iarilo by Iarila. The duality of the deity central to the festival demonstrates the need for the male and the female to complete the necessary circle, although at all times the importance of the female spirit far outweighed that of the male.

See also: Iarila; Iarilo; Kostroma; Kostromo (-Kostrobunko); Kupal'nitsa; Kupalo; Lada; Lado; Mother Earth; Rusaliia
References: Cross and Sherbowitz-Wetzor 1953; Mansikka 1922; Snegirev 1837–39; Zabylin 1880

IVAN SAVEL'EVICH
Russia
A young seal-hunter who lived in the city of Arkhangel'sk, in northern Russia, and who according to one story became captivated by the unearthly beauty of a russalka and spent one long winter in her company.

While seal hunting in winter on the bleak islands of Novaya Zemlya, well within the Arctic Circle, Ivan spent many lonely nights alone in his hut playing his balalaika. One night the oil in his lamp ran out and he continued to play in the dark. As he played, he heard the sound of someone dancing inside his hut. Knowing that he was alone, he was frightened and quickly refilled and relit his lamp. The hut was empty. The following night the same thing happened. Finally he hid the lit lamp behind a thick curtain, and as soon as the sound of dancing started, he drew back the curtain to reveal a young girl.

This girl explained to Ivan that she was a russalka but because she had a human father, she was able to remain out of the water for as long as she liked, provided she was in the presence of only one person. Ivan fell hopelessly in love with the russalka, and they

spent the winter together, during which time everything they ever wanted or needed magically appeared. However, when spring came Ivan had to return to his home to sell his catch. As they parted, the russalka gave him instructions on how he might find her again.

Some time later Ivan found he could not live without the russalka. Remembering what his lover had told him, he sought out her home: He climbed a tree that hung above the water, and at the stroke of midday, he dived into the water. As he reached the bottom of the river, his lover rushed out from the weeds and embraced him. Ivan stayed a long time beneath the waters of that river, but in the end he longed to return home. Remembering that anyone could be protected from the charms of the russalka by the holy cross, he made the sign and was immediately transported back home. However, having crossed himself, he could never again return to his russalka.

See also: Arkhangel'sk; Novaya Zemlya; Rus(s)alki (~ulki)

IVAN THE DRAGON KILLER
Ukraine
A young tsarevich who set out to rescue his neighbor who was at the mercy of a dragon that lived atop an ever growing glass mountain. Along the way he was bitten by an ant and was on the verge of squashing it, when it promised to help him if the young prince would spare its life. Ivan did so and continued on his journey, pondering the task that lay ahead of him. As he thought of the immense task he called out to the ant for help. The ant appeared and gave the prince a grain of wheat, telling him to place it at the foot of the glass mountain. Ivan thanked the ant and rode on.

Having introduced himself to the tsar, and told him his aim, Ivan rode to the foot of the glass mountain which by this time covered almost three quarters of the kingdom. Ivan tethered his horse to a tree and placed the grain of wheat at the base of the mountain. Then he hid amongst the trees and watched.

As he looked on, the grain of wheat began to glow, and as it did so a trickle of water began to flow from the base of the mountain. That trickle quickly became a raging torrent as the mountain continued to melt, and Ivan had to find higher ground or be swept away.

The dragon, on returning to his lair, saw the water gushing from the base of the mountain and swooped down to see what was causing it. As the dragon landed the torrent of water became even more intense, and a great wall of water dashed the dragon to its death and then carried its remains away. Ivan then rushed onto what remained of the mountain, released the princess, and together they hurried back to her father. Several days later Ivan and the princess were married, Ivan inheriting the kingdom some years later when the tsar abdicated in his favor.

See also: Dragon; Glass Mountain, The

IVAN THE FOOL
Russia
See Silver Roan

IVAN THE GREAT
Russia
The ruler and Grand Duke of Russia from 1462 to 1505, also known as Ivan III (1440–1505). Ivan successfully asserted authority over a number of Russian principalities and routed the Tatar occupiers, uniting these lands for the first time under a single Russian ruler. In 1472 he married Sophia, a niece of Constantine XI Palæologus Dragases (1404–1453, the last Byzantine emperor), assumed the title "Ruler of all Russia," and adopted the two-headed eagle—the emblem of the Byzantine Empire—as his royal crest.

See also: Byzantine Empire; Tatars

IVAN THE GUARD
Russia
When Nemal Chelovek, a sorcerer, kidnapped the only daughter of an unnamed tsar and his wife, the tsar immediately offered half his kingdom, and his daughter's hand in marriage, to whoever found her and brought her home. Many men tried and failed, and the tsar grew ever more despondent. One night a lowly guard named Ivan was standing watch in the tsar's garden when he overheard two crows talking. These crows talked about a sorcerer named Nemal Chelovek who had once visited the realm and made off with the daughter of the tsar, going so far as to name the kingdom in which the sorcerer lived and describe how he might be defeated.

Ivan listened intently, and when his watch came to an end, he asked the tsar's leave to search for his daughter. The tsar was less than responsive to the idea of a humble soldier going to look for his daughter, especially when so many nobler men had tried and failed. However, when Ivan assured the tsar that he would not fail, the tsar relented. However, he warned the soldier that if he failed, he would pay with his life.

Two days later Ivan set sail for the Southern Seas. En route he made a detour and came ashore at a small island on which lived two leshii who had jointly inherited the self-cutting Samosek Sword some thirty years before. As Ivan stepped onto the island he heard the two leshii fighting over whose the sword truly was. When he approached, they asked him to act as their judge. Ivan agreed. He proposed that he hold the sword and then shoot an arrow into the woods. Ownership of the sword would be awarded to the leshii who brought the arrow back to Ivan. The leshii readily agreed. Ivan then shot an arrow far into the woods, and the two leshii ran off and quickly found it, and then fell to fighting over whose it was. Ivan reboarded his ship and set sail with the Samosek Sword for the kingdom of Nemal Chelovek.

Two days later the ship landed and Ivan stepped ashore. He found Nemal Chelovek's mansion unguarded, for the sorcerer never imagined anyone would be foolish enough to enter his domain. Ivan slipped into the mansion and quickly located the daughter of the tsar, who told him that Nemal Chelovek intended her to become the bride of his nephew the Gorynich, a terrible dragon. Ivan told her not to worry, for he would deliver her. When she heard this, the princess gave Ivan her ring, a token that signified that they were betrothed and would become husband and wife upon returning home.

At that moment, Nemal Chelovek returned to his mansion and stormed into the great hall where Ivan stood with the princess. When the sorcerer saw Ivan, he cast a spell that made him grow until his head brushed the ceiling, and then he rushed to attack. Ivan, however, simply lifted the Samosek Sword, which flew through the air and neatly decapitated the oncoming giant. Then the sword went through the mansion and killed all of Nemal Chelovek's servants before returning neatly to Ivan's hand.

Several days later Ivan presented the tsar with his daughter, expressing the hope that they would soon marry. The tsar, however, tried to get out of his promise by saying that a foreign prince had asked for the princess's hand and would not look kindly upon being passed over for a mere soldier. The soldier was not to be put off, and he showed the tsar that he already wore the princess's ring, whereupon the tsar relented and called for the wedding preparations to begin.

During the wedding feast a messenger rushed into the hall and announced that the rejected prince had invaded the kingdom with a vast army. Amid the confusion, Ivan slipped out of the palace, strapped on the Samosek Sword, and rode out to meet the advancing army. Then, releasing the sword, he decimated the army, leaving only the prince and his generals alive. Ivan then returned to his new wife and calmly reported the news, and the feast continued.

A few weeks later news came that the prince had formed a new army and was again on the march. Ivan again rode out, annihilated the army, and returned unscathed; this time, only the prince survived. The prince wrote in secret to Ivan's wife, asking her to help him. The princess found out about the Samosek Sword and had the

palace armorer make an exact replica, which she substituted for the real sword. Soon Ivan rode out to attack the army of the prince a third time. Without the magical weapon, he had to fight as any normal soldier, and though he killed a great many of the enemy, in the end he was toppled from his horse and left for dead.

The tsar rejoiced that his daughter was at last free to marry a man of royal blood, and within hours the wedding had been arranged. That night, as the wedding feast progressed in the palace, Ivan awoke on the battlefield, surrounded by dead bodies. As he walked, he grew increasingly hungry. He came to a bush that had yellow berries, and without thinking, he ate two berries. Immediately his head began to ache terribly. When he put his hand to his head, he was horrified to find that it had sprouted two horns. Farther on, he came across another bush, this one with red berries, and as he was still hungry, he ate two berries. Once again he experienced a crushing headache, and when he felt his head, he was relieved to find that the horns had disappeared.

Realizing the potential of the berries, Ivan collected a pocketful of both yellow and red berries and set off toward the tsar's palace, where he could clearly hear the sounds of the wedding celebration. Back at the palace, Ivan disguised himself as a beggar and gave one of the palace maids some yellow berries to give to the princess in celebration of her marriage to the prince. The maid placed the berries on the princess's pillow. That night, when she came to her room, the princess ate the berries. As soon as she swallowed them, she had a splitting headache, and two horns sprouted from her forehead.

So distressed was the tsar that he offered half his kingdom to whoever would cure his daughter. Still disguised as a beggar, Ivan came to see the tsar and promised to cure the princess. The tsar himself led the beggar to his daughter's room; but before entering, the beggar stopped the tsar and told him that the cure might not be painless and that under no circumstances were they to be disturbed, for then the cure would not work. The tsar let the beggar into the room and told the palace guard to let no one else enter until the beggar came out again, no matter what noises they might hear inside.

Inside the room Ivan discarded his disguise and took a heavy wooden club out of his tunic. Then he approached the princess, who stared at him in disbelief and then screamed as Ivan began to beat her black and blue for her treachery. Then he told her that he had the cure for her affliction, but he would give it to her only if she returned the Samosek Sword to him. She ran to a cupboard, took out the sword, and gave it back to Ivan. He took the sword, ran to find the prince, and then unleashed it, watching in delight as the head of the prince rolled onto the floor. Then Ivan returned to the princess and gave her two red berries, and the horns instantly vanished.

The princess fell into Ivan's arms, but he pushed her away, telling her that as she had been unfaithful and as her father and mother were likewise dishonorable, he would banish them from the kingdom and rule in their stead. From that day forth Ivan ruled the kingdom with a fair hand; and thanks to the Samosek Sword, the kingdom remained safe from all would-be invaders.

See also: Leshii (~y); Nemal Chelovek; Samosek Sword

IVAN THE MARE'S SON
Siberia—Tungus

The hero of a story that comes from the Tungus people of Siberia. Ivan's mother was a mare that had escaped from a peasant couple who intended to eat her. As she ran through the forest, she came upon the corpse of a Tungus warrior, and licking his body, she instantly conceived a son, whom she called Ivan. She raised the boy alone. One day, she told him the time had come when he must fend for himself, adding that he should leave his arrow standing upright in the ground every night so that she would know he was

alive. If she found the arrow lying on the ground, then she would know that he was dead.

Ivan promised his mother that he would do so, and left. Several days later he came to a clearing in the forest. In the middle of this clearing was a young man on his hands and knees. When Ivan asked him what he was doing, the youth replied that he was looking for his arrow. Ivan found the arrow and handed it to the young man, who told him his name was Ivan the Sun's Son. The two agreed that from that day forth they would live as brothers.

A few days later the two Ivans returned to the clearing, where they found another youth searching the ground. He too had lost his arrow, and again Ivan the Mare's Son found it. This youth's name was Ivan the Moon's Son, and he too agreed to live as their brother. In the middle of the clearing they built themselves a home of wooden poles covered with the skins of the animals they had hunted. Every night each Ivan placed his arrow upright in the ground outside their home.

One morning, to their surprise, they found that during the night their arrows had been richly decorated. Ivan the Moon's Son said that he would keep watch that night and catch the culprit, but he fell asleep, and in the morning their arrows had been decorated once again. Exactly the same thing happened when Ivan the Sun's Son stayed on guard. The third night, Ivan the Mare's Son said he would stand watch.

On the stroke of midnight three herons flew down into the clearing, smashed themselves against the ground, and instantly became three beautiful maidens. Each plucked the arrow of the man she professed to love from the ground and set about decorating it. Ivan crept from his hiding place and hid their heron's wings and feathers. When the three maidens had finished the arrows, they could not find their heron skins. The eldest maiden called out for whoever had hidden them to come forward, saying that if he were older than they, then he would be their father. If he were younger, he would be their brother; but if he were the same age, then he would become her husband.

Ivan crept from his place of concealment and revealed himself to the eldest of the three maidens, who told him that her name was Marfida. The other maidens were Marfida's sisters, and the three agreed to become the wives of the three Ivans. All six lived happily in their home in the clearing.

However, one day when Ivan and his brothers returned from their day's hunting they noticed that their wives were becoming very pale and thin. On investigation they discovered several holes that had appeared in the ground beneath their home. Puzzled, Ivan and his brothers decided that instead of hunting the following day, they would stand guard. The following day, while his brothers dozed in the warmth of the sun, Ivan the Mare's Son saw a huge serpent crawl out of one of the holes beneath their home. Wrapping itself around the three wives, it started to suck their blood. Ivan drew his bow and shot the serpent, which quickly slithered back into the hole whence it had come, warning Ivan as it went that it would return three days later, riding on a cloud of fire.

For three days the three Ivans made as many arrows as they could before taking turns to watch for the approach of the cloud that would bring the serpent. Ivan the Moon's Son saw it first. Ivan the Sun's Son watched it approach. By the time Ivan the Mare's Son came to see, it was directly overhead, with the serpent in the middle, surrounded by his army of demons.

A mighty battle ensued. Ivan the Moon's Son was killed first. Some time later Ivan the Sun's Son was killed too. Ivan the Mare's Son fought on alone until he had reduced the army of demons to a third of its original size. Then he too was killed, his head cut clean from his body. The serpent gathered up the three maidens and disappeared with them down one of the holes beneath the house.

Ivan the Mare's Son's mother later found his arrow lying on the ground among the bodies of the demons. She located his body and his head, licked the body all over, and kicked it with her hind legs. The body became whole again. She licked and kicked the body again, and the body stirred. Once more she licked and kicked her son, and he jumped to his feet, fully revived. Next they sought out and found the bodies of the other two Ivans, whom the mare also brought back to life. She then left the three brothers discussing how they might rescue their wives.

After hunting for three days, they stitched a long rope from the hides they had collected. To one end of this rope they attached a leather cradle. Climbing into the cradle Ivan the Mare's Son was lowered down the hole through which the serpent had originally appeared. At the bottom he found himself in the underworld, the home of the serpent. Following a barren track, Ivan came to a lake. There he saw three women—Marfida and her sisters—coming to draw water. Ivan fired an arrow in front of his wife to tell her that he was there. After the sisters had drawn water, Marfida lagged behind the others, and she and Ivan were reunited.

Marfida told Ivan that he was to kill the serpent at exactly midday, while it slept in its hammock. Ivan did as she instructed, and he and the three maidens made their way back to the leather cradle. The wives of Ivan the Moon's Son and Ivan the Sun's Son were hoisted up first. When it was Marfida's turn, she beseeched Ivan the Mare's Son to go first, but he refused. Having raised Marfida, Ivan the Moon's Son and Ivan the Sun's Son cut the rope and threw the cradle back down the hole, thus trapping Ivan the Mare's Son in the underworld.

Once more his mother came to the rescue. Having discovered him lying dead at the bottom of the hole, she restored him to life as she had done before. Then she told him to hunt until they had enough meat for the journey back to the land of the living. Ivan did as instructed, and finally they set out. Each time the mare turned her head, Ivan fed her some meat. As they neared the exit, he ran out of meat; so he cut off a toe from his right foot and fed that to his mother. Next he cut off his calf, and finally, an ear. After they had left the underworld, Ivan's mother coughed up the pieces of her son that she had been fed, and licking his wounds, made him whole again.

Three days later Ivan came across Marfida, who was being made to drag a heavy load as punishment for remaining faithful to her husband. Ivan lifted her onto his shoulders, and then caught up with and killed his two false brothers. Taking the three heron skins from his pocket, he plucked a few feathers from each and made himself a pair of wings, on which he flew with the three maidens to their homeland, where they lived out their days in peace and happiness.

See also: Ivan the Moon's Son; Ivan the Sun's Son; Marfida; Siberia; Tungus; Underworld, The

IVAN THE MOON'S SON
Siberia—Tungus
Youth whose lost arrow was found by Ivan the Mare's Son, whom he thereafter treated as his brother. These two lived together, sharing a home with a third "brother"—Ivan the Sun's Son. During a battle with a huge serpent that had been sucking the blood of the three brothers' wives, the three Ivans were killed and their wives carried off to the serpent's underworld lair. All three were restored to life by Ivan's mother, the mare. Then the two other Ivans lowered Ivan the Mare's Son into the underworld to rescue their wives. After he had found and rescued the women, Ivan the Mare's Son was left for dead by his false brothers, who made off with all three wives. He was rescued by his mother, and killed both Ivan the Moon's Son and Ivan the Sun's Son.

See also: Ivan the Mare's Son; Ivan the Sun's Son; Underworld, The

IVAN THE MUTE
Russia
A young tsarevich, born without the ability to speak. At the age of twelve he was told by his favorite groom that he was about to have a sister, but was warned by the same groom that the girl would be a fearsome witch who would eat her family and everyone who came near her. The groom advised him to ask his father for a swift horse, the swiftest his father owned, so that he might escape before it was too late.

The tsar, delighted to hear his son speak for the first time, personally picked out the horse for his son. Having traveled quite a distance, the young tsarevich started to look for a place to live. First he came across two old seamstresses, who told him that they would be glad to take him in but they did not have long to live, for once they had finished the work they were doing, it would be time for them to die.

Brokenhearted, Ivan left and traveled on, next meeting a man whose task in life was to uproot massive trees. Called Uproot Oak, this man too would have been happy to take Ivan in, but he too only had a short time to live, for as he told the youth, when he had uprooted all the oaks in the forest he was clearing, then it would be his time to die.

Once more overcome with grief, Ivan journeyed on until he met a giant of a man who was busy tipping a range of mountains onto their sides. This man, whose name was Overturn Mountain, told Ivan that he would gladly take him in if it were not for the fact that his days would be at an end after he had overturned the entire mountain range.

Down at heart, Ivan rode on until he came to the home of Sun's Sister. She took the youth in and treated him as her own. After a while Ivan began to think about his family. He climbed a mountain, gazed far into the distance in the direction of his home, and cried. When he returned home to Sun's Sister, he said that the tears in his eyes were due to the wind. Twice more this happened. However, Sun's Sister had forbidden the wind to blow, so she knew that the tears had another cause. Ivan finally had to tell her what was wrong.

As Ivan prepared to leave, Sun's Sister gave him three items to help him on his journey: a comb, a brush, and two apples that had the power to rejuvenate whoever ate them. On his way Ivan met his friends once more. Overturn Mountain had only two mountains left to topple before he died. Ivan threw down the brush, and a massive mountain range sprang from the earth. Uproot Oak had only two trees left to uproot. Ivan threw down his comb, and a huge forest of oak trees appeared. Finally Ivan came to the two seamstresses, who were stitching the last seam of their piece. Ivan gave each of them an apple, and they were instantly young upon the very first bite. In return they gave Ivan a kerchief that they told him had magical properties.

At last Ivan came to his home and was welcomed by his sister, who asked him to play on the psaltery while she prepared a meal. After she went out, a mouse warned Ivan that his sister had really gone to sharpen her teeth. The mouse offered to run up and down the strings of the psaltery so that Ivan could make his escape.

When Ivan's sister discovered how she had been tricked, she set off in hot pursuit and was soon catching up with Ivan. Seeing her riding like the wind after him, Ivan threw down the kerchief, which immediately became a huge, deep lake. Swimming across it slowed Ivan's sister down and allowed him to increase his lead over her. Again she started to close the gap just as Ivan rode past Uproot Oak, who blocked the road with a huge pile of oak trees, which Ivan's sister had to gnaw her way through. Again she closed in on her brother just as he passed Overturn Mountain, who blocked the road with a pile of towering mountains. Finally Ivan made it safely back to the home of Sun's Sister, who locked him safely inside. Yet his sister would not give up.

Finally she suggested that they should be weighed on a huge pair of scales, the heavier having the right to destroy the other. Ivan sat on the scales first; then the witch, his sister, sat down. She was so heavy that Ivan shot off into the heavens, straight into the Sun's Sister's palace, where he remained secure from his sister's rivalry.

See also: Overturn Mountain; Sun's Sister; Uproot Oak

IVAN THE PEA
Russia

The youngest son of Tsar Svetozar and his wife, and brother to two other princes, both unnamed, and to a sister, Vasilissa of the Golden Braid. Ivan the Pea was miraculously conceived when his mother swallowed a small pea, which grew inside her until she gave birth to a son. Ivan the Pea grew at a very fast rate, and by the age of ten he was the strongest knight in all the kingdom. Learning of the fate of his sister, who had been carried away by a dragon, and his two brothers who had gone in search of her, Ivan the Pea vowed to find them and bring them home.

For three days he rode, until he came to a small wooden house on chickens' legs in the forest that rotated in the wind. The old crone that lived in that house gave him directions to the land of the dragon, in return for which Ivan the Pea promised to bring her some of the life-restoring water that the dragon owned.

Finally arriving at the dragon's golden palace, which rested on a single silver pillar, Ivan the Pea found his captive sister. He ignored his sister's pleas to run for his life, although his two brothers already lay dead in the vaults below the palace. Instead, Ivan the Pea had the court smith make him a huge mace that weighed five hundred poods (18,000 lbs or 8,190 kg). This mace took forty hours to make, and fifty men were needed to lift it; but Ivan the Pea lifted it easily with one hand and tossed it high into the air. So high did it fly that three hours passed before it came down again. Ivan the Pea easily caught it with one hand, the impact not harming him in the least, although it bent the mace slightly. Ivan the Pea simply laid the mace across his knees and straightened it out again.

Soon the dragon came home and leaped on Ivan the Pea; but Ivan simply stepped aside and killed the dragon with one throw of the mace, which flew through the palace walls and landed many hundreds of miles away. Ivan the Pea then found the Water of Life and Death, filled a flask with it for the old crone in the forest, restored his brothers to life by sprinkling some of the water over them, and then returned to his homeland with his sister and brothers, stopping en route to deliver the flask to the old crone. After the death of his father, Ivan the Pea became the tsar.

Although the old crone living in the forest is not named in this story, it is generally agreed that it is none other than the witch Baba-Yaga.

See also: Baba-Yaga (-Jaga, -Iaga); Dragon; Svetozar; Vasilis(s)a of the Golden Braid; Water of Life and Death, The

IVAN THE SOLDIER
Russia

A professional soldier who, after twenty-five years of service to an unnamed tsar, was discharged and sent on his way with nothing in his knapsack but a few meager rations. After several days' travel, when his rations had been exhausted, Ivan came across a flock of geese swimming on a lake. He killed three and hurriedly packed them into his knapsack. Then he made his way to the nearest town.

There he knocked on the door of a run-down farmhouse and asked the old woman who answered the door to roast a goose for him, keeping the second as payment for her trouble, and the third in exchange for a good quantity of wine. That night Ivan dined as if he were a tsar, and then he settled down to smoke his pipe. As he relaxed, he noticed a wonderful mansion a short distance away. He asked the old woman whose home it was, and she replied that it had been built by

the richest merchant in the town, though he had never dared live there. As soon as the house had been completed, a horde of evil demons had moved in and made the place uninhabitable.

Ivan asked the old woman how he might find the rich merchant, and then he bade her farewell. A little while later he entered the shop of the rich merchant and asked for permission to sleep in the empty house that night. The merchant was horrified, for he knew that sleeping in the house would mean certain death; but Ivan argued that as a soldier he had cheated death on several occasions, and at length the merchant agreed, supplying Ivan with a dozen candles, three pounds of dried walnuts, and one large boiled beetroot, which Ivan placed in his knapsack. Then he made his way to the empty house.

There he made himself comfortable, lit the candles, and settled down to see what might happen. As the town clock struck midnight, the first shriek filled the house. Soon the house was filled by a horde of demons with red, horned heads and green eyes that glowed with evil. When they saw Ivan they celebrated the fine meal they were soon to have, but Ivan simply stared back at them, and in a threatening voice, dared them to try it. The demons were taken aback and even frightened by this unexpected response; so the eldest demon stepped forward and challenged Ivan to a trial of strength. Ivan agreed.

The first test was to squeeze water from a stone. The eldest demon went first and squeezed his stone so hard that it crumbled into a heap of fine dust. Ivan applauded and then took the large boiled beetroot from his bag and slowly squeezed it with great deliberation so that all the demons could see the "blood" he was squeezing from it. The demons stared in disbelief; and in the silence, Ivan delved into his knapsack, took out a handful of walnuts, and began to munch on them.

The demons asked what he was eating, and he replied that he was eating walnuts, adding that none of them could even start to chew his walnuts. The eldest demon laughed and told Ivan to throw him one. Ivan reached down into his knapsack, took out a small stone, and threw this to the demon, who without looking at what he was putting in his mouth, began to chew. However, no matter how hard he chewed, he could not even start to crush the stone. All the while, Ivan stood there, popping one walnut after another into his mouth, chewing them up with ease.

Ivan then turned to the demons and derided them for the inability of their leader to beat him in these simple contests. He then suggested that they might redeem themselves a little by showing him how easily demons could squeeze into a small place—a space such as his knapsack, for example. The demons took the bait; and as soon as the last demon had crammed itself into the knapsack, Ivan bent down and quickly fastened it. Then Ivan settled down and slept soundly the rest of the night. The following morning he was awakened by two servants sent by the rich merchant, who were more than surprised to see Ivan still alive.

Ivan scoffed at them and asked them to show him the way to the local blacksmith, which they did. He set off with his knapsack. At the smithy he told the three smiths to hammer his knapsack flat. Before long, all three smiths were hammering at the knapsack with all their might, the demons inside squealing for mercy. Ivan refused to allow the smiths to give up until the demons promised never to trouble the town or the merchant again and declared that they would gladly pay a king's ransom for their freedom.

Ivan relented and let out all the demons except the leader, keeping him in return for the king's ransom promised. A short time later a small demon returned, carrying a small leather pouch. Ivan took the pouch and found that it contained nothing. Thinking that the demons were trying to trick him, Ivan turned to the smiths and told them to resume their hammering on the knapsack.

The demon still inside squealed in horror and hurriedly told Ivan that the pouch was no ordinary one. All Ivan had to do was think about what he wanted, and it would appear in the pouch. Likewise, if Ivan were to open the pouch and tell something to get into it, there was no way anything could resist his command. Ivan tried the pouch, and when he found that it worked, he declared himself satisfied and set the demon free— with a stern warning that the next time they met would be the demon's last.

Ivan then went to the rich merchant and told him that his new home was now free of demons and that he would never be troubled again. The merchant quickly moved into his house and threw a great banquet in honor of the soldier; but when he offered Ivan a reward, Ivan refused it, and the following morning he set off again toward his home village. Several days passed before Ivan reached his village, where he was greeted by his aged mother. She told him that his father had passed away five years before. That evening, with the aid of the pouch, Ivan and his mother ate a feast fit for a tsar.

The pouch helped Ivan restore the fortunes of his family. He used it to provide money to build a new home and buy new equipment; and if ever the cupboards were bare, all he had to do was use the pouch, and the cupboards were full once again. For seven years Ivan and his mother lived well; but then the old soldier fell ill, and after a few days he was confronted by Death himself. For several minutes Ivan and Death argued, but Death remained intransigent; so with the last of his feeble strength, Ivan reached for his pouch. Within seconds he had managed not only to trap Death inside his pouch but also to fully recover from his illness.

Ivan agreed to let Death out of the pouch only after Death promised to let him live another thirty years and not to take the life of any other living person during that time. For those thirty years, Ivan and his mother lived a comfortable life; but one day, thirty years to the day after Ivan had released

Death, Death came to him and told him that his time was up.

Ivan shrugged and told Death to bring him his coffin. Death grinned and brought the coffin to Ivan, telling him to jump in. However, Ivan replied that he was not prepared to get into his coffin without instructions on how to do so properly; he was a soldier, after all. So he asked Death to show him the correct manner in which one should enter a coffin. Death complied, whereupon Ivan slammed the lid of the coffin, nailed it down, took it to the nearby river, and cast Death adrift.

For several years Death floated, first down the river and then on the open sea. Then, during a particularly violent storm, the coffin was smashed against some rocks, and Death was released. He set out immediately to find the cunning old soldier. Back at Ivan's home, Death hid until he thought he could take Ivan by surprise, and then he leaped out of the shadows. However, Ivan was not to be outmaneuvered by Death, and he quickly grabbed an empty grain sack and brandished it at Death. Thinking the sack was Ivan's pouch, Death took to his heels. And that was the last anyone ever saw of Death (at least, according to one version of the legend). After that, Death took to creeping up on people unexpectedly; but he never again called on Ivan, who is said to be alive to this day.

Another version of the legend starts in the same way but differs after Ivan captures Death in his pouch. Instead of extracting a promise from Death, Ivan takes the pouch to the Briansk Woods and hangs it from the top branches of the tallest tree. From that day forward, no one in the whole world died. Ivan forgot all about Death hanging from the tree, and lived on in comfort with his mother. However, one day Ivan was traveling through a wood when he was stopped by a decrepit old crone who blamed him for not letting her die at her allotted time. Ivan immediately remembered Death. He went to the Briansk Woods; took the pouch with

Death inside, barely alive, down from the top of the tree; and carried it home with him. There he made his peace with his family, prayed for absolution from his sins, and then lay down and let Death out of the bag, telling him that his time had come and he would be Death's first victim. Death looked down at Ivan, laughed, and took to his heels, shouting after him that he would never come for Ivan, and Ivan could "go to hell."

Ivan reflected on his situation and decided that perhaps Death had the right idea. Saying goodbye to his family a second time, Ivan set out for Hell. At the gates of the infernal regions Ivan was stopped and asked what his purpose was. When he told his story to the gatekeeper, Ivan was astonished to find the gates immediately closed and barred to him. The gatekeeper hurried away and returned moments later with the Devil himself. Again Ivan explained the purpose of his visit, but the Devil would not permit him to enter. Ivan argued for some time, and then he realized that his situation was impossible.

Turning to leave, Ivan took his pouch from his pocket, and when the Devil saw it, he quickly backed away. Ivan then realized what it was that the Devil feared, and opening the pouch, he flourished it in the direction of the Devil, saying that if the Devil would not let him in, then maybe he should take the Devil to Heaven. The Devil pleaded with him, and after some time the two agreed that Ivan should have two hundred fifty souls to take with him to Heaven—souls that were quickly turned over to Ivan, who left.

As he approached the kingdom of Heaven, he was seen by the angel at the gates to the kingdom, who took the news of his approach to God. God told the angel to let the two hundred fifty souls into Heaven but then to close the gates and refuse Ivan entrance. However, after his run-in with the Devil, Ivan was prepared for some such ruse, so he let the souls out one by one, and when the last soul had been released from his pouch, he gave that soul the pouch and told him what to say once he had passed the gates and entered Heaven. However, the soul forgot what he had been asked to do; and so Ivan goes on living, growing older and older, only to die when the world itself is destroyed.

See also: Briansk Woods; Death; Devil, The

IVAN THE SUN'S SON
Siberia—Tungus

Youth whose lost arrow was found by Ivan the Mare's Son, whom he agreed to live with as a brother. They were later joined by Ivan the Moon's Son. All three lived in a clearing in a forest, where they had found and married three magical maidens. However, a serpent came and started to feed on the blood of their wives. In an epic battle all three Ivans were killed and their wives carried off to the underworld by the serpent.

Ivan the Mare's Son's mother restored all three to life, and then they lowered her son into the underworld to rescue the three wives. Having killed the serpent and rescued the maidens, Ivan the Mare's Son was left for dead by his false brothers, who made off with all three women. Restored to life once more by his mother, Ivan the Mare's Son escaped from the underworld, killed both Ivan the Moon's Son and Ivan the Sun's Son, and flew away with the three maidens to their homeland, where they lived their remaining days in peace and happiness.

See also: Ivan the Mare's Son; Ivan the Moon's Son; Underworld, The

IVAN THE TERRIBLE
Russia

Ivan IV (1530–1584), tsar of Russia from 1533, whose popular epithet *Groznyi* means "fearsome" or "threatening."

See also: Ivan IV; Ivan Groznyi

IVAN THE YOUNG
Russia

The youngest son of an unnamed tsar by one of that tsar's three concubines. The tsar could not decide which of his sons should be his heir; so he told them to go out into a field and shoot off arrows in different directions. Each son should first write his name on his arrow so that they could be identified. Wherever a son's arrow landed was where he would rule; and he would marry the daughter of the house in which his arrow landed. Ivan's arrow landed in a swamp, where he found it in the possession of a shape-changing frog who was, in reality, Vasilissa the Wise (some Ukrainian sources name the frog princess as Maria). After Ivan agreed to marry the frog, she revealed her full beauty to him and told him that she would be a frog by day and a beautiful maiden by night.

Engraving of the high priest Phillip rebuking Ivan the Terrible (Archive Photos)

Ivan fulfilled his promise and married the frog, and for some time they lived happily together. Then the tsar devised three tests for the wives of his three sons. Each time, the frog won, though the wives of Ivan's two brothers cheated by spying on her. Finally the tsar threw a banquet in honor of his three daughters-in-law at which the frog appeared in her human form. Seizing the opportunity to keep his wife in all her beauty, Ivan rushed home before she did and burned her frog skin. When she returned, she told Ivan her name for the first time, told him to seek her in the land of the eternal sun, and promptly vanished.

Ivan left his home and traveled until he came to the home of the witch Baba-Yaga. At first, the witch was annoyed at being disturbed; but with coaxing, Baba-Yaga eventually told him how he might capture Vasilissa the Wise, who flew in every day to visit her. Ivan hid and waited. When Vasilissa the Wise had arrived and made herself comfortable, he pounced on her; but she managed to wriggle free, rapidly changing her shape. Ivan then visited Vasilissa the Wise's middle sister, and exactly the same thing happened. Finally Ivan journeyed to the home of Vasilissa the Wise's youngest sister, and this time he managed to hold onto his wife as she changed her shape. When she changed into an arrow, Ivan broke it across his knee, and Vasilissa the Wise resumed her human form and told him that she would be his forever.

Together Ivan and Vasilissa the Wise returned home. There the tsar made Ivan his heir, and Ivan ruled in his father's stead.

See also: Baba-Yaga (-Jaga, -Iaga); Maria; Ukraine; Vasilis(s)a the Wise

IVAN TSAREVICH
Russia

A tsar's son named Ivan (*tsarevich* being a title that meant merely "son of the tsar"). The only Ivan Tsarevich referred to in the legends of early Russia was a son of Ivan Groznyi who was the subject of a story entitled *The Tsar Resolves to Kill His Son*. During a feast

Ivan Groznyi learned that his son, Ivan Tsarevich, was plotting against him. The tsar immediately had his son arrested and dragged off to the banks of the Moskva River where the executioner's block awaited him. The tsarina, Ivan Tsarevich's mother, rushed to her brother's house and told him what had occurred. Her brother, Nikita Romanov, hurried to the riverbank, where he stopped the execution. He found out who had betrayed his nephew, sought out the informer, and killed him. Ivan Groznyi later acknowledged his mistake and rewarded Nikita Romanov for preventing the death of his son. However, history records that this very tsarevich was killed by his father in 1581. If Nikita Romanov was successful in intervening on this occasion, Ivan Groznyi nevertheless eventually accomplished the evil deed by his own hand.

See also: Ivan Groznyi; Nikita Romanov
References: Chadwick 1964; Chistov 1967

IVAN VYSLAVOVICH
Russia

The son of Tsar Vyslav Andronovich, and brother of Dmitrii Vyslavovich and Vasilii Vyslavovich. Their father owned a wonderful garden in which there was an apple tree on which golden fruit grew. All was well until a Firebird took to visiting the garden and stealing the apples. Perplexed, the tsar promised half his kingdom to whichever of his three sons could catch the thief.

The first night, Dmitrii kept watch but fell asleep by the time the Firebird landed. The second night, Vasilii took his turn, but the same fate befell him. The third night, Ivan took his turn. After three hours the garden was filled with a wondrous light and the Firebird settled on the tree. Ivan crept up behind the Firebird and took hold of its tail. The Firebird struggled so hard that it managed to escape from Ivan, but in the process she lost one of her tail feathers to him. The following morning he presented that feather to his father, who treasured it above any of his other possessions.

A miniature on a black lacquer box depicts Ivan Vyslavovich and a princess being aided by a magical gray wolf. (Vakurov Isarevich / Sovfoto / Eastfoto / PNI)

As time passed, the tsar began to long for the Firebird itself rather than just one of its feathers. Once again he promised half of his kingdom to whichever of his sons could bring the Firebird back for him. All three set out on the quest, although none knew where they should look.

Ivan rode aimlessly for several days until he came to a crossroad that warned of death for anyone who took anything but the right-hand road, although this road would lead to the death of the rider's horse. Ivan took the right-hand road. After three days, he came across a huge gray wolf that tore his horse in half. Saddened by this loss, Ivan continued on foot until he was almost exhausted.

Just then the wolf that had attacked his horse rushed up, apologized for having killed the horse, and offered to take Ivan wherever he wanted to go. Ivan explained his quest to the wolf, which immediately sped off with Ivan on his back, much faster than any horse could have traveled. Soon

they came to a walled garden within which—so the wolf informed Ivan—the Firebird was kept in a gilded cage. The wolf warned Ivan to take only the Firebird and not to touch the cage; but when Ivan saw the beauty of the cage, he forgot the wolf's advice and took it down from its place in a tree. Immediately he was surrounded by guards, who hauled him off to confront the Firebird's owner, Tsar Dalmat.

The tsar was understandably furious, but gave Ivan a chance to redeem himself, telling him to ride to the kingdom of Tsar Afron and acquire for him the Horse with the Golden Mane. If Ivan achieved this, he would be rewarded with the Firebird. If not, he would be branded a common thief. Outside the palace Ivan apologized to the wolf for ignoring his advice, and asked his help in acquiring the Horse with the Golden Mane. The wolf told Ivan to jump on his back, and soon they were standing outside the stables of Tsar Afron.

The wolf told Ivan how he might bring the horse out unchallenged but warned him not to touch the horse's golden bridle. Once inside the stables, Ivan could not resist the bridle, and he was immediately arrested by the palace guards and dragged before Tsar Afron. Like Dalmat, Afron was furious; but he too gave Ivan a chance to save his good name. He told Ivan to bring him the princess Elena the Beautiful. If Ivan did this, his reward would be the Horse with the Golden Mane and its bridle.

Once more Ivan apologized to the wolf and asked its help. He jumped onto the wolf's back, and the two travelers soon found themselves in the land of Elena the Beautiful. Leaving Ivan on the edge of a plain, the wolf moved toward the railings that surrounded the palace gardens. That evening, as Elena the Beautiful strolled in the garden, the wolf captured her and ran off to where Ivan was waiting. Ivan leaped onto the wolf's back, and they sped back toward the land of Tsar Afron. Elena the Beautiful's servants were in hot pursuit, but the wolf easily outran them.

By the time they reached the palace walls of Tsar Afron, Ivan had fallen deeply in love with Elena the Beautiful, and vice versa. Now Ivan asked the wolf again for help, and the wolf agreed. He would become the image of Elena the Beautiful and would take her place with Tsar Afron while the two lovers made their getaway. When they were safely away, Ivan had only to think of the wolf, and the latter would return immediately to his side.

Tsar Afron was delighted when the false Elena the Beautiful was presented to him by Ivan. He kept his promise and gave Ivan the Horse with the Golden Mane and its bridle. Ivan rode off on the horse and met up with the real Elena the Beautiful, who was waiting for him in the forest. After traveling a short distance, Ivan thought of the wolf, which immediately appeared at their side.

When the travelers arrived at the palace of Tsar Dalmat, Ivan once again asked the wolf for his help, for he had grown very attached to the Horse with the Golden Mane. Once again the wolf transformed himself into the horse and was left in its stead, while Ivan left with the Firebird in its gilded cage. A short distance down the road, he thought of the wolf, who was instantly by their side.

Riding back toward Ivan's home, they came to the spot where the wolf had first attacked Ivan, killing his horse. Telling Ivan and Elena the Beautiful that he could go no farther, the wolf left them to continue their journey on the Horse with the Golden Mane. At the border of Ivan's homeland they passed Ivan's brothers Dmitrii and Vasilii. Jealous of Ivan's success, they ambushed him and killed him, dividing the booty by lot. Dmitrii won the Horse with the Golden Mane and Vasilii won Elena the Beautiful, whom the brothers swore to silence at sword's point.

For thirty days Ivan's body lay where he had been killed, until it was discovered by the wolf. Thinking of a way in which he could revive his young friend, the wolf caught a young raven (some versions say it was a crow) and threatened to tear it in half. The raven, or crow (named Voron Voronich), pleaded for mercy, to which the wolf replied that he would spare the young bird if the bird's mother would bring him some of the Water of Life and Death. The bird agreed and flew off. Three days later, she returned with two little bottles of the Water of Life and Death. To test the water, the wolf tore the mother bird in half and then sprinkled the water from one bottle over the carcass. Immediately the bird flew up into the sky, fully restored. The second bottle the wolf sprinkled over Ivan, who came back to life.

Ivan returned to the royal palace during the wedding feast of Vasilii. When Elena the Beautiful saw Ivan, she told the tsar the truth, upon which Dmitrii and Vasilii were cast into the palace dungeons. Elena the Beautiful then married Ivan, to whom ownership of the Horse with the Golden Mane was restored.

See also: Afron; Dalmat; Dmitrii (Vyslavovich); Elena the Beautiful; Firebird, The; Horse with the Golden Mane, The; Vasilii Vyslavovich; Voron Voronich; Vyslav Andronovich; Water of Life and Death, The

IVANOVICH, DUNAI
Russia
See Dunai Ivanovich.

IVANOVNA, KATRINA
Russia
See Katrina Ivanovna.

IVANUSHKA
Russia
The brother of Alenushka, Ivanushka was transformed into a kid after he drank from a lake near which some goats were grazing, although he had been warned by his sister not to drink. When Alenushka later was trapped at the bottom of the sea by an evil sorceress who had designs on Alenushka's husband, the tsar, Ivanushka pined for her by the edge of the sea. Worried that Ivanushka's actions would betray her secret, the sorceress—disguised as Alenushka—persuaded the tsar to kill Ivanushka. The desperate Ivanushka went three times to the edge of the sea to call for his sister. On the third occasion the tsar followed him and rescued Alenushka, with whom he returned to the palace. He immediately killed the sorceress by throwing her onto a huge bonfire.

See also: Alenushka

IVASHKO
Russia
The youngest son of an old peasant couple. Against his parents' better judgment, Ivashko persuaded them to let him go fishing. During the day his parents came to the water's edge and brought Ivashko food and drink. However, they did not go unobserved, for a witch witnessed everything and set about trapping the young boy for her supper.

Rushing to the local smith, the witch ordered him under threat of being eaten himself to forge her a voice so that she would sound just like Ivashko's mother. Equipped with her new voice, she hurried back to the lake and called for Ivashko to come to the shore. When he did, she grabbed the boy and made off to her home in the heart of the forest. There she ordered her daughter Alenka to heat up the stove and roast Ivashko, while the witch went to gather her friends for the fine feast of young human flesh.

Alenka did as her mother told her and heated up the stove, but when it came time to put Ivashko in to be cooked, the young boy tricked the girl, and it was she instead who was thrust into the heart of the stove. Ivashko left the house and hid in the canopy of the forest outside.

When the witch returned with her friends, she chided her absent daughter for leaving the house unattended. Judging from the aroma that their meal was ready, she and her companions sat down and ate until there was nothing left but a few bare bones. After they had eaten, the witch rolled around joyfully on the grass outside her home, shouting with glee about how she had enjoyed the roasted Ivashko. From the top of the trees, Ivashko whispered that the witch had enjoyed roasted Alenka. Looking up, the witch saw Ivashko. She tried to shake him down from the trees, but Ivashko hung on.

Furious that she had been tricked, the witch started to gnaw at the trunk of the tree, but she had gnawed only halfway through when her two top front teeth broke. Rushing to the smith, she had him fit her with steel teeth. Returning to the tree, she started to gnaw again, but now her two bottom front teeth broke. These too were replaced by the smith, and the witch returned again to her task. At last she gnawed through the tree; but Ivashko simply leaped to an adjoining one, and the witch had to start all over again.

Just then a flock of swans and geese flew overhead. Ivashko called out to them to carry him home. Two flocks passed over, but the third swooped down, picked up Ivashko, and carried him back to his anxious parents.

Although the witch in the story of Ivashko is unnamed, most authorities agree that it is none other than Baba-Yaga, the best known of all Russian witches.

See also: Alenka; Baba-Yaga (-Jaga, -Iaga)

References: Afanas'ev 1957

IVO

Croatia

Hero who lived in Senj, on the eastern coast of Croatia opposite the island of Krk. On one occasion he was reputed to have routed fifty thousand Turks with just eight hundred men. His death is recounted in a Croatian heroic ballad. His mother foresaw her son's death in a dream, which she recounted to the local priest. While she was in church, her son rode up to the door, his black horse covered in blood. Ivo was wounded in seventeen places and was holding his severed right hand in his left. His mother helped him down from his horse and bathed his wounds, whereupon Ivo told her that he and his men had been returning from Italy with a vast treasure when they were ambushed three times by Turks. The first two ambushes, Ivo and his men escaped without loss. The third, however, cost Ivo all his men. As he finished the story and was blessed by the priest, Ivo died in his mother's arms.

See also: Croatia

J

JANOS

Hungary—Magyar

The younger of the two sons of a poor widower, his younger brother being Istvan.

See also: Istvan
References: Biro 1980

JAZI BABA

Czech

The Czech name for the witch Baba-Yaga.

See also: Baba-Yaga (-Jaga, -Iaga); Czechs

JAZYGES

General

Ancient tribe of Sarmatians, who originally occupied the shores of the Black Sea.

See also: Black Sea; Sarmatians

JEZDA

Poland

One of the Polish names used to refer to the witch Baba-Yaga, signifying that the witch is associated with nightmares. The other name the Poles use to refer to this complex character is Ienzababa.

See also: Baba-Yaga (-Jaga, -Iaga); Ienzababa
References: Afanas'ev 1974

JUMALA

Ugric—Ural Mountains

The supreme being, mother of all things. The oak tree was her sacred symbol. Jumala bears a similarity to Mother Earth, but she is greater, for she alone created the universe. She is also one with the universe, for all that exists is contained within her body. In some regions Jumala is considered a male deity; but in fact Jumala is androgynous, at once both male and female. Jumala possibly developed from an ancient sky deity, as the name is cognate with the word for dusk.

See also: Mother Earth

JURAS MÀTE

Latvia

The sea goddess, respectfully called "Mother of the Seas."

K

KALINA

Russia

The name used by Katrina Ivanovna, the wife of Stavr Godinovich, while impersonating the ambassador of the King of Greece at the court of Prince Vladimir Bright Sun.

See also: Katrina Ivanovna; Stavr Godinovich; Vladimir Bright Sun, Prince

KALMUCKS (KALMYKS)

General

One of the major divisions of the Mongols. From the fifteenth to the seventeenth centuries, the Kalmucks were nomads who competed with China for control of Beijing. Later they migrated to the lower Volga River region in eastern Europe. In c. 1771, a group of some 300,000 Kalmucks decided to return to China to escape Russian domination. They took part in one of the largest and most difficult mass migrations in recorded history. They were attacked en route by Russian and Turkic bands, and only one-third of the group reached Chinese Turkestan. There they settled in the fertile basin of the Ili River. Some Kalmucks stayed on the steppes of the Volga region, and their descendants still live there. Kalmucks are also found throughout Central Asia.

The tsarist government of Russia attempted to settle the Kalmuck nomads on a reservation near Astrakhan', and the Soviet government established a republic for them in 1935. During World War II the Kalmucks collaborated with the invading Germans against the Soviets. In return the Soviet government abolished the Kalmuck Republic and exiled thousands of people to Siberia. However, many Kalmucks escaped to Europe and the United States. In 1958 the Kalmuck Autonomous Soviet Socialist Republic was reconstituted, and many of the people were returned to the Volga River region. Today they make up more than half of the total population of Russia's Kalmuck autonomous region. The people are engaged chiefly in farming, and are unique among Mongols in practicing Buddhism.

See also: Astrakhan'; Mongols; Siberia; Turkestan; Volga

KALVAITIS

Lithuania

The divine smith who daily forges the new sun. He also makes a wedding ring for the dawn goddess so that she can marry the sun every morning, and a silver belt and golden stirrups for Dievas and each of Dievas's sons, the Dievo suneliai.

See also: Dievas; Dievo suneliai; Sun

KAMS

Russia

The name sometimes given to the supernatural army with which the bogatyri attempted to do battle, in the epic poem *Why There Are No More Bogatyri in Holy Russia*. The poem explains that these bogatyri grew too confident of themselves and attacked a large, supernatural army. However, every time a supernatural warrior fell to the bogatyri, two more sprang up to take his place; and at last the bogatyri admitted defeat and fled to the mountains, where they were turned to stone.

See also: Bogatyr'; Il'ya Muromets; Mikhail Potyk; Mikula Selyaninovich; Sviatogor; Volkh Vseslav'evich
References: Evgen'eva and Putilov 1977; Nechaev and Rybakov 1959; Speranskii 1916; Ukhov 1957

KANDEK
Armenia

The youngest of the seven daughters of an unnamed man and his cannibal wife. Troubled by what she should do with all her daughters, the wife decided that she would cook them, and so she bundled them all into the stove—all except for Kandek, who hid. When the six daughters had been cooked, the woman began to moan that she should have kept one of them to help her with her chores, especially to make the long walk to the fields to take her husband his lunch. Kandek crawled out of her hiding place and offered to help her mother if she promised never to try to cook her.

Kandek's mother, being a lazy woman, readily agreed and sent Kandek off with her father's lunch. Kandek found her father and gave him his lunch, and then went for a walk. As she walked, she came to an apple tree on which were growing large, ripe, red apples. Kandek helped herself to one and sat down to eat. As she ate, an old, blind woman came up and asked Kandek to give her an apple. Kandek took down an apple and threw it to the old woman, who missed it and complained to Kandek that she was blind and that Kandek would have to bring the apple to her.

Kandek did so, whereupon the old woman took hold of her, threw her into a sack, and started for her home. A short while later Kandek asked if she might be allowed to stretch her legs. The old woman agreed and let Kandek out of the sack. Kandek quickly filled the sack with stones and then made off. When the old woman picked up the sack, she complained about the weight, but nonetheless she carried it all the way home. When she found that the sack contained nothing but a pile of rocks, the woman changed into a wolf and sought out Kandek. Changing back into the old crone, she captured Kandek, threw her back into the sack, and started for home.

Again Kandek asked to be allowed to stretch her legs, and again the old woman agreed. This time Kandek filled the sack with snow and then she made off. When the old woman picked up the sack, she complained that Kandek was making her wet, but nevertheless she carried it all the way home—only to find the snow instead of Kandek. Again she turned into a wolf and set off to find Kandek. Once again Kandek found herself in the sack, and yet again she was allowed to stretch her legs when she asked. This time Kandek filled the sack with the branches of a thorn bush; and even though the old woman complained that Kandek was pricking her, she carried the sack all the way home.

This time, however, after the old woman had recaptured Kandek, she ignored the young girl's request to be allowed to stretch her legs, and carried the sack straight back to her home, where she told her daughter to stoke the fire. Kandek cut her way out of the sack, killed the old woman's daughter, toppled her over into the cauldron, and then hid in the rafters of the house. Only after the old woman had devoured her daughter, leaving no more than a pile of cleanly picked bones, did Kandek call out, asking the old woman to help her down from the rafters.

The old woman first made a pile of wood; but clambering onto it, she fell down and hurt her back. Then she made a pile of metal combs, but fell down when the teeth cut into her feet. Finally she made a pile of salt sacks; but the salt got into the wounds on her feet, and she fell down in agony, writhing in pain, and died. Then Kandek climbed down and made her way home, telling everyone she met that the old werewolf was dead.

This story is interesting for the simple fact that it contains a female werewolf, whereas in almost all other instances a werewolf is masculine. It is also interesting to note that it contains only one element common to most werewolf legends—the ability to change shape at will—and that no special weapons, such as silver spears, are needed in order to kill the creature.

See also: Werewolf

References: Orbeli and Taronian 1959–67, vol. 3

KAPSIRKO
Russia

A poor but cunning peasant, who when caught stealing firewood from his master was threatened with being sent to the frozen wastelands of Siberia. However, his master decided that he would give Kapsirko a chance to redeem himself, and he assigned him a seemingly impossible task. Kapsirko was to steal his master's horse from a heavily guarded stable. He accomplished this task, but still his master was not satisfied; so the master told Kapsirko to steal his wife away from him.

Kapsirko achieved this by enticing the lady out of the house and bundling her into his waiting sleigh. He then made off with her down to a lake near which a vodianoi, or water demon, lived. The vodianoi asked Kapsirko to sell the lady to him, which Kapsirko did for a capful of money. The price having been negotiated, the vodianoi made off into the depths of the lake with the lady, telling his servant to fill Kapsirko's cap with money. Being a cunning man, Kapsirko cut a hole in his cap and placed it on the sleigh before the water sprite filled it. The cap leaked its contents into the sleigh, which was soon filled with coins.

Kapsirko then returned home. With his newfound wealth, he no longer had to be subservient to his old master. However, after a few weeks, his old master called him to his home, for he was missing his wife and wanted Kapsirko to get her back for him. The master promised Kapsirko half his estate and a large amount of money if he succeeded. Kapsirko agreed and rode down to the shores of the lake, where he built himself a shelter and spent hours twisting a rope.

One day while he was working on the rope, a water sprite appeared and asked Kapsirko what he was doing. Kapsirko replied that he was making a rope from which he would make the demons of the lake swing after he had drained it of water. Quickly the sprite disappeared and repeated Kapsirko's threat to the vodianoi, the water demon—chief of the demons and sprites who lived in the lake. He came to the surface and asked Kapsirko what he was doing. Again Kapsirko repeated his threat. The vodianoi asked what Kapsirko wanted of him.

When Kapsirko said that he wanted his old master's wife back, the vodianoi refused. Kapsirko then suggested three contests, the winner of all three to be awarded the lady. The vodianoi agreed. The first test was to stand together on the very edge of the lake, where each would whistle as loud as he could in an attempt to make the other fall into the water. The vodianoi went first, and Kapsirko almost fell in. When it was Kapsirko's turn, he whistled loud and long, but hit the vodianoi with a club so that the water demon fell headlong into the water, unaware that Kapsirko had hit him.

The second contest was to be a race, but Kapsirko derided the vodianoi, saying that he had a grandson who could easily beat the demon. The vodianoi accepted that Kapsirko's grandson was a hare, and said that as Kapsirko was so confident, maybe the hare should run rather than Kapsirko himself. Kapsirko readily agreed, for earlier he had trapped two hares. As the race started, Kapsirko let loose the first hare, which easily outran the vodianoi. When the vodianoi returned, out of breath, Kapsirko presented him with the second hare, which was as fresh as the morning dew.

The final contest was to be a wrestling match. Again Kapsirko tricked the vodianoi, saying that his grandfather, an old bear, could easily beat the demon. Again the vodianoi accepted this, and he was, of course, severely beaten as he attempted to wrestle the bear, which was displeased to have been awakened from hibernation.

In the end, the vodianoi submitted and returned the lady to Kapsirko, who took her back to his old master, who kept his promise and gave Kapsirko half his estate and a large sum of money.

See also: Siberia; Vodianoi (~nik)

KARACHAROVO
Russia

The village near Murom that was the birthplace of Il'ya Muromets.

See also: Il'ya Muromets; Murom

KARELIA
General

Karelia is an autonomous republic in northwest Russia, between the Finnish border and the White Sea. It was occupied in early times by nomadic Finnic settlers, who gave the area its Finno-Ugric language—still spoken today, despite the best efforts of the Russian government to enforce language laws mandating the use of Russian. Karelia came under Russian rule in the late Middle Ages. Sweden controlled a part of the region from the thirteenth to the late fifteenth centuries, and again from the seventeenth to the early eighteenth centuries. Subsequently Finland occupied a part of Karelia (from 1918 to 1920 and from 1941 to 1944).

See also: Finland; Finno-Ugric; White Sea

KARTA
Lithuania

The sister of Dekla and Laima-Dalia, though only in instances where there are three goddesses of fate. Usually Laima-Dalia was considered the sole goddess of fate. The three goddesses were believed to control the destinies of all living things, from a single blade of grass to a human being.

See also: Dekla; Laima(-Dalia)

KARTAGA
Tatar

A hero who appears in a poem recounting his struggle with the Swan Woman. For many years the couple wrestled, with neither gaining the upper hand. Meanwhile, Kartaga owned two horses, one piebald and one black, and both horses knew that the Swan

Woman did not carry her soul with her but rather kept it in a golden casket. That casket was hidden inside a black chest beneath a copper rock—a rock that rose from the earth to the heavens and marked the edge of the nine seas that flowed through the underworld, a point where the nine seas met and became one, rising to the surface of the earth.

The horses ran to the place where the copper rock emerged from the underworld, dug up the black chest, and removed the golden casket. Then the two horses carried the casket back to where Kartaga and the Swan Woman were still fighting. There the piebald horse transformed himself into a bald man, opened the casket, and killed the seven birds that flew out. These birds held the soul of the Swan Woman, who fell dead as the last bird was killed.

See also: Swan Woman; Underworld, The

KASHCHEI (THE DEATHLESS)
Russia
See Koshchei (the Deathless)

KATRINA IVANOVNA
Russia
The wife of Stavr Godinovich, who upon hearing of her husband's imprisonment did not become downhearted but instead rose to the challenge; gathered her retinue of thirty archers, thirty chess masters, and thirty minstrels; and set off for Kiev to free her unfortunate husband. She felt honor bound to do so, as her husband's plight had resulted from his boasting about her prowess.

A short distance from the walls of Kiev, Katrina and her retinue made camp. Katrina then proceeded alone into the city, disguised as a man. A short time later, she presented herself at the court of Prince Vladimir Bright Sun as "Kalina," ambassador of the King of Greece, saying that she had traveled to Kiev to exact tribute from Prince Vladimir Bright Sun under threat of a terrible war. Vladimir asked for three days and three nights to reflect on the demands of Kalina; but Katrina refused, saying that as ambassador "he" would accept the hand of the Princess Zabava in marriage in lieu of the tribute. Again Vladimir asked for time to think. Katrina said he could have twenty-four hours, and returned to her camp.

However, as she made her way back, she was secretly watched by Zabava and Evpraksiya, Vladimir's wife, who guessed that the ambassador from Greece was a woman. Thus, when Vladimir came to Zabava to tell her the news and to ask her to marry the ambassador to save them from a terrible war, Zabava and Evpraksiya told Vladimir about the ruse and sought to expose the fraud by challenging the ambassador to "manly" contests.

The following day, the ambassador returned to Kiev and asked Vladimir for his reply. Vladimir stalled, asking for more time, whereupon the ambassador grew very angry and demanded that Zabava become his wife there and then. Vladimir remained calm and suggested that while the wedding preparations were being made, they should sit a while and play the *gusli*. Katrina knew what was coming, and said that it had been a long time since "he" had played the *gusli,* but agreed to sit and play, as "his" own players were weary from the long journey from Greece. The ambassador outplayed and outsang all of the challengers in Prince Vladimir's court.

Vladimir was astounded. The ambassador could not possibly be a woman. Yet he decided to continue to stall, and so he challenged the ambassador to a game of chess. The ambassador replied that his own chess masters were weary from the journey to Kiev but that he had played chess as a child. Quickly Katrina outplayed every chess master Vladimir could produce, beating Vladimir himself in so few moves that the prince could not help but think that he was playing the greatest chess master in all the world. Convinced that the ambassador was a man, Vladimir continued with his plan and challenged the ambassador to an archery contest. Again Katrina said that

the archers in "his" camp were weary from the journey but that "he" would be glad to try.

Three times Vladimir shot an arrow at the target—composed of a ring and a knife—and on each occasion, he missed. Then the ambassador took aim and let fly a single arrow, which flew straight through the ring and split itself in two on the knife blade. Vladimir knew that he was beaten. The ambassador turned to Vladimir and told the prince either to produce the tribute required by Kalina or to have Princess Zabava taken to the cathedral in readiness for their marriage. With a heavy heart Vladimir went to his niece and commanded her to prepare herself for her wedding to the ambassador, and then he went back to where the ambassador waited to say that the bride was on her way.

The ambassador then issued a challenge of his own, saying that Vladimir and he should ride out onto the steppes and test their strength together. Vladimir replied that it would be a waste of time, as there was no man in all of Russia who could compete with the ambassador. The ambassador taunted Vladimir, saying that if the prince could not produce a champion and would not compete himself, then perhaps there was one in the palace dungeons who would compete.

Vladimir remembered Stavr Godinovich and his idle boast, and immediately he told his guards to release him and arm him for combat against the ambassador from Greece. Stavr soon rode out from Kiev, and hidden by the dust thrown up by their horses, Stavr and his wife were reunited. The pair then returned to Kiev, where Katrina Ivanovna revealed her true identity to Prince Vladimir Bright Sun. Then, laughing together, Stavr Godinovich and his wife Katrina Ivanovna rode out of Kiev, leaving Prince Vladimir Bright Sun thinking that Stavr had not made an idle boast.

See also: Evpraksiya (~ia), Princess; Kalina; Kiev; Stavr Godinovich; Vladimir Bright Sun, Prince; Zabava (Putyatichna), Princess

KATYA
Slav

A beautiful young peasant girl who had been orphaned and had inherited her parents' house. Over time she grew conscious of the fact that she was being helped around the house by a dvorovoi. As the years passed, she was able to see him clearly, a handsome youth who had obviously fallen in love with her. Katya invited the spirit to live with her. He plaited her hair and made her promise never to undo his handiwork.

Some years later Katya realized that her lover was incapable of physical affection. Yearning for human love and affection, she met and became engaged to Stefan. The night before her wedding, after she had bathed, Katya undid her hair, which had grown very long, and brushed it thoroughly before retiring. The following morning her neighbors broke into her house when their knocks went unanswered and found her still in bed. Her long hair had been twisted and knotted around her neck. She had fallen victim to her jealous dvorovoi lover, who had strangled her with her own hair.

See also: Dvorovoi

KAUKAI
Latvia

Subterranean spirits who are ruled by Puskaitis.

See also: Puskaitis

KAUKAS
Slav

One of the variant names applied to the domovoi, it might owe its origin to the Latvian name, kaukai.

See also: Domovoi; Kaukai

KAYEN
Armenia
Also: Cain

The ruler of Kilikia, or Cilicia, who had his palace in Adana. He is featured in the legend of Purto.

See also: Cilicia; Kilikia; Purto

KAZAKHSTAN
General

Among the former constituent republics of the USSR, Kazakhstan is unusual in that its indigenous people, the Kazakhs, are not a majority in their own country, being outnumbered there by other, nonindigenous ethnic groups. A large-scale influx of Russians took place in the nineteenth and twentieth centuries, as a result of which Kazakh society came under the influence of the Russian language and of Slavic ideas. However, the native Kazakhs did not completely assimilate with the Russians, and they retain their own unique culture. The official state language of Kazakhstan is Kazakh, a Turkic language, although Russian also is spoken by the majority of the population. Today the Slavic immigrants are concentrated in the northern part of the country and form a majority in Almaty (formerly Alma-Ata), the capital of Kazakhstan.

KAZAN'
Tatar

The capital of the Tatar republic, which lies on the Volga River about 500 miles (800 kilometers) east of Moscow. Kazan' is a cultural center of the Tatars, who founded the city in the fifteenth century. Ivan Groznyi, the first tsar of Russia, captured the city in 1552.

See also: Ivan Groznyi; Moscow; Tatars; Volga

KAZIMIROVICH, VASILII
Russia
See Vasilii Kazimirovich.

KEREMET
Votyak

A powerful but mischievous deity who—so the Votyak people of at least one village thought—caused famines through bad harvests because he was unmarried. After one particularly bad harvest, the village elders visited a neighboring village and arranged for Keremet to marry Mukylin, the earth mother.

When everything had been arranged, the village elders returned home and made the necessary preparations. They loaded wagons with food and drink, decorating the wagons brightly before driving them to the neighboring village as if they were bringing home a bride. There they cut a sod from the sacred grove and took it home with them, thus marrying Keremet to Mukylin. From that day forth the harvests were always good, though the harvests of their neighbors were forever bad—a state of affairs blamed on the unwilling marriage of the earth mother to Keremet.

See also: Mukylin; Votyaks

KHAN

Also: Khagan
General

Honorific title applied to a Mongol, Tatar, or Turkic ruler, perhaps most famously recalled from the historical Mongol leader Genghis Khan. In the legends of ancient Russia, the title is used indiscriminately to refer to the ruler of any foreign or supernatural power. In some versions of the legend of Dunai Ivanovich and the Princesses Nastas'ya and Evpraksiya, their father is said to be a Tatar khan instead of the king of Lithuania (as other legends have it).

A khan was seen, by Russian subjects, as being far removed from their own ruler, who was answerable to the people. The khan was above the law, an overlord and conqueror ruling over a subdued people. He was, therefore, the antithesis of a tsar or a grand prince and was regarded with disdain tinged with fear.

See also: Dunai Ivanovich; Evpraksiya (~ia), Princess; Genghis Khan; Lithuania; Mongols; Nastas'ya, Princess; Tatars

KHAN BOGHU

Armenia
See Boghu, Khan.

KHOR(S)

Russia

One of the triad of supreme deities in the earliest times, the others being Perun and Mokosh. Some authorities have suggested that Khor, or Khors, a sun god, was the offspring of Perun and Mokosh.

See also: Mokosh; Perun
References: Gimbutas 1971; Ivanov and Toporov 1965; Propp 1963; Tereshchenko 1848; Zemtsovskii 1970

KHORIV

Slav

The *Primary Chronicle* says that Kiev was founded by three Viking brothers named Kiy, Schek, and Khoriv, sometime before the founding of Novgorod. The legendary Kiy, Schek, and Khoriv may have a historical basis, but this cannot be confirmed. The *Primary Chronicle* places them in Kiev before Riurik founded Novgorod—because by that time, the descendants of these three were living in Kiev as tributaries of the Khazars. These descendants were killed when Oleg wrested Kiev from the Vikings, in 882.

See also: Kiev; Kiy; Novgorod; Oleg; *Primary Chronicle;* Riurik; Schek; Vikings
References: Cross and Sherbowitz-Wetzor 1953

KHOZIAIKA LESA

Russia

"Mistress of the forest," a title that usually applies to the witch Baba-Yaga but might equally be applied to any of the many woodland spirits.

See also: Baba-Yaga (-Jaga, -Iaga)
References: Wosien 1969

KIEV

Russia

The capital of Ukraine, situated at the confluence of the Desna and Dnieper Rivers. Founded in the fifth century, Kiev replaced Novgorod as the capital of Slav-dominated Russia in 882. It was also the center of the Orthodox faith after Vladimir I converted to Christianity in 988. As the seat of Prince Vladimir Bright Sun and his court, Kiev is the most important city mentioned in Russian legends.

Gold-topped buildings in Kiev, Ukraine (Archive Photos)

The *Primary Chronicle* says that Kiev was founded by three Viking brothers named Kiy, Schek, and Khoriv, before the founding of Novgorod. History supports an early date for the foundation of both Kiev and Novgorod, and the chroniclers who recorded their slightly dubious histories well after the events obviously did not have a true understanding of their subject. Kiev had been founded long before the Scandinavians came to Russia. The latter did not found the city but brought it prosperity and thus ensured its growth. Kiy, Schek, and Khoriv might actually have lived, but this is not certain. The *Primary Chronicle* places them in Kiev before Riurik founded Novgorod, by which time the descendants of the three Vikings were living in the city as tributaries of the Khazars. These descendants were killed when Oleg wrested Kiev away from the Vikings in 882.

See also: Desna; Dnieper; Khoriv; Kiy; Novgorod; Oleg; *Primary Chronicle;* Riurik; Schek; Ukraine; Vladimir I; Vladimir Bright Sun, Prince
References: Cross and Sherbowitz–Wetzor 1953

KIKIMORA
Slav

A female domestic spirit sometimes described as the wife of the domovoi. Depicted as having chicken's legs and a long, beaklike nose, Kikimora (also known as Domania and Domovikha) could be persuaded to perform household chores for busy wives by washing the kitchen utensils in a brew made from ferns. She would only assist competent housekeepers. Those who were lazy or sloppy would be punished. Kikimora would lose small items, spoil food, and wake the children at night by tickling them.

See also: Domovoi

KILIKIA
General
See Cilicia.

KING OF SNAKES

Armenia

Honorific title of Shah-Mar, who is featured in the story of the young hunter Purto.

> *See also:* Purto; Shah-Mar

KING OF THE FOREST

Armenia

The sworn enemy of the King of the Waters, featured in the story of Lusaghen.

> *See also:* King of the Waters; Lusaghen
> *References:* Orbeli and Taronian 1959–67, vol. 10

KING OF THE WATERS

Armenia

The father of Lusaghen, and the sworn enemy of the King of the Forest. Both kings are featured in the story of Lusaghen.

> *See also:* King of the Forest; Lusaghen
> *References:* Orbeli and Taronian 1959–67, vol. 10

KINGDOM BY THE SEA, THE

Russia

The kingdom in which Sviatogor was told that his bride-to-be lived. There, on a

An undated woodcut from a story of mortals bargaining with the King of the Forest (from the collections of Carol Rose; photo by David Rose)

dunghill in the City of the King, she had languished thirty years.

See also: City of the King, The; Sviatogor

KINGDOM OF DARKNESS, THE
Armenia

One of the lands crossed by Badikan during his journeys. It is reasonable to assume that this kingdom never saw the light of day (hence its name), and therefore, that it is an earthly representation of the darkness of the underworld.

See also: Badikan; Underworld, The

KINGDOM OF LIGHT, THE
Armenia

One of the lands crossed by Badikan during his journeys. It is reasonable to assume that this kingdom never knew the darkness of the night (hence its name), and therefore, that it is an earthly representation of heaven.

See also: Badikan

KINGDOM OF THE EAST, THE
Armenia

The kingdom in which the princess lived with whom the giant Khan Boghu fell in love. Badikan traveled there to abduct her on behalf of the giant, but the pair fell in love, and from that day forth they conspired to discover the secret of Khan Boghu's immortality. When they finally uncovered the secret, they quickly disposed of the giant, were duly married, and thenceforth ruled over the lands of Khan Boghu.

See also: Badikan; Boghu, Khan
References: Khatchatrian 1933

KINGS ARE NOT CREATED BY FLATTERY ALONE
Armenia

A proud peacock once strutted about, showing off his fine feathers to the birds who came to admire his beauty. Before long the peacock began to respond to their flattery and started to say that with his fine feathers he should be king of the birds in place of the eagle with its dull plumage. Some of the wiser birds warned the peacock that kings were born and did not owe their positions to their finery; but the peacock would not listen. News of the peacock's pretensions reached the ears of the eagle, which swooped down on the proud bird and stripped him and his family of their feathers. The peacock was not only reminded of the nature of a true king but lost his riches as well.

One of the fables of Mekhithar Gosh.

See also: Mekhithar Gosh

KIRBIT
Russia

The tsar of an unnamed kingdom and father of the beautiful maiden Vasilissa Kirbit'evna. His daughter was stolen from him by Ivan, whom it had been prophesied she would marry, and Bulat the Brave. Giving chase, Tsar Kirbit alone survived the onslaught of Bulat. Gathering twice as many men did him no good, for Bulat killed them all, again leaving only Kirbit alive to mourn the loss of his daughter.

See also: Bulat the Brave; Ivan; Vasilis(s)a Kirbit'evna

KIRBIT'EVNA, VASILIS(S)A
Russia

See Vasilis(s)a Kirbit'evna.

KIRGHIZ
Siberia

Ancient Siberian people who believe themselves the result of a divine conception. In a far-off land, so the legend goes, a ruler had a beautiful daughter whom he locked away so that no man might see her. The girl's only contact with the outside world was an old serving woman. When the girl had grown to adulthood she asked the old woman to show her the world outside her dark and gloomy prison, promising that she would not reveal her trip to anyone. The old woman agreed; but no sooner had the girl stepped outside the palace than she was seen by the gods, who immediately impregnated her. Her father was furious and had the unfortunate maiden locked in a golden casket and thrown into the sea. The casket floated across the sea until it was broken apart on a rocky coastline where the girl gave birth, her child being the first Kirghiz and the progenitor of the people. The ancient homeland of the Kirghiz is today known as Kyrgyzstan.

KIRNIS
Slav

Minor fertility deity who ensured that cherries ripened successfully.

KIY
Slav

The *Primary Chronicle* says that Kiev was founded by three Viking brothers named Kiy, Schek, and Khoriv, before the founding of Novgorod. Kiy, Schek, and Khoriv might actually have existed, although this cannot be proven. The *Primary Chronicle* places them in Kiev before Riurik founded Novgorod, by which time the descendants of these three were living in the city as tributaries of the Khazars. These descendants were killed when Oleg seized power in Kiev in 882.

> *See also:* Khoriv; Kiev; Kiy; Novgorod; Oleg;
> *Primary Chronicle;* Riurik; Schek; Vikings
> *References:* Cross and Sherbowitz-Wetzor 1953

KÖK CHAN
Tatar

The hero of a Tatar poem who gave a ring that held half his strength to a maiden. Sometime later Kök Chan was engaged in mortal combat and did not quite have enough strength to kill his opponent. Just then the maiden came by and dropped the ring into Kök Chan's mouth, and feeling his strength renewed, he quickly overcame and killed his opponent.

> *See also:* Tatars

KOKNAS
Armenia

The sister of Suren who was, in fact, a Ghovt, or she-devil. For the full story see the entry for Suren.

> *See also:* Ghovt; Suren
> *References:* Orbeli and Taronian 1959–67, vol. 4

KOLDUN
Russia

Thought to possess supernatural knowledge, the *kolduny* (pl.) of the Varangian period were considered direct successors to the ancient shamans. Unlike their female counterparts, the *volkhvy* (seers), who would only allow admittance of the opposite sex through blood lineage, the kolduny (or wizards) were open about their practices and welcomed all who wished to participate. In a patriarchal society, the kolduny might have held far greater sway than the volkhvy; but in ancient Russia, where women were the principal bearers of tradition and protectors of the community, the opposite was true. In later times, when wizardry was practiced by groups of men and women combined, sorcerers began to be called *znakhari*.

The kolduny, as the possessors of special knowledge, were often consulted in cases of community dispute or disaster, when they acted as mediators or as diviners of guilt. There is evidence that they might have favored men over women: For example, after a failed harvest in the regions of Rostov and Suzdal', in 1070, the women were blamed, with bloody results.

> *See also:* Shaman; Varangians; Znakhar'
> *References:* Tokarev 1957

KOLIADA
Russia

Winter solstice ceremony that began on or around 12 December. The word *Koliada* comes from *kolo* (round, or circle); and the name of Koliada's companion ceremony, *Sviatki,* is related to *svet* (light). (The festival known as Sviatki is only a small part of the ceremony of Koliada.)

The traditional festival of Koliada united an entire community in worship of its ancestors, thereby ensuring the rebirth of the land in the coming new year. Young women were central to the ceremonies. In the Sviatki ritual, they would divine their own futures as well as that of the larger community—the village and its farms. At the same time, the old women of the community would symbolically feed the dead ancestors. The winter solstice was seen as a time when the living and dead communed in a period of "half-light" as the sun approached its death surrounded by the forces of darkness. It was important to commune with dead ancestors in order to dislodge the evil forces that sought to kill the sun, ensuring both the sun's continuation and that of all life on earth.

In the Volga region the Koliada was known as Ovsen' or Vinograd, but the central core of the ceremonies remained the same. The name *Koliada* might also have been derived from the Greek *Kalanda,* or the Romanized *Calandæ.* The ancients believed that the rebirth of the sun goddess, whom they also called Koliada, was ensured by driving a young woman out of the village on a sled, while singing hymns invoking the sun. The woman on the sled symbolically "died" in this ritual, which might once have called for actual human sacrifice.

In some places, Koliada also has a masculine aspect (e.g., the festival once was connected with Saint Nikolai of Mozhaisk); but the most common form of practice was matriarchal, even going so far as to personify the festival as a childbearing goddess of wealth—though wealth in this case meant children rather than material riches. Sometimes both male and female aspects of the festival were combined; but whatever the gender and whatever the mix, the main purpose of the ritual was identical—to ensure the rebirth of the sun and of life on earth.

See also: Nikolai of Mozhaisk, Saint; Ovsen'; Sviatki; Vinograd; Volga

References: Afanas'ev 1865–69; de Beauplan 1732; Potebnia 1865; Propp 1963; Shein 1900

KORKA-MURT
Votyak
Literally, "man of the house," the spirit of the hearth that was central to any home.

KORYAKS
Siberia
Ancient maritime Siberian people about whom very little has been written and published. From the information that is available, they appear to have believed in the spirituality of animals. After they had killed and dressed a bear, they would garb themselves in the bearskin, dance around the bear's severed head, and repeat a formula laying the blame for the animal's death on someone else, usually a neighboring people. Likewise, when Koryaks caught a whale, they would feast on the dead spirit of the whale as they would any visiting dignitary. Both ceremonies were designed to ensure the success of future hunting. The Koryaks believed that if they did not show the proper respect, their prey would disappear and they would starve.

KOSHCHEI (THE DEATHLESS)
Russia
One of the most unpleasant of all the characters found in the Russian legends. The name *Koshchei* (in some variants, *Kashchei*) comes from *kost'* (bone). Koshchei could not be killed because his soul was not inside his body but was hidden elsewhere. Though the location of the hiding place varies quite widely from tale to tale, the soul itself was usually hidden inside an egg. This egg was, in turn, inside a duck or other bird, which was inside a rabbit. The three were then hidden in some remote and inaccessible place, such as beneath a large oak tree, on an island in the middle of a huge ocean, or under a tree on that island.

The egg is the symbol of life to many cultures, not just the Russian, as it is the female cell from which life will spring. Birds' eggs, so fragile and easily broken yet containing the power to create a new life, were held in awe by ancient peoples and were usually presented to new parents upon the birth of a child. The iconography of the egg continues even today among many cultures, a particular example being the giving of decorated eggs at Easter, representing the resurrection of Jesus Christ.

Koshchei the Deathless, who in some sources is described as a dragon and a male aspect of Baba-Yaga, finally met with his own death after he had kidnaped the beautiful Vasilissa Kirbit'evna. Bulat the Brave persuaded Vasilissa to find out where her captor Koshchei kept his soul. After recovering the egg, Bulat returned to the forest home of Koshchei, and breaking the egg on Koshchei's forehead, killed him.

An alternate version of the story of Koshchei the Deathless has him living in a magnificent golden palace where he keeps an unnamed princess prisoner, a princess whose lover continuously walks outside the walls of the palace, unable to find a way in. The princess sought to kill Koshchei but knew that he did not carry his soul with him, so she made up to him and asked him where his soul was hidden. Koshchei first said that his soul was in a broom in the kitchen, but this was a lie, as when the princess threw the broom onto the fire, Koshchei remained unharmed. So she tried again, and this time Koshchei told her that his soul was in a worm that lived beneath the largest of three oak trees in a field at the top of a high hill. The princess told her lover the news, and he sought out the field, cut down the largest of the three oaks, dug up the roots, and crushed the worm. Koshchei the Deathless remained unharmed.

The princess then tried again, and this time was told that the soul could be found hidden in an egg. That egg was in a duck which was in a hare, both animals in turn being within a basket that itself was locked in a steel chest that lay beneath a great oak that grew all by itself on a small island far out at sea. The princess related the story to her lover, who set off, found the oak, retrieved the egg, and came back to the palace, where he confronted Koshchei. Dismayed to see the egg in the young man's hand, Koshchei reached for a sword, and as he did so the young man squeezed the egg, whereupon Koshchei let out a piercing scream. Then the young man crushed the egg, and Koshchei instantly died.

There are many different versions of this story, but they all have a common theme in that the soul of the warlock is hidden in some bizarre and inaccessible place. The egg, however, is not the only vessel in which the soul is hidden. In one variant, where Koshchei appears as a serpent (possibly a dragon), the soul is contained within a pebble that could be found in the yolk of the egg, and death could only come to the serpent if that stone were smashed into his forehead. Needless to say, no matter where the soul is or what its vessel, Koshchei the Deathless always dies and the hero always rescues the maiden.

See also: Baba-Yaga (-Jaga, -Iaga); Bulat the Brave; Dragon; Vasilis(s)a Kirbit'evna
References: Afanas'ev 1865–69; Ivanov and Toporov 1965

KOSMA
Russia
Variant of Kuz'ma.

KOSMATUSHKA
Russia
One of the two names given to the magical horse of Il'ya Muromets, the other being Borushka Matushka.

See also: Borushka Matushka; Il'ya Muromets
References: Astakhova 1938–51

KOSTIA NIKITIN
Russia
One of the *druzhina* of Vasilii Buslayevich, Kostia stood guard over the stern of the pirates' ship while they sailed the waters of Lake Il'men'.

See also: Il'men', Lake; Vasilii Buslayevich

KOSTIA NOVOTORZHENI
Russia
The first bogatyr' to take the tests set by Vasilii Buslayevich and pass, and thus the first

member of Vasilii's *druzhina,* which eventually included thirty men.

> *See also:* Bogatyr';Vasilii Buslayevich

KOSTROMA
Russia

Fertility goddess who in tenth-century art is represented as a diamond-headed column in a temple, surrounded by horses enclosed in lozenge shapes. The horses are surmounted by human figures standing with their arms raised to the sky. Kostroma is the female counterpart of Kostromo and as such is connected with grain, both male and female aspects being seen as divine twins. They are, in fact, a part of a complex quadruple agrarian deity with male and female aspects considered as a single entity, the other pairings being Lado and Lada, Iarilo and Iarila, and Kupalo and Kupala. Sometimes the quadruple pairing within the deity was reduced to a single pairing, that pairing having different names in different regions. In Murom the pairing was Kostromo and Kostroma, whereas in Kostroma province it was Iarilo and Iarila.

Kostroma was celebrated each year on 29 June, St. Peter's Day, or the following Sunday, in a festival known as the "Funeral of Kostroma." Various versions of the festival were performed, according to region and regional consideration. Generally, however, a bonfire would be lit and a young maiden from the community chosen to represent Kostroma. She would be borne, with great reverence, to a local watercourse where she was ritually bathed. They would then return to the village to end the day with feasting, dancing, and games. Sometimes the maiden would be replaced with a straw effigy, but the rituals remained fairly constant.

> *See also:* Iarila; Iarilo; Kostromo
> (-Kostrobunko); Kupala; Kupalo; Lada; Lado;
> Murom
> *References:* Cross and Sherbowitz-Wetzor
> 1953; Mansikka 1922; Snegirev 1837–39;
> Zabylin 1880

KOSTROMO(-KOSTROBUNKO)
Russia

The male counterpart of Kostroma.

> *See also:* Kostroma

KOT BAYUN
Russia

A talking cat that lived in the Thrice-Ninth Kingdom within the Thrice-Ninth Land. Petrushka was sent to fetch Kot Bayun by a tsar who sought to be rid of Petrushka so as to marry his wife Masha. When the tsar assigned Petrushka this task, Petrushka returned home crestfallen. His wife told him to go to bed and sleep soundly that night and in the morning she would equip him for his task. As promised, Masha woke him in the morning and gave him three felt hats, a pair of pincers, and three metal rods. Petrushka followed Masha's advice to the letter. Before approaching the cat, he put the three felt hats on his head and took the first metal bar in one hand and the pincers in the other. The cat hissed and clawed viciously at Petrushka, but the hats protected him, though they were torn to shreds. Shortly before the cat tore away the third hat, Petrushka managed to catch the flaying leg in the pincers and started to beat the animal with the first metal rod, which was made of iron. When that bar broke, he seized the second, made of brass, and continued to beat the animal. When the second bar broke, he took up the last one, made of tin, and continued the punishment. This bar grew hot and bent but did not break, and in the end the cat and begged mercy and promised to go with Petrushka to his tsar.

When Petrushka again stood before the tsar, he bowed and told his ruler that he had accomplished his mission. The tsar looked at the cat and asked Petrushka how he could be sure that this was indeed Kot Bayun. Petrushka released the cat, which immediately bared its teeth, arched its back, spat, and flew at the tsar's throat. The tsar called out for help, whereupon Petrushka simply brandished the pincers and the tin bar, and the cat returned to his side. Petrushka then locked the cat in a cage within the palace and returned to the arms of Masha his wife.

This, however, was not the end of Petrushka's torment at the tsar's hands. For the remainder of the story see the entry for Petrushka.

See also: Masha; Petrushka; Thrice-Ninth Kingdom, The; Thrice-Ninth Land, The

KOTSKY, MR.
Ukraine

An aging tabby cat that lived with a bad-tempered farmer who drove him away from the farm when he grew too old to effectively hunt rats and mice. Mr. Kotsky took to wandering the forests, where he was befriended by a vixen who had never seen a domestic cat and therefore believed Mr. Kotsky when he said that he was the fiercest animal in the world.

The vixen took Mr. Kotsky back to her lair, and from that day on she did all the hunting, while Mr. Kotsky grew strong and rather fat. As Mr. Kotsky grew, so did his appetite, and before long the vixen was finding it difficult to catch all the food the cat needed. Thus she went out into the forest and told all the animals about Mr. Kotsky, his ferocity, and his appetite, adding that all the animals must help her hunt, otherwise Mr. Kotsky would be angry and would easily deal with them.

The following day, the animals of the forest caught a huge ox and dragged it back to the vixen's lair. Mr. Kotsky hurried out and leaped onto the carcass, tearing at its skin and shouting that he needed more to eat. As he set about the dead ox, a wild boar was hiding in a pile of leaves when it was bitten on the tail by a gnat. As the boar twitched, Mr. Kotsky saw the leaves move and, thinking that they hid a mouse, leaped into them with his claws extended. The boar was so terrified as Mr. Kotsky landed that he leaped out of the leaves, Mr. Kotsky being equally surprised and leaping into a tree where a huge bear was hiding. The bear

thought Mr. Kotsky was about to attack him, so he jumped down and ran off, meeting up with a huge wolf who was coming to see just what kind of animal Mr. Kotsky was. The boar and the bear told the wolf what had happened, and from that day forth all the animals of the forest lived in fear of the terrible Mr. Kotsky. All, that is, except for the vixen, for she had seen the fright in Mr. Kotsky's eyes, and having coaxed him down from the tree, she lived a life of luxury and ease as the other animals served their every need.

KRASNAIA GORA
Russia

"Red Mountain," a widespread springtime festival that, according to some authorities, stems from the ancient Slavic custom of burying the dead on hilltops or hillsides. The festival occurred at sunset, when young women and young men would come together and dance and sing about the coming of spring while holding bread and eggs. Often the ritual would be performed by young women alone who would dance around a single girl standing in their midst and holding bread and an egg that had been dyed red. The bread represented the fertility of the previous year; the egg symbolized the fertility of the earth waiting to be reborn; and the color red (*krasnoe*) signified the daily death and rebirth of the sun.

References: Afanas'ev 1865–69; Snegirev 1837–39

KREMARA
Slav

The patron spirit of adult pigs and possibly the brother of Kurwaichin in Poland, he is usually coupled with Priparchis, the patron of piglets in common Slavic belief. Kremara was believed to assume responsibility for the continued good health of adult pigs after Priparchis had overseen their successful birth and weaning. No true cult developed around Kremara; but the spirit's patronage was traditionally evoked by pouring beer onto a fire, which resulted in a pungent aroma thought to attract Kremara.

See also: Kurwaichin; Priparchis

KREMLIN
General

A fortified enclosure surrounding the administrative core of a Russian town, which generally consisted of a church or cathedral, a central plaza or marketplace, and in the larger towns and cities, a palace and other government buildings. The name comes from the Russian *kreml'*, which means "fortress." Many Russian cities have kremlins, but the most famous—known simply as the Kremlin—is the vast walled compound in Moscow.

Moscow's Kremlin has a long history as the seat of government in Russia. Beginning in the twelfth century, when Moscow was the administrative center of only one of many Russian states, its princes ruled from the Kremlin. The Kremlin was the headquarters of tsarist rule from the mid-sixteenth century until 1712, when Peter the Great moved the Russian capital to St. Petersburg. Moscow and the Kremlin again became the seat of government in 1918, shortly after the Bolsheviks took control of Russia, and remained the seat after the Soviet Union was created in 1922. With the breakup of the Soviet Union in 1991, the Kremlin became the seat of government of independent Russia.

The Moscow Kremlin is a triangular enclosure with a circumference of nearly 1.5 miles (2.4 kilometers). The first Kremlin on the site was built in 1156. The present Kremlin walls have stood since the late fifteenth century, when Moscow became the most powerful Russian city. At that time, architects from northern Italy and from throughout Russia were called to work on the Kremlin. Italian architects built the Cathedral of the Assumption (1475–1479), the Granovitaya Palace (1487–1491), the Bell Tower of Ivan the Great (1505–1508), and the Cathedral of the Archangel Michael (1505–1509). The architects carefully blended the Italian Renaissance classical style with more traditional Russian forms, such as those used in the Kremlin's Cathedral of the Annunciation (1484–1489).

During the seventeenth century, the towers and buildings of the Kremlin were enlarged and redecorated. The major Kremlin buildings of this period are the Terem Palace (1635–1636) and the Palace of the Patriarchs (1645–1655). In the eighteenth and nineteenth centuries construction continued, but this time in the baroque and later neoclassical styles. Notable buildings from this period include the Arsenal (1702–1736), the Menshikov Tower (1705–1707), the Senate (1776–1787), and the Grand Kremlin Palace (1838–1849). Buildings added during the twentieth century include the Presidium (1932–1934) and the Palace of Congresses (1960–1961), the great hall of which currently houses government meetings and performances of ballets and operas.

See also: Ivan the Great; Moscow; St. Petersburg

KRICCO
Slav

Minor fertility deity who protected the fruits of the field.

KRIMBA
Slav

A goddess of the house who was principally worshiped in Bohemia.

See also: Bohemia

KRUKIS
Slav

The patron spirit of blacksmiths, who according to some sources, also watched over the welfare of domestic animals along with Peseias.

See also: Peseias

KUL'
Ostyak

A water spirit who haunted large lakes and areas of deep water. His appearance always spelled misfortune—usually the drowning of some unfortunate individual who had been foolish enough to venture into the spirit's domain.

KUMSTVO
Russia

From *kum* (cousin), Kumstvo was a prelude to the major ceremonies of the festival of Semik. During the kumstvo a birch tree, known as the "Semik Birch," would be dressed with ribbons to stand like a goddess over the coming festivities, which were designed to confirm the unity of the community and reconfirm its link with deceased ancestors. Young girls were central to the kumstvo, and would wear garlands woven from birch twigs, the garlands representing the fertility of the maidens, which they would retain, unsullied, until they married. These girls would embrace, to signify the solidarity of the village, and pledge their eternal blood ties. These rituals completed, the festival of Semik could be brought to its ultimate conclusion.

See also: Semik
References: Afanas'ev 1865–69; Propp 1963; Rimsky-Korsakov 1951; Zemtsovskii 1970

KUPALA
Slav

The goddess of peace, water, magic, and herbs, who according to some sources, was married to Yarilo. The worship of Kupala involved ritual washing and the offering of flowers, which were thrown onto the water's surface. Curiously, the rites also involved fire, for fire was considered to have the same purifying qualities as water. Worshipers would run around fires and leap over the flames in order to purify themselves. Effigies of Kupala were either burned or thrown into the water. Kupala has been equated with the Celtic goddess Beltane. Kupala—in southern Russia, also known as Kupal'nitsa—was the female counterpart of Kupalo.

See also: Kupal'nitsa; Kupalo; Yarilo

KUPAL'NITSA
Slav

The name given to Kupala, the female counterpart of Kupalo, in southeastern and southwestern Russia.

See also: Kupala; Kupalo

KUPALO
Slav

The god of peace, magic, water, and herbs; one aspect of a quadruple fertility deity, the other aspects being Iarilo, linked with the Sun; Kostromo-Kostrobunko, linked with grain; and Lado, a name used in invocations of the fertility deity as a single entity. Each of these aspects also had a feminine personification—Kupalo's being Kupala, Kostromo-Kostrobunko's Kostroma, and Lado's Lada. Kupalo and Kupala, like the other aspects of the fertility deity, were considered divine twins, and their effigies were often burned together in order to stimulate the fertility and potency of the aspect they represented—in the case of Kupalo and Kupala, water.

See also: Iarilo; Kostroma; Kostromo (-Kostrobunko); Kupala; Lada; Lado; Sun
References: Snegirev 1837–39; Vernadsky 1959

KUPIATITSKAIA
Russia

A twelfth-century religious icon that was "miraculously" found in a Ukrainian wood by a girl in 1182. It was common between the eleventh and fifteenth centuries for icons to be found in woods and forests, the peasants declaring that they had been left there by God to signify his potency. However, the truth was far more mundane, for the icons were placed in the woods and forests by the clergy who knew that if they were found as if by magic, the peasants would be more likely to convert to Christianity than they would by more conventional means.

KURKE
Russia

The spirit of the grain, who was envisioned in the form of a cockerel. During the harvest festival a young cockerel was sacrificed to Kurke and a few ears of grain were left standing in the field to feed the spirit.

See also: Rugiu Boba

KURWAICHIN
Poland

The patron spirit of sheep, and according to some sources, the brother of Kremara. Both were offered beer poured into the fireplace.

See also: Kremara

KUSH-PARI
Armenia

From the Turkish *kush* (bird) and the Persian *pari* (winged spirit), Kush-Pari was exactly that, a winged spirit in the form of a bird. The legend from Armenia concerning the Kush-Pari exhibits many Turkish and Anatolian influences and shows how during the expansionist years of the Russian Empire, these influences came to be regarded as an integral part of their heritage.

An unnamed king in an unnamed realm was going blind as he grew older. This king had three sons, and one by one he sent them to find a cure for his affliction—a cure that could only be found where no horse had ever trod. The first son traveled to a tree that miraculously came to life overnight, bearing huge apples—apples that he took back to his father, who was disappointed, for he had already been to that place and the apples could not provide his cure.

The second son traveled past the tree and came to a mountain, the top of which was awash in precious stones. Convinced that no one had ever set foot on the mountain—for if they had, surely all the gems would have been carried away—the son filled a saddlebag with them and returned to his father. Yet his father had visited that mountain many years before, and now, just as had happened then, the gems had turned to colored glass.

Finally the youngest son was called upon by his father to seek out the cure. In a dream the young man was advised to set out equipped with his father's ring and sword

and riding his father's horse. This he did; and whereas it had taken his brothers many months to travel, it took him a matter of hours. As night fell on the very first day, having already passed the apple tree and the mountain of gems, the young man came to the crest of a hill and saw two suns in the valley below him, one in the sky, and one on the ground.

Riding down into the valley, the young prince discovered that the sun on the ground was a magnificent golden feather, which he picked up, and ignoring the warning of his horse, tucked into his hatband. Then he rode on, and before long he came to a city. He was seen by the palace guard, who brought the king news of the approach of a rider with the sun on his head. As soon as the prince arrived at the city he was led to see the king, who took the feather from him, and without even a word of thanks, dismissed the young man and set the feather on his wall. From that day forth the king had time only for the feather, all other affairs of the city having to be handled by his advisers.

One day the king started to yearn for more than just the feather, and so he called for the young man who had found the feather to be brought before him. There the young prince was told to go and fetch the whole bird to whom the feather belonged. Failure would result in his execution by beheading. The prince told his troubles to his horse, and the next day the horse led him to a forest that had a white poplar tree growing in its midst. Under the tree, so his horse advised him, was a white marble pool in which a Houri-Pari, a nymph from paradise, came to bathe. The horse told the young man to wait until the maiden had bathed and had donned her golden feathers again before he seized her by the legs.

The prince did as he was instructed, and before long he was riding back to the city with the Houri-Pari for the king. The king took the bird from the prince and summarily dismissed him, and then set the bird in a golden cage, and from that day forth spent every day and every night in the presence of the bird.

Before long the Houri-Pari spoke to the king, saying that she would become the most beautiful maiden in all the world if the king would fetch for her her handmaiden, who was being held prisoner by a red demon somewhere between the Black Sea and the White Sea. (In this case the White Sea was not the Russian *Beloe More*. If not entirely imaginary, the White Sea in Anatolia would have been the Mediterranean Sea, which is *Akdeniz,* "White Sea," in Turkish.) The king agreed and once again sent for the hapless young prince, whom he commanded upon pain of death to bring back the handmaiden.

The following morning the young prince allowed his horse to take him to the shores of the Black Sea. Once there, on the advice of his horse, the young man unsheathed his father's sword and pointed it out across the waters, which immediately divided, leaving him a dry path across. After crossing the sea, the prince quickly came to the home of the red demon, whom he decapitated. He rescued the handmaiden and then rode back to the king. Once again the king did not thank the young prince but simply took the handmaiden and dismissed the young man.

The king presented the Houri-Pari, whose name was Kush-Pari, with the handmaiden and told her to cast off her feathers and become his wife. She refused, saying that if she did, he would surely die. Yet if he would bring her the forty fiery mares that lived by the Red Sea, and if he bathed in their milk, he too would become a Houri-Pari, and they could then be united.

Once again the king sent for the unfortunate prince and sent him on this latest quest under threat of beheading. The prince was once again guided and helped by his horse, which turned out to be one of the forty fiery horses (for although the stories spoke of forty mares, there were in fact only thirty-nine mares, and one stallion). At the edge of the Red Sea the stallion lay down, and before long his mother came to him. The prince

leaped onto the back of the mare and rode her until she quieted and followed his every command. Then the prince led the mare and her thirty-nine offspring to the city of the king. There, under the guidance of his horse, the prince hung the ring his father had given him into the middle of a vat, from a thread tied to his sword, which he laid over the top of the vat. Then he milked each of the thirty-nine mares into the vat.

The prince then undressed, bathed in the milk, redressed, resheathed his sword, and put his father's ring on his finger. Having done so he sent the message to the king that his bath of mares' milk, which would transform him into a Houri-Pari, was ready. The king hurried to the vat and stepped in, and was immediately boiled to a pulp. The young prince then dressed himself as king and took his place.

Kush-Pari knew what had happened and immediately cast off her feathers and ran to the side of the young man who now was king; the couple was married before the next day dawned. That morning, however, the young king remembered his father, and he told his new wife the story of his original quest. She knew of the affliction, for she herself had caused it when her husband's father had failed to take her captive. Together they rode back to the blind king, and there Kush-Pari cured his blindness, and she and the young prince became the new rulers in his stead.

The bird with golden plumage is encountered among myths and legends of a great many peoples around the world, and elements of the legend of the Kush-Pari are strikingly similar to that of the Firebird.

See also: Black Sea; Firebird, The; Houri-Pari; White Sea

References: Orbeli and Taronian 1959–67, vol. 1

KUZ'MA, SAINT
Russia

Russian Orthodox saint who, according to some legends, collaborated with Saint Dem'-

yan in forging the first plow (other versions of this legend name the two saintly smiths as Saints Boris and Gleb). Kuz'ma and Dem'yan, however, had nothing at all to do with smithing; they were doctors who had been martyred. Their connection with the legends surrounding smiths stems simply from the fact that Kuz'ma sounds similar to the Russian word for a smithy, *kuznya*. As a result, in the Russian Orthodox calendar of saints, they became the patrons of smiths and craftsmen. Churches dedicated to them were often to be found in the part of a town in which smiths and craftsmen carried out their business.

The plow reputedly forged by Kuz'ma and Dem'yan was of enormous proportions, and was forged with implements of like size. The two smiths were reported to have used twelve golden hammers, and tongs that weighed almost four hundredweight, or twelve poods (a pood is an old Russian measure roughly equivalent to 36 pounds or 16.38 kilograms). One story, apparently of Ukrainian origin, tells how this plow was first used.

For some reason not told in the story, the people of southern Russia angered God so greatly that he sent a fierce dragon to wreak havoc throughout their land. Every day, in a futile attempt to appease the dragon, a different family was obliged to sacrifice a son. Finally it was the tsar's turn to sacrifice his son; and though many of his loyal subjects offered to send their son in the place of the tsarevich, the dragon would not agree to this. Reluctantly the tsar led his son to the appointed place, where he left him to await his fate. While the boy was waiting, an angel appeared to him and offered him a means of escape. Teaching the tsarevich the Lord's Prayer, the angel told the youth to run as fast as he could, all the time reciting the Lord's Prayer.

For three days and nights the boy ran as fast as his legs would carry him, continually reciting the prayer, for every time he stopped his recitation, he could feel the hot breath of the dragon on his neck. Finally, on the fourth day, almost totally exhausted, he came to the smithy where the saints Kuz'ma and Dem'yan were putting the finishing touches on the first plow that mankind would have. The tsarevich ran straight into the smithy, and the two saints immediately slammed shut the massive iron doors in an effort to protect him.

From outside, the dragon demanded that the two saints relinquish the boy to meet his fate. The saints refused, so the dragon licked the iron doors, his tongue penetrating them on the fourth lick. However, as the dragon's tongue appeared through the doors, the two saints caught hold of it with their red-hot pincers, and thus captive, they harnessed the dragon to the plow and made him plow a deep furrow, the great mounds of earth that he threw up thereafter being known as "dragons' ramparts."

Kuz'ma and Dem'yan, as the magical smiths of legend, were also believed capable of forging nonmaterial objects: Russians, in their wedding songs, would ask Kuz'ma and Dem'yan to forge them a wedding with links so strong that they would last forever. In this way Kuz'ma and Dem'yan came to be regarded as the patron saints of marriage. 1 November was Koz'ma and Dem'yan Day (also known as Matushka Kozma-Demian), an important agricultural feast day. On this day young women would go out to seek their future husbands.

See also: Boris, Saint; Dem'yan, Saint; Dragon; Gleb, Saint; Matushka Kozma-Demian
References: Chicherov 1957

L

LADA

Slav

Also: Liuli

The goddess of beauty, female counterpart of Lado. Lado and Lada are commonly referred to in unison, in the songs sung by women while planting grain or at wedding ceremonies. As a pair, the divine twins Lado and Lada form one aspect of a quadruple fertility deity, the other aspects being Kupalo, who is linked with water; Kostromo-Kostrobunko, linked with grain; and Iarilo, linked with the Sun. Each of these aspects also has a feminine personification—Kupalo's being Kupala, Kostromo-Kostrobunko's Kostroma, and Iarilo's Iarila.

Lada has been tentatively linked with a Latvian goddess, though it also has been suggested that she derived from the Finno-Slavic Mokosh, or the Great Goddess of the northern Letts and Mordvins. Other authorities identify her with Loduna, the Scandinavian goddess of fire, the hearth, and herds. She may, however, have a more southerly origin in the classical Leto, the mother by Zeus of Apollo and Artemis. Lada and Lado are also connected with the twin deities Zizilia and Didilia worshiped by the Poles, who also venerate Lada and Lado—though in this instance she appears connected with the classical Leda, the mother of the twins Castor and Polydeuces. One seventeenth-century chronicler extenuates this connection by naming Lada as the mother of Lel and Polel, both of whom have been directly connected with Castor and Poly-

deuces. Lada, here without Lado, is venerated as the Great Goddess, the parthenogenetic mother of Dido, who is either her son or her consort (or perhaps simply Lado by another name).

An eighteenth-century text seems to confirm that by that time, Lada had assumed an ascendancy over Lado, who was then seen as her son-consort, though here Lado is referred to as Dido or Dida (although the latter name has a feminine ending, Dida is almost always referred to as a male).

See also: Dida; Didilia; Dido; Great Goddess; Iarila; Iarilo; Kostroma; Kostromo (-Kostrobunko); Kupala; Kupalo; Lado; Lel; Mokosh; Polel; Zizilia

References: Afanas'ev 1865–69; Haase 1939; Snegirev 1837–39; Vernadsky 1959; Znayenko 1980

LADO

Slav

The male counterpart of Lada.

LADOGA, LAKE

Russia

Lake Ladoga in northwestern Russia is the largest lake in all of Europe, covering 6,835 square miles (17,703 square kilometers). Ladoga is situated 40 miles (64 kilometers) northeast of St. Petersburg. Along with Lake Onega to its northeast, Lake Ladoga forms part of a canal system that links the Baltic and White Seas. Ownership of Lake Ladoga was divided between the Soviet Union and Finland until 1940, when the Soviet Union took possession of the lake after war against Finland. The lake now belongs to the Russian Federation.

See also: Baltic; Finland; St. Petersburg; White Sea

LAIMA(-DALIA)

Lithuania

The goddess of fate, to whom lime trees were sacred. Her name is cognate with *laim,* "happiness"; she was sometimes referred to as Laima-Dalia (meaning "Happiness-Fate"). Lithuanian in origin, the goddess later gained cult status throughout the Baltic countries. She was believed to control the fate of all life-forms—animal, plant, and human. Some stories refer to three, or even seven, goddesses of fate, though Laima is usually conceived as a single deity. In instances where there are three goddesses of fate, Laima's sisters are named Karta and Dekla. All three jointly controlled the destinies of each and every living thing, from the single blade of grass to humankind. Laima was responsible for choosing the moment of an individual's death and had special responsibility for the lives of women, from conception through birth, marriage, and childbirth—when, perversely, her responsibility came to an end. Laima would favor the chaste and would punish those whom she considered unchaste (or those whom the village gossips deemed so) by pinching or poking them.

See also: Dekla; Karta

LAME
Russia
One of the two servants of Whirlwind. He and his companion, One-Eye, are so called because that is exactly what they were. Endowed with magical powers, they helped Ivan Belyaninovich return home after he killed Whirlwind, and they later helped Elena the Fair prove the treachery of Ivan's brothers Peter Belyaninovich and Vasilii Belyaninovich.

See also: Elena the Fair; Ivan Belyaninovich; One-Eye; Peter (Belyaninovich); Vasilii Belyaninovich; Whirlwind

LAPLAND
General
Lapland is located in the extreme northern part of Europe, above the Arctic Circle. The region is called Lapland because it is the homeland of a people who are known as Lapps. However, the territory is not an inde-

pendent country; it is shared among Norway, Sweden, Finland, and Russia. Lapland covers about 150,000 square miles (388,000 square kilometers) and has no definite boundary to the south, ending approximately at the Arctic Circle.

See also: Finland; Lapps; Russia

LAPPS
General
Though currently the Lapps are very much a minority race—possibly numbering fewer than 20,000—they once occupied the entire territory that is today's Finland. Starting around the first century B.C., the Lapps were driven northward by Finnic invaders from Asia. Their current homeland in the far north is known as Lapland. Having no political definition or precise boundaries, Lapland is situated roughly within the Arctic Circle and belongs to four different countries—Norway, Sweden, Finland, and Russia. The correct name for the Lapp people is *Saami,* though for simplicity's sake the more common term *Lapp* has been used in this book.

See also: Finland; Lapland; Russia; Saami

LATVIA
General
European nation situated on the eastern shore of the Baltic Sea. Latvia was an independent state between 1918 and 1940, when the Soviet Union occupied it and made it one of the fifteen Soviet republics. Latvia regained its independence in 1991.

An ancient people lived in what is now Latvia as early as 7000 or 8000 B.C. They were forced out about the time of Christ by invaders who became the ancestors of today's Latvians. In time, these people established trade with Arabs, Estonians, Lithuanians, Romans, and other groups, and developed their own language and culture. The Vikings raided Latvia during the eighth century, and Russian forces attacked Latvia several times in the tenth century. The Teutonic Knights, an organization of German crusaders, invaded Latvia during the thirteenth century, and war between the two sides followed, lasting until late in the century, when the Latvians surrendered.

For more than 200 years the Knights governed Latvia as part of a larger state called Livonia; but by 1562, most of Latvia had fallen under the control of Poland and Lithuania. Sweden conquered northern Latvia in 1621; Russia took control of this area in 1710, and by 1800, Russia ruled all of Latvia. During the late nineteenth century the Latvians began to organize an independence movement—a movement that became stronger as Russian and German authority steadily declined. On 18 November 1918, just after the end of World War I, Latvia proclaimed itself independent. At first Russia and Germany tried to maintain control, but they eventually recognized Latvia's independence in 1920.

In 1939, shortly before World War II began, the Soviet Union and Germany secretly agreed to divide much of eastern Europe between themselves. The Soviet Union made Latvia sign a treaty that permitted the Soviets to build military bases there, and Soviet troops occupied Latvia in June 1940, while Latvian Communists took over the government. In August 1940, the Soviets made Latvia a republic of the Soviet Union. German forces invaded Latvia in 1941 and occupied the country until 1944, when Soviet troops recaptured it. Soviet rule continued until the breakup of the Soviet Union in 1991, when Latvia regained its independence.

See also: Baltic; Estonia; Lithuania; Livonia; Poland; Russia; Teutonic Knights; Vikings

LAUKPATIS
Lithuania

The patron deity of agriculture, whose name means "Lord of the Fields." He is sometimes wrongly called Lauksargis (the latter is his subordinate).

See also: Lauksargis

LAUKSARGIS
Lithuania

A patron deity of agriculture whose name means "Guardian of the Fields." He was considered subordinate to Laukpatis, whose responsibilities were for all aspects of agriculture. Lauksargis had the specific task of protecting crops and livestock in the fields, hence his name.

See also: Laukpatis

LAWKAPATIM
Poland

One of the three patron deities of the field, the others being Datan and Tawals.

See also: Datan; Tawals

LAY OF IGOR'S CAMPAIGN
Russia

Russia's first national epic, dating from the twelfth century, tells of the attack and defeat of the Riurik princes by the Turkic Polovtsy, or Kumans. This epic reflects the political and social atmosphere of Russia at a time when the general populace was calling for a curbing of the autocratic powers of the rulers, believing that the latter should serve the people and the country, rather than the other way around.

See also: Riurik
References: Mann 1979; Rambaud 1879; Zenkovsky 1963

LAZAR
Serbia

The sole survivor of an attack by invading Turks. All the people of his village in southern Macedonia escaped into a tunnel in the hills—all except one girl. She laughed at the invaders, telling them that the villagers had eluded them, and then she made the mistake of revealing where they were hiding. The Turks lit fires at the entrance to the tunnel and asphyxiated all those inside with the exception of Lazar, who pressed himself into the ground and crawled with such force that his tracks became the bed of a stream that later flowed through the mountain and into the next valley. Lazar founded the village of Lazaropolje at the spot where he crawled from the hillside.

See also: Macedonia

LEL

Russia

One of the twin offspring of Lada, the other being Polel. These twins have been identified with the divine twins Castor and Polydeuces of classical Greece (or Castor and Pollux, as they became known in Rome).

See also: Lada; Polel
References: Afanas'ev 1865–69; Znayenko 1980

LENA, RIVER

Russia

The chief waterway of a large district of eastern Siberia, in Russia. The river rises on the slopes of the Baikal Mountains and flows northeast 2,734 miles (4,400 kilometers) before emptying into the Arctic Ocean through the Laptev Sea. Along its middle course, the Lena flows through a region that is inhabited by the Yakuts, a Turkic people who fish, farm, and raise livestock.

See also: Siberia; Yakuts

LEONTII

Russia

A priest from Rostov and the father of Alesha.

See also: Alesha; Rostov

LESHACHIKHA

Slav

The wife or female counterpart of the Leshii.

See also: Leshii (~y)

LESHII (~Y)

Slav

Also: Ljeschi(e)

A demon-god, the spirit of the forest from which it takes its name, for *les* means "wood" or "forest." A leshii resembled an old man, being extremely wizened, and had skin that usually was tinged with blue because of his

blue blood and as rough as the bark on a tree. However, not much of his skin could be seen because he was covered from head to foot with a long, shaggy coat of hair, almost always green in color. His hair was long and tangled, and he had strange, protruding, pale green eyes. Some representations of the leshii show him (a leshii was almost always male) with horns and cloven hooves. To make recognition easier for mere mortals, the leshii wore his shoes on the wrong feet and cast no shadow.

The leshii had the ability to change his size or shape at will, and to appear or disappear in an instant. His flair for changing size meant that in one moment he could be small enough to hide behind a single blade of grass, but the next be so tall as to tower above the tallest tree in the forest that was his home. The shape-changing ability of the leshii meant that he could instantly become any one of the animals in the forest, especially the wolf or the bear (which enjoyed his special protection)—or even a human.

As the leshii almost never left the forest, only those who entered the forest were likely to encounter him. Since the leshii was the spirit that controlled the forest, people left him votive offerings in the form of eggs and pancakes. Particularly active in the spring, having hibernated or taken a winter holiday with his wife, the Leshachikha, and their children, the leshii returned with wild shrieks to enjoy leading people astray in the thickest parts of his forest home. The leshii could, however, be foiled by a traveler who removed all his clothes and put them on again back to front, with shoes on the wrong feet, thus imitating the leshii's style of dress. Cowherds were even reported to have made pacts with leshiis to prevent their cattle from straying.

One such story tells of a peasant who built his smallholding in a remote and lonely part of the countryside. One night this peasant welcomed a passing traveler, fed him well, and gave him a good bed to sleep on, and the next morning refused the man's offer of payment. The traveler then promised the peasant that from that day forth he would no longer have any trouble with his cattle. They would no longer wander off or be attacked by wild beasts, and no longer would the peasant have to tend them. Instead, all he had to do was to chase them out of the yard every morning, and every evening they would return well fed and give a plentiful supply of milk.

Everything went just as the traveler had said for three years, until one day the peasant could no longer quell his curiosity and followed his cattle out of the yard. After a while, they stopped and started to graze in a lush meadow, where they were watched over by an old crone who leaned heavily on her stick as she dozed, rocking gently from side to side. As the peasant spoke to her, the crone became still and then disappeared. Perplexed, the man went home again; but from that day on the cattle once again needed his attention, for the crone had been the leshii's helper, and the curiosity of the peasant had broken the spell that the traveler, a leshii, had cast.

The leshii's favorite trick seems to have been the abduction of babies who had not been baptized or had been left unattended. Young children who entered the forest to fish or to gather nuts or berries were particularly at risk from the antics of the leshii.

In some regions there were whole tribes of leshiis. Every spring they would run amok through the woods, yelling and screeching with the sheer pleasure of simply being alive. Every autumn, like the leaves on the trees among which they lived, they would die.

See also: Leshachikha
References: Ivanov and Toporov 1965; Pomerantseva 1975

LETTS

General

Indigenous inhabitants of Latvia, closely related to their neighbors the Lithuanians. Their language is Baltic and resembles Lithuanian.

See also: Latvia; Lithuania

LIAR, THE

Armenia

A bored king once proclaimed that he would give the man who could prove himself the most outrageous liar an apple made of gold. Many people came and lied to the king, but he remained unimpressed. Finally a man came to the palace claiming that the king owed him a pot of gold. The king laughed and called him an outrageous liar—whereupon the man said that if that was the case, the king owed him the golden apple. The king realized that the man was trying to trick him and tried to take back his words. The man retorted that if he was not a liar, then the king should pay him the pot of gold he owed. The king knew he had been beaten and handed over the golden apple.

LIKHO, ONE-EYED

Russia

A personification of evil (*likho* is Russian for "evil"). Two good men, one a tailor and the other a blacksmith, once went on a journey to see if they could discover the whereabouts of Evil, which neither had ever encountered. They traveled far and wide. One night they sought shelter with a wizened old crone. She sat them down, and they were immediately transfixed, for the old crone was none other than One-Eyed Likho herself. She cackled and crowed and told the two men that she would eat them.

Likho then prepared her stove, cut the throat of the tailor, cooked him, and ate him, picking his bones clean. When she turned her attention to the blacksmith, he told her his profession and said that he could forge her any item she might require. She asked for a new eye, which the smith consented to make, provided Likho allowed herself to be bound, as he would have to hammer the new eye in and any sudden movement would be disastrous.

Once Likho was securely bound, the smith took a red-hot poker from the fire, and deftly put out Likho's one good eye. Evil twisted and fought until the rope snapped, and the smith found his exit barred. That night Likho drove her sheep into the hut, and the smith was forced to spend an uncomfortable night in the company of Evil and her sheep. The following morning Likho drove her sheep out of the hut, feeling each one as it passed her. The smith took off his sheepskin coat, turned it inside out, and safely crept past Likho; she thought he was simply another of her flock.

Once outside, the smith jeered at Likho and then made his way off through the forest. After a good distance the smith saw a wondrous golden ax sticking out of a tree stump. He felt strangely compelled to take hold of it; but when he did, he found that the ax would not move. Worse than that, his hand had become fixed to the handle, and no matter how hard he pulled he could not free himself. Then the smith heard Likho hurrying through the forest toward her ax, and without a moment's hesitation the smith took a sharp knife from his pocket, cut off his hand, and ran for home as fast as his legs could carry him.

The moral of this post-Christian tale is clear: Although it is relatively easy to find evil, it is much harder to escape evil's clutches; and it is better not to meddle with what one does not understand.

See also: Evil

LION'S SHARE, THE
Armenia

A lion, a wolf, and a fox once formed a team to hunt. At the end of the first day they had killed a ram, a ewe, and a lamb—spoils that the lion told the wolf to divide among them. The wolf gave the ram to the lion, as it was the largest; the lamb to the fox, as it was the smallest; and he took the ewe for himself. The lion roared his disapproval and hit the wolf so hard that one of his eyes fell out, for he knew that the ram would be old and tough, the lamb tasty but very small, and that the best meat would be that of the ewe.

The lion then told the fox to divide the spoils. The fox told the lion that the ram was

for his breakfast, the ewe for his lunch, and the lamb for his dinner. The lion laughed and asked the fox who or what had taught him to give such fair shares. The fox simply replied that it had been the eye of the wolf that had guided him.

One of the fables of Vardan.

See also: Vardan

References: Marr 1894–99

LITHUANIA
General

One of the three Baltic countries (with Latvia and Estonia). The Lithuanian language has retained many features of the Indo-European family of languages and is one of only two Slavic languages surviving today in the Baltic region (Estonian being of Finno-Ugric origin, and more closely related to Finnish and Swedish than to the Slavic languages).

Scholarly opinion is divided as to when the ancient Lithuanian people first occupied the country today known as Lithuania. Some believe they arrived around 2500 B.C.; others, that they migrated to the area sometime around the beginning of the first century A.D. The first reference to the people by name, however, comes much later—in 1009, in a medieval Prussian manuscript known as the *Quedlinburg Chronicle*.

With the rise of the medieval lords in adjacent Prussia and Russia, Lithuania acted as a buffer between Germany to the west and the Mongols and Tatars to the east, constantly being subjected to invasion and attempted conquest over a number of centuries. As a result, a loose confederation of Lithuanian tribes was formed in the early Middle Ages and subsequently became the Kingdom of Lithuania in 1251. In the thirteenth century A.D., when the Teutonic Knights, a German militaristic religious order, were establishing their power, the Lithuanians resisted, and c. 1260 they defeated the order. About a century later a dynasty of grand dukes called the Jagiellons established, through conquest, a Lithuanian empire that reached from the

Baltic to the Black Sea. The Lithuanian Prince Gedimin occupied Belorussia and western Ukraine, and his son Grand Duke Olgierd added the territory between Ukraine and the Black Sea. Jagiello, the son of Olgierd, succeeded his father in 1377. In 1386 he married Jadwiga, queen of Poland, and after accepting Christianity, he was crowned Wladyslaw II Jagiello, king of Poland.

Jagiello's cousin Witold revolted against him in 1390 and forced Jagiello to recognize him as vice regent two years later. Witold made the grand duchy into a prestigious state, and in 1401 Jagiello made him a duke. Together the reconciled cousins decisively defeated the Teutonic Knights in 1410. In 1447, under Jagiello's son Casimir IV, Lithuania and Poland formed an alliance. With the accession of Casimir's son Alexander I in 1501, the countries had a single, common ruler, and in 1569 they agreed to a common legislature and an elective king. Although the political union of Poland and Lithuania was induced by the threat of Russian conquest, it actually provided little protection. Poland was partitioned in 1772, 1793, and 1795, and Lithuania became a part of Russia, except for a small section that was awarded to Prussia. Unhappy with tsarist rule, Lithuanians staged large-scale nationalist insurrections in 1812, 1831, 1863, and 1905.

During World War I the German army occupied Lithuania, but at the end of the war nationalists established the country's independence. Lithuania's independence was recognized by the Treaty of Versailles in 1919, and in August 1922 the Lithuanian constituent assembly, which had been in session since May 1920, approved a constitution that proclaimed the country a democratic republic.

With the outbreak of World War II and the partition of Poland by Germany and the USSR, the Lithuanian and Soviet governments concluded a mutual-assistance treaty in October 1939. A pro-Soviet government assumed power in Lithuania the following June and shortly afterward began a campaign for Lithuania's inclusion in the USSR. In July 1940 the new parliament unanimously approved a resolution requesting incorporation of Lithuania in the USSR. Soviet forces withdrew following the German invasion of Russia, whereupon the Germans pillaged Lithuanian resources, and as a national resistance movement developed, killed more than 200,000 people. In summer 1944 the Soviets reoccupied Lithuania and reestablished it as a Soviet republic, and Lithuania settled into comparative calm.

Multiparty elections were held in February 1990 and independence was declared the following month. The USSR used economic, political, and military pressure to keep Lithuania within the union as long as it could; but after the Soviet state collapsed in August 1991, the central government granted independence to Lithuania, Estonia, and Latvia on September 6, and all three Baltic republics were admitted to the United Nations later that month.

See also: Baltic; Belarus'; Black Sea; Estonia; Latvia; Mongols; Poland; Prussia; Tatars; Teutonic Knights; Ukraine

LITO
Bohemia

The personification and spirit of summer, ritually carried into a village every year in the form of a newly cut sapling with a good covering of leaves. The tree was decorated with ribbon of many colors, and a female doll was hung among its branches.

LITTLE BEAR
General

The common name for the constellation Ursa Minor.

See also: Ursa Minor

LIULI
Slav

Related to Lada, the goddess called Liuli is the mistress of growth—a fertility aspect far beyond Lada's role as the goddess of beauty. Liuli could be called upon by reluctant brides in the hope that she would intervene and prevent an unhappy union; or if she could not prevent the ceremony from taking place, at least to ensure that the marriage would be happy.

See also: Lada
References: Shein 1900; Zemtsovskii 1970

LIVONIA
General
Livonia was a region of Europe on the eastern coast of the Baltic Sea that covered most of present-day Latvia and Estonia. Conquered in the early part of the thirteenth century and converted to Christianity by the Livonian Knights, a crusading order, Livonia remained independent until 1583 when it was divided between Poland and Sweden. In 1710 it was occupied by Russia, and in 1721, ceded to Peter the Great. The Latvian portion of Livonia was inhabited by people who spoke a Slavic language, and the Estonian part by people who spoke a Finnic language called Livonian. Livonian is still spoken by a few inhabitants of the region.

See also: Baltic; Estonia; Finno-Ugric; Latvia; Poland

LJESCHIE
Slav
Alternative name for the leshii.

LOMPSALO
Lapp
A sorcerer who once owned a sejda that enabled him to catch huge quantities of fish. On the opposite bank of the river lived another sorcerer who stole Lompsalo's sejda and thus obtained the power of the sejda and the ability to catch large quantities of fish. Lompsalo countered the theft by procuring a more powerful sejda, so once more the fish returned to his side of the river—until his rival destroyed the new sejda.

See also: Sejda

LONZARIC, PETAR
Croatia
See Petar Lonzaric.

LOQMÂN THE WISE
Armenia
Also: Luqmân the Wise
Loqmân, or Luqmân, the Wise is a legendary physician and sage celebrated throughout the Middle East, where he is said to be a son of Job's sister or aunt and a disciple of David; by others a judge in Israel; and by others an emancipated Ethiopian slave. In Armenia Loqmân the Wise was the name given to Purto.

See also: Purto

LUKA
Russia
One of two boyar brothers who passed the test set by Vasilii Buslayevich to see if they were worthy of becoming members of his *druzhina*. His brother was Moisei. Both passed the test, and with twenty-seven others, joined Vasilii Buslayevich.

See also: Moisei; Vasilii Buslayevich

LUKA ZINOVIEV
Russia
One of the two governors of the city of Novgorod, the other being Foma Nazariev. The pair accepted the wager of thirty thousand rubles made by Sadko when he boasted that he had amassed fortune enough to buy everything that was for sale in the city. Sadko ultimately lost the bet because as soon as he had bought something, replacement goods would be brought in.

See also: Foma Nazariev; Novgorod; Sadko

LULIZAR
Armenia
"Pearly face," a talking mare that belonged to an unnamed king. This king once lost his daughter. The princess was found wandering alone in the forest by an old woman and her daughter, who took her in. The king announced that he would grant any wish to whoever returned his daughter. The old woman learned of the proclamation and sent word to the king that the princess was safe and with her in the forest.

Immediately the king sent one of his ministers, who rode Lulizar. The old woman embraced the princess and sent her on her way, the old woman's daughter accompanying the princess and the minister in the guise of a boy. En route Lulizar spoke to the old woman's daughter, advising her to ask no reward other than ownership of Lulizar. This she did after the king had been reunited with his daughter. The king not only consented to the gift of Lulizar but also granted the youth he saw before him his daughter's hand in marriage.

The wedding feast lasted seven days and seven nights; and on the last night, the princess realized that her new husband was a woman, and ran to tell her mother, the queen. Alarmed at the news, the queen told the king. The royal parents were at a loss. The king finally decided that they should send their "son-in-law" on a mission from which there would be no return.

The king sent for his "son-in-law" and told him to fetch the brother of Lulizar. In the stables the "boy" told Lulizar of his mission; but all Lulizar would say was that there was nothing to worry about, for with her to help, they would accomplish the quest with ease. Thus they rode out from the palace, found Lulizar's brother, captured him, and brought him back to the palace, where they presented him to the king. The king consulted his chamberlain about what to do next. The chamberlain suggested that the "boy" should be sent to the house of the demons, to collect the seven years' back taxes they owed.

The king summoned his "son-in-law" and dispatched him again on a mission from which there was sure to be no return. Once again Lulizar brought the quest to a satisfactory conclusion by decimating the marble quarry of the demons, who rushed out to see what all the commotion was; and while they were gone, the "boy" entered the house and took the back taxes. They then rode back to the palace and gave the king the money he was owed. Again the king consulted his

chamberlain, and this time it was suggested that the "boy" should reclaim the rosary of the king's grandfather that had fallen into the hands of a terrible she-devil.

The king sent his "son-in-law," again riding Lulizar, to the castle of the demoness. There Lulizar told her that she should catch the rosary before it fell into the she-devil's hand and then leap into the ravine that ran past the castle, and Lulizar would catch her on her back. The "boy" did as instructed; but the noise of her escape woke the she-devil, who saw the fleeing figure of Lulizar and her rider. The she-devil knew that she could never catch Lulizar, so instead she shouted a curse after them, saying that if the rider be a man, then he should become a woman, and if the rider be a woman, then she should become a man. Thus when Lulizar returned to the palace, all was well, for the princess found that her husband was now indeed a young man; and she implored her father to stop sending him on perilous missions.

Thus the princess and her husband were reconciled, and the king gave them dominion of their own, and Lulizar lived in their stables and advised them whenever the need arose.

References: Orbeli and Taronian 1959–67, vol. 1

LUQMÂN THE WISE
Armenia
Variant of Loqmân the Wise.

LUSAGHEN
Armenia
"Radiant," a water sprite, the daughter of the King of the Waters. A young man who was down on his luck and who remains nameless in the legends once sat down beside the well in which Lusaghen and her parents lived. Lusaghen immediately fell in love with the young man. She told him to return to his parents so that his mother might come and ask her father, the King of the Waters, for her hand in marriage, as was the custom.

A fountain at Petrodvorets in St. Petersburg features a gilded statue of the water sprite Lusaghen. (C. Arnesen/Allstock/PNI)

The young man could not believe his ears. He asked who had spoken to him and why he could not see them. Lusaghen told the young man her name but said she could not show herself—for reasons that he would later understand—but that if he returned home he would believe that she spoke the truth, for his home would have walls and a roof of gold and silver, and the table would be laid with a banquet fit for a king.

The young man did as he was asked, and he found that his home had indeed been magically transformed. As for the banquet, he had never beheld such fine food and such an elegant setting in all his life. Believing, therefore, that Lusaghen had been telling him the truth, the young man took his mother to the well to ask for the hand of Lusaghen in marriage. At the well the young man's mother looked into the waters and called out to the King of the Waters, who immediately rose from the water. A tall, imposing man with a crown of gold and wearing robes of deepest purple, the King of the Waters had eyes as green as grass and a beard of flowing green hair, and carried a staff made of mother-of-pearl.

The King of the Waters listened to the young man's proposal, and then he told the youth's mother that he would permit the marriage on one condition. Some time earlier, the King of the Forest, the sworn enemy of the King of the Waters, had stolen all Lusaghen's clothes in a chest. Only if the young man could recover the stolen items would the King of the Waters give his consent, as without her clothes Lusaghen could never show herself to anyone.

The mother told her son the condition, and he set off into the forest without a moment's delay on a horse supplied by his prospective father-in-law. This horse was the most magnificent animal anyone in the whole of Armenia had ever beheld, with a saddle of mother-of-pearl, a bridle of silver, golden horseshoes, and a wonderful sword and scabbard. His mother bade him mount and then told him that the King of the Forest would try everything to make him look behind him. On no account should he turn around, as if he once did so, he would be turned into a tree in the great forest.

Thus armed and warned, the young man rode into the forest and began to search for the chest containing Lusaghen's clothes. Before long, having divined the purpose of the youth's journey to the forest, the King of the Forest commanded his trees to attack. The young man unsheathed his sword and laid into the trees, the steel blade slashing left and right until he managed to behead the King of the Forest himself. As the king died the forest fell quiet, and it was an easy task for the youth to recover the chest containing Lusaghen's apparel.

Returning to the well, where his mother was waiting, the young man presented the King of the Waters with the chest of clothing. With profuse gratitude, the king thanked him and immediately gave his blessing to the marriage of Lusaghen and the youth. Lusaghen then dressed and rose from the well, and by nightfall she and the gallant youth were married.

See also: King of the Forest; King of the Waters
References: Orbeli and Taronian 1959–67, vol. 10

LYTUVONIS
Lithuania
The Lithuanian god of rain.

MAAN-ENO

Estonia

The consort of the supreme being Ukko, and joint creator of man. She had specific responsibility for the success of the harvest and the fertility of women.

See also: Ukko

MACEDONIA

General

A region on the Balkan Peninsula of southeastern Europe that includes the territory of today's Republic of Macedonia (formerly a part of Yugoslavia), plus parts of northern Greece and southwestern

Coin of Philip II, king of Macedonia (Bibliothèque Nationale, Paris, France; Giraudon/Art Resource, NY)

Bulgaria. The Republic of Macedonia has an area of 9,928 square miles (25,713 square kilometers). Greek Macedonia covers 13,206 square miles (34,203 square kilometers), and Bulgarian Macedonia 2,502 square miles (6,480 square kilometers). The kingdom of Macedonia was powerful in ancient times, .when the Macedonian ruler Alexander the Great conquered much of Asia and spread Macedonian and Greek culture throughout his empire.

The earliest known settlements in Macedonia were villages established about 6200 B.C. A number of different peoples settled in the region over the next several thousand years. The people living there eventually came to be known as Macedones, and the region as Macedonia. The name *Macedones* comes from the Greek word *makednon,* meaning "high"—a reference to the group's mountainous homeland.

The earliest known rulers of the Macedonians were members of the Argead dynasty, founded by King Perdiccas I about 650 B.C. During the sixth and fifth centuries B.C., the Argeads expanded Macedonian rule into nearby regions. King Philip II continued this expansion, and by 338 B.C., he controlled all of Greece. Philip was assassinated in 336, and his son Alexander became king (he subsequently became known as Alexander the Great). Alexander died in 323 B.C., without leaving a strong successor.

Macedonia became a Roman province c. 140 B.C. and a part of the Byzantine Empire in A.D. 395. In the sixth century, Slavs from eastern Europe raided and settled in Macedonian towns, and in the late ninth century, Bulgars from central Asia conquered Macedonia. In 1018, the Byzantine Empire regained control and ruled the region until it became part of Serbia in the early fourteenth century. However, in 1371, the Ottoman Empire again conquered the region, after which it remained part of the Ottoman Empire for more than 500 years.

By the late nineteenth century the Ottoman Empire had begun to collapse. Bulgaria controlled Macedonia for a brief period in 1878, before most of the region was returned to Ottoman rule. At the end of the Second Balkan War (1913), Macedonia was divided among Serbia, Greece, and Bulgaria. Serbian Macedonia became the Yugoslav republic of Macedonia in 1946 and an independent country in 1991.

See also: Alexander the Great; Bulgaria; Byzantine Empire; Serbia

MADER AKKA
Finno-Ugric—Lapp

The wife of Mader Atcha, she was responsible for the creation of the body of man, whereas her husband created the soul.

See also: Mader Atcha

MADER ATCHA
Finno-Ugric—Lapp

The divine creator, husband of Mader Akka. He created the soul, the life force of man, whereas his wife created the body. If the child to be born was a boy, then Mader Atcha sent it to his daughter Uks Akka for completion and placement in a human woman; if it was a girl, he sent it to another daughter, Sar Akka, for the same purpose.

See also: Mader Akka; Sar Akka; Uks Akka

MAGYARS
General

The Magyars are the largest single ethnic grouping in Hungary. Of mixed Ugric and Turkic origin, the Magyars arrived in Hungary from western Siberia toward the end of the ninth century. They are generally regarded as a Finno-Ugric–speaking people due to their place of origin, though their language today more closely resembles a Turkic language. Hungary was over-

run by Turkish invaders during the sixteenth century and remained a Turkish kingdom until the end of the seventeenth century, when the Turks were driven out by the Habsburgs and Hungary came under Austrian rule.

Magyar, the native tongue of Hungary, is still spoken in isolated parts of Czechoslovakia, Yugoslavia, Romania, and Moldova. The Magyar kingdom was first established in the late ninth century, when the ten Magyar tribes overran the country—until then inhabited by Celts and Slavs—under a chief named Arpád. Like most of the region, Hungary has had a very turbulent history that unfortunately has nearly erased the ancient customs and beliefs of the Siberian Magyar people.

See also: Czechoslovakia; Finno-Ugric; Hungary; Moldova; Romania; Siberia

MAIN
Siberia—Evenk

A hero who returned light to the world after it was stolen by a mighty elk that lived in the upper world. The theft plunged mankind, which lived in the middle world, into darkness. Main put on a pair of winged skis and traveled to the upper world, where he shot the elk with an arrow, released the sun, and returned light to the middle world. Main himself did not return to the middle world because every day the elk returns to life and steals the sun, and every night Main has to kill it again to ensure that daylight will return to mankind in the morning.

MAJAHALDAS
Slav

One of the various alternate names for the domovoi.

See also: Domovoi

MAJAS KUNGS
Latvia

God of the home, the Latvian version of the Lithuanian Zemepatis.

See also: Zemepatis

MAJASGARS

Slav

One of the various alternate names for the domovoi.

See also: Domovoi

MAKAR'EVSKAIA

Russia

Religious icon of the Virgin Mary found near a pagan sacred spring in 1442. Between the eleventh and fifteenth centuries many such icons "miraculously" appeared. It has now been generally accepted that the Christian clergy placed the icons at various sites where they could be "found," thus indicating the potency of the Christian faith and particularly of the Virgin Mary. When the icons appeared at pagan sacred sites, such as springs or groves, the people understood them as

This fourteenth-century religious icon, "The Virgin of Tlog," is one of many such as the Makar'evskaia that appeared between the eleventh and fifteenth centuries. It is now on display in a Russian Orthodox church. (Sovfoto/Eastfoto/PNI)

signs that the pagan gods had accepted the inevitability of Christianity. The credulous were thus more readily converted than they might have been by verbal persuasion alone.

References: Matorin 1931

MAKOSH

Finno-Slavic

Simple variant of Mokosh.

MAL, PRINCE

Russia

The peaceful leader of the Derevliane, he courted the widowed Olga in an attempt to marry her and thus to acquire the Kievan kingdom. What happened then is related in a folktale known as *Olga's Revenge*.

Upon hearing the suit of Prince Mal, Olga sends messengers to the Derevliane asking them to send royal envoys to her so that they might discuss a possible marriage alliance. When those envoys arrive, however, Olga has them immediately thrown into a deep trench and buried alive. Next Olga sends for further envoys to visit her, inviting them to a great feast at which the proposed alliance would be discussed. When these envoys arrive, Olga invites them to refresh themselves in the bathhouse. Then she has her men set fire to the bathhouse with her guests inside.

Now Olga turns her thoughts against Prince Mal and the Derevliane. She and her entourage travel to the grave of Igor, her husband, which happens to lie within the realm of the Derevliane. There she invites the Derevliane to a feast in honor of Igor, and when all her guests are drunk, her men hack them to pieces. She assumes command of the army of the Derevliane and demands three pigeons and three sparrows as tribute from every household. When these have been delivered, she fixes firebrands to their claws and sets them free so that they might fly back to their homes and burn the homes of the Derevliane. Olga proceeds to vanquish Prince Mal and to assume rule over the lands of the Derevliane.

See also: Derevliane; Igor; Kiev; Olga
References: Cross and Sherbowitz-Wetzor
1953

MARENA

Russia

"Winter" or "Death," the name given to the tree used in the ceremonies of Kupalo.

See also: Kupalo

MARFA VSESLAV'EVNA

Russia

The mother of Volkh Vseslav'evich. Volkh was conceived when Marfa stepped on a serpent, which wound itself around her and impregnated her. Born in Kiev, he became a great wizard.

See also: Kiev; Volkh Vseslav'evich

MARFIDA

Siberia—Tungus

The wife of Ivan the Mare's Son. One of three sisters with whom she used to fly, wearing heron skins, to decorate the arrows of Ivan the Mare's Son and his two "adopted" brothers, Ivan the Moon's Son and Ivan the Sun's Son. When Ivan the Mare's Son hid their heron skins, she swore to marry him. Her sisters married the other two Ivans.

All was well until a serpent started to visit their home during the day and suck their blood. All three Ivans were killed during a battle with the serpent, who carried Marfida and her sisters off to its underworld lair. Ivan the Mare's Son was restored to life by his mother along with his two brothers. Lowered into the underworld, Ivan the Mare's Son killed the serpent and rescued the three maidens. However, Ivan the Moon's Son and Ivan the Sun's Son left Ivan the Mare's Son in the underworld and made off with all three women. Ivan the Mare's Son was restored to life once more and rescued from the underworld by his mother. He killed his false brothers, and having made himself wings from feathers he had plucked from the heron skins he had hidden earlier,

he flew away with Marfida and her sisters to their homeland.

See also: Ivan the Mare's Son; Ivan the Moon's Son; Ivan the Sun's Son; Underworld, The

MARFUSHA

Russia

The eldest daughter of an aging peasant, stepdaughter to his second wife, and stepsister to the couple's two younger daughters. Although she was her father's favorite, Marfusha was hated by her stepmother, who called her lazy and idle and made her do all the household chores, though her own two daughters did nothing from morning to night. Finally the stepmother decided that Marfusha should marry. One winter's morning she made the girl carry all her belongings out to the sleigh and told her browbeaten husband to take the girl out into the forest and leave her to her future husband—the husband she had in mind being Morozko, the frost demon.

Saddened by the thought of what would become of his daughter, the man obeyed his wife and left Marfusha in the middle of the forest. Growing colder by the minute, Marfusha heard Morozko approaching. As he arrived he asked her three times if she was warm enough, and each time, although frozen half to death, she replied that she was quite warm. Finally Morozko took pity on the girl, wrapped her in warm furs, and gave her wondrous gifts.

The following morning Marfusha's father reappeared, certain that he would find her frozen. To his delight, he instead conveyed the still living and wondrously clothed Marfusha back to the house. The stepmother was horrified that her plan had backfired; but seeing the finery that Morozko had bestowed on Marfusha, she insisted that her own daughters must now be left in exactly the same place.

This they were; but when Morozko came to them, they both bitterly complained about the cold, and so he froze them to death. Of these two girls only the name of the eldest is known—Parakha. When the father brought their bodies home, his wife berated him for killing her daughters; but the man could no longer stand her scolding, and he finally made her realize that it was all her fault. From that day forth, his wife treated Marfusha lovingly and did all the work the unfortunate girl had been made to do before.

Marfusha finally married the son of a neighbor and lived happily for many years on the gifts Morozko had given her, which became her dowry.

See also: Morozko; Parakha

MARIA

Ukraine

The shape-changing daughter of the Sea King. She is known in Russia as Vasilissa the Wise and appears in a story that is basically the same as that of Vasilissa, though the way her husband reclaims her is markedly different.

An unnamed tsar had three sons who all came of age and asked their father, as was the custom, for his permission to seek wives. He agreed, saying that the sons should each fire a single arrow, and where that arrow landed they should seek their wife. The eldest son went first. His arrow fell into the courtyard of a neighboring ruler. The ruler's daughter picked up the arrow and agreed to the young prince's proposal.

The second son went next. His arrow fell into the courtyard of a rich merchant, where that merchant's daughter found it and picked it up. Thus the second prince became betrothed. The youngest son, whose name was Ivan the Young, went next. His arrow flew through the clouds, so no one saw where it landed, and Ivan had to set out to look for it. For three days Ivan looked for his arrow without any success. He was about to head for home when he passed through a swamp, and there, sitting on a lily pad, he saw a large green frog holding his arrow. The frog spoke to Ivan saying that she would return the arrow only if he agreed to marry her. Ivan was horrified and hurried back to his father, who told him that although his arrow had been retrieved by a frog, Ivan was honor-bound to marry her.

All three brothers were married at the same service followed by a banquet at which the beauty of the two human wives was praised and the frog princess was made the butt of many cruel jokes. Ivan the Young and his new bride left the banquet early to the sounds of hilarity and hurried to their new home.

Some time later the tsar decided to put his three daughters-in-law through a series of tests to discover which was the best. The first test was to embroider a *rushnik* (a towel—pl. *rushniki*). The two human wives set to work with needle and thread, while the frog princess told Ivan to sleep soundly and not worry about the fact that his wife was a frog. The following morning Ivan awoke to see the *rushnik* his wife had embroidered with the help of the animals of the forest, and knew that she was no ordinary frog. The *rushnik* was the finest anyone had ever seen, and Ivan's wife was easily adjudged the best seamstress of the three wives.

The tsar then decided to see which of his three daughters-in-law was the best baker. He told his three sons to tell their wives to bake him a loaf of bread. Convinced that the wife of Ivan the Young had had magical assistance in completing the first test, the two human wives watched through the kitchen window this time. They saw the frog open the door and step outside to call the animals of the forest to her assistance. However, as she stepped outside, the frog princess caught the aroma of the two women's perfume; and so she mixed flour, water, and soot together and placed the mixture in the oven. Certain that they had her secret, the two human wives went home and copied what they had seen. Meanwhile the frog princess had thrown away the foul mixture and with the help of her forest friends, had produced the most exquisite loaf of bread any had ever seen.

Thus, while the two human wives were cleaning out their ovens and starting over again, Ivan was presenting the loaf to his father, who again judged in favor of Ivan's unusual wife. When the two human brides produced their best results, the tsar immediately sent the bread to his swineherd to be fed to the pigs, but even they would not eat it.

Finally the tsar decreed that he must find out which of his daughters-in-law was the best dancer, and he announced that a banquet and grand ball would be held in seven days. Now the two human wives felt certain that they would get the better of Ivan's wife, as they saw no way on earth that a frog could do more than hop, let alone dance. However, Ivan's wife told him that on the night of the ball, he was to go alone and tell his father that his wife would arrive late. Then, she told him, they would hear three loud claps of thunder. On the third he was to leave the ball and escort her inside. Ivan did as he was instructed, and after enduring almost two hours of cruel jokes, he left the hall on hearing the third clap of thunder.

Outside he stopped dead in his tracks. At the foot of the steps sat a magnificent carriage from which the most beautiful woman was stepping down. He hurried down the steps to her. She told him that she was his wife, the Princess Maria, the daughter of the Sea King. As Ivan the Young led her into the hall and introduced her to his father, all eyes fell on Maria, and the hearts of all the men present ached with jealousy.

Ivan, however, knew that his wife had taken off her frog skin. Making some excuse, he hurried home, found the skin, and burned it, because he thought that if the skin were gone when his wife returned, she would not be able to become a frog again and would always be beautiful. However, when Maria returned from the ball and found her frog skin burned, she told Ivan that she had been placed under a spell by her father, and if Ivan had waited only a little while longer, the spell would have been broken. Now he would have her only until daybreak; and if he ever wanted to find her again he would have to

travel to the Thrice-Ten Kingdom and enlist the help of Baba-Yaga, her aunt.

As the sun rose, a dark cloud gathered around the home of Ivan and Maria. Maria was suddenly transformed into a cuckoo and flew away. Ivan the Young pined for his beautiful wife, unable to either eat or sleep. At length he decided to go in search of his beloved. After almost a year's travel, Ivan came to the Thrice-Ten Kingdom and the forest in which Baba-Yaga lived. Fighting his way through the thick undergrowth, Ivan came to a clearing as the sun began to set; and there, on four chicken's legs, stood Baba-Yaga's little house. Entering the house, he found the witch asleep on her stove, woke her, and told her the purpose of his visit.

Maria had already told her to expect him, and she had slept a whole year on the stove for fear of missing him. Ivan stayed the night with Baba-Yaga, and in the morning she gave him a ball of thread with instructions to follow it wherever it went and to stop whenever it stopped. Ivan thanked Baba-Yaga and set off in pursuit of the ball of thread. At length the thread came to rest beside the sea. Ivan settled down to rest in a thicket and soon fell asleep. A bit later he was awakened by the rustling of feathers. Sitting up, he saw thirty swans land on the beach, discard their feathers, and start to bathe in the sea. Ivan saw that his wife was among them, and when their backs were turned, he hurried out of his hiding place and hid Maria's feathers.

When the maidens had finished bathing, they changed back into their feathers and flew away, leaving only Maria standing on the beach. Ivan made himself known to his wife, who embraced him and told him that he must come to the undersea kingdom of her father that night, and when the Sea King asked him what he wanted, he should say that he simply wanted to see what the bottom of the ocean looked like.

Thus, as the sun sank below the horizon, Ivan the Young walked into the sea and continued walking until he came to the palace of the Sea King. There, when the Sea King asked Ivan what he wanted, Ivan replied as he had been instructed, and the Sea King invited Ivan to stay. In his room in the palace, Ivan was visited by Maria, who told him that the next morning her father would offer Ivan the choice of thirty black fillies, each of which would be identical, and she would be the one that tapped one hoof.

The following morning the Sea King led Ivan into a paddock in which thirty black fillies were lined up. The Sea King told Ivan to choose one as a gift. Ivan walked around the fillies, but not one of them moved. He walked around them a second time, and again they all remained motionless. Ivan walked around them a third time, and this time he noticed an almost imperceptible movement of a hoof, and he immediately indicated his choice.

That night Maria came back to Ivan and told him that her father would again give Ivan a choice, this time of thirty white doves, twenty-nine of which would be her sisters and the thirtieth herself. All would look identical, but she would be the one that turned its head to the left.

Just as she had said, the Sea King led Ivan the Young to a dovecote and gave the prince the choice of thirty beautiful birds. Ivan walked around the dovecote once, but not one bird stirred. He walked around a second time, and they all remained motionless. Ivan then walked around the dovecote a third time, and this time one bird moved its beak a fraction to the left, and Ivan immediately made his selection.

Yet again Maria visited Ivan in the middle of the night and told her husband that the Sea King would give him the choice of thirty maidens, each the image of herself, and that she would be the one upon which a fly alighted. Thus it was that Ivan was given his choice the following morning, and the third time he walked around the thirty identical maidens, he saw the small fly and immediately chose the real Maria, claiming her as his wife.

As Ivan the Young spoke, the Sea King scowled and grew angry, banging his fists on his throne. As his anger grew, the seas began to boil. Maria took Ivan by the hand, and the pair fled along the seabed and upward until they fell exhausted on the beach. Behind them the storm raged, but they had escaped the fury of the Sea King and were free to return to their home in Ivan's kingdom.

See also: Baba-Yaga (-Jaga, -Iaga); Ivan the Young; Sea King; Sea Tsar; Thrice-Ten Kingdom, The; Vasilis(s)a the Wise

MARIA MORENA
Russia

The bride of an unnamed youth. When Maria Morena is taken prisoner by an unnamed captor, her husband is told that he must travel to Baba-Yaga's home to secure a horse that will help him release his bride. When the young man arrives at the witch's home, he is startled by the bone fence that surrounds it. On closer inspection, however, he sees that one spike on the fence has no skull on top. As he examines the fence more closely, he is confronted by Baba-Yaga, who informs him that the last picket has been reserved for his skull. However, he can escape death and obtain what he came for if he completes a simple task—controlling the witch's forty mare-daughters for twenty-four hours. Needless to say, the hero of this story completes the task, receives a supernaturally empowered steed from the witch, and succeeds in his quest to free his bride.

See also: Baba-Yaga, (-Jaga, -Iaga)
References: Afanas'ev 1957

MARINKA
Russia

A powerful sorceress who assumed the guise of Princess Evpraksiya in Kiev, where she came to the attention of Dobrynya Nikitich. Although he had been warned by his mother that she was a powerful witch, Dobrynya took no notice of the warning, and he soon fell under Marinka's spell. Dobrynya returned to his mother to ask her permission to marry, but his mother withheld her blessing. Dobrynya nevertheless married Marinka and was soon transformed by her sorcery into a golden bull.

This magical transformation triggered a great battle between Marinka and Dobrynya's mother—a battle not fought with conventional weapons but rather with magic. Dobrynya's mother finally overcame Marinka and released her son from the spell. According to some sources, Dobrynya then tore Marinka in two.

See also: Dobrynya Nikitich; Evpraksiya (~ia), Princess; Kiev

References: Evgen'eva and Putilov 1977; Gil'ferding 1949

MARKO, PRINCE
Serbia

A historical figure who became a legendary hero of the Serbs. A man of enormous strength (the mace he wielded in battle weighed more than 180 pounds) and cunning, Marko had an inexhaustible capacity for alcohol. He was chivalrous, fearless, and passionate, though he was also capable of the most ruthless brutality, even to women. Marko was in league with the supernatural mountain nymphs, the *vile,* and owned a horse named Sarac that was the fastest in the world and had the power of speech. Sarac, like his master, had a considerable liking for alcohol and Marko often shared his wine with the horse.

Marko is traditionally depicted as a very large man, with very dark, almost black eyes and a black mustache as large as a six-month-old lamb. He wears a *kalpak,* a fur hat, and a cloak made of wolf-skins. His spear is slung across his back, and a damascened sword hangs from his belt. From Sarac's saddle hangs Marko's huge mace and a large wineskin.

In poetry and popular tradition Marko was identified with the resistance against the invading Turks. He was the exemplar of heroic valor and the embodiment of the spirit of true independence. In historical fact Marko became, like many other Serbs, a vassal of the Turkish invaders, fighting for the Sultan against the Christians at the Battle of Rovine in Romania in 1394. Popular legend says that before that battle he prayed to God to give the Christians the victory, even if that meant he would lose his life.

Legend tells of his death in this manner. One morning he was riding Sarac along a road when the normally surefooted horse stumbled and wept, omens that Marko immediately recognized as evil. Instantly a *vila* appeared and told him that because none could kill Marko and none should own Sarac but Marko, the time had come for both horse and rider to die.

Marko recognized this as a message from God. He had attained the age of 300, and Sarac was 160; they accepted that their time had come. Marko killed Sarac and gave his trusted friend an elaborate burial. He then broke his sword and spear and threw his mace over the mountains and far out to sea before lying down to die.

A continuation of this legend says that a priest found his body and took it to Mount Athos for burial. A more popular belief says that Marko never died but instead, like King Arthur, sleeps in a cave in the mountains, to rise again in a time of great need. One Bulgar variant embroiders this idea, saying that Marko sleeps in the cave with his beard wound several times around him.

See also: Arthur, King; Athos, Mount; Romania; Sarac; Vila

MARTHA (~FA)
Russia

The sister of Mary in the biblical story.

MARTIROS
Armenia

A young merchant from Yerevan who had promised his father as the old man lay dying that he would never trade in Aleppo. However, finding that he could not get a fair price for his wares and hearing that the people of Aleppo paid exorbitant prices, especially for boxwood, he asked for his mother's blessings, bought forty bales of boxwood, and set off toward Aleppo. Late in the evening and still some distance from Aleppo, Martiros stopped at a tavern for the night.

After the merchant went to sleep, a thief stole one of the bales of boxwood, piled half of it in the fireplace, and liberally spread the rest around the tavern. When the merchant came down to eat, the thief asked the merchant what he was traveling to Aleppo to sell. When Martiros said that it was boxwood, the thief pointed to the wood lying all around them and offered Martiros seven pots of gold for the wood, which was so common there that the people used it as firewood.

Martiros was not to be put off, realizing that if he sold the boxwood without actually traveling to Aleppo, he would not be able to tell his mother what he had seen there. Thus Martiros entered the city the following day and was told that boxwood was so scarce there that it could bring a king's ransom. Hearing this, Martiros told an old shopkeeper what had happened to him at the inn. The shopkeeper advised him to ask the cook at the inn for help. Martiros did this and was told to listen at his wall that night, for the room next to his was occupied by three thieves.

Martiros did as he was advised and learned that he could only get out of his predicament if he demanded a really unusual payment for the boxwood. The following morning the merchant offered to sell his bales of boxwood for seven pots of fleas—a price that the thieves had no ability to pay. Thus they decided to deceive Martiros a different way, so they hired a man to learn all he could about the young merchant. When the one-eyed thief met Martiros as he walked through the streets of Aleppo, he was able to inquire after Martiros's mother and neighbors, and to speak of many other subjects that only Martiros himself could possibly have known.

When Martiros asked the thief how he came to know these things, the thief told Martiros that he had once lived with the young merchant and his family, and that when Martiros had lost an eye, he had gladly given him one of his. Now that he was old he needed it back. Martiros was astonished. Thinking quickly, he suggested that they go to the local magistrate the following morning and have him decide. That night Martiros again listened at his wall, and when they saw the magistrate the next day he told the official that he would give up his eye if it weighed the same as the one-eyed thief's other eye.

The thief fled from the court, realizing that the only way this could be accomplished was if they took out his one good eye. He returned to his two thieving friends, and when they heard what had happened, they all fled the area. Martiros took his boxwood into Aleppo and sold it for a large amount of gold before returning home to live a life of luxury.

See also: Aleppo
References: Khatchatrian 1933

MARUSYA

Ukraine

Marusya and her young brother Vasilko lived far out on the steppes with their trapper father and mother. One day, in order to sell the furs they had trapped during the long winter months, the parents set off for a fair, leaving Marusya in charge of her young brother. They instructed Marusya to stay indoors with Vasilko at all times, as a flock of wild geese had been carrying off small children and they feared for Vasilko's safety.

At first the two children obeyed their parents, but soon the house became so hot and stuffy that Vasilko had his sister open the door, saying that if they heard the geese coming they could easily close the door. Still the house remained hot and sultry, and it wasn't long before Vasilko was asking his sister whether they could sit outside, saying that if they heard the geese coming they could easily hurry back inside. Marusya agreed, and the two sat down in the hot sunshine. Before long Vasilko asked Marusya if she would fetch a pitcher of water. Marusya agreed and went into the house. While she was filling the pitcher, she heard the honking of geese and Vasilko's scream.

Marusya ran out of the house and saw the geese flying away with her little brother. Carefully locking the door behind her, Marusya set off after the geese. Although she soon lost sight of the geese, Marusya continued in the direction she had last seen them flying, and after some time she came to a river of honey with banks made of *kisel'* (a pudding of puréed fruit thickened with cornstarch). Marusya asked the river if it had seen the geese. The river replied that it had but it would not tell Marusya the direction in which they had flown until she had drunk some of its honey and eaten her fill of the *kisel'*. Marusya did this, and then tidied up the riverbanks. The river then told the young girl the direction the geese had taken, and Marusya hurried off after she had thanked the river for its assistance.

At length Marusya came to a forest, but she did not know where to look. In the middle of the forest stood an ancient apple tree laden with sour, green apples, its branches crawling with hundreds of caterpillars. Marusya asked the tree if it had seen the geese and her brother Vasilko, which it had. Yet when Marusya asked the tree to tell her where they had gone, the tree refused, saying that Marusya must first taste its sour apples. Marusya ate several of the apples until her eyes streamed and her toes began to curl, and then she cleared all the caterpillars from the tree and swept up all the fallen leaves. The tree then told Marusya which path to follow. Thanking it, Marusya hurried after her brother.

The path took her far out onto the steppe, toward a range of mountains in the far distance. As she began to wonder if she was indeed following the right path, she came to an old stove beside the path—a stove that was filthy, covered in rubbish, and full of hard, cold buckwheat biscuits. Marusya asked

the stove if it knew which way the geese had flown with her brother, and when the stove replied that it did, Marusya ate some of the cold, hard buckwheat biscuits and then cleaned the stove and cleared away all the rubbish. The stove then pointed out the particular mountain where the geese had their nest and told Marusya to hide in the bushes until all the geese were fast asleep, and then make away with her brother as fast as she could.

Marusya thanked the stove and ran to the mountain and hid and waited until she was quite certain that all the geese had fallen asleep. She then crept into their nests and found Vasilko, and the pair made away as quickly as they could. When day broke, the geese discovered that Vasilko was gone, and they set off in hot pursuit. As Marusya and Vasilko heard the geese honking behind them, they came to the stove, which told them to climb into its oven. This they did. They sat quite still inside while the stove pointed the geese in the wrong direction. When the geese had flown away, Marusya and Vasilko climbed out of the oven, thanked the stove, and hurried off toward the forest.

As they reached the apple tree in the center of the forest, they again heard the honking of the geese, which had realized they were headed the wrong way. The apple tree told the two children to stand close to its trunk. Then it shook its branches and covered them in a pile of leaves. When the geese arrived, the tree pointed them in the direction opposite to the one that Marusya and Vasilko would be taking. When the geese had left, the two children shook off the leaves, thanked the tree, and hurried toward the river.

Just as they reached the banks of the honey river, Marusya and Vasilko heard the geese approaching. The river told them to jump in, and then it covered them with *kisel'* so that they were well hidden when the geese arrived. The river sent the geese in the wrong direction, and Marusya and Vasilko climbed out, thanked the river, and made it home just as the geese were swooping down on them. They managed to close the wooden door in the nick of time, and the geese thudded into it.

That evening their parents came home, chased away the geese that were circling the house, and listened to the story their children told them. The following morning the family awoke to three carts coming toward the house, the first laden with wonderfully sweet biscuits; the second with delicious, ripe, red apples; and the third with two huge pots, one full of honey and the other full of *kisel'*. For many weeks the family feasted on those foods, and no one was ever again troubled by the geese.

See also: Vasilko
References: Oparenko 1996

MARY (~IIA)
Russia
Sister of Martha. The two women, both widows, met each day on the road between Byzantium and Murom. One night as they slept, an angel appeared to them both, giving gold to Mary and silver to Martha and instructing them to give the gold and silver to the first three men they met on the road the next day as they traveled to see each other. Both women did exactly as they were instructed, telling the men to use the gold and silver to build the church dedicated to Archangel Michael in Murom, which they did. This church later housed the Golden Cross given to the city by Byzantium.

This story is generally accepted as a parable of the political union between Murom, a well-known pagan city, and Byzantium, and thus also for the conversion of the pagan city to Christianity.

See also: Byzantium; Martha (~fa); Murom
References: Gudzii 1962

MARYSHIA
Russia
Alternative name sometimes applied to Vasilissa the Beautiful.

See also: Vasilis(s)a the Beautiful

MARZAN(N)A
Poland
The goddess of fruit and fruit trees, though in some parts of Poland she is seen as the goddess of death. Every year during Lent, in a ceremony resembling the dismemberment of Goik, an effigy of the goddess would be made in the house where the most recent death had occurred. This effigy would then be carried on the end of a pole to the outskirts of the village, where it would either be burned or thrown into a pond. This ceremony, known as "carrying out Death," was meant to protect people against sudden, untimely death—though they could do nothing to save themselves from the inevitable death of old age and natural causes.

See also: Goik

MASHA
Russia
The wife of Petrushka, she appeared to her future husband as a Dove Maiden. Petrushka wounded the bird but took pity on it and brought it home to nurse it back to health. Petrushka patched up the broken wing and set the bird on his windowsill so that it might rest. As the bird fell asleep, Petrushka tapped it with a finger, as he had been instructed, whereupon the bird fell from the sill and instantly became the most beautiful maiden in all of Russia. For the remainder of the story see the entry for Petrushka.

See also: Dove Maiden; Petrushka

MASHEN'KA
Russia
An eight-year-old girl who was abducted by a lonely bear. Though her parents feared she had been eaten, the bear simply wanted someone to live with him and keep him company. The bear felt sorry for Mashen'ka as she pined for her parents. He told the young girl to bake some pies for her parents and he would deliver them for her. Mashen'ka baked the pies and then hid herself in the bottom of the basket, after warn-

ing the bear not to sneak any pies for himself because she would see him.

On his way to the village where Mashen'ka's parents lived, the bear sat down to eat one of the pies. From inside the basket came Mashen'ka's voice, warning him that she could still see him; so the bear put the pie back and hurried on his way. Three times this happened. At last the bear reached the village and left the basket outside Mashen'ka's house before running back into the forest. As Mashen'ka's parents opened the basket, their daughter leaped out.

For some time Mashen'ka would not leave the house for fear that the bear would return. When the bear came back one day, however, it was only to say goodbye and to tell Mashen'ka he forgave her for tricking him. As he left, he threw a leather bag into the house. For several days neither Mashen'ka nor her parents would touch the bag; but in the end curiosity overcame fear. When they opened the bag, a large quantity of gold and silver coins poured out. From that day on, Mashen'ka and her parents lived a life of ease.

MASLENITSA
Russia
A festival held at the end of February, marking the start of Lent. The name comes from *maslo* (butter or fat). A celebration of the earth's awakening, Maslenitsa involved the making of a straw doll, or the dressing of a young woman to play the role of the doll, and the decorating of a tree. Following a feast of traditional foods, the ceremonies would culminate with newly married couples sledding down artificially constructed slopes. Those who slid the farthest would be assured the best crops in the coming year. The spinners in the community also sledded down the hills, and the one that slid the farthest would be assured the best crop of flax for her spinning.

Maslenitsa also was the name given to the goddess of spring, whom the festival welcomed at her return from winter exile. The

feast was seen as feeding the goddess, and the sledding was a means of securing the pleasure of the goddess, who would then ensure the fertility of the ground and a good crop.

Having been serenaded and fed, the straw doll would be taken out into the fields, where it would be torn apart. Food would spill from the doll, which would then be burned. The ashes would be scattered over the fields to further the influence of the goddess. This tearing apart of the doll and burning of its remains has been seen as a way of scaring away winter with the warmth of spring—the fate of the doll perhaps demonstrating what the village people would do to winter if he stayed too long.

References: Afanas'ev 1865–69; Propp 1963; Tereshchenko 1848; Vsevolodskii-Gerngross 1929; Zemtsovskii 1970

MATERGABIA
Slav
Female spirit who directed the housekeeping and who was always offered the first piece of bread from the kneading trough. Failure to make this offering would lead to certain disaster.

MATI-SYRA-ZEMLYA
Slav
Also: Zemes Màte; Zemyna
The earth goddess whose name is literally "Moist Mother Earth." She is not often referred to by name in the myths of ancient Russia, nor was she ever given form, being worshiped simply as the earth itself. She was often called upon to witness oaths and contracts, a common method being the placing of a handful of soil on the head before taking a vow. This made the vow sacred, for Mother Earth could not be cheated. Her cult dated from very early times, as in most agrarian cultures; however, relative to similar cults, hers was undeveloped.

The Slavs once believed that they could communicate with the goddess by digging a hole in the ground, speaking into it, and then listening for her reply. It also was common practice to kiss her before setting out on a journey, and then again at journey's end. Beneficent to all, the goddess was particularly benevolent to women. She oversaw the fertility of the world every spring, at which time bread was buried for her to eat and wine or beer was poured into a hole for her to drink. She was also the patroness of the harvest. In times of plague, she could be called upon to keep a household free of the pestilence if a furrow was dug around the house at night—a furrow that Mati-Syra-Zemlya would fill with her potency, preventing the infection from entering the home.

See also: Mother Earth

MATRIOSHKA

Russia

Traditional Russian nested doll, hollow and made of wood, with the largest, exterior doll concealing a smaller one inside it, which in turn conceals an even smaller one, and so on. The matrioshka is usually brightly painted in traditional peasant garb—a head kerchief, an embroidered peasant blouse, and a dress similar to a jumper, called a *sarafan*. The first syllable of the doll's name is aptly derived from

"Matrioshka," or Russian stack dolls (Russell Thompson/Archive Photos)

Matriona (affectionate form of "mother"): In its traditional, feminine form, the matrioshka may be seen as a representation of Mother Russia, whose maternal love for her people, especially the humblest, is expressed by a doll that bears more dolls and thus ensures the continued existence of not just the people but also the country itself.

References: Pronin and Pronin 1975

MATUSHKA

Russia

Matushka is a Russian term of endearment meaning "dear mother." The Russian word is applied not only in its literal sense to human mothers but also figuratively, as a poetic epithet indicating affection for and emotional attachment to natural phenomena, such as the river Volga.

See also: Volga

MATUSHKA KOZMA-DEMIAN

Russia

One of the names given to the feast of 1 November, an important agricultural festival also known as Kuz'ma and Dem'yan Day. Traditionally on this day unmarried women would go out and search for a husband.

See also: Dem'yan, Saint; Kuz'ma, Saint

MATUSHKA KRASNOGO SOLNTSA

Russia

"Mother of the Red Sun," the personification of the mother of the sun god Dazhbog, and by association, possibly the wife of the sky god Svarog.

See also: Dazhbog; Sun; Svarog

MATUSHKA ZEMLIA

Russia

"Mother Earth," the literal Russian name for the goddess of the earth who usually remains unnamed in the myths and legends. When she is named, she is usually called Mati-Syra-Zemlya, "Moist Mother Earth."

See also: Mati-Syra-Zemlya; Mother Earth
References: Levin 1967

MAVKI

Russia

One of many names applied to russalki.

> *See also:* Faraony; Navki; Rus(s)alki (~ulki);
> Vodianiani
> *References:* Pomerantseva 1975

MEDEINE

Lithuania

Goddess of the forest whose name is only known from thirteenth-century texts.

MEKHITHAR GOSH

Armenia

Born c. 1140 in Gandzak (modern Kirovabad), Mekhithar Gosh was a jurist and monk of the Getik and New Getik monasteries. The contemporary of Vardan of Aygek, he collected and wrote a great number of Armenian fables before his death in 1213, several of which are described in this book. Like Vardan, Mekhithar often incorporated contemporary historical figures, such as Alexander the Great, into his fables. The fable in which Alexander the Great is mentioned went as follows:

Having had a new palace built for himself, Alexander the Great rewarded the blacksmith far more generously than the carpenter and the gardener. Envious of the smith, the carpenter and the gardener complained to the emperor that they had both done far more work on the palace than the blacksmith. Alexander the Great consulted his advisers, who told him that before the carpenter could do his work he needed the tools of the blacksmith, and before the gardener could do his work he needed the skills of both the carpenter and the blacksmith. Thus the blacksmith deserved the greatest reward. The carpenter and the gardener readily accepted this reasoning and were no longer jealous.

> *See also:* Alexander the Great; Vardan

MENESS (~ULIS)

Latvia

The moon god, the Latvian equivalent of the Lithuanian Menuo. Meness was said to have married the Weaver of the Stars—although he might also have had earlier marriages, as did Menuo.

> *See also:* Menuo; Moon; Weaver of the Stars

MENUO

Lithuania

The moon god, known in Latvia as Meness. Wearing a starry robe, he traveled across the night sky in a chariot drawn by gray horses. He married Saule but later fell in love with Ausrine, the Morning Star, for which he was punished by Perkunas, who broke him into two pieces. Instead of learning from this punishment, Menuo continued his affair with Ausrine, as a consequence of which he suffered the same fate each and every month.

> *See also:* Ausrine; Meness (~ulis); Moon;
> Morning Star; Perkunas; Saule

MESYATS

Slav

Also: Myesyats

Mesyats, the moon god, appears widely throughout Slavic mythology and legend, though later stories tend to leave him nameless. In Ukrainian myth, Mesyats marries the sun goddess, although the sun is almost always thought of as masculine (perhaps this is why later storytellers left the name out). Later Russian belief only adds to this gender confusion.

Early Russian belief said that Mesyats was the old, balding adviser to Dazhbog, the sun. Later belief changed the gender of Mesyats and made him a young moon goddess who married Dazhbog in the summer, left him in winter, and was reunited with him the following spring. She and Dazhbog were believed to be the parents of all the stars, and their marital spats were thought to cause earthquakes.

> *See also:* Dazhbog; Moon; Sun; Ukraine

METHODIUS, SAINT

Slav

See Cyril and Methodius, Saints.

METSIK

Estonia

"Wood spirit," the personification of the spirit of the woods and forests, patron deity of cattle and herds. Once a year, on the eve of Shrove Tuesday, an effigy of the metsik would be fashioned of straw, or sometimes of stalks of grain. In alternating years the effigy would represent either the male aspect of the spirit, and thus be dressed with a man's hat and coat, or the female aspect, dressed in a hood and petticoat. Then, fastened to the end of a pole, the effigy of the metsik would be carried out of the village and affixed to the top of a tall tree where it could watch over the people and warn them of impending danger. The effigy would remain at the top of the tree for a whole year, every day being given prayers and votive offerings that were thought to strengthen the metsik's protection over the village and its herds.

MIDNIGHT

Slav

The unnamed sister of Zorya Utrennyaya and Zorya Vechernyaya. All three were daughters of Dazhbog; however, only the goddesses of dawn and of dusk were referred to by name, Midnight being a shadowy character who appears only in a few references.

See also: Dazhbog; Zorya Utrennyaya; Zorya Vechernyaya

MIKHAIL POTYK

Russia

Also: Mikhailo Ivanovich Potok

A knight, or bogatyr', who made a pact with his wife Avdot'ya at their wedding feast that when one of them died the other would follow into the tomb. Soon after the wedding Avdot'ya died, and Mikhail, true to his word, had himself lowered into the tomb beside her. However, Mikhail took with him a rope that was attached to the church bell, so that if he changed his mind, he could ring the bell and summon assistance. Some versions say that he provided himself a secret exit and took his horse with him.

Lighting a candle, Mikhail sat down beside the body of his wife. Around midnight he saw many snakes entering the tomb, one of which turned into a dragon spouting fire and smoke. Unafraid, Mikhail drew his saber and cut off the beast's head, which he rubbed onto his dead wife's body; magically she was brought back to life. Mikhail and Avdot'ya rang the bell and were released from the tomb to spend many happy years together.

See also: Avdot'ya; Bogatyr'

MIKHAILO, PRINCE

Russia

A Muscovite prince who married against his mother's wishes. While he was away on business, his mother lured his wife to the bathhouse and boiled her to death. When Prince Mikhailo returned home and learned of his wife's death, he died of shock, and his mother realized that through her intolerance she had killed her entire family, including her unborn grandchild.

References: Chadwick 1964

MIKOLA MOZHAISKI, SAINT

Russia

See Nikolai of Mozhaisk, Saint.

MIKULA SELYANINOVICH

Russia

A legendary plowman, favorite of Mati-Syra-Zemlya, who imbued him with great strength and allowed him to ride across her faster than anyone else. His association with Mother Earth indicates that he possibly owes his origins to Volos. His story appears fairly late, possibly as late as the fifteenth century. However, its foundation seems much older and might have some historical basis, though Mikula started his life in legend as a god and was only later (after the advent of the Christian era) downgraded to a bogatyr'. The story of Mikula Selyaninovich illustrates quite clearly how peasants regarded their rulers, for the prince in this story, Vol'ga Sviatoslavovich, is much less a hero than the

A Russian lacquer painting of Prince Sviatoslavovich's soldiers straining to move a massive plow as Mikula looks on (Sovfoto/Eastfoto/PNI)

humble Mikula—though Mikula is by no means an ordinary peasant.

Vol'ga Sviatoslavovich was the nephew and godson of Prince Vladimir Bright Sun, grand prince of Kiev. His uncle had given him dominion over three towns, along with the peasants who lived on the surrounding lands. As was his right, Vol'ga periodically demanded and collected taxes from his subjects, and on one such trip around his domain he encountered Mikula.

As they rode through the countryside, Vol'ga and his entourage heard the sounds of a plowman whistling and calling to his horse and of the plow cutting its furrow, and the grating of the plowshare as it struck a stone. However, no matter how fast they rode, they were unable to catch up with the plowman. For two and a half days they rode hard, chasing the elusive sounds, until they finally came upon him.

Whistling as he went, the plowman Mikula tore up tree stumps that lay in his path, roots and all, and cast aside huge boul-

ders. A light bay mare pulled the plow, which was made of maple and had a coulter of damask steel, a share of silver, handles of red gold, and traces made of silk. Mikula himself is described as a man of tremendous masculine beauty, with eyes as keen as a falcon's, hair in tight ringlets, and brows as black as sable. He wore a black velvet tunic, a soft felt cap, and boots of green Morocco leather with extremely pointed toes and very high heels.

Mikula and Vol'ga exchanged greetings. When Vol'ga told Mikula the purpose of his journey, the plowman warned the prince that a band of robbers were camped along his chosen route. These robbers lay in wait by a bridge over the river Smorodina, the planks of which they had sawn through so that travelers would fall into the water and drown. Mikula told the prince that he had been that way just three days before and that these robbers had attempted to waylay him as he traveled home carrying two skins filled with salt that weighed 100 poods (roughly 3,600 lbs, or 1,638 kg) each. When the robbers had demanded money from Mikula in return for safe passage, he simply mowed down 1,000 of their men.

Hearing this, Prince Vol'ga invited Mikula to join his party. Mikula willingly agreed and unharnessed his horse. However, after a short ride, Mikula began to worry about his plow, for he had left it in the open where it might easily be stolen. Vol'ga sent five of his men back to hide the plow, but they could not even begin to move it. Ten men went back, and they had no more success than the original five. Finally Vol'ga's entire company attempted to move the plow, but it still would not move. Seeing this, Mikula walked into the field, lifted the plow from the ground with one hand, and hid it himself behind a willow bush after he had carefully cleaned it off.

With the plow safe, Mikula urged his little mare forward. When the mare broke into a trot, Vol'ga had to urge his steed into a gallop. When Mikula gave his mare her head, Vol'ga was left far behind. Calling out for Mikula to stop, Vol'ga caught up with him. Having been duly impressed with Mikula's strength and prowess, the prince made Mikula lord of his three towns and bade him collect the taxes in his place.

See also: Kiev; Mati-Syra-Zemlya; Mother Earth; Smorodina; Vladimir Bright Sun, Prince; Vol'ga Sviatoslavovich; Volos
References: Chadwick 1964; Nechaev and Rybakov 1959

MILKY WAY, THE
Slav
Russian peasants believed that the souls of their departed loved ones crossed the celestial bridge of the Milky Way to reach the moon, which was to be their eternal abode. A similar belief existed in Lithuania, where the Milky Way was known as the Bird's Way, and was believed to be a bridge across which the souls or spirits of the dead traveled to reach their eternal abode, the realm of Dausos, which lay beyond the slippery high

hill of the sky (some authorities equate Dausos with the moon). This was one of several routes by which the departed could make their journey, other options being to climb up the slippery high hill of the sky, to ride on horseback, to travel in the smoke of the cremation fire, or to travel in a boat such as that used every day by the sun as it returned home for the night.

See also: Bird's Way, The; Dausos; Moon; Sun

MILOSERDNIA
Russia
Post-Christian name given to one of the three female spirits that oversaw all the functions of human life—the Russian equivalents of the Greek Fates. Her companions were Alleluiah and Miloslaviia. Popular legend of the flight from Jerusalem of Mary the Mother of God says that she placed the infant Jesus in the care of an elderly woman called both Miloserdnia and Miloslaviia. This woman had a child of her own, whom she sacrificed in order to hide the baby Jesus. When Mary returned for Jesus, the generous woman found that her own child had been resurrected.

See also: Alleluiah; Miloslaviia
References: Afanas'ev 1865–69; Bezsonov 1861; Haase 1939

MILOSLAVIIA
Russia
Post-Christian name given to one of the three female spirits that oversaw all the functions of human life—the Russian equivalents of the Greek Fates. Her companions were Alleluiah and Miloserdnia.

See also: Alleluiah; Miloserdnia
References: Afanas'ev 1865–69; Bezsonov 1861; Haase 1939

MISFORTUNE, THE IMPS OF
Ukraine
Invisible spirits that arbitrarily choose a victim and cause that person bad luck throughout their life, going so far as to climb into the coffin of their victim after they have died so

that they might continue their influence in the afterlife. Their influence is recorded in a story concerning two brothers, one a carpenter who had a large number of children and grew steadily poorer, and the other a rich merchant who had no children and grew steadily richer.

One year, as Christmas approached, the poor brother went cap in hand to his rich brother and asked for charity, but his brother would not help him. However, as he made his way home again, he started to sing in order to keep up his spirits, and he heard many voices join his in song. When he asked who was there, the voices told him that they were the Imps of Misfortune, whose goal was to ruin a man's life and ensure that whatever he did would end in failure. Having learned exactly what was causing his life of misery, the man returned home and made himself a coffin, telling his distraught wife and family that he had decided to end his life. The Imps of Misfortune told the man that even then he would not escape them, for they would lie in his coffin with him. That was exactly what he had hoped.

Bidding his family farewell, the man took his coffin into the fields and dug a hole, into which he lowered the open casket. Then the man asked the Imps of Misfortune to test the coffin for him, especially to make certain that the lid fit tightly enough. The Imps of Misfortune climbed into the open coffin, whereupon the man screwed down the lid and filled in the hole. Then he returned to his wife and family and told them what had happened. From that day forth their fortunes changed, and within a year they had amassed a considerable fortune and had built themselves a fine new home.

The rich man was traveling through his brother's village one day and was astonished to see the riches he had managed to amass. He stopped to call on his brother and was told what had transpired. Jealous of his brother's good fortune, he hurried out into the countryside to release the Imps of Misfortune so that his brother's good fortune

might once again turn to ill. However, when the rich brother released the Imps of Misfortune, they refused to return to their former victim because he had tried to kill them, and instead decided to stay with the rich brother, who soon became as poor as his brother had once been. However, when he called on his brother and asked for charity, he was received warmly, and from that day forth could always rely on his brother when the need arose.

This story should be compared with that of Misha, which—apart from a few minor differences—is identical.

See also: Misha

MISHA
Russia

The poorer of two brothers who lived in a village near Smolensk. The name of Misha's brother is unknown. The two brothers had been left equal riches by their late father; but for reasons not recorded, Misha steadily became poorer while his brother grew ever richer. At length Misha was forced to go cap in hand to his brother, but the only help Misha got was to be invited, along with his wife and family, to a great banquet that his brother was hosting.

Misha and his wife duly went to the party, and there Misha sang; but when he sang, his voice sounded like two voices. Finally it dawned on him that he was being accompanied by Sorrow, who swore that from that day forth they would be constant companions.

Returning from the party, Sorrow asked Misha for vodka, but Misha had none, nor did he have the money to buy any. Sorrow simply shrugged and told Misha that they could sell Misha's fur coat, as in six months it would be summer and he would no longer need it. Thus they took Misha's fur coat to the market the following day and sold it for enough to buy two bottles of vodka. That night, with the vodka gone, Sorrow told Misha that the following day they would sell his sled, for in six months, when summer came, he would have no need for it. So it went, day after day, until Misha had nothing left that they could sell.

Sorrow told Misha to go to his neighbor and borrow his ox and cart. Misha did so, and before long he and Sorrow were stopped in a field in which a huge boulder lay. Sorrow and Misha climbed down from the cart, and after much exertion, moved the boulder aside, uncovering a huge cache of money. When they loaded the money onto the cart, it was filled to the brim. As Sorrow made ready to climb up onto the cart, Misha asked him to have one last check in the hole; and Sorrow, thinking only of the vodka he might miss if even one coin were left behind, gladly climbed down. As he did so, Misha leaned all his weight against the rock and rolled it over the hole, trapping Sorrow inside.

Misha then drove home, unloaded the money, and returned the cart to his neighbor. Before long Misha had built a beautiful new home and was living a life of luxury and leisure. It was then that his brother came to call on his new, rich neighbor and found to his surprise that it was none other than his brother who had, not six months before, come to him for money. When Misha told his brother what had happened, the brother became green with envy and set out to release Sorrow so that Misha might once again have his company.

However, when the brother moved the rock to one side, Sorrow leaped out and clung to his hair, sneering and saying that he would never be free of him. Sorrow laughed loudly and called the brother a liar when he attempted to tell Sorrow that he was not Misha. Thus the greedy brother was stuck with Sorrow, who soon started to whittle away at his fortune. The brother thought long and hard about his predicament, and then he invited Sorrow to play a game of hide and seek with him. Sorrow agreed, and he easily found the brother. The brother then challenged Sorrow to hide in the hub of a wheel. Sorrow agreed. No sooner had Sorrow squeezed into the open hub of a cartwheel than the brother plugged the hub.

He then carried the wheel down to the river and cast it adrift; and from that day forth neither brother saw Sorrow again. They were soon reconciled and lived ever after as brothers should.

See also: Misfortune, The Imps of; Sorrow

MOCKER KING, THE
Armenia
The title given to an unnamed ruler of an unnamed realm who took great delight in laughing at those less fortunate than himself. One day, seated at his window, he beheld the most hideously deformed woman he had ever seen, and almost split his sides in ribald laughter. The old woman heard his mockery, and there and then she determined that she would have the last laugh.

The old woman was a powerful witch, and that evening she transformed herself into a beautiful maiden and found employment at the palace as one of the queen's maids. When she touched the queen as she stepped from her bath, the queen changed into a deformed old crone. The maid then disappeared, and the queen had to call out to the king for assistance. He did not know which way to turn or where to look for the witch, and so he sat comforting his wife, though he found her repulsive.

The witch left the couple to reflect on their misfortune for a couple of days before she returned to the palace. The king recognized the old woman as the one he had mocked from his window. The witch explained to the king that his mockery had rebounded on him, and promised that if he would hold his mockery in check, she would restore his wife. The king readily agreed, and pleaded with the witch to restore his wife. The witch laughed and touched the queen, who immediately became as she had been before. From that day forth, the king only laughed when it was appropriate to do so, and never again mocked the afflictions of others.

References: Orbeli and Taronian 1959–67, vol. 10

MODEINA
Poland
One of the two patron deities of the forest, the other being Siliniets.
  See also: Siliniets

MOISEI
Russia
One of two boyar brothers (the other was Luka) who passed the test put to them by Vasilii Buslayevich in an attempt to discover whether they were worthy of joining his *druzhina.* The two men joined twenty-seven other members, completing Vasilii Buslaye-vich's band of thirty. (Vasilii himself was the thirtieth.)
  See also: Boyars; Luka; Vasilii Buslayevich

MOKOSH
Finno-Slavic
Also: Makosh
A fertility goddess widely worshiped in the regions immediately north of the Black Sea. Close to Mati-Syra-Zemlya, possibly serving as her handmaiden, Mokosh, whose name comes from *mokosi* or *mokryi,* both meaning "moist," ensured that men's semen was rich in sperm, and protected women and sheep and their offspring during labor and birth. She was unique in the earliest pantheon, being the only goddess; and she appears to have been the oldest of the deities in this pantheon. Mokosh is usually represented in the company of the bird-dog Simorg. The dog's name is of Iranian origin, which suggests that Mokosh too may have originated in that region.

Many authorities, however, rely on the sound of the word *Mokosh* to determine her origins, as with the Finno-Ugric tribes, and perhaps even with the Finno-Ugric Moksha. However, such etymological reasons are extremely thin, and it now seems increasingly certain that Mokosh should be regarded as an autochthonous goddess of the Poliane and other Slavic peoples from the Kievan region. Mokosh, however, developed into a Great Goddess with a truly phenome-nal range, as she was the most widespread of all the Russian Slavic deities. In Novgorod, for example, she was worshiped as the goddess of spinners, childbirth, animals, the moon, and rain. After the advent of Christianity her office was handed over to the Virgin Mary or Saint Paraskeva.
  See also: Black Sea; Finno-Ugric; Great Goddess; Mati-Syra-Zemlya; Moksha; Paraskeva, Saint; Simorg (~argl, ~urg)
  References: Boba 1967; Brückner 1823; Gimbutas 1971; Grekov 1959; Haase 1939; Ivanov and Toporov 1965; Matorin 1931

MOKSHA
General
The southern branch of the Mordvin people, their northern counterparts being the Erzya.
  See also: Erzya; Mordvins

MOLDAVIA
General
One of the six provinces of which Romania is comprised, the others being Transylvania, Bukovina, Walachia, Banat, and Dobruja. The former principality of Moldavia is situated in northeastern Romania and extends from Transylvania to the Prut River along the border with Moldova (the former Soviet republic). Walachia, in the south, stretches from the southernmost mountains to the Danube. Banat, in western Romania, extends from the western mountains to Yugoslavia and Hungary.
  See also: Danube; Hungary; Moldova; Romania; Transylvania

MOLDOVA
General
Not to be confused with the Romanian province that is also called Moldova or Moldavia. A country in south-central Europe, bordered by Romania in the west and by Ukraine on its other sides, formerly known as Bessarabia. From 1940 to 1991, Moldova was a republic of the Soviet Union, when it was called the Moldavian Soviet

Socialist Republic, or simply Moldavia. With the collapse of the Soviet Union in 1991, the republic declared its independence.

From c. 700 B.C. until c. A.D. 200, the region that is now Moldova was under the control of Iranian peoples from central Asia—first the Scythians and later the Sarmatians. From about A.D. 200 until the thirteenth century, various other peoples from the west and east invaded and ruled the area, including the Goths, Huns, Avars, and finally the Mongols or Tatars. The people of Moldova gradually united, and by the mid-fourteenth century they had formed an independent state under a single ruler. The state was called the principality of Moldavia and included present-day Moldova—then called Bessarabia—as well as an area between the Moldavian Carpathian Mountains and the Prut River in modern Romania.

The Ottoman Empire gained control of the principality of Moldavia by the early sixteenth century and ruled the region until 1812, when Russia took control of Bessarabia. The Treaty of Paris that ended the Crimean War in 1856 gave southern Bessarabia to the principality of Moldavia, following Russia's defeat in that war. In 1861, the principality of Moldavia united with the principality of Walachia to form the new nation of Romania. Russia regained southern Bessarabia in 1878.

After World War I (1914–1918), all of Bessarabia became part of Romania. However, the Soviet Union refused to recognize Bessarabia's unification with Romania, and in 1924, the Soviets established the Moldavian Autonomous Soviet Socialist Republic (ASSR) in the Trans-Dniester region. In 1940, during World War II, the Soviet Union seized Bessarabia and merged most of Bessarabia with part of the Moldavian ASSR to form the Moldavian Soviet Socialist Republic. Bessarabia became part of Romania again in 1941, but the Soviet Union regained it in 1944.

In 1990 the Moldavian Supreme Soviet declared that its laws took precedence over those of the Soviet Union, and changed the name of the country from Moldavia to Moldova. In August 1991 Moldova and several other republics declared their independence, which was confirmed by the dissolution of the Soviet Union at the end of that year.

See also: Avars; Bessarabia; Carpathian Mountains; Mongols; Romania; Sarmatians; Scythia; Tatars; Ukraine

MONGOLS

General

Pastoral people now found in east-central Asia, including parts of China and Russia, who speak one of the Altaic languages. Their written language, Mongolian, dates from at least the eleventh century. The Mongols are thought to have been a loose confederation of peoples until the Mongol conqueror Genghis Khan united them into one formidable nation in the early thirteenth century. Under his leadership, they developed a powerful army that swept west into Europe and east into China, eventually forming a widespread Eurasian empire. The descendants of Genghis Khan ruled large areas of China, East Asia, Russia, Iran, and Turkey for long periods of time. The Mongols were subsequently overcome, and they returned to relative political obscurity. The Mongols now number approximately one million, with most of the population practicing Buddhism and the remainder embracing shamanism. They are still largely a nomadic people, and their wealth consists of sheep, horses, cattle, camels, and goats.

See also: Genghis Khan; Golden Horde, The

MONTENEGRO

General

Montenegro is one of the two republics of present-day Yugoslavia, Serbia being the other. Montenegro's name in Serbo-Croatian, the republic's language, is Crna Gora, which means "black mountain."

Present-day Montenegro became part of the Roman Empire in about 11 B.C. Slavs settled the region in the seventh century, and Montenegro became part of Serbia in the late twelfth century. The Ottoman Empire defeated the Serbs at the Battle of Kosovo Polje in 1389, and from that date until 1516, local nobles ruled the country on behalf of the Ottomans. That year, Serbian Orthodox bishops of the monastery at Cetinje began to rule part of Montenegro, and by the late eighteenth century their rule extended to the entire country. In 1852, Montenegro's ruler took the title of prince, and the position of bishop reverted to a separate office. In 1878, the Congress of Berlin formally recognized Montenegro as independent and granted the state new lands that almost doubled its size. Prince Nicholas took the throne in 1860 and declared himself king in 1910.

In the early twentieth century a movement to unite Serbs and other Slavic peoples gathered strength in the region, and in 1918 townspeople deposed the king, and Montenegro became part of the new Kingdom of the Serbs, Croats, and Slovenes. In 1946, Montenegro became one of the six republics of Yugoslavia.

In 1990, Montenegro held its first multiparty elections, and between June 1991 and March 1992, four Yugoslav republics—Croatia, Slovenia, Macedonia, and Bosnia-Herzegovina—declared their independence. In April 1992, Serbia and Montenegro formed a new, smaller Yugoslavia.

See also: Bosnia; Croatia; Herzegovina; Macedonia; Serbia; Slovenia

MOON
Slav and Baltic

Like the sun and elemental forces such as frost or wind, the moon is not usually given a name in later Russian folktales. Earlier tales call him (or her, for the moon is sometimes described as feminine) Mesyats. Some say that the sun and the moon were brother and sister, and that every spring they would come together to talk about what they had been

doing and what they had seen. Sometimes, however, the moon would be angry with her brother and would block out his light. (Early peoples thought the moon had eaten the sun and then spat him out.) Such occurrences were usually short-lived, for the moon could not remain angry long. The sun and the moon both feature in the story of Raven Ravenson, though this story has more to do with man's stupidity than with either celestial object.

The moon is also widely regarded as an eternal abode for the souls of the dead, each soul crossing the celestial bridge of the Milky Way to reach its final resting place.

The Russians believed that the moon was the realm of the dead, as did the ancient Lithuanians, who believed that the souls of the departed crossed the Bird's Way (the Milky Way) to reach their eternal abode. As the realm of Dausos was also considered the land of the dead, positioned as it was beyond the slippery high hill of the sky, this has led to conjecture that Dausos was the Lithuanian name for, though not a deification of, the moon. The latter honor was reserved for Menuo, who is described as traveling across the night sky in a chariot drawn by gray horses and wearing a starry robe. He married

View of the moon, taken from Apollo 11 (NASA)

Saule, the sun goddess, but later fell in love with Ausrine, the Morning Star, for which he was punished by Perkunas, who broke him into pieces (the ancient explanation for the lunar phases). The Latvian equivalent of the Lithuanian Menuo was Meness, who was said to have married the Weaver of the Stars.

See also: Ausrine; Bird's Way, The; Dausos; Frost; Meness (~ulis); Menuo; Mesyats; Milky Way, The; Morning Star; Perkunas; Raven Ravenson; Saule; Sun; Weaver of the Stars; Wind

MORAVIA
General

Moravia was an Avar territory from the sixth century until it was conquered by the Holy Roman Empire of Charlemagne. In 874 the Slavic prince Sviatopolk founded the kingdom of Great Moravia, which he ruled until 894. The Magyars invaded and conquered Great Moravia in 906, and the kingdom became a fief of Bohemia in 1029. In 1526 it was passed to the Habsburgs; and in 1849 it became an Austrian crown land. Moravia was incorporated into the new republic of Czechoslovakia in 1918, remaining a province of that country until 1949. Today Moravia is a region in the eastern Czech Republic.

See also: Avars; Bohemia; Czechoslovakia; Magyars

MORDVINS
General

People speaking one of the Finno-Ugric languages and forming a large part of the population of the Mordvinian autonomous region, an internal division of Russia. The Mordvins number about one million and are divided into two groups with different dialects—a northern branch called the Erzya, and a southern branch known as the Moksha. Their chief occupation is agriculture, but carpentry, the manufacture of wooden vessels, and beekeeping are also important to their economy. Many of the women wear a distinctive traditional cos-

tume of profusely embroidered jackets and skirts, elaborate coiffures, large earrings, and numerous necklaces. Although Christianity is common, ancient forms of nature worship are still practiced. The chief divinity of the non-Christian faith is Shkay, a sun god. The moon, trees, water, frost, and thunder are also deified, and altars are sometimes built in homes for the purpose of animal sacrifice.

See also: Erzya; Finno-Ugric; Moksha; Shkay

MORNING STAR
Slav and Baltic

The Slavic personification of the Morning Star, the planet Venus when seen in the dawn sky, was called Zvezda Dennitsa, one of the two Auroras. She and her sister Zvezda Vechernyaya, the Evening Star, were daughters and attendants of the sun god Dazhbog, with the specific task of grooming their father's horses. They were sisters of the two, or three, Zoryi, though the Zoryi and Zvezdy may be interchangeable. The Morning Star was believed to give birth to Dazhbog each morning, whereas the Evening Star welcomed him to his death.

The Latvian personification of the Morning Star was Ausrine, and her Lithuanian counterpart was Auseklis.

See also: Auroras; Dazhbog; Evening Star; Sun; Venus

MOROZKO
Russia

The frost demon who features most notably in the story of Marfusha, on whom he took pity when she was left to be his bride, although he froze her two spoiled stepsisters to death when they complained of the cold.

Another story concerning the frost does not name Morozko directly. In this tale a peasant pays homage to the Wind, who appears as a man with tousled hair, disheveled clothing, and a swollen face and lips. This homage paid to the Wind offends both the Sun, who appears as a chubby man with rosy cheeks, and Frost, who appears as a thin man with gray hair and bushy white eyebrows. The Wind, however, promises the peasant that neither shall ever harm him. That winter the peasant feared because of the frost to venture from his home; but he was forced to go out when he ran out of firewood. As he walked through the forest, he felt Frost attacking him, so he broke into a run. Soon he was warm and thanked Frost for making him move more quickly to keep himself warm. Angered by this, Frost swore that he would make the man suffer horribly; so when the peasant removed his hat and gloves in order to chop wood, Frost froze them solid. Returning to his garments, the man saw that they were frozen, so he began to pound them with the blunt edge of his axe. Frost barely managed to escape the onslaught, and he crept away badly beaten and bleeding. The Wind stayed quiet throughout this episode, for it knew that Frost was not really dangerous without his collaboration.

The Wind also helped the peasant the following summer when the Sun tried to scorch him—blowing gentle, cooling breezes and making small clouds scurry across the sky to blot out the Sun and drop a quenching rain on the man. Neither Frost nor Sun ever bothered the peasant again.

See also: Frost; Marfusha; Sun; Wind

MORSKOI
Russia

The Russian name of the Sea Tsar with whom Sadko had dealings, and from whom that merchant managed to escape only with the help of Saint Nikolai of Mozhaisk.

See also: Nikolai of Mozhaisk, Saint; Sadko; Sea Tsar

MOSCOW
General

Capital of Russia, located about 400 miles (640 km) southeast of St. Petersburg. Founded as the city-state of Muscovy in 1127, it was destroyed by the Mongols during the thirteenth century and rebuilt in 1294 by Prince Daniel (d. 1303) as the capi-

tal of his principality. During the fourteenth century, under the rule of Alexander Nevski, Ivan I, and Dmitri Donskoi, the city became the foremost political and religious center in Russia. The city was burned in 1571 by the khan of the Crimea and ravaged again by fire in 1739, 1748, 1753, and 1812. In the last instance the fire might have been deliberately set in an attempt to stop Napoleon's troops from taking the city. In 1918 Moscow became the capital of the RSFSR (Russian Soviet Federated Social Republic), and in 1922 it was named the administrative capital of the USSR (Union of Soviet Socialist Republics).

See also: Crimea; Khan; Mongols; Russia; St. Petersburg

MOTHER EARTH
Russia

Mother Earth, personified as Mati-Syra-Zemlya, is essential to Russian legend. In the story of Dobrynya Nikitich, the hero calls upon her to open up and swallow the vast lake of dragon's blood he finds himself stranded in after he slays a hideous, twelve-headed she-dragon.

Mother Earth came into existence, so the legends tell us, when a little duck laid an egg on a small island that rose out of the primeval ocean. The egg rolled off the island and broke into two, the lower half forming the earth and the upper half the sky. This legend bears comparison with the remarkably similar Finno-Ugric story of Ilmater Luonnotar and the duck that laid its eggs on the goddess's knees in the primeval ocean.

See also: Dobrynya Nikitich; Dragon; Finno-Ugric; Mati-Syra-Zemlya; Matushka Zemlia
References: Afanas'ev 1865–69; Fedotov 1960, 1966; Matorin 1931; Pilnyak 1968; Tokarev 1957

MOTHER OF THE SEAS
Latvia

Respectful name by which Juras Màte, the sea goddess, was known.

See also: Juras Màte

MOTOVUN
Croatia
Town on the peninsula of Istria (in northern Croatia) that was the home of Veli Joze, a giant who, in a fit of temper, shook the town tower with such force that it was badly cracked and began to lean—a condition in which it remains to this day.

See also: Croatia; Veli Joze

MOUNTAIN OF GOLD
Russia
A mountain made of solid gold that lay on an island that was the home of a greedy merchant who would hire men from a mainland town, ship them out to the island, and then, after they had put in a hard day's labor at the top of the insurmountable mountain, leave them there to die. The merchant, however, met more than his match when he hired a young man by the name of Grishka. The merchant's daughter fell in love with Grishka at first sight, and she gave him a magical tinderbox to help him escape the difficulties she knew he would encounter.

As the mountainsides were too sheer to permit an ascent on foot, the merchant had devised a clever means of transporting his laborers to the top: He gave the young men a drink that was drugged, and when they had fallen asleep, he sewed them up inside the carcass of a horse. Two enormous black crows would then alight, pick up the carcass, and carry it to the top of the mountain, where they would pick the bones clean, leaving the young man within the bare bones, hopefully to awaken before the crows pecked his body clean as well. The merchant would then promise to bring the young man down in return for a cartload of gold dug from the mountain. However, when the day came to a close,

the merchant would drive away with the gold and leave the young man to be killed by the crows.

See also: Grishka.

MOZHAISKI, MIKOLA, SAINT
Russia
Alternative name of Saint Nikolai of Mozhaisk.

See also: Nikolai of Mozhaisk, Saint

MUKYLIN
Votyak
The Votyak earth mother. According to one Votyak village tale, Mukylin ensured that particular village a good harvest after she married Keremet. However, because the marriage was made against her will, she brought bad harvests on all the villages that had acquiesced to her marriage without trying to protect her virgin status.

See also: Keremet

MUROM
Russia
Russian city famous for its fervent paganism and resistance to missionaries and Christianity. Situated to the east of Moscow and southwest of Gorky, the city was the home of Il'ya Muromets (whose epithet literally means "of Murom").

See also: Il'ya Muromets; Moscow

MUXDI
Siberia—Tungus
Alternative name for Dzuli.

See also: Dzuli

MUZEM-MUMI
Votyak
The name given by the Votyak to Mother Earth.

See also: Mother Earth; Votyaks

NADANOJLA

Slav

The leader of the *vile*. Her headdress and wings were stolen by Prince Marko. Nadanojla and Prince Marko were married and lived happily together until Marko foolishly boasted that his wife was a *vila*. Nadanojla immediately gathered up her headdress and wings and flew away. After she was recaptured by Marko, she remained his wife forever, reacting only with laughter when her husband boasted of her supernatural origins.

See also: Marko, Prince; Vila

NAINAS

Russia

The personification of the northern lights, the aurora borealis. He was betrothed to Niekia, the daughter of the Moon, but he never married her, due to the intervention of Peivalké and his father, the Sun.

See also: Aurora Borealis; Moon; Niekia; Peivalké; Sun

NASTASIIA

Russia

Alternative spelling of Nastas'ya.

NASTAS'YA, PRINCESS

Russia

Daughter of the king of Lithuania and sister of Princess Evpraksiya (some sources identify both as daughters of the Tatar khan). When Dunai Ivanovich and Dobrynya Nikitich traveled from Kiev to Lithuania to request Evpraksiya's hand for Prince Vladimir Bright Sun, Nastas'ya was away hunting. When she returned to find that her sister had been taken away, she followed them, vowing to bring her sister home or to die in the attempt. She quickly caught up with Dunai Ivanovich, Dobrynya Nikitich, and her sister; however, for some unknown reason she did not attack them and instead turned and rode away. She was followed and unseated from her horse by Dunai Ivanovich. Her courage so impressed Dunai that he asked her to be his wife. Nastas'ya rode with the party to Kiev, and she and Dunai were married at the same ceremony as Vladimir Bright Sun and Evpraksiya.

During the wedding feast Nastas'ya's new husband boasted that there was no finer archer in all of Kiev than he. Nastas'ya rose to this bait and challenged her husband, proposing that a silver ring be set up on the head of one and that the other fire an arrow along the blade of a knife and then through the ring. Dunai Ivanovich invited his wife to try first. Three times she successfully performed the feat. However, as Dunai Ivanovich prepared to take his turn, Nastas'ya implored him not to pursue their dangerous game and to forgive her foolishness. Dunai Ivanovich refused to listen. Nastas'ya again begged him to abandon the contest—if not for her sake, then for that of their unborn child, whom she said would be the most wondrous babe ever born: He would have arms of pure gold from the shoulders to the elbows and legs of pure silver from the hips to the knees; stars would cluster around his temple; the moon would shine from his back; and the sun would radiate from his eyes.

Dunai Ivanovich still refused to listen. Dipping the tip of his arrow in snake venom, he let it fly. The arrow accidentally pierced Nastas'ya's heart. As she lay dying, the child was cut from her womb. He proved to be just as Nastas'ya had described him. Grief-stricken, Dunai Ivanovich planted his spear in the ground and threw himself onto its point. Where the two died, two rivers sprang up: the Nastas'ya and the Dunai, the latter of which is better known today as the river Danube.

In another version of the legend, Nastas'ya was chosen as a suitable bride for Dunai Ivanovich by his mother; but in order to win Nastas'ya's hand, he had to defeat her in battle. Instead, Nastas'ya triumphed over Dunai. She placed him in her bag, stating that if he were younger than she, then he would become her brother; if he were older, she would kill him; but if he were of the same age, she would marry him. Dunai was the same age as Nastas'ya, and the two were subsequently married.

In later times the story of Princess Nastas'ya became linked with that of Nastas'ya Nikulichna, although the two stories had separate origins.

See also: Danube; Dobrynya Nikitich; Dunai Ivanovich; Evpraksiya (~ia), Princess; Khan; Kiev; Lithuania; Nastas'ya Nikulichna; Tatars; Vladimir Bright Sun, Prince
References: Astakhova 1961; Evgen'eva and Putilov 1977; Khudiakov 1964

NASTAS'YA NIKULICHNA
Russia

A polianitsa whom Dobrynya Nikitich came across as she spurred her jet-black horse across the plains. Dobrynya quickly strung an arrow in his bow and fired at the maiden, the arrow flying straight and true and striking her on the side of her helmet.

However, rather than hurting the rider, the arrow simply fell to the ground and the woman rode on as if nothing had happened. Dobrynya let a second arrow fly, with exactly the same result. The third arrow struck the woman on her helmet, causing her to stop and look around. She caught sight of Dobrynya and rode up to him, lifted him from his saddle by his hair, and thrust him into a deep pouch she carried with her. For

three days he brooded there in silence as they rode across the steppes. On the fourth day, the woman's horse stumbled and complained that it could no longer continue to carry a polianitsa and a bogatyr'.

The woman immediately climbed down from her horse and took Dobrynya out of her pouch, demanding to know who he was, and saying that if he was older than her, she would kill him; if he were younger, she would consider him her brother; and if they were the same age, she would marry him. Dobrynya refused to tell the woman anything. However, her horse recognized him and told the woman that his name was Dobrynya Nikitich and that he was the same age as the woman. The latter then told Dobrynya that her name was Nastas'ya Nikulichna, and that as they were the same age, they should marry. Dobrynya agreed, and the two of them rode back to Kiev.

Dobrynya's mother, the widow Amelfia Timofeyevna, welcomed Nastas'ya to their home. Before long, a huge wedding was arranged which was attended by Prince Vladimir Bright Sun and his wife Evpraksiya. For three days and three nights the wedding feast wore on, and afterward Dobrynya and his new wife Nastas'ya returned to live with Amelfia Timofeyevna. Thereafter Nastas'ya stayed at home like any other Russian wife. When Dobrynya left to wage war in behalf of the king of Lithuania, his wife promised that she would wait faithfully for him. However, after many years had passed and news of her husband's death had reached Kiev, Nastas'ya agreed to marry Alyosha Popovich—even though she had promised Dobrynya that Alyosha would be the last man she would ever consider marrying.

Dobrynya Nikitich heard of the wedding plans and rode quickly back to Kiev, where he disguised himself as a minstrel and sang for the wedding guests. When his identity was revealed, Dobrynya forgave his wife for her errant ways but made ready to kill Alyosha Popovich—his sword being stayed by Il'ya

Muromets. Dobrynya and Nastas'ya lived the rest of their lives in peace and happiness and never again spoke of (or to) Alyosha Popovich.

See also: Alyosha Popovich; Amelf(i)a Timofe(y)evna; Bogatyr'; Dobrynya Nikitich; Evpraksiya (~ia), Princess; Il'ya Muromets; Kiev; Lithuania; Polianitsa; Vladimir Bright Sun, Prince
References: Astakhova 1961; Evgen'eva and Putilov 1977; Gil'ferding 1951; Rambaud 1879

NASTAS'YA OF THE GOLDEN BRAID
Russia

Wife of Bel Belyanin and mother of Peter Belyaninovich, Vasilii Belyaninovich, and Ivan Belyaninovich. She was abducted by Whirlwind and rescued many years later by her youngest son Ivan, although Peter and Vasilii tried to claim the credit for themselves.

See also: Bel Belyanin; Ivan Belyaninovich; Peter (Belyaninovich); Vasilii Belyaninovich; Whirlwind

NAUI
Russia

A great, mythical bird into which Vol'ga Buslavlevich turned himself in order to drive all the birds in a forest into the nets strung up by his men. The exact shape and form of the Naui bird are not revealed, but some have suggested that it was a cross between an eagle and a dragon.

See also: Dragon; Vol'ga Buslavlevich

NAVA
Russia

A name for the underworld, the land of the dead (a land also known as Rai, or Peklo). Also the name of a sea in the underworld that the dead must cross in order to reach their eternal abode.

See also: Peklo; Rai; Underworld, The
References: Afanas'ev 1865–69; Haase 1939

NAVII DEN'
Russia

A festival day shortly after Easter and Radunitsa that marked the time of the year when the russalki moved from their watery winter homes to spend the summers in the trees of the woods and forests.

See also: Radunitsa; Rus(s)alki (~ulki)

NAVKI
Russia

One of the various names applied to the russalki, which appears to owe its origins to Nava, the name of the underworld sea. Other names for the russalki include mavki, faraony, and vodianiani.

See also: Faraony; Mavki; Nava; Rus(s)alki (~ulki); Underworld, The; Vodianiani
References: Snegirev 1837–39

NAZARIEV, FOMA
Russia
See Foma Nazariev.

NEDELIA, SAINT
Russia

One of the two saints commonly associated with Saint Paraskeva, the other being Saint Sreda. Saint Nedelia was also linked with Saint Anastasia. The three saints—Paraskeva, Nedelia, and Sreda—are considered Christian personifications of the pagan goddesses of fate. They were worshiped either as a triune entity or individually and interchangeably.

See also: Anastasia, Saint; Nedelia, Saint; Paraskeva, Saint; Sreda, Saint
References: Afanas'ev 1865–69; Bezsonov 1861; Haase 1939; Ralston 1872

NEMAL CHELOVEK
Russia

"The Big Man," a sorcerer who, in the guise of a rich merchant, kidnapped the only daughter of an unnamed tsar and his wife by luring the young woman onto his ship with promises of untold riches, such as a self-playing lute, a talking cat, a self-laying tablecloth, and a host of other objects never before seen. The tsar immediately offered half his kingdom and his daughter's hand in marriage to whoever could find her and return her home again.

Many men tried and failed, and gradually the tsar grew more and more despondent. Then one night a lowly guard named Ivan was standing watch in the tsar's garden when he overheard two crows talking. These crows talked about a sorcerer named Nemal Chelovek who had once visited the realm and made off with the daughter of the tsar. In the course of their conversation, the crows named the kingdom in which the sorcerer lived and described how he might be defeated.

Ivan listened intently, and when his watch had come to an end, he went to ask permission of the tsar to search for his daughter. The tsar was less than responsive to the idea of a humble soldier going to look for his daughter, especially when so many valiant and noble men before him had failed. When Ivan assured the tsar that he would not fail, the tsar relented and provisioned and equipped Ivan for his journey. However, the tsar warned the soldier that if he failed he would pay with his life.

Two days later Ivan set sail for the Southern Seas. En route he made a detour and came ashore at a small island on which two leshie lived who had jointly inherited the self-cutting Samosek Sword some thirty years before. As Ivan the guard stepped onto the island, he heard the two leshie fighting over whose the sword truly was, and seeking the two out, he offered to act as their judge. Ivan thought for a moment, and then proposed that he should hold the sword himself. He would shoot an arrow into the woods, and the leshii that brought the arrow back to him would be awarded ownership of the sword. The leshie readily agreed and gave the sword to Ivan. Ivan then shot an arrow far into the woods, and the two leshie ran off. They quickly found the arrow but then began fighting over whose it was. Ivan laughed to himself as he reboarded his ship and set sail with the Samosek Sword for the kingdom of Nemal Chelovek.

Two days later the ship landed and Ivan stepped ashore to find Nemal Chelovek's mansion totally unguarded, for the sorcerer never imagined anyone would be foolish enough to enter his domain. Ivan entered the mansion and quickly located the tsar's daughter, who told him that Nemal Chelovek intended her to become the bride of the Gorynich, a terrible dragon that was also the nephew of the sorcerer. Ivan told her not to worry, for he would deliver her. When she heard these brave words, the princess gave Ivan her ring as a token of their betrothal.

Just then Nemal Chelovek returned to his mansion and stormed into the great hall where Ivan was standing with the princess. When the sorcerer saw Ivan, he cast a spell that made him grow until his head brushed the ceiling, and then he rushed at Ivan. Ivan simply lifted the Samosek Sword, which flew through the air of its own volition and neatly decapitated the oncoming giant. Then the sword went through the mansion and killed all of Nemal Chelovek's servants before returning neatly to Ivan's hand. Ivan and the princess then went home, and no one in the world was ever troubled again by Nemal Chelovek.

See also: Dragon; Gorynich; Ivan the Guard; Leshii (~y); Samosek Sword

NESTOR
Russia
A monk of the Pechersky cloister in Kiev who was once considered the author of the *Nachal'naya Letopis'*, one of several extant versions of the *Primary Chronicle*. However, it is now generally accepted that Nestor was simply an editor of or a contributor to the chronicle.

See also: Kiev; *Primary Chronicle*
References: Cross and Sherbowitz-Wetzor 1953; Vernadsky 1948

NICHOLAS, SAINT
Russia
Anglicized name for Saint Nikolai of Mozhaisk.

See also: Nikolai of Mozhaisk, Saint

NIEKIA

Russia

The daughter of the Moon, betrothed to Nainas. Because the Sun wanted her to marry his son Peivalké, the Moon sent her daughter to be raised on earth by an elderly couple. Eventually the Sun discovered the whereabouts of Niekia and took her up to meet his son, a journey that left her badly burned. She refused to marry Peivalké. In his fury, the Sun threw the unfortunate Niekia back into her mother's arms. The Moon pressed Niekia to her breast, leaving an imprint that is still visible to this day on the lunar surface.

See also: Moon; Nainas; Peivalké; Sun

NIGHT

Russia

There are no Slavic legends specifically devoted to Night; however, the legends of Baba-Yaga the witch describe him as being under her command, like Sun and Day. In these tales Night is described as a horseman with a black face, dressed from head to foot in black, and riding a horse of the deepest black imaginable, complete with a black saddle and harness. Night is the brother of Day—his exact opposite—but Night's relationship to Sun is never revealed. Some say that Sun may be the father of both Day and Night, but this idea is not confirmed by any of the stories in which Night appears.

See also: Baba-Yaga (-Jaga, -Iaga); Day; Sun

NIGHTINGALE

Russia

A brigand, half bird and half man, whose Russian name was Solovei Rakhmatich. Solovei lived in a nest, in a tree beside the stream called Smorodinka. For thirty years he had controlled the road between Chernigov and Kiev, killing any who tried to pass with his shrill whistle. When Il'ya Muromets traveled down this road, Solovei tried to unseat the great knight but only succeeded in making his horse stumble. Quickly regaining his balance, Il'ya Muromets shot an arrow at the brigand, which struck him in the temple, knocking him senseless and dislodging him from his perch. Il'ya Muromets then bound the brigand and took him back to Kiev, where he paraded him before Prince Vladimir Bright Sun. Then he took Solovei out onto the steppe, where he was beheaded.

See also: Chernigov; Il'ya Muromets; Kiev; Smorodinka; Solovei (~y) Rakhmatich; Vladimir Bright Sun, Prince

NIKITA

Russia

The husband of Amelfia Timofeyevna and father by her of Dobrynya Nikitich. Legends indicate that Amelfia Timofeyevna was also married at one time to Buslai, and it would thus appear either that Buslai died and Amelfia Timofeyevna subsequently married Nikita, or vice versa.

See also: Amelf(i)a Timofe(y)evna; Buslai (~y); Dobrynya Nikitich

NIKITA ROMANOV

Russia

The brother-in-law of Ivan Groznyi. He is featured in a story by the title of *The Tsar Resolves to Kill His Son*. This bylina opens during a feast held in Moscow in honor of the state's male and female warriors. During the course of the feast, Ivan Groznyi learns that his son Ivan Tsarevich has conspired against him, and the tsar immediately has this son arrested and dragged off to the banks of the Moskva River where the executioner's block awaits him. The tsarina, Ivan Tsarevich's mother, rushes to the house of her brother and tells him what has occurred. The brother, named Nikita Romanov, hurries to the banks of the river, where he stops the execution. He then seeks out the informer who betrayed his nephew, and kills him. Ivan Groznyi acknowledges his mistake and rewards Nikita Romanov for preventing the death of his son. However, it is this very tsarevich whom history records as having been killed by his father in 1581. Regardless of Nikita Romanov's success in warding off disaster, Ivan Groznyi eventually accomplishes the evil deed by his own hand.

See also: Bylina; Ivan Groznyi; Ivan Tsarevich; Moscow; Nikita Romanov

References: Chadwick 1964; Chistov 1967

NIKITICH, DOBRYNYA

Russia

See Dobrynya Nikitich.

NIKITIN, KOSTIA

Russia

See Kostia Nikitin.

NIKOLAI OF MOZHAISK, SAINT

Russia

One of the patron saints of Russia and a patron saint of sailors, as well as one of the most popular saints worldwide. He is known in English as Saint Nicholas. Very little is known about the true Saint Nicholas other than that he was a bishop of Myra in Lycia (southwest Turkey) during the fourth century. As the patron saint of children, Saint Nicholas became inextricably linked with the tradition of giving and receiving pres-

ents, especially at Christmas. His feast day is 6 December.

Saint Nikolai is featured in the story of Sadko. The saint was credited by Sadko with having helped him escape imprisonment beneath the sea by the Sea Tsar. As a gesture of thanks to Saint Nikolai, Sadko—the richest merchant in Novgorod—built a magnificent cathedral in Novgorod and dedicated it to him.

The protective nature of Saint Nikolai is also well demonstrated in the story of Ivan the merchant's son. Ivan was placed under the protection of Saint Nikolai of Mozhaisk and then made to keep vigil over the body of the local tsar's daughter, who was a witch. By reading the Psalms, and with the help of Nikolai, Ivan captured the witch when she rose from her coffin and made her pray to God for absolution. Even though she did this and was resurrected, she was still possessed by evil. Seeing this, Saint Nikolai pushed the girl into a bonfire and pulled her burning body apart. Hordes of frogs, snakes, and other reptiles—the source of her evil—crawled from her severed limbs and were burned in

Detail of Saint Nikolai of Mozhaisk, from a mosaic in Cappella Palatina, Palazzo Reale, Palermo, Italy (Alinari/Art Resource, NY)

the fire. Saint Nikolai then restored the princess to life, baptized her, and married her to Ivan. Many years later, after his father-in-law died, Ivan ascended to the throne.

See also: Nicholas, Saint; Novgorod; Sadko; Sea Tsar

References: Magarshack 1968

NIKULICHNA, NASTAS'YA

Russia

See Nastas'ya Nikulichna.

NO BIGGER THAN A FINGER

Russia

A tiny boy who was born when his mother cut off her little finger while baking an apple pie. When the boy went out to the fields to help his father plow, he told his father that should anyone offer to buy him, he should be sold for as high a price as his father could get. Then the boy told his father to rest. The little fellow climbed up to the horse's ear to whisper instructions as he quickly finished the plowing.

Just then a rich landowner came by and was amazed to see the horse plowing the field, apparently by itself. When the father explained that his diminutive son was giving it instructions, the landowner paid a very high price for him and put the tiny boy in his pocket. No Bigger than a Finger gnawed a hole in the pocket, jumped to the ground, and started for home.

That night, resting behind a blade of grass, he overheard three thieves who were planning to steal a bull. He persuaded them that he could be of help, so they took him along to the bull pen. No Bigger than a Finger entered the pen and led out the finest bull, which the thieves then shared among themselves, leaving only the offal for No Bigger than a Finger, who lay down to sleep beside it. During the night a hungry wolf came along and swallowed the offal and the tiny fellow.

Alive in the wolf's stomach, No Bigger than a Finger gave it a very hard time, for each time it stalked a flock of sheep, a tiny voice rang out to warn the shepherd. Finally the wolf pleaded

with No Bigger than a Finger to crawl out of his stomach. The boy agreed on condition that the wolf take him home. Back at the village, No Bigger than a Finger crawled out of the wolf and took hold of it by the tail. Too weak to run away, the wolf was easily killed by No Bigger than a Finger's old parents, with whom the boy was then reunited.

NOBODY

Russia

The name of the invisible being commonly known as I-Know-Not-What, who lived at I-Know-Not-Where and who was brought thence by Petrushka.

See also: I-Know-Not-What; I-Know-Not-Where; Petrushka

NOVAYA ZEMLYA

Russia

A group of Russian islands in the Arctic Ocean that separate the Barents Sea from the Kara Sea. The Russian name, which means "new land," most commonly refers to the two largest islands. The northernmost of these covers about 20,000 square miles (52,000 square kilometers) and is blanketed by glaciers. The Soviet Union tested nuclear bombs here in the 1950s, and the island still registers harmful levels of radiation today. The large, southern island has an area of about 15,000 square miles (38,800 square kilometers), most of which is a treeless plain.

Early Russians first discovered Novaya Zemlya between the eleventh and twelfth centuries, but the islands remained uninhabited until 1877, when the Samoyeds established the first permanent settlements there. Today a few Russians and Samoyeds live on the southern island.

See also: Samoyeds

NOVGOROD

Russia

City on the Volkhov River in northwest Russia. A major trading city in medieval times and the original capital of Russia, Novgorod was founded by the Viking chieftain Riurik in 862. The Viking merchants who went there quickly became fully assimilated into the native Slav population. The Russian capital was moved to Kiev in 912, but this did little to harm the prosperity of Novgorod. It developed a strong municipal government that was run by the leaders of the various craft guilds, and until the thirteenth century, it flourished as a major commercial center— a fact illustrated by the legend of Sadko.

Novgorod became a principal member of the Hanseatic League, but by then its economy had started to decline. This decline was hastened by the rule of the boyar nobles who wrested power away from the guilds in 1416. In 1476 Novgorod came under the control of Ivan the Great, and it was sacked in 1570 by Ivan Groznyi.

See also: Hanseatic League; Ivan Groznyi; Ivan the Great; Kiev; Riurik; Sadko; Vikings

NOVOTORZHENI, KOSTIA
Russia
See Kostia Novotorzheni.

NUM
Samoyed
God of the sky, who had no form other than that of the air. The very first being, he subsequently created the universe from a beak full of mud that one of the birds he sent out over the primordial ocean brought back to him.

NYA
Slav
God of the dead and ruler of the underworld realms of Rai, Peklo, and Nava. His name comes from the root *ny,* which expresses the idea of death.

See also: Nava; Peklo; Rai; Underworld, The

OBIDA
Russia

A swan-maiden whose appearance was supposed to be the precursor of bad times for the people and a barren period for agriculture. She is connected with Div and the personification of grief as a triune deity. Unless Obida was invoked and appeased with the correct rituals, she would fly over the land, laying it to waste.

See also: Div
References: Mann 1979; Zenkovsky 1963

OBIN-MURT
Votyak

"Rain man," the god of rain.

OD(LEK)
Mongolia

Variant name(s) for Tengri.

ODZ-MANOUK
Armenia

"Serpent Child," the dragon born to an unnamed king and queen. One week after his birth the child, who had been born as a snake, became a dragon, and had to be locked away in a special chamber for fear of what he might do if allowed to roam free. Odz-Manouk was offered all the finest foods in the kingdom, but he did not touch any of it, and before long his roars of hunger threatened to shake the very palace apart. Then, by chance, the daughter of the king's chamberlain went to see Odz-Manouk, who snatched her up and quickly ate her.

From that day forth, Odz-Manouk had to be fed with maidens at the rate of one a day. Every morning the palace guards would go out into the countryside and drag back an unsuspecting maiden who would be lowered to her death through a hole in the roof of Odz-Manouk's chamber. One day the guards brought back the most beautiful maiden in all the land, a girl by the name of Arevhat, whom they lowered through the roof of the chamber before they hurried away.

Later that day the king went to look in on his son and was astonished to find the girl still alive. His astonishment turned to bewilderment when he saw that Odz-Manouk was no longer a dragon but had been transformed into a handsome prince. This transformation came about because Arevhat had spoken kindly to him and had not been frightened by his appearance. Released from the chamber, Odz-Manouk and Arevhat soon were married.

Some days later, Odz-Manouk asked his new wife exactly who she was. She told him that she was an orphan and had not always been the radiant woman he saw before him. Once she had been an ordinary girl. One day, while she sat on a hillside sewing, her bobbin fell down a narrow ravine. She reached down into the crevice but could not reach the bobbin. Then she saw an old woman standing at the bottom. The woman told her how she could enter and retrieve the lost item.

Once Arevhat was inside, however, the entrance disappeared. The girl realized that she was in the presence of a witch. The witch first asked Arevhat to clean her home, which she did, and then to comb her hair. Arevhat performed these tasks with kindness. Then she allowed the old woman to rest her head in her lap while she slept, having first given Arevhat instructions to wake her when she saw yellow water flowing. Arevhat did as she was instructed; and when the old woman awakened, she took Arevhat by the ankles and plunged her into the yellow water. Then she sent her on her way, transformed into a radiant beauty; and it was thus that she had been brought to the palace.

See also: Arevhat

References: Orbeli and Taronian 1959–67, vol. 1

OHAN

Armenia

The laborer father of an unnamed youth who became known as the Apprentice.

See also: Apprentice, The

OKA

Russia

A river that barred the passage of Il'ya Muromets on his journey from Murom to Kiev. He was able to cross the river only after he asked her permission and thanked her for the fertility she brought to the surrounding land. That alone would not have been enough: The Oka allowed him passage also because his mother had blessed his journey and because he was riding his wondrous horse, Borushka Matushka or Kosmatushka.

See also: Borushka Matushka; Il'ya Muromets; Kiev; Kosmatushka; Murom

OLEG

Russia

Historical prince of Kiev who died in 912. He was successor to Riurik and had a daughter named Olga. According to the Russian chronicles, Oleg asked his wizards how he would meet his death. They told him that he would be killed by his favorite horse. Reluctantly Oleg banished the animal from the court and had it released far out on the steppe. Many years later Oleg heard that the horse had died and rode out to the place, where he was shown the animal's skeleton. Dismounting, he placed one foot onto the skull of the animal—upon which a poisonous viper shot out of one eye socket and bit him on the ankle. Several days later Oleg died, fulfilling the prophecy. After his death

the throne passed to Igor, his son-in-law, and then to his daughter Olga after the murder of Igor.

See also: Kiev; Olga; Riurik

References: Chadwick 1964; Cross and Sherbowitz-Wetzor 1953; Waliszewski 1926

OLGA

Russia

The wife of Igor, and the daughter of Oleg. Following the murder of her husband, Olga was courted by Prince Mal, the peaceful leader of the Derevliane, who sought her hand in an attempt to acquire the Kievan kingdom. What happened then is related in a folktale known as *Olga's Revenge.*

Upon hearing the suit of Prince Mal, Olga sent messengers to the Derevliane asking them to send envoys so that they might discuss a possible marriage alliance. When those envoys arrived, however, Olga immediately had them thrown into a deep trench and buried alive. Next Olga sent for further envoys to visit her, inviting them to a great feast at which the proposed alliance would

An undated illustration of Prince Oleg (RIA-Novosti/Sovfoto)

be discussed. When these envoys arrived, Olga invited them to refresh themselves in the bathhouse and then had her men set fire to the bathhouse with her guests inside.

Now Olga turned her wrath directly upon Prince Mal and the Derevliane. She and her entourage traveled to the grave of Igor, her husband, which happened to lie within Derevlian territory. There she invited the Derevliane to a feast in Igor's honor. When all her guests were drunk, her men hacked them to pieces. Then she assumed command of the army and demanded three pigeons and three sparrows as tribute from every Derevlian household. When these were delivered, she fixed firebrands to their claws and set them free so that they might fly back to their homes and burn the Derevlian houses. Olga went on to vanquish Prince Mal. Not only did the Derevliane fail to gain the Kievan kingdom, but Olga conquered the Derevlian land.

See also: Derevliane; Igor; Kiev; Mal, Prince; Oleg

References: Cross and Sherbowitz-Wetzor 1953

ONCE A WOLF, ALWAYS A WOLF
Armenia

A wolf once walked the hills above a flock of sheep and called down his blessings on them. The oldest sheep of the flock listened to the blessing and then turned to the remainder of the flock and warned them not to listen, for a wolf would always be a wolf, no matter what he said or did to the contrary.

One of the fables of Vardan.

See also: Vardan
References: Marr 1894–99

ONE-EYE
Russia

One of the two servants of Whirlwind. He and his companion, Lame, are so called because that is exactly what they were. Endowed with magical powers, they helped Ivan Belyaninovich to return home after he killed Whirlwind, and once there, to com-

plete the tasks set by Elena the Fair, which revealed the treachery of Ivan's brothers Peter Belyaninovich and Vasilii Belyaninovich.

See also: Ivan Belyaninovich; Lame; Peter (Belyaninovich); Vasilii Belyaninovich; Whirlwind

OPSIKION
Slav

Slav colony that was at one time under the governorship of Methodius, the brother of Saint Cyril.

See also: Cyril and Methodius, Saints

ORSEL
Slav

Variant name for Ursula.

ORT
Finno-Ugric—Cheremiss

Cheremiss word for the spirit or soul with which all things, animate and inanimate, are imbued. Among the Votyaks this soul is called the urt.

See also: Cheremiss-Mordvin; Urt; Votyaks

OSSETES
Russia

People descended from the ancient Alans, who speak Ossetic, a language of the Iranian branch of the subfamily of Indo-Iranian languages. Ossetic has two dialects, Iron and Digor, both of which are written using the Latin alphabet (previously, the Armenian alphabet was used). The Ossetes traditionally inhabited Ossetia, a region in the central Caucasus (part of Caucasia), the northern areas of which are in Russia and the southern areas in the republic of Georgia. Ossetians presently number about 600,000. The northern Ossetians are Sunnites. They export timber and cultivate various crops, especially maize. The southern Ossetians are Eastern Orthodox Christians and are chiefly pastoral, herding sheep, goats, and cattle. Traditional industry includes the manufacturing of leather goods, fur caps, daggers, and metalware. Christianity was introduced to Ossetia in the twelfth century. The region was conquered by Russia in 1802–1806. These people tell a very similar story to that of the passing of King Arthur—a story that might have been carried to the area by the Romans, though this connection has not been proved.

See also: Alans; Arthur, King; Caucasus; Georgia

OSTYAKS
General

Ancient indigenous people from western Siberia closely related to the Voguls. They speak Ostyak, a language of the Ugric branch of the Finno-Ugric language family, and inhabit the upland valleys of the Ural Mountains, principally the basin of the Ob' River. The name is also applied to a group of peoples of different languages, the so-called Ostyak-Samoyeds, living between the Urals and the Yenisey River. Ostyaks live chiefly by hunting and fishing. Their handicrafts include carving in wood, bone, and birch bark. As with many early peoples of Asiatic Russia, very little remains of the customs and beliefs of these people. They were almost totally assimilated by the invading and conquering Russians.

See also: Finno-Ugric; Samoyeds; Siberia; Ural Mountains; Voguls

OTHERWORLD
General

A concept common to many cultures. To some it is the land of the dead; to most it is a spiritual land where strange beings and creatures abide. It can usually be reached by the living after a long, torturous journey; but only those of extreme cunning—or luck— ever return. In that respect it is a sort of limbo, a land between life and death through which all must pass and from which only those with the knowledge, ability, or help of the gods can ever hope to return.

OVERTURN MOUNTAIN
Russia

A giant who appears in the story of Ivan the Mute. During Ivan's flight from home to escape his unborn sister, who he had been told would be a terrible witch, Ivan sought to live with Overturn Mountain. The giant told Ivan that he would take him in if it were not for the fact that the giant did not have long to live; he would die as soon as he had overturned the mountain range he was working on.

Later, as Ivan returned home from the sanctuary given him by Sun's Sister, he found that Overturn Mountain only had two mountains left to topple. As Ivan the Mute did not want to see his friend die, he threw down a brush that Sun's Sister had given him, which caused a huge mountain range to spring up from the earth. These mountains Overturn Mountain later toppled into the path of the witch as she chased Ivan back to the home of Sun's Sister, thus delaying the witch long enough to allow Ivan to reach safety.

See also: Ivan the Mute; Sun's Sister

OVINNIK
Slav

The spirit of the barn—from *ovin* (barn)— who looked like a large black cat with fiery eyes but had a fierce bark like a dog. If fed, the Ovinnik would protect the barn and its occupants. If forgotten, the spirit would become malevolent and help itself to the livestock housed in the barn.

OVSEN'
Russia

"Garden," an archaic name for the festival of the Koliada in the Volga region, along with Vinograd. Ovsen' may have been named after the goddess of spring, Vesna.

See also: Koliada; Vesna; Vinograd; Volga
References: Afanas'ev 1865–69; Potebnia 1865

P

when Vol'ga Buslavlevich gathered together his bogatyri and marched into Turkey. Volga and his bogatyri killed the sultan and his men, released Queen Pantalovna, and then divided the rich spoils equally among themselves.

See also: Bogatyr'; Vol'ga Buslavlevich

PARAKHA

Russia

The eldest of the two stepsisters of Marfusha, and the only one of the two to be named. Unlike Marfusha, she and her unnamed sister died when they were left to be married to the frost demon Morozko.

See also: Frost; Marfusha; Morozko

PARASKEVA, SAINT

Russia

Apocryphal saint who appears to have adopted many functions of Mokosh. One of the few truly Russian saints, Paraskeva is of pagan origin. She was usually referred to in her dual identity as Paraskeva-Piatnitsa, or "Saint Friday." The epithet of "Friday" applied to this most popular Russian saint appears to have come from the translation of the Greek word *paraskeva,* meaning the day before the Sabbath, or Friday. Friday was sacred to the goddess Zhiva, and it would seem that the connection being sought by Christian missionaries was again one of assimilation by association.

Celebration of Saint Paraskeva, however, remained pagan, being condemned in 1589 by the patriarch of Constantinople. Twelve Fridays throughout the year were believed sacred to Paraskeva, and on these days, men and women, both young and old, would strip naked and jump and shake, saying that they had seen Saints Paraskeva and Anastasia and had been ordered to honor them with their lascivious dances. The Stoglav Council, set up during the latter half of the sixteenth century by Ivan Groznyi, also condemned the festivals, calling them orgies. However,

PANNONIA

General

Ancient country of Illyria, bounded on the north and east by the Danube River, on the south by Dalmatia, and on the west by Noricum and parts of upper Italy. Pannonia included parts of modern Austria, Hungary, Croatia, and Slovenia. It received its name from the Pannonians, a people probably of Illyrian origin, who lived there in ancient times. Octavian, who later became the Roman emperor Augustus, invaded Pannonia in 35 B.C. but was unable to subdue the country until 9 B.C., when he made it a part of Illyricum, a colony established by the Romans in 168 B.C. The Pannonians moved to the north of the region after an insurrection in A.D. 6 was suppressed, and in A.D. 10 this area became the separate Roman province of Pannonia. In the early second century the Roman emperor Trajan divided the province into Upper Pannonia and Lower Pannonia, but by the end of the fourth century the region was abandoned by Rome. Subsequently Pannonia was held successively by the Huns, Ostrogoths, Lombards, Avars, and Slavs. The Magyars took possession of most of the area at the end of the eleventh century.

See also: Avars; Croatia; Danube; Hungary; Magyars; Slovenia

PANTALOVNA, QUEEN

Russia

At one time held captive by a sultan of Turkey, Queen Pantalovna was released the cult continued, especially in Ukraine, where Friday was considered the Sabbath over Sunday until well into the eighteenth century.

The Stoglav Council issued a decree, known unsurprisingly as the Stoglav document, denouncing Saint Paraskeva as the goddess of fate connected with two other saints with pagan roots—Saints Sreda and Nedelia. All three were seen as the triune Fates, spinners who wove the course of mankind's life, and as mistresses of the cosmic order. This, of course, the Christian church could not accept, as it would place the three saints on the same plane as God.

Paraskeva was represented in folklore and icons as a tall, thin woman with long, flowing hair, the hair being an uncharacteristic trait in a country where long hair was usually plaited. She was surrounded by her twelve "apostles"—another aspect of her cult that brought it into direct conflict with the Stoglav Council. The members of the Council considered the cult a mockery of the Christian faith and an unveiled attempt to assimilate Christianity with paganism, rather than the other way around. Paraskeva's icons were even said to have been "miraculously" discovered, as various Christian icons had—claims that were again an open challenge to the Orthodox faith because they explicitly identified Paraskeva with the Tree of Life. So widespread and well integrated was her cult that at one time, right in the heart of the Russian Empire, in Red Square in Moscow, there stood a chapel dedicated to Paraskeva that was open only to women, who came there to worship on Fridays.

Worship of Paraskeva was perhaps the most entrenched pagan tradition of all and it proved the most difficult for the Orthodox church to eradicate, particularly among the peasantry. The saint was as feared as Baba-Yaga, being associated with death and the underworld, but at the same time was as revered as the Virgin Mary. Paganism and Christianity came into direct conflict through the cult of Paraskeva, giving way eventually to an uneasy coexistence of the two, called "double faith" (dvoeverie). Only after many generations did Paraskeva's pagan influence begin to wane, giving the advantage to the Orthodox rite. Paraskeva was not only worshiped as a saint but was also remembered in folklore, where she has two names—Paraskeva Griaznaia, "Muddy Paraskeva" or "Dirty Paraskeva," and Paraskeva L'nianitsa, "Flaxen Paraskeva." In these two guises she was identified with Mother Earth and the bounty she provided.

See also: Anastasia, Saint; Baba-Yaga (-Jaga, -Iaga); Constantinople; Dvoeverie; Ivan Groznyi; Mokosh; Moscow; Mother Earth; Nedelia, Saint; Paraskeva Griaznaia; Paraskeva L'nianitsa; Paraskeva-Piatnitsa; Sreda, Saint; Tree of Life, The; Ukraine; Underworld, The; Zhiva
References: Afanas'ev 1916 and 1865–69; Bezsonov 1861; Chicherov 1957; Dal' 1957; Haase 1939; Kologrivof 1953; Meyer 1931; Potebnia 1865; Ralston 1872; Warner 1976

PARASKEVA GRIAZNAIA

Russia

"Muddy Paraskeva" or "Dirty Paraskeva," a name given to Saint Paraskeva in popular Russian belief that seems to identify this aspect of the pagan goddess-saint as Mother Earth.

See also: Mother Earth; Paraskeva, Saint
References: Chicherov 1957; Dal' 1957; Potebnia 1865

PARASKEVA L'NIANITSA

Russia

"Flaxen Paraskeva," a name given to Saint Paraskeva that identifies the pagan goddess-saint with the bounty provided by Mother Earth, who is represented by Paraskeva Griaznaia.

See also: Mother Earth; Paraskeva, Saint; Paraskeva Griaznaia
References: Chicherov 1957; Dal' 1957; Potebnia 1865

PARASKEVA-PIATNITSA

Russia

Dual aspect of Saint Paraskeva in which she represented the duality of Paraskeva Griaznaia and Paraskeva L'nianitsa, at once Mother Earth and the bounty she provided. As the mistress of animals, she granted mankind the right to hunt, provided that they did not violate the sanctity of Friday, her day. She was the patroness of marriage as well as the provider of children, acting as a protectress of women during childbirth, thus ensuring her continuing popularity among women long after Christianity had been adopted and accepted by most.

See also: Mother Earth; Paraskeva, Saint; Paraskeva Griaznaia; Paraskeva L'nianitsa
References: Chicherov 1957

PATRIMPAS

Slav

The god of rivers, streams, and springs, but not of lakes.

PAUL

Russia

The Christian ruler of Murom. His wife, euphemistically referred to as the Dark Princess, was visited by the Devil in the form of a serpent, though only she could recognize the Devil and those around her saw the image of Paul. When she told her husband of the visit she had received in her bedchamber, Paul advised her to discover from the Devil the manner of his death. She did as he asked, and found out that Paul's brother Peter of Murom would kill him. However, when Peter came to do the dirty deed, he only succeeded in killing the serpent that had assumed Paul's guise. Even though Peter only managed to kill the semblance of his brother, all reference to Paul disappears from the legend at this point; perhaps by killing his brother's image Peter did indeed manage to dispatch Paul himself.

For a full account of this legend see the entry for Fevroniia or Peter of Murom.

See also: Dark Princess, The; Devil, The; Fevroniia; Murom; Peter of Murom
References: Zenkovsky 1963

PEASANT, THE PRIEST, AND THE GOLD, THE

Russia

A very poor, very old peasant who had no money to bury his beloved wife went cap in hand to his neighbors to ask them to help him dig a grave. No one would help, so the peasant went to the local priest to ask him to bury his wife. The priest was a greedy man and he immediately asked the old peasant who was going to pay for the service. The peasant replied that he had no money but he would gladly work for the priest in repayment. The priest laughed and told the old man to bury his wife himself.

As the snow fell, the old man wielded his spade against the frozen soil. Hour after hour he toiled, until his spade hit something hard in the ground, something that shone in the light of the old man's lantern. Minutes later, his tools discarded, the old man hurried home with a chest of gold under his thin cloak.

The very next day the old man went back to the priest and this time was able to pay him a gold coin to bury his wife. After the funeral service, the priest and his retinue went to the humble home of the peasant for the *pominki* (the name given to the traditional Russian feast in memory of the dead), and there the peasant told the priest what he had found. Greed flashed across the face of the priest, who immediately made plans to deprive the old man of his gold.

When the priest returned home, he had his wife kill and skin their goat, making sure that the horns remained attached to the pelt, and then he had her sew him up inside it. Satisfied that he could never be recognized, the priest made his way to the home of the peasant and introduced himself as the Devil, come to reclaim the gold that he had buried in the graveyard. The peasant gave up the chest and the priest hurried home, sure that he had become a very rich man. However, when his wife came to cut away the goatskin, she could not, for it had become part of the priest, and every time she cut the skin, she cut her husband as well.

The priest prayed for forgiveness and returned the gold to the peasant, who lived the rest of his life in comfort. The priest remained trapped in the goatskin and was thus punished by both God and the Devil, as he had offended both.

See also: Devil, The

PECHENEGS
General

An ancient, warlike, nomadic tribe of the Black Sea steppes.

See also: Black Sea

PECHERSKAIA LAVRA
Russia

The very first Russian monastery, built during the tenth century, in Kiev. Pecherskaia Lavra consisted of a series of caves connected by a honeycomb of tunnels bored into the limestone cliffs above the city. The site was thought to be guarded by the Virgin Mary.

See also: Kiev
References: Bezsonov 1861

PEIVALKÉ
Russia

The Sun's son. When he announced to his father that he had attempted to find a bride, his father replied that he had heard that the Moon had just had a daughter and that he would approach the Moon about a betrothal. The Moon was horrified at the prospect and protested that the Sun would scorch her delicate daughter, but the Sun simply waved the Moon's objections aside. She then told the Sun that her daughter was already betrothed to Nainas. At this the Sun became so angry that everyone on earth had to take cover.

To protect her daughter, the Moon sent her to be raised on earth by an elderly couple who called her Niekia. Finally the Sun became aware of Niekia's existence and carried her up to meet his son, but she was severely scorched and adamant that she would not marry Peivalké. Furiously, the Sun flung Niekia back into the arms of the Moon, her mother, who pressed her to her heart. Tradition has it that Niekia's face is visible to this day on the surface of the moon.

See also: Moon; Nainas; Niekia; Sun

PEKLO
Russia

One of many names applied to the underworld, *Peklo* is associated with *pech'* (a verb meaning "to bake," and a noun meaning "oven" or "furnace"). In ancient times this word evoked the comforting warmth of paradisal realms rather than the scorching heat of hell—the modern, post-Christian interpretation.

See also: Nava; Rai; Underworld, The
References: Afanas'ev 1865–69; Haase 1939

PERKONIS
Prussia

The thunder god, the Prussian version of the Lithuanian Perkunas. His sanctuaries contained a fire that was never allowed to go out.

See also: Perkunas

PERKONS
Latvia

The Latvian thunder god, the equivalent of the Lithuanian Perkunas and the Prussian Perkonis.

See also: Perkonis; Perkunas

PERKUNAS
Lithuania

The thunder god who was known as Perkons in Latvia, Perkonis in Prussia, and Perun in Russia and the Czech lands. Perkunas was perceived as a vigorous red-bearded man brandishing an ax as he rode across the sky in his rattling chariot drawn by a billy goat. These attributes are remarkably similar to those of the Norse god of thunder,

Thórr, which leads to the conjecture that Perkunas is a Lithuanian variant of that deity.

Perkunas lives in a castle on the top of the slippery slope of the sky (see Dausos), where as the agent of good and justice, he attacks the Devil with his thunderbolt. He also dispenses justice on mankind, either striking down evil men with his thunderbolt or striking their homes with lightning. The thunderbolt of Perkunas is, as in many other mythologies, conceived of as a symbol of fertility, and in spring the thunder of Perkunas is believed to purify the earth of the evil spirits of winter and bring it back to life.

See also: Dausos; Devil, The; Perun

PERMYAKS
General

Indigenous people from a region to the east of the Ural Mountains, related to the Votyaks and Zyrians, who have been almost totally assimilated by the Russians. Their Finno-Ugric language is still spoken in a few isolated places, but virtually nothing remains of their ancient traditions and beliefs.

See also: Finno-Ugric; Ural Mountains; Votyaks; Zyrians

PEROM (~N)
Slovakia

Literally, "Curse." The Slovak name for Perun, the god of thunder and rain.

See also: Perun

PERPERUNA
Russia

Virgin goddess who invokes rain. Perperuna is identified as a feminine personification of the great god Perun.

See also: Perun
References: Frazer

PERUN
Slav

Also: Perom; Peron; Pikker; Piorun; Pyerun
The god of thunder and rain, known as Perkonis in Prussia, Perkons in Latvia, Perkunas in Lithuania, Perusan in Bulgaria, Peron ("curse") in Slovakia, and Perun in Russia and the Czech lands. His name is possibly cognate with that of Paranjanya, an epithet of the Hindu storm god Indra. Perun was depicted with a head of silver and a gold mustache. In the tenth century an idol of Perun stood in Novgorod near Lake Il'men', around which six eternal fires burned. Regarded as the lord of the universe, Perun lived in the sky and had absolute control over the weather. When he was angry, he caused thunderstorms and sent lightning to strike down people who had offended him. Belemnite fossils, which formed around the arrow-like internal bone of a creature similar to the cuttlefish, traditionally were regarded by those who found them as missiles flung down by Perun, and they were thus called "thunder arrows." Perun's thunderbolts also were considered a potent fertility symbol because they were thought to awaken the earth in spring from its death-like winter sleep.

God of war as well as thunder, Perun was believed to ride across the sky in an iron chariot pulled by an enormous billy goat and to carry a bow and arrows as well as a heavy cudgel, a spear, and a battle-ax that always returned to his hand after it was thrown. The protector of soldiers, the god could bestow victory on those he favored. For this reason, when military or commercial treaties were concluded, it was by their naked swords and by Perun that the Russians swore to keep their word. Very much an exclusive deity, Perun had no priests, his rites being performed by princes and military leaders. However, the common populace did regard him as necessary to their everyday existence, for without his intervention every morning, Darkness would hold the Sun prisoner in a cell whose door was impregnable to everything but Perun's lightning.

Cockerels and other animals were offered as votives to Perun, and human sacrifices in his honor also were common. One recorded example of the latter was a Viking living in Kiev who was chosen by Vladimir I to be the sacrificial victim following a successful raid. The Viking, a Christian, refused to be the votive for a pagan god, but he was nonetheless sacrificed as Vladimir I had ordered. Perun was especially honored in pre-Christian times at a spring festival where young maidens would dance themselves to death in his honor, a practice that later became the inspiration for Stravinsky's *The Rite of Spring*. Over time, the rite was modified to become a ceremonial ring-dance in which all the virgins of a village or a nomadic group took part.

In 988, when Vladimir I made the political decision to accept Christianity as part of a pact with the Byzantine emperor Basil II, Vladimir ordered that all the pagan idols be destroyed. The statue of Perun that stood outside his palace in Kiev was tied to a horse, beaten with metal rods, and finally cast into the waters of the Dnieper. Even though Christianity was the new official faith in Russia, Christian missionaries found it enormously difficult to stamp out worship of this king of the gods. In Novgorod he was apparently tolerated well into the Christian era, as records show that the statue of Perun was solemnly flogged each year to rid it of demonic forces. In other areas Perun was simply amalgamated with the prophet Elijah—or Il'ya, as he was known in Russia—because according to the Old Testament, Elijah shared many of Perun's powers, including the ability to call down rain or fire from heaven. Some say that Perun became Il'ya Muromets, the bogatyr', although separate legends of Perun and Il'ya Muromets appear to have sprung up side by side.

Perun and two other ancient gods, Khors and Mokosh, together form a trinity.

See also: Anna; Basil II, Bulgaroctonus; Bogatyr'; Darkness; Dnieper; Il'men', Lake; Il'ya; Il'ya Muromets; Khor(s); Kiev; Mokosh; Novgorod; Perkunas; Sun; Vikings; Vladimir I
References: Gimbutas 1971; Ivanov and Toporov 1965; Potebnia 1865

PERUSAN
Bulgaria
The Bulgar name for Perun, the god of thunder and rain.
See also: Perun

PESEIAS
Slav
One of the two patrons of domestic animals, the other being Krukis.
See also: Krukis

PETAR LONZARIC
Croatia
A notorious gambler from the thirteenth century who was playing cards outside the church of St. Vid in Rijeka (Vid being the Slav form of Vitus) and losing badly. Enraged by his bad luck, he began to blaspheme, blaming the saint for his misfortune. Throwing yet another losing hand of cards onto the ground, he raced into the church and began hurling accusations at God. Not content with that, he snatched up a large stone and hurled it at the crucifix hanging above the altar. The figure on the cross began to bleed, and Petar Lonzaric suffered divine retribution for his actions: As he left the church, the ground opened up and swallowed him, except for one hand, which remained thrust from the ground in a spasm of death. The governor of the city ordered the hand cut off and cremated.

This legendary event is commemorated in the church of St. Vid by a bronze hand dangling from the cross above the altar and by a stone, attached to the figure of Christ, bearing an inscription to the effect that Petar Lonzaric's attack took place in 1296.

PETER (BELYANINOVICH)
Russia
Son of Bel Belyanin and Nastas'ya of the Golden Braid, and brother to Vasilii Belyaninovich and Ivan Belyaninovich. After Ivan rescued their mother from Whirlwind, Peter and Vasilii left their young brother stranded and returned home to claim credit

for the rescue. The truth eventually came out and their father wanted to have them executed, but Ivan interceded. Peter then married the tsaritsa of the Silver Kingdom and Vasilii the tsaritsa of the Copper Kingdom, and Ivan married Elena the Fair, the tsaritsa of the Golden Kingdom—all three maidens having been rescued by Ivan Belyaninovich when he freed his mother.

See also: Bel Belyanin; Copper Kingdom, The; Elena the Fair; Golden Kingdom, The; Ivan Belyaninovich; Nastas'ya of the Golden Braid; Silver Kingdom, The; Vasilii Belyaninovich; Whirlwind

PETER OF MUROM
Russia

The brother of Paul, who was a Christian ruler of the city of Murom. Paul's wife, euphemistically referred to as the Dark Princess, was visited by the Devil in the form of a serpent. Only she could recognize the Devil in this serpent, whereas those around her saw only the image of Paul. When she told her husband of the visit she had received in her bedchamber, Paul advised her to discover from the Devil the manner of his death. She did as he asked, and found out that Paul's brother Peter would kill him. However, when Peter came to do the dirty deed he succeeded only in killing the serpent that had assumed Paul's guise. It is worth pointing out that at this point in the legend all references to the Dark Princess stop, and it can only be assumed that she was, in fact, a servant of the Devil, and when she had accomplished her purpose, she returned to eternal damnation.

Peter, however, had been tainted by the blood of the serpent. Covered in sores, he set out in search of a cure for himself and his kingdom, which had been struck down as a result of his apparent fratricide. Traveling with a large coterie, Peter arrived at a village called Charity, where he was carried to an isolated cottage in which a very beautiful, half-naked woman sat spinning. The spinner told Peter that she lived alone as her family had died

long before and that she would cure him of his affliction on the condition that he marry her. Peter immediately agreed; and no sooner had he done so than his sores disappeared and his strength was renewed. However, Peter now saw no reason to marry the maiden, and he made to leave the cottage. As he did so, his strength sapped away and the sores again erupted. Convinced that he had no choice in the matter, Peter agreed to the union, and the couple were duly married.

At their wedding the woman told Peter that her name—or rather the name she had chosen to use as his wife—was Fevroniia. Together Peter and Fevroniia traveled back to Murom, where the influential boyars, angered that Peter had married a mere peasant, accused Fevroniia of bad manners at the feast thrown in honor of their prince. Fevroniia retaliated by performing a series of miracles, such as turning crumbs from the table into frankincense and myrrh. These acts, however, did not alleviate the anger of the boyars, who demanded that she be banished from court because she was a powerful sorceress and would hold their wives in her power. Fevroniia agreed to leave Murom, provided Peter accompany her.

So Peter, Fevroniia, and their retinue set out from Murom by boat. As they made camp that evening, Peter expressed worry about their exile. Fevroniia assuaged his fears by performing another miracle: She picked up the branches that had been cut to fuel the cooking fire and blessed them, saying that by morning they would be great trees. True enough, the following morning Peter and his coterie awakened to find themselves in the middle of a great forest, whereas they had been on the edge of a small wood the night before. Peter and Fevroniia remained there until news was brought to them of a fratricidal war that had broken out among the boyars in Murom, who were asking Peter and Fevroniia to return and rule over them. This they did; but while Peter was the figurehead, the true ruler of Murom was Fevroniia.

Many years passed, and the couple ruled Murom wisely. After Peter died and was buried in the cathedral, Fevroniia died by her own will on the feast of Kupalo. She was buried outside the city walls, in emphasis of her pagan and peasant origins; but the following morning the boyars discovered her grave was beside that of her husband, inside the cathedral grounds.

Fevroniia, as symbolized by her legendary transformation of the cut branches into a fully grown forest, is a personification of the pagan tree goddess. This story, which was recorded by the fifteenth-century monk Ermolai-erazm, demonstrates the willingness of the Christian faith to accept certain central aspects of the ancient pagan religions and shows that the two belief systems lived happily side by side so long as Christianity was demonstrably the more potent (as was well illustrated by the burial of Peter in the cathedral and Fevroniia outside the city walls). The magical movement of Fevroniia's grave to the cathedral demonstrates that no matter whether pagan or Christian, God accepts all into his kingdom after death.

See also: Boyars; Charity; Dark Princess, The; Devil, The; Fevroniia; Kupalo; Murom; Paul
References: Zenkovsky 1963

PETROV DEN'
Russia
Saint Peter's Day, the Christianized festival that preceded the harvest and thus welcomed the degenerative powers of autumn. The festival was popularly referred to as "Petrovki." Women, married and single, were central to the festival. On the eve of Petrov Den' the whole village would stay up to welcome the sun, called Lado, as it appeared from beneath the horizon, born again. The women would then gather and swing beneath trees, in imitation of the russalki. As they swung, they would sing about the declining power and vitality of the sun, about the ancestral spirits in the underworld, and about the departure of the water and woodland spirits, who were leaving for their winter homes.

See also: Lado; Petrovki; Rus(s)alki (~ulki); Underworld, The
References: Snegirev 1837–39; Sokolov 1945; Zabylin 1880

PETROVKI
Russia
Popular name for the pagan festival held on Petrov Den', Saint Peter's Day, just before harvest time.
See also: Petrov Den'

PETRUSHKA
Russia
The favorite archer of an unnamed tsar, he was relied upon to supply the finest meat for the tsar's table. One day, however, Petrushka was having no luck at all. All day long he had neither seen nor heard any prey suitable for his master. Trudging wearily back to the palace, thinking about the punishment the tsar might mete out, Petrushka saw a white dove seated in a tree. Carefully notching an arrow to his bow, Petrushka shot and wounded the bird, which fell to the ground. Petrushka ran up to the bird, picked it up, and was about to wring its neck when the bird cried out to Petrushka to spare its life in return for a wondrous reward. Petrushka agreed, and the dove gave him instructions on how he might obtain this reward.

Petrushka took the bird home, patched up its broken wing, and set it on his windowsill so that it might rest. When the bird fell asleep, Petrushka tapped it with a finger as he had been instructed, whereupon the bird fell from the sill and instantly became the most beautiful maiden in all Russia. Petrushka stared in amazement at the apparition before his eyes. Masha the Dove Maiden (for that is how she was known) said they should immediately marry, and Petrushka agreed.

Their life together was extremely happy, though the tsar paid Petrushka little and the couple lived a life of abject poverty. Petrushka's entire life savings amounted to a mere hundred rubles. One day Masha told her husband to take those hundred rubles

A 1990 ballet depicting the story of Petrushka by the Kirov Opera Company in 1996 (Sovfoto/Eastfoto)

and buy her one hundred skeins of silk. Petrushka did as his wife asked; and while Masha worked the silk, Petrushka went to bed. The following morning he awoke to find his wife asleep at the table, and the most beautiful silk carpet he had ever seen stretched out in front of her. The work on the carpet seemed to live, and Petrushka embraced his wife.

She told him to take the carpet into the city and sell it for the first price he was offered, warning him not to ask any price but to let those interested give what they thought was fair. Petrushka did not question his wife, as he knew there were forces afoot that he did not understand. He simply gathered up the carpet and went to the market. There he was soon surrounded by a good number of people who marveled at the carpet. Many asked him what price he would take, but Petrushka

would not name a price. Finally, hearing the commotion, the tsar's counselor came to see the carpet and immediately offered Petrushka five thousand rubles for it. Petrushka accepted the money, and the counselor set off for the palace with the carpet under his arm.

At the palace the counselor showed the tsar the new carpet. The tsar immediately recognized it as a woven tableau of his kingdom. So impressed was the tsar with the carpet that he bought it from his counselor for fifty thousand rubles. The counselor decided that there was a great deal of money to be made from dealing with Petrushka. After the tsar retired to admire his new acquisition, the counselor rode to Petrushka's lowly home and knocked on the door. However, when Masha opened the door, he was so dumbstruck by her beauty that he could not utter a single word, and so Masha closed the door, thinking that an idiot had called on her.

The counselor rode back to the tsar and reported the beauty of Petrushka's wife to his master. The tsar decided to see whether his counselor was speaking the truth, and he rode out to Petrushka's home. He was equally stunned by Masha's beauty. That evening the tsar summoned his counselor and promised him half his kingdom if he could dispose of Petrushka so that the tsar could make Masha his wife.

The counselor pondered the problem, and was still pondering it when he was approached by a rough peasant who offered his assistance in return for a goblet of wine. The counselor gave the peasant the required payment, whereupon the peasant told the counselor to advise the tsar to ask Petrushka to travel to the underworld to see how the tsar's father was faring in that land—for there was never any return from the land of the dead. The counselor so advised the tsar, who commanded the hapless Petrushka to do as bidden or be put to death. Petrushka could do nothing but agree. He went home to tell Masha the news.

She told him to sleep soundly. The following morning she gave him a gold ring, which she told him to roll along the ground: It would take him straight to the underworld. She also advised him to take the tsar's counselor along as a companion because otherwise the tsar would never believe Petrushka's report. Thus Petrushka set out, accompanied by the tsar's counselor. Together they followed the gold ring all the way to the underworld. As they entered that dark realm they encountered an old man pulling a cart laden with wood, goaded by two red-horned demons.

Petrushka recognized the old man as the tsar's father. He called to the demons to allow the old man ten minutes to talk with him. The demons agreed, but only if the counselor took his place; so for ten minutes the old tsar talked with Petrushka, while the counselor hauled the cart under a relentless beating by the demons.

Petrushka and the counselor then returned to the tsar's palace and met with the tsar, who was furious to see Petrushka back in his realm. At first the tsar refused to believe Petrushka's story, especially when the latter told him that his father advised him to be kinder to his subjects. The tsar was on the verge of ordering his guards to take Petrushka away, when the counselor revealed the marks from the beating he had received at the hands of the demons. The tsar reluctantly allowed Petrushka to return home, and then set about berating his counselor for failing him, demanding that he devise a new plan.

Once more the counselor sought the advice of the old peasant, who again accepted a goblet of wine in payment for his counsel. The peasant told the counselor to instruct the tsar to send Petrushka to the Thrice-Ninth Kingdom, which lay in the Thrice-Ninth Land, to capture Kot Bayun, the talking cat, and bring him back.

The tsar followed his counselor's advice, and once again Petrushka returned crestfallen to his wife, who told him to sleep soundly for in the morning she would equip him to safely undertake his task. Sure enough

Masha woke him in the morning and gave him three felt hats, a pair of pincers, and three metal rods. Petrushka followed Masha's advice to the letter. As he drew near the cat, he put the three felt hats on his head and grasped the first metal bar in one hand and the pincers in the other. The cat hissed and clawed viciously at Petrushka; but the hats protected him, although they were torn to shreds. Shortly before the cat tore away the third hat, Petrushka managed to catch the flaying leg in the pincers and started to beat the animal with the first metal rod, which was made of iron. When that bar broke, he picked up the second bar, made of brass, and continued to beat the cat; and when that bar broke, he took the last one, made of tin, and continued the punishment. This bar grew hot and bent, but it did not break, and in the end the cat begged mercy and promised to go with Petrushka to his tsar.

When he stood again before the tsar, Petrushka bowed and told his ruler that he had accomplished his mission. The tsar looked at the cat and asked Petrushka how he could be sure that this was indeed Kot Bayun. Petrushka released the cat, which immediately bared its teeth, arched its back, spat, and flew at the tsar's throat. The tsar called out for help, whereupon Petrushka simply brandished the pincers and the tin bar, and the cat returned to his side. Petrushka then locked the cat in a cage within the palace and returned to the arms of Masha his wife.

The tsar nursed his wounds and then called for his counselor, telling him that if he did not rid him of the troublesome Petrushka once and for all, the counselor would lose his head. The counselor immediately sought out the rough peasant and bought a plan from him as he had done twice before, the payment once again being a single goblet of wine. The peasant this time advised the counselor to tell the tsar to send Petrushka to I-Know-Not-Where, with instructions to return with I-Know-Not-What.

The counselor relayed the plan to the tsar, who in turn passed on these instructions to

Petrushka, who again returned home and told Masha of his plight. This time Masha was at a loss; but she sent her husband off the following morning with an embroidered towel and a ball of wool that he was to roll on the ground and follow to the home of the only person in all the world who might help. Petrushka did as he was instructed and followed the ball of wool. After a long journey the ball of wool came to rest beside the fence that surrounded a curious hut that stood on chicken's legs, a hut that Petrushka immediately recognized as the home of the witch Baba-Yaga.

As Petrushka entered the compound that surrounded the hut, it stopped revolving in the wind, and the witch came out to see who had dared enter her dominion. When she saw Petrushka she cackled and sang about the fine meal of Russian man she would dine on that night. Unperturbed, Petrushka faced the witch and told her that she would not enjoy him as he was, grimy from his journey, and perhaps she would at least allow him to wash before she ate him. Baba-Yaga led him to a barrel of water, and Petrushka washed off the grime of the journey, taking out the towel Masha had given him to dry himself on.

When Baba-Yaga saw the towel, she asked Petrushka where he had come by it; and when he said that Masha his wife had given it to him, Baba-Yaga embraced Petrushka and welcomed him as her son-in-law, for Masha was Baba-Yaga's daughter. Baba-Yaga led Petrushka into her unusual home, and there she laid out a feast fit for any tsar. After they had eaten, Petrushka explained his mission to his mother-in-law. She knew nothing of I-Know-Not-Where or of I-Know-Not-What, but she told Petrushka that he should sleep and she would work on the problem that night.

As soon as Petrushka had fallen asleep Baba-Yaga took her pestle and mortar and sailed through the night sky to the boundaries of the Green Marsh. There she stood on the edge and called out to Babushka-Lyagushka-Skakushka ("Grandmother Hopping Frog"),

the oldest living creature. The marsh stirred and the frog appeared. Baba-Yaga asked the frog if it knew the place I-Know-Not-Where and the thing I-Know-Not-What; and when the frog replied that it did, the witch asked it to take Petrushka there.

Babushka-Lyagushka-Skakushka said that she would do so, provided Petrushka first carried her in a jug of fresh milk to the River of Fire; for she was old, and without the rejuvenating powers of that river, she would not have the strength to undertake the journey. Baba-Yaga agreed and took the frog back to her home in her pestle and mortar. There she prepared a jug of fresh milk, placed the frog in the jug, and woke her son-in-law and told him what to do.

Petrushka took the jug with the frog in it, mounted Baba-Yaga's swiftest horse, and within a matter of a few minutes, stood beside the River of Fire. There Petrushka took the frog out of the jug and placed her on the ground. Placing one foot in the River of Fire, Babushka-Lyagushka-Skakushka started to grow until she was the size of Petrushka's horse. The frog told the archer to climb on her back and hold tight, which Petrushka did, waiting while the frog continued to grow until it was higher than the tallest tree in any forest. The frog made certain that Petrushka was holding on tightly and then leaped high into the air. When they came to earth, they found themselves in a foreign land. The frog slowly exhaled until she resumed her normal size.

Babushka-Lyagushka-Skakushka informed Petrushka that they were now in I-Know-Not-Where. The frog then told Petrushka that he should go to the lowliest hut in a nearby village and hide there behind the stove, for within that hut lived I-Know-Not-What. Petrushka thanked Babushka-Lyagushka-Skakushka and set out. He found the hut with little difficulty and hid himself inside, as instructed.

A short time later an old man came in and told Nobody to bring him food. Instantly a banquet appeared. The old man called out again, this time for drink, and a jug of wine appeared. After the old man had eaten and drunk his fill, Petrushka crept out from behind the stove and called to Nobody to accompany him. Then he left the hut with his mysterious companion and started back toward the kingdom of the tsar and the arms of his beautiful wife.

After a short walk they came across a bandit who owned an enormous club. The bandit asked Petrushka for food, whereupon Petrushka ordered Nobody to supply the bandit with food and drink. The bandit was so impressed that he offered his club to Petrushka in exchange for Nobody, adding that his club, unaided, would kill anyone its master ordered it to kill. Petrushka agreed to the exchange and then continued on his way. After he had gone a short distance, he commanded the club to kill the bandit, which it did; and then he ordered Nobody to return to him.

A distance farther on, Petrushka came across a second bandit, this one carrying a *gusli* slung over his shoulder. Again Nobody fed the man, and again Petrushka agreed to the exchange of Nobody for the *gusli,* which had the power to create a vast sea when the first string was plucked and a huge fleet of ships when the second was plucked; and to cause those ships to fire their cannons whenever the third string was plucked. However, a short distance away, Petrushka ordered his club to kill the bandit and to return Nobody to him. Then he continued his journey homeward.

After many weeks of travel, Petrushka returned home. To his dismay, he found the door broken from its hinges and his wife gone. Cursing the tsar, Petrushka saw a white dove fly down toward him, and then before his eyes, change back into Masha, his wife. The couple embraced. Masha told him that she had been forced to hide from the tsar. Petrushka then commanded Nobody to build him an impenetrable palace, which Nobody did with amazing speed.

Some weeks later the tsar was traveling through his kingdom when he came across

the palace and asked a local woodsman whose it was. When he was told that the owner of the palace was Petrushka, the tsar commanded ten of his men to enter the palace and drag Petrushka and his wife out; but when the tsar's men advanced, the club flew from a window and quickly killed all ten. The tsar then called out his entire army, but Petrushka saw what was happening, opened the *gusli,* and plucked the first string. A vast sea appeared between the palace and the tsar's army. Petrushka then plucked the second string, and a fleet of ships appeared. He then plucked the third string time and time again, and within a few short minutes the tsar's army was no more.

The tsar, horrified by these events, called out to Petrushka to stop, whereupon Petrushka closed the *gusli,* and the ships and the ocean vanished. Then Petrushka called out to the tsar to have his counselor put to death, for it was his evil that had led to their problems; but when the counselor heard this, he took to his heels and fled. Petrushka sent his club after the counselor, and the latter fell as he ran for cover, his head caved in.

From that day on, the tsar and Petrushka were close friends. The tsar gave his old archer half the kingdom in recompense for his service. Great banquets were often held in the palace of Petrushka and Masha. When Petrushka was asked where Nobody came from, he would reply "I-Know-Not-Where," and when asked what kind of being he was, he would reply "I-Know-Not-What."

See also: Baba-Yaga (-Jaga, -Iaga); Babushka-Lyagushka-Skakushka; Dove Maiden; Green Marsh; I-Know-Not-What; I-Know-Not-Where; Kot Bayun; Masha; Nobody; River of Fire, The; Thrice-Ninth Kingdom, The; Thrice-Ninth Land, The; Underworld, The

PIKKER
Russia
One of the variant names applied to Perun, the god of thunder and rain.
See also: Perun

PIORUN

Russia

One of the variant names applied to Perun, the god of thunder and rain.

See also: Perun

PLENKOVICH, CHURILO

Russia

See Churilo Plenkovich.

POKROV

Russia

The veil or dress of the Virgin Mary, allegedly brought from Jerusalem to Byzantium sometime during the fifth century and placed in a church specially dedicated to it. On Pokrov Day (Pokrovskaia Subbota) in October, which was inextricably linked to pagan fertility worship, it was believed that peasant girls of marriageable age would be granted favors by the Virgin Mary as she wandered through the countryside. In some areas, the day would be marked by these young women coming together to weave a veil to adorn the local icon of the Mother of God, behind whom stood Saint Paraskeva, associated with the pagan goddess of childbirth, Mokosh. By thus invoking the matriarchal powers of the Virgin, the young women would be assured a suitable marriage, protection from the tirades of their future husbands, and most importantly, children. It was also a time when the women would ask for a good harvest, though this was not the primary function of the festival of Pokrov Day.

See also: Byzantium; Mokosh; Paraskeva, Saint; Pokrovskaia Subbota
References: Afanas'ev 1865–69; Haase 1939; Kondakov 1914–15; Potebnia 1865

POKROVSKAIA SUBBOTA

Russia

Literally, "Sabbath of Protection" or "Sabbath of Intercession." The true name of Pokrov Day, a festival in October at which women (in the main) paid homage to the veil of the Virgin Mary and were thus ensured fertility and a good, safe marriage. Pokrovskaia Subbota coincides on the modern Christian calendar with the Harvest Festival.

See also: Pokrov

POLAND

General

Poland is a large central European nation that borders the Baltic Sea and is bounded to the east by Russia, to the south by the former Czechoslovakia, and to the west by Germany. It is named for the Poliane, a Slavic tribe that lived more than a thousand years ago in what is now Poland. The name *Poliane* comes from a Slavic word meaning "inhabitants of the fields," which aptly describes a country that is mostly covered in flat plains and gently rolling hills. Poland has had a long and varied history.

Slavic tribes probably lived in what is now Poland as early as the second millennium B.C. The various tribes were first united under one ruler in the tenth century A.D., under the Christian prince Mieczyslaw. In 1025, Boleslaw was crowned the first king of

Engraving of Thaddeus Kosciuszko, a Polish patriot (1746–1817), in battle (Archive Photos)

Poland, but after his death later that year, Poland went through periods of warfare and disunity. By the mid-twelfth century, it had broken up into several sections, each ruled by a different noble. Mongols devastated the country in 1241. Some time later, German and Jewish refugees began to migrate into Poland and settle among the Slavic indigenes. In 1386, Queen Jadwiga of Poland married Wladyslaw Jagiello, the Grand Duke of Lithuania—a move that combined both countries' rule under a single monarch, though each remained largely self-governing. Jagiellonian kings ruled Poland for nearly 200 years, and under their leadership Poland expanded its territory and made important advances in its cultural, economic, and political development. The Polish empire reached its height during the sixteenth century, when it covered a large part of central and eastern Europe, including Ukraine and Belorussia. In 1493, the first national parliament of Poland was established, and in 1569, Poland and Lithuania were united under a single parliament. At that time, Poland was the largest country in Europe. It would not long be so. In 1648, Poland lost much of its territory in Ukraine as a result of a rebellion there, and in 1655, Sweden won control over most of Poland's Baltic provinces. The dramatic decline of Poland continued into the eighteenth century. In 1772, Austria, Prussia, and Russia took advantage of Poland's weakness and partitioned Polish territory among themselves. Austria seized land in the south, Prussia took land in the west, and Russia took land in the east. As a result, Poland lost around one-third of its territory and half of its population. In 1793, Prussia and Russia seized additional territory in eastern and western Poland, which led to an uprising among Poles in 1794. Polish forces under Thaddeus Kosciuszko fought Russian and Prussian troops but were defeated, as a result of which Austria, Prussia, and Russia divided what remained of the country among themselves in 1795.

In 1815 a small, self-governing Kingdom of Poland was created under Russian control. In 1830, Poles in the Kingdom of Poland rebelled against the Russians, but Russia crushed the revolt. Other unsuccessful revolts were launched against Austria and Prussia, and after a second revolt in the Kingdom of Poland in 1863, Russia tried to destroy Polish culture by making Russian the official language there. After 1871, when Prussia formed the German Empire, Poles under Prussian control were forced to adopt the German language. Not until after World War I did Poland regain its status as a sovereign state.

See also: Baltic; Belorussia; Czechoslovakia; Lithuania; Mongols; Prussia; Ukraine

POLEL
Russia

One of the twin offspring of Lada, the other being Lel. These twins have been identified with the divine twins Castor and Polydeuces of classical Greece—or Castor and Pollux, as they were known in Rome.

See also: Lada; Lel
References: Afanas'ev 1865–69; Znayenko 1980

POLEVOI (~IK)
Slavic

Masculine spirit of the fields whose appearance varied according to geographical location. Sometimes he was dressed all in white, sometimes he had grass for hair, and sometimes he was a dwarf with skin the color of the earth. Drunkards or travelers who slept in his fields were likely to be attacked or even murdered, for the polevoi jealously guarded the sanctity of his home.

POLIANITSA
Russia

(pl. polianitsy) Word describing a female warrior in the byliny, related to *pole* (field). She was the feminine counterpart of the bogatyr', rivaling or even bettering the bogatyri in every respect, from skill in weapons handling to guile, speed, intuition, and other legendary attributes. Many polianitsy are described by ancient legends, among them the Princess Nastas'ya.

See also: Bogatyr'; Bylina; Nastas'ya, Princess
References: Barker 1986

POLUDNITSA
Russia
Also: Pudnitsa

(pl. poludnitsy) The goddess(es) of the fields (from *polden'* or *poluden',* meaning "midday"). Represented as a tall, beautiful woman dressed in white, she was attended by the polevoi. Although she was a patron deity of agriculture, the poludnitsa was also a mischievous spirit who would punish those who worked in the fields at midday, an hour sacred to her, for she had decreed it a time of rest. She would pinch them and pull their hair; and if the workers failed to greet her cordially, then she would lure the young children of the workers into fields of grain, where they would lose their way. In Ukraine, poludnitsy were considered moon maidens who directed the rays of the sun to ensure the fertility of the fields.

See also: Polevoi (~ik); Ukraine

POPOVICH, ALYOSHA
Russia
See Alyosha Popovich.

POREVIK (~IT)
Baltic Coast

Literally, "Power"; an alternative name for Svantovit, used in the cult in which the god's iconography depicts him with five faces rather than the usual four.

See also: Svantovit (~dovit)

POTANIA, TINY
Russia

One of the *druzhina* of Vasilii Buslayevich, and the man placed to guard the stem of the pirates' ship while they sailed the waters of Lake Il'men'.

See also: Il'men', Lake; Vasilii Buslayevich

POTOK, MIKHAILO IVANOVICH
Russia
See Mikhail Potyk.

POTYK, MIKHAIL
Russia
See Mikhail Potyk.

PRIGIRSTITIS
Slav

A spirit whose hearing was so acute that he could distinguish even the faintest whisper. He so loathed shouting that if he was near someone who was speaking too loudly, he would immediately retaliate.

PRIMARY CHRONICLE
Russia

Eleventh-century chronicle that is an invaluable source of early Russian myths and legends. Recorded within 150 years of the adoption of Christianity as the state religion, the *Primary Chronicle* relates the legends in the spirit of dvoeverie; thus, although the legends obviously reflect a Christianized view of pagan religious beliefs, they retain enough of their original character to enable the pagan elements to be reconstructed. The *Primary Chronicle* is also considered an extremely useful source of early Russian history. There are several versions of the text. One, *Povest' vremennykh let,* is known as the Laurentian. Another, called *Nachal'naya Letopis',* is known as the Nestorian Chronicle due to an earlier belief that it was composed by the monk Nestor of the Pecherskaia Lavra in Kiev. It is now generally accepted that Nestor was simply an editor of or a contributor to the chronicle. The most important extant versions are the Laurentian, of the late fourteenth century, and the Hypatian, of the early or mid-fifteenth century.

See also: Dvoeverie; Kiev; Nestor; Pecherskaia Lavra
References: Cross and Sherbowitz-Wetzor 1953; Vernadsky 1948

PRINCE AND THE FLEA, THE
Armenia

A prince was tormented by a flea, the torment continuing until the prince managed to catch the offending insect under his shirt. The flea begged for mercy, saying that the harm it had done the prince was very small. The prince replied that the flea had done all the harm that it was in his power to do, and then squashed him.

One of the fables of Vardan.

See also: Vardan
References: Marr 1894–99

PRIPARCHIS
Slav

Usually coupled with Kremara, Priparchis was the patron of piglets who ensured that they were safely born and successfully weaned, whereupon responsibility passed to Kremara, who ensured their continued good health until it was time for them to be slaughtered. Unlike Kremara, no cult or ceremonial tradition developed around Priparchis.

See also: Kremara

PRUSSIA
General

This northern German duchy founded in 1525 became a state in 1618 when it was united with Brandenburg. Prussia became a kingdom in 1701 under Frederick I, around which time the Baltic language of Prussian fell into disuse. Silesia, East Frisia, and West Prussia were annexed by Frederick II between 1740 and 1786, the lost territory being restored after the Congress of Vienna in 1815, along with lands in the Rhineland and Saxony. A war in 1864 with Denmark resulted in the acquisition of Schleswig-Holstein. In 1867 Prussia became a dominant power in the North German Confederation, and in 1871, the core of the German Empire, under the Prussian king Wilhelm I. After World War I, Prussia became a republic, but it soon lost its independence in 1932. Prussia ceased to exist as a state in 1947, after World War II, when the Allies divided its territories among East and West Germany, Poland, and Russia.

See also: Poland; Silesia

PSKOV ICON, THE
Russia

A cherished icon that was found floating on a lake in 1420. It was one of many Orthodox icons "miraculously" discovered in nature. Modern thinking attributes the appearance of these holy relics to the early clergy who recognized the importance of associating the Virgin Mary with the nature goddesses that pervaded pagan religious belief. They might have reasoned that icons found near pagan holy trees and water bodies would be readily accepted by the folk and revered even by those least likely to convert to Christianity. The available evidence suggests that this ruse was successful.

References: Matorin 1931

PTITSY-SIRINY
Russia

Magical maidens, half human and half bird—perhaps best described as a cross between the classical Greek harpies and sirens.

PU-ORT
Cheremiss

The soul of the tree. *Ort* is the name given by the Cheremiss people to the soul that they believe everything, animate or inanimate, possesses.

See also: Cheremiss-Mordvin; Ort

PUCHAI
Russia

An extremely fast-flowing river that rose in the Sorochinsk Mountains and above which a terrible twelve-headed she-dragon, who lived in the mountains, liked to fly so that she could pick off unsuspecting people who bathed in the river. On one such occasion the dragon attacked Dobrynya Nikitich, but he almost killed her. Later, after the dragon had broken her pact with Dobrynya and abducted the Princess Zabava, the knight came to her lair and killed her, thus releasing the princess and all of the dragon's other captives.

See also: Dobrynya Nikitich; Dragon; Sorochinsk Hill; Zabava (Putyatichna), Princess

PUDNITSA
Russia
Variant form of poludnitsa.

PURTO
Armenia
A young hunter who at the age of fifteen happened to stray into the cave of Shah-Mar, the king of snakes, to seek shelter from the rain. The king of snakes was a strange being with the head of a man but the body of a huge serpent. Trying to ignore his situation, Purto lit a fire and sat down to dry himself, and he did not feel the king of snakes reach out and place his mark on the young man's back. Purto placed some of his catch on a spit and roasted it over his fire, and having only taken a small portion for himself, offered the rest to the king of snakes and his four serpent attendants.

After he had eaten, the king asked Purto for some water. Purto left the cave and returned a short time later with a basin of water from a nearby spring. Then Purto set to work, and six days later he had finished digging a channel from the spring so that clear water now flowed into a basin he had prepared in the cave. Thanking him for his kindness, Shah-Mar gave Purto a small stone of great value and then adopted the young hunter as his son.

Purto thanked Shah-Mar and went his way, sold the stone for a great price, settled all his debts, and built himself a fine mansion. Then he bought a flock of forty sheep and returned to the cave, where he regally entertained Shah-Mar and his attendants. In return Shah-Mar gave Purto another stone of great value and an escort back to his mansion.

Meanwhile Kayen, or Cain, the ruler of Kilikia, or Cilicia, who had his palace in Adana (in south-central Turkey, above the "tail" of Cyprus), had fallen ill with terrible ulcers all over his body that were slowly eating him away. The king called his most trusted doctor to his side and asked him if there was any cure for his illness. The doctor knew of Purto, and by magic means, also of his association with Shah-Mar. He told the king that only the power of Shah-Mar could cure him and that he would see to it that Purto brought the king of snakes to his assistance.

The doctor had Purto brought to him and told him to bring Shah-Mar to the palace. Purto refused, whereupon the doctor had Purto flogged. Still Purto refused, so the doctor had Purto's ears sliced open and salt and pepper rubbed into the wounds. Still Purto remained resolute, so the doctor set to the unfortunate hunter with pincers, tearing off large chunks of his flesh until finally Purto consented.

Purto made his way painfully to the cave of Shah-Mar, who already knew of the torment his adopted son had suffered. Shah-Mar quickly consented to travel with him to Adana. On the way they came to Mount Nauriz, where Shah-Mar plucked a flower and told Purto to swallow it. Then he picked a whole bunch of different flowers and told Purto to make a brew of them, which would imbue him with the power of telling the properties of every flower and herb. Purto did as he was told and then fell asleep. When he awoke, he found that he did indeed know the healing qualities of every plant in existence.

Shah-Mar then told Purto that he must now make him drunk on red wine that was exactly seven years old. Then he was to cut off his head, bury his body, and make two potions—one from the brains in the left side of his head, and one from those in the right side, the former potion being healing and the latter poisonous. Purto did as he was instructed and then set out for the palace with the two potions. There Kayen told the doctor to test the medicine, so Purto gave him the concoction made from the right-hand brains of Shah-Mar. As soon as the doctor tasted the brew, he screamed the most hideous scream anyone had ever heard, and he died before his body hit the floor. The king was petrified; but when Purto explained what had happened, the king was happy to drink the other potion. He was immediately cured of his vile illness. From that day forth, he decreed, Purto would be known as Loqmân the Wise, the Father of Medicine.

All went well for a while, but then one of the snakes that had once attended Shah-Mar learned of the king of snakes' death, and he sent word to all the snakes of the world to come together and attack Adana. When the king heard what was happening, he sent for Loqmân the Wise, who promised to quickly settle the situation. Loqmân the Wise then made a potion from the liver of Shah-Mar and set out to visit the snakes, wearing the prayer beads that had once belonged to Shah-Mar. When they saw these beads and received the potion made from Shah-Mar's liver, the snakes accepted Loqmân the Wise as their king and made their peace.

Loqmân the Wise took a deaf and dumb youth as his assistant. Unsure that the youth was really afflicted as he appeared, Loqmân made sure that the youth did not learn any of his secrets, at the same time as he attempted to trick him into talking. For seven years the youth remained dumb, but Loqmân continued to try to make him speak.

One day they were summoned by a man who suffered intolerable headaches. Loqmân brewed the man a potion that rendered him unconscious and then removed the top of the man's head. There he saw an eight-legged creature crawling inside the man's brain; but try as he could, he could not get a grip on it with his pincers. The young man, forgetting his subterfuge, told Loqmân to heat the tongs, which Loqmân did and so cured the man. However, knowing that his secret was out and that his life was in peril, the assistant took to his heels and hid, and no matter how hard Loqmân searched for him, he could not find him.

Many years later, as Loqmân grew old and knew death was close at hand, he called for the youth's mother to come to him and persuade her son to give himself up, for Loqmân meant him no harm. Several days passed. Finally the assistant came back, and the two were reconciled. Then Loqmân had the youth brew a potion that would restore his life, but the assistant managed to pour only one drop into Loqmân's mouth. Loqmân gasped, and then died.

Thereafter the assistant was beset with haunting nightmares of Loqmân and took to wandering the countryside. For twenty-five years he wandered sleeplessly, until he came to a richly appointed house, the home of a bishop whose wife was in labor but could not deliver. The youth went to her aid, and with the knowledge he had gained from Loqmân, delivered the baby. Having thus proved his worth, the young man conquered his nightmares, and from that day to his death he slept peacefully.

See also: Cain; Cilicia; Kayen; Kilikia; King of Snakes; Loqmân the Wise; Shah-Mar
References: Hakyuni 1901

PUSKAITIS
Latvia

A subterranean deity who lived beneath an elder bush and ruled over the barstukai and kaukai. He rewarded those who worshiped him and left him votive offerings, sending his subjects to his worshipers with gifts of grain.

See also: Barstukai; Kaukai

PUTYATICHNA, ZABAVA, PRINCESS
Russia

See Zabava (Putyatichna), Princess.

The egg in both cases symbolizes rebirth: It was a seemingly inert or dead object from which life would eternally emerge—life that would later be reborn in a future egg, and so on, with the cycle being endlessly repeated.

See also: Babii Prazdnik; Rus(s)alki (~ulki)
References: Mansikka 1922; Snegirev 1837–39

R

RADIGAST
Baltic Coast

A deity whose attributes and characteristics are similar to those of Svantovit. Radigast is only known through the writings of Saxo Grammaticus, the Danish chronicler who lived between c. 1150 and c. 1220. Radigast was the god of good advice, sound thinking, and the honoring of promises. He carried a two-headed battle-ax and wore two important symbols—a swan on his head, symbolizing thought, and a bull's head on his chest, symbolizing unshakability.

See also: Saxo Grammaticus; Svantovit (~dovit)

RADUNITSA
Russia

Ancient spring feast occurring the day after Easter that commemorated the dead and was dedicated to the russalki. The name appears to be related to *rad,* meaning "gladness," or to *rod,* meaning "birth" or "offspring." Celebrated in the main by women, Radunitsa was concerned with the damaging aspects of fertility and rebirth, and was held in direct contrast to, and to counteract the effects of, the Rusaliia, which was held slightly later in the year. It has been argued that russalki, with whom the festival is closely linked, were once known as radunitsy.

In Kievan Rus', Radunitsa was also called Babii Prazdnik ("Old woman's holiday"). During the festival it was customary to paint eggs, a practice that was later transferred to the Christian festival of Easter.

RAI
Russia

One of various names applied to the underworld, others being Nava and Peklo. Rai was believed to be the home of Alkonost', a terrible bird-woman whose song tortured the souls of the dead and gave them no rest. It was also the place where the sun set each evening and whence it was reborn the following morning, and the abode of those who had died and were to be reborn.

The underworld appears, through the three names given to it, to have been organized in much the same way as the classical Greek realm of Hades, with definite regions allocated to the various classifications of dead. Peklo was a paradisal realm that could be associated with the Elysian Fields of Hades. Nava could be equated with the rivers of Hades, while Rai would seem to be closest to Tartarus. However, from the latter infernal region there was never any possibility of return—a trait not shared by the realm of Rai, the inhabitants of which had a hope of achieving eternal peace and blessing, perhaps after a number of earthly lives.

See also: Alkonost'; Nava; Peklo; Underworld, The
References: Afanas'ev 1865–69; Haase 1939

RAKHMAT
Russia

The father of Solovei Rakhmatich, the half-man, half-bird brigand known in English as Nightingale.

See also: Nightingale; Solovei (~y) Rakhmatich

RAKHMATICH, SOLOVEI
Russia
See Solovei (~y) Rakhmatich.

RATAINITSA
Slav
Spirit who looked after the welfare of the stables and horses.

RAVEN RAVENSON
Russia
A raven who, along with the sun and the moon, helped an old peasant pick up a measure of rye grain after he had carelessly spilled it. As a reward, each of the three was to receive one of the man's three daughters as his wife. Raven Ravenson chose the youngest girl, the moon chose the middle daughter, and the sun chose the eldest one. After the girls left home to live with their new husbands, the father set out to see each in turn.

First he traveled to see his eldest daughter, who was living happily with the sun. She cooked pancakes for her father, using the heat from her husband's head to cook them. When the old man tried the same thing at home, nothing happened. Next he visited his middle daughter and the moon. There he took a bath, the light he needed to see by being provided by one of the moon's fingers. Again he tried the same thing at home, using his own finger, and got the expected result—nothing. Finally he went to visit his youngest daughter and Raven Ravenson. There he spent the night securely tucked under the wing of the raven. When he tried the same thing at home, sleeping in the chicken coop, he was all right while he stayed awake but he immediately crashed to the ground when he fell asleep.

This story serves but a single purpose—to illustrate the stupidity of man.
See also: Moon; Sun

RIURIK
Scandinavia and Russia
Viking chieftain who founded the city of Novgorod, the original capital of Russia.

Legend has it that Riurik, or Rurik, came to rule Russia at the invitation of the people, and that is how he became the first Varangian ruler of a kingdom that embraced both Novgorod and Kiev. The Russian chronicles indicate that Riurik was succeeded by Oleg. It is generally less known that Riurik was the eldest of three brothers, all of whom settled in Russia. Sineus settled at Beloozero, and Truvor in Izborsk—the *Primary Chronicle* dating their settlement at between 860 and 862. Two years later Sineus and Truvor died and Riurik became the sole ruler, being assigned various regencies, including those of Polotsk, Rostov, and Beloozero. The Hypatian *Primary Chronicle* gives a different account, saying that Riurik first settled at Lake Ladoga, Sineus at Beloozero, and Truvor in Izborsk. After the death of Sineus and Truvor, Riurik assumed sole authority and moved his seat of power to the city he had founded on the banks of the river Volkhov—Novgorod. The *Primary Chronicle* also gives information about the foundation of Kiev, a city that Riuruk is always popularly believed to have ruled but that might have remained independent until the reign of Oleg.

> *See also:* Kiev; Ladoga, Lake; Novgorod; Oleg; *Primary Chronicle;* Rostov; Sineus; Truvor; Varangians; Vikings
> *References:* Cross and Sherbowitz-Wetzor 1953

RIVER OF FIRE, THE
Russia
The river to which Petrushka carried Babushka-Lyagushka-Skakushka in a jug of fresh milk. There Petrushka let the frog out of the jug and placed her on the ground. Placing one foot in the River of Fire, Babushka-Lyagushka-Skakushka started to grow until she was the size of Petrushka's horse. The frog told Petrushka to climb onto her back and hold tight, which he did, while she continued to grow until she was higher than the tallest tree in any forest. The frog made certain that Petrushka was

holding on tightly, then leaped through the air, landing in a foreign land and breathing out slowly until she resumed her normal size. Thus Petrushka was carried to I-Know-Not-Where, the home of I-Know-Not-What.

See also: Babushka-Lyagushka-Skakushka; I-Know-Not-What; I-Know-Not-Where; Petrushka

ROD(Ú)

Slav

Also: Chur

An ancient rain and fertility god who, along with his female counterparts, the rozhanitsy, and the spirits of dead ancestors, protected the home. Rod was originally the god of husbandmen, though his attributes went far beyond this role. He was a universal deity, the god of heaven, rain, and the thunderbolt, who had created the world and all forms of life in it. He created man by sprinkling dust or gravel over the surface of the earth, established the importance of the family, and united his devotees into a unified nation. His wife was called Rozhanitsa (also spelled Rozanica). The frequent use of the word with the plural ending -*y* (rozhanitsy) implies that Rod had many wives; appropriately, polygamy was a common trait among pagan Slavs. Later, Rod was toppled from his position at the head of the pantheon by Perun and was reduced to his role as protector of the home and guardian of ancestors. Rod is the Eastern Slavic equivalent of the Baltic deity Svantovit.

See also: Perun; Rozanica; Rozhanitsa; Svantovit (~dovit)
References: Ivanov and Toporov 1965

ROMAN VASIL'EVICH

Russia

Legendary despotic ruler of Moscow who murdered his unnamed wife. When his young daughter, also unnamed, came to ask him where her mother was, he refused to tell her. She went into the gardens, and there an eagle swooped down and dropped the hand of the young girl's mother. The girl recognized the hand by the ring that still adorned one finger. She followed the eagle to the river, and there she found the remains of her mother, which she gathered up and buried. At that point some of the legends end, whereas others say that the mother was resurrected and accepted the Christian faith. The latter variants obviously owe their origins to the continuing struggle the state was having in converting women from pagan ways.

See also: Moscow
References: Ukhov 1957

ROMANIA

General

Country in southeastern Europe on the Black Sea, bounded to the north and east by Russia, to the south by Bulgaria, to the southwest by the former Yugoslavia, and to the northwest by Hungary. The earliest known inhabitants of Romania merged with invaders from Thrace to form an indigenous people who became subject to Rome when their land was conquered by Emperor Trajan around A.D. 106 and became the Roman province of Dacia. Most of the inhabitants, known as Daci, had originally emigrated from Thrace in northern Greece. Following the withdrawal of the Romans in 275, Romania was occupied by Goths. Later, between the sixth and the twelfth centuries, it was overrun by Huns, Bulgars, Slavs, and others. Through intermarriage and gradual assimilation with Slavic tribes, these people developed into a distinct ethnic group called Walachians, or in Slavonic, Vlachs. Their nomadic habits and warlike conduct made them a constant threat to the neighboring Byzantine Empire.

Under Bulgarian rule, in the ninth century, the Orthodox form of Christianity was introduced to Dacia. Around the end of the thirteenth century, Hungarian expansion by Magyars drove many of the people from the western provinces to settle south and east of the Carpathians. There they established the principality of Walachia and later that of Moldavia, each ruled by native princes or *voivodes* (from the Russian *voevoda,* "leader of an army"), many of whom acknowledged the suzerainty of the kings of Hungary or Poland. With the defeat of the Hungarians by the Ottoman Empire at the Battle of Mohács in 1526, Moldavia and Walachia came under Turkish rule, which lasted three centuries. At the close of the sixteenth century, Moldavia, Transylvania, and Walachia were temporarily united by Prince Michael of Walachia, who made continual war on the Turkish sultan in an attempt to gain and maintain independence. For a time Michael successfully opposed the Ottomans, conquering Transylvania in 1599 and Moldavia in 1600, but he was assassinated the following year, and the spirit of independence waned thereafter.

The Ottomans restored their control over the principalities after Michael's death, imposing severe political restrictions. Finally the Romanians turned to Russia for help. In an effort to fend off the growing influence of Russia in the early eighteenth century, Moldavia and Walachia were ruled by Turkish-appointed *hospodars* (Old Slav *gospodî,* "lords"), usually members of Greek families from the Phanar district of Constantinople.

Russian influence became preeminent after 1750 and remained so for a century. In 1774 Russia defeated Turkey, which was then forced to promise lenient treatment of Moldavia and Walachia. In 1802 Russia obtained a voice in the appointment of *hospodars.* In 1812, having defeated Turkey in the Russo-Turkish War of 1806–1812, Russia obtained Bessarabia, which had previously been part of the principality of Moldavia. The weakening of Turkish influence became more evident after the start of the Greek War of Independence in 1821. By the Treaty of Adrianople, which ended the Greek war in 1829, Moldavia and Walachia, while remaining nominally under Turkish control, became more autonomous. The Phanariot system was ended, and Russia became the unacknowledged suzerain of the two states—a situation disapproved of by the great European powers, which had begun to intervene in Balkan affairs during the Greek war.

The country has existed within its current borders since 1859.

> *See also:* Bessarabia; Black Sea; Boyars; Bulgaria; Byzantine Empire; Dacia; Hungary; Magyars; Moldavia; Poland; Russia; Transylvania; Walachia

ROSSIYA
General
"Land of the Rus'," the Russian name for the country of Russia.

ROSTOV
General
Port on the river Don in southwest Russia, some 14 miles (23 kilometers) east of the Sea of Azov. Modern Rostov dates from 1761 and is linked by river and canal to Volgograd on the river Volga.

ROT
Lapp
The god of the underworld and the dead.
> *See also:* Underworld, The

ROZANICA
Slav
The wife of Rod. After Rod was displaced as the head of the pantheon by Perun, Rozanica appears to have been replaced—especially in Russia—by the rozhanitsy (plural form of Rozanica).
> *See also:* Perun; Rod; Rozhanitsa

ROZHANITSA
Russia
Usually referred to in the plural form (rozhanitsy). A group of female deities who along with Rod and the spirits of dead ancestors protected the home. They also presided over the birth of children and animals and ensured that the land was always

fertile, in this respect resembling the goddesses of fate. At their festival in September,
offerings of bread or porridge, honey-mead,
and cheese were made to them in a ceremony similar to today's harvest festival.

In the Balkan states, right up to the twentieth century, the cult of the rozhanitsy
involved a ceremony in which three women
(usually elderly) drank from a horn, or rhy-
ton, and predicted the fate of a newborn
child.

See also: Rod
References: Arbatskii 1956; Zabylin 1880

RUGAVIT (~IEVIT)
Baltic Coast
A deity whose attributes and characteristics
are similar to those of Svantovit. He is
known only through the writings of Saxo
Grammaticus, the Danish chronicler who
lived between c. 1150 and c. 1220, and
would appear to be the same as Radigast,
who is similarly described. Rugavit was an
ancient god of war who was especially associated with the island of Riigen. Saxo
Grammaticus wrote that Rugavit was
chiefly remembered for his savagery—a trait
that was visually evidenced by depictions of
the god's savage glances from his seven faces
and of his wearing seven swords while brandishing an eighth.

See also: Saxo Grammaticus; Svantovit (~dovit)

RUGIU BOBA
Lithuania
A female votive made from the last sheaf of
the harvest. Her name means "Old One of
the Rye." She was the guest of honor at a
feast held during the harvest festival. She
would then be kept for a year until a new
figure was made to replace her. What became
of the old figure is unknown; but one scholar
has suggested that this figure was buried in
the last field to be harvested.

RUJEVIT
Baltic Coast
Simple variant of Rugavit.

RUKHS-AS
Russia
A tribe of the Alans of southern Russia. The
tribal name is believed by some to be the
origin of the word *Rus'*, which is in turn the
root of the modern name of Russia.

See also: Alans; Russia

RUS'
General
One of the names applied to the early
Scandinavian traders who helped the Slavs
develop the first Russian state (the native
peoples of Russia are reported to have invited
Riurik, a Scandinavian chief, to become the
ruler of Novgorod in A.D. 862). From *Rus'*,
which some believe comes either from
Rukhs-As (the name of a tribe of Alans in
southern Russia) or from *ruotsi* (the Finnish
name for Swedes), comes the modern name
Rossiya, or Russia, which means "land of the
Rus'." The word *Rus'* is still used to describe
the first true Russian state (Kievan Rus').

See also: Kiev; Novgorod; Riurik; Rossiya;
Rukhs-As; Slavs

RUSALIIA
Russia
Part of a weeklong cycle of rituals that lasted
from Whitsun to the Intercession of the
Trinity that was known as Trinity Week, or
Zelenie Sviatki. The other two parts were the
Semik, the central part of the week's cere-
monials, and the Troitsa, which occurred on
the Christian festival of Trinity Sunday.
During the Rusaliia, worship of Lada was
performed, and the potent powers of the russalki were invoked by young women. During
the festival, two straw dolls would be made,
representing the russalki, and then taken out
into the fields by the women of a community. There the women would split into two
groups—the mothers and the unmarried
women. The young, unmarried women
would protect the dolls, while the married
women would "attack" them in a series of
dances, *khorovody,* that mimicked war. Finally
the dolls would be captured from their pro-

tectors, torn to pieces, and then scattered across the fields to ensure the land's fertility. The young women would lament the "death" of the dolls, let their hair down and wail, and finally fall to the ground as if dead.

The Rusaliia was essentially a female ceremony. In Ukraine no woman would dare bathe on the eve of the Rusaliia for fear of offending the spirits, the punishment for which might be floods, or plagues spreading among their cattle.

See also: Lada; Rus(s)alki (~ulki); Semik; Troitsa; Ukraine; Zelenie Sviatki

References: Propp 1963; Ralston 1880; Snegirev 1837–39; Vsevolodskii-Gerngross 1929; Zabylin 1880; Zemtsovskii 1970

RUS(S)ALKI (~ULKI)
Slav

Water nymphs, sometimes malevolent, sometimes benevolent, who, like the leshie, lived in the forest. Although they principally lived in the waters that flowed through the forest, they would quite often climb out and lie on the banks of the river or lake, or climb a tree that hung over the still waters below. Their favorite pastime was combing their flowing golden or green hair while admiring their beauty in the water. On clear, moonlit nights they would assemble to dance and sing, weaving garlands out of the forest flowers. A russalka could not live long out of the water; but as long as she carried her comb, she was not in danger, for her comb gave her the magical ability to conjure up water when she needed it, no matter where she was.

Russalki were thought to be the spirits of drowned girls, so they were depicted as almost human, though their characteristics depended on their surroundings: Russalki of soft and sunny southern rivers were described as nubile and attractive, while those from the cold north were stern, cruel, and ugly. Their skin was exceptionally translucent and pale, and they sometimes had tails; the latter characteristic indicates that they might have originated as mermaids. Like leshie they possessed the power to transform their

appearance; but they were severely limited in this ability, for they could only change into animals that lived in the water, such as fish or toads and frogs. Some accounts say that during the winter the russalki lived in the water, coming ashore during the summer to live in the forest.

The russalki are spinners who weave the cycle of the seasons and the weather and who regulate human and animal fertility. They are mistresses of the woodland; guardians of streams, lakes, and other waterways; and representatives of Mother Earth. They were the goddesses of the horse, and could change their shape at will into that of any animal—though if they were not in human form, they would most commonly appear as a horse. In the underworld they were said to inhabit Nava, the ocean that the dead had to traverse upon entry into the afterlife. Depending on the region, the russalki had various names, such as mavki, navki, vodianiani, and faraony; but no matter what name they were known by, they shared common attributes, if not appearance. They were inextricably linked to the festivals of Radunitsa and Rusaliia, and they may be equated with the Germanic Lorelei, the French Ondine, and the classical Greek sirens and harpies.

Often represented as sad and lonely figures, russalki might well attempt to find human companions who could be lured to their deaths and thus join the russalki in their underwater crystal palaces. Young children were fair game, and legends describe the russalki as attempting to lure them into the water with baskets of fruit and nuts or biscuits. However, what every russalka really desired was a young man. In order to lure young men into their power they would leave the water and call out young men's names at random. If a young man in the forest was foolish enough to call out in reply, then the russalka had him in her power. The russalka would then make him join her in her games and eventually would drown him in the water. If this did not work—for some men appeared to have a resistance to the charms of a russalka—the russalka would tease and tickle him until he fell down out of exhaustion and then she would drag him down into the water. Peasants who believed in the existence of russalki always remembered to wear a cross, or to cross themselves when swimming or crossing a stretch of water, for this would render the russalka powerless to harm them.

Some stories tell of men who were captivated by the unearthly beauty of russalki and who tried to live an ordinary life with them. One such story concerns a young seal hunter by the name of Ivan Savel'evich, who came from Arkhangel'sk. Spending the winter seal hunting on the bleak island of Novaya Zemlya, in the Arctic Circle, he spent many nights alone in his hut playing his balalaika. One night the oil in his lamp ran out and he continued to play in the dark. As he played, he heard the sound of someone dancing inside his hut. Knowing that he was alone, he became frightened and quickly refilled and relit his lamp. He was indeed alone. The following night, the same thing happened. Finally he hid the lit lamp behind a thick curtain, and as soon as the sound of dancing started, he drew back the curtain, revealing a young girl.

This girl explained to Ivan that she was a russalka but that as she had a human father, she was able to remain out of the water as long as she liked, so long as she was only in the presence of one person. Ivan fell hopelessly in love with the russalka and they spent the winter together. However, when spring came Ivan had to return to his home to sell his catch. On parting the russalka gave him instructions on how he might find her again.

Some time later Ivan found he could not live without the russalka. Remembering what the russalka had told him, he sought out her home, climbed a tree that hung above the water, and on the stroke of midday, dived into the water. As he reached the bottom of the river, his love rushed out from the weeds and embraced him. Ivan stayed quite

some time beneath the waters of that river, but in the end he began to long for home. Remembering that anyone could be protected from the charms of the russalka by the holy cross, he made the sign and was immediately transported back home—though having crossed himself, he would never be able to return to his love. In the words of Alexander Pushkin (1799–1837) in his poem *Russalka:*

> She looked at him and shook her hair,
> Threw kisses, laughed
> And like a child,
> Cried to the monk: "Come to me,
>   here. . . ."

Some authorities have sought to connect the russalka with *Rosa,* the Latin for "rose," and thus say that the name is a reflection of the wedding garlands worn by newly married women.

See also: Arkhangel'sk; Faraony; Ivan Savel'evich; Leshii (~y); Mavki; Mother Earth; Nava; Navki; Novaya Zemlya; Radunitsa; Rusaliia; Underworld, The; Vodianiani
References: Afanas'ev 1865–69; Branston 1980; Gimbutas 1982; Haase 1939; Mansikka 1922; Moszynski 1967; Oinas 1969; Paulson 1971; Pomerantseva 1975; Pushkin 1964; Ralston 1880 and 1872; Snegirev 1837–39; Vasilenko 1960

RUSSIA

General

The Russian Empire in the nineteenth century comprised parts of Europe and western and northern Asia—a vast territory that was inherited by the Bolshevik regime after the revolution of October 1917 and subsequently renamed the Union of Soviet Socialist Republics (USSR). Today *Russia* commonly refers specifically to the Russian Federation, the largest and most influential of the fifteen former constituent republics of the USSR, and an independent nation since Christmas Day 1991. The term *Russia* also is used more broadly to denote the former Russian Empire. At its greatest extent, in

1914, the Russian Empire included about 8.5 million square miles (22 million sq km), an estimated one-sixth of the land area of the earth, divided into four general regions: Russia proper, comprising the easternmost part of Europe and including the Grand Duchy of Finland and most of Poland; the Caucasus; Siberia; and Russian Central Asia, which was further subdivided into the steppe regions of the southwest and Russian Turkestan in the southeast. It is roughly this historical area that is represented within this book, along with a few fringe areas that have come under, or exhibit, Slavic and/or Russian influences.

During the pre-Christian era the vast territory that became Russia was sparsely inhabited by groups of wandering, nomadic tribes, many of which were described by Greek and Roman writers. The largely unknown north, a region of extensive forests, was inhabited by tribes later known collectively as Slavs—the ancestors of the modern Russian people. Far more important was the south, where the indeterminate region known as Scythia was occupied by a succession of Asian peoples, including the Cimmerians, Scythians, and Sarmatians.

In the early centuries of the Christian era, the Asian peoples of Scythia were displaced by the Goths, who established a kingdom on the Black Sea. In the fourth century A.D. the invading Huns conquered and expelled the Goths, destroying Scythia. The Huns held the territory constituting present-day Ukraine and the region of Bessarabia until their defeat in western Europe in 451. Later came the Avars, followed by the Magyars and the Khazars, who remained influential until about the mid-tenth century.

Meanwhile, during this long period of successive invasions, the Slavic tribes dwelling northeast of the Carpathian Mountains had begun a series of migratory movements. As these migrations took place, three distinctive subdivisions evolved. The western tribes evolved as the Moravians, Poles, Czechs, and Slovaks; the southern tribes as the Serbs,

Croats, Slovenes, and Bulgars; and the eastern tribes as Russians, Ukrainians, and Belorussians. The Eastern Slavs became renowned traders and established a number of trading posts, notably the cities of Kiev in the south and Novgorod in the north.

The political organization of the Eastern Slavs was largely tribal. According to Russian tradition recorded in the *Primary Chronicle,* internal dissension and feuds among the Eastern Slavs around Novgorod became so violent that they voluntarily chose to call upon a foreign prince who could unite them into one strong state. Their choice was Riurik, a Scandinavian chief, who in 862 became ruler of Novgorod. Two other Scandinavians, Dir and Askold—possibly legendary figures—gained control of Kiev; A.D. 862 is thus considered the beginning of the Russian Empire. From the Scandinavians, called Varangians, or Rus', came the name *Rossiya,* or Russia, meaning "land of the Rus'." The establishment of Riurik and the dynasty he founded initiated a period of consolidation and expansion of Slavic populations, notably toward the northeast and northwest, where indigenous Finnic groups were largely absorbed or replaced by Slavs.

Riurik was succeeded in 879 by his son Igor (reigned 912–945), a child for whom Oleg ruled as regent. Prince Oleg, realizing the value of the Kiev region, had the Varangian rulers of that city killed in 882 and united the two centers, establishing his capital at Kiev. He extended Russian rule considerably, subduing neighboring tribes, and led his raiders as far south as Constantinople, where he concluded a treaty with Byzantium in 911—the first event in Russian history that bears a date verified by non-Russian sources. In the years that followed, Russian relations with the Byzantine Empire became continually closer. Igor assumed power in 912, and in 945 he was succeeded by his widow, Olga, who became a Christian in 955. In 964 Olga abdicated in favor of her son, Sviatoslav, the first prince of the house of Riurik to bear a Slav name. With his government centered in Kiev, Sviatoslav devoted himself to strengthening the Russian position in the south. He led his troops against the Khazars in the southeast, against the Pechenegs, and against the Bulgars. Sviatoslav built a great empire, and commerce and crafts increased under his reign.

The empire was divided among the prince's three sons, causing dynastic conflicts that were ended in 980 when the youngest son, Vladimir I, later known as Vladimir the Great, became sole ruler. The most significant event of his reign was his conversion to Christianity (the Byzantine rite) in 988 and the institution of that religion as the official religion of the Russian people. After casting off his several pagan wives, Vladimir married Anna, a sister of the Byzantine emperor Basil II. Early Russian monasteries and churches were built in the Byzantine style, and Byzantine culture ultimately became the predominant influence in such fields as architecture, art, and music.

Upon the death of Vladimir in 1015, his dominions were divided among his sons, and strife immediately developed. Vladimir's eldest son, Sviatopolk, called The Accursed (reigned 1015 and 1018–1019), held the supreme power; but in order to secure his position, he murdered his brothers Boris and Gleb. Sviatopolk in turn was defeated and deposed by his brother Yaroslav the Wise, prince of Novgorod. Yaroslav attempted to re-create the empire of his grandfather Sviatoslav, and by 1036 he had succeeded in making himself ruler of all Russia. During his reign, the state of Kiev reached its greatest power. Yaroslav made Kiev an imperial capital with magnificent buildings, including the notable Hagia Sophia. Schools were opened; and the grand duke revised the first Russian law code, the *Russkaia pravda*. To consolidate the position of his heirs, Yaroslav devised a system of precedence, grading the various principalities from the smallest to Kiev, the most powerful, so that when a grand duke of Kiev died, each vassal below

him was moved to a larger principality, ending with the throne of Kiev.

Although this unique pattern of precedence was nominally practiced, Yaroslav's death in 1054 signaled Kiev's decline. One final attempt was made to unite the country by Yaroslav's grandson, Vladimir II Monomachus; but his death in 1125 ended efforts to form an alliance, and the division continued, with other states challenging Kiev's supremacy. Russia became a loose federation of city-states held together by a common language, religion, traditions, and customs and ruled by members of the abundant house of Riurik, who were usually involved in internecine wars.

In the early thirteenth century a greater danger than any that Russia previously had faced came from the east. In 1223 the Mongol armies of Genghis Khan appeared in the southeast, and in the Battle of the Kalka River (now Kalmius River), completely routed Russian forces. For twelve years after this Mongol victory, however, the khan's armies remained in their homelands. In 1237, Batu Khan, grandson of Genghis Khan, led the Mongols again to eastern Russia; this time, on their march northward, they captured and destroyed most of the major cities on their route.

In 1240 Batu Khan swept the southwest, destroying Kiev despite the city's desperate effort at self-defense, and in 1242 he established his capital at Sarai on the lower Volga (near modern Volgograd), where he founded the khanate known as the Golden Horde.

Although the Mongols did not attack Novgorod, northwestern Russia was menaced by invaders from the west at the same time. In 1240 a Swedish army landed on the banks of the Neva. Prince Alexander Yaroslavevich led a Russian army to meet them, and his forces so completely defeated the Swedes that he was thenceforth known as Alexander Nevsky (the epithet means "of the Neva"). Two years later the Teutonic Knights advanced from the west, but again Alexander's troops routed the enemy. Faced with continuing danger in the west, Alexander adopted a policy of loyal acquiescence to the Golden Horde and conciliation with the khan. In 1246 Alexander succeeded his father as grand prince of Novgorod, and in 1252 he was invested by the khan as grand prince of Vladimir and Suzdal'.

In 1263 Alexander Nevsky gave Moscow to his younger son, Daniel, the progenitor of a line of powerful Muscovite dukes, who as Mongol favorites, gradually extended their lands by annexing surrounding territories. In 1328 Daniel's son Ivan I became duke of Muscovy. Beginning with Ivan, the dukes of Muscovy styled themselves "princes of all Russia."

In the mid-fourteenth century internal dissension weakened the power of the Golden Horde. Taking advantage of this weakness, Grand Duke Dmitrii led the first successful revolt against the Mongols. Dmitrii's important victory over the Mongols on the banks of the Don River in 1380 won him the honorary title *Donskoi* (of the Don) and marked the turning point of Mongol power.

When Constantinople fell to the Ottoman Turks in 1453, Moscow became the center of Christian Orthodoxy. The grand duke Ivan III Vasilevich, who added to Muscovy the states of Novgorod in 1478 and Tver' in 1485, began to regard himself as the tsar. In 1480 he refused to pay the annual tribute to the Golden Horde, a date that is regarded as the end of Tatar domination. Once free of Tatar rule, Ivan invaded Lithuanian territory, in 1492 and 1500. Ivan's son and successor, Basil III Ivanovich, followed his father's aggressive policy of expansion to the west—he annexed Pskov in 1510, captured Smolensk in 1514, and absorbed the grand duchy of Riazan' in 1521.

Ivan IV Vasilevich, better known as Ivan Groznyi ("the Terrible"), became ruler in 1533 at the age of three. In 1547 Ivan assumed the throne and became the first Muscovite grand duke to be formally crowned as tsar. In 1549 he convened the first Zemsky Sobor (National Assembly), and in December 1564, Ivan left Moscow and announced that he had abdicated. He returned the following January, however, having agreed to resume the throne after receiving absolute powers. He then seized half of Muscovy as his personal property—a territory called the *oprichnina,* which was a separate administrative unit ruled directly by the tsar. Ivan distributed these holdings among his supporters as rewards for military and personal service, thereby establishing a new service corps of *oprichniki* who acted as Ivan's personal police. In 1552 Muscovite armies conquered and annexed the Tatar kingdom of Kazan', while Astrakhan' became a Russian territory in 1556.

Ivan's son, Fyodor I, was sickly and feebleminded, and during his reign (1584–1598) he was dominated by his brother-in-law, the boyar Boris Godunov. In 1598, when Fyodor died childless, ending the house of Riurik, Boris was elected tsar by a Zemsky Sobor. Although he ruled with ability, his hold on the throne was uneasy because of the widely held belief that he had murdered Dmitrii Ivanovich, a son and legal heir of Ivan the Terrible. Dmitrii's mysterious death in 1591 made possible the subsequent appearance of pretenders to his name and ranks, inaugurating a period of unrest and revolt known in Russian as the *smutnoe vremia* (Time of Troubles).

In 1604 a pretender to the throne calling himself Dmitrii I, and known as the False Dmitrii, gained the support of a number of Polish and Lithuanian nobles and Cossacks. Three months after the death of Boris in 1605, Dmitrii I entered Moscow and was crowned tsar. He was murdered by boyars who subsequently elevated Prince Basil Shuisky to the throne. This move was opposed by the Cossacks and rebellious peasants who supported a second pretender, Dmitrii II, who was already advancing on Moscow. At the same time King Sigismund III of Poland invaded from the west. At Basil's request, Sweden sent in armed support. After a long period of fighting and intrigue, in 1610, Basil was deposed and the country fell into a state of anarchy. The situation was at last resolved in 1613 when a Zemsky Sobor elected Michael Romanov, grandnephew of Anastasia Romanovna, as tsar. Michael founded the ruling house of Romanov.

Under the first two Romanovs—Michael and his son Alexis I, who succeeded him as tsar in 1645—Russia advanced to the status of a European power. In 1654 the Cossacks of Ukraine, rebelling against Polish rule, offered their allegiance to Tsar Alexis; and in the resulting war with Poland (1654–1667) Russia regained Smolensk (lost in 1611) as well as eastern Ukraine, including Kiev.

Alexis was succeeded by his son Fyodor III, and he in turn was replaced in 1682 by his half brother, Peter I (the Great). Peter's older half sister Sophia Alekseyevna succeeded in having her own brother, the weak-minded Ivan V, declared senior co-regent with herself acting as regent. Sophia was forced to resign all power in 1689 after an attempt to deprive Peter of his right to the throne and to assassinate both him and his mother.

The accession of Peter I to the tsardom in 1682 marked the beginning of a period during which Russia became a major European power. Peter was greatly attracted by the culture of western Europe, and in 1697 he led a technical and diplomatic mission to the West. He was absent from Russia for eighteen months. On his return, Peter attempted to transform Russia into a Western society and to make the Russian state a major power in Europe. Moreover, during his reign Russia began a series of great territorial acquisitions. In 1703 Peter began construction of a new capital city, St. Petersburg, on marshy territory taken from Sweden. The seat of government was moved there from Moscow in 1714. By the terms of the Treaty of Nystad (30 August 1721), Russia acquired Livonia, Estonia, Ingria, part of Karelia, and several Baltic islands. Having achieved Russian dominance in northern Europe, Peter was

Peter the Great of Russia (1672–1725) (Archive Photos)

formally proclaimed emperor in 1721, and the Muscovite state was renamed the Russian Empire.

Peter left no direct heir. His son Alexis had been charged with treason and died in prison in 1718. The throne thus went to Peter's second wife, Catherine I. After her death in 1727 the accession passed to a succession of rulers. Peter II, the son of Alexis, was chosen emperor after Catherine, and was succeeded in 1730 by Anna Ivanovna, daughter of Ivan V. Anna ruled as a despot and was succeeded by Ivan VI, an eight-week-old grandnephew. A palace conspiracy the next year placed Elizabeth Petrovna, youngest daughter of Peter the Great, on the throne, and under her rule (1741–1762) a national revival took place. Her nephew and successor, Peter III, was swiftly deposed and murdered. His wife, a German princess by birth, ascended the throne as Catherine II, and became better known as Catherine the Great.

Catherine successfully carried out ambitious plans for Russian expansion. In the Russo–Turkish Wars of 1768–1774 and 1787–1792, Russia acquired territory in the Crimea. Catherine II also looked to the west: As a result of the three partitions of Poland (1772, 1793, and 1795), Russia gained 180,000 square miles (468,000 sq km) of land and around six million inhabitants.

Catherine II was succeeded in 1796 by her son Paul I. A despotic and unbalanced ruler, he was assassinated in his palace in 1801, the same year that Russia annexed Georgia. Paul was succeeded by his son Alexander I, who had been Catherine's favorite grandson.

In 1805 Russia joined Great Britain, Austria, and Sweden against Napoleon I, but switched sides in 1807. After the Russo–Turkish War of 1806–1812, Russia received Bessarabia from Turkey, and in 1813 Russia acquired Dagestan and other areas. In 1815, at the Congress of Vienna, most of the duchy of Warsaw was awarded to Russia.

Tsar Nicholas II with his three daughters, under arrest after his abdication (Popperfoto / Archive Photos)

Catherine II ("the Great") of Russia (1729–1796) (Archive Photos)

When Alexander died in 1825 without an heir, the throne passed to his youngest brother, Nicholas I. After the revolutions that occurred throughout Europe during 1848, Nicholas began a vigorous campaign against liberal ideas in education and in intellectual circles in general. Nicholas also made some efforts to expand his empire. A war with Iran began in 1826 and ended two years later with the Russian acquisition of part of Armenia, including the city of Yerevan.

During the Crimean War (1853–1856) Russia was faced by British, French, Sardinian, and Turkish troops and was utterly defeated.

Nicholas died in 1855, and peace was concluded a year later by his son and successor, Alexander II. Alexander was assassinated in 1881 by a bomb thrown by revolutionaries. Alexander II was succeeded by his son, Alexander III, who was, in turn, succeeded by his eldest son Nicholas II, in 1894. Nicholas proved a weak ruler, out of touch with his people and easily dominated by others—most notably Grigory Yefimovich Rasputin.

On Sunday, 22 January 1905, thousands of petitioners, led by Georgy Apollonovich Gapon, a priest, marched to the Winter Palace to present their demands to the tsar and were fired on by imperial troops. Hundreds were either killed or wounded on that day, which subsequently became known as Bloody Sunday. The massacre acted as a catalyst for revolution—a process only temporarily halted by the outbreak of World War I, in 1914.

In February 1917, riots began in Moscow, and when the imperial troops were ordered to fire on rioters, they instead joined in the rioting. The abdications of Nicholas II and his son were announced on 15 March, and the imperial government was replaced by a temporary provisional government. In October, the Bolshevik coup put an end to this transitional state; and a few years later, the Union of Soviet Socialist Republics (Soyuz Sovetskikh Sotsialisticheskikh Respublik) was formed.

> See also: Alans; Avars; Batu Khan; Bessarabia; Black Sea; Bulgaria; Byzantine Empire; Crimea; Croatia; Desna; Dnieper; Don; Estonia; Finland; Gleb, Saint; Golden Horde, The; Hanseatic League; Karelia; Kiev; Lithuania; Livonia; Magyars; Moldova; Mongols; Montenegro; Moravia; Pechenegs; Poland; *Primary Chronicle;* Prussia; Riurik; Sarmatians; Scythia; Serbia; Slovakia; Slovenia; Sviatopolk; Tatars; Teutonic Knights; Turkestan; Varangians; Volga

RUSSIAN AND THE TATAR, THE
Russia—Tatar

An unnamed Russian and an unnamed Tatar had become traveling companions as they made their way across the southern steppes of Russia. The Russian was riding a thin white horse and the Tatar a sturdy black one.

As night fell, the two made camp. After they ate, they argued over who should keep watch over their horses. The Russian argued that he had no need to watch his horse, because it was white and therefore easy to see; so it was only fair that the Tatar should guard his own mount. The Tatar, hoping to get the better end of the bargain, exchanged his horse for the Russian's—whereupon the Russian said that he had no need to watch over a black horse, which could not be seen at night. The Tatar stood guard and fumed.

After a while he led the Russian's horse to a nearby swamp and pushed it in before returning to their camp and falling asleep. The Russian had only been pretending to sleep, and as soon as the Tatar fell asleep, he led that man's horse to the swamp, rescued his own, and pushed the Tatar's horse in. He then returned to the camp and went to sleep. At dawn the Tatar shook the Russian awake and said that he had had a dream in which the Russian's horse had wandered into a swamp and drowned. The Russian countered that he had dreamed that the Tatar's horse had broken loose and died in a swamp. The Tatar rushed to the swamp, but the horse had been dead several hours.

Feigning compassion, the Russian sold his horse ostensibly so that they would be equal, and the two continued on their way on foot. Before long the Tatar suggested that they should take turns carrying each other. The Russian agreed and suggested that to measure the distance, the one being carried should sing a lullaby, and when the singer fell asleep, it would be time to trade places. Thus the Tatar climbed onto the Russian's back and began to sing a sweet lullaby in his fine baritone, and before long, he had fallen fast asleep.

The Russian put the Tatar down; and when the Tatar awakened, he climbed onto his back and began to sing. Though he had a fine voice, the Russian sang in a raucous voice that sent the birds fluttering from the trees and would have awakened the dead. All day long he sang, and all day long the Tatar carried the Russian, until the time came to make camp.

However, when they went to prepare their meal, they discovered that they had but one small chicken. The Tatar suggested that they both go to sleep, and whoever had the best dream should have the chicken all to himself. The Russian agreed, and they both settled down. While the Tatar thought up his story, the Russian ate the chicken and then fell fast asleep. An hour later the Tatar shook the Russian awake and told him that he had dreamed that he floated up to the heavens, where he was greeted by beautiful angels who led him straight into paradise.

The Russian replied that he had had precisely the same dream, and thinking that the Tatar would never return, he had naturally eaten the chicken. The Tatar had, by now, had enough of the Russian's trickery. He packed his bag and took to the road; and from that day forth, he always traveled alone.

See also: Tatars

RUSSKAIA PRAVDA
Russia
Eleventh-century legal code compiled by Vladimir Monomakh that reflected the continuing significance of matrilineal and matrilocal custom in Kievan society.

See also: Vladimir II; Vladimir Monomakh

RUTHENES
General
The inhabitants of Ruthenia, or Carpathian Ukraine, a region of central Europe on the southern slopes of the Carpathian Mountains. Dominated by Hungary from the tenth century, the Ruthenes remained under the influence of Austria and Hungary until World War I.

See also: Carpathian Mountains; Hungary; Ukraine

RYURIK
Scandinavia and Russia
Variant spelling of *Riurik,* the name of the Scandinavian chieftain elected to become the ruler of Novgorod.

been eaten and all the beer had been drunk. The bones of the birds would then be given to the dogs; and if they left anything, the remains would be buried under the dung in the cattle stall.

All this was done to celebrate and give thanks for the harvest and to ensure a similarly good harvest in the coming year. This complex ritual was performed in December to rekindle the fertility of the earth at a time when everything would appear dead and thus to ensure that the following year the earth would spring back to life. The ritual was widely practiced until about the start of the nineteenth century, and a variant of it is still practiced in rural areas today.

SADKO

Russia

Originally an ancient water deity, Sadko reemerged after the advent of Christianity as a poor musician from Novgorod who played the *gusli,* a stringed instrument similar to a psaltery—essentially, a flat wooden box that was laid across the knees and plucked with the fingers. Sadko earned his living by playing at banquets. One day he fell into disfavor, for a reason that is not given. Saddened and worried by this, he went to the shores of Lake Il'men', where he began to play. He played all day long and into the dusk—until he saw a huge wave forming out on the lake. Greatly frightened, he ran all the way back to Novgorod.

Three days later, still out of favor, he returned to the shores of Lake Il'men' and sat down to play. Again a huge wave formed on the lake and he ran away. Another three days passed before Sadko had plucked up enough courage to return to the lake. Once more he played until the huge wave appeared, and this time he did not turn and run but sat and waited.

Out of the wave came the Sea Tsar—perhaps the personification of Lake Il'men'—to thank Sadko for so regally entertaining his

SAAMI

Lapp

The name the Lapp people use to refer to themselves.

SABARIOS

Lithuania

Harvest celebration that occurred after all the grain had been gathered and threshing had just begun. The farmer would take nine handfuls of grain, one of each type of crop gathered—wheat, barley, oats, and so on—and then divide each handful into three smaller portions. Each of the twenty-seven portions would then be thrown into a heap and mixed together. Half of this mixture would be ground into flour and made into small loaves, one for each member of the family. The remainder would be mixed with more barley and brewed into beer. Then, on an evening at the beginning of December, when farmers could expect that they would not be interrupted, they would celebrate the harvest.

First the farmer would pour a jug of the beer over the bung of the barrel and take the beer through to where his wife and family were waiting with a black, white, or speckled (never red) cock and hen. With the jug of beer in his hand, the farmer would kneel and give thanks for the harvest. Then he would take a wooden spoon and beat the cock and hen to death. His wife would then boil the birds in a new pot, and the cooked meat and small loaves would be set out. The farmer and his family would then drink the beer and eat the flesh and the loaves, until everything had

Olga Markova-Mikhailenko performs in a Kirov Opera production of Sadko *at the Edin Festival in Scotland, 1995. (Robbie Jack/Corbis)*

The following day, just as he had been told, Sadko was invited to play at a magnificent banquet. As the rich men began to become drunk, they started to boast. In a loud voice Sadko made the boast he had been told to. When the rich men poured scorn on Sadko, he challenged the men as he had been instructed to, wagering his head against the men's shops and merchandise. Six men took Sadko up on his wager. Having procured a silken net, Sadko led the men to the shores of Lake Il'men', where he cast the net three times into the waters, each time hauling it in with a fish with golden fins struggling in its mesh.

The men were obliged to keep their end of the wager, and soon Sadko became one of the richest merchants in all Novgorod. In keeping with his wealth, Sadko decided to hold a banquet for all the merchants and free men of the city. As the meal ended, the customary time came for those present to boast. Sadko was the first to do so, boasting that he had sufficient wealth to buy up everything that was for sale in the city of Novgorod, wagering thirty thousand rubles should he fail to do so. The wager was accepted by Foma Nazariev and Luka Zinoviev, governors of the city.

For three days Sadko's men bought up everything in the city; but as they cleared the shops and stalls, more goods arrived from Moscow, and Sadko began to realize the folly of his boast. Thus he settled his wager of thirty thousand rubles and set sail in a fleet of thirty boats to sell all the goods he had bought. He sailed from Novgorod to the River Volkhov, and from there to Lake Ladoga. From Lake Ladoga the fleet sailed to the River Neva, and thence across the sea to the land of the Golden Horde.

As Sadko was returning from this long sea voyage, during which he had sold all of his merchandise and had reloaded his fleet of ships with gold, silver, precious gems, and pearls, the fleet became strangely becalmed on the open sea. Although the sails flapped in the wind and the waves lapped against the

guests. As a reward, he told Sadko, the very next day he would be invited to play at a banquet at which some of the richest men of Novgorod would be present. At this banquet the rich men would start to boast about their wealth and their possessions. The Sea Tsar told Sadko that he too should make a boast, stating that he could tell them where to find a fish with golden fins swimming in the waters of Lake Il'men'.

ships' hulls, the ships did not move forward. Sadko immediately guessed what was wrong and ordered that a barrel filled with red gold be thrown into the sea as a tribute to the Sea Tsar, whom they had forgotten to honor on their countless previous voyages.

Still the ships did not move, even after they had tossed numerous other barrels filled with valuables over the side. Finally Sadko suggested that they draw lots and make a human sacrifice; but Sadko tried to trick his men by writing his name on a twig while the men wrote theirs on gold coins. The human sacrifice would be the name that was on the first lot to reach the bottom of the sea. Sadko fully expected his lot to float, but to his dismay it sank while the gold coins floated. Realizing that the Sea Tsar wanted him alone, he called for writing materials so that he could write his will. Then, having lowered an oak raft into the sea and taking only his *gusli* with him, he bade farewell to his men and was cast adrift. Immediately the ships were released and sailed off toward Novgorod, leaving Sadko alone.

Having nothing else to do, Sadko lay back on the raft and quickly fell asleep. When he awoke, he found himself on the seabed close to a white palace that was the home of the Sea Tsar. As soon as the Sea Tsar had chided Sadko for having failed earlier to pay him tribute, he ordered Sadko to play his *gusli*. As Sadko played, the Sea Tsar began to dance until the sea was whipped into a frenzy, causing many people to die. Soon people began to pray to Saint Nikolai of Mozhaisk, the patron saint of sailors, also called Mikola Mozhaiski, to save them.

Beneath the sea Sadko continued to play and the Sea Tsar continued his frenzied dance. As he played, Sadko was confronted by an old man who bade him stop; but Sadko could not stop, as he was under the spell of the Sea Tsar. The old man then instructed Sadko to break the strings and the pegs of his *gusli* so that it would be impossible to continue playing. This Sadko did, and the storms abated.

Seeing that Sadko could no longer play because his *gusli* had been ruined, the Sea Tsar tried another way of keeping Sadko forever beneath the sea. He offered him a wife from hundreds of beautiful maidens. As instructed by the old man, Sadko chose the very last maiden, a beautiful girl by the name of Chernava—though some sources name this maiden as Volkhof—and did not consummate the marriage but instead fell into a deep sleep.

When he awoke, Sadko found himself on the banks of the river Chernava, his fleet sailing toward him down the river Volkhov into Novgorod. Released from the grip of the Sea Tsar, Sadko kept a promise to the old man who had appeared to him on the ocean bed, and built a cathedral in honor of Saint Nikolai of Mozhaisk, in Novgorod, for it had been none other than the saint himself who had appeared to and had helped Sadko. This was the last time Sadko ever sailed the seas, for he had decided instead to stay safely at home in Novgorod. Some sources say that Sadko not only built a cathedral to Saint Nikolai but also built another in honor of the Virgin Mary; but this assertion appears to be a much later addition.

An alternative version of events says that the storm created when the Sea Tsar danced to the music of Sadko's *gusli* sank Sadko's ships, and that when Sadko escaped from the undersea palace he found himself penniless. As a result he had to take work as a barge hand, a job he stayed in for twelve years, eating nothing but bread and salt. Then Sadko decided that the time had come to return home; but recalling the Sea Tsar's wrath, this time Sadko remembered to give thanks to the spirit of the river that had provided his livelihood for the past twelve years. The river spirit responded by asking Sadko to take a message to his brother, the spirit of Lake Il'men'. Sadko agreed and dutifully carried the message to the lake. The lake responded by telling Sadko to take a boat to its center and to cast out a net three times there. Sadko did as he was instructed, hauled in three nets teeming with fish, and then returned to shore. As soon as the keel of the boat touched dry land, the fish turned into silver coins, and Sadko once again found himself a rich man.

The story of Sadko is best known outside Russia in the version presented in Rimsky-Korsakov's opera *Sadko*.

See also: Chernava; Foma Nazariev; Golden Horde, The; Il'men', Lake; Ladoga, Lake; Luka Zinoviev; Mikola Mozhaiski, Saint; Moscow; Nikolai of Mozhaisk, Saint; Novgorod; Sea Tsar

References: Barker 1986; Gil'ferding 1951; Ukhov 1957

SAFAT

Russia

River near the banks of which Dobrynya Nikitich and his bogatyri did battle with a heathen army and encountered a supernatural power that could not be defeated. This final battle of the last of the bogatyri is described in the poem *Why There Are No More Bogatyri in Holy Russia*, which explains that the knights became too confident of their abilities. Their overconfidence led them to attack a large supernatural army—a force that is identified in some versions of the story as the Kams. Every time a supernatural warrior fell to the bogatyri, two more sprang up to take his place. At last the bogatyri admitted defeat and fled to the mountains, where they were turned to stone.

See also: Bogatyr'; Dobrynya Nikitich; Kams

SAINT GEORGE AND THE DECEITFUL FOX

Armenia

A fox was swimming across a swiftly flowing river when he was caught in the current and swept away. He cried out to Saint George to rescue him, promising to burn an ounce of incense in his honor. Saint George immediately plucked the fox out of the river and set him down on the bank beneath a huge rock. There the fox began to complain and berate the saint for only responding to prayers in return for a bribe. However, as he complained, the rock began to slide toward him, as though it might crush him.

Once more the fox called out to the saint for help, this time promising to burn one and a half ounces of incense, and again the saint plucked him from the jaws of death. Again, as soon as he had recovered from shock, the fox began to complain about the saint, saying that martyrdom had done nothing to lift the saint beyond the enticement of a bribe, and if he wanted incense then he could buy it himself. As he moaned, a group of hunters came across the fox and set their dogs on him.

This time, when the fox called out to Saint George, the saint stood by and watched as the dogs set about the fox, and then as the hunters flayed him for his pelt and threw his bloody carcass away. When the hunters had left, Saint George appeared and scolded the fox, saying that as it had broken its oaths, it would never be a martyr and would die unabsolved.

One of the fables of Vardan of Aygek.

See also: George, Saint; Vardan

SAITE (~VO)

Lapp

Alternative names for the sacred sejda stone.

SALTYK

Russia

In the legend of Volkh Vseslav'evich, the king of India who was killed by the hero of the tale.

See also: India; Volkh Vseslav'evich

SAMOSEK SWORD

Russia

A self-cutting sword that was jointly inherited by two leshie who lived on a small island. The leshie constantly argued over whose the sword truly was. Their argument had lasted thirty years since the sword came into their possession and was still raging when Ivan the Guard visited the island. Ivan sought out the leshie and offered to act as their judge. He proposed that he should hold the sword and then shoot an arrow into the woods, and that ownership of the sword would be awarded to the leshii that brought the arrow back to Ivan. The leshie readily agreed and gave the sword to Ivan the Guard. He shot an arrow far into the woods, and the two leshie ran off and quickly found it but then fell to fighting over whose it was. Ivan the Guard laughed to himself, reboarded his ship, and set sail with the Samosek Sword for the kingdom of Nemal Chelovek.

Ivan used the sword to great effect at the mansion of the giant Nemal Chelovek, who as soon as he saw Ivan, cast a spell that made himself grow until his head brushed the ceiling. The giant then rushed at Ivan, who simply lifted the Samosek Sword, which flew through the air and neatly decapitated the oncoming giant. The sword then flew through the mansion and killed all of Nemal Chelovek's servants before returning neatly to Ivan the Guard's hand.

See also: Ivan the Guard; Leshii (~y); Nemal Chelovek

SAMOYEDS
General
People inhabiting the extreme north of Russia between the Kanin and Taymir peninsulas. They live in small communities around the Ob' and Yenisey Rivers or in scattered nomadic clans. The settled groups generally subsist by farming; and the nomads, by fishing, hunting, and trapping. Samoyeds breed reindeer to provide themselves with food, clothing, and skins for shelter. Until recent times, all Samoyeds believed in and practiced a form of shamanism. Their ancient language, known as Samoyed, is part of the Uralic language family and is related to the Finno-Ugric languages. However, Russian and various Turkic dialects have replaced the Samoyed tongue in much of the region. Scholars hypothesize that the Samoyeds originated in southwestern Siberia. They appear to have reached northernmost Russia by the twelfth century, migrating there under pressure from various other peoples moving into their original homeland.

See also: Finno-Ugric; Siberia

SAMSON
Armenia
The hero of a post-Christian legend who obviously owes his origins to the biblical hero of the same name. Samson was the son of a poor, unnamed peasant who saw a maiden in a dream and fell in love with her. At the same time, the maiden, who actually existed, had a dream in which she saw Samson, and she fell in love with him. For a whole month Samson pined for the mysterious maiden he had dreamed of. One day he fell asleep briefly, and when he awoke, he felt imbued with tremendous strength. Feeling so empowered, Samson first went into the village near his home where he floored an ox with which several men were struggling by taking hold of a horn in one hand and punching it with his other fist.

Then Samson went to the local blacksmith and had him make a sword weighing thirty *litr* (a *litr* is an indeterminate weight that varies between twelve and twenty pounds, so this sword might have weighed anywhere between 360 and 600 pounds). Thus armed, Samson set off on foot, and after many days' travel met a lone man traveling in the opposite direction. After they had exchanged the customary greetings, each wishing the other good health and a long life, Samson told the man that he was en route to Anatolia in search of his "dream maiden." The man told Samson that he could not possibly accomplish the journey on foot. Rather, Samson should buy a bridle and make his way to the sea. There, under a tree, he would find a fountain. Every evening a horse that lived beneath the sea came to the fountain to take a drink. While it was thus engaged, Samson should place the bridle over its head, and it would become his.

Samson followed this advice to the letter, and snared the horse. At first, the animal threatened to dash him to death under its hooves, but Samson sat steadfastly on its back, and before long the horse consented to do Samson's bidding. Samson told the horse to take him where his heart most desired, and immediately the horse leaped upward and flew swiftly through the sky until its path was blocked by two mountains. The horse told Samson to strike its belly with his stirrups, and as he did so, the horse reared up and cleared the peaks, losing only a few hairs from its tail. On and on the horse and Samson flew until they came to a magnificent garden where the horse alighted to graze. As Samson sat eating his own meal, a gardener came up to him and told him that he had settled in the private garden of the king of the devils and that he should be gone before the king found out.

Samson replied that he would welcome the attention of the king and all his army, and then gave the gardener a shove. Some time later the gardener regained consciousness and ran to his master, who drew his army around him and marched toward Samson. Samson saw them coming, drew his sword, mounted his horse, and killed each and every demon, including the king of the devils himself. Then Samson flew onward.

After several days Samson saw a huge stone slab blocking the entrance to a cave— a cave in which Samson knew his beloved "dream maiden" was captive. Samson had the horse land, easily moved aside the stone slab that a hundred normal men could never have hoped to move even a fraction of an inch, and entered the cave. There, seated on a carpet, he saw his "dream maiden," and he knew that his journey had come to an end. The two embraced, and the maiden told Samson that her name was Gulinaz (a Persian name denoting a young rose), adding that she had been carried off and imprisoned in that cave by Tapagöz.

Samson had never heard of Tapagöz, though Gulinaz actually refers to this creature as *a* Tapagöz, rather than *the* Tapagöz, signifying that there was a race of giants and her captor was just one example of that race. Gulinaz told Samson how he might kill the Tapagöz, and then she asked her beloved to replace the stone slab and hide in the cave. As night fell, the ground began to shake, and

peeping out from his hiding place, Samson saw the Tapagöz returning, driving a mixed flock of bison, sheep, cows, and oxen in front of him, using an uprooted tree as his staff.

The Tapagöz entered the cave, made a vast meal of the animals he had driven before him, and then went to sleep. As his snores filled the cave, Samson crept out and was amazed by the size of the Tapagöz. Samson estimated that his head weighed fifty poods, his nose fifteen poods, and each tooth between four and five poods. Taking the spit from the Tapagöz's fire, Samson climbed onto the giant's nose, and gathering all his strength, thrust the point of the spit into the single eye in the middle of the Tapagöz's forehead. With a mighty sigh, the giant keeled over and died.

Setting out on the back of Samson's flying horse, Samson and Gulinaz flew for several days until they alighted in a beautiful palace garden. While Samson and Gulinaz rested in the shade of a tree and the horse fed on the lush grass, a gardener discovered them and asked them what they thought they were doing. Samson calmly replied that he was the one who would put out the eye of the gardener and the king. The gardener hurried to the king and gave him the message. Worried, the king called for his *lala* (a Turkish tutor or servant that has charge of a young prince or gentleman). The *lala* suggested that the young man's anger had been brought about by hunger, so the king had the *lala* take the young man and the young lady some food. Samson responded by drawing fifteen camels laden with gold on a piece of paper, and he sent the picture back to the king with the *lala*.

The king realized that the young man was demanding fifteen camels laden with gold in exchange for leaving the palace gardens. He responded by sending his *lala* back with two eggs, signifying that he would put out the young man's eyes for being so insolent. Samson responded by sending the *lala* back with two walnuts to show that he was as hard a nut to crack.

Knowing that he was being toyed with, the king sent the *lala* back with a handful of grain. Samson knew this meant that the king had an army as numerous as grains of wheat. Thus he responded by sending the *lala* back with a chicken, to show that no matter how large the army was, this chicken would soon gobble them up. Seeing that reasoning was hopeless, the king assembled his army and marched out to do battle with the impudent young man.

Samson saw the army approaching. Taking up his sword, he leaped onto his horse and completely decimated the unfortunate soldiers. Seeing his army dead on the battlefield, the king summoned three demons that lived within his kingdom and sent them against Samson. Within minutes the three demons lay dead; so the king assembled all his advisers and asked them how he might overcome or escape this violent youth.

One of these counselors advised the king to consult a local sorcerer. The king immediately summoned the sorcerer, who divined the situation and told the king that the young man had slain the Tapagöz and rescued the daughter of King Aslan. When the king heard this, he sent thirty camels laden with gold to Samson, and news to King Aslan of the safe return of his daughter. King Aslan hurried to the palace and was reunited with his daughter. He then took Samson and his daughter back to his own kingdom, where he married his daughter to her rescuer and then abdicated in favor of his new son-in-law.

See also: Aslan; Gulinaz; Tapagöz

References: Orbeli and Taronian 1959–67, vol. 4

SAR AKKA
Lapp

One of the daughters of Mader Atcha and Mader Akka. If an unborn child—created by Mader Atcha and Mader Akka—was to be a girl, Sar Akka completed the child's creation and placed the fetus in the womb of its human mother. If it was to be a boy,

then that task was carried out by Sar Akka's sister, Uks Akka.

See also: Mader Akka; Mader Atcha; Uks Akka

SARAC
Serbia

Prince Marko's horse. The name means "piebald." Described as the fastest horse in the world, Sarac had the gift of speech and a capacity for alcohol equivalent to that of his master, whose wine he always shared. Sarac was 160 years old when he was killed by Marko, who was 300 years old at the time. Marko gave the horse an elaborate burial before lying down to die.

See also: Marko, Prince

SARACEN HILL
Russia

A mountain, also called Sorochinsk, that lay on an uninhabited island. The place was visited by Vasilii Buslayevich and his men, who climbed the mountain. Halfway up the mountainside, Vasilii Buslayevich came across a pile of human bones and idly kicked the skull aside. As he did so, the skull warned him that he would die on that very mountain. Vasilii refused to believe this, kicked the skull to one side, and continued to climb. At the top of the mountain the men came to a huge stone slab that had an inscription on it saying that any who dived across it would surely die. This slab is described by some sources as being three fathoms high (24 feet), three *arshins* and a quarter wide (an *arshin* equals 28 inches), and a whole ax-throw across. Vasilii and his men read the words, laughed at them, and then crossed the stone, though none dared to dive across. However, since they found nothing else on that island, they returned to their ship and set their course again toward Jerusalem.

Vasilii Buslayevich and his men visited the island again, on their way back to Novgorod. Again Vasilii Buslayevich and his men climbed the mountain and crossed the stone slab at the top, although this time Vasilii decided he would take a risk and dive head-long from one side to the other. He took a good run up and leaped into the air. However, as his legs crossed the edge of the stone, one foot caught on the lip, and Vasilii Buslayevich crashed down onto the slab, splitting his head open and spilling his brains. Vasilii's men gave him a Christian burial and then returned home to Novgorod, where they went their separate ways.

See also: Novgorod; Sorochinsk Hill; Vasilii Buslayevich

SARMATIANS
Russia

An ancient barbarian people who inhabited Russia during the Roman epoch. Their descendants, the Ossetes, still inhabit the Caucasus. The Ossetes have a story about their hero Batradz that bears great similarity to the tale of the passing of King Arthur—a story that was possibly brought to them by Roman soldiers.

See also: Arthur, King; Batradz; Caucasus; Ossetes

SAULE
Lithuania

The sun goddess who was believed to live with her daughters in a castle located either at the far end of the sea or beyond the tops of the slippery high hill of the sky (see Dausos). Every day she would drive her gleaming copper chariot, drawn by tireless fiery steeds, across the sky. As evening approached, she would rest her horses and wash them in the sea before retiring to her castle home. Sometimes she would ride down the slopes of the slippery high hill of the sky to her apple orchard in nine chariots drawn by one hundred horses. The red, setting sun was said to be one of her precious apples slipping from her hand, the goddess weeping fiery red tears that would shine from the mountainside and fall to earth as red berries.

Sometimes Saule was described as sailing the seas in a golden boat, or as a jug from which light was poured, her daughters washing it every evening in the sea. Saule was closely associated with the moon god Menuo, or Meness, and the unnamed sons of Dievas, known as the Dievo suneliai. General Baltic belief (as opposed to purely Lithuanian) holds that Saule became the consort of the moon and that the stars and the earth are their offspring. However, because Saule spent every day with the sky, the marriage is not a happy or peaceful one. Eclipses were interpreted as the rare occasions when Saule and the moon made up and hung a cloth over themselves to hide their lovemaking.

See also: Dausos; Dievas; Dievo suneliai; Meness (~ulis); Menuo; Moon; Sun

SAVEL'EVICH, IVAN
Russia

See Ivan Savel'evich.

SAXO GRAMMATICUS
General

Danish chronicler (c. 1150–c. 1220) who compiled the *Gesta Danorum,* a Latin history of the legendary and historical kings of Denmark up to 1186, in sixteen volumes that were probably written between 1185 and 1216. The writings of Saxo Grammaticus and other obscure contemporary chroniclers contain the only known historical references to several Baltic coast deities, such as Svantovit.

See also: Baltic; Svantovit (~dovit)

SBRODOVICH
Russia

A family of seven brothers, all of whom passed the tests set by Vasilii Buslayevich and as a result became members of Vasilii's thirty-strong *druzhina*. Other members of this group were Kostia Novotorzheni, the first to pass; the brothers Luka and Moisei; and the men of Zalyoshen. Twenty-nine members of the *druzhina* were picked through the tests, Vasilii Buslayevich himself being the thirtieth. Those who failed the tests were killed and simply thrown over a wall.

> *See also:* Kostia Novotorzheni; Luka; Moisei; Vasilii Buslayevich; Zalyoshen

SCHEK
Slav

The *Primary Chronicle* says that Kiev was founded by three Viking brothers named Kiy, Schek, and Khoriv. Kiy, Schek, and Khoriv might actually have existed, but this is not certain. However, the *Primary Chronicle* places them in Kiev before Riurik founded Novgorod, and reports that by that time, the descendants of these three were living in the city as tributaries of the Khazars. These descendants were killed when Oleg seized power in Kiev, in 882.

> *See also:* Khoriv; Kiev; Kiy; Novgorod; Oleg; *Primary Chronicle;* Riurik; Schek; Vikings
> *References:* Cross and Sherbowitz-Wetzor 1953

SCYTHIA
General

Region to the north of the Black Sea between the Carpathian Mountains and the river Don, the original inhabitants of which, after the middle of the fourth century, were slowly superseded by the Sarmatians.

> *See also:* Black Sea; Carpathian Mountains; Don; Sarmatians

SEA KING
Russia

Alternative name for the Sea Tsar.

SEA TSAR
Russia
Also: Sea King

The god of the oceans, in one account equated with the spirit of Lake Il'men'. The Sea Tsar also features in the story concerning the poor musician Sadko, who became the richest merchant in Novgorod, with his help. No matter how often Sadko sailed the open seas, he forgot to pay tribute to the Sea Tsar. One day his ships were strangely becalmed, even though the wind still filled their sails and the waves still lapped at their hulls.

Set adrift on an oak raft, Sadko fell asleep, only to find himself under the sea in the presence of the Sea Tsar when he awoke. The Sea Tsar ordered Sadko to play his gusli (a stringed musical instrument), which he did. The Sea Tsar began a frenzied dance, which whipped the seas into a fury. Many people drowned in the storm, while those who survived prayed for salvation to Saint Nikolai of Mozhaisk, the patron saint of sailors. Saint Nikolai helped Sadko to escape from the Sea Tsar by telling him to break his instrument. The Sea Tsar then attempted to hold onto Sadko by having him marry one of his daughters. As instructed by Saint Nikolai, Sadko chose the very last maiden offered to him, a girl by the name of Chernava. Also as Nikolai had directed him, Sadko did not consummate the marriage, and when he awoke the morning after his wedding he found himself on the banks of the river Chernava near his home city of Novgorod.

> *See also:* Chernava; Il'men', Lake; Nikolai of Mozhaisk, Saint; Novgorod; Sadko

SECOND ALMAFI
Hungary—Magyar
See: Almafi.

SEJDA
Lapp
Also: Saivo, Saite

A sacred stone that also acted as a talisman. A sorcerer named Lompsalo once owned a sejda that enabled him to catch copious quantities of fish. On the opposite bank of the river lived another sorcerer who stole Lompsalo's sejda, and thus obtained the power of the sejda and the ability to catch large quantities of fish. Lompsalo countered the theft by procuring a more powerful sejda; so once more the fish returned to his side of the river—until his rival destroyed the new sejda.

> *See also:* Lompsalo

SELYANINOVICH, MIKULA
Russia
See Mikula Selyaninovich.

SEMIK
Russia
Festival that was central to the weeklong cycle that started with the Rusaliia and ended with the Troitsa (from Whitsun to Trinity Sunday). The root of Semik is *sem'*, which associates the festival with the words for "seed," "sperm," "family," and "seven." The festival was celebrated on the seventh Thursday after Easter, and was immediately preceded by a ritual called kumstvo. During this prelude, a birch tree known as the "Semik Birch" would be dressed with ribbons like a goddess to preside over the coming festivities. This ritual and others were designed to confirm the unity of the community and reconfirm its link with deceased ancestors and the society of the past. Young girls were central to kumstvo, during which they would wear garlands woven from birch twigs, representing their fertility, which they would retain unsullied until they married. The girls would embrace, signifying the solidarity of the village, and pledge their eternal blood ties. These rituals of kumstvo completed, the festival of Semik could begin.

Once the kumstvo was completed, the birch tree would be cut down and brought into the village, where its boughs would be used to decorate every house. Then the tree would be feasted as a goddess of the dead. Then, having been well fed, the tree would be carried down to the banks of a local river where it would be ceremonially "undressed" and cast into the water to drown. During this time the unmarried women of the village would select their future husbands, and having done so, would cast their birch-branch garlands into the water. If a garland sank, its owner was fated to die; but if it floated, she would marry, be happy, and bear healthy children.

Semik lasted two days, Thursday and Friday, and was followed by Troitsa, which at that time was celebrated on Saturday.

See also: Kumstvo; Rusaliia; Troitsa
References: Afanas'ev 1865–69; Propp 1963; Rimsky-Korsakov 1951; Zemtsovskii 1970

SENMURV
Slav
Alternative name for the Simorg.

SERAPION
Russia
Historical thirteenth-century bishop of Vladimir who vociferously denounced women for clinging to pagan beliefs, calling them witches. However, he opposed the drowning of witches, as he saw this as confirming their power over the natural world.

SERBIA
General
During the sixth and seventh centuries A.D., various groups of Slavs, including the ancestors of the Serbs, settled on the Balkan Peninsula in the area of present-day Serbia (then the Roman province of Moesia), at the invitation of the emperor Heraclius. These people adopted Christianity about two hundred years later. Each group had its own leader until the late twelfth century (c. 1169), when Stefan Nemanja, a warrior and chief, formed the first united Serbian state. During the fourteenth century, Emperor Stefan Dusan (1331–1355) led the country in successful wars against the Byzantine Empire, but the Serbian Empire began to break up after his death in 1355. The Ottoman Empire conquered Serbia in the Battle of Kosovo Field in 1389, annexed the country in 1459, and subsequently ruled Serbia for more than three hundred years, throughout which time the Serbs never lost their national pride. Djordje Petrovic, a Serbian peasant nicknamed Black George, led an uprising against the Ottomans in 1804, while another Serbian peasant leader, Milos Obrenovic, led a second revolt in 1815, after which Turkey recognized Serbia as an autonomous principality. Serbia regained independence in 1878 following the Ottoman Empire's defeat by

Russia in the Russo-Turkish War of 1877–1878.

During the early twentieth century, various economic and political conflicts developed between Serbia and Austria-Hungary. In June 1914, the heir to the throne of Austria-Hungary, Archduke Francis Ferdinand, was assassinated by Gavril Princip, a Serbian student. The assassination sparked World War I, which began a month later when Austria-Hungary declared war on Serbia. After the war ended in 1918, Serbia spearheaded the formation of the Kingdom of the Serbs, Croats, and Slovenes, which was renamed Yugoslavia in 1929.

Following World War II, Tito and the Communists founded the socialist state of Yugoslavia with a new federal system of government, and Serbia became one of the country's six republics. A bloody conflict in the late 1980s led to the breakup of Yugoslavia, and in April 1992 Serbia and Montenegro formed a smaller Yugoslav confederation.

See also: Bosnia; Byzantine Empire; Herzegovina; Montenegro

SERGIUS OF RADONEZH, SAINT
Russia
National hero and patron of the fourteenth-century monastery named in his honor—the Troitse-Sergiyeva Lavra at Sergiyev Posad (Zagorsk)—which became the center of Muscovite religious life.

References: Kazanskii 1855

SHAH-MAR
Armenia
King of the snakes, a strange being with the head of a man and the body of a huge serpent. The legends connected with Shah-Mar are outlined in the entry for Purto.

See also: King of Snakes; Purto

SHAMAN
General
The term *shaman* originated with the Tungus people of the Siberian Arctic, who gave the name to their priestly magicians and seers who practiced a form of what is now popularly known as "charismatic religion." The female counterpart of the shaman is the shamanka. The word means "one who is excited" or "one who is exalted." The priest or priestess on whom the title was bestowed was said to have the power of entering the spirit world at will and to bring its denizens under his or her command. In some instances the journey of the shaman is symbolized by his climbing a tree or a ladder, a symbology that connects the rites of the shaman to the World Tree. In others he or she is spoken of as flying, usually in bird form, or riding on a magical horse. The shaman is also believed to have the ability, like the gods he or she could communicate with, to send his or her spirit out at will to summon other spirits and to exorcise those who caused illness or other harm.

Though in certain cases the role of shaman might be inherited from generation to generation, the shaman was usually "chosen" by a spirit that would inhabit the body of the unwilling individual until it could be driven out. While the spirit was within its host, that person would take to living in the woods, until at length he or she underwent an ecstatic enlightenment during which the secrets of the universe were revealed. These individuals then accepted their particular roles in life and acknowledged their spirit aids. The spirits inhabiting their bodies then return to the spirit world, where they wait to be contacted by the new shamans.

See also: Shamanka; Siberia; Tungus; World Tree

SHAMANKA
General
A female shaman.

SHKAY
Mordvin
The sun god, head of the non-Christian pantheon of the Mordvin people.

SHUNDI-MUMI

Votyak

"Mother of the sun," the sun goddess.

SIBERIA

General

A vast, thinly populated region in northern Asia that accounts for about three-quarters of the total area of Russia but contains only about 20 percent of Russia's population. Ice and snow cover most of the region about six months a year, and the temperature sometimes drops below −90 degrees F (−68 degrees C). Siberia covers about 4,929,000 square miles (12,766,000 square kilometers) and includes three different primary geographic regions—the West Siberian Plain, the Central Siberian Plateau, and the East Siberian Highlands. The West Siberian Plain, the largest level region in the world, extends from the east side of the Ural Mountains to the Yenisey River. The Central Siberian Plateau lies between the Yenisey and Lena Rivers. The plateau's southern edge is the site of Lake Baikal, the world's deepest lake, with depths up to 5,315 feet (1,620 meters). The East Siberian Uplands consist of a series of mountain ranges between the Lena River and the Pacific coast and contain Siberia's highest point—an active volcano named Klyuchevskaya that rises to 15,584 feet (4,750 meters).

People were living in Siberia by about 30,000 years ago. Asian nomads called Tatars, under the Mongolian emperor Genghis Khan, conquered the southern steppes during the early thirteenth century and drove many of the original tribes into the northern forests. In the late sixteenth century a band of Cossacks led by Yermak defeated the Tatars, and by 1700, the Russians controlled almost all Siberia. Siberia is perhaps best known for its labor camps, to which the Communist regime of the old USSR exiled political dissidents and criminal prisoners.

See also: Cossacks; Genghis Khan; Lena, River; Mongols; Tatars; Ural Mountains

People walking in a snowy street, Siberia (Archive Photos)

SICKSA

Slav

A mischievous forest spirit that could alter its shape at will, and was thus akin to the leshii.

See also: Leshii (~y)

SIELA

Baltic

The living spirit, or power of life, that does not depart with the dead spirit, or vele, but instead is reincarnated in animals or plants, especially trees.

See also: Vele(s)

SILESIA

General

A region of southwestern Poland, eastern Germany, and the northern part of the Czech Republic, Silesia includes the upper Oder river valley and the Sudeten Mountains. The region became part of Poland in the tenth century. Austria took over Silesia in 1526, and Prussia seized northern Silesia from Austria in 1742. In 1919 Germany and Poland divided northern Silesia, and southern Silesia became a part of Czechoslovakia. Poland gained control of the entire northern part in 1945, and in 1993 the Czechoslovak section became a part of the Czech Republic.

See also: Czechoslovakia; Czechs; Poland

SILINIETS

Poland

One of the two forest spirits, the other being Modeina.

See also: Modeina

SILVER CITY, THE

Armenia

One of the succession of cities that the princess wife of Habërmani traveled through on her quest to find her husband and restore him to her side.

See also: Habërmani
References: Orbeli and Taronian 1959–67, vol. 4

SILVER KINGDOM, THE

Russia

One of the three kingdoms of Whirlwind, located on a plateau at the top of tremendously high mountains. The tsaritsa of this kingdom, a prisoner of Whirlwind, lived in a silver palace that was guarded by dragons. She was set free by Ivan Belyaninovich, along with her sisters, the tsaritsas of the Copper Kingdom and the Golden Kingdom, when he killed Whirlwind and released his mother Nastas'ya of the Golden Braid. She married Peter Belyaninovich, one of the two brothers of Ivan. Her sister the tsaritsa of the Copper Kingdom married Vasilii Belyaninovich, and her other sister Elena the Fair, the tsaritsa of the Golden Kingdom, married Ivan.

See also: Copper Kingdom, The; Golden Kingdom, The; Ivan Belyaninovich; Nastas'ya of the Golden Braid; Peter (Belyaninovich); Vasilii Belyaninovich; Whirlwind

SILVER ROAN

Russia

A magical horse whose eyes spark fire and whose nostrils breathe fire. An old man once instructed his three sons to guard his grave for three nights after his death. When the time came, the two eldest sons ignored his instructions and sent their younger brother, Ivan the Fool, to take their place. At midnight on the third night, the old man rose from his grave and rewarded Ivan the Fool with Silver Roan.

Shortly afterward the local tsar announced that he would marry his daughter to any man who could snatch her veil from a great height. Ivan the Fool muttered a spell to Silver Roan, climbed into its ear, and emerged as a handsome youth. At the third try he snatched the veil and won the contest. He then returned home and changed back into his normal, squalid self. The tsar looked high and low for the youth. Finding no trace of him, he arranged a feast and ordered the entire local population to attend. Ivan the Fool sat in a corner in the banqueting hall and remained unnoticed until he wiped the rim of his glass with the veil and was recognized. The tsar welcomed him as a man would welcome a lost son, and duly married him to his daughter, much to the displeasure of Ivan's brothers.

SIMIZAR
Armenia

The daughter of King Zarzand who was abducted by Tapagöz, the oldest of the demons, who carried the maiden to his lair, the Devil's Castle, and there, for forty days and forty nights, besought her to become his wife. She refused, whereupon Tapagöz went mad for three days, calling her name endlessly, and then had the maiden handed over to his mother, who was a witch. The latter imprisoned Simizar in a cave, allowing her to wander outside only at midnight. It was on one of these occasions that she encountered Aslan, who promised to free her.

For the remainder of the legend see the entry for Zurab.

See also: Aslan; Devil's Castle; Tapagöz; Zarzand; Zurab

SIMORG (~ARGL, ~URG)
Slav

Also: Senmurv

Possibly having originated with the ancient Persian *Simarghu,* Simorg was a dragon, a hybrid bird-dog that guarded the Tree of Life, on which could be found the seeds of every living plant on earth. There was, however, one problem: The Tree of Life looked like any other tree, and Simorg was invisible, a ruse that was meant to protect the Tree of Life from the attentions of mankind. Thus, the act of cutting down a tree was fraught with danger, lest one fell the Tree of Life. To alleviate this danger, an elaborate ritual was performed, propitiating Simorg, who in response would ensure the safety of the tree.

Often mentioned alongside the goddess Mokosh, Simorg was described as the protector of the home and the family and has been linked with the ancient Sumerian god-dess Ishtar. In Ukraine, Simorg was depicted as seated on a tree, on an island guarded by voracious fish. In the tenth century, especially in Ukraine, Simorg was a popular embellishment on women's jewelry.

See also: Dragon; Mokosh; Tree of Life, The; Ukraine

References: Afanas'ev 1957; Ivanov and Toporov 1965

SINEUS
Scandinavia and Russia

One of the two younger brothers of Riurik, the other being Truvor. When Riurik was chosen as the first Varangian ruler of Novgorod, Sineus settled at Beloozero and Truvor at Izborsk, the *Primary Chronicle* dating their settlement at between 860 and 862. Two years later Sineus and Truvor died and Riurik became the sole ruler. The Hypatian *Primary Chronicle* gives a different account, saying that Riurik settled first at Lake Ladoga. After the deaths of Sineus and Truvor, Riurik assumed sole authority and moved his seat of power to the city on the banks of the river Volkhov—Novgorod.

See also: Ladoga, Lake; Novgorod; *Primary Chronicle;* Riurik; Rostov; Truvor; Varangians

References: Cross and Sherbowitz-Wetzor 1953

SIRIN
Russia

A water nymph that may be directly equated with the classical Greek siren and the Germanic Lorelei. She was a paradisal bird with the face of a beautiful young maiden. Unlike her Greek and German counterparts, the sirin was not known for luring unsuspecting travelers to a watery death through their enchanting song: The russalka adequately filled that role. Instead the sirin was a bird of happiness and beauty who rewarded the virtuous by flying down from heaven and singing to these fortunate few. Any who heard the song of the sirin would instantly forget everything and die.

See also: Rus(s)alki (~ulki)

SIVUSHKO

Russia

The wondrous horse of Il'ya Muromets that galloped like the wind and according to some sources, cleared mountains in a single leap. These sources state that a single leap of this wondrous animal covered fifty versts—a distance approximately equivalent to thirty-three miles.

See also: Il'ya Muromets

SJADAEI

Siberia—Samoyed

A wooden or stone idol that had a human (*sja*) or semihuman appearance. The sjadaei were dressed in reindeer skins and decorated with scraps of colored cloth.

SKAZKA

Russia

(pl. skazki) One of the three major categories of Russian legend, along with the bylina and the bylichka. Unlike the byliny, the skazki are pure fantasy. The commonest name for the hero in these stories is Ivan, one of the most widespread of Russian proper male names. No matter whether the hero comes from a royal or noble family or is a peasant or even the offspring of an animal, he is always brave and kind and is usually beset with some personal misfortune that he ultimately overcomes.

See also: Bylichka; Bylina

SLAVS

General

The most numerous of the various European peoples, with a vast population of more than 250 million distributed principally in eastern and central Europe. The Slavic language group with its many dialects is a part of the Indo-European language family and can be divided into three linguistic subgroups: the East Slavic branch, consisting of Russian, Belorussian, and Ukrainian; the West Slavic branch, including Polish, Czech, and Slovak; and the South Slavic branch, including Slovenian, Serbo-Croatian, Macedonian, and Bulgarian.

The early Slavs were farmers and herders living in the marshes and woodlands of what is now eastern Poland and western Russia, Belorussia, and Ukraine. From about A.D. 150 the Slavs began to expand in all directions. To the north they followed the rivers through the forests of Russia, occupying territory populated by Finnish and Baltic peoples, many of whom they absorbed. To the west they encountered Germanic and Celtic groups as they occupied much of central Europe. By the seventh century the Slavs had reached as far south as the Adriatic and Aegean Seas. During the next two centuries they settled in most of the Balkan Peninsula, then part of the Byzantine Empire, dislocating indigenous populations or slavicizing newcomers, such as the Bulgarians. To the east, by the end of the sixteenth century, the Russians had already secured a permanent foothold beyond the Ural Mountains in Asia; and by the nineteenth century, Slavic culture had reached the Pacific Ocean.

Whereas the ancient Slavs probably exhibited considerable racial and cultural homogeneity, the modern Slavic peoples are united mainly by their linguistic affinity and a sense of common origins. Extensive contact with a variety of peoples has profoundly influenced the racial and cultural develop-

A woman cries over the grave of her husband, who was killed by a grenade in downtown Sarajevo. (Reuters/Corinne Dufka/Archive Photos)

ment of the Slavs. Today, the Slavic groups show a far greater range of diversity in physical type and in culture than other European ethnic groups.

Christianity was initially introduced to the Slavs by Greek missionaries during the ninth and the tenth centuries. Their religious development, however, was altered by the separation of the Eastern and Western churches in 1054. The Slavs quickly became the focus of intense rivalry between Roman Catholicism and Eastern Orthodoxy. Catholicism and Western culture triumphed among the Poles, Slovaks, and Czechs; later, however, the Czechs were significantly affected by the Reformation, and because of this, they are today the only Slavic people with a large Protestant minority. In the Balkans, the Slovenes and Croats also gave their allegiance to Roman Catholicism and fell into the sphere of central European civilization. Serbs, Macedonians, Bulgarians, and a majority of the Eastern Slavs (Belorussians, Russians, Ukrainians) joined the Orthodox Church and adopted many aspects of Byzantine culture, including an adaptation of the Greek alphabet—what is known today as the Cyrillic alphabet.

During the fourteenth century the Ottoman Turks conquered much of southeastern Europe. Parts of what are now Bosnia and Herzegovina, Bulgaria, Croatia, the former Yugoslav Republic of Macedonia, Serbia and Montenegro, and Slovenia remained under Ottoman rule until 1912. Centuries of Turkish domination had a profound effect on the Balkan Slavs, many of whom were forced to convert to Islam. Today the majority of Slavic Muslims are in Bosnia and southern Bulgaria.

Although the Slavs created a number of medieval kingdoms between the ninth and the eleventh centuries, much of their subsequent history was characterized by subjugation within foreign states. The present Slavic nations are to a great extent the results of the dissolution of the Austro-Hungarian and Ottoman Empires following World War I.

With the exception of the Czechs, the Slavs remained a predominantly agrarian people until the mid-twentieth century. After World War II most of the Slavic nations came under the Soviet sphere of influence, and their Marxist governments embarked on ambitious programs of industrialization and urbanization. In the late 1980s and early 1990s, with the breakdown of the Soviet Union, the various East European nations moved toward setting up independent democratic governments. In some areas, particularly the former Yugoslavia, this transition ignited conflict among Slavs of different national and religious groups.

See also: Belorussia; Bosnia; Bulgaria; Byzantine Empire; Croatia; Cyrillic alphabet; Czechs; Herzegovina; Macedonia; Montenegro; Poland; Russia; Serbia; Slovakia; Slovenia; Ukraine; Ural Mountains

SLOVAKIA

General

A newly independent country in central Europe that is bordered by Poland to the north, Ukraine to the east, Hungary to the south, and Austria and the Czech Republic to the west. A Slavic people called Slovaks make up most of Slovakia's population.

From 1918 until 31 December 1992, Slovakia and the Czech Republic were partners in the larger nation of Czechoslovakia. Hungary had ruled Slovakia from the tenth century until 1918 when the Slovaks joined with the Czechs and other local groups to form Czechoslovakia. In mid-1992, Czech and Slovak leaders decided to split Czechoslovakia into two nations, one for Czechs and one for Slovaks; and on 1 January 1993, the Czech Republic and Slovakia were created to replace Czechoslovakia.

See also: Czechoslovakia; Czechs; Hungary; Poland; Ukraine

SLOVENIA

General

Under the Roman Empire (27 B.C.–A.D. 476), Slovenia was part of the provinces of

Pannonia and Noricum. During the sixth century A.D., the region was invaded by the Mongolian Avars, and later, by Slavs who threw off Avar domination. A period of Bavarian rule ensued, during which most of the people converted to Roman Catholicism. In A.D. 623, the chieftain Franko Samo created the first independent Slovene state, which stretched from Lake Balaton (now located in Hungary) to the Mediterranean. It lasted until late in the eighth century, when the region became part of the Frankish Empire. In the tenth century it was reorganized as the duchy of Carantania by Holy Roman Emperor Otto I. From 1335 until 1918, except for a brief interlude from 1809 to 1814, Slovenes were governed by the Habsburgs of the Austro-Hungarian Empire in the Austrian crown lands of Kärnten (Carinthia), Carniola, and Steiermark (Styria), except for a minority in the republic of Venice. During the Napoleonic Wars, the region was taken from Austria by France and reorganized as the Illyrian Provinces from 1809 to 1814. This brief period of liberal rule fostered the Slovene and South Slav nationalism that triumphed at the close of World War I in 1918 in the formation of the Kingdom of the Serbs, Croats, and Slovenes (renamed Kingdom of Yugoslavia, which means "Land of the South Slavs," in 1929). In 1941, during World War II, Germany, Hungary, and Italy divided the territory among themselves. In spite of forced transfers of populations during the war, since 1945 most Slovenes have lived in the Slovenian republic, which became autonomous in 1946, and a year later also acquired Slovenian-speaking districts on the Adriatic Sea (in Istria) from Italy. Slovenia voted to secede from Yugoslavia in 1989.

The term *Slovene* refers to the Slavic inhabitants of Slovenia and parts of the Austrian alpine provinces of Styria and Carinthia.

See also: Avars; Croatia; Mongols; Pannonia; Serbia

SMORODINA

Russia

River that Vol'ga Sviatoslavovich was intending to cross in order to collect the taxes due him. However, Mikula Selyaninovich warned him of a band of robbers that lay in wait under the bridge over the river, watching those who crossed through the cracks between the planks. Instead of crossing the river, Vol'ga Sviatoslavovich sent Mikula Selyaninovich in his place.

See also: Mikula Selyaninovich; Vol'ga Sviatoslavovich

SMORODINKA

Russia

A stream that ran across a road that led from Chernigov to Kiev. Beside this stream lived the brigand Nightingale, who killed all who attempted to pass with his whistle. Having blocked free passage on the road over this stream for thirty years, he was finally defeated by Il'ya Muromets.

See also: Chernigov; Il'ya Muromets; Kiev; Nightingale

SNOWSTORM, GRANNY

Ukraine

A personification of Mother Earth as a benevolent fertility deity who controls not only the fertility of the soil but also the weather, especially in winter. None of the characters in the most popular legend that concerns Granny Snowstorm are named, as it is the moral of the legend that is the most important point—a moral that is immediately apparent from the story.

An aging couple, each of whom had a daughter from a previous marriage, married and moved into a single house on the edge of a village. The woman grew to hate her stepdaughter, who was far more beautiful than her own, and treated her increasingly like a servant, while her own daughter was allowed to laze away the days. One day the old man's daughter dropped the bucket down the well and had to tell her stepmother. The stepmother flew into a terrible rage and made the unfortunate girl climb down the well to fetch it.

The girl climbed over the lip of the well and dropped into the water, where she sank to the bottom. There she saw a door, which she opened, and walked into a beautiful garden, where all the flowers were in full bloom and the sun shone in a brilliant blue sky, even though the village she had left had been gray and wet. Right in the middle of the garden was a small house, and standing in the doorway was a woman dressed all in white. The girl asked this woman if she had seen her bucket. The woman replied that she had, and if the girl wanted it back she would have to work to earn its return.

The girl agreed, as it did not matter to her where she worked, and she settled down to do the chores the old woman assigned her. One of these was to shake the old woman's mattress. While she was shaking the mattress, she looked out the window and saw her home and the well in her garden. All around the snow was falling, and the people of the village seemed pleased to see it settling on the ground. The old woman walked into the room and saw the puzzled expression on the girl's face. She explained that she was Granny Snowstorm; and each year, if she was pleased, she sent a hard winter so that the following year would produce a good harvest, the snow ensuring the fertility of the soil.

Three weeks passed, and the young girl worked for Granny Snowstorm and completely forgot about her real home. However, one night she dreamed that her father was grieving for her, and the following morning she asked Granny Snowstorm if she might take her bucket and go home. Though she was sad to see the young girl leave her, Granny Snowstorm said she could go, and gave the girl her bucket, which she had filled with gold coins. The young girl climbed back up the well and was reunited with her father, much to the

chagrin of her stepmother, who had thought the girl gone for good. She was so jealous of the young girl's good fortune that the very next morning she decided that her own daughter should descend into the well so that she too might return with a bucket of gold.

Deliberately dropping the bucket down the well, the old woman's daughter climbed down and was soon in the employment of Granny Snowstorm. However, the girl did not know how to do any of the household chores she was assigned, and Granny Snowstorm grew increasingly tired of her. After just a few days, she told the girl that she could go. The girl asked to be paid for the work she had done, though in fact she had not done any—whereupon Granny Snowstorm took her to a storeroom full of gold, silver, diamonds, and pearls. The girl took her bucket and started to fill it, then stopped and asked Granny Snowstorm what was the most valuable thing in the room. Granny Snowstorm told her that it was a single, immense pearl. The girl emptied her bucket and put the pearl in it. Then she climbed back up the well, took the pearl out of the bucket, and ran to show her mother and all the people in the village. However, as she ran the pearl began to melt: It was nothing more than a large snowball.

From that day on the woman's daughter was the laughingstock of the village. The old man's daughter, on the other hand, was soon being courted by the son of a nobleman; and as the village gathered in the harvest, the couple married—the riches of Granny Snowstorm acting as the young girl's dowry.

See also: Mother Earth
References: Oparenko 1996

SOLOVEI (~Y) RAKHMATICH
Russia
The name literally means "Nightingale, Son of Rakhmat." This brigand was described as half man, half bird.

See also: Nightingale; Rakhmat

Mosaic image of the Madonna from the Cathedral of Saint Sophia in Kiev, Ukraine (Konstantin Starodub/Art Resource, NY)

SOPHIA, SAINT
Russia

The patron saint of a great number of churches throughout Russia, notably the great cathedral in Kiev where a sixteen-foot-high image of the Mother of God, with her arms upraised in a strikingly pagan gesture, hangs over the altar. Sophia, whose name is Greek and means "wisdom," symbolized both the feminine aspect of God and the continued importance of matriarchy in Russian Christianized peasant society.

See also: Kiev

SOPHIA PAL(A)EOLOGUE
Russia

A niece of Constantine XI Palæologus, she married Ivan III (better known as Ivan the Great) in 1472, whereupon he assumed the title "Ruler of All Russia" and adopted the symbol of the Byzantine *basileus,* the two-headed eagle, and the mantle of the

Defender of Orthodoxy. Moscow became the capital of the new state.

See also: Ivan the Great; Moscow

SOROCHINSK HILL
Russia

Alternative name for the Saracen Hill, located on a remote island and climbed by Vasilii Buslayevich and his men, and the place where Vasilii Buslayevich, in at least one account, met his death.

See also: Saracen Hill; Vasilii Buslayevich

SOROCHINSK MOUNTAINS
Russia

Mountain range that was the home of a twelve-headed she-dragon that was killed by Dobrynya Nikitich after she had abducted the Princess Zabava from the court of Prince Vladimir Bright Sun in Kiev. The mountain range was the source of the Puchai, an extremely fast-flowing river above which the dragon liked to fly and pick off unsuspecting people who foolishly bathed in its waters.

See also: Dobrynya Nikitich; Dragon; Puchai; Vladimir Bright Sun, Prince; Zabava (Putyatichna), Princess

SORROW
Russia

The personification of bad luck that attached itself to Misha and refused to leave him. Misha finally tricked Sorrow and buried him in a hole from which a great quantity of gold had been dug. When Misha's unnamed brother found out about his brother's new-found wealth, jealousy got the better of him and he dug up Sorrow in the hope that Misha would again fall on hard times. Instead Sorrow attached himself to the brother, and Misha continued to live a life of luxury. The brother was as resourceful as Misha, and he managed to capture and seal Sorrow in the hub of a wheel, which he threw into a river. From that day forth neither brother saw Sorrow again. They were soon reconciled and lived thereafter as brothers should.

See also: Misha

SREDA, SAINT
Russia
The patron saint of Wednesday, who was associated with Paraskeva-Piatnitsa and Saint Nedelia.

> *See also:* Nedelia, Saint; Paraskeva-Piatnitsa
> *References:* Afanas'ev 1865–69; Bezsonov 1861; Marr 1894–99

ST. PETERSBURG
General
Russia's second largest city, St. Petersburg is a major port situated in northwestern Russia, at the eastern end of the Gulf of Finland, an arm of the Baltic Sea. The city has had three names: Tsar Peter I (the Great) founded it in 1703 as Sankt-Peterburg (St. Petersburg). After Russia went to war against Germany in 1914, at the start of World War I, the name was changed to Petrograd in order to get rid of the Germanic ending -*burg*. In 1924, the Communist government renamed the city Leningrad in honor of V. I. Lenin. However, when the Communist state disintegrated in 1991, the people of the city voted to restore the name St. Petersburg—a decision officially approved in September of that year.

> *See also:* Baltic

STAND YOUR GROUND
Armenia
A lame warrior once went to war with his able-bodied compatriots. One of his comrades asked him what he thought he was doing in a battle he could not hope to run away from if things turned against them. The old warrior replied that in battle one should stand his ground and not run and hide at the first hint of defeat.

One of the fables of Vardan.

> *See also:* Vardan
> *References:* Marr 1894–99

STARINA
Russia
Alternative name for the bylina, the plural form being *stariny*.

> *See also:* Bylina

Colored engraving of the view of the Imperial Bank and environs, St. Petersburg (Nationale, Paris, France; Giraudon/Art Resource, NY)

STAVR GODINOVICH

Russia

During a great banquet at the palace of Prince Vladimir Bright Sun in Kiev it was noticed that one bogatyr', Stavr Godinovich, was sitting quietly and not joining in the custom of boasting. When asked what was the matter, Stavr replied that he had nothing to boast about. All the company laughed, saying that everybody had something to boast about, and if he could not think of a boast about himself, then why not boast about his wife.

Stavr rose to the bait. His wife, so he said, was as brave and skillful as any polianitsa. She was the best archer in all the land, the finest *gusli* player, and a master at chess. The boast went on to say that even Prince Vladimir Bright Sun himself would find it hard to outshine his young wife.

The room fell silent as Stavr made the last part of his boast. The silence lasted only a few seconds before Vladimir commanded his guards to seize Stavr Godinovich and throw him into a dungeon for his impudence. Stavr sat in the cold stone dungeon pondering his fate and the foolishness of his boast. As he sat there, a face appeared at the window—a face everyone in Kiev knew well, for it was that of Zabava Putyatichna, better known simply as Princess Zabava, the favorite niece of Prince Vladimir Bright Sun.

She asked how the brave bogatyr' had come to be thrown into the dungeons. When he told her his sorry tale, she took pity on him and went out to get a basket of fine food and mead, which she lowered down to him. She then went to her chambers and told her pet raven the story, telling the bird to fly to the home of Stavr Godinovich and tell his wife, Katrina Ivanovna, the sorry news. The raven did as it was commanded and flew straight to the chamber of Stavr's wife and told her the story.

Katrina Ivanovna was not crestfallen, as might have been expected, but rather she rose to the challenge and gathered her retinue of thirty archers, thirty chess masters, and thirty minstrels, and set off for Kiev to free her unfortunate husband, feeling honor-bound to do so as his plight resulted from his boasting about her prowess.

A short distance from the walls of Kiev, Katrina and her retinue made camp, Katrina herself to go alone into the city, disguised as a man. So it was that a short time later she entered the hall of Prince Vladimir Bright Sun and announced that she was the Ambassador of the King of Greece, whom she named as Kalina, and that she had traveled to Kiev to exact tribute from Prince Vladimir Bright Sun under threat of a terrible war. Vladimir asked for three days and three nights to reflect on the demands of Kalina; but Katrina, in her disguise, refused, and instead said that "he" would accept the hand of the Princess Zabava in marriage in lieu of the tribute. Again Vladimir asked for time to think. Katrina said he could have twenty-four hours, and then she returned to her camp.

However, as she returned to her camp she was secretly observed by Zabava and Evpraksiya, Vladimir's wife, and they guessed that the Ambassador from Greece was a woman. Thus, when Vladimir came to Zabava to tell her the news and to ask her to marry the Ambassador to save them from a terrible war, Zabava and Evpraksiya told Vladimir they suspected a ruse. They suggested the fraud might be exposed by challenging the Ambassador to "manly" contests.

The following day the Ambassador returned to Kiev and asked Vladimir for his reply. Vladimir stalled and asked for more time, whereupon the Ambassador grew very angry and demanded Zabava as his wife there and then. Vladimir remained calm and suggested that while the wedding preparations were being made, they should sit a while and play the *gusli*. Katrina divined Vladimir's intent and said that it had been a long time since "he" had played the *gusli* but agreed to sit and play, as "his" players were weary from the long journey from Greece.

Vladimir was astounded. The Ambassador could not possibly be a woman. But he decided to put the Ambassador to another challenge—this time, a game of chess. The Ambassador replied that his chess masters were weary from the journey to Kiev, but that he had played chess as a child. Quickly Katrina outplayed every chess master Vladimir could produce, beating Vladimir himself in so few moves that the prince could not help but think that he was playing the greatest chess master in all the world. Convinced that the Ambassador was a man, Vladimir nonetheless continued with his plan and challenged the Ambassador to an archery contest. Again Katrina said that the archers in "his" camp were weary from the journey but that "he" would be glad to try his hand.

Three times Vladimir fired his arrow at the target, a ring and a knife, and on each occasion missed. Then the Ambassador aimed and let fly a single arrow, which flew straight through the ring and split itself in two on the knife blade. Vladimir knew that he was beaten. The Ambassador turned to Vladimir and told the prince to either produce the tribute required by Kalina, or to have the Princess Zabava taken to the cathedral in readiness for their marriage. With a heavy heart Vladimir went to his niece and commanded her to prepare herself for her wedding to the Ambassador. Then he went back to where the Ambassador waited to say that the bride was on her way.

The Ambassador himself then issued a challenge, saying that Vladimir and "he" should ride out onto the steppes and test their strength together. Vladimir Bright Sun replied that it would be a waste of time, as there was none in all Russia who could compete. The Ambassador taunted Vladimir, saying that if the prince could not produce a champion and refused to compete himself, then perhaps there was one in the palace dungeons who would compete.

Vladimir remembered Stavr Godinovich and his idle boast, and immediately he told his

guards to release him and arm him for combat against the Ambassador from Greece. Stavr rode out from Kiev, and hidden by the dust thrown up by their horses, Stavr and his wife were reunited. The pair then returned to Kiev, where Katrina Ivanovna revealed her true identity to Prince Vladimir Bright Sun. Then, laughing together, Stavr Godinovich and his wife Katrina Ivanovna rode away from Kiev, leaving Prince Vladimir Bright Sun musing that Stavr had not made an idle boast.

See also: Bogatyr'; Evpraksiya (~ia), Princess; Kiev; Polianitsa; Vladimir Bright Sun, Prince; Zabava (Putyatichna), Princess

STEEL CITY, THE
Armenia
One of the succession of cities that the princess wife of Habërmani traveled through on her quest to find her husband and restore him to her side.

See also: Habërmani
References: Orbeli and Taronian 1959–67, vol. 4

STEFAN
Slav
Peasant who became engaged to Katya, who on the night before their wedding, was strangled in bed with her own hair by her jealous dvorovoi lover.

See also: Dvorovoi; Katya

STEPHEN (OF HUNGARY), SAINT
Hungary
The patron saint of Hungary, whose feast day is 16 August. Born c. 975 in Asztergom, Stephen was the son of Geza, the duke of the Magyar community that had recently settled in Hungary. At least partially Christianized, Stephen was baptized along with his father in Prague by Saint Adalbert in 985. Ten years later he married Gisela, sister to Duke Henry III of Bavaria, and in 997 he succeeded Geza as ruler of the Magyars. Although he faced some opposition, Stephen consolidated his position and implemented the Christianization of his people. He had himself crowned the first king

of Hungary in 1001, a title sanctioned by Pope Sylvester II, who sent a crown for the coronation. This crown was captured by the U.S. Army during World War II and not returned until 1978.

During his reign, King Stephen concentrated on establishing an independent Hungary and converting his people to Christianity, even going so far as to make it illegal to blaspheme or to marry a pagan. In 1031 his son and heir, Emeric, was killed in a hunting accident, and the latter years of his reign were marred with ill health and squabbles over the succession. Stephen died in 1038. His relics were enshrined at the Church of Our Lady in Buda in 1083, and he was canonized by Pope Gregory VII the same year.

See also: Adalbert of Prague, Saint; Hungary; Magyars

STRENGTH DOES NOT ALWAYS COME IN NUMBERS
Armenia

Once, all the stars in the heavens held a meeting to discuss why they were outshone by the sun and the moon. The eldest star said it was because they were not united, and so they decided to come together to outshine the sun as it rose the following morning. However, as they did so they found that their light was obliterated by that of the rising moon. They reluctantly went back to their original places in the sky, as they realized that if they did not have the power to outshine the moon, they stood no chance of competing with the sun.

A fable of Mekhithar Gosh, the moral of which is that even though a group may consist of many members, if the members are all weak, they cannot hope to overcome an enemy who is strong.

See also: Mekhithar Gosh

STRIBOG
Russia

"Wind Lord," the god of air, or more specifically of wind, and the grandfather of all particular winds. In some areas Stribog was also con-

sidered the god of wealth, which he spread as far as his winds blew. In areas with harsh winter weather, Stribog also came to be considered the winter king, whose gusts carried the snow and chilled the bones of Mother Earth.

See also: Mother Earth

SUAIXTIS
Prussia

The god of light, but not the sun god. His name probably means "Star."

SUKHMAN
Russia

Knight at the court of Prince Vladimir Bright Sun. During a feast, Sukhman boasted that he would catch for his prince a snow-white swan without harming it. Riding away, he was disappointed to find that where the wild fowl usually gathered, on that day there was not even the smallest duck to be found. Riding on farther, to the Dnieper, he was surprised to find that the river, usually a racing torrent, was meandering at a snail's pace, its waters silted up with sand. When Sukhman asked the river the meaning of this, the river replied that a Tatar army some forty thousand strong was camped upstream and continually tried to build bridges across the river, and that she had used up almost all of her strength washing these bridges away.

Sukhman realized that if the Tatar army managed to cross the river, then Kiev would be lost. Goading his horse into an enormous leap, he cleared the river in a single bound. There he uprooted a huge tree—said in some accounts to have weighed ninety poods (a pood roughly equals 36 lbs or 16.38 kg), which he wielded as a huge club as he decimated the Tatar army, killing all but three warriors. These three hid and ambushed Sukhman as he rode back toward Kiev, their arrows striking him in his side. Pulling the shafts out, Sukhman killed the three Tatars and then plugged his wounds with leaves and herbs before riding back to Kiev.

There he was greeted by Vladimir Bright Sun, who asked for his swan. Sukhman related what had happened, but Vladimir thought he was simply making excuses, so he had him thrown into a deep dungeon. Nevertheless he sent Dobrynya Nikitich to investigate Sukhman's claims. When Dobrynya Nikitich returned with conclusive proof of their truth, Vladimir Bright Sun released Sukhman and apologized to him. Sukhman refused to accept the apology, and riding away from Kiev, unplugged his wounds, from which his blood gushed to form the fast-flowing river that bears his name.

See also: Dnieper; Dobrynya Nikitich; Kiev; Tatars; Vladimir Bright Sun, Prince

SUN
Slav

Though many Russian folktales are told about the sun, none refer to Dazhbog, the ancient god of the sun. As paganism was forgotten, the sun had become connected with death, as had the moon. Russians would always try to bury their dead just before sunset so that the sun on its downward journey might carry away the departing soul.

One Russian folktale describes the sun as a beautiful maiden with wings like an angel. This story says that a peasant once came to a cottage at the end of the world, where the earth and the sky meet. He asked whether he could stay the night. Welcomed into the house, he retired before sunset but awoke in the night, hearing the old woman talking to her daughter. Peering through a crack in the curtain, he saw the maiden sitting at the table eating her supper, her dress radiating a brilliant light that warmed the room. After her meal, the girl hung up her dress and her mother covered it with a thick cloth, and darkness immediately fell. The following morning the maiden put on her dress and left the house, and as she did so, the night became day.

In other Russian folktales the Sun marries human girls, while in others he either warms men who have honored him or tries to scorch men who have offended him. In one such story (see Morozko) he appears as a chubby man with rosy cheeks. However, stories of the

witch Baba-Yaga say that the Sun is under her command, along with Day and Night, and in these stories the Sun is described as a scarlet horseman, dressed from head to foot in that color and riding a scarlet stallion. He starts his journey from Baba-Yaga's cottage, and returns there when his day's work is done.

Lithuanian legend held that at the end of the Sun's daily journey across the sky, he would travel from west to east in a boat across the night sky in order to be ready for the following day's journey. Other Lithuanian legends assign a feminine gender to Sun, naming Saule as the sun goddess. Others still say that the new sun was forged every morning by the divine smith Kalvaitis.

On the Baltic coast, the god of the sun remains unnamed but is said to be the offspring of Svantovit. This bears comparison with the Lithuanian sun goddess Saule, who in this context might be seen as the daughter of Svantovit.

See also: Baba-Yaga (-Jaga, -Iaga); Day; Dazhbog; Kalvaitis; Lithuania; Moon; Morozko; Night; Saule; Svantovit (~dovit)

SUN'S SISTER
Russia

Given no specific name, Sun's Sister appears in the story of Ivan the Mute, which tells how she helped the young tsarevich escape from the cannibalistic clutches of his sister, a fearsome witch. Though in this story Sun's Sister lives on earth, the story also tells of a palace she has in the heavens—the sun itself.

See also: Ivan the Mute

SUPREME DEITY
General

The head of any pantheon; usually—though not always—a celestial deity, such as Dazhbog.

See also: Dazhbog

SUREN
Armenia

The young son of an old peasant couple, he was driven from his home by his mother after he told his parents that he had seen his infant sister Koknas stealing the family's food; his parents did not believe her old enough to be capable of such an act. Suren traveled for some time until he came to a tumbledown house where he found an old, blind couple. The couple marveled that he had managed to make his way to their home past the three vicious vishaps (dragons) that lived in the area and kept all the local people prisoner so that they could eat them one by one. Only the old couple remained free because they milked the goats and sheep belonging to the dragons. The dragons had plucked out their eyes and hidden them so that they would not run away.

Suren said he would live with and help the old couple, who immediately adopted him as their own. From that day on, Suren led the sheep and the goats out to pasture every day and brought them home again in the evening. One day, while sitting in the shade of a tree, Suren saw a huge lion approaching. He leaped to his feet, club in hand, ready to protect the sheep and goats. The lion, however, spoke to Suren, telling him that he meant no harm and that he had come to Suren only to give him two lion cubs, which he did, and then departed. The cubs grew in one day as much as a normal lion would grow in a month. Within fifteen days, they had grown into enormous, mature lions. Suren called the two lions Zangi, or "Blackie," and Zarangi, or "Goldie."

One day, while Suren, Zangi, and Zarangi were sitting in the shade of a tree watching the sheep and goats, Zangi and Zarangi suddenly leaped to their feet and ran off toward a huge shape that was slithering toward the tree. Suren rightly guessed that this was one of the three vishaps that were holding the people captive. The dragon spoke to Suren, asking him to call off his lions, as she meant the youth no harm and had a favor to ask. Suren called to Zangi and Zarangi, who settled down beside their young master, while remaining poised to spring into action should the need arise.

The dragon asked Suren if he would be kind enough to comb her mane and look for nits. Suren, suspecting a trick—for the dragon had hunger in her eyes—said that he would, and he invited her to join him under the tree. Placing the dragon's head on his knee, Suren pretended to search for nits while the dragon lay there sharpening her teeth. In reality, however, Suren was tying the dragon's mane to the tree. When he was sure that the dragon could not jump after him, Suren got up and said that he had to fetch a goat that was wandering away. The dragon let him go, and then tried to spring after him, only to find herself unable to.

Suren gathered up the goat that was indeed about to wander, and then stood a short distance from the dragon, which seemed perplexed as to why Suren had tied her to the tree. Suren told the dragon that he would let her go if she told him where she and her sisters had hidden the eyes of his adoptive parents. The dragon told Suren that she could not, for her big sister held the key. Hearing this, Suren set Zangi and Zarangi on the dragon with the command that not one drop of her blood should fall to the ground. Zangi and Zarangi tore the dragon to pieces, and within minutes there was no evidence that she had ever existed.

Several days passed before Suren saw the second dragon coming his way. This dragon, too, asked Suren to check her mane for nits, and Suren tied her to the tree. Once more the young man gathered up a goat that was about to stray and then asked this dragon for the eyes of his adoptive parents. When the dragon replied that her little sister had the key, Suren told her that her little sister was no more, whereupon the dragon told Suren that her big sister held the key. Suren then set Zangi and Zarangi on the dragon, and within minutes there was nothing left of her—not so much as a single drop of blood.

Two months passed before Suren encountered the third dragon. She was so large that her form blocked the light of the sun, and the earth trembled as she walked. Again

Suren made a pretext of combing the dragon's mane looking for nits, while he actually tied her to a tree and then went off after one of his goats. With the dragon firmly tied to the tree and thus unable to move, Suren was finally able to obtain from her the keys to the caskets in which the eyes of his adoptive parents had been locked away, as well as the key to the storehouse in which the three dragons had locked all the people of the city. With the keys safely in his possession, Suren set Zangi and Zarangi on the dragon, and within minutes there was nothing left to indicate that there had ever been a dragon tied beneath the tree.

Suren took the three keys and went to find the home of the dragons. Before long he came to two huge buildings. In the first he found two small caskets, and unlocking these with the smaller two of the three keys, he removed the eyes of his adoptive parents. Then he went to the other building and freed all the people, who immediately elected Suren to become their new ruler, their true king having been one of the first eaten by the dragons. Suren accepted their offer, but said that he had a couple of other matters to attend to first. When these tasks had been completed, he would return.

First Suren returned to his adoptive parents and restored their eyesight. Then he set out for his true home village, wondering what had become of his real parents and his little sister. He took along a single hair from each of his two lions. It did not take many days to ride back to his old home village; but when he arrived, he found it deserted. Remembering where he had once lived, Suren made his way to the house of his true parents, and after stabling his horse, went in. There, in front of the stove, was his sister Koknas, who had become a ghovt, or she-devil.

Koknas turned around as Suren entered the house, and greeted her long-lost brother, asking him if he had come on horseback. When Suren said that he had, his sister told him to sit by the stove and warm himself while she went to feed his horse. In the stables Koknas tore off one of the horse's legs and ate it. She then returned to the house and asked Suren if he had really ridden a horse with just three legs. When he replied that he had, Koknas returned to the stable, tore the remaining three legs from the horse, and ate them. Returning once more to the house, Koknas asked Suren if he had ridden on a horse with no legs. Suren knew what was going on, and replied that he had. Koknas returned to the stable and devoured what was left of the horse before returning to the house and asking her brother if he had walked.

Suren said that he had; then, saying that he had to stretch his legs, Suren went out of the house, locked the door behind him, and climbed up onto the roof, where he pondered his predicament—for he knew that his sister surely intended to eat him next. Suren devised a plan and removed his trousers. He then tied the bottom of each leg and filled them with handfuls of ashes scooped from the chimney. So stuffed, he dangled the trousers down through the skylight.

When Koknas found the door locked, she knew that she could get out of the house through the skylight. When she walked over to the skylight, she saw the stuffed trouser legs dangling. Thinking these to be Suren, she leaped up and took them in her teeth, whereupon they exploded in a shower of ashes that left Koknas reeling, coughing, and gagging. Furious, Koknas started to break down the locked door; but as she did so, Suren took the hairs of Zangi and Zarangi from his pocket, and as soon as he did so, his lions appeared beside him. Then, as Koknas finally managed to hack the door down, Zangi and Zarangi leaped on her, and within seconds all that was left of the ghovt was a single drop of blood on the ground.

Suren cleaned up the blood with his handkerchief, and then, with Zangi and Zarangi by his side, he set off to return to the city he was due to become the ruler of. En route he came across a group of people gathered around a log that was filled with gold. When he asked what they were doing, Suren was told that the gold could be released from the log only if the name of the tree could be guessed. Suren tried a couple of guesses, but to no avail. Then he wiped his forehead with his handkerchief, and seeing the blood, sighed for his sister Koknas. This time when the log was struck, it split open and the gold spilled out, for the tree was the yellow fir, or *Köknar* (the Turkish name for the yellow fir).

Thus, when Suren finally arrived at his new home city, exhausted from his travels, he was able to restore the inhabitants' fortunes. The people then chose Suren the most beautiful maiden in the city to become his wife, and Suren settled down to rule the city, his faithful lions Zangi and Zarangi ensuring its safety from attack.

See also: Dragon; Ghovt; Koknas; Vishap; Zangi; Zarangi

References: Orbeli and Taronian 1959–67, vol. 4

SVANTOVIT (~DOVIT)

Baltic Coast

Also: Sventovit, Iarovit ("wrath"), Porevit ("power"), Rujevit ("rutting time"), Triglav "Energy," the principal deity of the peoples inhabiting the Baltic coastal districts, controller of the fertility of the world, lord of prophecy and war, god of gods and father of all gods, particularly Sun and Fire. His chief temple was at Arcona, with another on the island of Riigen containing a statue some eight meters high, depicting Svantovit in four aspects, one for each cardinal point, on a carved wooden pillar. The god held a bull's horn cup in his right hand that was annually filled with wine, which would seep away or evaporate. The amount left in the cup at the end of the year was believed to portend the coming year's prosperity. No wine left in the cup spelled disaster.

A white stallion, sacred to Svantovit, was kept in his temple, and beside his statue hung its saddle and bridle along with Svantovit's sword and war banner. The stallion, like the wine, was a means of divination, being driven by the god's priests through a twisting course made up of spears stuck into the ground. The forecast for the coming year was good if the horse did not disturb any of the spears, but bad if any spears were dislodged— the degree of bad luck depending on the number of spears uprooted. The statue and inner shrines of Svantovit's temple were so sacred that they were guarded day and night, and even the high priests—who were the only people ever to be allowed past the armed guards—had to hold their breath while inside.

Early chroniclers, such as Saxo Grammaticus, are the only sources of testimony regarding the cult of Svantovit, and the information they provide is sketchy at best. Similar deities—Radigast, Rugevit, and Yarilo—also are described in these early texts. While each has attributes like Svantovit's, they are all plainly different, and might be understood as the various, contrasting aspects of Svantovit.

One statue of Svantovit, discovered in the nineteenth century near the river Zbrucz on the Russo-Galician border, shows an aspect that appears female, having breasts. No other statue of the god with this aspect has been discovered; and it may well be that this was a later representation of the deity designed to show acceptance, or at least tolerance, of women within the god's sanctuary.

See also: Arcona; Baltic; Iarovit; Porevik (~it); Radigast; Rugavit (~ievit); Rujevit; Saxo Grammaticus; Sun; Triglav; Yarilo

References: Grammaticus 1886

SVAREVICHI

Russia

A group of deities identified as the sons of Svarog. The Svarevichi are linked with the powers of fire and sunlight, and are generally assumed to be of Iranian origin. Today the word is used as a collective name for Dazhbog and Svarozhich.

See also: Dazhbog; Svarog; Svarozhich (~gich)

References: Gimbutas 1971; Ivanov and Toporov 1965

SVAROG
Russia

"Very Hot," god of the sky, his name is cognate with the Sanskrit *svar* (meaning "bright," "clear," or "shining"). The father of the two most important elemental deities, Dazhbog, the god of the sun, and Svarozhich, the god of fire, Svarog traditionally was considered the father of all gods. His position as head of the pantheon was later inherited by his two sons, while Svarog himself became a remote albeit benevolent presence. Svarog is the equivalent of the Baltic deity Svantovit. Many temples dedicated to Svarog once existed, in which the standards of armies would be laid after military campaigns. These temples were also the sites of animal sacrifices by Svarog's priests, and—some records suggest—human sacrifices as well.

See also: Dazhbog; Sun; Svantovit (~dovit); Svarozhich (~gich)

SVAROZHICH (~GICH)
Russia

The god of fire and prophecy, the son of Svarog, and the brother of Dazhbog, god of the sun. He and his brother were considered the two most important elemental deities, for, in a land where it is cold many months of the year, the sun and fire provided the people with warmth and light. As Dazhbog retired for the night, Svarozhich would take his place, warming the people and lighting their homes.

Svarozhich lived in an oasthouse where a fire burned in a deep pit over which sheaves of grain had been laid to dry prior to threshing. Grain was the usual votive offering to Svarozhich until well into the nineteenth century. Another custom that survived well after paganism had died out was the taboo on anyone cursing while the domestic fire was being lit, for it was believed that as Svarog had given fire, he could also take it away.

See also: Dazhbog; Sun; Svarog

SVENTOVIT
Baltic Coast

Variant of *Svantovit.*

SVETOZAR
Russia

The father of Vasilissa of the Golden Braid, her two unnamed brothers, and of Ivan the Pea. The latter was conceived when Svetozar's wife, the tsaritsa, inadvertently swallowed a small pea. Tsar Svetozar was succeeded after his death by Ivan the Pea.

See also: Ivan the Pea; Vasilis(s)a of the Golden Braid

SVIATKI
Russia

Solstice ceremony, from *svet* (light), that along with the Koliada took place each year around 12 December. For all intents and purposes, Sviatki and Koliada were one and the same.

See also: Koliada

SVIATOGOR
Russia

Also: Svyatogor

The last of the giants. His name is a compound of two roots: *sviat,* or "holy"; and *gor,* or "of the mountains." There are two accounts of how Sviatogor met his end. In the first, his strength was put to the test by Il'ya Muromets, who rode to the Holy Mountains to find the giant, for he had heard that Sviatogor was one of the mightiest of men.

As he neared the Holy Mountains, Il'ya Muromets saw a huge man, larger than any he had ever seen before, riding toward him. Realizing at once that this was the giant Sviatogor, Il'ya spurred on his horse and struck the giant a mighty blow with his huge mace. Sviatogor did not even wince and rode lazily on. Again Il'ya struck him, and again the giant did not even flinch. The third time Il'ya struck, however, the giant jerked upright in his saddle. Seeing who had hit him, he deftly picked Il'ya up by the hair and dropped him into his pouch.

Some time later, Sviatogor's horse stumbled and complained that carrying two knights was too much, even for him. Sviatogor took Il'ya out of his pouch, and seeing that he was a knight of Holy Russia, suggested that the two of them ride together as brothers. This they did for many days, until they came to a huge stone coffin lying beside a tree.

Il'ya leaped off his horse and lay down in the coffin. It was much too large for him, but it fit Sviatogor perfectly. Even though Il'ya Muromets pleaded with him not to put the lid on, Sviatogor did just that. However, when he asked Il'ya to remove the lid, Il'ya found it far too heavy. Three times he hit it with his mace, but each time he hit it a steel band closed around the coffin, securing the lid.

Sviatogor blew some of his strength into Il'ya so that he could use the giant's own sword; but this just made matters worse, for two steel bands closed around the coffin every time it was hit with the sword. Resigning himself to his fate, Sviatogor had Il'ya tie his horse to the tree, to die there beside its master. Il'ya did as asked and sadly rode away from the coffin, knowing that Sviatogor, the last of the giants, would shortly be no more.

The second account of Sviatogor's demise is possibly the older of the two: Sviatogor often boasted of his great strength, going so far as to say that he could even lift Mother Earth. One day while he was out riding, he came across a small bag lying in his path. Unable to move it with the tip of his staff, Sviatogor dismounted, and with tremendous effort, managed to raise the bag as high as his knees. In doing so, he sweated so heavily that his sweat became blood. Sinking deep into the earth under the weight of the bag, he could not save himself.

Interestingly, there is a further legend concerning Sviatogor and his attempt to lift Mother Earth. In this story, Sviatogor is out riding, trying to find a means by which to test his great strength. While riding, he spots a stranger carrying a small bag slung over one shoulder; but no matter how hard he spurs his mount, he cannot catch up with the stranger. Finally, Sviatogor calls out to the stranger, who stops and waits for the giant to catch up.

When the two finally meet, Sviatogor asks the stranger where he is going in such a hurry and what he is carrying. The stranger places the bag on the ground and tells Sviatogor that if he wants to see what is in the bag, he should lift it up and take a look. Sviatogor accepts the challenge, climbs down from his horse, and takes hold of the bag. However, no matter how hard Sviatogor strains, he cannot move the bag even a fraction of an inch. Sviatogor admits defeat and asks the stranger what is in the bag. The stranger replies that the bag contains the weight of the world.

Sviatogor is impressed and asks the stranger his name. The stranger replies that his name is Mikulushka Selyaninovich but that most people call him Mikula. Sviatogor has heard of Mikula, and asks him how he might learn his fate. Mikula tells the giant to ride to the Northern Mountains, and there under the tallest tree he will find a smithy where the blacksmith will tell him all that will come to be.

Sviatogor thanks Mikula and rides as hard as he can toward the Northern Mountains. When he reaches the mountains, he finds the blacksmith hard at work in his smithy, forging two thin hairs. Sviatogor asks him what he is doing, and the smith replies that he is forging the fates of all those destined to marry. Interested, Sviatogor asks whom he is destined to wed; but the reply he receives is not what he expects. The smith tells him that his bride lives in the Kingdom by the Sea, dwelling in the City of the King, where she has lain for the past thirty years on a dunghill.

Although he is disgusted by the thought, Sviatogor quickly seeks out the woman fate has decreed he will marry. When he finds her, the sight repulses him. There, in a poor and lowly hut, the woman lies on a dunghill, her skin as black and as thick as the bark of a fir tree. Sviatogor cannot imagine marrying the maiden; so instead he takes five hundred rubles from his purse and lays them on a table before drawing his sword and stabbing the maiden through the breast.

As Sviatogor rides away, the maiden stirs from her deep sleep; and as she stands up, the bark that has protected her for the past thirty years falls away, revealing her true beauty, the likes of which have never been seen before—or since. Finding the money on the table, she quickly sets herself up as a merchant and amasses a great fortune, sailing all over the then-known world, trading as she goes. Finally her ships land at the edge of the Holy Mountains, and Sviatogor comes to see the woman that everyone is talking about. As soon as he sees her, he is smitten, and before long he has persuaded her to marry him. On their wedding night Sviatogor notices the scar on her breast and asks his new bride what caused it.

She replies that she had slept for thirty years on a dunghill in the City of the King that lay within the Kingdom by the Sea. When she awakened from her deep sleep, she found five hundred rubles on a table, the scar on her breast, and that she was no longer covered in fir bark. It is then that Sviatogor realizes that this is the woman he was destined to marry and that there is no way of avoiding the fate decreed by God.

Later accounts seem to confuse the relationship between Sviatogor and Il'ya Muromyets, tending to make the two one and the same—Sviatogor being the pre-Christian personification, and the bogatyr' the post-Christian one. Evidence does not, however, support these theories, which appear to be due to confusion caused by the passage of time.

See also: Bogatyr'; City of the King, The; Il'ya Muromets; Kingdom by the Sea, The; Mikula Selyaninovich; Mother Earth
References: Chadwick 1964

SVIATOPOLK
Russia
Also: Svyatopolk
The brother of Boris and Gleb, both of whom willingly submitted to their deaths at his hand—so history records—in 1015.
See also: Boris, Saint; Gleb, Saint
References: Cross and Sherbowitz-Wetzor 1953

SWAN WOMAN
Tatar
A mysterious bird-woman who appears in a poem along with the hero Kartaga. For many years the couple wrestled, neither gaining the upper hand. Kartaga owned two horses, one piebald and one black, and they knew that the Swan Woman did not carry her soul with her but kept it in a golden casket. That casket was hidden in a black chest beneath a copper rock, a rock that rose from the earth to the heavens, marking the point where the nine seas of the underworld met and became one, rising to the surface of the earth.

The horses ran to the place where the copper rock emerged from the underworld, dug up the black chest, and removed the golden casket. Then the two horses carried the casket back to where Kartaga and the Swan Woman were still fighting. There the piebald horse transformed itself into a bald man, opened the casket, and killed the seven birds that flew out. These birds held the soul of the Swan Woman, who fell dead as the last bird was killed.
See also: Kartaga; Underworld, The

A Kholui lacquer miniature by N. Kurchatkina depicts the Swan Woman befriending two swans during a banquet. (Sovfoto/Eastfoto/PNI)

T

TALKING MOUNTAIN, THE
Hungary—Magyar
A magical mountain to which Third Almafi journeyed in order to obtain directions to the well of the sorcerer called Deceit. Third Almafi traveled to a vast forest in the middle of which rose a lofty mountain, on which he found a cave. Within that cave he found a marble slab that gave him instructions on how to awaken the voice of the mountain. Third Almafi went out of the cave and tore up twelve tall pine trees from the forest below, dragged them into the cave, and set fire to them as the instructions told him to. Then he waited until the last embers died away, whereupon the mountain spoke, telling Third Almafi how to find the well of Deceit.

See also: Almafi; Deceit

TAPAGÖZ
Armenia
A terrible, three-headed giant who was one of seven, all apparently called Tapagöz (as Gulinaz refers to the giant as *a* Tapagöz rather than *the* Tapagöz). However, in the legend of Zurab, who later became known as Aslan, there is just one giant—though that giant does have six brothers who remain unnamed. In this legend, where Tapagöz abducts Simizar, the daughter of King Zarzand, and carries her off to his lair, the Devil's Castle, he is confronted and killed by Aslan.

In the legend of Samson and Gulinaz, it is Samson who kills a Tapagöz, but which Tapagöz is never made clear. Perhaps it was one of the six brothers of the Tapagöz killed by Aslan. If this is the case, then it is safe to assume that Tapagöz was a family name rather than a personal one. The Tapagöz in the legend of Aslan and Simizar had three heads, but that in the legend of Samson and Gulinaz had just one. Both had a common attribute, however: a single eye in the center of the head. One need only put out that eye to kill the giant. The legend also contains an allusion to the size of the Tapagöz, with estimates that the head weighed fifty poods, his nose fifteen poods, and each tooth between four and five poods.

See also: Aslan; Devil's Castle; Gulinaz; Simizar; Zarzand; Zurab
References: Orbeli and Taronian 1959–67, vol. 4

TATARS
General
A Turkic, mainly Muslim people who are the descendants of the followers of Genghis Khan. They live mainly in Tatarstan and Uzbekistan, having been deported there from the Crimea in 1944, and in southwestern Siberia. Their language belongs to the Altaic grouping.

See also: Crimea; Genghis Khan; Siberia; Uzbekistan

TAWALS
Poland
One of the three gods of the field, the other two being Datan and Lawkapatim.

See also: Datan; Lawkapatim

TENGRI
Mongolia
Also: Od(lek)
The creator of the universe, which before his intervention existed only in a state of utter chaos. He created people from fire, wind, and water, and then breathed life into them. His wife was Itugen, Mother Earth, or Umai, Mother of All, and his children, who

Engraving of a battle scene showing a Tatar invasion (Archive Photos)

were all known as Tengri, came to live on earth as the spirits of everything in the world—from visible objects such as trees and the flames of a fire, to abstract notions such as law, order, and human nature. Tengri himself still rides across the surface of the earth on his storm horses, and storms announce his arrival to right wrongs and to punish those who have broken the law.

See also: Itugen; Mother Earth; Umai

TEUTONIC KNIGHTS
General

The name of an organization of German crusaders that arose in Europe during the twelfth century. The Teutonic Knights were organized for service in the Holy Land, and modeled their organization after two earlier crusading orders—the Knights Templars and the Knights Hospitalers. In the thirteenth century the Teutonic Knights shifted their activities to central Europe, where they tried to convert and control the people in the

lands that later became known as Prussia, Lithuania, Latvia, and Estonia. In the fourteenth century the Teutonic Knights lost much of their power, and finally the Poles and Lithuanians overthrew them. In 1525, the Grand Master, Albert of Hohenzollern, became a Protestant and changed the order from a religious to a civic organization; and in 1618 the order's territory passed to the Hohenzollern elector of Brandenburg.

See also: Estonia; Latvia; Lithuania; Prussia

THIRD ALMAFI
Hungary—Magyar
See: Almafi.

THRICE-NINTH KINGDOM, THE
Russia

An unidentified kingdom that according to some sources was (at least partly) the land of Tsar Afron. The Thrice-Ninth Kingdom, unsurprisingly, lay within the Thrice-Ninth Land—a land that is equally unidentified and

Tomb of Konrad von Thueringen, Grand Master of the Order of Teutonic Knights, 1240–1245, Elisabeth Church, Marburg, Germany (Erich Lessing/Art Resource, NY)

unidentifiable. Another distinguishing feature of the Thrice-Ninth Kingdom was that it was home to the talking cat Kot Bayun, which Petrushka sought to capture for his tsar. The tsar had assigned Petrushka this mission in order to get rid of him so as to take Petrushka's wife as his own.

See also: Afron; Kot Bayun; Petrushka; Thrice-Ninth Land, The

THRICE-NINTH LAND, THE
Russia
An unidentified country within which lay the Thrice-Ninth Kingdom, home to Kot Bayun. Some sources have sought to identify the Thrice-Ninth Land with Turkey, but this seems dubious.

See also: Kot Bayun; Thrice-Ninth Kingdom, The

THRICE-TEN KINGDOM, THE
Ukraine
According to the legend of Maria, the Thrice-Ten Kingdom was the homeland of the witch Baba-Yaga.

See also: Baba-Yaga (-Jaga, -Iaga); Maria

TIME
Armenia
Personified as an old man sitting on a stone throne at the foot of Mount Biledjan. Time controlled Death and could, if so disposed, free men of their fear of Death and enable them to live a full life.

See also: Death

TIMOFE(Y)EVNA, AMELF(I)A
Russia
See Amelf(i)a Timofe(y)evna.

TIPI
Armenia
The name Aslan gave his horse.

See also: Aslan; Zurab

TO EACH ITS OWN
Armenia
A wolf once seized a lamb from a pen and made off with it. The lamb asked the wolf to serenade her before he ate her, as her parents had told her that wolves had the most beautiful voices. The wolf was flattered and immediately began to howl with all its might. The noise woke the shepherd's watchdogs, which attacked the wolf and bit it severely. The wolf managed to escape and crawled away to lick its wounds, blaming itself for thinking that it could succeed in something it had never tried before.

One of the fables of Vardan of Aygek.

See also: Vardan

References: Marr 1894–99

TOAD, DR.

Armenia

A large toad once hung a pestle and a mortar around his neck, took a jar of ointment in his hand, and proudly announced to all the animals that he was a doctor. All the animals flocked to him to be treated, including a wily fox, who after he had a look at the toad, refused to be treated. When the toad asked why, the fox replied that if the toad could not cure his own warts and spots, then he could hardly be qualified to treat anyone else. The moral of the story is that many a man gives advice while forgetting his own defects.

One of the fables of Vardan.

See also: Vardan
References: Marr 1894–99

TOBIAS

Magyar

A poor man who through human initiative and ingenuity got the better of not just a whole family of dragons but a whole region inhabited by these creatures.

Having no food to feed his ever-increasing family, Tobias set out to see what employment he could find to earn their keep. During his travels he stopped in a large field that belonged to a seven-headed dragon. Instead of showing his fear of the monster, Tobias challenged the dragon to see what they could squeeze out of a rock. The dragon went first and quickly reduced a large rock to dust. Tobias then bent down to pick up a rock, and with his back turned toward the dragon, swapped it for a lump of cheese he had in his pocket. Thus, when Tobias squeezed the "rock," whey ran out of it. The dragon was so impressed that he suggested that the two become friends. Tobias agreed on condition that the dragon treat him as his elder brother.

Thus the two set off across the field toward a cherry tree. There, as Tobias directed, the dragon held down the tree so that his elder brother might eat his fill. When Tobias could eat no more, he said that he would hold the tree down for the dragon;

but when the dragon let go of the tree, Tobias was naturally catapulted through the air and landed in the middle of a large bush under which a hare was hiding. Before the hare could run away, Tobias took hold of it and held it up, saying that he had seen the hare hiding and had leaped over the cherry tree in order to catch it.

The dragon was so impressed that he invited Tobias to return with him to meet his family. Shortly thereafter Tobias and the dragon entered the dragons' village, and he was soon presented to the dragon's mother, father, and two brothers. When the dragon explained to his family just what Tobias could do, they immediately invited him to stay, and from that day forth Tobias did little more than eat and sleep. The dragons tolerated their guest's indolence for a short while, and then one day they said that it was Tobias's turn to fetch water in the family's huge bucket made of the skins of twelve oxen.

Tricking the dragon into carrying the huge bucket, Tobias went to the well, picked up a spade, and immediately began to dig a trench around the well. When the dragon asked what he was doing, Tobias replied that he was going to take the well back with them so that they no longer had to fetch and carry their water. The dragon was alarmed, as the well served the whole village, and so he quickly filled the huge bucket and carried the water back home.

The following day the mother dragon asked Tobias to fetch firewood from the forest. Tobias went down to the forest with his dragon brother. There he wove a rope and began to stretch it around the whole forest. When the dragon asked what he was doing, Tobias replied that he intended to take the entire forest home so that they no longer had to fetch and carry their firewood. The dragon was horrified, as the forest supplied the needs of seven villages of dragons; so he quickly pulled up enough trees to serve their requirements and hurried home with them.

When they arrived home, the mother dragon was furious to see that her son was again doing the work Tobias had been asked to do. She told her son to get rid of the troublesome human, so the dragon suggested that they should fight. Tobias agreed, and asked how he would be rewarded if he won. The dragon said that he would give Tobias a barrel of gold if he won; but Tobias would have to go home if he lost. Then the dragon suggested that they fight with sticks. The dragon chose a huge poplar tree, and Tobias a small sapling. Then Tobias, who had the right by way of tradition, said that they should fight in the pigsty. There, of course, the dragon could hardly move, let alone swing his club, whereas Tobias set about the dragon with ease and soon had him begging for mercy.

Having won the fight, and with one barrel of gold already secured, Tobias thought he was safe. However, the dragon now suggested a sneezing competition, again offering a barrel of gold to Tobias if he won, and again saying that if he lost, Tobias must go home. Tobias agreed, and they went indoors. The dragon sneezed first and blew Tobias all around the room. Picking himself up, Tobias went around the walls and started to plug up any holes he found. When the dragon asked what he was doing, Tobias said that if he did not plug up the holes the house would not collapse, and if the house did not collapse, the dragon would not be certain who had sneezed the best.

The dragon was horrified, begged Tobias not to sneeze, and gave him the second barrel of gold. Still determined to beat Tobias, the dragon then suggested a shouting competition. Tobias immediately agreed and asked to be taken to the local blacksmith. The dragon was naturally curious as to the reason for such a visit. Tobias told him that it was to have seven hoops made, one for each of the dragon's seven heads, as without them his shout would crack the dragon's heads like eggs. The dragon again begged for mercy and measured out a third barrel of gold for Tobias.

Knowing that he had now amassed more than enough wealth to last a lifetime, Tobias

told the dragon that he wished to return home, provided the dragon would carry him on his back. The dragon was only too happy to oblige, so that he could finally be rid of Tobias. Thus it was that Tobias rode the dragon home like a horse. At the gate to Tobias's house the dragon made its farewells and set off for home. En route he came across a fox that was rolling on the ground laughing. When the dragon asked what was so funny, the fox told him that he was laughing at the dragon-horse he had seen the human riding.

The dragon was furious and asked the fox what he might do to retrieve the three barrels of gold. The fox brokered a bargain with the dragon, saying that he would help in return for a cock and nine hens; and the two set off toward Tobias's house. Tobias saw them coming and shouted to the fox in an angry voice, saying that he had been promised nine dragon skins, so why had the fox brought him just one? The dragon was so scared that he took to his heels and ran all the way home. As for Tobias, he built a fine mansion with the gold and lived in peace and comfort for the rest of his natural days.

See also: Dragon
References: Biro 1980

TONX

Vogul
Collective name for benevolent water spirits who brought men luck when hunting or fishing, and who could be propitiated to cure illness and disease.

TRANSCAUCASIA

General
A geographic region that between 1936 and late 1940 was divided among the republics of Azerbaijan, Armenia, and Georgia.

See also: Armenia; Azerbaijan; Georgia

TRANSYLVANIA

General
A region of Romania, near the Hungarian border, that covers about 39,000 square miles (101,000 square kilometers). The Carpathian

Bela Lugosi as the fictitious Count Dracula in 1931 (The Museum of Modern Art Film Stills Archive)

Mountains and Transylvanian Alps separate the region from the rest of Romania. For years, Romanians and Hungarians quarreled over Transylvania. Magyars conquered the region in the tenth century, and from 1526 to 1699, Transylvania was part of the Ottoman Empire. It was under Hungarian control from 1699 to 1867, when it again became part of Hungary. After World War I, Transylvania became part of Romania, and after World War II it lost its political identity.

Transylvania is the main site of the legend about the famous vampire Dracula. The character of Dracula is based on Vlad Tepes, a cruel prince of the fifteenth century who lived in Walachia, a region south of Transylvania. Vlad executed many of his enemies by driving a sharpened pole through their bodies and thus earned the common epithet of "the Impaler." A belief in vampires formerly held by many Romanian peasants added details to the legend, and *Dracula* (1897), a novel by English author Bram Stoker, made the legend internationally famous.

See also: Carpathian Mountains; Hungary; Romania; Vampire; Vlad (the Impaler), Prince; Walachia

TREE OF LIFE, THE
Slav

An alternative name for the World Tree, which among the Yakut of Siberia is the world pillar of Yryn-al-tojon, the "white creator lord." Though the Tree of Life is not given a particular name, it does appear in one Yakut myth when a youth is nourished by Ajysyt from her milk-laden breasts after she has arisen from the roots of the tree. This myth combines the cosmic Tree of Life and the mother goddess into one sustaining and nourishing entity.

See also: Ajysyt; Siberia; World Tree; Yakuts; Yryn-al-tojon

TRIGLAV
Slovenia

Name by which Svantovit was worshiped in Slovenia, his iconography there having just three faces rather than the usual four.

See also: Svantovit (~dovit)

TRIGLAV, MOUNT
Slovenia

The highest mountain of the Julijske Alps in northeastern Slovenia, and the highest peak in the former Yugoslavia. Mount Triglav lies about eight miles south of the Austrian border, to the east of Bled. It was considered by the Slovenes the home of the gods, a sort of Mount Olympus on which the legendary chamois with golden horns, Zlatorog, was hunted.

See also: Slovenia; Zlatorog

TROITSA
Russia

The final day of a weeklong cycle of festivals that started at Whitsun. The other festivals that made up the week were the Rusaliia and the Semik. On the Orthodox calendar, Troitsa became Trinity Sunday, though it was more usually referred to as Mother Troitsa. On this day a young woman would stand inside a marked ring and make predictions regarding marriage and fertility, complain, and listen to complaints about misfortune. The unmarried women of a community would then sing about relinquishing their carefree youth for the responsibilities of marriage and a family.

See also: Rusaliia; Semik
References: Snegirev 1837–39

TRUVOR

Scandinavia and Russia

One of the two younger brothers of Riurik, the other being Sineus. When Riurik was chosen as the first Varangian ruler of Novgorod, Sineus settled at Beloozero and Truvor at Izborsk, according to the *Primary Chronicle,* which dates their settlement at between 860 and 862. Two years later Sineus and Truvor died and Riurik became the sole ruler. (The Hypatian *Primary Chronicle* says that Riurik first settled at Lake Ladoga.) After the deaths of Sineus and Truvor, Riurik assumed sole authority and moved his seat of power to the city he founded on the banks of the river Volkhov—Novgorod.

See also: Ladoga, Lake; Novgorod; *Primary Chronicle;* Riurik; Rostov; Sineus; Varangians
References: Cross and Sherbowitz-Wetzor 1953

TSMOK

Belorussia

The personification of the domovoi in the form of a snake that depended on the blessings of a house, and in particular on that of the women of the house, for its sustenance, and thus for its life.

See also: Domovoi

TUGARIN

Russia

A vile, heathen monster who is described as a giant with the girth of two fully grown oak trees. His eyes were set wide—some accounts say a full arrow's length apart—and his ears were almost eight inches long. While he was at the court of Prince Vladimir Bright Sun at

Kiev, during a banquet, he was insulted by Alesha, whom he then attempted to kill by throwing his knife at him. Ekim, Alesha's squire, caught the knife. Tugarin then challenged Alesha to meet him out on the steppe.

Alesha went out on the steppe in the guise of a pilgrim. Tugarin thought he would have the upper hand, for he had made himself a pair of wings out of paper on which he flew while sitting astride his powerful horse. Alesha, however, prayed for rain. The rain indeed came, ruining the giant's wings. Crashing to the ground, Tugarin rushed at Alesha on horseback, fully intending to trample him into the ground; but Alesha hid in the horse's flowing mane and struck Tugarin's head from his shoulders with the heavy staff he was carrying. Alesha then stuck Tugarin's head onto the end of the staff and rode back into Kiev on Tugarin's horse.

Tugarin is a prime example of the way the traditional dragon developed in the later epic stories, the byliny, for he was human in form but had the power to fly like a dragon—albeit on paper wings.

See also: Alesha; Bylina; Dragon; Ekim; Kiev; Vladimir Bright Sun, Prince

TUNGUS

Siberia

Ancient indigenous people from one of the coldest regions on earth, who endured the rigors of life in the tundra of Siberia. Only one of the major Tungus legends has survived—which is unfortunate, as this story, that of Ivan the Mare's Son, is particularly fine.

See also: Ivan the Mare's Son; Siberia

TURKESTAN

General

A vast region in Asia that has no definite boundaries. The name refers to the Turkic-speaking tribes that have lived in this region since as early as the fifth century A.D. Turkestan (also spelled Turkistan), stretches from Siberia on the north to Iran, Pakistan,

India, and Tibet on the south. The Mongolian Desert lies to the east, and the Caspian Sea to the west.

Turkestan consists of three primary regions: Western Turkestan, formerly also called Soviet Turkestan, lies between the Caspian Sea and the Tian Shan mountain range and includes the countries of Kazakhstan, Kyrgyzstan, Tajikistan, Turkmenistan, and Uzbekistan. Chinese Turkestan, also called Eastern Turkestan, in the heart of Asia, extends eastward from Western Turkestan to the Gobi Desert and Tibet, and forms part of China's Xinjiang region. This region is bordered by the Tian Shan range on the north and by the Kunlun Mountains on the south. Afghan Turkestan is bounded on the north by the Amu Darya (Oxus River) and on the northwest by Western Turkestan.

Russia began to extend its rule to Western Turkestan soon after the conquest of Siberia, during the seventeenth century, and most of Western Turkestan was Russian territory by the nineteenth century. The government created the province of Turkestan and made Tashkent its capital. In 1887, an Anglo-Russian commission established the boundary between Afghanistan and Russian Turkestan. During the 1920s and 1930s, Western Turkestan was divided into five separate states of the Soviet Union: the Kazakh, Kyrgyz, Tajik, Turkmen, and Uzbek Soviet Socialist Republics. In 1991, following the dissolution of the Soviet Union, each of the five republics became independent.

See also: Caspian Sea; Kazakhstan; Siberia; Turkmenistan; Uzbekistan

TURKMENISTAN

General

A mostly desert country in west-central Asia. Russia began a conquest of the region in the mid-1870s, and by 1885, all Turkmen lands were under Russian control. In 1924, after much resistance from local tribes, Turkmenistan became a republic of the Soviet Union and was named the Turkmen Soviet Socialist Republic, or Turkmenia. In 1990, Turkmenistan declared that its laws overruled those of the Soviet Union; and in October of the following year the republic declared its independence. That December, after the Soviet Union was dissolved, Turkmenistan became independent and joined a loose association of former Soviet republics called the Commonwealth of Independent States.

UKKO

Estonia

The supreme being, consort of Maan-Eno, and the joint creator of man.

See also: Maan-Eno

UKRAINE

General

A constituent republic of the Soviet Union since 1923, the capital of which is Kiev. Ukraine is the second-largest European country in area, exceeded only by Russia, its neighbor to the east. The Ukrainian language is a member of the Slavic branch of the Indo-European family and is closely related to Russian.

During the ninth century A.D., Kiev became the center of a Slavic state referred to as Kievan Rus'. In the fourteenth century, most of Ukraine came under Polish and Lithuanian control. Cossacks freed that portion of Ukraine from Polish rule in 1648 (eastern Ukraine was absorbed by Russia in 1667) and liberated the remainder of the country from Austrian rule in 1793.

In 1923, Ukraine became a constituent republic of the Soviet Union and was renamed the Ukrainian Soviet Socialist Republic. In 1991, Ukraine declared its political independence, and later that year, after the breakup of the Soviet Union, received diplomatic recognition as an independent country.

Human settlement in Ukraine began almost 300,000 years ago. By about 1500 B.C., nomadic herders, including the warlike, horse-riding Cimmerians, occupied the region. The Scythians conquered the Cimmerians about 700 B.C., and between 700 and 600 B.C., Greek colonies appeared on the northern coast of the Black Sea, although the Scythians controlled most of the region until c. 200 B.C., when it fell to the Sarmatians. The region was invaded by Germanic tribes from the west in A.D. 270 and by the Huns in 375.

During the ninth century a Slavic civilization called Rus' sprang up around Kiev, the resultant East Slavic state being known as Kievan Rus'. Scandinavian merchant-warriors known as Varangians, or Vikings, played an important role in organizing the East Slavic tribes into the Kievan state.

Vladimir I, the ruler of Novgorod, conquered Kievan Rus' in 980, and under his rule the state became a political, economic, and cultural power in Europe. In 988, Vladimir became a Christian and made Christianity the state religion. In 1240, Tatars swept across the Ukrainian plains from the east and conquered the region. After the fall of Kievan Rus', several principalities emerged in the region. The state of Galicia-Volhynia, in what is now western Ukraine, grew in importance. In the fourteenth century, Poland took control of Galicia, while Lithuania seized Volhynia, and later, Kiev. By 1569, Poland ruled the entire region. In 1648, a Cossack named Bohdan Khmelnitsky led an uprising that freed Ukraine of Polish control, and in 1654 he formed an alliance with the Russian tsar against Poland.

Ukraine was divided between Poland and Russia in 1667, with Poland gaining control of lands west of the Dnieper River, while Ukrainian lands east of the Dnieper came under Russian protection but retained self-rule. By 1764, Russia had abolished Ukrainian self-rule, and in the last decade of the eighteenth century, it gained control of all of Ukraine except Galicia, which Austria ruled from 1772 until 1918. Ukraine became one of the four original constituent republics of the Soviet Union in 1922, and it did not return to independent status until the dissolution of the Soviet Union in 1991.

See also: Black Sea; Cossacks; Dnieper; Kiev; Lithuania; Novgorod; Poland; Rus'; Tatars; Sarmatians; Scythia; Varangians; Vikings; Vladimir I

UKS AKKA
Lapp
One of the daughters of Mader Atcha and Mader Akka. If an unborn child—created by Mader Atcha and Mader Akka—was to be a boy, Uks Akka completed the creation and placed the fetus in the womb of its human mother. If it was to be a girl, then that task was carried out by her sister, Sar Akka.

See also: Mader Akka; Mader Atcha; Sar Akka

ULGAN
Siberia and Lapp
The sky god, known as Yryn-al-tojon among the Yakuts, who created the earth by setting a huge saucer of land on the backs of three fish that he found frisking about in the waters of the primordial ocean. The three fish did not take kindly to having the weight of the earth on them, and their violent movements as they tried to shake it off caused earthquakes. As a result, the earth fractured, and pieces both large and small floated off and continued to move freely around until Ulgan anchored them to the seabed. One of the smallest specks he found floating on the surface of the waters startled Ulgan when it spoke to him, complaining that it did not want to be permanently fixed, nor did it have any intention of letting plants grow on it. Ulgan took the small speck, and rather than turning it into an island, created Erlik, the first being.

See also: Erlik; Yakuts; Yryn-al-tojon

UMAI
Mongolia
Mother-of-All, the wife of Tengri, though some sources name his consort as Itugen.

See also: Itugen; Tengri

UMILENIE
Russia
"Lady of Tender Mercy," one of the three most representative styles of popular iconography of the Virgin Mary. The other two were "Mary Orans" and the Christianized pagan goddess shown surrounded by her human and animal creations. Each of these three forms declares the panoptic oversight of the Mother of God over all creation, from the heavens to the underworld.

UNDERWORLD, THE
General
Though the underworld is not a recognized domain of the dead in Russian legend, it does appear in the Siberian Tungus story about Ivan the Mare's Son. There it is described as the realm of a huge serpent who feeds on the blood of Marfida and her sisters. Three days after the serpent is wounded by Ivan the Mare's Son, it returns, riding in a cloud of fire surrounded by its army of demons.

Some Russian legends connect the witch Baba-Yaga with the realm of the dead, though this is never specifically called the underworld. Some authorities go so far as to say that her cottage, with its chicken legs, stands where the land of the living meets that of the dead. In this context Baba-Yaga may be seen as protecting the entrance to the underworld, her role being similar to that of the Greek Cerberus. However, instead of keeping outsiders from entering the underworld, she is there to stop the dead from escaping. In the story of Ivan the Mare's Son, her role seems to have been replaced by the heroic Ivan; for his house, and that of his false brothers, also stands in a clearing in the middle of a forest.

In Lithuanian folklore the underworld is described as the realm of Puskaitis and the subterranean barstukai and kaukai. Though it was not necessarily considered the land of the dead, it certainly was considered a realm whose occupants affected the fertility of the ground, for the barstukai were believed to influence the harvest.

See also: Baba-Yaga (-Jaga, -Iaga); Barstukai; Ivan the Mare's Son; Kaukai; Lithuania; Marfida; Puskaitis; Siberia; Tungus

UPINIS
Lithuania

The god of rivers to whom white suckling pigs were sacrificed to ensure the purity of the waters.

UPIR
Russia

A fantastical creature described as either a vampire or a werewolf, which connected the creature with wise women and witches, and possibly with the moon goddess, as wolves, werewolves, swans, vampires, and serpent women all were thought to issue from the goddess. Some sources theorize that the word *vampire* derives from *upir,* though the multiple attributes of the upir do not seem to support this theory.

See also: Vampire; Werewolf
References: Dontenville 1973; Perkowski 1976

UPROOT OAK
Russia

A giant who appears in the story of the young tsarevich Ivan the Mute. When Ivan flees his home (for he has discovered that his sister, who is about to be born, will be a cannibal witch), he asks Uproot Oak to take him in. Uproot Oak would have done so, but he was due to die when he had cleared the forest he was working on. Later, after Ivan found sanctuary with Sun's Sister, he was returning home to find out what had happened to his family. On the way, he met up with Uproot Oak, and seeing that he had but two trees left to topple, Ivan threw down a comb that had been given him by Sun's Sister, from which a huge forest of sturdy oak trees sprang up. These trees later delayed the witch as she pursued Ivan, for Uproot Oak blocked the road with a huge pile of their trunks, and the witch had to gnaw her way through them before she could continue the chase.

See also: Ivan the Mute; Sun's Sister

URAL MOUNTAINS
General

The Ural Mountains extend about 1,500 miles (2,400 kilometers) through the western part of Russia and run south from near the Arctic Ocean to around the Kazakhstan border. The highest peak of the Ural Mountains is Mount Narodnaya (6,217 feet, or 1,895 meters).

URSA MAJOR
General

Familiar constellation of the northern celestial hemisphere that is perhaps better known as the Great Bear. It is also known as the Big Dipper, the Plow, Charlie's Wain, and the Wagon. Ursa Major is a circumpolar constellation that can be seen from northern latitudes all night, every clear night. It can never be seen from southern latitudes.

The five central stars are part of an associated group that also includes stars from other parts of the sky. These stars form an open cluster that is approximately 75 light-years away—and is the nearest open cluster to Earth.

See also: Great Bear

URSA MINOR
General

Constellation of the northern celestial hemisphere that is also known as the Little Bear. The constellation contains the Pole Star, Polaris, which lies very close to the celestial north pole.

See also: Little Bear

URSULA
Slav

Also: Horsel and Orsel

Goddess of the moon, feasted on 21 October. Following the advent of Christianity her importance continued to be recognized, and she became Saint Ursula.

URT
Finno-Ugric—Votyak

The Votyak name for the concept or belief that all things, animate and inanimate, possess a soul or spirit. Among the Cheremiss this soul is called the ort.

See also: Cheremiss–Mordvin; Ort; Votyaks

UZBEKISTAN

General

A country in central Asia that extends from the foothills of the Tian Shan and Pamir Mountains to the land just west of the Aral Sea. The country covers 172,742 square miles (447,400 square kilometers). It became an independent state in 1991, after nearly 70 years as a republic of the Soviet Union.

In the sixth century, Arabs invaded the area that is now Uzbekistan and introduced Islam. Mongols led by Genghis Khan conquered the region in the early thirteenth century, and in the late fourteenth century the Mongol conqueror Tamerlane founded the capital of his vast Asian empire in Samarqand. A group of Turkic tribes known as the Uzbeks invaded in the sixteenth century, and over a period of time political states called khanates were established in the region. In the nineteenth century, the khanates were either conquered by Russia or came under Russian influence; and in 1924, Uzbekistan became a republic of the Soviet Union. In 1990, the Uzbek government declared that its laws superseded those of the Soviet Union, and with the dissolution of the Soviet Union in 1991, Uzbekistan became an independent country.

See also: Genghis Khan; Mongols

V

VA-KUL'
Zyrian

A malevolent water spirit who was depicted as either a man or a woman with long, unkempt hair.

VAHAGN
Armenia

The warrior and creator god who was accidentally born at the dawn of creation. Sky and earth had coupled in an attempt to create life, but their violent actions caused a red reed that had been floating on the surface of the primordial ocean to fly up into space. As it flew through space, its motion caused the red color of the reed to concentrate at one end, and a tail of sparks to fly from the other; and thus the comet-like fiery being dubbed Vahagn was created. As he moved through the sky, sparks flew from his tail, filling the night sky with stars. The Milky Way was formed, by some accounts, as slivers of the reed flew off, or from wisps of straw that Vahagn dropped from the bale of straw he had gathered to feed his chariot horses. Vahagn also covered the surface of the earth with all kinds of plants and animals, and then went on to create humankind. Vahagn was married to Astlik, goddess of the stars—a marriage to his own offspring, for the stars were his creation.

See also: Astlik; Milky Way, The

VAMPIRE
Slav

In Slavic demonology the vampire was a corpse that returned to life at night to suck the blood of the living. The victim of the vampire's bite in turn would become one of the "living dead." This is, of course, the source of the famous novel *Dracula* by Bram Stoker. The vampire seems to have originated as a dragon who ate the moon—such occurrences being believed to bring the dead back to life. The name itself is borrowed from the Serbian *vampir,* which is in turn related to the Turkisk word *ubir,* "undead," though some sources assert an association with the Slavic *upir.* In certain cases the vampire had the ability to shift shape at will, its favorite animal manifestation being the wolf, though bats were also common. These vampires were known as *vukodlak,* which literally translates as "wolf's hair," a word that is still in common usage. Common superstition still holds that when a werewolf dies, it becomes a vampire.

Christopher Lee as Dracula bares his fangs. (The Museum of Modern Art Film Stills Archive)

The origin of the vampire myth is obscure, but it may come from ancient Black Sea beliefs about ghosts that were persuaded to return from the underworld by pouring warm blood onto the ground. These ghosts then required fresh blood if they were to be kept from returning to the underworld—a trait that was to follow through to the legends of corpses rising from their graves to suck the blood of the living and thus to save them from the corruption of death. During the sixteenth century a belief arose that vampires were the spirits of suicide victims and could only be killed if they were exposed to daylight, or stabbed through the heart with the sharpened point of a wooden crucifix, after which they would, in a matter of a few seconds, crumble from a living being to a heap of dust. They were also believed to be the servants of the Devil and were thought to rape their virgin victims while they gorged themselves on their blood. As a result, suspected victims were executed just as often as, if not more often than, suspected vampires.

Modern belief, based to a great degree on the novel *Dracula,* has added a great many aspects to the vampire myth. Bram Stoker based the novel not only on local superstitions but also on history, for parts of the story are based on the life and times of the fourteenth-century Transylvanian warlord named Vlad, better known as "Vlad the Impaler," for the punishment he inflicted on his enemies. These unfortunates would be balanced at the top of a sharpened post and tied by their hands and feet to four more posts. Then they were slowly rocked back and forth until the point of the post impaled them gradually through the stomach. Stoker also added the idea that vampires were shape-changers who were in fact half human and half bat and could change from one form to the other at will. Since the advent of cinema, and later, television, the vampire has gone through countless changes; but still the vampire retains the basic elements of ancient Slavic belief, and as such may be considered as one of the longest-lived superstitions of modern times.

> *See also:* Black Sea; Devil, The; Dragon; Underworld, The; Upir; Vlad (the Impaler), Prince; Werewolf
> *References:* Perkowski 1976; Summers 1929

VARANGIANS
General
The name given by the Slavs to the Scandinavian traders who were known as Russes, Rhos, or Rus' to the Greeks. The traders built towns and trading posts such as Novgorod and Smolensk in Russia, and Chernigov and Kiev in Ukraine. The Scandinavians exacted tribute from the Slavs and carried many of them off as slaves (the root of the word indicates how closely Slavic people were identified with servitude). However, some Scandinavians also settled in Slavic regions, intermarried, and adopted Slavic customs. More often, the traders were peripatetic and had semipermanent settlements without domains or fields.

> *See also:* Chernigov; Kiev; Novgorod; Rus'; Ukraine

VARDAN
Armenia
Born (c. 1160) near Aleppo, Syria, and studied at Drazark Monastery, near Sis (modern Kozan, Turkey). Vardan then entered the monastery at Aygek, near Antioch (modern Antakya, Turkey), where he remained until his death (c. 1230). Vardan of Aygek was, in many respects, the Armenian version of the more famous Aesop. He wrote many Armenian fables in which he incorporated local folklore that he had collected. His fables also concerned contemporary figures from history, such as Alexander the Great. A number of the fables of Vardan of Aygek may be found interspersed throughout this book. That concerning Alexander the Great went as follows:

A poor man once went to Alexander the Great and asked him for charity. Being well known for his generosity, Alexander the

Great gave the man a city and its income. When told by his ministers that the man did not deserve such a gift, Alexander the Great replied that when one is known for his generosity, his gifts must be truly memorable.

See also: Aleppo; Alexander the Great; Mekhithar Gosh
References: Marr 1894–99

VARPULIS
Czech
The god of the storm wind and an attendant of the thunder god Perun, whose chariot he ran alongside as it galloped across the sky. As a result Varpulis was often out of breath, and his panting was perceived in the rumbling of thunder.

See also: Perun

VASILII II, GRAND PRINCE
Russia
Historical ruler of Muscovite Russia who adopted the patronage of Saint George in 1415.

See also: George, Saint
References: Cherniavsky 1969

VASILII BELYANINOVICH
Russia
Son of Bel Belyanin and Nastas'ya of the Golden Braid, and brother to Peter Belyaninovich and Ivan Belyaninovich. After Ivan rescued their mother from Whirlwind, he and Peter left their young brother stranded and tried to claim credit for the rescue themselves. The truth finally came out, and their father wanted to have them executed. Ivan interceded; and Peter married the tsaritsa of the Silver Kingdom, Vasilii married the tsaritsa of the Copper Kingdom, and Ivan married Elena the Fair, the tsaritsa of the Golden Kingdom, the three maidens having been rescued by Ivan when he freed his mother.

See also: Bel Belyanin; Copper Kingdom, The; Elena the Fair; Golden Kingdom, The; Ivan Belyaninovich; Nastas'ya of the Golden Braid; Peter (Belyaninovich); Silver Kingdom, The; Whirlwind

VASILII BUSLA(Y)EV
Russia
Alternative name for Vasilii Buslayevich, the son of Buslai and Amelfia Timofeyevna.

VASILII BUSLAYEVICH
Russia
The son of Buslai, as his name indicates, Buslayevich simply meaning "son of Buslai," and the sorceress Amelfia Timofeyevna. Although the legends do not explicitly state the relationship, Vasilii must have been a half brother of Dobrynya Nikitich, as Amelfia Timofeyevna is also said to be the mother of that great bogatyr' and the widow of Dobrynya's father Nikita.

At the age of seven, Vasilii Buslayevich was sent to learn to read and write, which he accomplished with aplomb, and then to write and sing hymns, which he again achieved without equal in all of Novgorod, his home city. However, when he grew up, Vasilii began to consort with a drunken and rowdy crowd, and soon he gained a reputation as a lout who would do harm to others simply for the fun of it. The law-abiding citizens of Novgorod went to see the widow Amelfia Timofeyevna to complain about the conduct of her son, and she, in turn, scolded her son for his behavior.

However, the scolding did nothing to Vasilii Buslayevich other than make him resolve to live his life as he saw fit. He sent out a challenge to all those in Novgorod that if they could pass two tests he would set them, they would become members of his *druzhina* (retinue) and live a life of luxury at his expense.

Word of the challenge quickly spread, and it was not long before a huge crowd had gathered in front of Vasilii Buslayevich's home. Vasilii faced the crowd and told them that the two tests consisted of drinking, in a single quaff, a cup of green wine—no normal cup, but one holding the equivalent of one and a half *vedro*. The second test would be to stand, unwavering, under a single blow from Vasilii Buslayevich's huge mace, which was made of elm wood and filled with lead and weighed more than twenty poods (approximately 720 pounds).

The first to take the tests and pass was Kostia Novotorzheni. He was followed by two boyar brothers by the names of Luka and Moisei, then by the men of Zalyoshen, the seven Sbrodovich brothers, and so on, until there were twenty-nine members of the *druzhina,* Vasilii Buslayevich himself being the thirtieth. Those who failed the tests were killed and simply thrown over a wall.

Several days later Vasilii Buslayevich heard that the men of Novgorod were organizing a large party in honor of one Nikolai, so he and his men went along to see if they could gain entry, which they did when Vasilii Buslayevich paid five rubles for each of them and twenty-five for himself. As the evening wore on, great quantities of alcohol were consumed, and a fight broke out during which Vasilii Buslayevich was set upon and came close to being strangled. He called out for help, whereupon Luka, Moisei, and Kostia Novotorzheni came to his aid, killing their ataman's attackers.

The fighting continued until the partygoers begged Vasilii Buslayevich and his men for mercy. Vasilii Buslayevich considered the problem for a moment and then wagered the townsfolk that his followers could take on the entire city and win. He added that if he did win, then the city would pay him and his men a tribute of three thousand rubles a year, until the very last member of his *druzhina* was dead; but if he lost, then he would pay the city three thousand rubles a year until his death. The men of Novgorod accepted the challenge and agreed that the fight should start the very next day.

Quickly it became apparent that Vasilii Buslayevich and his men were the more powerful; so several of the leaders of Novgorod went to the widow Amelfia Timofeyevna and pleaded with her to take her son in hand. The widow considered various courses of action and then had her handmaiden bring her son to her. Amelfia

Timofeyevna gave her son a drugged drink, then had her handmaiden lock him in a strong dungeon with thick iron bars at the windows and several locks on the many doors between the dungeon and the outside.

The battle now turned in favor of the men of Novgorod, who steadily forced Vasilii Buslayevich's men back toward the river Volkhov. There the handmaiden of the widow Amelfia Timofeyevna came across the fight and was beseeched for help by Vasilii Buslayevich's men. She immediately cast the buckets from the yoke about her neck, and brandishing the yoke, plowed into the men of Novgorod, killing a great many and knocking a great many more senseless. Then, with the odds slightly evened, she ran to the dungeon where she had incarcerated Vasilii Buslayevich and set him free.

Vasilii Buslayevich rushed to the aid of his men, only to find his way blocked by an aged pilgrim carrying a huge gold bell that weighed over three hundred poods (10,800 pounds). The pilgrim warned Vasilii Buslayevich to refrain from attacking the men of Novgorod, for he said that the men of Novgorod would be victorious in the end. Disinterested and disbelieving, Vasilii Buslayevich told the pilgrim to stand aside, and when he did not, he struck out at him, whereupon the pilgrim disappeared.

Vasilii Buslayevich hurried back into the battle. Soon he and his men once more had the upper hand. Seeing that they were losing the battle, the men of Novgorod went to the widow Amelfia Timofeyevna and told her that they would accept defeat and gladly pay the tribute her son had demanded. Amelfia sent the handmaiden to fetch Vasilii Buslayevich, and over glasses of wine the two sides made their peace.

Peace, however, was not what burned in Vasilii Buslayevich's heart. Still, he had signed a pact with the city of Novgorod, and so he had to seek adventure farther afield. To this end he built a sturdy ship, painted it blood red, and took to a life of piracy on the waters of Lake Il'men'. As they sailed, Kostia

Nikitin guarded the stern and Tiny Potania the stem, while Vasilii Buslayevich paced up and down looking for a new target to attack. At length, Vasilii Buslayevich felt the burden of age bearing down on him, and so he and his men decided to make a pilgrimage to Jerusalem to seek divine forgiveness before they died.

Setting sail from Novgorod, they sailed three weeks before sighting another ship. When the two ships drew abreast, they asked the other sailors, who all had heard of Vasilii Buslayevich and his *druzhina,* the most direct route to Jerusalem. The sailors told them that the city they sought lay seven weeks' sail away by the most direct route, or a year and a half by the indirect one. Vasilii Buslayevich told them he would follow the quickest route to his salvation; but the sailors warned him that this meant they would have to pass the island of Kuminsk in the Caspian Sea, where three thousand Kazakh atamans barred the way, robbing and sinking any ship that attempted to pass.

Undeterred, Vasilii Buslayevich and his men sailed on until they came to an island on which they beached their ship. They began to climb the central mountain, which was called the Sorochinsk, or the Saracen, Hill. Halfway up the mountainside, Vasilii Buslayevich came across a pile of human bones and idly kicked the skull aside. The skull warned Vasilii Buslayevich that he would die on that very mountain; but Vasilii refused to believe it, kicked it again to one side, and continued to climb.

At the top of the mountain they came to a huge stone slab that had an inscription on it saying that any who dived across it would surely die. This slab is described by some sources as three fathoms high (24 feet), three *arshins* and a quarter wide, and a whole ax-throw across. Vasilii and his men read the words, laughed at them, and then crossed the stone, though none dared dive across. However, they found nothing else on that island, so they returned to their ship and resumed their course for Jerusalem.

Sailing on into the Caspian Sea, the ship came to the island of Kuminsk and docked under the watchful eye of over a hundred Kazakh pirates. Vasilii Buslayevich paid them no attention, calmly moored the ship, and then leaped ashore, carrying his huge elm mace. So intimidated were the Kazakhs by his casual indifference that they scattered to tell their atamans of the arrival of Vasilii Buslayevich and his *druzhina*. The atamans came out to greet their visitor, who simply asked them to point out to him the most direct route to Jerusalem. They invited him to dine with them, which he did, and then, amazed by his prowess and calm among a company feared by all others, the Kazakh atamans provided Vasilii Buslayevich a young guide and bade him a safe journey—glad to see him go and to have escaped his legendary wrath.

Vasilii Buslayevich and his men sailed across the Caspian Sea and entered the confines of the river Jordan, where they tied up the ship, Vasilii Buslayevich going on into Jerusalem by himself. There he prayed and took communion in the Church of the Holy Sepulchre. While he was away, his men waited patiently on their ship and bathed in the waters of the Jordan. While bathing they were approached by an old woman, who told them that only Vasilii Buslayevich might bathe in the same waters that Jesus Christ had been baptized in and that they would lose their valiant leader before long.

The men laughed at the old woman's superstition and continued to bathe in the river. Vasilii Buslayevich completed his prayers in Jerusalem and returned to his boat, and then set sail, retracing his course back to Novgorod. On the way he again stopped and feasted with the Kazakh pirates, and moored his ship again at the island of the Sorochinsk, or Saracen, Hill. Again Vasilii Buslayevich and his men climbed the hill, and crossed the stone slab at the top. This time Vasilii decided to defy the prophecy engraved on the slab and dove headlong from one side to the other. He took a good run up and leaped into the air. However, as his legs crossed the edge of the stone, one foot caught the lip, and Vasilii Buslayevich crashed down onto the slab, splitting his head open and spilling his brains. He died instantly.

His men quickly gave Vasilii Buslayevich a Christian burial and then returned to Novgorod, where they broke the news of his death to the widow Amelfia Timofeyevna. Vasilii's mother offered each of his men an equal share of her dead son's fortune, but they all refused and drank a simple toast before going their separate ways.

This is not the only account of the death of Vasilii Buslayevich. Another legend, which is a post-Christian attempt to stamp out the remembrance of these great heroes and demigods, says that seven bogatyri once assembled to go on a journey together. The seven were Vasilii Buslayevich, Godenko Bludovich, Vasilii Kazimirovich, Ivan Gostinyi Syn, Alyosha Popovich, Dobrynya Nikitich, and Il'ya Muromets. Setting out together on horseback, the seven rode out toward the river Safat. At the junction of three roads, not far from the banks of the Safat, the seven men made camp and settled down for the night.

The following morning Dobrynya Nikitich was the first to wake and went down to the Safat to bathe and give thanks to God. As he made to leave he noticed a white tent pitched on the opposite bank that he recognized as belonging to a Tatar—a Muslim, and thus a sworn enemy of every bogatyr'. Dobrynya called out a challenge to the Tatar, who rushed from his tent fully armed and leaped onto his horse to meet Dobrynya Nikitich in battle on the plain. For a long time the two fought before Dobrynya was toppled from his horse. The Tatar leaped down and cut out Dobrynya's heart and liver.

As Dobrynya Nikitich died, Alyosha Popovich rose from his bed and came to the Safat to bathe and make ready for the day. There he saw Dobrynya Nikitich's horse wandering aimlessly, and catching the sad look in the horse's eyes, he knew that some-

thing was wrong. Quickly he mounted his own horse and rode across the plain, looking for his comrade. Before long he came to the tent of the Tatar, and there he saw the dismembered body of Dobrynya Nikitich lying on the ground. Alyosha roared a challenge and was quickly met by the Tatar. The two fought long and hard until Alyosha managed to unseat the Tatar, leaped upon him, and made ready to cut out his heart. As he kneeled over the body, knife poised, a black raven swooped down and beseeched Alyosha to spare the life of the Tatar, saying that if his life was spared, then the raven would fetch the Water of Life and Death so that Alyosha might restore his fallen comrade to life.

Alyosha agreed, and before long the raven returned with two vials of water, one containing the Water of Death and the other the Water of Life. Alyosha first anointed the body of Dobrynya Nikitich with the Water of Death, and his body became whole again. Then he anointed the body with the Water of Life, and Dobrynya came back to life and embraced his comrade. They then set the Tatar free and returned to the banks of the Safat to wash and give thanks to God.

As they rose from their ablutions they saw a huge Tatar army approaching the river and called to the other bogatyri to join them in the coming battle. For three hours and three minutes they rode through the Tatar army, and by the end of that time had killed each and every Tatar warrior. As they rode back to the banks of the river to wash off the blood of the battle, the seven began to boast about their accomplishments. As they boasted that none could ever defeat them, they were confronted by two strange warriors, who challenged them.

Alyosha Popovich took up the challenge first and rushed at the warriors, cutting each in half as he rode past them; but as he turned his horse to boast to his comrades, he saw that the two had now become four. Dobrynya Nikitich was the next to charge, and he too cut all the warriors in half; but as he turned, he found that the four had now become eight. Il'ya Muromets then charged, but with the same result. For the first time in their lives, the seven felt fear, and deciding that living was better than certain death, they all fled for the mountains. There, as each of the seven entered the foothills, he was immediately turned to stone. That is why, after this encounter, there were no more bogatyri left in all Russia.

It is interesting to note in this story that the Water of Life and Death is depicted as two separate elements, whereas it is usually referred to as a single solution. It is also interesting to note that the deaths of the heroes vary from those described in the tales of their individual lives.

See also: Alyosha Popovich; Amelf(i)a Timofe(y)evna; Boyars; Buslai (~y); Caspian Sea; Dobrynya Nikitich; Godenko Bludovich; Il'men', Lake; Il'ya Muromets; Ivan Gostinyi Syn; Kostia Nikitin; Kostia Novotorzheni; Luka; Moisei; Nikita; Nikolai of Mozhaisk, Saint; Novgorod; Potania, Tiny; Safat; Saracen Hill; Sbrodovich; Sorochinsk Hill; Tatars; Vasilii Kazimirovich; Water of Life and Death, The; Zalyoshen
References: Speranskii 1916; Ukhov 1957

VASILII KAZIMIROVICH
Russia
One of seven bogatyri who once assembled to go on a journey together. The other six were Vasilii Buslayevich, Godenko Bludovich, Ivan Gostinyi Syn, Alyosha Popovich, Dobrynya Nikitich, and Il'ya Muromets. This legend, which attempts to explain why the bogatyri disappeared from Holy Russia, may be found in the entry for Vasilii Buslayevich.

See also: Alyosha Popovich; Bogatyr'; Dobrynya Nikitich; Godenko Bludovich; Il'ya Muromets; Ivan Gostinyi Syn; Vasilii Buslayevich
References: Speranskii 1916; Ukhov 1957

VASILII VYSLAVOVICH
Russia
Son of Tsar Vyslav Andronovich and brother of Dmitrii and Ivan Vyslavovich. He and Dmitrii waylaid their brother Ivan when he was returning home with the Firebird, the Horse with the Golden Mane, and Elena the Beautiful, and killed him. Vasilii won Elena the Beautiful when he and Dmitrii cast lots, while his brother received the Horse with the Golden Mane. They presented the Firebird to their father as proof that they had completed the quest for the fabulous bird. After Ivan was restored to life with the Water of Life and Death and returned to the royal palace, Vasilii and Dmitrii were thrown into the deepest dungeon by their father for their treachery.

See also: Dmitrii (Vyslavovich); Elena the Beautiful; Firebird, The; Horse with the Golden Mane, The; Ivan Vyslavovich; Vyslav Andronovich; Water of Life and Death, The

VASILIS(S)A, PRINCESS
Russia
A daughter of the Sea Tsar, sometimes referred to as Vasilissa the Wise, and described by some as an incarnation of the witch Baba-Yaga. In an unnamed realm, an unnamed tsar sought to sacrifice his son to an eagle in return for great wealth, but the youth was rescued by Princess Vasilissa. The tsar called on the Sea Tsar to return his son to him, but Princess Vasilissa overcame and killed her father, married the youth, and ruled in the Sea Tsar's stead.

See also: Baba-Yaga (-Jaga, -Iaga); Sea Tsar; Vasilis(s)a the Wise

VASILIS(S)A KIRBIT'EVNA
Russia
The beautiful daughter of Tsar Kirbit. She lived in a tower with a gilded roof from which she was abducted by Bulat the Brave and Ivan, the latter of whom it had been prophesied she would marry. En route she was kidnapped by the terrible Koshchei the Deathless.

Bulat the Brave and Ivan came to the home of Koshchei to rescue her. With her help, they found out where Koshchei had hidden his soul—for without it, he could not be killed. After Bulat the Brave and Ivan had successfully collected Koshchei's soul and killed him, Vasilissa returned with Ivan to his homeland, where in fulfillment of the prophecy, she became his wife.

See also: Bulat the Brave; Ivan; Kirbit; Koshchei (the Deathless)

VASILIS(S)A OF THE GOLDEN BRAID

Russia

The beautiful daughter of Tsar Svetozar. For the first twenty years of her life she lived alone, save for her maids and ladies-in-waiting, in her room at the top of a tall tower. She earned her epithet from her hair, which reached to her ankles and which she wore in a single plait. News of her wondrous beauty had gradually spread far and wide, and soon offers of marriage were received. Her father was in no hurry and waited until the appropriate time to announce that she would choose a husband.

As Vasilissa had never been outside her room, she longed to see the fields and the flowers that lay beyond the palace. Finally her father agreed to let her out just once. As she strolled around, picking the pretty flowers, she wandered away from her ladies-in-waiting. Just then, a strong wind sprang up, lifting the unfortunate girl from the ground and carrying her far away to the domain of a fierce dragon, who imprisoned her in a golden palace that stood on a single silver pillar.

Heartbroken by her disappearance, her parents sent her two brothers to find her. After two years they came to the land of the dragon and saw Vasilissa behind a barred window inside the strange palace. As they entered the palace the dragon returned. Confronted by the two young men, he deftly picked up one and dashed him against his brother, thus killing both.

Vasilissa at first starved herself; but then she vowed that rather than die, she would escape from the palace. Pretending to be nice to the dragon, she learned that there was only one who could overcome him, and he was named Ivan the Pea. The dragon laughed as he told her this, for he did not believe that such a person existed. Indeed, at that time, Ivan the Pea had not yet been born.

Back at her home, Vasilissa's mother was heartbroken for the lack of news of her children. Walking in her garden one hot day, she became thirsty and drank from a small stream that ran through the garden, failing to see that she also swallowed a small pea that was in the water. The pea started to swell inside the tsarina, and after the appropriate time she gave birth to a son, whom she called Ivan the Pea.

Ivan the Pea grew at a tremendous rate. At the age of ten, he was the strongest and fattest knight in all the kingdom. Learning of the fate of his brothers and sister, Ivan the Pea set out to find them. After traveling three days, Ivan the Pea came to a house on chickens' legs that revolved in the wind. The old crone who lived in the house gave Ivan the Pea directions to the land of the dragon, on the condition that he bring back some of the magic water owned by the dragon, which would make her young again.

After a lengthy journey, Ivan the Pea arrived at the palace of the dragon. When Vasilissa found out who he was, she begged him to leave and save his life. Ivan the Pea would not hear anything of the sort. Instead, he went to the palace smithy and asked the old smith to make him a mace weighing five hundred poods (18,000 lbs or 8,190 kg). The mace took forty hours to make, and fifty men were needed to lift it; but Ivan the Pea picked it up in one hand and tossed it into the air, where it disappeared from sight. Ivan the Pea returned to the palace and asked to be told when the mace was sighted. Three hours later, a frightened messenger told Ivan the Pea that the mace had been spotted, and he deftly caught it in one hand, the impact having no effect on him but making the mace bend slightly. Ivan the Pea simply laid it across his knee and bent it straight again.

Shortly afterward the dragon returned to the palace, which normally would have begun to revolve on its single silver pillar as he approached. This time it did not even move an inch, warning the dragon that there must be something, or someone, extremely heavy inside.

The dragon, who had the body of a man but the head of a serpent, flew in through one of the windows, riding a winged black horse. Spying Ivan the Pea, the dragon leaped at him, but Ivan the Pea jumped nimbly to one side. As the dragon crashed to the floor, Ivan the Pea launched his enormous mace at it. As the mace made contact, it smashed the dragon into thousands of tiny pieces. However, the mace did not stop at that, and continued through the walls of the palace, coming to rest many hundreds of miles away.

Refusing the requests of the beleaguered kingdom that the dragon had ruled over to become their tsar, Ivan the Pea appointed the smith who had made his mighty mace. Next, remembering the promise he had made to the old crone in the forest, he located the magic water owned by the dragon, the Water of Life and Death. He carefully filled a flask with the water and then sprinkled some over the bodies of his dead brothers, who came back to life, rubbing their eyes as if they had just awakened from a deep sleep.

All four then returned home, stopping en route to deliver the flask of the magic water to the crone in the forest. Once home, Vasilissa took a husband, and following the death of their father, Ivan the Pea became tsar.

Even though the crone in the forest in this story is not named, most authorities agree that she is none other than the witch Baba-Yaga.

See also: Baba-Yaga (-Jaga, -Iaga); Dragon; Ivan the Pea; Svetozar; Water of Life and Death, The

VASILIS(S)A THE BEAUTIFUL
Russia
Also: Maryshia.

Vasilissa the Beautiful was the only daughter of a merchant whose wife died when the girl was just eight years old. As she lay dying her mother gave Vasilisushka, her pet name for Vasilissa, her blessings and a doll, saying that if ever Vasilissa needed guidance all she had to do was feed the doll and it would tell her what to do. A short time later the merchant married for the second time, this time marrying a widow who had two daughters of her own.

Vasilissa's stepmother and stepsisters were jealous of her beauty and did everything they could to make her life miserable. They gave her all the hardest jobs to do and yet were always complaining about her. However, Vasilissa completed each task with ease, for all she had to do was feed the doll her mother had given her, and while she passed the time picking flowers or walking in the meadows, the doll did all the work that had been assigned.

The years passed and the merchant spent much of his time away from home. On one such occasion the stepmother moved the entire family to the edge of a very dark forest in the middle of which Baba-Yaga had her home. Every day some excuse would be found to send Vasilissa into the forest; but every time, the doll guided her and kept her clear of Baba-Yaga's house. One night in autumn the stepmother and her daughters let all the fires in the house go out, and ordering Vasilissa to fetch light from Baba-Yaga, they pushed her out of the house.

After talking with her doll, who told her that no harm would come to her as long as she kept the doll with her, Vasilissa left the house and started into the forest. A short way down the path, just as dawn was breaking, she was passed by a galloping horseman whose face and clothes were white, as were his horse and its harness. Just as the sun was rising, she were passed by a second racing horseman. This time the rider's face and clothes were scarlet, as were his horse and harness. Vasilissa walked deeper and deeper into the forest, well into the evening, until she came to the clearing in which Baba-Yaga's house stood.

The sight she saw froze her to the spot. A high fence of human bones circled the cottage, which revolved slowly in the slight breeze. Human skulls adorned the fence posts. The gate consisted of a pair of human legs, the bolts of a pair of human hands, and the lock of a mouth with razor-sharp teeth. As Vasilissa stood there, a third horseman passed her, riding swiftly through the gates, which magically opened to admit him. This rider was entirely black and rode the blackest horse Vasilissa had ever seen. As horse and rider passed through the gate, they disappeared from view, and night instantly fell. Light soon returned to the scene, however, for the eyes in the skulls that sat atop the fence started to glow until the clearing was lit as brightly as it would have been in the middle of the day.

As Vasilissa stood in the strangely lit clearing, she heard an awful noise coming from the forest. Suddenly Baba-Yaga herself came into view, riding in a mortar that she rowed with a pestle, and brushing away all traces of her passage with a broom. Stopping at the gates, she saw Vasilissa and asked her why she had come. When Vasilissa told her that she had come for a light, Baba-Yaga said that she would give her one provided she worked for her for a time, warning that her failure to complete any assigned task would result in her being eaten.

For two days Baba-Yaga assigned Vasilissa seemingly impossible tasks, such as extracting earth from poppy seeds, or fennel from wheat; but each task was carried out with ease by the doll. All Vasilissa had to do was cook for the witch, a task she enjoyed and the doll did not, for fear of falling into the fire and burning up. On the third evening Baba-Yaga told Vasilissa that as her mother had blessed her, she was free to leave. First, however, Vasilissa asked whether she might know the answer to a single question. The witch agreed. Vasilissa wanted to know who the three horsemen were whom she had seen. Baba-Yaga explained that they were her servants, Day, Sun, and Night. Leading the girl to the gate, she took one of the skulls down from the fence and placed it on a pole

before handing it to Vasilissa, who then made her way back to the cottage where her stepmother and stepsisters awaited her return.

Outside the cottage Vasilissa made to throw away the skull, but it told her not to. Entering the cottage, Vasilissa was warmly welcomed, because since she had left they had been unable to light anything in the cottage and had spent five miserable days in the dark and the cold. However, when they took the skull from Vasilissa, it stared straight into their eyes. No matter where they hid the skull managed to fix its gaze on them, and by morning all three had been burned to a cinder.

Leaving the cottage the next morning, Vasilissa buried the skull and returned to town to await her father. While she waited, her doll wove some spectacular thread, which a seamstress took to the tsar. When he saw it he asked for the spinner of such a thread to be brought to him. When he saw Vasilissa, the tsar fell instantly in love with her and made her his wife.

This story, whose theme is well known in such stories as that of Cinderella, shows both the benevolent and the malevolent nature of the witch Baba-Yaga. Authorities have identified the mother of Vasilissa as a sister of Baba-Yaga who is jealous of Vasilissa's beauty, or as one of Baba-Yaga's aspects that is equivalent to the third aspect of the triune goddess—that of death. Baba-Yaga herself represents the second aspect of the triune goddess—that of fate, neither good nor bad, and the doll, her first aspect—that of protectress and life-giver.

See also: Baba-Yaga (-Jaga, -Iaga); Day; Night; Sun; Vasilisushka

References: Afanas'ev 1957

VASILIS(S)A THE WISE
Russia

A princess from a remote, unnamed kingdom who had the ability to change her shape at will, though she usually chose to assume that of a frog. It was in this guise that Ivan the Young found her.

Ivan was the youngest son of an unnamed tsar and one of his three concubines, each of whom had presented the tsar with a son. Unsure which son should succeed him, the tsar told each to go into a field and to shoot a single arrow, with the son's name written on it, each in a different direction. Wherever the arrow landed, that son would rule, and he would marry the daughter of the house the arrow landed in. Each prince did as instructed and set off to find his arrow.

Ivan was at first unable to locate his arrow. However, after three days of searching he came across a small hut made of reeds, in the middle of a swamp. Inside sat a large green frog with Ivan's arrow in its mouth. The frog saw Ivan the Young and bade him enter, changing the hut into a pretty summerhouse so that it was large enough to accommodate him.

The frog then magically conjured up a table fully laden with food, and when Ivan had eaten, told him that unless he consented to marry her he would never leave the swamp. Realizing that the frog was an enchantress, Ivan the Young agreed. With that, the frog discarded its skin and stood before him in its real form—that of a beautiful maiden. The maiden told Ivan that she would wear her frog skin during the day but would appear every night as he now saw her.

When he returned home, Ivan the Young was at first ridiculed for wanting to marry the frog; but finally his father consented and the two were wed. The frog kept her word and appeared as a beautiful woman every night. For a long time Ivan and his wife lived happily. Then the tsar devised three tests for each of his son's wives. The first was to sew a fine shirt. The frog easily won, for she had had the garment magically made. The second test was to embroider a tapestry in a single night. Again the frog easily won, for she commanded the winds to bring her the finest tapestry from her father's kingdom. Finally the tsar commanded each to bake him a loaf of bread. This time the two other wives tried to cheat by spying on the frog; but each only produced disastrous results, while the frog produced the finest loaf ever seen.

To congratulate each of his daughters-in-law the tsar organized a huge banquet in their honor. Distraught, Ivan the Young knew he would be the laughingstock of the kingdom if he brought a frog to the banquet. Telling him to go on ahead, the frog changed into the beautiful maiden and arrived at the banquet in the finest horse and carriage anyone in that kingdom had ever seen. As the feast drew to a close, Ivan made an excuse and left early to arrive home ahead of his wife. There, in an attempt to keep his wife in her womanly form, he found and burned her frog skin. When his wife returned, she told him that had he waited just a while longer, she would have been his forever. She told him that her name was Vasilissa the Wise and that she must now disappear; and she gave him instructions on how to travel to the land of eternal sunlight if he wished to find her.

Ivan the Young set out to find his wife. After a long journey he found himself in front of a small wooden hut on chicken's legs that revolved slowly in the wind—the home of the witch Baba-Yaga. Entering the hut he was confronted by the angry witch; but when he explained the purpose of his visit, the witch agreed to help him. She told him that his wife flew in every day to see her. After she had made herself comfortable, Ivan was to take hold of her firmly and not let go even when she changed her shape. Finally she would turn into an arrow, which Baba-Yaga told Ivan to break over his knee. Then, and only then, would Vasilissa be his forever.

Shortly afterward Vasilissa flew in on her magic carpet. Making herself comfortable, she did not see Ivan as he leaped out of his hiding place and caught hold of her. Instantly she began to change her shape, and in surprise, Ivan let her wriggle free and fly away. Baba-Yaga then advised Ivan the Young to visit Vasilissa's middle sister, for the witch knew that Vasilissa also visited her. Ivan thanked the witch and made his way to the home of Vasilissa's middle sister. There the very same thing happened, so the middle sister sent Ivan on to visit their youngest sister.

There he was told that this time he must not fail, for if he did, he would never see Vasilissa again. After Vasilissa had arrived, Ivan pounced on her and hung on with all his might. Finally realizing that she could not escape him, Vasilissa changed herself into an arrow, which Ivan broke across his knee. Instantly Vasilissa assumed her human form and told him that she was his forever. Together they rode on Vasilissa's flying carpet back to the home of Ivan, and there they lived happily together, Ivan eventually inheriting his father's domain.

In the Ukrainian version of this tale, the shape-changing frog is named Maria and identified as the daughter of the Sea King.

See also: Baba-Yaga (-Jaga, -Iaga); Ivan the Young; Maria; Sea King

VASILISUSHKA
Russia

The pet name given to Vasilissa the Beautiful by her mother.

See also: Vasilis(s)a the Beautiful

VASILKO
Ukraine

The younger brother of Marusya.

See also: Marusya

VED'MA
Russia

The Russian word for a witch, which comes from "to know"—a root that indicates the importance of witches such as Baba-Yaga, who were not only the doers of magical deeds but also the repositories of all knowledge.

See also: Baba-Yaga (-Jaga, -Iaga)

VELE(S)
Baltic

Spirits of the dead. They are believed to live in another world, referred to as the Sand Hills, in families and villages similar to those they lived in on earth.

VELES
Russia

A nature deity who was regarded as the patron of cattle and of merchants. Following the adoption of Christianity by Vladimir I, Veles became Saint Vlasii, who is depicted in Russian iconography as being surrounded by sheep, cows, and goats.

See also: Vladimir I; Vlas(i)i, Saint

VELI JOZE
Croatia

Literally, "Big Joe." Veli Joze was a giant and a valiant warrior who lived at Motovun, on the Istra peninsula of northern Croatia. Once, in a fit of fury against a tyrannical feudal lord, he wrapped his arms around Motovun tower and shook it with all his might. The tower cracked and began to lean to one side—a state it remains in to this day. Veli Joze did not escape unpunished. Two iron rings were fixed to the side of a nearby canyon from which Veli Joze was suspended, though whether or not he died there was not recorded.

See also: Motovun

VELNIAS
Baltic

A malevolent spirit of the dead.

VENUS
General

The nearest planet to Earth. Venus lies nearer the Sun than does Earth, and thus it appears in phases. It is most famous as the Morning Star or the Evening Star—the first "star" visible in the dusk sky, or the last star to disappear at dawn. Many cultures around the world have connected the planet Venus with deities personifying the daily death of the Sun and its wondrous rebirth the following morning.

See also: Evening Star; Morning Star; Sun

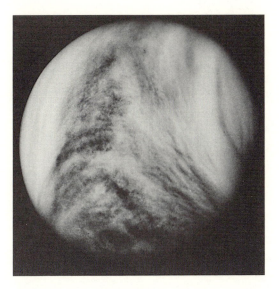

Full-disc image of Venus, taken by the Pioneer Venus Orbiter, March 3 1979 (NASA)

VESNA
Russia

A goddess of spring whose name appears to have given rise to Ovsen', an archaic name used for the Koliada festival in the Volga region—though the inverse might also be the case.

See also: Koliada; Ovsen'; Volga
References: Afanas'ev 1865–69; Potebnia 1865

VESNIANKA
Russia

In certain parts of Russia, this goddess was considered the personification of spring. She might owe her origins to Vesna, or vice versa.

See also: Vesna

VIKHOR'
Russia

The Russian name of the character referred to as "Whirlwind" in English translations of the story of the tsarevich Ivan Belyaninovich. A wicked enchanter who, in the guise of a whirlwind, abducted either the mother or the sister of the tsarevich. Popular belief held that if a knife could be thrust into the very center, or heart, of a whirlwind, it would injure or kill the wizard or devil riding there.

See also: Ivan Belyaninovich; Whirlwind

VIKINGS
General

Also called Norsemen, and known as "Danes" in England and Ireland, the Vikings were Scandinavian sea warriors who raided Europe between the eighth and eleventh centuries. Many Vikings eventually settled in the lands they raided and conquered—for example, the province of Normandy, in France. The Vikings conquered England in 1013 under Sweyn I, whose son Canute was later crowned king of England, Denmark, and Norway. In the east they created the first state in Russia (Kievan Rus') as well as either founding the city of Novgorod or helping to establish it on a firm footing. Excellent mariners, the Vikings sailed as far as the

Detail of the prow of the ninth-century Viking Oseberg ship (Museum of the Viking Ship, Oslo, Norway; Knudsens-Giraudon/Art Resource, NY)

Byzantine Empire in the south, and Ireland, Iceland, Greenland, and North America in the west.

Noted for the barbarity of their raids, the Vikings were able to penetrate far inland in their shallow-draft, highly maneuverable longships. They plundered villages and towns in order to obtain gold and other riches, killing men and children with abandon before raping the women and putting them to the sword as well. It was the need for organized resistance against the Vikings that accelerated the development of the feudal system. The Vikings actually successfully invaded Britain twice: first as Vikings proper, and second in 1066, under the leadership of William the Conqueror, as Normans.

See also: Byzantine Empire; Novgorod

VILA
Slav

(pl. *vili* or *vile*) A woodland nymph who is possibly similar in characteristics to the Baltic vele. In some cases, the vili were seen as male versions of the russalki; but more often the vila and russalka were interchangeable. One particular story concerning the *vile* involves Prince Marko, who saw a group of them singing and dancing. Marko released his falcon to capture the headdress and wings of their leader Nadanojla, who set off in hot pursuit of Marko as he rode away with the captured items. Marko explained to all who saw him that the woman following him was a shepherdess who was to become his wife. Duly married, the couple lived for some time in peace and contentment, until one day Marko boasted that his wife was a vila, whereupon she put on her wings and flew away. Only after she was recaptured by Marko did Nadanojla accept her role as Marko's wife. Thereafter, she reacted only with laughter when her husband boasted of her supernatural origins.

See also: Marko, Prince; Nadanojla; Rus(s)alki (~ulki); Vele(s)

VINOGRAD
Russia

Literally, "Vine" or "Grapes"—an archaic name sometimes used to refer to the Koliada festival in the Volga region of Russia.

See also: Koliada; Volga

VISAPAKLAL
Armenia

Vahagn's name when he is referred to in his dragon-slaying aspect—a function of the god about which nothing further is known.

See also: Dragon; Vahagn

VISHAP
Armenia

Armenian word for dragon.

VIXEN AND THE LIONESS, THE
Armenia

A lioness once gave birth to a cub, and all the other animals came to offer her their congratulations. Into the midst of their gathering walked a vixen that berated the lioness as only being able to produce one offspring at a time, whereas she could produce a whole litter. The lioness retorted that while the vixen was indeed telling the truth, at least her child was a lion.

One of the fables of Vardan of Aygek, which possibly owes its origins to the classical Greek story of Niobe and Leto. In this tale, Niobe boasted that she had six sons and six daughters (some sources say seven of each), whereas Leto had only produced the twins Apollo and Artemis.

See also: Vardan
References: Marr 1894–99

VIZI-ANYA
Magyar

The wife of Vizi-ember.

VIZI-EMBER
Hungary—Magyar

An extremely unlikable and unattractive water god who lived in rivers and lakes and regularly demanded human sacrifices—the counterpart of the vu-murt of the Votyak people. When human sacrifices were slow in being offered to Vizi-ember, those living along the banks of the rivers in which he lived would hear his voice, after which someone was certain to be drowned. Vizi-ember was one of three similar water deities, the others being his wife, Vizi-anya, and his daughter, Vizi-leany.

See also: Vizi-anya; Vizi-leany; Votyaks; Vu-murt

VIZI-LEANY
Hungary—Magyar
The daughter of Vizi-ember.

VLAD (THE IMPALER), PRINCE
Romania
A historical prince of the fifteenth century whose true name was Vlad Tepes. This tyrant lived in Walachia, a region south of Transylvania, and was known for executing his enemies by driving a sharpened pole slowly through their bodies. Vlad was nicknamed Dracula, which in Romanian means "son of the devil" or "son of a dragon," and he was the prototype for the fictional vampire of the 1897 novel *Dracula,* by Bram Stoker (1847–1912).

See also: Transylvania; Vampire; Walachia

VLADIMIR I
Russia
Also known as Saint Vladimir or Vladimir the Great, the first Christian sovereign of Russia. Born c. 956, the son of Sviatoslav, Grand Prince of Kiev, and thus grandson of Olga (the daughter of Oleg), he became Prince of Novgorod in 970, and seized Kiev from his brother in 980. Consolidating the Russian realm from the Baltic to the Ukraine, he extended its dominions into Galicia, Lithuania, and Livonia, making Kiev his capital city. Until 987 he, like his people, worshiped pagan gods such as Perun; but in 987 or 988, he formed a pact with the Byzantine emperor Basil II, married Basil's sister Anna, and accepted Christianity. He was, with his great-grandson, Vladimir II, amalgamated into the legendary hero Vladimir Bright Sun.

See also: Anna; Baltic; Basil II, Bulgaroctonus; Byzantine Empire; Kiev; Lithuania; Livonia; Novgorod; Olga; Perun; Ukraine; Vladimir II; Vladimir Bright Sun, Prince

VLADIMIR II
Russia
Correctly known as Vladimir Monomakh or Vladimir Monomachus, Vladimir II was born in 1053, the great-grandson of Vladimir I. He became Grand Prince of Kiev in 1113 by popular demand, and therefore became ruler of Russia instead of the prior claimants of the Sviatoslav and Iziaslav families, thus founding the Monomakhovichi dynasty. A popular, powerful, and peaceful ruler, he ruled until his death in 1125. Over the course of time, the popular imagination subsequently conflated Vladimir Monomakh with his forebear Vladimir I, creating the legendary hero Prince Vladimir Bright Sun.

The fourteenth-century Bran Castle in Romania, home of Vlad Tepes ("the Impaler") (Reuters/Radu Sigheti/Archive Photos)

During his reign, Vladimir Monomakh compiled the *Russkaia pravda,* the first code of law in Kievan society, which placed great importance on the matriarchal role.

> See also: Kiev; Vladimir I; Vladimir Bright Sun, Prince; Vladimir Monomakh

VLADIMIR BRIGHT SUN, PRINCE
Russia

A legendary figure created from two historical princes of Kiev, Vladimir I (c. 956–1015) and Vladimir Monomakh (1053–1125). According to the legends, the bogatyri, or Holy Russian knights, gathered at his court before setting off on their adventures in defense of their country.

> See also: Bogatyr'; Kiev; Vladimir I; Vladimir Monomakh

VLADIMIR MONOMACHUS
Russia

Latinized form of Vladimir Monomakh.

VLADIMIR MONOMAKH
Russia

The name by which Vladimir II, the founder of the Monomakhovichi dynasty and ruler of Russia from 1113 to 1125, was known.

> See also: Vladimir II

VLAS(II), SAINT
Russia

Saint created from the older pagan patron of cattle and merchants, Volos. In Russian religious iconography he was depicted as surrounded by cows, sheep, and goats.

> See also: Volos

VLASTA
Russia

The bravest of the polianitsy who lived in a castle on the banks of the river Vltava (a river of the Czech Republic, on whose banks the city of Prague is situated) and remained undefeated by all the bogatyri who challenged her. Thus she came to be regarded as the leader of the polianitsy, though in truth neither the polianitsy nor the bogatyri were ever organized in a fashion that required a leader.

> See also: Bogatyr'; Polianitsa

VLKODLAK
Slav
Also: Vookodlak

"Wolf hair," one of the many names applied to a werewolf.

VODIANIANI
Russia

One of the many variant names applied to the russalki, others being mavki, navki, and faraony.

> See also: Faraony; Mavki, Navki; Rus(s)alki (~ulki)
> References: Pomerantseva 1975

VODIANOI (~NIK)
Russia

The chief of the water demons (from *voda,* meaning "water") that inhabit any particular stretch of water, whether river or lake. He is usually portrayed as a fat, jolly man with a long beard and tangled green hair, although he could assume any shape, from a log to a beautiful maiden. His true form, however, was green-skinned, covered in weeds, slime, bumps, and hideous warts. He was believed to live in an underwater home with his wife and children and to have total control over the other water sprites and demons, such as the sad russalki, who lived in the same tract of water. Sometimes his babies would stray from home and be caught in fishermen's nets. If the fishermen gently returned them to the water, he would reward them with a good catch; but if they did not, he would vent his anger on them, tearing their nets and capsizing their boats.

Some legends said that the vodianoi tended a herd of his own cattle on dry land and would creep out at night to pasture them on the peasants' land. On these occasions he would be dressed as an ordinary peasant but was nonetheless instantly recognizable, for his clothes were always damp and he left a trail of wet footprints wherever he went.

Usually a jolly, benevolent being—his favorite sport being to ride on the backs of large fish—the vodianoi could also become angry, such as when humans tampered with his possessions or forgot to return his offspring to the water. Early legends said that a vodianoi would claim a life in compensation every time a new water mill was built, for the vodianoi tended to favor the still waters of the millpond. To safeguard the mill, the peasants would slaughter a chicken or a horse and throw it into the water. They also crossed themselves before swimming or stepping into the water to bathe, just in case the vodianoi was angry and tried to drown them. However, as the story of Kapsirko demonstrates, the vodianoi were not omniscient and might easily be tricked. And although the vodianoi were immortal, they aged like humans and were rejuvenated according to the phases of the moon.

See also: Kapsirko; Rus(s)alki (~ulki)

VOGULS
General
Ancient indigenous people from western Siberia closely related to the Ostyaks. As with many early peoples of Asiatic Russia, very little remains of the customs and beliefs of these people, as they have been almost totally assimilated by the invading and conquering Russians.

See also: Ostyaks; Siberia

VOLGA
Russia
The longest river in Europe, the Volga flows approximately 2,250 miles, or 3,600 kilometers. It rises in the Valdai plateau about 200 miles (320 kilometers) southeast of St. Petersburg, drains most of central and eastern Russia, and flows into the Caspian Sea 55 miles or 88 kilometers below Astrakhan'. It is 748 feet (228 meters) above sea level at its source, and 92 feet (28 meters) below sea level where it empties into the Caspian. In Russian legends the river is affectionately referred to as *matushka,* which translates as "dear mother."

See also: Astrakhan'; Caspian Sea; St. Petersburg

VOL'GA BUSLAVLEVICH
Russia
A mighty shape-changing warrior and bogatyr' who is the subject of a bylina. Born to unnamed parents, Vol'ga Buslavlevich was obviously destined to be a great warrior from an early age, for when he was just five it is said that even Mother Earth trembled when he walked and animals fled as he approached—though there is no evidence that he was a giant. For the next seven years Vol'ga Buslavlevich traveled throughout the known world and learned everything there was to learn about people—their history, their language, and everything else. Then he traveled to Kiev and gathered a group of twenty-nine other bogatyri around him, himself acting as their ataman, or chieftain.

Vol'ga Buslavlevich's first command to his men was to make nets of silk and set them in the forest, and then hunt through the forests and catch him martens, sables, foxes, hares, and any other creatures they might come across, driving the animals into the nets. His men obeyed his command; but no matter how hard they hunted, not one animal was driven into the nets. Then Vol'ga Buslavlevich himself went into the forest, turned himself into a lion, and drove just about every animal in the forest into the nets.

Back in Kiev, Vol'ga Buslavlevich commanded his men to make him more nets, and this time he told them to place the nets between the branches of tall trees, hunt for three days, and drive all the birds of the forest into the nets. His men again followed his commands to the letter; but no matter how hard they hunted, not one bird flew into the nets. Then Vol'ga Buslavlevich himself went into the forest, turned himself into the great naui bird, and drove all the flying animals of the forest into his nets.

Once more assembled in Kiev, Vol'ga Buslavlevich told his men to make him yet more nets of silk and to build him a great boat from which they were to fish for three days on the sea. After three days of intensive fishing, not one fish had been caught. Vol'ga Buslavlevich therefore turned himself into a great pike, and soon he had driven all the fish for miles around into the nets.

Knowing by these tests that his men would do exactly as he commanded, he told them that he had learned that the sultan of Turkey was planning to invade Russia and that he would travel there to discover the intentions of that ruler. Vol'ga Buslavlevich turned himself into a fast-flying bird, and quickly flew to the palace of the sultan. He landed on the windowsill of the throne room, whence he could hear the sultan speaking. The sultan was telling his prisoner, Queen Pantalovna, of his plans to invade Holy Russia. As Vol'ga Buslavlevich listened, he heard the sultan say that he intended to take nine cities for his nine sons and to bring back the finest sable coat in all Russia.

Queen Pantalovna replied that she had had a dream. In that dream a tiny white bird had met in aerial combat with a mighty black raven, the white bird triumphing and scattering the feathers of the raven to the four winds. She added that the white bird was none other than Vol'ga Buslavlevich, while the raven was the sultan of Turkey. The sultan was furious and struck the queen, whereupon Vol'ga Buslavlevich turned himself into a wolf and quickly ran to the royal stables, where he tore the throats of all the horses there. Then he turned himself into a weasel and ran through the palace, breaking bows and arrows, shattering swords and spears, and smashing steel maces. Then Vol'ga Buslavlevich resumed his form as a tiny white bird and flew quickly back to Kiev.

There he gathered together his bogatyri, and the thirty of them marched into the lands of the sultan of Turkey, killed the sultan and all his men, released Queen Pantalovna, and then divided the rich spoils equally among them.

This story should be compared with the story of Volkh Vseslav'evich, which apart from the numbers and the country involved, is similar.

See also: Bogatyr'; Bylina; Kiev; Mother Earth; Naui; Pantalovna, Queen; Volkh Vseslav'evich

VOL'GA SVIATOSLAVOVICH
Russia
Nephew and godson of Prince Vladimir Bright Sun, who had bestowed on him a domain that included three towns and their surrounding lands, and lordship over all the inhabitants of this domain. He is best known from a legend, possibly dating from as late as the fifteenth century, that describes him as setting out to collect taxes from his subjects, and being warned of robbers in the vicinity by the plowman Mikula Selyaninovich. The latter so impresses the prince with his strength and prowess that Vol'ga makes him lord of his domain, empowering him to collect taxes in Vol'ga's behalf.

See also: Mikula Selyaninovich; Vladimir Bright Sun, Prince

VOLGA VSESLAV'EVICH
Russia
See Volkh Vseslav'evich.

VOLGA YAROSLAVICH
Russia
One of three heroes with whom Il'ya Muromets was advised never to do battle, the other two being Sviatogor and Mikula Selyaninovich. Il'ya was given this advice by pilgrims who cured him of his disabilities. The pilgrims told him that although he might defeat Volga Yaroslavich in battle, the cunning of Volga would be sure to defeat him in time.

See also: Il'ya Muromets; Mikula Selyaninovich; Sviatogor

VOLKH VSESLAV'EVICH
Russia
Also: Volga Vseslav'evich.
One of the most ancient Russian heroes, a mighty wizard and hunter, the son of Tsar-

evna Marfa Vseslav'evna and a snake who impregnated his mother when she stepped on him. His birth was hailed as that of a great man, for the sky was lit up by the brightest moon ever seen, and a huge earthquake rocked the land and made all the animals of both land and sea seek a safe hiding place.

At the age of just one and a half hours, he spoke his first words, telling his mother not to swaddle him but rather to equip him with a suit of shining armor and a helmet of solid gold. He also told her to give him a heavy lead mace. By the age of ten, Volkh was fully educated and possessed many special skills, such as the ability to change his shape at will. At twelve he began to gather an army of youths, a task that took him three years. By the age of fifteen, he had assembled an army some seven thousand strong—all the same age as he.

A short time later, a rumor reached Kiev that the king of India was threatening to invade Russia. Immediately Volkh and his army set out for the far-off land. Each night as his troops slept, Volkh would change himself into a vicious wolf and hunt down the animals that were needed to feed his army. Some nights, wanting to give his men a change from red meat, Volkh would change himself into a falcon and harry swans, geese, and ducks.

As they neared the border of India, Volkh changed himself into a wild ox and bounded away from his army to survey the land ahead. When they crossed the border, Volkh changed himself into a falcon and flew straight to the palace of King Saltyk, whom he overheard talking to his wife, who was warning him of Volkh's approach. Knowing that his advance on India had been reported, Volkh changed himself into a stoat and ran all over the palace, seeking out the king's armaments. He gnawed through bow strings, removed the flints from firearms and buried them, and ruined as much as he could find. Then he changed himself back into a falcon and flew back to where his men were waiting.

Marching inexorably into the heart of India, they finally arrived at the walls of the capital city. There appeared to be no entry; but Volkh changed himself and his entire army into ants, and they crawled through tiny gaps until they were all inside the city. After changing his men back into their human form, he commanded them to slaughter everyone, save for seven thousand beautiful maidens—one for each of them. He himself went straight to the royal palace. There he forced his way into King Saltyk's chamber, swung him into the air, and smashed him onto the floor, shattering his bones.

Volkh then divided the spoils of battle among his men, who married the seven thousand maidens who had been spared; and Volkh and his men settled in that land, Volkh ruling wisely over them and taking the captive queen as his wife.

Some accounts of the story of Volkh say that Volkh first defeated the infidel forces as they sought to destroy the churches of Kiev and then went to India to take control of that country. His name is post-Christian, though it could also be pre-Christian, as *Volkh* means both "priest" and "sorcerer."

See also: India; Kiev; Marfa Vseslav'evna; Saltyk

VOLKHV
Russia
Best described as seers, the volkhvy (pl.) are generally believed to have been female shamans, or shamankas—female counterparts of the kolduny. The volkhvy would allow admittance of the opposite sex only through blood lineage, whereas the kolduny were reportedly more open about their practices and welcomed all who felt disposed to join their number. In later times the volkhvy and the kolduny were combined in an open society of male and female sorcerers known as znakhari.

See also: Koldun; Shaman; Shamanka; Znakhar'
References: Tokarev 1957

VOLOS

Slav

Also: Veles, Vyelyes

A god of war who may simply have been an aspect of Perun. The Russians considered him the provider of individual wealth (thus, he was the god of farm animals as well as of war) and an attendant of Perun's. With the advent of Christianity, Volos became a shepherd figure and was absorbed into the cult of Saint Vlasii (Saint Blaise). When disease attacked farm animals, a sheep, a cow, and a horse would be tied together by their tails and driven over a ravine and finished off with boulders. This sacrificial offering to Volos continued well into the Christian era, perpetuating remembrance of the pagan god.

> *See also:* Perun; Vlas(i)i, Saint
> *References:* Ivanov and Toporov 1974

VOLSHEBNYE SKAZKI

Russia

The largest subdivision of skazki. Literally translated as "wonder tales," these take place in fantasy lands which are inhabited by fabulous beings such as Baba-Yaga, Koshchei the Deathless, and Morozko the frost demon. The stories all follow the same basic plot. The hero of the story must find some way to enter the fantasy world, which may lie beyond the horizon, under the sea, or in the sky, and there overcome any number of obstacles until he wins the prize he seeks, such as the release of a beautiful maiden, the return of his mother or wife, or a fabulous, magical object like the Water of Life and Death. Like the skazki, they have no historical grounding and are pure make-believe—unlike the byliny, which have at least some historical background. Stories that deal with the underworld may appear to be skazki or volshebnye skazki, but they are in fact a specific grouping of bylichki that deal with the supernatural.

> *See also:* Baba-Yaga (-Jaga, -Iaga); Bylichka; Bylina; Koshchei (the Deathless); Morozko; Skazka; Underworld, The; Water of Life and Death, The

VORON VORONICH

Russia

Literally, "Raven Ravenson"—the young bird that in some versions of the legend of Ivan Vyslavovich is said to have been caught by the shape-changing wolf. The wolf threatened to tear Raven in half if the mother bird did not fetch him some of the Water of Life and Death.

> *See also:* Ivan Vyslavovich; Water of Life and Death, The

VORONEYUSHKA

Russia

"Little Raven," the wondrous horse of Dobrynya Nikitich.

VOTYAKS

General

Indigenous people from a region to the east of the Ural Mountains, related to the Permyaks and Zyrians, who have been almost totally assimilated by the Russians. Their Finno-Ugric languages are still used in a few isolated locales, but very little remains of their ancient traditions and beliefs.

> *See also:* Finno-Ugric; Permyaks; Ural Mountains; Zyrians

VSESLAV

Russia

A shamanic, shape-changing werewolf that appears in the twelfth-century *Lay of Igor's Campaign*. Vseslav was a historical eleventh-century prince of Polotsk (now in Belorussia). Sources suggest that he was born with a caul over his head and that his birth coincided with an eclipse of the sun. Legend has it that his mother was a princess who was raped by a snake, and that as Vseslav grew up he rapidly learned all the magic arts and became a most skillful hunter and warrior. As an adult he was never beaten in battle; but he enjoyed his greatest successes at night, when—so the legends would have us believe—he transformed himself into a wolf.

> *See also:* Belorussia; Shaman
> *References:* Mann 1979

VSESLAV'EVICH, VOLGA

Russia

See Volkh Vseslav'evich.

VSESLAV'EVNA, MARFA

Russia

See Marfa Vseslav'evna.

VU-KUTIS

Votyak

A water spirit whom the Votyak would propitiate in order to fight illness and disease.

VU-MURT

Votyak

"Man of Water"—the god of water, whether it be sea, lake, river, stream, or puddle.

VU-NUNA

Votyak

"Water Uncle," a protective water spirit who ensured that the yanki-murt left the Votyak people alone.

See also: Yanki-murt

VU-VOZO

Votyak

A malevolent water spirit who lived in the springs and wells from which the Votyaks drew their drinking water. The Votyaks, taking water from a new source or from a source that belonged to a neighboring community, would protect themselves from the vu-vozo by asking him to spare them and take a Cheremiss or Russian woman instead. The vu-vozo had a counterpart in the yanki-murt, from whom the Votyaks were protected by vu-nuna.

See also: Vu-nuna; Yanki-murt

VUK

Serbia and Bosnia

A historical fifteenth-century ruler who was known as Despot Vuk and who came to be equated with Zmag Ognjeni Vuk, a legendary werewolf.

See also: Werewolf; Zmag Ognjeni Vuk

VULTURES ARE LIKE PRIESTS, WHY

Armenia

A family of young vultures once asked their parents why they only ever had dead things to eat, whereas the children of eagles and hawks dined on live prey. The parents replied that it had been ordained by God that they should never kill anything. Thus, they were like priests, and not like princes, who preyed on the living.

One of the fables of Mekhithar Gosh.

See also: Mekhithar Gosh

VYELYES

Russia

Also: Veles

The Russian god of war, known elsewhere as Volos.

See also: Volos

VYSLAV ANDRONOVICH

Russia

The tsar of an unnamed realm, he had three sons—Dmitrii Vyslavovich, Vasilii Vyslavovich, and Ivan Vyslavovich (the second name, Vyslavovich, is a patronymic meaning "son of Vyslav"). The tsar coveted the Firebird and sent his three sons on a quest for it. Ivan Vyslavovich succeeded in snaring the creature and at the same time secured Elena the Beautiful and the Horse with the Golden Mane. However, Ivan's brothers killed him and claimed his trophies as their own. Ivan Vyslavovich was restored to life by a shape-changing wolf that had helped him by using the Water of Life and Death. When Vyslav Andronovich learned of the treachery of Dmitrii Vyslavovich and Vasilii Vyslavovich, he had them thrown into his deepest dungeon.

See also: Dmitrii (Vyslavovich); Elena the Beautiful; Firebird, The; Horse with the Golden Mane, The; Ivan Vyslavovich; Vasilii Vyslavovich; Water of Life and Death, The

VYSLAVOVICH, IVAN

Russia

See Ivan Vyslavovich.

W

WAIZGANTHOS
Prussia
Fertility deity and patron of crops who was propitiated in a ceremony where the tallest girl in a community would stand on one leg and toast the god with brandy, beseeching him to make the crops grow at least as tall as she was. She would drink the first cup of brandy and then pour a second on the ground for the god. If the girl remained steady throughout the ceremony, good crops would follow; but if she faltered and her raised foot touched the ground, even for the briefest moment, it was feared that the harvest would be doomed.

WALACHIA
Romania
An ancient region of southern Romania that stretches from the southernmost mountains to the Danube. The original inhabitants of Walachia gradually united and formed an independent state under a single ruler before the region was conquered by Ottoman Turks in 1476. Walachia was united with Moldavia in 1861 to form the modern country of Romania. Bucharest, the capital of Romania, is situated in Walachia.

See also: Danube; Moldavia; Romania

WALG(A)INO
Poland
The patron god of cattle.

WATER OF LIFE AND DEATH, THE
Russia
A magical water that was owned by the dragon that abducted Vasilissa of the Golden Braid. It was used by Ivan the Pea to restore his two brothers to life after he rescued his sister Vasilissa from the dragon. Ivan the Pea, keeping a promise, also gave some of the life-restoring water to an old crone who lived in a small wooden house on chicken's legs in a forest, for she had given him directions to the land of the dragon.

The Water of Life and Death also makes an appearance in the story of Ivan Vyslavovich. Here it was used by a shape-changing wolf to restore Ivan to life after he had been ambushed and killed by his brothers, Dmitrii and Vasilii Vyslavovich, who were jealous because Ivan had not only obtained the Firebird but also had managed to secure the Horse with the Golden Mane and the maiden Elena the Beautiful.

See also: Dmitrii (Vyslavovich); Dragon; Elena the Beautiful; Firebird, The; Horse with the Golden Mane, The; Ivan the Pea; Ivan Vyslavovich; Vasilii Vyslavovich; Vasilis(s)a of the Golden Braid

WEAVER OF THE STARS
Latvia
The wife of Meness the moon god.

See also: Meness (~ulis); Moon

WENCESLAS, SAINT
Czech
The patron saint of the Czech Republic, whose feast day is 28 September. He is best known from the famous Christmas carol by J. M. Neale, a reworking of the medieval carol *Tempus adest floridum*. Wenceslas was the son of Duke Wratislaw of Bohemia, but his upbringing was handled in the main by his grandmother Ludmilla. In c. 920 Wratislaw died during a battle against the

Heinrich Parler, Scenes from the Life of St. Wenceslas, *1353, Cathedral of Saint Vitus, Prague, Czech Republic (Erich Lessing/Art Resource, NY)*

Magyars, and Wenceslas's mother Drahomira seized power. She had Ludmilla murdered and adopted the role of regent, establishing an anti-Christian government. Her reign ended in a popular revolt c. 922, and Wenceslas then succeeded to the duchy.

Wenceslas proved a fair, if somewhat strict ruler. He quickly re-Christianized the court and the people. He invited German missionaries into the country and accepted the overlordship of Henry the Fowler, King of Germany, whom he recognized as the successor to Charlemagne. The political and religious reforms inaugurated by Wenceslas provoked a strong reaction. Wenceslas's own brother Boleslav, whose dissatisfaction at his birthright grew into open revolt after the birth of Wenceslas's son and heir, was among the pagan traditionalists who rebelled.

Wenceslas was murdered by Boleslav and his followers on 20 September 929. He was immediately venerated as a martyr. Boleslav had his relics transferred to the Church of St. Vitus in Prague, which soon became a popular place of pilgrimage; and Wenceslas was quickly elevated to the position of patron saint of Bohemia.

See also: Bohemia; Czechs; Magyars

WENDS

General

An ancient Slavic people who were called Wends by the Germans in medieval times, when they occupied the territory that roughly lay between the Elbe and Saale Rivers on the west and the Oder on the east. From about the sixth century onward, German rulers waged war against the powerful Wends, conquering and converting them to Christianity in the twelfth century. Their descendants, today known as Sorbs (sometimes confusingly spelled Serbs), still inhabit the region of Lusatia in southwestern Poland and eastern Germany (which includes the cities of Cottbus and Bautzen), and still speak a West Slavic language similar to Polish and Czech.

WEREWOLF
General
Also: Vlkodlak; Vookodlak

The legends that surround a person who metamorphoses into a wolf at night but reverts to human form by day may have come from the Berserkirs, the warriors dedicated to Odínn, who wore bear- or wolf-skin shirts into battle and who drove themselves into a martial frenzy. The English name, however, comes from the Saxon *wer* (man) and *wulf* (wolf). Werewolves were born to human mothers, were particularly hairy at birth, and might have extra folds of skin on their heads or even a wolf's claws and fangs, with which they bit and scratched their mothers as they

Scene from The Wolfman *(The Museum of Modern Art Film Stills Archive)*

suckled. Often as not, they were twins. Although some werewolves were thought to have the ability to change their form at will, others changed involuntarily under the influence of the full moon. This latter form of metamorphosis has become the most popular in modern tales of werewolves. Some werewolves were thought to be invulnerable to mortal weapons, though most could be wounded with silver weapons—originally arrows, but later bullets—and others could be hurt as could any mortal human being. Wounded werewolves resumed their human form before they died. Common superstition still holds that when a werewolf dies it becomes a vampire, although the soul of the werewolf would be reborn to another human mother and thereby perpetuate the survival of this supernatural race.

The belief in werewolves dates back at least three millennia but had its heyday in late medieval and renaissance Europe. During these times, werewolves received as much attention as did the other emissaries of the Devil—demons and witches. Any signs of lycanthropy, with a recognized series of symptoms, were met with the severest punishment. No woman could ever be persecuted for being a werewolf, as all werewolves were male; but women had to contend with witch-hunts, which were common at that time. Characteristics of the werewolf included an excessive hairiness; a port wine–colored birthmark known as the "mark of Cain"; short, stubby fingers with sharp nails; excessive and often threatening sexuality; and in the most extreme cases, cannibalism. No factually substantiated record of a werewolf exists; but from the first quarter of the sixteenth century to the first quarter of the seventeenth century, more than 30,000 suspected werewolves were put to death in France.

See also: Devil, The; Vampire

WHIRLWIND
Russia

The personification of a whirlwind, sometimes referred to as Vikhor'. In one story he abducts

Nastas'ya of the Golden Braid, the wife of Bel Belyanin and mother of Peter Belyaninovich, Vasilii Belyaninovich, and Ivan Belyaninovich, and keeps her in a wondrous palace encrusted with diamonds and other precious stones on a plateau atop a high mountain range. There he also holds three maidens captive as the tsaritsas of his three kingdoms—the Copper Kingdom, the Silver Kingdom, and the Golden Kingdom, the tsaritsa of the latter being Elena the Fair. Each of the four palaces in Whirlwind's realm was guarded by a multi-headed dragon that could only be placated with water drawn from a well nearby.

Whirlwind renewed his strength periodically from a barrel that contained a magical water that bestowed great strength on anyone who drank it. He also kept a second barrel, which contained a water that sapped the drinker's strength. These two barrels ultimately were his downfall.

Ivan and his two brothers set off to search for their lost mother. Ivan finally found her, after climbing the tall mountains and passing through the three kingdoms. Nastas'ya of the Golden Braid told Ivan of Whirlwind's secret, and by drinking of the strength-increasing water and then swapping that with the strength-sapping one, Ivan was able to defeat Whirlwind, cutting off his head with a single blow, burning his body, and scattering the ashes in the wind.

Whirlwind had two servants, Lame and One-Eye, who could work wondrous magic. After Whirlwind's death, these two served Ivan.

See also: Bel Belyanin; Copper Kingdom, The; Dragon; Elena the Fair; Golden Kingdom, The; Ivan Belyaninovich; Lame; Nastas'ya of the Golden Braid; One-Eye; Peter (Belyaninovich); Silver Kingdom, The; Vasilii Belyaninovich; Vikhor'

WHITE GOD
Slav

Known as Belobog or Belun in Russia, the White God is the personification of goodness, light, and life. He is opposed by Chernobog, the Black God, the personification of evil and the cause of all misfortune. White God is the literal translation of the root words of the name *Belobog, belyi* (white) and *bog* (god).

See also: Belobog; Belun; Black God; Chernobog

WHITE RUSSIA
General

Literal English translation of *Belorussia* (Belarus', in the indigenous language), formerly a constituent republic of the Soviet Union and today an independent state.

See also: Belorussia

WHITE SEA
General

(*Russ.* Beloe More) An arm of the Arctic Ocean that reaches into northwestern Russia, the White Sea is icebound from September until June. The port city of Arkhangel'sk is located on its shore.

See also: Arkhangel'sk

WHITE YOUTH
Finno-Ugric—Yakut

The father of mankind, known as the White Youth, who was nourished by the spirit of the World Tree. Possible parallels to White Youth are the Russian Belobog and the Norse Heimdallr.

See also: Belobog; World Tree

WIND
General

In many Russian folktales the wind is referred to simply as that, and has no name. Earlier stories named the god of the wind Stribog. In one such story (see Morozko), the wind appears as a nameless man with tousled hair, a swollen face and lips, and wearing disheveled clothing. He can be either benevolent or malevolent and is said to give rise to demons whenever he blows hard. The following Russian legend, "In Favor of the Wind," aptly demonstrates the benevolent aspect of the Wind:

A peasant was walking along a country lane one day when he was met by Sun, Frost, and Wind. The peasant said "good morning" and continued on his way, though that innocuous remark almost caused the three elements to come to blows, as they could not decide which of them the peasant had been addressing. Before resorting to physical force, the three decided to ask the peasant, and they hurried to catch up to him.

When the peasant replied that he had been greeting Wind, Sun became furious and threatened to burn up the peasant, but Wind said that his breezes would keep the peasant cool.

Then Frost vented his anger and threatened to freeze the peasant; but Wind told him that he could do no harm if there was no breeze, thus proving that the peasant had been right in giving Wind precedence over Sun and Frost.

Later legends name not merely one god of the wind but three: the gods of the North, East, and West winds. Of these winds, which lived on the oceanic island of Buyan, only the West wind is given a name—Dogoda.

The Czechs also had more than one god of the wind, but their god of the storm wind was potentially the most dangerous. An attendant on the thunder god Perun, he was named Varpulis.

See also: Buyan; Czechs; Dogoda; Frost; Morozko; Perun; Stribog; Sun; Varpulis

WORLD TREE
Slav

Also known as the Tree of Life. Common to many mythologies and religions is the concept of a World Tree whose roots reach down to the underworld and whose branches reach up to heaven. It was generally believed that this tree grew in the exact center of the world. Later traditions tended to treat the World Tree with contempt. In Siberia, however, the legends of the tree retained their importance for a much longer time, for it was this tree that aspiring shamans climbed in order to gain their magical powers.

One post-Christian story illustrates the manner in which the World Tree was treated

long after the disappearance of paganism. This story tells of a peasant couple who were so poor that they were reduced to living off acorns from the forest. One of the acorns they had gathered rolled out into their cellar, where it began to grow. When the sapling reached the floor of their home, they simply cut a hole for it to grow through. They did the same when it reached the roof. Now they had a tree growing straight through their home.

Finally the time came when they could find no more acorns in the forest, so the man climbed the tree to gather acorns from it instead. Among its uppermost branches he found a magnificent cockerel and a handmill. Quickly he seized both and climbed back down to his wife. Wondering what they would have to eat that day, the old woman turned the handle on the mill. To the couple's delight, pies and pancakes began to tumble from the mill. From that day forth they no longer felt the pangs of hunger.

Some time later a wealthy merchant was passing through the forest and stopped at their house, where he was hospitably welcomed and fed from the mill. Seeing the mill, the merchant offered a high price for it, but the couple would not sell it. The merchant stole the mill and quickly made his way home. Knowing that they could not go after the merchant, for no one would believe their word against his, the couple sent the cockerel out after the mill. The bird flew off to the home of the merchant, perched on his gate, and began to crow, saying that the merchant should return the mill. Hearing this, the man ordered his servants to throw the cockerel into the well. There the cockerel simply drained the water and flew onto the man's balcony, where it repeated its demands. This time the man had his cook throw the cockerel into the stove. In the midst of the flames, the cockerel spat out all the water from the well and flew right into the heart of the man's house. As the man ran away, the cockerel seized the mill and flew back to the old couple in the woods.

See also: Shaman; Siberia; Tree of Life, The; Underworld, The

Pacino da Bonaguida, Tree of the Cross, *fourteenth century, Accademia, Florence, Italy (Alinari/Art Resource, NY)*

Y

world of mortal men. Its entrances were located where rivers flowed into the frozen wastes of the Arctic Ocean. Some stories describe Yambe-akka as supporting the world on her upturned hands, explaining that earthquakes are tremors in her hands, caused by the continual strain.

See also: Underworld, The

YAKUTS

General

Ancient Siberian people who speak a Turkic language (in the Uralic-Altaic linguistic family) and who live near the Lena River in northeastern Siberia—one of the coldest regions on earth—where they constitute the majority of the population of the Yakut autonomous region. Although many were converted to Christianity after their subjection by the Russians in the beginning of the eighteenth century, shamanist traditions still color their religious life, particularly in the north. The Yakuts have not decreased in number as have other Siberian peoples; on the contrary, they have increased considerably. Their economy is a mixture of the traditional and the modern. Some still pursue a nomadic life of hunting, trapping, and fishing. Others, under Russian influence, have adopted modern methods of agriculture and have collectivized activities such as cattle raising. Fishing also has been commercialized to some extent. Today there is an institute in Yakutsk, the coldest point of the Arctic, for studying the permafrost.

See also: Finno-Ugric; Lena, River; Shaman; Siberia

YAMBE-AKKA

Lapp

"Old woman of the dead," goddess of the underworld, whose realm was described as a vast ice kingdom situated beneath the

YANKI-MURT

Votyak

The counterpart of the vu-vozo, and from whom the Votyaks were protected by vu-nuna.

See also: Votyaks; Vu-nuna; Vu-vozo

YARILO

Slav

Also: Erilo

A goddess of peace who later became the god of spring, fertility, and erotic or sexual love. The name is derived from *yary* (passionate). Depicted as a handsome, barefoot youth dressed in a white cloak and adorned with a crown of wildflowers, Yarilo rode on a white horse, his left hand holding a bucket of wheat seed, the duality of his role as god of sex and spring being visible in the eagerness of the earth to receive his seed in springtime. Ceremonies honoring Yarilo were commonplace as recently as the eighteenth century. These included a springtime planting rite, during which a beautiful young girl was crowned with flowers as Yarilo's queen, and an autumn ritual burning of his effigy after the harvest—accompanied by an orgy of eating, drinking, and lovemaking—after which the ashes of the effigy were scattered on the fields to ensure a good crop the following year.

YAROSLAVICH, VOLGA

Russia

See Volga Yaroslavich.

YAROVIT

Baltic Coast

A deity with attributes similar to those of
Svantovit; possibly, simply an aspect of that
deity. His legendary existence is known only
through the writings of the Danish chronicler Saxo Grammaticus.

> *See also:* Saxo Grammaticus; Svantovit
> (~dovit)

YRYN-AL-TOJON

Siberia—Yakut

The "white creator Lord," the supreme being
of the Yakut people. He lives in, or above, the
Tree of Life, the cosmic pillar in whose roots
the mother goddess Ajysyt lives and whence
she rises to suckle those in need of nourish-
ment and sustenance.

> *See also:* Ajysyt; Tree of Life, The

Z

ZABAVA (PUTYATICHNA), PRINCESS

Russia

The favorite niece of Prince Vladimir Bright Sun. Princess Zabava was abducted from the gardens of the royal court at Kiev by a twelve-headed she-dragon and carried away in the dragon's jaws to a lair in the Sorochinsk Mountains. She was later rescued by Dobrynya Nikitich, who killed the dragon after an epic, three-day battle.

See also: Dobrynya Nikitich; Dragon; Kiev; Sorochinsk Mountains; Vladimir Bright Sun, Prince

ZALTYS

Lithuania

The grass snake, believed to be lucky. Aitvaras was sometimes depicted as having the head of a grass snake.

See also: Aitvaras

ZALYOSHEN

Russia

A family whose men took and passed the tests set by Vasilii Buslayevich when he was seeking twenty-nine members for his new *druzhina*. Others who passed the tests included Kostia Novotorzheni, Luka, Moisei, and the seven Sbrodovich brothers.

See also: Kostia Novotorzheni; Luka; Moisei; Sbrodovich; Vasilii Buslayevich

ZAMORYSHCHEK

Russia

The youngest of the forty sons of an aged peasant couple. He and his brothers were miraculously born from eggs. Under the parentage of the old couple, they grew up to be strong young men who labored effortlessly in the fields. For several weeks the forty brothers noticed that some of the hay they had baled was being stolen. For thirty-nine days the brothers sat and watched the hay; but each time, the guard fell asleep and the hay was stolen. However, when Zamoryshchek's turn came, he stayed awake and caught the mare who was stealing the hay.

As soon as the mare was caught and the thirty-nine other brothers came back to the field, the mare changed into Baba-Yaga. The witch gave each of the thirty-nine brothers a mare to ride and then returned to her equine form so that Zamoryshchek could ride her. The forty brothers rode out to search for suitable wives. Before long, they were offered the forty daughters of a witch. The mare resumed her guise as Baba-Yaga and warned the brothers that the forty daughters of the witch intended to kill them; so the brothers killed their new wives on their wedding night and then set out to find true wives, finally marrying the forty daughters of a tsar.

Though two witches appear in this legend, it is generally agreed that both witches are Baba-Yaga, the mare being her benevolent aspect as the horse goddess, and the witch with forty daughters being her malevolent aspect as the goddess of death.

See also: Baba-Yaga (-Jaga, -Iaga)
References: Afanas'ev 1957

ZANGI

Armenia

"Blackie," one of two lions given to Suren as cubs that grew to full maturity within fifteen days. The other was Zarangi. For the story of Zangi and Zarangi see the entry for Suren.

See also: Suren; Zarangi

ZARANGI
Armenia
"Goldie," one of the two lions given to Suren, the other being Zangi.
> *See also:* Suren; Zangi

ZARZAND
Armenia
"Terror," a king whose daughter Simizar was abducted by a Tapagöz who locked her away in his lair, the Devil's Castle. She had been placed under a spell by the giant's mother, who kept her imprisoned in a cave except for a short period every midnight, when she could wander outside. It was on one such occasion that she encountered Zurab, who eventually set her free and restored her to her father, and having married Simizar, became the heir to the kingdom of Zarzand. For the full story see the entry for Zurab.
> *See also:* Devil's Castle; Simizar; Tapagöz; Zurab

ZELENIE SVIATKI
Russia
Trinity Week, the Christianized festival that displaced—albeit gradually and incompletely—the pagan Rusaliia.
> *See also:* Rusaliia

ZEMEPATIS
Lithuania
Also: Zemininkas
The brother of Zemyna, Zemepatis is the god of the homestead, sometimes being called Dimstipatis, this latter name being derived from *dimstis* (home) and *patis* (father). His Latvian equivalent is Majas Kungs.
> *See also:* Dimstipatis; Majas Kungs; Zemyna

ZEMES MÀTE
Latvia—Lett
The name given to Mother Earth by the Lett people of Latvia. The Lithuanian equivalent to Zemes Màte is Zemyna.
> *See also:* Letts; Mother Earth; Zemyna

ZEMININKAS
Lithuania
Alternative name for Zemepatis.

ZEMYNA
Lithuania
The Lithuanian name for Mother Earth. Sometimes referred to as the sister of Zemepatis, god of the home, Zemyna is also known as "Mother of the Fields," "Mother of Springs," "Mother of Forests," "Blossomer," and "Bud Raiser."
> *See also:* Mother Earth; Zemepatis

ZHIROVITSKOI
Russia
An icon of the Virgin Mary that was discovered in a pagan sacred tree by a shepherd in 1191. It was one of many religious icons that were "miraculously" discovered in natural settings. Modern thinking attributes the appearance of these holy relics to the early clergy who recognized the importance of associating the Virgin Mary with the nature goddesses that pervaded pagan religious belief. They would have reasoned that icons found near pagan holy trees and water would be more readily accepted and revered by those least likely to convert to Christianity. All available evidence suggests that the ruse was successful.
> *References:* Matorin 1931

ZHIVA
Russia
Goddess of fertility and of the dead whose name comes from *zhit'* (to live), she was worshiped principally in the region surrounding the Elbe. Mentioned in the twelfth century by the Saxon priest Helmhold, worship of Zhiva appears to have involved an entire community and to have taken place deep in a forest, near a sacred spring, river, or lake. Friday was sacred to the goddess, although this day later became dedicated to the worship of Paraskeva.
> *See also:* Paraskeva, Saint
> *References:* Afanas'ev 1865–69; Ivanov and Toporov 1965

ZINOVIEV, LUKA

Russia

See Luka Zinoviev.

ZIZILIA

Poland

One of a pair of fertility deities, the other being Didilia. The twin mothers of divine twins, Didilia and Zizilia were venerated as goddesses of love both erotic and maternal.

> *See also:* Didilia
> *References:* Afanas'ev 1865–69; Znayenko 1980

ZLATOROG

Slovenia

A white chamois with golden horns that lived on the slopes of Mount Triglav in northeastern Slovenia. Once Zlatorog was pursued by hunters, who were after the animal's golden horns. Zlatorog outwitted the hunters by leading them to the edge of a precipice over which all but one of the hunters fell. This survivor managed to wound Zlatorog, but from this wound sprang a red flower that Zlatorog ate and that immediately cured the wound. Some accounts say that this flower was a red carnation, the emblem of Slovenia.

> *See also:* Slovenia; Triglav, Mount

ZMAG OGNJENI VUK

Serbia and Bosnia

"Fiery Dragon Wolf," a legendary werewolf who in later songs became equated with a fifteenth-century ruler known as Despot Vuk. In these songs, Despot Vuk is depicted as having been born with a birthmark (either in the shape of a saber, or colored blood red and on his fighting arm), tufted with wolf hair, and able to breathe fire. Growing up at amazing speed and quickly becoming a formidable warrior, Despot Vuk is the only person in the kingdom who can defeat the fiery dragon that might have fathered him, his success being attributed solely to his ability to change into Zmag Ognjeni Vuk at will.

> *See also:* Vuk; Werewolf

ZNAKHAR'

Russia

Znakhari (pl.) were sorcerers similar to the earlier kolduny and volkhvy, and considered direct successors to the early Slavic shamans.

> *See also:* Koldun; Shaman; Volkhv
> *References:* Tokarev 1957

ZORYA UTRENNYAYA

Slav

One of two—or in some accounts, three—daughters of Dazhbog, she is goddess of dawn, wife of Perun, and sister to Zorya Vechernyaya. Zorya Utrennyaya (*utro* means "morning") opens the gates to her father's palace so that he can ride forth at the start of the sun's journey. Her sister, the goddess of dusk, closes them again after Dazhbog has returned home. There is sometimes a third sister, the goddess of midnight, who oversees the darkness of the night, but she remains nameless. As the wife of Perun, Zorya Utrennyaya accompanies her husband when he rides out to do battle, and amid the fray lets down her veil to protect those warriors she favors and save them from death. The two, or three, sisters are collectively known as the Zoryi, and are sisters to Dazhbog's other daughters, Zvezda Dennitsa and Zvezda Vechernyaya, who in turn are collectively known as the Zvezdy. Eventually Zorya Utrennyaya eclipsed her sisters, and *zorya*, which originally meant "light," came to mean "dawn."

> *See also:* Dawn; Dazhbog; Dusk; Great Bear; Little Bear; Midnight; Perun; Sun; Ursa Major; Ursa Minor; Zorya Vechernyaya; Zvezda Dennitsa; Zvezda Vechernyaya

ZORYA VECHERNYAYA

Slav

One of the two, sometimes three, daughters of Dazhbog. The goddess of dusk and sister to Zorya Utrennyaya, Zorya Vechernyaya (*vecher* means "evening") closes the gates to her father's palace after he returns home at the end of the day. There is sometimes a third sister, the goddess of midnight, but she remains nameless. The two, or three, sisters are collectively known simply as the Zoryi and are sisters to Dazhbog's other daughters, Zvezda Dennitsa and Zvezda Vechernyaya, who in turn are known collectively as the Zvezdy.

See also: Dazhbog; Midnight; Zorya Utrennyaya; Zvezda Dennitsa; Zvezda Vechernyaya

ZORYI

Slav

Also: Zaryi

Collective name describing the two daughters of Dazhbog—Zorya Utrennyaya, the goddess of dawn, and Zorya Vechernyaya, the goddess of dusk. Some accounts describe three daughters; but the third, the goddess of midnight, remains nameless. Although each Zorya has a specific task to carry out in her father's palace, the three share the responsibility of guarding an unnamed deity who is chained to the constellation Ursa Major (the Great Bear); for if he breaks loose, the world will come to an end. Some accounts say that the Zoryi watch over the constellation in case the bear, or hound, imprisoned within breaks free; and some identify the constellation as Ursa Minor (the Little Bear). The Zoryi are sisters of the Zvezdy (Zvezda Dennitsa and Zvezda Vechernyaya).

See also: Dawn; Dazhbog; Dusk; Great Bear; Little Bear; Midnight; Ursa Major; Ursa Minor; Zorya Utrennyaya; Zorya Vechernyaya

ZOSIM

Slav

The god of bees, named for the sound they make. Zosim was also the god of mead, a drink made from fermented honey, and the source of the ribald songs that those who drank his potent brew often sang.

ZROYA

Slav

The virgin goddess of war, closely associated with Perun in his various incarnations.

See also: Perun

ZURAB

Armenia

The son of a poor peasant couple, Zurab lost his father when he was just four years old, his father having been crushed by a heavily laden cart. Just five years later, when he was nine, Zurab's mother died of a plague that swept through their village, and he was thenceforth known as the Orphan Zurab. His neighbor, a well-to-do farmer, took the lad in, thereby gaining a pair of able hands as well as the right to annex the meager land that Zurab had inherited from his mother and father.

The farmer took to calling the young boy Zuro and put him in charge of the sheep and cattle. Zuro led the animals to pasture every morning and brought them back again every evening. At the age of twelve, Zuro also was put in charge of the young lambs, for he had constantly proved his worth in fights with the older children of the village. Though he was small for his age, Zuro already had the strength of any grown man. His strength was put to the test one day when a wolf sneaked in among the lambs he was tending, snatched one, and made off with it. The other shepherds in the fields saw what had happened and blocked the wolf so that it had to turn around and run back toward Zuro. Zuro stood his ground; and when the wolf came within reach, he darted forward and snapped the wolf's neck as if it were a piece of dried kindling.

All the other shepherds witnessed the event and shouted their approval. One suggested that from that day forth he should be known as Zuro the Wolf-Strangler, but another shouted that he should be called Aslan, the Lion—and from that day forth Zurab, who had already become known as Zuro, was known as the Orphan Aslan.

When Aslan reached the age of twenty-one, he was put in charge of all the farmer's livestock, and in the summer evenings he took to herding the sheep into a cave and sleeping across the entrance, his water jug and satchel of rations, *baghadj* (unleavened bread) and eggs, hanging above his head. On more than one occasion he noticed that some of his rations were missing, and so one night he kept watch instead of sleeping, his *kulab* (shepherd's cloak) pulled over his head to shield his open eyes. In the middle of the night, as Aslan was fighting to stay awake, a radiant maiden approached the cave, took down Aslan's satchel, ate half his rations, and drank half his water.

As she turned to leave, Aslan caught hold of her and demanded to know who she was. She pleaded to be released, but Aslan was smitten; and rather than let her go, he pleaded with her to remain with him and become his wife. The maiden told him that she would bring Aslan nothing but bad luck; but Aslan was resolute. Seeing that his mind was made up, the maiden told him that she was the daughter of King Zarzand, who for the past four or five years had been embroiled in a bitter war with seven kings who had formed an alliance against him. Her father had ridden off to war, leaving the maiden and her two brothers behind.

All would have been well had not the terrible giant, the three-headed demon Tapagöz, arrived with his six brothers, attacked the palace, and carried her off. Her two brothers had raised an army and hurried in pursuit. For ten days the two sides fought, and by the eleventh day four of the demons and the maiden's eldest brother had been killed. On the thirteenth day another demon and the maiden's younger brother had been killed. Now leaderless, the army had scattered and returned to their homes.

Tapagöz, who was the oldest of the demons, carried the maiden to his lair, the Devil's Castle, and there, for forty days and forty nights, besought her to become his wife. She refused, whereupon Tapagöz went mad for three days, calling her name, Simizar, endlessly, and then had the maiden handed over to his mother, a witch, who had imprisoned her in the cave, allowing her to wander forth only at midnight. Thus the maiden was condemned to live until one who truly loved

her found the swallows that knew how she might be freed.

There and then Aslan promised Simizar that he would seek out the swallows and return for her. The next morning, he drove the sheep back down to the village, asked for the money due him, and set out. Before long he came to the intersection of three roads. Unsure which road to take, he prayed to God and then threw his staff in the air. When the staff landed, Aslan picked it up and followed the road it had lain across. All day he walked, until just as the sun was about to dip beyond the horizon, he came to a village, and there he saw some swallows nesting above the door of a cottage.

The cottage belonged to an old woman who was only too glad to receive Aslan as her guest. She fed him bread and whatever else came to hand; and after he had eaten, she prepared him a bed. All night Aslan lay awake thinking about Simizar and wondering whether the swallows he had seen would indeed provide him the information he required. As day broke, Aslan climbed a ladder to where the swallows had their nest, praying to God for the ability to understand their language. God answered his prayer in an instant, and soon Aslan understood exactly what he had to do.

Following the guidance of the swallows, Aslan descended the ladder and went to the old woman who had provided him with food and lodging. Aslan kissed the woman's hand three times and thanked her three times, just as the swallows had said, and the old woman embraced him. She gave Aslan fourteen hazelnuts, two walnuts, a small bottle of water, a small quantity of flour in a cloth, and explicit instructions on how it should all be used.

Aslan profusely thanked the old woman and departed. A short distance from the village, he sat down and ate one of the hazelnuts. Instantly all thoughts and pangs of hunger left him. Aslan cracked open one of the two walnuts, and before him stood a magnificent horse of fire and air, with wings that were invisible to mere mortal eyes. Aslan then cracked open the second walnut, and from it came a steel-tipped spear, a sword sharp enough to cut through wrought iron, a shield under which a man could shelter in safety, and the finest clothes in all the world.

Aslan dressed himself in the clothes, picked up the weapons, and mounted the horse, and for seven days he rode like the wind until he came to the Devil's Castle. There, following the instructions he had been given, Aslan sprinkled water from the bottle over the sleeping form of the ogre's mother, climbed down the well in which Tapagöz slept, took a green wand from the water, climbed back up the well, and leaped onto the back of Tipi, the name he had given his horse. Aslan spurred his horse on and rode toward the cave and his beloved Simizar.

For three days he rode, as fast as the wind, and on the fourth he looked back and saw a huge dust cloud following him, being thrown up by Tapagöz and his mother in hot pursuit. As Aslan spurred on his horse, Tipi spoke to him for the first time and told him to throw the flour he had been given into the air. Aslan did as he was told, and as the flour settled on the ground, a great forest sprang up—a forest so thick that Tapagöz and his mother quickly became entangled in its undergrowth.

For two more days Aslan and Tipi rode on. On the third day Aslan turned around in alarm as he heard the approach of Tapagöz and his mother. Tipi told them that they must stand their ground and fight, so Aslan prepared himself to do battle.

Tapagöz was the first of the giants to reach Aslan. His first punch, which would have smashed Aslan to a million pieces, missed when Aslan neatly stepped to one side, the force of the blow causing Tapagöz to stumble and fall. Aslan seized this chance to cut off one of the giant's three heads. Again the giant came at him, and again his blow missed its

mark, giving Aslan the chance to almost completely sever a second head, which then lay useless against the ogre's chest. Tapagöz realized he was losing the battle, so he raised himself to his full height, and heaving a huge boulder over his head, he launched it at Aslan, who simply parried it with his shield and then lunged at the giant with his spear. The steel point found its mark, penetrating Tapagöz's head through its single eye and appearing again on the opposite side of his skull.

With Tapagöz dead, Aslan turned to face his mother, but she was nowhere to be seen. Instead there was a huge lake where none had been before. Tipi told Aslan that the lake had been formed from the ogress's spittle and that she herself was now a duck swimming on its surface. Tipi then told Aslan to pluck three hairs from his mane and throw them on the lake. Aslan did so, and instantly a bridge appeared, over which Aslan safely rode.

Two days later Aslan reached the cave in which Simizar was imprisoned, and tapping the wand three times on the rock, he released his beloved. Together they rode to the village of the old woman who had given Aslan the help he needed to accomplish his mission, and they invited her to accompany them as their mother. She was delighted, and after she gathered together her meager possessions, she took a small carriage from beneath her dress and blew it up. Aslan and Simizar rode Tipi toward the kingdom of King Zarzand, the old woman following in her carriage a short distance behind, some invisible force carrying it along.

After many days' travel the three came to the border of Zarzand's kingdom, where they encountered an army that barred their way. Aslan was all for fighting, but neither Simizar nor the old woman thought it a good idea, Simizar for fear that Aslan would receive a mortal blow, and the old woman, because she knew it was unnecessary. She took her shawl from around her neck and spread it on the ground. Then she and Simizar sat on it and it rose into the air, and Tipi unfurled his wings, and he too rose into the sky with Aslan on his back.

As the travelers reached the edges of Zarzand's capital city, they landed, and on the advice of the old woman, they waited outside the city walls while she went to gain approval for the marriage of Simizar and Aslan. At first neither the king nor queen would believe that their daughter was still alive; but at length, having been shown a talisman Simizar had given the old woman, Zarzand and his wife came to the city gates and greeted their daughter and her betrothed.

Several days later, following the wedding feast, Simizar and Aslan retired to their quarters while the old woman, aware that they were in danger, stationed herself outside their door with a three-pronged spear in her hand. Just as she had expected, on the stroke of midnight, a huge snake slithered into view. The old woman sprang to her feet and thrust the spear through the snake's head. The beast was killed and instantly transformed itself back into the mother of Tapagöz, one of each of the three prongs of the spear through each eye of the ogress's three heads.

King Zarzand was so delighted by the marriage his daughter had made that he immediately abdicated, and so began the reign of King Orphan Aslan.

See also: Aslan; Devil's Castle; Simizar; Tapagöz; Zarzand

References: Orbeli and Taronian 1959–67, vol. 4

ZURO
Armenia
See Zurab.

ZUTTIBUR
Slav
An obscure deity of the forests who is thought to be a spirit of the same type as the leshii, though obviously of far less potency and lesser importance.

See also: Leshii (~y)

ZVEZDA DENNITSA
Slav
The Morning Star, sister to Zvezda Vechernyaya and the two, or three, Zoryi—all four, or five, being the daughters of Dazhbog. She and her sister Zvezda Vechernyaya (the Evening Star) are both described as having married Mesyats (the moon) and having given birth to the stars by him. The specific task of Zvezda Dennitsa and her sister was to groom the horses that daily pulled their father's chariot across the sky.

See also: Dazhbog; Evening Star; Mesyats; Moon; Morning Star; Zoryi; Zvezda Vechernyaya

ZVEZDA VECHERNYAYA
Slav
The Evening Star, daughter of Dazhbog, and sister to Zvezda Dennitsa as well as the two, sometimes three, Zoryi. She is said to have married Mesyats (the moon) and to have been the mother of the stars by him, but her sister Zvezda Dennitsa is also said to have done this. Zvezda Vechernyaya and Zvezda Dennitsa had the specific job of grooming their father's white horses. In some cases Zvezda Vechernyaya is referred to as Vechernyaya Zvezda.

See also: Dazhbog; Evening Star; Mesyats; Moon; Zoryi; Zvezda Dennitsa

ZYRIANS
General
Indigenous people from a region to the east of the Ural Mountains, related to the Permyaks and Votyaks, who have been almost totally assimilated by the Russians. Their native Finno-Ugric languages are still in use today in a few isolated locales, but virtually nothing remains of their ancient traditions and beliefs.

See also: Finno-Ugric; Permyaks; Ural
Mountains; Votyaks

ŽYTNIAMATKA

Prussia

The goddess of the grain whose continued fertility was ritually observed each year by the simulated birth of a child in the recently harvested fields. A woman in the guise of Žytniamatka would lie down in the fields, and a newborn child that previously had been hidden beneath her skirt would be drawn out and held aloft. This ritual, which symbolized the life brought to the village by the fields, and thus by Žytniamatka, was thought to ensure a good crop each year.

REFERENCES AND FURTHER READING

The main sources that I consulted in compiling this work or that might be appropriate for further study are listed below. Some of these sources are core texts in various European languages, a number of which have been translated wholly or partly into English but many of which have not. Even though these texts might be extremely difficult to obtain, they are essential literature for further research on the subject, and their inclusion here therefore seems warranted.

Afanas'ev, A. N. (ed. and trans. N. Guterman). *Russian Fairy Tales.* New York, 1974.

———. *Narodnye russkie skazki A. N. Afanas'eva* (3 vols.). Moscow, 1957.

———. *Narodyne russkie skazki i legendy.* Berlin, 1922.

———. *Narodnye russkie legendy.* Moscow, 1916.

———. *Poeticheskie vozzreniia slavian na prirodu* (3 vols.). Moscow, 1865–69.

Alexander, A. E. *Bylina and Fairy Tale: The Origins of Russian Heroic Poetry.* The Hague, 1973.

Anisimov, A. F. *Kosmologicheskie predstavleniia narodov-severa.* Moscow and Leningrad, 1959.

Arbatskii, Iu. *Etiudy po istorii russkoi muzyki.* New York, 1956.

Arbman, Holger. *Svear i österviking.* Stockholm, 1955.

Arne, T. J. *La Suède et l'Orient.* Uppsala, 1914.

Astakhova, A. M. (ed.). *Byliny severa* (2 vols.). Moscow and Leningrad, 1938–51.

Astakhova, A. M., et al. *Byliny pechory i zimnego berega.* Moscow, 1961.

Azadovskii, M. (ed.). *Russkaia skazka.* Moscow and Leningrad, 1931–32.

Baktin, V. *Skazki Leningradskoi oblasti.* Leningrad, 1976.

Balodis, F. *Handelswege nach dem Osten und die Wikinger in Russland.* Stockholm, 1948.

Barker, A. M. *The Mother Syndrome in the Russian Folk Imagination.* Columbus, Ohio, 1986.

Baroja, J. C. (trans. N. Glendinning). *The World of the Witches.* London, 1964.

Barsov, E. V. *Drevnerusskie pamiatniki sviashchennogo venchaniia tsarei na tsarstvo.* Moscow, 1883.

Behr-Sigel, E. *Prière et sainteté russe dans l'église russe.* Paris, 1950.

Bezsonov, P. (ed.). *Kalieki perekhozhie.* Moscow, 1861.

Biro, Val. *Hungarian Folk-tales.* Oxford, 1980.

Boba, I. *Nomads, Northmen, and Slavs in Eastern Europe in the Ninth Century.* The Hague, 1967.

Branston, B. *Gods of the North.* New York, 1980.

Brückner, A. (trans. J. Dicksteinowna). *Mitologia slava.* Bologna, 1823.

Brudnyi, V. I. *Obriady vchera i segodnia.* Moscow, 1968.

Bulgakov, S. (trans. E. S. Cram). *The Orthodox Church.* London, 1944.

———. *L'Orthodoxie.* Paris, 1932.

Chadwick, N. K. *Russian Heroic Poetry.* New York, 1964.

———. *The Beginnings of Russian History.* Cambridge, 1946.

Cherniavsky, M. *Tsar and People: Studies in Russian Myths.* New York, 1969.

Chicherov, V. I. *Zimnii period russkogo narodnogo zemledel'cheskogo kalendaria XVI–XIX vekov.* Moscow, 1957.

Chistov, K. V. *Russkie narodnye sotsial'no-utopicheskie legendy XVIII–XIX vv.* Moscow, 1967.

Cross, S. H., and O. P. Sherbowitz-Wetzor (eds. and trans.). *The Russian Primary Chronicle: Laurentian Text.* Cambridge, Mass., 1953.

Dal',V. I. *Poslovitsy russkogo naroda.* Moscow, 1957.

Davidson, H. R. Ellis. *The Viking Road to Byzantium.* London, 1976.

de Beauplan, S. A. *Description of Ukraine.* London, 1732.

Delehaye, H. *Les Légendes hagiographiques.* Brussels, 1927.

Dontenville, H. *Histoire et géographie mythiques de la France.* Paris, 1973.

Downing, Charles. *Armenian Folk-tales and Fables.* Oxford, 1972.

———. *Russian Tales and Legends.* Oxford, 1956.

Dvornik, F. *The Slavs: Their Early History and Civilization.* Boston, Mass., 1956.

Esping, Mikael. *The Vikings.* London, 1982.

Everyman Dictionary of Non-Classical Mythology. London and New York, 1952.

Evgen'eva, A. P., and B. I. Putilov (eds.). *Drevnie rossiiskie stikhotvoreniia sobrannye Kirsheiu Danilovym.* Moscow, 1977.

Fedotov, G. P. *The Russian Religious Mind* (2 vols.). New York, 1960 (vol. 1) and 1966 (vol. 2).

Frazer, Sir J. G. *The Golden Bough.* Various editions.

Funk and Wagnalls Standard Dictionary of Folklore, Mythology and Legend (2 vols.). New York, 1949.

Ghananalian, A. T. *Aratsani.* Erevan, 1960.

Gil'ferding, A. P. *Onezhskie byliny zapisannye A. P. Gil'ferdingom letom 1871.* Moscow, 1951.

Gimbutas, Marija. *The Goddesses and Gods of Old Europe: 6500–3500 B.C.* London, 1982.

———. *The Slavs.* New York, 1971.

———. *The Balts.* London, 1963.

———. *Ancient Symbolism in Lithuanian Folk Art.* Philadelphia, 1958.

Golubinskii, E. E. *Istoriia kanonizatsii sviatykh v russkoi tserkvi.* Moscow, 1903.

Green, Miranda. *The Sun-Gods of Ancient Europe.* London, 1991.

Grekov, B. D. *Kiev Rus'* (English version). Moscow, 1959.

Gudzii, N. K. *Khrestomatiia po drevnei russkoi literature XI–XVII vv.* Moscow, 1962.

Haase, F. *Volksglaube und Brauchtum der Ostslaven.* Breslau, 1939.

Hakyuni, S. *Eminian Azgagrakan Zhoghovatsu.* Moscow and Leningrad, 1901.

Hapgood, I. *Service Book of the Holy Orthodox Church.* Boston, Mass., 1906.

Hubbs, Joanna. *Mother Russia: The Feminine Myth in Russian Culture.* Bloomington, Ind., 1988.

Ivanits, Linda J. *Russian Folk Belief.* Armonk, N.Y., 1989.

Ivanov, V. V., and V. N. Toporov. *Issledovaniia v oblasti slavianskikh drevnostei.* Moscow, 1974.

———. *Slavianskie iazykovye modeliruiushchie semioticheskie sistemy.* Moscow, 1965.

Jones, G. A. *A History of the Vikings.* Oxford, 1984.

Kazanskii, P. *Istoriia pravoslavnogo russkogo monashestva.* Moscow, 1855.

Khatchatrian, Y. *Armianskie skazki* (2nd edition). Moscow and Leningrad, 1933.

Khudiakov, I. A. (ed. V. G. Bazanov). *Velikorusskie skazki v zapisiakh I. A. Khudiakova.* Moscow, 1964.

———. *Materialy dlia izucheniia narodnoi slovesnosti.* St. Petersburg, 1863.

Kirby, W. F. (trans.). *Kalevala: The Land of Heroes* (2 vols.). Everyman's Library 259 and 260. London, 1907.

Kologrivof, I. *Essai sur la sainteté en Russie.* Bruges, 1953.

Kondakov, N. P. *Ikonografiia Bogomateri* (2 vols.). St. Petersburg, 1914–15.

Kovalevsky, M. *Modern Customs and Ancient Laws of Russia.* London, 1891.

Lalayan, E. *Margaritner hay banahiusuthean.* Tiflis and Vagharshapat, 1914–15.

Larousse Encyclopedia of Mythology, The. London, 1959.

Lebedev, A. *Razlichie v uchenii vostochnoi i zapadnoi tserkvei o Presviatoi Deve Marii.* Moscow, 1881.

Léger, L. *Les Anciennes civilisations slaves.* Paris, 1921.

Leroy-Beaulieu, A. (trans. Z. A. Rogosin). *The Empire of the Tsars and the Russians.* London, 1905.

Levin, S. (trans. M. Samuel). *Forward from Exile: The Autobiography of Shmarya Levin.* Philadelphia, 1967.

Lönnrot, Elias. *Kalevala.* Various translations.

MacCulloch, John A., and Louis H. Gray. *The Mythology of All Races* (13 vols.). New York, 1922.

Magarshack, D. (trans.). *Mirgorod: Four Tales by Nikolai Gogol.* New York, 1968.

Mann, R. *The Song of Prince Igor: A Great Medieval Epic.* Eugene, Oreg., 1979.

Mansikka, V. J. *Die Religion der Ostslaven*. Helsinki, 1922.

Marr, N. *Sbornik pritch Vardana*. St. Petersburg, 1894–99.

Matorin, N. *Zhenskoe bozhestvo v pravoslavnom kul'te*. Moscow, 1931.

McLeish, Kenneth. *Myth: Myths and Legends of the World Explored*. London, 1996.

Meyer, C. H. *Fontes historiae religionis slavicae*. Berlin, 1931.

Moszynski, K. *Kultura ludowo slowian* (2 vols.). Warsaw, 1967.

Nechaev, A. A., and N. Rybakov (eds.). *Russkie narodnye skazki*. Moscow, 1959.

Newell, V. (ed.). *The Witch Figure*. London, 1973.

Novikov, N. V. (ed). *Russkie skazki v rannikh zapisiakh i publikatsiiakh XVI–XVIII vekov*. Leningrad, 1971.

———. *Russkie skazki v zapisiakh i publikatsiiakh pervoi poloviny XIX veka*. Leningrad and Moscow, 1961.

Oinas, Felix J. *Essays on Russian Folklore and Mythology*. Columbus, Ohio, 1985.

———. *Studies in Finnic-Slavic Folklore Relations*. Helsinki, 1969.

Oinas, Felix J. (ed.). *Heroic Epic and Saga*. Bloomington, Ind., 1978.

Oinas, F. J., and S. Soudakoff. *The Study of Russian Folklore*. The Hague, 1975.

Oparenko, Christina. *Ukrainian Folk-tales*. Oxford, 1996.

Orbeli, I., and S. Taronian. *Hay zhoghovrdakan heqiathner* (10 vols.). Erevan, 1959–67.

Paulson, I. *The Old Estonian Folk Religion*. Bloomington, Ind., 1971.

Pears Encyclopedia of Myths and Legends (4 vols.). General editors: Mary Barker and Christopher Cook. *Vol 2. Western and Northern Europe: Central and Southern Africa*. London, 1978.

Perets, V. N. *Materialy k istorii apokrifa i legendy*. St. Petersburg, 1899.

Perkowski, Jan L. *The Darkling: Vampires of the Slavs*. Columbus, Ohio, 1989.

———. *Vampires of the Slavs*. Cambridge, Mass., 1976.

Pilnyak, B. (trans. V. T. Reck and M. Green). *Mother Earth and Other Stories*. Garden City, N.Y., 1968.

Pomerantseva, E. V. *Mifologicheskie personazhi v russkom fol'klore*. Moscow, 1975.

Popovic, Tatyana. *Prince Marko: The Hero of South Slavic Epic*. Syracuse, N.Y., 1988.

Potebnia, A. A. *O mificheskom znachenii nekotorykh obriadov i poverii*. Moscow, 1865.

Pronin, A., and B. Pronin. *Russian Folk Arts*. New York and London, 1975.

Propp, V. Iy. *Russkia agrarnae prazdniki*. Leningrad, 1963.

——— (ed.). *Byliny*. Leningrad, 1957.

Pushkin, A. S. (trans. G. R. Aitken). *The Complete Prose Tales of Alexander Sergeyevitch Pushkin*. New York, 1966.

———. *Sochineniia* (3 vols.). Moscow, 1964.

Ralston, W. R. S. *Russian Folktales*. New York, 1880.

———. *Songs of the Russian People*. London, 1872.

Rambaud, A. *La Russie épique*. Paris, 1879.

Riasanovsky, N. V. *A History of Russia*. New York, 1963.

Rimsky-Korsakov, N. A. *Sto russkikh narodnykh pesen*. Moscow and Leningrad, 1951.

Shein, P. *Velikorusy v svoikh pesniakh, obriadakh, obychaiakh, verovaniiakh, skazkakh, legendakh*. St. Petersburg, 1900–2.

Snegirev, I. M. *Russkie protonarodnye prazdniki i obriady* (2 vols.). Moscow, 1837–39.

Sokolov, Iu. (trans. G. Welter). *Le Folklore russe*. Paris, 1945.

Speranskii, M. (ed.). *Russkaia ustnaia slovesnost' byliny*. Moscow, 1916.

Summers, M. *The Vampire in Europe*. London, 1929.

Tereshchenko, A. V. *Byt' russkogo naroda* (7 vols.). St. Petersburg, 1848.

Tokarev, S. A. *Religioznye verovaniia vostochno-slavianskikh narodov XIX–nachala XX vekov*. Moscow, 1957.

Ukhov, P. D. *Byliny*. Moscow, 1957.

Vasilenko, V. M. *Russkaia narodnaia rez'ba i rospis' po derevu XVIII–XX vv*. Moscow, 1960.

Vernadsky, G. *Kievan Russia*. London, 1973; New Haven, 1948.

———. *The Origins of Russia*. Oxford, 1959.

———. *Ancient Russia*. New Haven, 1943.

Vsevolodskii-Gerngross, V. N. *Istoriia russkogo teatra*. Moscow and Leningrad, 1929.

Waliszewski, K. *La Femme russe*. Paris, 1926.

Warner, Elizabeth. *Heroes, Monsters and Other Worlds from Russian Mythology*. London, 1985.

Warner, M. *Alone of All Her Sex: The Myth and Cult of the Virgin Mary*. New York, 1976.

Wosien, M. G. *The Russian Folktale*. Munich, 1969.

Zabylin, M. *Russkii narod: Ego obychai, obriady, predaniia, sueveriia, i poeziia*. Moscow, 1880.

Zemtsovskii, I. I. (ed.). *Poezii krest'ianskikh prazdnikov*. Leningrad, 1970.

Zenkovsky, A. (ed.). *Medieval Russia's Epics, Chronicles, and Tales*. New York, 1963.

Znayenko, M. T. *The Gods of the Ancient Slavs: Tatishchev and the Beginnings of Slavic Mythology*. Columbus, Ohio, 1980.

APPENDIX 1: GLOSSARY OF TERMS

arshin   28 inches

ataman   A leader or chieftain, usually of a robber band, though not always; for example, the word is used in reference to Volga Buslavlevich, who led a band of *bogatyri*. Sometimes the term *ataman* is used to refer to a Cossack.

babushka   grandmother

batiushka   father, old man

bogatyr'   hero or knight

boyan   a bard or poet

boyar   nobleman

druzhina   bodyguard or retinue

gusli   psaltery or zither

izba   peasant hut

kisyel'   Also *kissel*. A traditional pudding made of puréed fruit cooked with cornstarch, often served with cream.

mirza   Tatar prince

muzhik   peasant

polianitsa   female warrior

pood   approximately 40 Russian pounds, or 36 English pounds (approximately 16.35 kg)

rushnik   A narrow linen cloth, sometimes referred to as a towel, that was embroidered at both ends, and that held a place of great importance in traditional Ukrainian households. The *rushnik* was ceremonially bound around the joined hands of a young couple during the marriage ceremony. It was also used in the traditional greeting ceremony, when an offering of bread and salt would be made on the *rushnik*. When not being used ceremonially, the *rushnik* would be draped over the icons in the home.

tsar or **czar**   Russian emperor. The title was first used c. 1482 by Ivan Vasilevich, Grand Duke of Muscovy—better known as Ivan Groznyi, or Ivan the Terrible. Thereafter, it was used by the emperors of Russia until the 1917 Revolution. The word *tsar* is derived from the Latin *Cæsar*.

tsarevich or **czarevich**   The son of a tsar. Historically the tsarevich was the eldest son, but the word applies to any son, not just the heir.

tsarevna or **czarevna**   The daughter of a tsar. Like the tsarevich, the tsarevna was usually the eldest daughter of the tsar; but the word may be correctly applied to any daughter.

Tsargrad   Constantinople

tsarina or **czarina**   The wife of a tsar; an empress, but not necessarily a ruler in her own right. (Unlike a tsaritsa, she is empress merely by virtue of her marriage.)

tsaritsa or **czaritsa**   A woman who is empress and rules in her own right, regardless of whether she is married to a tsar.

ulan   Tatar lancer

–ushka   diminutive suffix

vedro   a bucketful—2.75 gallons

verst   approximately two-thirds of a mile

yaga   a witch, as in Baba-Yaga

APPENDIX 2: TRANSLITERATION
FROM CYRILLIC TO LATIN LETTERS

Cyrillic	Latin	Pronunciation
А	a	a as in *far* (accented syllable) or a as in *alone* (unaccented syllable)
Б	b	b, p (at the end)
В	v	v, f (at the end)
Г	g	g, k (at the end)
Д	d	d, t (at the end)
Е	e, ye, ie, je	ye as in *yet* (accented syllable) or i as in *fit* (unaccented syllable)
Ё	e, yo, io, jo	yo
Ж	zh	zh or sh (at the end of a word)
З	z	z or s (at the end of a word)
И	i	ee as in *feet* (accented syllable) or i as in *fit* (unaccented syllable)
Й	j	y as in *yet*
К	k	k
Л	l	l
М	m	m
Н	n	n
О	o	o as in *hotel* (accented syllable) or as in *son* (unaccented syllable)
П	p	p
Р	r	r
С	s	s
Т	t	t
У	u	oo as in *boot*
Ф	f, ph	f
Х	h, kh	kh
Ц	ts, cz	ts
Ч	ch	ch
Ш	sh	sh
Щ	shch	shch
ъ	"	follows a nonpalatalized sound
Ы	y	æe
ь	'	follows a palatalized sound
э	e	e as in *get*
Ю	yu, iu, ju	as in *you*
Я	ya, ia, ja	ya

APPENDIX 3: THE RULERS OF RUSSIA

PRE-TSARIST ERA

Ruler	Lived	Reigned
Riurik	d. 879	gpN 862–879, gpK 879
Dir and Askold		gpK c. 862
Igor	c. 877–945	gpN 879–945, gpK 912–945
Oleg	d. 912	gpN 879–912, gpK 882–912 [ruled as regent for Igor]
Olga	c. 890–964	gpN/K 945–964 (co-ruled)
Sviatoslav I	d. 972	gpN/K 945–972, 945–964
Vladimir I	c. 956–1015	gpN c. 969, gpK 980–1015
Sviatopolk		1015, 1018–1019
Yaroslav the Wise	980–1054	gpN 1019, gpN/K 1036–1054
Vladimir II Monomachus	1053–1125	gpK 1113, gpN/K –1125
Yaroslav Vsevolodovich		gpN until 1236, gpN/K 1236–1246
Alexander Nevsky	1218–1263	gpN 1236, gpK 1246, gpV 1251
Andrei		gpV until 1251
Daniel		gpM 1263
MONGOL RULE		1240–1480
Yurii		gpM ?1318
Ivan I Danilovich (Kalita ["Moneybags"])	c. 1304–1341	gpM 1328–1341
Ivan II		gpM 1353–1359
Dmitrii Donskoi		1380–1382
Basil II (Vasilii II)		gpM until 1462
Ivan III Vasilevich (the Great)	1440–1505	gpM 1462–1505, gpN 1478
Basil III (Vasilii III)	1479–1533	gpM 1505–1533
Ivan IV Vasilevich	1530–1584	gpM 1533–1547

Key: gpN = Grand Prince of Novgorod
       gpK = Grand Prince of Kiev
       gpM = Grand Prince of Moscow
       gpV = Grand Prince of Vladimir

TSARS AND EMPRESSES OF RUSSIA

Ruler	Lived	Reigned
Ivan IV Vasilevich (the Terrible)	1530–1584	1547–1584
Theodore I (Fyodor I)	1557–1598	1584–1598
Irina		1598
Boris Fyodorovich Godunov	1552–1605	1598–1605
Theodore II (Fyodor II)	d. 1605	1605

False Dmitrii (Dmitrii III)	d. 1606	1605–1606
Basil Shuisky (Basil or Vasilii IV)		1606–1610
INTERREGNUM		1610–1613

House of Romanov

Michael (Mikhail Fyodorovich Romanov)	1596–1645	1613–1645
Alexis I	1629–1676	1645–1676
Theodore III (Fyodor III)	d. 1682	1676–1682
Ivan V	1666–1696	1682–1696 ⎫ co-ruled 1682–1689 under
Peter I (the Great)	1672–1725	1682–1725 ⎬ the regency of Sophia d.
		1704
Catherine I	1684–1727	1725–1727
Peter II	1715–1730	1727–1730
Anna Ivanovna	1693–1740	1730–1740
Ivan VI	d. 1741	1740–1741
Elizabeth Petrovna	1709–1762	1741–1762
Peter III	1728–1762	1762
Catherine II (the Great)	1729–1796	1762–1796
Paul	1754–1801	1796–1801
Alexander I	1777–1825	1801–1825
Nicholas I	1796–1855	1825–1855
Alexander II	1818–1881	1855–1881
Alexander III	1845–1894	1881–1894
Nicholas II	1868–1918	1894–1917

APPENDIX 4: TOPIC FINDER

The following guide divides each of the entries up into topic categories so that related articles on similar subjects may be located with comparative ease.

BY COUNTRY

Russia

Afron
Alans
Alenka
Alenushka
Alesha
Aliosha
Alkonost'
Alleluiah
Alyosha
Alyosha Popovich
Amelfia Timofeyevna
Amur
Anastasia, Saint
Andrew, Saint
Andronovich, Vyslav
Anna
Apraksi(i)a
Arkhangel'sk
Askold
Aurora Borealis
Auroras
Avdot'ya
Baba Latingorka
Baba-Yaga (-Jaga, -Iaga)
Bab'e leto
Bab'ia Kasha
Babii Prazdnik
Babushka-Lyagushka-
    Skakushka
Badnik

Bald Mountains
Basil, Saint
Basil II, Bulgaroctonus
Basil the Great, Saint
Batradz
Batu Khan
Bel Belyanin
Belun
Bereginy
Black Mire
Black Stream
Bludovich, Godenko
Bogatyr'
Bogoroditsa
Boris, Saint
Borushka Matushka
Boyars
Bozhena
Briansk Woods
Bright Sun
Bulat the Brave
Buslaev, Vasilii
Buslai (~y)
Buslavlevich, Vol'ga
Buslayevich, Vasilii
Bylichka
Bylina
Charity
Chernava
Chernigov
Chudo-Yudo
Churilo Plenkovich
City of the King, The
Copper Kingdom, The
Dalmat
Danilo, Prince
Dark Princess, The
Darkness
Dawn

Day
Dazhbog
Death
Ded Moroz
Dedy
Demian, Saint
Dem'yan, Saint
Derevliane
Desna
Devil, The
Devil and the Soldier, The
Dir
Div
Dmitrii (Vyslavovich)
Dnieper
Dobrynya Nikitich
Dormition, The
Dove Maiden
Dragon
Dunai, River
Dunai Ivanovich
Dunay (-ushka)
Dusk
Dvoeverie
Ekim
Elena the Beautiful
Elena the Fair
Eletskoi
Elias
Ermolai-erazm
Evil
Evpraksiya (~ia), Princess
Faraony
Fevroniia
Firebird, The
Foma Nazariev
Fool and the Birch Tree, The
Frost
George, Saint

Tungus
Ulgan
Yryn-al-tojon

Prussia
Adalbert of Prague, Saint
Autrimpas
Bardoyats
Perkonis
Prussia
Suaixtis
Waizganthos
Žytniamatka

Poland
Adalbert of Prague, Saint
Baba
Dadzbog
Datan
Didilia
Dilwica
Dziewona (~wan[n]a)
Goik
Ienzababa
Jezda
Kurwaichin
Lawkapatim
Marzan(n)a
Modeina
Poland
Siliniets
Tawals
Walg(a)ino
Zizilia

Hungary
Almafi
Ambrose
Budapest
Deceit
First Almafi
Hungary
Istvan
Janos
Magyars
Second Almafi
Stephen (of Hungary), Saint
Talking Mountain, The
Third Almafi
Tobias
Vizi-anya
Vizi-ember
Vizi-leany

Romania
Vlad (the Impaler), Prince
Walachia

Slovenia
Slovenia
Triglav
Triglav, Mount
Zlatorog

Slovakia
Perom (~n)
Slovakia

Estonia
Estonia
Maan-Eno
Metsik
Ukko

Bohemia
Lito

Mongolia
Itugen
Od(lek)
Tengri
Umai

Ukraine
Glass Mountain, The
Golden Mountain, The
Ivan the Dragon Killer
Kotsky, Mr.
Maria
Marusya
Misfortune, The Imps of
Snowstorm, Granny
Thrice-Ten Kingdom, The
Ukraine
Vasilko

Croatia
Croatia
Ivo
Motovun
Petar Lonzaric
Veli Joze

Bulgaria
Bulgaria
Perusan

Bosnia
Bosnia
Vuk

Zmag Ognjeni Vuk

Latvia
Auseklis
Debestevs
Juras Màte
Kaukai
Latvia
Majas Kungs
Meness (~ulis)
Mother of the Seas
Perkons
Puskaitis
Weaver of the Stars
Zemes Màte

Scythia
Atrimpaasa
Scythia

Serbia
Athos, Mount
Dazhbog
Diiwica
Dodola
Dojran, Lake
Ivan Crnojevic
Lazar
Marko, Prince
Sarac
Serbia
Vuk
Zmag Ognjeni Vuk

Norse
Askold
Riurik
Sineus
Truvor

Baltic
Arcona
Iarovit
Moon
Morning Star
Porevik (~it)
Radigast
Rugavit (~ievit)
Rujevit
Siela
Svantovit (~dovit)
Sventovit
Veles

White Youth
Yryn-al-tojon

Romany
Alako
Dundra

Magyar
Almafi
Ambrose
Deceit
First Almafi
Istvan
Janos
Second Almafi
Talking Mountain, The
Third Almafi
Tobias
Vizi-anya
Vizi-ember
Vizi-leany

Ostyak
As-Iga
Kul'

Votyak
Busi-urt
D'u-urt
Gudiri-mumi
Keremet
Korka-murt
Mukylin
Muzem-mumi
Obin-murt
Shundi-mumi
Urt
Vu-kutis
Vu-murt
Vu-nuna
Vu-vozo
Yanki-murt

Tungus
Dzuli
Eskeri
Ivan the Mare's Son
Ivan the Moon's Son
Ivan the Sun's Son
Marfida
Muxdi

Samoyed
Hahe

Hahengan
Num
Sjadaei

BY CATEGORY
General
Alexander the Great
Armenia
Arthur, King
Astrakhan'
Avars
Azerbaijan
Azov, Sea of
Balkan(s)
Baltic
Belarus'
Belorussia
Bessarabia
Black Sea
Blaise, Saint
Blasius, Saint
Bohemia
Bosnia
Bulgaria
Byzantine Empire
Byzantium
Carpathian Mountains
Caspian Sea
Caucasus
Cheremiss-Mordvin
Cherkess
Cilicia
Circassians
Constantinople
Cossacks
Crimea
Croatia
Cyrillic alphabet
Czechoslovakia
Czechs
Dacia
Dalmatia
Danube
Don
Donets
Dvina
Earth Mother
Erzya
Estonia
Fairy
Finland
Finno-Ugric

Genghis Khan
Georgia
Gilyaki (Nivkhi)
Golden Horde, The
Great Bear
Great Goddess
Hanseatic League
Herzegovina
Hungary
Istanbul
Jazyges
Kalmucks (Kalmyks)
Karelia
Kazakhstan
Khan
Kilikia
Kremlin
Lapland
Lapps
Latvia
Letts
Lithuania
Little Bear
Livonia
Macedonia
Magyars
Moksha
Moldavia
Moldova
Mongols
Montenegro
Moravia
Mordvins
Moscow
Ostyaks
Otherworld
Pannonia
Pechenegs
Permyaks
Poland
Prussia
Pu-ort
Romania
Rossiya
Rostov
Rus'
Russia
Ruthenes
Samoyeds
Saxo Grammaticus
Scythia
Serbia

Baltic
Belorussia
Bessarabia
Black Mire
Black Sea
Black Stream
Bohemia
Bosnia
Briansk Woods
Budapest
Bulgaria
Byzantium
Carpathian Mountains
Caspian Sea
Caucasus
Chernigov
Cilicia
Circassians
Constantinople
Cossacks
Crimea
Croatia
Czechoslovakia
Czechs
Dacia
Dalmatia
Danube
Desna
Dir
Djandjavaz, Mount
Dnieper
Dojran, Lake
Don
Donets
Dunai, River
Dvina
Estonia
Finland
Finno-Ugric
Genghis Khan
Georgia
Gilyaki (Nivkhi)
Golden Horde, The
Herzegovina
Hungary
Il'men', Lake
Istanbul
Ivan Crnojevic
Kalmucks (Kalmyks)
Karacharovo
Karelia

Kazakhstan
Kazan'
Kiev
Kirghiz
Kremlin
Ladoga, Lake
Lapland
Lapps
Latvia
Lena, River
Lithuania
Livonia
Macedonia
Magyars
Matushka
Moldavia
Moldova
Mongols
Montenegro
Moravia
Mordvins
Moscow
Motovun
Murom
Novaya Zemlya
Novgorod
Oka
Opsikion
Ossetes
Ostyaks
Pannonia
Pecherskaia Lavra
Permyaks
Poland
Prussia
Puchai
Riurik
Romania
Rostov
Russia
Ruthenes
Safat
Samoyeds
Sarmatians
Scythia
Serbia
Siberia
Silesia
Slavs
Slovakia
Slovenia

Smorodina
Smorodinka
Sorochinsk Mountains
St. Petersburg
Talking Mountain, The
Transcaucasia
Transylvania
Triglav, Mount
Tungus
Turkestan
Turkmenistan
Ukraine
Ural Mountains
Uzbekistan
Vikings
Voguls
Volga
Votyaks
Walachia
White Russia
White Sea
Yakuts
Zyrians

Bogatyri
Alesha
Alyosha Popovich
Bogatyr'
Buslai (~y)
Churilo Plenkovich
Dobrynya Nikitich
Dunai Ivanovich
Godenko Bludovich
Goryshche
Il'ya Muromets
Ivan Gostinyi Syn
Kostia Nikitin
Kostia Novotorzheni
Luka
Mikhail Potyk
Moisei
Nightingale
Potania, Tiny
Sbrodovich
Stavr Godinovich
Sukhman
Sviatogor
Vasilii Buslayevich
Vasilii Kazimirovich
Vladimir Bright Sun, Prince
Vol'ga Buslavlevich

Vol'ga Sviatoslavovich
Zalyoshen

Variant Names
Aliosha
Alyonka
Alyonushka
Apraksi(i)a
Belarus'
Belorussia
Blasius, Saint
Bouyan
Buslaev, Vasilii
Cain
Chur
Dadzbog
Demian, Saint
Domania
Domovik
Dunai Ivanovich
Dunay (-ushka)
Earth Mother
Faraony
Helen
Horsel
Iarovit
Ivan Crnojevic
Ivan Savel'evich
Ivan Vyslavovich
Kashchei (the Deathless)
Kaukas
Kilikia
Kosma
Ljeschie
Luqmân the Wise
Majahaldas
Majasgars
Makosh
Maryshia
Mavki
Mikola Mozhaiski, Saint
Mikula Selyaninovich
Muxdi
Nastasiia
Navki
Od(lek)
Orsel
Pikker
Piorun
Porevik (~it)
Pudnitsa

Rujevit
Ryurik
Saite (~vo)
Sea King
Selyaninovich, Mikula
Senmurv
Sorochinsk Hill
Sventovit
Triglav
Vasilii Busla(y)ev
Vasilis(s)a Kirbit'evna
Vasilisushka
Vlkodlak
Vodianiani
Volkh Vseslav'evich
Vseslav'evich, Volga
Vyslav Andronovich
Vyslavovich, Ivan
Zemininkas
Zuro

Sacred Places and Objects
Alatnir
Alka
Badnik
Bozhena
Dzuli
Goik
Golden Book of Fate, The
Hahe
Hahengan
Kumstvo
Kupiatitskaia
Lompsalo
Makar'evskaia
Marena
Pskov icon, The
Saite (~vo)
Sejda
Sjadaei
Zhirovitskoi

Demons and Demonesses
Alkonost'
Aznavor
Badikan
Devil, The
Devil and the Soldier, The
Evil
Frost
Ghovt
Ivan the Soldier

Koknas
Leshii (~y)
Likho, One-Eyed
Misfortune, The Imps of
Misha
Morozko
Sorrow
Suren
Vampire
Vodianoi (~nik)

Spirits, nymphs, and fairies
As–Iga
Bannik
Barstukai
Bereginy
Busi–urt
Death
Ded Moroz
Dedy
Devil, The
Dievo suneliai
Domovikha
Domovoi
Dove Maiden
Dove Maidens, The
D'u–urt
Dvorovoi
Evil
Fairy
Frost
Giwoitis
Gramovitsa
Houri
Houri-Pari
Kams
Kapsirko
Kartaga
Katya
Kaukai
Kaukas
Khoziaika lesa
Kikimora
Korka-murt
Kremara
Krukis
Kul'
Kurke
Kurwaichin
Kush-Pari
Lel

INDEX